Oracle Developer's Guide

David McClanahan

Osborne **McGraw-Hill**

Berkeley New York St. Louis
San Francisco Auckland Bogotá Hamburg London Madrid
Mexico City Milan Montreal New Delhi Panama City
Paris São Paulo Singapore Sydney Tokyo Toronto

Osborne **McGraw-Hill**
2600 Tenth Street
Berkeley, California 94710
U.S.A.

For information on translations or book distributors outside the U.S.A., or to arrange bulk purchase discounts for sales promotions, premiums, or fundraisers, please contact Osborne **McGraw-Hill** at the above address.

Oracle Developer's Guide

1234567890 DOC 99876

ISBN 0-07-882087-1

Acquisitions Editor	**Computer Designer**
Cynthia Brown	Lance Ravella
Project Editor	**Illustrator**
Linda Comer	Rhys Elliot
Copy Editor	**Series Design**
Jan Jue	Jani Beckwith
Proofreader	**Quality Control Specialist**
Pat Mannion	Joe Scuderi

This book is dedicated to my family
Kyle Russell, Kristen Kay, and Patricia Ann McClanahan

About the Author

David McClanahan is a consultant who specializes in the design and development of Client/Server systems. He has been involved with every phase of development, including feasibility studies, design, data modeling, and coding for large Client/Server projects and is one of the most widely published experts in the field. He is currently a columnist for DataBase Advisor and PowerBuilder Advisor magazines. He has written several books, including *PowerBuilder 4: A Developer's Guide* published by M&T Books.

As a database specialist he has worked with most of the major database systems including Oracle, Sybase, SQL Server, Informix, Ingres, Progress, Ontos, and Versant. He has also developed with a wide range of front-end tools including PowerBuilder, Visual Basic, SQLWindows, Delphi, Access, and has extensive C and C++ experience in the UNIX and Windows environments. He is also a technical reviewer for Oracle Press and teaches a number of seminars related to Client/Server development and database design.

David McClanahan can be reached through CompuServe at 72517,1124 or email at mcclanah@ix.netcom.com.

Contents

Acknowledgments

 technical book like this one, involves many people.

   I would like to thank Scott Urman and Bill Floyd for their major contributions to this book. Thanks to Technalysis Corporation for their support of this project. Everyone there has my best wishes.

   I would like to thank all those involved at Osborne that worked with me on this project. Special thanks go to Cynthia Brown, Linda Comer, Terese Tatum, and Bradley Shimmin.

Introduction

This book is a guide to the development of database applications that use Oracle as the database management system. Databases are an increasingly important component of most application development projects. Oracle, which is available on a very wide range of hardware and software systems, is the leading, most wide-spead database management system, and is generally the best choice for a corporate system.

This book assumes that the reader is fluent in at least one of the standard programming languages. All the examples in this book are given in the C language, but since the focus is on the database functionality, programmers using other languages will have little problem following the code examples and adapting that code to their needs. I also assume a basic understanding of relational database systems. I do provide an introduction to basic database concepts, development techniques for the Oracle system, distributed databases, and the Client/Server architecture. If you need additional introductory information then I recommend another book in the Oracle Press series, *Oracle: A Beginner's Guide* by Michael Abbey and Michael Corey published by Osborne McGraw-Hill (ISBN 0-07-882122-3).

If you are developing database applications, this book will provide everything you need when working with an Oracle system. There are several approaches to adding database functionality to your application using different Oracle tools.

I cover each of these methods in detail. Several chapters are dedicated to embedded SQL which is the most popular method for development. Other chapters are dedicated to PL/SQL which is Oracle's procedural extensions to SQL, and the Oracle Call Interface (OCI) which is an Application Program Interface that is called directly from your application programs. I provide an explanation of each technique and discuss the advantages and disadvantages of each to assist you in making the decision as to which approach to use for your application development. There are many detailed code examples throughout the book, and I cover the process of developing applications with each method in detail.

Chapter 1 also contains an introduction to Personal Oracle7, a new Oracle product, which is a Windows version of Oracle. Personal Oracle7 contains almost the full capability of the full-fledged Oracle DBMS that runs on mini and main-frame systems. Personal Oracle7 is an excellent tool for development and is a tremendous value for educating oneself about Oracle.

This book is also intended to serve as a reference manual; the chapters dedicated to Pro*C, PL/SQL, the OCI, and the appendixes contain a great deal of information that you will find useful as you develop your applications.

CHAPTER 1

An Introduction to the Oracle Database System

This chapter presents an overview of the Oracle system for developers of database applications. It covers the following topics:

- Basic database concepts and terminology
- Developing applications with Oracle 7
- Oracle System Architecture
- Personal Oracle 7

Relational Database Basics

A *database* is a collection of sharable information (data). A *database management system* (DBMS) is a program (or set of programs) that manages one or more databases. The DBMS is the mechanism through which you access and modify the data. The DBMS also provides such functionality as database security and transaction processing to ensure data integrity. Throughout this book, the DBMS will be referred to as Oracle, or simply the *server*.

A *database application* is an application that uses a DBMS such as Oracle 7 for data access. This book focuses on developing database applications and how you can add database functionality to your applications.

A *relational database* is organized according to the relational data model created by E. F. Codd in 1970. The relational model has the advantage of providing a natural (conceptually simple) view of the structure of the data in the system while being based on sound mathematical principles. The relational data model defines three aspects of the system:

- **Architecture**   The way data objects are structured.

- **Data operations**   The methods for manipulating those data objects.

- **System constraints**   The rules that govern the operations and ensure that the result of each operation is absolutely predictable.

Database Objects

Database objects are structures defined by the Oracle system. Your application program will reference various database objects in SQL statements. The most common object is the table.

Tables

The basic storage structure in a relational system is a *table*, a two-dimensional matrix consisting of columns and rows of data elements. All Oracle data exists as data items (column values) in tables in the database. Each table contains information of a certain type and represents an entity or a relationship. An entity could be a person, place, thing, or concept. Examples of tables you might create are employee, department, invoice, appointment, inventory, and work_assignment. Each row in a table contains the information needed to describe one instance of the entity; each column represents an attribute of the entity (a single data value).

Figure 1-1 is an example of a relational table with 12 elements of data, organized into three columns and four rows. Each column has a label, called its *column name*, that describes the information (data items) in the column and allows

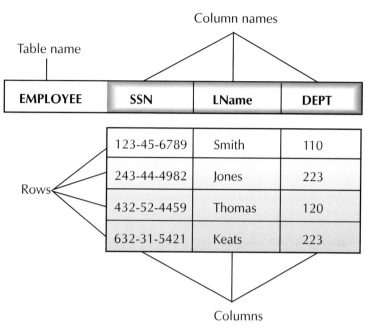

FIGURE 1-1. *A database table*

you to refer to values in a specific column. Each column entry consists of a field of data called a *column value* (or data item) drawn from a set of possible values known as the *domain* of the column. This domain has a data type, such as numeric or character, as well as a specific format. All data items in a column have the same data type.

NOTE
The relational model uses the term relation to describe the construct shown in the figure. This book uses the more common term table throughout. Though the terms actually have a slightly different meaning--a table is an occurrence of a relation in the database system--this is not significant for our discussion.

In this example, "SSN" is a column name. This column contains the Social Security Number that uniquely identifies each employee in the database. "123-45-6789" is a column value drawn from the domain of possible values ranging from 000-00-0000 to 999-99-9999.

The rows in a table are all of the same type; that is, they are based on the same table definition. Each row consists of one value drawn from each column's domain.

There is exactly one column value for each column in a row. Sometimes a value for a certain column is unknown or does not apply to a certain row. In this case, a *null* value is placed in the column. A null indicates that the value is unknown, is unnecessary, or does not apply in this case. You cannot assign a null value to any of the key fields in a table. If you don't have a value for all the key fields, then you don't have enough information to enter a row of data.

Figure 1-2 shows another table, DEPT, which contains the department number (Dept_no) and other information related to each department.

A fundamental characteristic of relational database systems is the relationship between logically associated tables. In the examples shown in Figures 1-1 and 1-2, if you wanted to know the name of a certain employee's manager, you would look up the employee's department number (Dept_no) in the EMPLOYEE table. You then look at the DEPT table, using Dept_no to locate the manager. In the example in Figure 1-3, you can see that employee Smith's manager is McClanahan.

Indexes

Indexes are special objects that Oracle creates to provide rapid access (lookups) to tables in the database. Most of your applications' database retrievals will be based on column values. For example, you may retrieve the employee information where the employee's name is Kyle Russell. Internally, Oracle maintains a binary value, called a *ROWID*, that uniquely represents the location of each row of data in the database. A ROWID is the fastest way to retrieve a row in the Oracle system. An index contains two entries for each row in a table: The first entry is a key value, and the second is the corresponding ROWID. The key value is the value of one or more columns in a table (for example, LAST_NAME or LAST_NAME + FIRST_NAME). Given a key value, Oracle can quickly locate the row(s) of data in which you are interested using as an index.

DEPT	Dept_no	Manager
	110	McClanahan
	120	Fox
	130	Russell
	223	Beethoven

FIGURE 1-2. *The DEPT table*

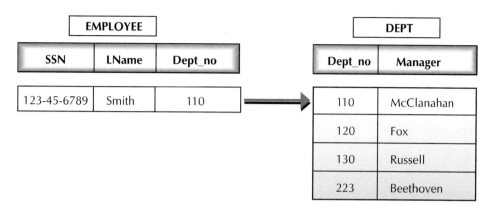

FIGURE 1-3.   *The EMPLOYEE table's relationship to the DEPT table*

Views

EMPLOYEE is a table that exists and is stored in the database system. Another type of database object, a *view*, is based on one or more tables in the database. A view is a *virtual table*; it does not actually exist in the database, but is accessed in your SQL code just like a normal table. Views often allow a filtered look at a table. For example, you could create a view, EMP_INFO, that is based on the EMPLOYEE table but is designed to allow only certain columns of the EMPLOYEE table to be viewed. Views can be used to allow someone to see the employee's name, address, and SSN but not more sensitive information, such as salary.

Your applications will use views in virtually the same manner as tables. You can retrieve rows from views with the SELECT statement and, in most cases, update, insert, and delete rows in the database by using views. Some views do not permit updates to the database.

Sequences

In your applications, you will often need to generate a series of unique numbers such as invoice numbers or customer ID numbers. Oracle provides for this using a *sequence*, a series of numbers Oracle generates for a particular table in the database. Sequences are stored in the data dictionary (discussed later) and managed by Oracle so that two applications requesting a sequence number at the same time will be given correct values. When you define a sequence, you can specify the starting value, a maximum value, and whether or not the numbers are to be recycled after reaching the maximum. Besides being very useful, sequences are more robust and easier to deal with than if you were to program the same functionality in your applications.

Synonyms

A synonym is an alternate name (or alias) for a database object, such as a table or view. Synonyms are useful for simplifying references, providing security, or avoiding physical dependencies; a user only needs to know an object's synonym to access it. The user does not need to know other details, such as the location or owner of the object.

Data Dictionary

Tables store two types of information in the database: *user data* and *system data*. Your applications will access user data most often; this is data that is inserted, updated, or deleted through the database applications that you create for your enterprise.

Oracle needs to maintain a large amount of system data, which describes the database system and is used by Oracle during its operation. Oracle stores this information in system tables—that is, tables that are created and managed by Oracle. This happens automatically; you will scarcely notice the process.

System data is used to manage the database. It contains descriptions of all the objects in the system, including tables, columns, views, indexes, and synonyms. The set of tables that Oracle uses for the system data is called the *data dictionary*. You won't usually need direct access to the data dictionary, but you can query the data dictionary when necessary (for example, to get a list of the columns in a particular table in the database).

Users and Schemas

Oracle controls and limits access to the data in the database. It provides a security system that prevents the unauthorized use of the information. You must have a username and password before you can access an Oracle database. A *user* (often called a user account) is a name (identification) that has been granted a set of Oracle privileges. Normally, the DBA (database administrator) sets up user accounts, creating a user ID and password. When Oracle is installed, however, it creates two initial user accounts: SYSTEM and SYS. The DBA uses these accounts to administrate the database.

Each user owns a set of database objects (including tables, views, and indexes). This set of objects is called a *schema*. The SYS user account owns the data dictionary tables described earlier. The SYSTEM user account owns a number of views based on the data dictionary tables. You should never use the SYS account and, in general, should not need to use the SYSTEM account in your applications.

Developing Database Applications

C is a standard language designed for general programming purposes. It has everything needed to create most applications, but database access is a specialized requirement and, therefore, not part of the C language. Accessing an Oracle database requires some additional tools. This section looks at the choices you have when developing database applications.

SQL

Accessing a relational database system (RDBMS) requires the use of a data access language. The data language Oracle uses is called SQL (originally an abbreviation for Structured Query Language; pronounced "S.Q.L." rather than "sequel"). SQL is a sublanguage that contains only the statements necessary to access a database system (DBMS). It can be used interactively or programmatically.

Oracle's SQL*Plus utility provides an interactive interface to the database. You can execute SQL statements directly against the database using SQL*Plus. You can use it to create database objects and data and to verify the functioning of your applications.

Embedded SQL

One way of using SQL in your applications is through a technique called *embedded SQL*. When you embed SQL statements, you place them directly into your C (or C++) application code. C programs can use embedded SQL statements to access and manipulate the data stored in an Oracle database. This requires the use of an Oracle precompiler called Pro*C. Pro*C makes a pass through the source code to convert the SQL statements to function calls, then produces a new C source-code file as output. You compile this output file with your standard C compiler and link the object code with Oracle libraries to create the executable program.

PL/SQL

As mentioned earlier, SQL is a sublanguage; it only contains the statements and constructs required to allow data access. Oracle has developed a procedural version of SQL, called PL/SQL, that adds a set of procedural statements (similar to those in C). Those statements allow SQL to be used as a programming language. PL/SQL can also be embedded in Pro*C programs.

Stored Procedures

You can create stored procedures from blocks of PL/SQL code. Stored procedures are compiled and then stored in the database (specifically, in the data dictionary) so you can call them from your applications. This is a way to create code that is shared across applications; it also moves the processing from the client machine to the server.

Stored procedures can also be used to provide data security. You can create these procedures and allow users to execute them without giving the users direct access to the tables and the views used by the procedure. In this way, you can control access to these tables.

Packages
You can bundle procedures, functions, and other related objects to create a larger construct called a *package*. Packages let you specify the logical groupings for procedures and build packages to perform administrative or processing tasks. Packages are compiled and stored in the database (in Oracle's data dictionary), like procedures or functions.

Triggers
You can define procedures that will be initiated by certain events (triggers) in the database, such as the insertion or deletion of a record. This is most useful for maintaining data integrity, performing additional processing automatically, or providing for security.

Oracle Call Interface (OCI)
Besides embedded SQL, another option is to use an Application Programming Interface (API) to develop your applications. Oracle provides a set of functions, called the Oracle Call Interface, in a run-time library that can be called directly from your C program to access the Oracle system. You make the OCI accessible to your application simply by linking to a library available from Oracle.

SQL*Net and Database Links
SQL*Net is an optional Oracle product that provides database communications between nodes on the network. Database links are names that you create to reference different access paths on the network; they simplify these references and remove any physical dependency from the reference. For example, you can create a database link to an INVENTORY database that resides at a remote site (say, in Atlanta). If the database is later moved (perhaps to Cincinnati), the code that uses that link will still work correctly because the link contains no reference to the location. Of course, the DBA would need to redefine the link to point to the new location, but that would not be visible to your applications.

The Oracle Server

The Oracle Server is a set of programs that manages one or more databases and allows concurrent database access by multiple users. Oracle also provides transaction management, security, monitoring, open connectivity to other systems, and a number of management utilities.

The internal structure of Oracle is not discussed here—that topic is covered in other books in this series—but there are a few details you need to understand.

The Oracle database system is built on the client-server architecture. In this architecture, a *server* program provides services to other programs in the system, called *clients.* The Oracle database system acts as the database server to all clients that need access to an Oracle database. Your database application is a client program.

The server must be running before a database can be accessed. There are several steps involved in getting to the point where your application can actually access a database: Oracle must be loaded into memory, processes started, initialization files read, and communications initiated between the server and the client applications. A DBA probably performs these steps for your company.

Specifically, the steps involved in starting up Oracle are:

- **Starting the server**   Oracle is loaded into memory and initialized so that it can function. An Oracle *instance* is a set of processes and their memory allocations. At that point, the Oracle server (or an instance) is said to be *running.*

- **Opening the database**   Once Oracle is running, a database must be opened. This will make it available (accessible) to the users (your applications).

- **Connecting to the database**   After the database is open, your application must connect to it using a user account (logon ID and password). This step makes a schema available to your application.

Personal Oracle

Personal Oracle 7 is a Windows version of Oracle and part of the Workgroup/2000 suite of products, which includes the DBMS system, SQL*Loader, SQL*Plus, and the Import and Export utilities. Personal Oracle 7 has most of the power and functionality of Oracle 7, except that it does not implement the distributed database and data replication options. This is only a minor drawback when you consider the advantages of being able to develop your applications with a local version of Oracle; Personal Oracle 7 gives you full access to Oracle's stored procedures, referential integrity, security, datatypes, and cursor processing.

If you are new to Oracle, Personal Oracle 7 is an excellent way to gain hands-on experience and an excellent investment, if only for your own education. You can also use Personal Oracle 7 to develop applications that may later be deployed to run against Oracle on other platforms (such as a UNIX system). Doing the initial development with the Oracle database on a PC can save a great deal of time and simplify life for the developer, who can focus on application development and ignore the intricacies of the network database system. When the application is finished, or when you need to add distributed capabilities, you can switch to the target Oracle system with little effort.

You can make Personal Oracle 7 the database for your applications by using ODBC (Open DataBase Connectivity, a database interface standard for Windows applications), native Oracle drivers, or Oracle's Objects for OLE. Objects for OLE is an OLE2 implementation that provides Oracle access to the Windows development environment; you can use it with programming languages (such as C, C++, or Visual Basic) to give your applications database functionality.

Database Administration Tools

Personal Oracle contains a number of graphical database administration tools—Database Manager, Database Expander, Object Manager, Session Manager, and User Manager—that assist in the configuration and maintenance of the system. These tools make the system easier to handle, allowing a developer who is not a DBA to manage the system. These are the same tools provided with the Workgroup Server.

The installation program creates a Personal Oracle 7 program group, as shown in Figure 1-4. Double-clicking on these icons launches various tools. You use the Database Manager (see Figure 1-5) to start the database. This is simply a matter of selecting the desired database from the drop-down list box, then clicking on the Startup button. You would also use this tool to shut down the database, check the current status, and perform configuration functions. You then use the User Manager (see Figure 1-6) to add or modify user accounts. This includes creating or deleting users in the system, changing the user password, and controlling database privileges. You can list the users, view their roles, change passwords and privileges and so forth in the dialog box shown in Figure 1-6. Another dialog box, shown in Figure 1-7, displays the privileges for each user.

Occasionally you will need to increase the size of the database. The Database Expander (see Figure 1-8) provides a simple interface for doing that. The space allocation and use are shown in a pie chart, so you can see at a glance the available space for any table. The expansion can take place while the system is

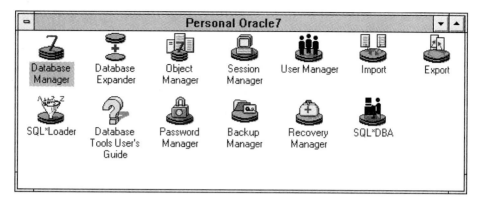

FIGURE 1-4. *The Oracle program group*

running, so you don't need to know the exact syntax of the ALTER TABLESPACE SQL statement.

The Object Manager (see Figure 1-9) simplifies the administration of various objects in the Oracle system, including tables, indexes, synonyms, views, and database links. You select the type of object in a drop-down list box and the owner in another list box. The Objects list box then displays the objects associated with that user. You can create, update, and delete any of these objects in the Object

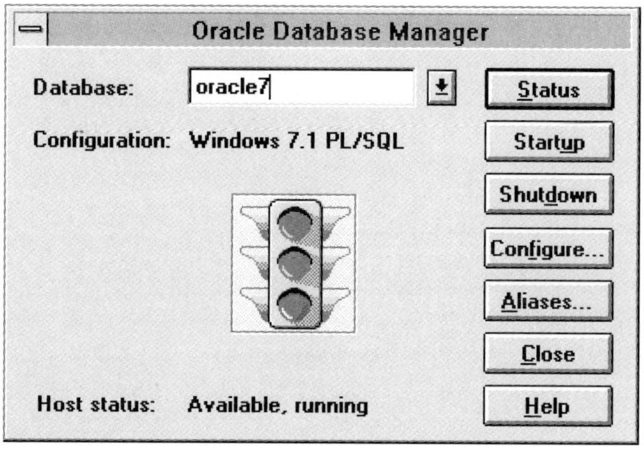

FIGURE 1-5. *The Database Manager*

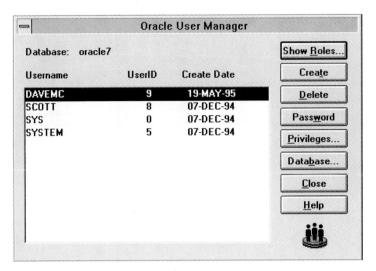

FIGURE 1-6. *The User Manager*

Manager. You can also grant and revoke privileges against those objects in this utility (see Figure 1-10).

You can also access the object's definition through the Object Manager. To do that, you just select the object in the list box, then click on the Show command button to open the related Management dialog box. For example, the Table

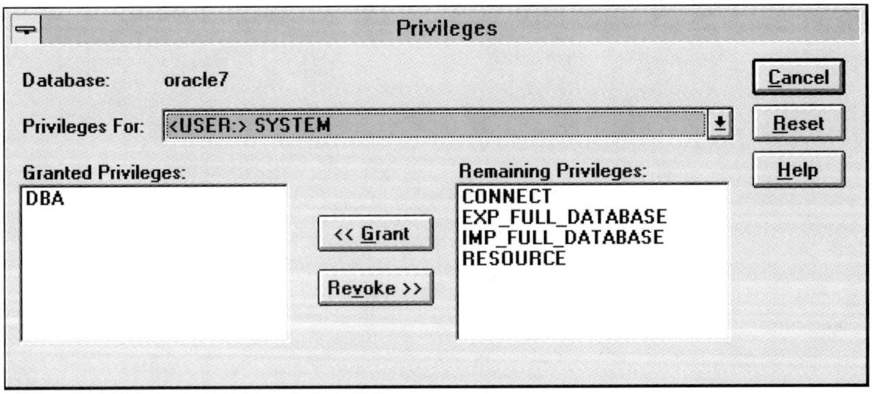

FIGURE 1-7. *Viewing user privileges*

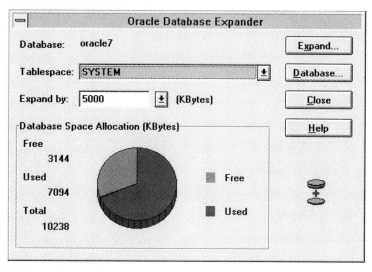

FIGURE 1-8.   *The Database Expander*

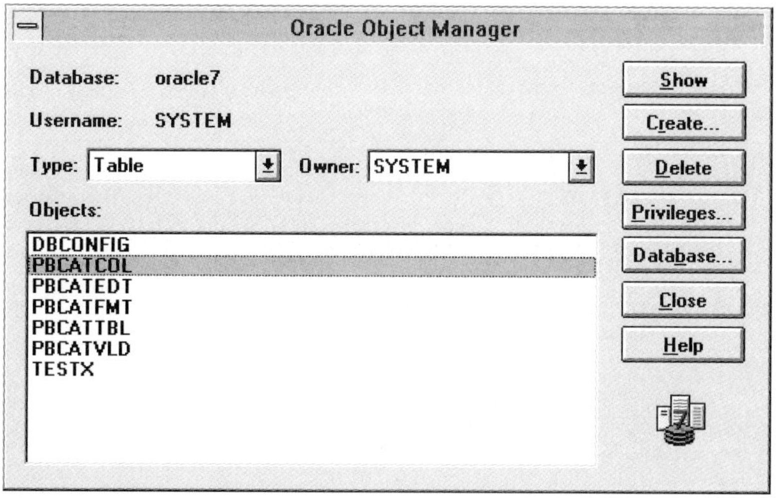

FIGURE 1-9.   *The Object Manager*

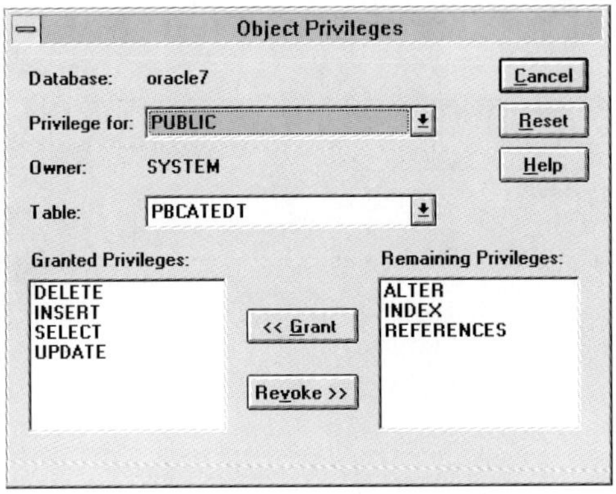

FIGURE 1-10. *The Object Privileges dialog box*

Management dialog box (see Figure 1-11) has a grid in which you can update a table's definition.

The Oracle Session Manager (see Figure 1-12) provides information on every session in each database, including the username, SID, serial number, and status. You can also disconnect any of the sessions using this dialog box.

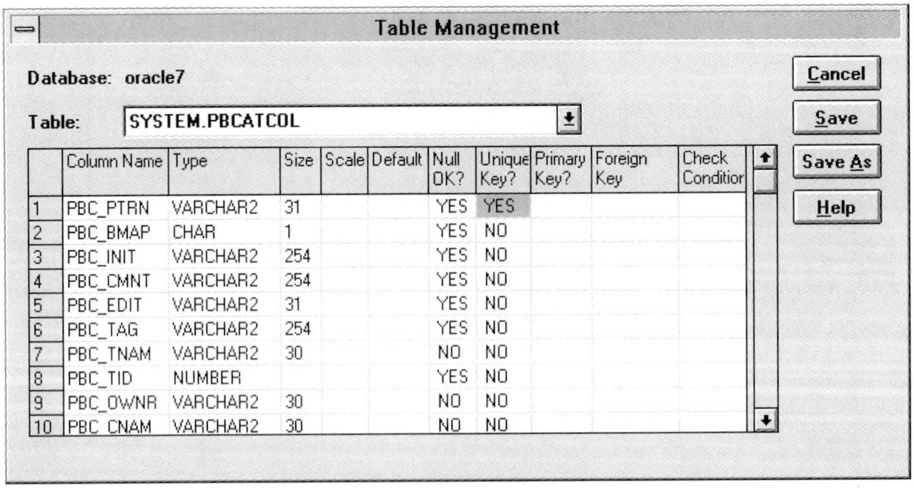

FIGURE 1-11. *The Table Management dialog box*

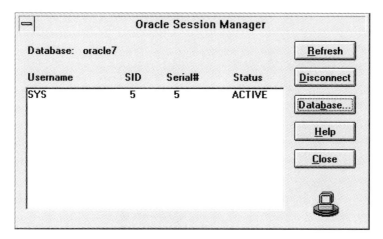

FIGURE 1-12.   *The Session Manager*

Product Information

Personal Oracle 7 requires a minimum configuration of 8 MB of RAM (16 MB is recommended) and 30 MB of disk space. A fully functional version is available for a free 90-day trial from Oracle's Internet server; the World Wide Web address is http://www.oracle.com.

Summary

In this chapter we presented a basic overview of the Oracle database system. It provided basic definitions and a brief look at some of the options available for developing Oracle database applications. Finally, it introduced Personal Oracle 7, which you may use to develop the sample applications in this book.

CHAPTER 2

An Overview of Application Development

This chapter presents an overview of the development of database applications using the C language. Though our examples always use C, much of the material in this chapter (and throughout this book) also applies to the development process for other languages. This chapter covers the following topics:

- Database application architecture
- SQL—the data access language

■ Embedded SQL and the Pro*C precompiler

■ The Oracle Call Interface (OCI)

■ The PL/SQL language

Creating Database Applications

An *application program* is a collection of software components designed to do one or more specific tasks. Most applications need to access and manipulate data; a *database application* uses a database management system (DBMS) such as Oracle 7 for data access. This book focuses on developing database applications and adding database functionality to your applications.

Developers partition applications into major divisions called *systems,* which in turn are broken up into subcomponents, or *subsystems.* The number and size of these subsystems will vary depending on the scope and complexity of the system. Database application programs usually consist of the following major components:

■ A **high-level programming language** to encode logic and processing. This book focuses on using the C/C++ programming language to create program modules.

■ A **user interface** that allows programs to interact with the person using the application. You may implement the interface to the user with a simple terminal interface or with a more modern graphical interface, the latter by using Microsoft Windows on PCs or X Window (and Motif) on UNIX workstations. The examples in this book use either a DOS (text) interface or a Windows interface.

■ A **DBMS** to create, access, and administrate data. This is provided by the Oracle 7 relational database management system (RDBMS).

■ A **data language** to access the Oracle system. This is provided by SQL using a variety of development techniques available in the Oracle 7 environment.

■ An **operating system access** mechanism to interface with the operating system. This is provided through operating-system–specific calls on the *host computer.*

A typical application program's major components can be structured as shown in Figure 2-1.

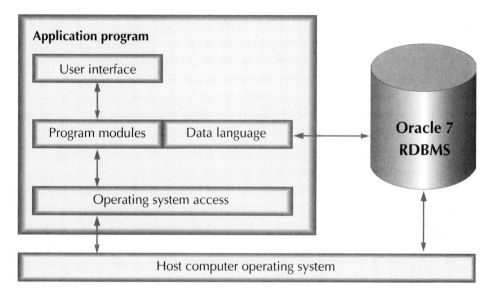

FIGURE 2-1.   *A typical database application*

SQL

C is a standard programming language that was designed for general programming purposes. It has everything you need to create most applications. Since not all applications require database access, however, this functionality is not part of the C language. Accessing an RDBMS therefore requires the use of a data access language. The most popular data language, and the one used by Oracle, is SQL. *SQL,* which originally stood for *Structured Query Language,* is properly pronounced "S-Q-L" but is also commonly pronounced "sequel" (for historical reasons).

SQL is a sublanguage in that it only contains the statements necessary to access a DBMS. It can be used interactively or programmatically. The SQL*Plus and SQL*DBA utilities provide an interactive interface to the database. You can execute SQL statements directly against the database using these tools. As a database application developer, you should be familiar with SQL*Plus. You will find it essential for accessing the database during the development process, and you can use it to verify the functioning of your applications. In addition to SQL statements, SQL*Plus can execute statements to control various environment parameters. These statements are not available programmatically but are essential for setting up configuration and report details.

With a technique called *embedded SQL*, C programs can use SQL to access and manipulate the data stored in an Oracle database. SQL lacks the procedural structures of the C language, so the logical flow of the application is defined using C's procedural constructs. SQL only provides for the database access. It does that in a *nonprocedural* manner—that is, it specifies a set of data and states what action should take place with that set of data, but it does not state exactly how those actions should be accomplished. In other words, you use SQL to say what you want done, then leave it up to Oracle to decide how to do the work. We will cover the details of embedded SQL in the next section.

SQL is the standard relational database language; it has been standardized by several organizations. The Oracle precompilers meet the initial ANSI (American National Standards Institute), ISO (International Organization for Standardization), and NIST (National Institute for Standards and Technology) standards. Oracle's implementation also provides a number of additions and extensions to SQL.

Accessing Oracle

A database application is an application that uses a DBMS (such as Oracle 7) for its data requirements. The rest of this chapter introduces the methods available for adding Oracle database functionality to your applications. Oracle provides several methods for programmers:

- **Embedded SQL**   This allows you to place SQL statements directly into your program code. It requires an Oracle precompiler called Pro*C. The precompiler reads and modifies the C source code (with the embedded SQL statements) and produces a new C source-code file as output. You can then compile this output file with your standard C compiler and link the object code with Oracle libraries to create the executable.

- **API**   Another option is to use an *application program interface* (API) to develop your application. Oracle provides a set of functions in a run-time library that can be called directly from your C program to access the Oracle system. Oracle calls this interface the *OCI* (Oracle Call Interface). Your application can access it simply by linking to a library available from Oracle.

- **PL/SQL**   The third option, PL/SQL (Procedural Language Extensions to SQL), is Oracle's procedural version of SQL. Oracle has added a set of procedural statements, similar to the procedural statements in C, that allow SQL to be used as a programming language.

Your application isn't limited to using just one of these methods; you can combine them in your applications. Each technique is introduced in the following sections and also has a dedicated chapter later in the book.

Embedded SQL

Embedded SQL involves placing SQL statements directly into a program's source code. The application that contains the embedded SQL is called the *host program,* and the language in which the application is written (such as C) is called the *host language.* You design and code your C application in essentially the same manner as other applications you've written. To access the Oracle system, you place SQL statements into your application.

Your C compiler doesn't understand SQL and wouldn't be able to compile the source-code modules successfully. Therefore, the source code must be preprocessed using the Pro*C precompiler. The precompiler translates the embedded statements into Oracle run-time library calls, or function calls, that can be handled by the C compiler (given a set of include files for the function specifications and a set of libraries to resolve the function calls). You can see that using embedded SQL adds a step to the normal process of developing C applications.

Figure 2-2 shows the steps involved in creating an embedded SQL program. The next sections step you through the process.

Editing the Source Code

You edit the C source code to add the embedded SQL statements. You can place embedded SQL statements almost anywhere within your C program (though the application's database interface is often placed in a well-defined layer in structured systems). You can mix C statements and SQL statements in the same functions and can also reference the C program's variables directly from the SQL statements. However, you must keep the following requirements in mind.

To use embedded SQL statements in your C program, you must tag each one so that the precompiler can locate the code to be preprocessed. To do this, you precede each SQL statement with the EXEC SQL keyword. For example, to change the name of an employee's manager, you would add the following statement to your program:

```
EXEC SQL UPDATE emp SET mgr = "Kyle Russell" WHERE empno = 1234;
```

EXEC tags the statement for the precompiler. The semicolon indicates the end of the SQL statement.

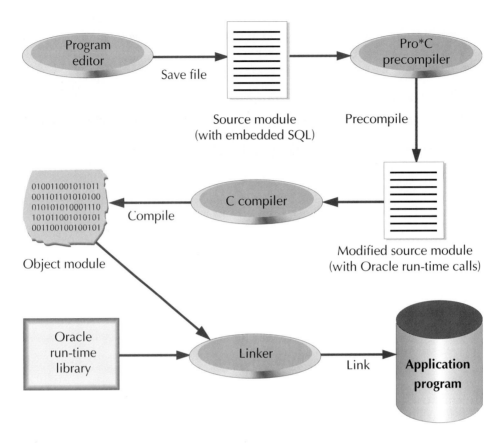

FIGURE 2-2. *Developing an embedded SQL application*

To reference program variables from within an SQL statement, you must prefix the variable name with a colon (:). To reference an integer variable **nEmployee**, for example, you would use **:nEmployee**. To modify the previous example to use a variable rather than hardcoding the employee's ID number, you would use the following code:

```
int nEmployee
nEmployee = 1234;
EXEC SQL UPDATE emp SET mgr = "Kyle Russell" WHERE empno =
    :nEmployee;
```

Precompiling the Source Code

After editing the source files to add the SQL statements, you process each file with the Pro*C precompiler. This precompiler generates a C host language file that replaces the embedded SQL statements with code that can be compiled by a standard C compiler. Pro*C may generate error messages if it encounters problems with the source code. The convention is to use the suffix PC (for *Pro*C*) for the name of the source file. For example, a module could be named DEMO.PC, and the output of the precompiler would then be DEMO.C.

The precompiler translates the embedded SQL into function calls to the Oracle run-time library and/or other C code. It processes statements beginning with EXEC SQL and ignores all other statements. Your original SQL statement will still be visible in the generated C file, but it will be commented out and used for documentation purposes only. You need not be able to read and understand every detail of the generated code, but you at least must be able to recognize the relationship between the source and generated code. An example of the generated code would be

```
/* SQL stmt #19

                EXEC SQL
                DELETE FROM emp
                WHERE CURRENT OF emp_cursor;
*/
{

                sqlstm.stmt = "DELETE FROM EMP WHERE ROWID=:b1";
                sqlstm.iters = (unsigned long  )1;
                sqlstm.offset = (unsigned short)193;
                sqlstm.cud = sqlcud0;
                sqlstm.sqlest = (unsigned char  *)&sqlca;
                sqlstm.sqlety = (unsigned short)0;
                sqlcex(&sqlctx, &sqlstm, &sqlfpn);
}
```

This code is extracted from a C file generated by Pro*C, which has retained the original SQL statement (DELETE) as a comment. The generated code assigns the elements of the **sqlstm** structure (an Oracle C structure), then executes the statement by calling the **sqlcex** function. This function is part of the Oracle run-time library. The precompiler has also generated and used its own variables. Note that the actual generated code may vary among different versions of Oracle and across different platforms.

Compiling the Source Code

The next step is to compile the generated C code with your compiler. This is not a compiler supplied by Oracle; it is whatever compiler you use to build C applications on the target platform. This step produces one or more object modules that must be linked to create the final application executable.

Linking the Application

You must link the application's object modules with the Oracle run-time libraries to create the executable. Again, this step uses the standard linker for the platform on which you are developing. This is not an Oracle-supplied linker; the most important tools you need from Oracle are the Pro*C precompiler and the run-time libraries.

At this point (assuming a successful link), you have created the executable and can run and test the application. Oracle does provide platform-specific makefiles or scripts that tell you which run-time libraries are necessary.

Summary of Embedded SQL

Using embedded SQL statements is one way to add Oracle access to your applications. The major disadvantage is that it requires an additional step—the use of the Pro*C precompiler. Thus, every time you change the source code, you must precompile it before submitting it to the compiler. The advantages are that it's convenient, it's easy to understand the meaning of each embedded statement, and the precompiler translates the SQL statement (as opposed to the OCI method, where *you* have to). Another major advantage is that embedded SQL is standardized and widely used. It's available on all platforms, and the process is essentially the same as for other database vendors. See Chapter 8, The Pro*C Precompiler, for more information on using embedded SQL.

The OCI (Oracle Call Interface)

A second technique for creating an Oracle database application is to use the OCI. Instead of embedding SQL statements into your C program code, you can use a set of API calls to the OCI library. These calls perform exactly the same functions as embedded SQL, but this technique doesn't require the Pro*C precompiler; you just need to link the application with the OCI library, so you save a step in the development process.

The disadvantages are that OCI call usage is not as intuitive as embedded SQL (assuming you're fluent in SQL), and it requires some additional effort to learn the syntax of the OCI calls and to format your code to use the calls. When you create an OCI application, you're responsible for doing some of the work that is done automatically when you use the Pro*C precompiler. Figure 2-3 shows the steps involved in creating an OCI application; the following sections explain the process.

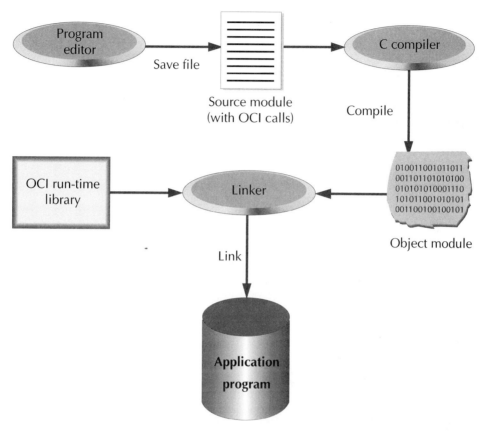

FIGURE 2-3. *Creating an OCI application*

Editing the Source Code

You edit the C source code to add the OCI function calls and other statements to set up OCI data structures. With OCI you must define and use data structures to give the OCI the information it needs to execute a function. The OCI chapter (Chapter 11) will cover the details of these structures. Basically, these structures track the session information and are used to move data and code between the database and the application. You can place OCI calls almost anywhere within your C program, just as you would calls to any other run-time libraries. OCI calls include functions such as **oopen**, **oparse**, and **obndrn**.

In the application, you must connect to Oracle, open cursors as required, process SQL statements, close the cursors, and finally disconnect from Oracle. The following is a code excerpt, limited for simplicity, from an OCI application; Chapter 11, which is dedicated to OCI, provides a complete example and all the details.

```
SetupUpdate(szUpdate)
if (oopen(DML_CURS, LDA, (char far *)0, -1, -1,
    (char far *)0, -1))
{
    /* place error-handling code here */
    return rc;
}
if (oparse(DML_CURS, (char far *)szUpdate, -1))
{
    /* place error-handling code here */
    return rc;
}
if (obndrv(DML_CURS, (char far *)":rid_row", -1,
        (char far *)&((SEL_CURS)->rid), 14, ROWID,
        -1, (short far *)0, (char far *)0, -1, -1))
{
    /* place error-handling code here */
    return rc;
}
if (obndrv(DML_CURS, (char far *)":nEmployee", -1,
        (char far *)emp_empno, sizeof(emp_empno),
        NULLTERM, -1, (short far *) &ind_emp_empno,
        (char far *)0, -1, -1))
{
    /* place error-handling code here */
    return rc;
}
```

In this example, the **oopen** function opens a cursor for the UPDATE that follows. If the **oopen** was successful, the **oparse** function parses the UPDATE SQL statement. The first **obndrv** function binds the host variable **:rid_row** to the rowid in the cursor used for the SELECT statement. The next **obndrv** function binds the columns in the EMP table to their respective host variables where the updated data resides.

Compiling the Source Code

The next step is to compile the C code with your standard compiler. This would be the same compiler that you use to build other C applications on the target platform.

This step will produce one or more object modules that must be linked to create the final application executable.

Linking the Application

You must link the application's object modules with the Oracle run-time libraries to create the executable. Again, this step uses the standard linker for the platform on which you are developing. Oracle provides the platform-specific makefiles or scripts, listing the necessary libraries. At this point (assuming a successful link), you will have created the executable and can run and test the application.

Summary of OCI

Using OCI calls is one way to add Oracle access to your applications. The major disadvantage is that it requires additional effort to learn the OCI calls, procedures for setting up the data structures, and other details. OCI is Oracle-specific and is not available from other database vendors; the advantage is that it avoids the use of the precompiler required for embedded SQL.

PL/SQL (Procedural Language Extensions to SQL)

PL/SQL is Oracle's SQL extension that adds procedural constructs, variables, and other features. Earlier you learned that SQL is a nonprocedural language that must be used with a standard procedural language (such as C). SQL also uses the host language's variables. Oracle's extensions add both features, along with more robust error handling, to PL/SQL. This makes PL/SQL a more complete language than SQL (though SQL was never intended to be more than a sublanguage). You can create blocks of code using PL/SQL statements, then embed these blocks into your applications to improve performance over embedded SQL. A block of PL/SQL is sent to the server and executed as a unit, rather than a line at a time (as is the case with embedded SQL). This reduces the network load and results in better processing.

Because PL/SQL was designed by Oracle, it provides better integration with the Oracle system than is possible with the ANSI version of SQL. The process of creating a PL/SQL program is essentially the same as creating an embedded SQL program.

You can create procedures and functions in PL/SQL that combine multiple SQL statements with procedural processing. These procedures and functions can be called by your application program, reducing the number of calls to the Oracle database.

You can create and store PL/SQL packages—which contain procedures and functions—in the Oracle database, where they can be reused by multiple application programs. These packages and their contents (data, procedures, and functions) can be standardized for reuse. Packages can also use stored procedures and functions to enforce data integrity for all applications that access the same database. This eliminates the need for the application developer to build data integrity processing into each application program that accesses the database.

Editing the Source Code

One of the uses of PL/SQL is to include blocks of PL/SQL in your embedded SQL. In this case, you edit the C source code to add the embedded SQL statements. The blocks are labeled with the BEGIN and END statements (as in Pascal). An example of a PL/SQL block is

```
EXEC SQL EXECUTE
    DECLARE
        dAmount NUMBER(9,2);
    BEGIN
        SELECT total INTO dAmount FROM  payment
            WHERE id = :nAccount;
        UPDATE account SET balance =  balance - dAmount
            WHERE id = :nAccount;
    END;
END-EXEC;
```

In this example, the SQL statements and one variable are in the block.

Precompiling the Source Code

After editing the source files to add the SQL statements, you process the file with the Pro*C precompiler to generate the C code. The precompiler translates the embedded SQL into function calls to the Oracle run-time library and/or other C code.

Compiling the Source Code

The next step is to compile the generated C code with the compiler you use to build C applications on the target platform. This step produces one or more object modules that must be linked to create the final application executable.

Linking the Application

Finally, you link the application's object modules with the Oracle run-time libraries to create the executable. Oracle provides the required makefiles (or scripts) and include files.

Other PL/SQL Programs

You can also use PL/SQL outside an application to create stored procedures (or functions), triggers, and packages. These objects are compiled and stored in the database (this process is covered in Chapter 9, PL/SQL—The Procedural Data

Language). Once in the database, your application can execute these PL/SQL programs by making a call to the database.

Summary of PL/SQL

PL/SQL is another way to add Oracle access to your applications. The major disadvantage is that it is not a standard language and is specific to Oracle. The advantages are improved performance and tighter integration with the Oracle system.

CHAPTER 3

The C Application Program

In this chapter we will begin to explore how you can construct an application program using the elements of the Oracle development tools discussed in the previous chapter. For illustrative purposes, a working application program is provided with this book. This sample application program is constructed of various modules, each containing elements of a real application program. The key elements of this example are explained to help you understand the program's content and purpose. The key elements of this sample program are

- Program variables
- Include files

- Connecting to the database
- Embedded SQL
- Transaction processing
- Error processing

Before examining the details of each of these program elements, let's discuss the general format of a typical application program.

Format of a C Application Program

All C application programs consist of one or more functions. Each program function provides a specific service that is combined with the services of other functions to accomplish the overall processing of the application program.

Every C application program must contain a **main** function, the first function invoked when the program begins execution. In a well-designed application program, the **main** function contains what is essentially an outline of the processing that occurs in the overall program. This outline appears as a set of processing statements and function calls, which in turn perform a major service for the application program. Each function may also appear as an outline of processing for the service that the function provides. The function outline also appears as a set of processing statements and function calls. When the processing of all the statements and functions is complete, the application can terminate execution.

Generally, a C application program consists of the following elements:

- C include files
- Global and static variable declarations
- Main and subfunction definitions
- Function-specific variable declarations
- Program-processing statements
- Function calls
- Program end

The following listing shows how these C program elements can be constructed into an application program.

```
C include files
global variable declarations
static variable declarations

<return-datatype> main (parameter list)
    {
    local variable declarations

    program processing statements
    ...
    function call (func1)
    program processing statements
    ...
    function call (funcn)
    ...
    return (return-datatype)
    }

<return-datatype> func1(parameter list)
    {
    local variable declarations

    program processing statements
    ...
    function call (funcx)
    ...
    return (return-datatype)
    }

<return-datatype> funcn(parameter list)
    {
    local variable declarations

    program processing statements
    ...
    function call (funcy)
    ...
    return (return-datatype)
    }
```

An application program that accesses an Oracle database follows the same general format as a C application program, but it consists of several additional elements:

- Oracle include files

- Oracle-specific variable declarations

- Database connection statements

- Embedded SQL statements

- Transaction-processing statements

- Error-processing statements

The following listing shows how these program elements are added to the general format of a C application program (Oracle program elements are in **boldface**).

```
C include files
Oracle include files
global variable declarations
static variable declarations
Oracle global variable declarations
Oracle static variable declarations

<return-datatype> main (parameter list)
    {
    local variable declarations
    Oracle variable declarations

    program processing statements
    ...
    embedded SQL statements
    error processing statements
    ...
    transaction processing statements
    ...
    function call (func1)
    ...
    program processing statements
    ...
    embedded SQL statements
    error processing statements
    ...
```

```
transaction processing statements
...
function call (funcn)
...
embedded SQL statements
error processing statements
return (return-datatype)
}


<return-datatype> func1(parameter list)
    {
    local variable declarations
    Oracle variable declarations
    ...
    program processing statements
    ...
    embedded SQL statements
    error processing statements
    ...
    transaction processing statements
    function call (funcx)
    ...
    embedded SQL statements
    error processing statements
    return (return-datatype)
    }


<return-datatype> funcn(parameter list)
    {
    local variable declarations

    program processing statements
    ...
    function call (funcy)
    return (return-datatype)
    }
```

As this listing shows, the same general format applies to both C and Oracle application programs. When access to an Oracle database is required, just add the necessary statements as outlined earlier. These statements will perform such actions as connecting to the database, accessing data, and committing transactions. Now let's take a look at a sample application program that illustrates each of these program elements.

Sample Application Program

The sample application program contained on the diskette available for this book is a Windows-based application; Figure 3-1 shows its initial window.

Windows-based applications use a programming paradigm called *event-driven programming*, so called because the program responds to the events that are triggered when the user selects a menu option, clicks a command button, and so on. The program is constructed by placing program statements or function calls in the sections of the program that are executed when an event is triggered. For example, when the Connect menu entry is selected, the Connect menu event is triggered and the Database Logon window is displayed and processed (see Figure 3-2).

The application program is also constructed using *modular programming* techniques. Logically related functions and other programming elements that provide services for a common area of the application program are organized into separate source-code modules. For example, the functions and program elements necessary to process the main window and the Employee Record window are organized into different source modules. The main window processing is in the EXAMPLES source module, and the employee window processing is in the EMPLOYEE source module.

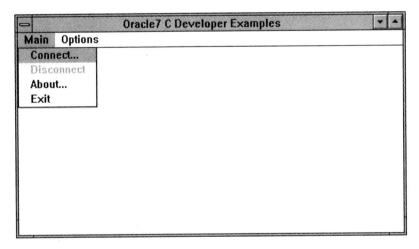

FIGURE 3-1. *Sample application's main window*

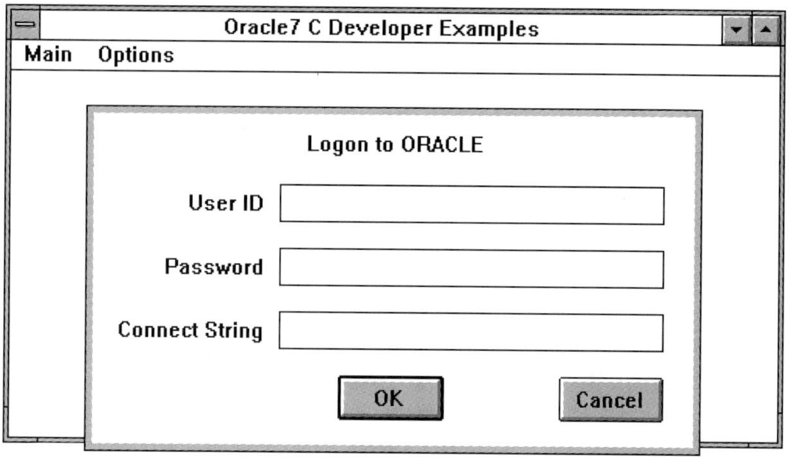

FIGURE 3-2. *Database Logon response window*

The following sample program illustrates the basic elements of an Oracle database application program. It allows the user to perform the following operations:

■ Connect to the Oracle database

■ Disconnect from the Oracle database

■ Exit the program

Examine the listing and note the elements in **boldface**; these are required to access the Oracle database. The full listing is in the EXAMPLES.PC source module.

```
/* Main Window listing */
#include <windows.h>
#include "examples.h"
#include "examprot.h"
#include <string.h>
#include "sqlproto.h"
/*
*********************************************************************
**              Pro*C Declaration Section - Module Scope
*********************************************************************
```

```
**    The Pro*C DECLARE section cannot contain 'C' typedefs or macro
**    facilities.
**********************************************************************
*/
EXEC SQL BEGIN DECLARE SECTION;
    /*
    ** Host variables for logging into the Oracle database.
    */
    VARCHAR vcConnect[21];
    VARCHAR vcPassword[21];
    VARCHAR vcUserId[41];
EXEC SQL END DECLARE SECTION;

/*
** Include the SQLCA and SQLDA structures necessary for Pro*C
** processing.
*/

EXEC SQL INCLUDE SQLCA.H;
EXEC SQL INCLUDE SQLDA.H;
extern SQLDA *sqlald();
Database_status zDbStatus;

/*
** Declare Windows resource variables.
*/
char scAbout[MAX_ABOUT_STRING + 1];
char scAppName[MAX_APPNAME_STRING + 1];
char scMainMenu[MAX_MAIN_MENU_STRING + 1];
char scTitle[MAX_TITLE_STRING + 1];

static HANDLE hInst;
HWND hWndMain;

/*
** Declare the Main Window processing callback.
*/
#ifdef __BORLANDC__
#pragma warn -par
#pragma warn -aus
LRESULT CALLBACK MainWndProc(HWND, UINT, WPARAM, LPARAM);
#else
```

```
long FAR PASCAL MainWndProc(HWND, unsigned, WORD, LONG);
#endif


/*
************************************************************************
** WinMain - Main function for the example application.
**
** Description:
**
**     This function is the main entry point invoked from windows
**     when the application is executed.
**
** Parameters:
**
**     hInstance              INPUT
**         Application instance handle.
**
**     hPrevInstance          INPUT
**         Application instance handle of an existing application
**         instance. (The application is already running.)
**
**     lpscCmdLine            INPUT
**         Window dialog command message.
**
**     iShowCmd               INPUT
**         Show command.
**
** Return:
**
**     Function Status
**         Function status.  Possible values:
**
**             TRUE  - The function completed correctly.
**             FALSE - The function encountered an error.
**
************************************************************************
*/
int PASCAL WinMain(HANDLE hInstance, HANDLE hPrevInstance,
   LPSTR lpscCmdLine, int iShowCmd)
{
   HMENU hMainMenu;
   HWND  hWnd;
```

```
MSG     msgMessage;

/*
** If a previous instance of the application is running, return an
** abnormal end to the application.
*/

if (hPrevInstance)
   return( FALSE );

/*
** Initialize the application. If the initialization fails,
** end the application abnormally.
*/
if (!ExampleInit(hInstance))
   return( FALSE );

/*
** Initialize the database connection status structure.
*/

zDbStatus.bConnected = FALSE;
zDbStatus.bOpened = FALSE;

/*
** Assign the application instance handle to the global
** variable so that it is accessible throughout the application.
*/

hInst = hInstance;

/*
** Load and assign the main menu.
*/

hMainMenu = LoadMenu(hInst, "MAINMENU");

/*
** Create the main window instance. Show the window and process
** events from the window.
*/
```

```
    hWndMain = hWnd = CreateWindow((LPSTR)scAppName, (LPSTR)scTitle,
        WS_OVERLAPPEDWINDOW, CW_USEDEFAULT, CW_USEDEFAULT,
        CW_USEDEFAULT, CW_USEDEFAULT, (HWND)NULL, (HMENU)NULL,
        (HANDLE)hInst, (LPSTR)NULL);

    ShowWindow(hWnd, SW_SHOWNORMAL);
    UpdateWindow(hWnd);

    while (GetMessage((LPMSG)&msgMessage, NULL, 0, 0))
        {
        TranslateMessage((LPMSG)&msgMessage);
        DispatchMessage((LPMSG)&msgMessage);
        }

    return((int)msgMessage.wParam);
}


/*
************************************************************************
** MainWndProc - Process the command dialog for the Main window.
**
** Description:
**
**      This function is used to process the command dialog
**      for the Main window.
**
** Parameters:
**
**      hWnd        INPUT
**          Window handle.
**
**      uiMessage   INPUT
**          Window dialog command message.
**
**      wParam      INPUT
**          Window parameter.
**
**      lParam      INPUT
**          Window parameter.
**
** Return:
**
```

```
**      bDialogStatus
**          Dialog status.   Possible values:
**
**              TRUE  - A command was processed.
**              FALSE - The default was processed.
**
*************************************************************************
*/
#ifdef __BORLANDC__
LRESULT CALLBACK MainWndProc(HWND hWnd, UINT uiMessage,
    WPARAM wParam, LPARAM lParam)
#else
long FAR PASCAL MainWndProc(HWND hWnd, unsigned uiMessage,
    WORD wParam, LONG lParam)
#endif
{
    static HWND hInst;
    HMENU hMainMenu;

    /*
    ** Process the event message passed in from the main window.
    */

    switch (uiMessage)
        {
        /* Window create event. */
        case WM_CREATE :
            hInst = ((LPCREATESTRUCT) lParam)->hInstance;
            return (TRUE);

        /* Only process menu commands from the main window. */
        case WM_COMMAND :
            if (LOWORD(lParam) == 0) /* Message is from a menu. */
                {
                switch (wParam)
                    {
                    /* Process the Connect menu command. */
                    case IDM_MAIN_CONNECT :
                        if (LogonProc(hInst, hWnd) == TRUE)
                            {
                            hMainMenu = GetMenu(hWnd);
                            EnableMenuItem(hMainMenu, IDM_MAIN_CONNECT,
```

```
            MF_GRAYED);
        EnableMenuItem(hMainMenu, IDM_MAIN_DISCONNECT,
            MF_ENABLED);
        EnableMenuItem(hMainMenu, IDM_MAIN_ABOUT,
            MF_ENABLED);
        EnableMenuItem(hMainMenu, IDM_MAIN_EXIT,
            MF_ENABLED);
        }

    return(TRUE);

/* Process the Disconnect menu command. */
case IDM_MAIN_DISCONNECT :
    if (DisconnectProc(hWnd) == TRUE)
        {
        hMainMenu = GetMenu(hWnd);
        EnableMenuItem(hMainMenu, IDM_MAIN_CONNECT,
            MF_ENABLED);
        EnableMenuItem(hMainMenu, IDM_MAIN_DISCONNECT,
            MF_GRAYED);
        EnableMenuItem(hMainMenu, IDM_MAIN_ABOUT,
            MF_ENABLED);
        EnableMenuItem(hMainMenu, IDM_MAIN_EXIT,
            MF_ENABLED);
        }
    return(TRUE);

/* Process the About window. */
case IDM_MAIN_ABOUT:
    AboutProc(hInst, hWnd);
    return(TRUE);

/*
** Process the Exit command by executing the
** Close command.
*/
case IDM_MAIN_EXIT :
    SendMessage(hWnd, WM_CLOSE, 0, 0L);
    return(TRUE);

/*
** Process the Employee menu entry.
```

```
                            */
                    case IDM_EXAMPLE_EMPLOYEE :
                        EmployeeProc(hInst,  hWnd);
                        return(TRUE);


                    ...


                    default :
                        break;
                    }
                }
            break;

        /* Process the Close application command. */
        case WM_CLOSE :
            /* Disconnect before ending the application. */
            if (zDbStatus.bConnected)
                DisconnectProc(hWnd);

            break; /* Break here so default operation can occur. */

        case WM_DESTROY :
            PostQuitMessage(0);
            break;

        default:
            break;
        }


    /*
    ** Perform default command processing.
    */

    return(DefWindowProc(hWnd, uiMessage, wParam, lParam));
}


/*
**************************************************************************
** LogonProc - Process the Logon window.
**
** Description:
**
```

```
**      This function is used to display and process the Logon window.
**
** Parameters:
**
**      hInst       INPUT
**          Application instance handle.
**
**      hWnd        INPUT
**          Window handle.
**
** Return:
**
**      iStatus
**          Dialog status.   Possible values:
**
**              TRUE  - A window processed without error.
**              FALSE - An error occurred in the window.
**
**************************************************************************
*/
int LogonProc(HANDLE hInst, HWND hWnd)
{
    FARPROC lpprocLogon;
    /*
    ** Check to see if the database is already connected.
    */

    if (zDbStatus.bConnected)
        return(TRUE);

    /*
    ** Create the Logon window instance.
    */

    lpprocLogon = MakeProcInstance(LogonWndProc, hInst);

    /*
    ** Continue to retry the Logon until CANCELed or successful.
    */

    while (!zDbStatus.bConnected)
        {
```

```
/*
** Open the Logon window.
**
** If the Cancel button is pushed, break out of the while loop.
** Otherwise attempt to log on to the database.
*/

if (DialogBox(hInst, MAKEINTRESOURCE(LOGONBOX), hWnd,
    lpprocLogon) == 0)
    break;

/*
** Set the length of the input strings.
*/

vcUserId.len = strlen(vcUserId.arr);
vcPassword.len = strlen(vcPassword.arr);
vcConnect.len = strlen(vcConnect.arr);

/*
** Execute the Pro*C CONNECT statement...
**     one of several possible forms.
*/

EXEC SQL CONNECT :vcUserId
    IDENTIFIED BY :vcPassword
    USING :vcConnect;

/*
** Process the results of the CONNECT statement.
*/

if (!ProcErrorCode(hWnd))
    {
    if (MessageBox(hWnd, "Retry Logon to Database?", "Oracle",
        MB_RETRYCANCEL) != IDRETRY)
        break;
    }
else
    {
    MessageBox(hWnd, "Logon Successful!", "Oracle", MB_OK);
    zDbStatus.bConnected = TRUE;
```

```
            }
        }

    FreeProcInstance(lpprocLogon);
    return(zDbStatus.bConnected);
}


/*
***************************************************************************
** LogonWndProc - Process the command dialog for the Logon window.
**
** Description:
**
**     This function is used to process the command dialog
**     for the Logon window.
**
** Parameters:
**
**     hWnd        INPUT
**         Window handle.
**
**     uiMessage   INPUT
**         Window dialog command message.
**
**     wParam      INPUT
**         Window parameter.
**
**     lParam      INPUT
**         Window parameter.
**
** Return:
**
**     bDialogStatus
**         Dialog status.  Possible values:
**
**             TRUE  - A command was processed.
**             FALSE - The default was processed.
**
***************************************************************************
*/
#ifdef __BORLANDC__
BOOL CALLBACK LogonWndProc(HWND hWnd, UINT uiMessage,
```

```
      WPARAM wParam, LPARAM lParam)
#else
BOOL FAR PASCAL LogonWndProc(HWND hWnd, unsigned uiMessage,
    WORD wParam, LONG lParam)
#endif
{
    /*
    ** Process the event message from the Logon window.
    */

    switch (uiMessage)
        {
        /* Process the command from the window event. */
        case WM_COMMAND :
            switch (wParam)
                {
                /* Process the Logon OK command button. */
                case ID_LOGON_OK :
                    GetDlgItemText(hWnd, ID_LOGON_USERID,
                        (LPSTR)vcUserId.arr, MAX_USERID);

                    GetDlgItemText(hWnd, ID_LOGON_PASSWORD,
                        (LPSTR)vcPassword.arr, MAX_PASSWORD);

                    GetDlgItemText(hWnd, ID_LOGON_CONNECT,
                        (LPSTR)vcConnect.arr, MAX_CONNECT);

                    EndDialog(hWnd, 1);
                    return(TRUE);

                /* Process the Logon Cancel command button. */
                case ID_LOGON_CANCEL :
                    EndDialog(hWnd, 0);
                    return(TRUE);

                default :
                    break;
                }

            break;

        case WM_INITDIALOG :
```

```
                    return(TRUE);

            default :
                return(FALSE);
            }

        return(FALSE);
}



/*
****************************************************************************
** DisconnectProc - Process the disconnect.
**
** Description:
**
**     This function is used to process the disconnect.
**
** Parameters:
**
**     hInst      INPUT
**         Application instance handle.
**
**     hWnd       INPUT
**         Window handle.
**
** Return:
**
**     iStatus
**         Dialog status.  Possible values:
**
**             TRUE  - A window processed without error.
**             FALSE - An error occurred in the window.
**
****************************************************************************
*/
int DisconnectProc(HWND hWnd)
{
    /*
    ** Check to see if the database is already disconnected.
    */
```

```
    if (!zDbStatus.bConnected)
       return(TRUE);


   /*
   ** Commit any open transaction and release the
   ** current connection.
   */

   EXEC SQL COMMIT WORK RELEASE;

   /*
   ** Process the results of the COMMIT statement.
   */

   if (ProcErrorCode(hWnd))
      {
      MessageBox(hWnd, "Disconnect Successful!", "Oracle", MB_OK);
      zDbStatus.bConnected = FALSE;
      }

   /*
   ** Return the status of the disconnect process.
   */

  return((zDbStatus.bConnected == FALSE) ? TRUE : FALSE);
}

/*
***********************************************************************
** ProcErrorCode - Process database errors and display
**                 error messages.
**
** Description:
**
**    This function is used to process and display errors
**    returned from database operations. This function
**    should be called after each database operation.
**
** Parameters:
**
**    hWnd        INPUT
**        Window handle.
```

```
**
** Return:
**
**     bErrorStatus
**         Error code status.   Possible values:
**
**             TRUE  - No error was processed.
**             FALSE - An error was processed.
**
** ********************************************************************
*/
BOOL ProcErrorCode(HWND hWnd)
{
    /*
    ** Check the SQLCA structure for a database error.
    ** Database errors are less than zero.
    */

    if (sqlca.sqlcode < 0)
       {
       MessageBox(hWnd, sqlca.sqlerrm.sqlerrmc, "Database Error", MB_OK);
       return(FALSE);
       }

    return(TRUE);
}
```

This module only processes the main window; the following listing processes the Employee Record window (see Figure 3-3). This window is displayed when the Options | Employees menu entry is selected.

The following listing allows the user to perform several operations:

- Insert employee records into the database

- Select the employee records from the database

- Update employee records

- Delete employee records

- Commit and roll back changes to the database

For a complete listing, see the EMPLOYEE.PC source module.

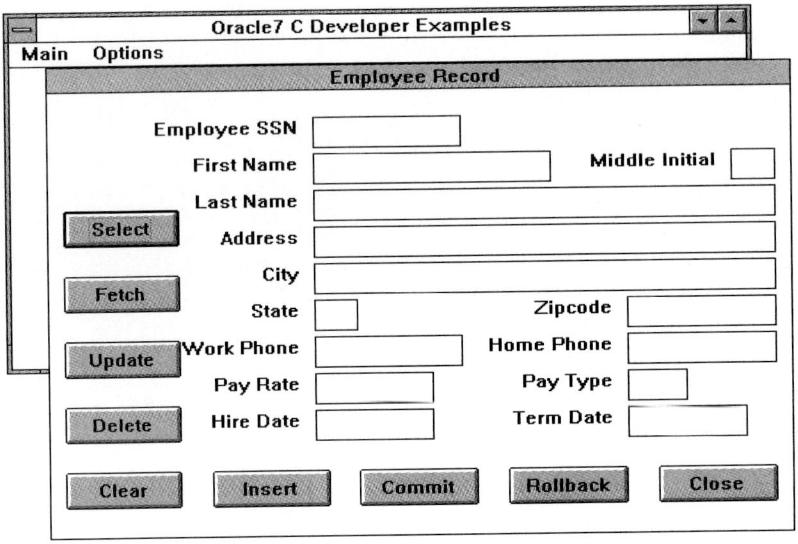

FIGURE 3-3. *Employee Record window*

```
/* Employee Record listing */
#include <windows.h>
#include "examples.h"
#include "examprot.h"
#include <string.h>
#include "sqlproto.h"


/*
**********************************************************************
**          Pro*C Declaration Section - Module Scope
**********************************************************************
**    The Pro*C DECLARE section cannot contain 'C' typedefs or macro
**    facilities.
**********************************************************************
*/


EXEC SQL BEGIN DECLARE SECTION;
    /*
    ** Host variables for accessing the EMPLOYEE table.
    */
```

```
        VARCHAR vcEmpSSN[12];
        VARCHAR vcFName[41];
        VARCHAR vcLName[41];
        VARCHAR vcMiddleInit[2];
        VARCHAR vcAddress[41];
        VARCHAR vcCity[41];
        VARCHAR vcState[3];
        VARCHAR vcZipcode[11];
        VARCHAR vcWPhone[13];
        VARCHAR vcHPhone[13];
        VARCHAR vcPayRate[10];
        VARCHAR vcPayType[3];
        VARCHAR vcHireDate[11];
        VARCHAR vcTermDate[11];

        /*
        ** Indicator variables for the host variables defined above.
        */

        short indEmpSSN;
        short indFName;
        short indLName;
        short indMiddleInit;
        short indAddress;
        short indCity;
        short indState;
        short indZipcode;
        short indWPhone;
        short indHPhone;
        short indPayRate;
        short indPayType;
        short indHireDate;
        short indTermDate;

EXEC SQL END DECLARE SECTION;

/*
** Declare the employee cursor for later processing in this module.
*/

EXEC SQL DECLARE employee_cursor CURSOR FOR
    SELECT EMPLOYEE.EMPLOYEE_SSN, EMPLOYEE.FIRST_NAME,
```

```
            EMPLOYEE.MIDDLE_INITIAL,  EMPLOYEE.LAST_NAME,
            EMPLOYEE.ADDRESS,  EMPLOYEE.CITY,
            EMPLOYEE.STATE,  EMPLOYEE.ZIPCODE,  EMPLOYEE.WORK_PHONE,
            EMPLOYEE.HOME_PHONE,  EMPLOYEE.PAY_RATE,  EMPLOYEE.PAY_TYPE,
            EMPLOYEE.HIRE_DATE,  EMPLOYEE.TERMINATION_DATE
    FROM EMPLOYEE
    /*
    ** The "FOR UPDATE OF" clause is necessary so that the
    ** "FOR CURRENT OF" clause can be used with the UPDATE and
    ** DELETE statements.
    */

    FOR UPDATE OF EMPLOYEE.EMPLOYEE_SSN, EMPLOYEE.FIRST_NAME,
            EMPLOYEE.MIDDLE_INITIAL,  EMPLOYEE.LAST_NAME,
            EMPLOYEE.ADDRESS,  EMPLOYEE.CITY,
            EMPLOYEE.STATE,  EMPLOYEE.ZIPCODE,  EMPLOYEE.WORK_PHONE,
            EMPLOYEE.HOME_PHONE,  EMPLOYEE.PAY_RATE,  EMPLOYEE.PAY_TYPE,
            EMPLOYEE.HIRE_DATE,  EMPLOYEE.TERMINATION_DATE;

/*
** Define the SQLCA as an external reference and include
** the SQLCA and SQLDA structures necessary for Pro*C processing.
*/

#define SQLCA_STORAGE_CLASS extern

EXEC SQL INCLUDE SQLCA.H;
EXEC SQL INCLUDE SQLDA.H;
extern SQLDA *sqlald();

/*
** Declare Windows resource variables.
*/

extern Database_status zDbStatus;

/*
****************************************************************************
** EmployeeWndGet - Get the values from the Employee window.
**
** Description:
**
```

```
**      This function is used to get the values from the fields of the
**      Employee window.
**
** Parameters:
**
**      hWnd        INPUT
**          Window handle.
**
** Return:
**
**      None.
**
*****************************************************************************
*/
void EmployeeWndGet(HWND hWnd)
{
    /*
    ** Initialize the indicator variables to zero (0).
    */

    indEmpSSN = indFName = indMiddleInit = indLName = indAddress =
       indCity = indState = indZipcode = indWPhone = indHPhone =
       indPayRate = indPayType = indHireDate = indTermDate = 0;


    /*
    ** Get the values from each field of the Employee window. If the
    ** length of the value returned is zero (0), set the indicator variable
    ** to -1 (NULL).
    */

    if ((vcEmpSSN.len = GetDlgItemText(hWnd, ID_EMPLOYEE_FLD_EMPSSN,
       (LPSTR)vcEmpSSN.arr, 12)) == 0)
       indEmpSSN = -1;

    if ((vcFName.len = GetDlgItemText(hWnd, ID_EMPLOYEE_FLD_FNAME,
       (LPSTR)vcFName.arr, 41)) == 0)
       indFName = -1;

    if ((vcMiddleInit.len = GetDlgItemText(hWnd, ID_EMPLOYEE_FLD_MI,
       (LPSTR)vcMiddleInit.arr, 2)) == 0)
       indMiddleInit = -1;
```

```
if ((vcLName.len = GetDlgItemText(hWnd, ID_EMPLOYEE_FLD_LNAME,
    (LPSTR)vcLName.arr, 41)) == 0)
    indLName = -1;

if ((vcAddress.len = GetDlgItemText(hWnd, ID_EMPLOYEE_FLD_ADDR,
    (LPSTR)vcAddress.arr, 41)) == 0)
    indAddress = -1;

if ((vcCity.len = GetDlgItemText(hWnd, ID_EMPLOYEE_FLD_CITY,
    (LPSTR)vcCity.arr, 41)) == 0)
    indCity = -1;

if ((vcState.len = GetDlgItemText(hWnd, ID_EMPLOYEE_FLD_STATE,
    (LPSTR)vcState.arr, 3)) == 0)
    indState = -1;

if ((vcZipcode.len = GetDlgItemText(hWnd, ID_EMPLOYEE_FLD_ZIPCODE,
    (LPSTR)vcZipcode.arr, 11)) == 0)
    indZipcode = -1;

if ((vcWPhone.len = GetDlgItemText(hWnd, ID_EMPLOYEE_FLD_WPHONE,
    (LPSTR)vcWPhone.arr, 13)) == 0)
    indWPhone = -1;

if ((vcHPhone.len = GetDlgItemText(hWnd, ID_EMPLOYEE_FLD_HPHONE,
    (LPSTR)vcHPhone.arr, 13)) == 0)
    indHPhone = -1;

if ((vcPayRate.len = GetDlgItemText(hWnd, ID_EMPLOYEE_FLD_PAY_RATE,
    (LPSTR)vcPayRate.arr, 11)) == 0)
    indPayRate = -1;

if ((vcPayType.len = GetDlgItemText(hWnd, ID_EMPLOYEE_FLD_PAY_TYPE,
    (LPSTR)vcPayType.arr, 3)) == 0)
    indPayType = -1;

if ((vcHireDate.len = GetDlgItemText(hWnd, ID_EMPLOYEE_FLD_HIRE_DATE,
    (LPSTR)vcHireDate.arr, 11)) == 0)
    indHireDate = -1;

if ((vcTermDate.len = GetDlgItemText(hWnd, ID_EMPLOYEE_FLD_TERM_DATE,
```

```
            (LPSTR)vcTermDate.arr, 11)) == 0)
            indHireDate = -1;


    return;
}


/*
*************************************************************************
** EmployeeWndSet - Set the values in the Employee window.
**
** Description:
**
**      This function is used to set the values in the fields of the
**      Employee window.
**
** Parameters:
**
**      hWnd        INPUT
**          Window handle.
**
** Return:
**
**      None.
**
*************************************************************************
*/
void EmployeeWndSet(HWND hWnd)
{
    /*
    ** NULL terminate each string variable.
    */

    vcEmpSSN.arr[vcEmpSSN.len] = EOS;
    vcFName.arr[vcFName.len] = EOS;
    vcMiddleInit.arr[vcMiddleInit.len] = EOS;
    vcLName.arr[vcLName.len] = EOS;
    vcAddress.arr[vcAddress.len] = EOS;
    vcCity.arr[vcCity.len] = EOS;
    vcState.arr[vcState.len] = EOS;
    vcZipcode.arr[vcZipcode.len] = EOS;
    vcWPhone.arr[vcWPhone.len] = EOS;
    vcHPhone.arr[vcHPhone.len] = EOS;
```

```
    vcPayRate.arr[vcPayRate.len] = EOS;
    vcPayType.arr[vcPayType.len] = EOS;
    vcHireDate.arr[vcHireDate.len] = EOS;
    vcTermDate.arr[vcTermDate.len] = EOS;

    /*
    ** Set the values of each field in the Employee window.
    */

    SetDlgItemText(hWnd, ID_EMPLOYEE_FLD_EMPSSN, (LPSTR)vcEmpSSN.arr);
    SetDlgItemText(hWnd, ID_EMPLOYEE_FLD_FNAME, (LPSTR)vcFName.arr);
    SetDlgItemText(hWnd, ID_EMPLOYEE_FLD_MI, (LPSTR)vcMiddleInit.arr);
    SetDlgItemText(hWnd, ID_EMPLOYEE_FLD_LNAME, (LPSTR)vcLName.arr);
    SetDlgItemText(hWnd, ID_EMPLOYEE_FLD_ADDR, (LPSTR)vcAddress.arr);
    SetDlgItemText(hWnd, ID_EMPLOYEE_FLD_CITY, (LPSTR)vcCity.arr);
    SetDlgItemText(hWnd, ID_EMPLOYEE_FLD_STATE, (LPSTR)vcState.arr);
    SetDlgItemText(hWnd, ID_EMPLOYEE_FLD_ZIPCODE, (LPSTR)vcZipcode.arr);
    SetDlgItemText(hWnd, ID_EMPLOYEE_FLD_WPHONE, (LPSTR)vcWPhone.arr);
    SetDlgItemText(hWnd, ID_EMPLOYEE_FLD_HPHONE, (LPSTR)vcHPhone.arr);
    SetDlgItemText(hWnd, ID_EMPLOYEE_FLD_PAY_RATE, (LPSTR)vcPayRate.arr);
    SetDlgItemText(hWnd, ID_EMPLOYEE_FLD_PAY_TYPE, (LPSTR)vcPayType.arr);
    SetDlgItemText(hWnd, ID_EMPLOYEE_FLD_HIRE_DATE, (LPSTR)vcHireDate.arr);
    SetDlgItemText(hWnd, ID_EMPLOYEE_FLD_TERM_DATE, (LPSTR)vcTermDate.arr);

    return;
}


/*
***********************************************************************
** EmployeeWndClear - Clear the values in the Employee window.
**
** Description:
**
**    This function is used to clear the values in the fields of the
**    Employee window.
**
** Parameters:
**
**    hWnd        INPUT
**        Window handle.
**
** Return:
```

```
**
**      None.
**
*************************************************************************
*/
void EmployeeWndClear(HWND hWnd)
{
    /*
    ** Set the length of each string variable to zero (0).
    */

    vcEmpSSN.len = 0;
    vcFName.len = 0;
    vcMiddleInit.len = 0;
    vcLName.len = 0;
    vcAddress.len = 0;
    vcCity.len = 0;
    vcState.len = 0;
    vcZipcode.len = 0;
    vcWPhone.len = 0;
    vcHPhone.len = 0;
    vcPayRate.len = 0;
    vcPayType.len = 0;
    vcHireDate.len = 0;
    vcTermDate.len = 0;

    /*
    ** Set the Employee window fields.
    */

    EmployeeWndSet(hWnd);

    return;
}

/*
*************************************************************************
** EmployeeWndProc - Process the command dialog for the Employee
**                   window.
**
** Description:
**
```

```
**      This function is used to process the command dialog
**      for the Employee window.
**
** Parameters:
**
**      hWnd         INPUT
**         Window handle.
**
**      uiMessage  INPUT
**         Window dialog command message.
**
**      wParam       INPUT
**         Window parameter.
**
**      lParam       INPUT
**         Window parameter.
**
** Return:
**
**      bDialogStatus
**         Dialog status.   Possible values:
**
**             TRUE  - A command was processed.
**             FALSE - The default was processed.
**
*************************************************************************
*/
#ifdef __BORLANDC__
BOOL CALLBACK EmployeeWndProc(HWND hWnd, UINT uiMessage,
    WPARAM wParam, LPARAM lParam)
#else
BOOL FAR PASCAL EmployeeWndProc(HWND hWnd, unsigned uiMessage,
   WORD wParam, LONG lParam)
#endif
{
   BOOL bReturn = TRUE;

   /*
   ** Process the event message from the Employee window.
   */

   switch (uiMessage)
```

```
{
/* Process the command from the window event. */
case WM_COMMAND :
    switch (wParam)
        {
        /* Process the Close command button. */
        case ID_EMPLOYEE_CLOSE :
            EndDialog(hWnd, 1);
            break;

        /* Process the Select command button. */
        case ID_EMPLOYEE_SELECT :

          /*
          ** Check the cursor open status.
          ** If it is open, close it, then reopen.
          */

          if (zDbStatus.bOpened)
             EXEC SQL CLOSE employee_cursor;

          EXEC SQL OPEN employee_cursor;

          /*
          ** Process the error from the OPEN command.
          ** If an error occurred, skip the following processing.
          ** Otherwise, drop into the FETCH processing to
          ** retrieve the data.
          */

          if (!ProcErrorCode(hWnd))
             break;

          zDbStatus.bOpened = TRUE;

        case ID_EMPLOYEE_FETCH :
          /*
          ** Check the cursor open status.
          ** If it is not open, report an error.
          */

          if (!zDbStatus.bOpened)
```

```
        {
        MessageBox(hWnd, "Cursor not open, no active set!",
            "Oracle", MB_OK);
        break;
        }

/*
** FETCH the data from the cursor into the host
** variables.
*/

EXEC SQL FETCH employee_cursor
    INTO :vcEmpSSN:indEmpSSN,
        :vcFName:indFName,
        :vcMiddleInit:indMiddleInit,
        :vcLName:indLName,
        :vcAddress:indAddress,
        :vcCity:indCity,
        :vcState:indState,

        :vcZipcode:indZipcode,
        :vcWPhone:indWPhone,
        :vcHPhone:indHPhone,
        :vcPayRate:indPayRate,
        :vcPayType:indPayType,
        :vcHireDate:indHireDate,
        :vcTermDate:indTermDate;
/*
** Check the SQLCA for no more data in the active set.
*/
if (sqlca.sqlcode == 1403)
    {
    MessageBox(hWnd, "No data left in the active set!",
        "Oracle", MB_OK);
    break;
    }

/*
** Process the error code. If no error is encountered,
** set the values in the Employee window.
*/
if (ProcErrorCode (hWnd))
```

```
        EmployeeWndSet(hWnd);
    break;

/* Process the Insert command button. */
case ID_EMPLOYEE_INSERT :

  /*
  ** Get the values from the Employee window.
  */

  EmployeeWndGet(hWnd);

  /*
  ** Insert the values from the Employee window into
  ** the database.
  */

  EXEC SQL INSERT INTO EMPLOYEE
      (EMPLOYEE.EMPLOYEE_SSN, EMPLOYEE.FIRST_NAME,
       EMPLOYEE.MIDDLE_INITIAL, EMPLOYEE.LAST_NAME,
       EMPLOYEE.ADDRESS, EMPLOYEE.CITY,
       EMPLOYEE.STATE, EMPLOYEE.ZIPCODE, EMPLOYEE.WORK_PHONE,
       EMPLOYEE.HOME_PHONE, EMPLOYEE.PAY_RATE,
       EMPLOYEE.PAY_TYPE,
       EMPLOYEE.HIRE_DATE, EMPLOYEE.TERMINATION_DATE)
  VALUES (:vcEmpSSN:indEmpSSN,
          :vcFName:indFName,
          :vcMiddleInit:indMiddleInit,
          :vcLName:indLName,
          :vcAddress:indAddress,
          :vcCity:indCity,
          :vcState:indState,
          :vcZipcode:indZipcode,
          :vcWPhone:indWPhone,
          :vcHPhone:indHPhone,
          :vcPayRate:indPayRate,
          :vcPayType:indPayType,
          :vcHireDate:indHireDate,
          :vcTermDate:indTermDate);

  /*
  ** Process the error code.
```

```
        */

      ProcErrorCode(hWnd);
    break;

/* Process the Update command button. */
case ID_EMPLOYEE_UPDATE :
    /*
    ** Check the cursor open status.
    ** If it is not open, report an error.
    */

    if (!zDbStatus.bOpened)
       {
       MessageBox(hWnd, "Cursor not open, no active set!",
          "Oracle", MB_OK);
       break;
       }

    /*
    ** Get the values from the Employee window.
    */

    EmployeeWndGet(hWnd);

    /*
    ** Update the values from the Employee window in
    ** the database.
    */

    EXEC SQL UPDATE EMPLOYEE
       SET EMPLOYEE_SSN = :vcEmpSSN:indEmpSSN,
          FIRST_NAME = :vcFName:indFName,
          MIDDLE_INITIAL = :vcMiddleInit:indMiddleInit,
          LAST_NAME = :vcLName:indLName,
          ADDRESS = :vcAddress:indAddress,
          CITY = :vcCity:indCity,
          STATE = :vcState:indState,
          ZIPCODE = :vcZipcode:indZipcode,
          WORK_PHONE = :vcWPhone:indWPhone,
          HOME_PHONE = :vcHPhone:indHPhone,
          PAY_RATE = :vcPayRate:indPayRate,
```

```
              PAY_TYPE = :vcPayType:indPayType,
              HIRE_DATE = :vcHireDate:indHireDate,
          TERMINATION_DATE = :vcTermDate:indTermDate
      WHERE CURRENT OF employee_cursor;


  /*
  ** Process the error code.
  */

  ProcErrorCode(hWnd);
  break;

/* Process the Delete command button. */
case ID_EMPLOYEE_DELETE :
  /*
  ** Check the cursor open status.
  ** If it is not open, report an error.
  */

  if (!zDbStatus.bOpened)
     {
     MessageBox(hWnd, "Cursor not open, no active set!",
        "Oracle", MB_OK);
     break;
     }

  /*
  ** Delete the current record from the employee cursor.
  */

  EXEC SQL DELETE FROM EMPLOYEE
      WHERE CURRENT OF employee_cursor;

  /*
  ** Process the error code.
  */

  if (ProcErrorCode(hWnd))
     EmployeeWndClear(hWnd);
  break;

/* Process the Clear command button. */
```

```
        case ID_EMPLOYEE_CLEAR :
           EmployeeWndClear(hWnd);
           break;

        /* Process the Commit and Rollback command button. */
        case ID_EMPLOYEE_COMMIT :
        case ID_EMPLOYEE_ROLLBACK :

          if (wParam = ID_EMPLOYEE_COMMIT)
             EXEC SQL COMMIT WORK;
          else
             EXEC SQL ROLLBACK WORK;

          /*
          ** The COMMIT and ROLLBACK operations release all locks,
          ** so the employee cursor should be closed.
          */

          if (zDbStatus.bOpened) then
             {
             EXEC SQL CLOSE employee_cursor;
             zDbStatus.bOpened = FALSE;
             }

          /*
          ** Process the error code.
          */

          ProcErrorCode(hWnd);
           break;
        default :
           bReturn = FALSE;
           break;
        }
     break;
   case WM_INITDIALOG :
      break;
   default :
      bReturn = FALSE;
      break;
   }
return(bReturn);
```

```
}

/*
**********************************************************************
** EmployeeProc - Process the Employee window.
**
** Description:
**
**     This function is used to display and process the Employee window.
**
** Parameters:
**
**     hInst      INPUT
**         Application instance handle.
**
**     hWnd       INPUT
**         Window handle.
**
** Return:
**
**     iStatus
**         Dialog status.  Possible values:
**
**             TRUE  - A window processed without error.
**             FALSE - An error occurred in the window.
**
**********************************************************************
*/
int EmployeeProc(HANDLE hInst, HWND hWnd)
{
    FARPROC lpprocEmployee;
    int iReturn = 0;

    /*
    ** Check to see if the database is connected.
    */

    if (!zDbStatus.bConnected)
       return(FALSE);

    /*
    ** Create the Employee window instance.
```

```
*/

lpprocEmployee = MakeProcInstance(EmployeeWndProc, hInst);

/*
** Open the Employee window.
*/

iReturn = DialogBox(hInst, MAKEINTRESOURCE(EMPLOYEEBOX), hWnd,
    lpprocEmployee);

FreeProcInstance(lpprocEmployee);
return(iReturn);
}
```

Now let's discuss some of the elements of the previous sample application programs.

Oracle Include Files

In Chapter 2 we discussed the process of creating a Pro*C program, which requires that all the source modules in an application program be precompiled in preparation for compilation and linking. Thus, the **#include** C compiler directive cannot be used to include files that contain any Oracle precompiler statements. This includes precompiler files that Oracle provides (such as SQLCA.H and SQLDA.H) and user-defined include files. To provide the same function as the **#include** compiler command during the precompiler step, the Oracle precompiler uses the INCLUDE statement.

The INCLUDE statement allows precompiler-specific files to be inserted into source modules so that common information can be shared among modules, similar to files included with the **#include** C statement. The following excerpt from the Main Window listing shows how to use the INCLUDE statement:

```
EXEC SQL INCLUDE SQLCA.H;
EXEC SQL INCLUDE SQLDA.H;
```

When a source module is precompiled, each EXEC SQL INCLUDE statement is replaced by a copy of the file named in the statement. Any file can be INCLUDEd into a source module if it contains correct syntax. If an include file contains Pro*C declarations or embedded SQL statements, you must INCLUDE it. Only INCLUDEd files are precompiled; files included with the **#include** C statement are not included until the compiler processes a source module.

If a file extension is not specified with the filename in the INCLUDE statement, the precompiler assumes the default file extension for a C include file, *.H.

The default directory, where the precompiler will look for INCLUDE files, can be specified with the following precompiler option (precompiler options are discussed in Chapter 12):

```
INCLUDE=path
```

where **path** is the operating system directory in which the precompiler looks for the specified file. If a path is not specified, the default is the current working directory.

The precompiler uses the following order of precedence when searching for an INCLUDEd file on the operating system:

1. The precompiler always searches the current working directory, even if you have specified a directory with the INCLUDE precompiler option.

2. The precompiler searches the directory specified by the INCLUDE precompiler option. If not specified, the default is the current working directory.

3. The precompiler searches a directory for standard include files. As a result, a directory path for standard include files is unnecessary.

In summary, the INCLUDE precompiler option specifies a directory path for nonstandard include files unless the files exist in the current directory.

If the host operating system is case-sensitive (UNIX, for example), be sure to specify the same upper/lowercase filename that exists on the operating system.

Program Variables

To process information in an application program, you declare program variables of different types. Program variables reserve locations in memory that allow the storage and modification of data values in an application program. The C language requires all program variables to be declared in an application program before they are used. The following listings use examples from the Main Window listing to show how C program variables and Oracle precompiler program variables are declared differently.

```
char scAbout[MAX_ABOUT_STRING + 1];
char scAppName[MAX_APPNAME_STRING + 1];
char scMainMenu[MAX_MAIN_MENU_STRING + 1];
char scTitle[MAX_TITLE_STRING + 1];
```

```
static HANDLE hInst;
HWND hWndMain;

EXEC SQL BEGIN DECLARE SECTION;
    /*
    ** Host variables for logging into the Oracle database.
    */
    VARCHAR vcConnect[21];
    VARCHAR vcPassword[21];
    VARCHAR vcUserId[41];
EXEC SQL END DECLARE SECTION;
```

C Variables

The C language provides five basic datatypes that are used to declare program variables:

- Character (**char**)
- Integer (**int**)
- Floating-point (**float**)
- Double-precision (**double**)
- No value (**void**)

The **void** datatype is not typically used to declare variables in a C program; it is most often used to declare that a function returns no value. However, it can be used to declare generic pointer variables, which allow the memory address of any datatype to be assigned to a pointer. These basic datatypes will fill many of the requirements to process data values in an application program. A C variable is declared with the following syntax:

```
<datatype> <variable_name>;
```

or

```
<datatype> <variable1, variable2,...>;
```

where **datatype** is any valid C language datatype (**char**, **int**, **float**, or **double**) and **variable_name** or **variable1** represents a uniquely defined variable name. A variable name must be alphanumeric and can contain underscores. However, it cannot begin with a number or an underscore. In C, variables are case-sensitive; a variable must be declared and used with exactly the same spelling and case.

The size and range of the basic C datatypes can differ with each type of computer processor and with each C compiler. This is because the ANSI C standard only specifies the minimal range for each of these datatypes. If an application program is compiled on multiple hardware and software platforms, you can make no assumptions about the size or range of the datatypes. For example, a single character is normally one byte (eight bits) long and an integer is two bytes long, but these may differ on various computer systems.

The C language provides *datatype modifiers* to control the size and range of variables when they are declared. The datatype modifiers available in C are

- **signed**
- **unsigned**
- **long**
- **short**

Table 3-1 shows all the combinations of datatypes and modifiers allowed in ANSI Standard C, as well as the typical size of each datatype in bits and its minimal range.

C program variables are declared in three locations in an application program:

- Inside function definitions
- In function parameter lists
- Outside functions

Respectively, these variables are called *local variables, formal parameters,* and *global variables.*

Local Variables

Local variables are declared inside the *control block* of any function. More specifically, local variables can be declared inside any program control block in a function. In C, a control block is any section of code that begins with a curly brace ({) and ends with a curly brace (}). Therefore, a local variable declaration is valid after the beginning of a control block inside a function—before any other executable statements occur (in C++, this restriction doesn't exist). The following listing, taken from the Main Window listing, shows how local variables are declared at the beginning of a function control block.

Datatype and Modifier	Typical Size in Bits	Minimal Range
char signed char	8	-127 to 127
unsigned char	8	0 to 255
int signed int short int signed short int	16	-32,767 to 32,767
unsigned int unsigned short int	16	0 to 65,535
long int signed long int	32	-2,147,483,647 to 2,147,483,647
unsigned long int	32	0 to 4,294,967,295
float	32	6 digits of precision
double	64	10 digits of precision
long double	128	10 digits of precision

TABLE 3-1.   *Datatypes and modifiers allowed in ANSI Standard C*

```
/* Local Variable Declarations listing */
int PASCAL WinMain(HANDLE hInstance, HANDLE hPrevInstance,
    LPSTR lpscCmdLine, int iShowCmd)
{
    HMENU  hMainMenu;
    HWND   hWnd;
    MSG    msgMessage;
    . . .
```

In practice, all the local variables in a function are declared immediately after the opening curly brace of the primary function control block. This makes all the declared local variables valid within the scope of the entire function and avoids confusion.

Local variables are also known as *automatic variables*. All local variables are declared, by default, with the **auto** storage class identifier. Because the **auto** identifier is the default, in practice it is rarely specified explicitly (you won't see it specified in this book). The **auto** identifier specifies that a variable is automatically allocated in memory when the control block in which the variable is declared is entered. Also, the variable is automatically deallocated from memory when the control block is exited. Therefore, local variables are not valid outside the control block where they are declared; they can only be referenced inside that control block. This is referred to as the variable's *scope*.

Because local variables are allocated when a control block is entered and deallocated when the control block is exited, the value assigned to a variable is lost upon exit from the control block. If the variable must retain a value after the control block is exited, you can declare the variable with the **static** storage class identifier. That name doesn't imply that the value assigned to the variable is static and not modifiable; it simply specifies that space for the variable is allocated at compile time and is permanent. An example from the Main Window listing shows how a static variable is declared:

```
static HANDLE hInst;
```

When a value is assigned to a static local variable, that value is retained after the control block is exited. In fact, it is retained until a new value is assigned or the application program is exited. Therefore, if the control block is reentered, the variable will have the value that was assigned to it before the control block was last exited.

Formal Parameters

Formal parameters are declared in the parameter list of a function. If a function uses parameters, the datatype and variable name for each parameter are declared in the function's parameter list. These formal parameters behave just like the local variables that are declared at the beginning of a primary function control block; the only difference is that the values assigned to the formal parameters are passed to the function as parameters when the function is called and can be returned if the parameters are declared as pointers.

Local variables are not assigned values until after the function is entered. Remember, like local variables, the values assigned to the formal parameters are lost when the function is exited. See the Local Variable Declarations listing for an example of how the formal parameters of a function are declared.

Global Variables

Global variables are declared outside any function definition in a source module (source file). Although global variable declarations are valid anywhere in a source module except a function definition, you typically place the declarations at the top of the module before any function declarations. That way the global variables are declared before they are referenced in any functions. The following is an example of a global variable from the Main Window listing:

```
Database_status zDbStatus;
```

Global variables are accessible in all functions within the scope of the global variable declaration. Because they're stored in a reserved memory location throughout the execution of your program, they retain their value until the application program terminates.

If an application program consists of multiple functions and/or source modules, global variables can be declared so that their values are available to all functions and modules in the program. A global variable is declared once inside a single source module; in all other source modules, the variable is assigned the **extern** storage class identifier. The **extern** identifier specifies that a global variable declaration exists in another source module but is accessed in this source module. Therefore, you declare all global variables in a single source module (whether or not you reference them in that module), then declare them as **extern** in all other source modules. The following example from the Employee Record listing shows how to use the **extern** identifier:

```
extern Database_status zDbStatus;
```

If you want to restrict access to a global variable to all the functions within a source module, assign the global variable the storage class identifier **static**. For global variables, the **static** identifier specifies that the global variable is only valid within the scope of the source module that contains its declaration. The global variable can be referenced by all functions inside that source module but cannot be referenced outside that module. A static global variable declaration is just like a static local variable except that you declare it outside any function.

Global variables declared with the **static** identifier can be useful when many functions use the same data inside a single source module in an application program. However, global variables accessible throughout an application program are somewhat taboo in practice, and you should avoid them for the following reasons:

- Global variables are stored in memory throughout an entire program and use up precious memory resources.

- A function that references a global variable causes that function to be dependent on that global variable; the function cannot be generalized for reuse by other modules or application programs.

- Global variables can cause innocuous errors in an application program; the global variable can be modified unknowingly anywhere in the program, causing undesired side effects in other parts of the program. These errors are very difficult to debug.

If you need to use global variables, use *data encapsulation* techniques to hide the specifics of the global variables (datatype, variable name, and so on) and protect them from unwanted modification. Data encapsulation means that a single source module contains a set of functions that are used to reference and modify the global variables. These functions are used in the program when the global variable values need to be accessed and modified.

Now that you understand the rules and syntax for declaring C language variables, let's discuss how to declare variables to interact with the Oracle database.

Host and Indicator Variables

In this section, you'll see how to declare host variables in a program and how they are used, both in a program and in embedded SQL statements. In Chapter 4, all the details of host and indicator variables are discussed, including some advanced topics.

Host Variables

Host variables are the key to communication between an application program and the Oracle database. Each variable used to communicate with the Oracle database must be uniquely declared in an application program. A host variable is declared in an application program so that it can be shared with Oracle, allowing both to access the value of the host variable.

Host variables are used for both input to and output from the database. An input host variable is used to pass a data value from the application program to the database. An output host variable is used to return a data value from the database to the application program. A single host variable can be used for both input and output in a program, though not in a single SQL statement.

Indicator Variables

When a host variable in an application program is either passed to or retrieved from the database, often there is a need to know the host variable's status. *Indicator variables* are integer variables that indicate the status of an associated host variable on either input or output.

An indicator variable can be optionally associated with any host variable. Indicator variables are used to assign a null value to an input host variable or to detect a null or truncated value assigned by the database to an output host variable.

The DECLARE Section

Each host and indicator variable is declared in a special section of an application program called the *DECLARE section*. Oracle understands and interprets the contents of this section. Host and indicator variables are declared much like C variables. However, *any* variable declared in this section is treated by Oracle as a host or indicator variable. This lets Oracle automatically convert the host variable datatype to one that's compatible with the Oracle database. The syntax to create a DECLARE section anywhere in an application program is

```
EXEC SQL BEGIN DECLARE SECTION;
    ...
EXEC SQL END DECLARE SECTION;
```

In this section (between these two statements), the following statements are allowed:

- Host and indicator variable declarations
- EXEC SQL INCLUDE statements
- Equivalence datatypes
- C and ANSI style comments

Like C language variables, DECLARE sections can be used to declare host and indicator variables as local function variables, static global variables (global to a source module), or global variables. Multiple DECLARE sections can be placed anywhere in a function or source module as long as there are no conflicting variable declarations.

Declaring Host and Indicator Variables

Host and indicator variables are declared in the DECLARE section using the same set of rules that apply to C variables. Host variables can be declared using the basic C datatypes; Oracle automatically converts the basic C datatypes into datatypes compatible with the database. In addition to the basic C datatypes, Oracle provides support for *external datatypes*. The external datatypes are understood by Oracle and are compatible with the Oracle database. For example, Oracle supports the VARCHAR datatype, which is used to process variable character data.

An indicator variable must be declared as a **short** integer. It can be declared anywhere in the DECLARE section and need not precede or directly follow the declaration of its associated host variable. The following example from the Employee Record listing illustrates how you declare host and indicator variables:

```
EXEC SQL BEGIN DECLARE SECTION;
    /*
    ** Host variables for accessing the EMPLOYEE table.
    */

    VARCHAR vcEmpSSN[12];
    VARCHAR vcFName[41];
    VARCHAR vcLName[41];
    VARCHAR vcMiddleInit[2];
    VARCHAR vcAddress[41];
    VARCHAR vcCity[41];
```

```
VARCHAR vcState[3];
VARCHAR vcZipcode[11];
VARCHAR vcWPhone[13];
VARCHAR vcHPhone[13];
VARCHAR vcPayRate[10];
VARCHAR vcPayType[3];
VARCHAR vcHireDate[11];
VARCHAR vcTermDate[11];

/*
** Indicator variables for the host variables defined above.
*/

short indEmpSSN;
short indFName;
short indLName;
short indMiddleInit;
short indAddress;
short indCity;
short indState;
short indZipcode;
short indWPhone;
short indHPhone;
short indPayRate;
short indPayType;
short indHireDate;
short indTermDate;
```

```
EXEC SQL END DECLARE SECTION;
```

The rules for declaring host and indicator variables are discussed in Chapter 4. Let's look at how they're used in an application program.

Using Host and Indicator Variables

Host and indicator variables can be referenced in regular C language statements and in embedded data-manipulation SQL statements in an application program. However, when host and indicator variables are used in embedded SQL statements, they must be prefixed by a colon (:). The following example from the Employee Record listing shows how this is done:

```
EXEC SQL INSERT INTO EMPLOYEE
    (EMPLOYEE.EMPLOYEE_SSN, EMPLOYEE.FIRST_NAME,
     EMPLOYEE.MIDDLE_INITIAL, EMPLOYEE.LAST_NAME,
```

```
        EMPLOYEE.ADDRESS, EMPLOYEE.CITY,
        EMPLOYEE.STATE, EMPLOYEE.ZIPCODE, EMPLOYEE.WORK_PHONE,
        EMPLOYEE.HOME_PHONE, EMPLOYEE.PAY_RATE,
        EMPLOYEE.PAY_TYPE,
        EMPLOYEE.HIRE_DATE, EMPLOYEE.TERMINATION_DATE)
VALUES (:vcEmpSSN:indEmpSSN,
        :vcFName:indFName,
        :vcMiddleInit:indMiddleInit,
        :vcLName:indLName,
        :vcAddress:indAddress,
        :vcCity:indCity,
        :vcState:indState,
        :vcZipcode:indZipcode,
        :vcWPhone:indWPhone,
        :vcHPhone:indHPhone,
        :vcPayRate:indPayRate,
        :vcPayType:indPayType,
        :vcHireDate:indHireDate,
        :vcTermDate:indTermDate);
```

Note that an indicator variable directly follows its associated host variables in the SQL statement; they cannot be separated by anything but a space.

Host and Indicator Arrays

Host variables are used to process single-valued variables when accessing the Oracle database. However, Oracle is a *set-oriented* relational database; the database is designed specifically to operate on sets of data.

How can an application program be set-oriented as well? This is typically accomplished using arrays. An array is a set of variables of the same datatype that are accessed by a single variable name. Each variable in the array is called an *element*. Oracle allows the declaration of *host arrays* and *indicator arrays*, which are used to access sets of data in the Oracle database. A host or indicator array is declared in the DECLARE section of an application program, just like host and indicator variables.

A host and indicator array is declared in the DECLARE section of a program and is assigned a datatype, a unique name, and a size (or length), called the array *dimension*. Most host arrays can have only one dimension; character arrays can have two dimensions.

An indicator array declaration must be of the **short** datatype. An indicator array is used in conjunction with a host array for exactly the same reason an indicator variable is used with a host variable—to set or obtain the status of a host array element. A host array and its associated indicator array must be declared with the same dimension. There are no examples of host arrays in the Main Window or Employee Record listings, but host arrays are discussed in depth in Chapter 4.

Database Access

It may not be apparent at this point how an application program is connected to the Oracle database system. A database context must exist before any database operations (SQL statements) can be executed in an application program.

A database context is established by creating a communication link, called a *database connection*, between the application program and the target Oracle database. A database connection is critical to the operation of an application program. Through this connection all communication with the Oracle database takes place. For example, each SQL statement is packaged, sent to the database, and processed by the database and the results returned to the application program using this connection.

Establishing a connection to an Oracle database is called a *database session*. An Oracle session is established with the CONNECT statement. The following example from the Main Window listing shows how to use the CONNECT statement in an application program:

```
EXEC SQL CONNECT :vcUserId
    IDENTIFIED BY :vcPassword
    USING :vcConnect;
```

Once a database session is established, Oracle makes database access virtually transparent to the application program.

Before an SQL statement is executed in an application program, a database connection must be requested to establish a session. The CONNECT statement must be the first executable SQL statement in the application program. Obviously, the DECLARE section needs to precede this statement. Other declarative SQL statements can also exist.

The details of accessing local Oracle databases are discussed in Chapter 5. The details of accessing remote and distributed Oracle databases are discussed in Chapter 13.

Embedded SQL

SQL is the standard data language for easily and consistently accessing and manipulating data in relational databases. SQL statements can exist directly in an application program, in which case they are called *embedded* SQL statements. Embedded SQL allows any SQL statement to exist in an application program. This provides all the power of the SQL language to access data in a database and process that data in the application program.

Primarily, data-manipulation SQL statements exist in an application program to access and manipulate data in a database. Data-manipulation SQL statements consist of the following:

- **INSERT** Allows data to be inserted into a database table.

- **SELECT** Allows data to be selected in many combinations from individual and multiple database tables.

- **FETCH** Allows data to be obtained a row at a time.

- **UPDATE** Allows existing columns of data in rows to be updated in a database table.

- **DELETE** Allows existing rows of data to be deleted from a database table.

Embedded SQL statements can be used in any logical combination and can be intermixed with C language statements. The only requirement is that each embedded SQL statement be prefixed with the following syntax:

```
EXEC SQL statement;
```

The Employee Record listing contains several examples of embedded SQL statements. For example, the following statement is used to FETCH an employee record:

```
EXEC SQL FETCH employee_cursor
    INTO :vcEmpSSN:indEmpSSN,
        :vcFName:indFName,
        :vcMiddleInit:indMiddleInit,
        :vcLName:indLName,
        :vcAddress:indAddress,
        :vcCity:indCity,
        :vcState:indState,
        :vcZipcode:indZipcode,
        :vcWPhone:indWPhone,
        :vcHPhone:indHPhone,
        :vcPayRate:indPayRate,
        :vcPayType:indPayType,
        :vcHireDate:indHireDate,
        :vcTermDate:indTermDate;
```

The format of the SQL statement, the host variables, and the format of the data being processed are known when the program is compiled. The format of the embedded SQL statement doesn't change while you execute your application program. As discussed in Chapter 2, this is referred to as *static embedded SQL*.

Some application programs are designed so that the format of the SQL statement is not fully specified, or the entire SQL statement may be unknown when the program is developed. The complete SQL statement, the host variables, and the data to be processed are determined at run time when your application executes. This is called *dynamic embedded SQL*. A dynamic embedded SQL statement allows your program to process an SQL statement passed to the application program at run time and allows the statement to be constructed on the fly. Dynamic embedded SQL is an advanced application development technique that can be very complex. This method is not used in our sample program.

Transaction Processing

A *transaction* is a set of logically related SQL statements that make up an atomic unit of work. A transaction is called an atomic unit of work because all the changes brought about by the SQL statements that constitute a transaction can either be *committed* (made permanent) to the database or *rolled back* (undone) from the database, all at the same time.

Oracle employs transactions to ensure data integrity and is classified as a transaction-oriented system. If all the SQL statements in a transaction perform the task successfully, the changes performed by the unit of work commit to the database at the same time. If any one of the SQL statements fails or something occurs (a software, hardware, or network failure) to interrupt the transaction, the changes performed by the unit of work roll back. If a transaction rolls back, the database is restored to its state prior to the transaction and it's as if the transaction never occurred.

A transaction begins when the first SQL statement is executed in an application program, and all subsequent SQL statements execute within the context of that transaction. A transaction ends when the changes caused by the SQL statements in the transaction commit or are rolled back. The next executable SQL statement begins the next transaction, and so on.

Changes are committed in a transaction using the COMMIT statement. The changes are ignored or rolled back with the ROLLBACK statement. The following example from the Employee Record listing shows how these statements are used in the sample program.

```
if (wParam = ID_EMPLOYEE_COMMIT)
   EXEC SQL COMMIT WORK;
else
   EXEC SQL ROLLBACK WORK;
```

Transactions are controlled by the placement of the COMMIT and ROLLBACK statements in a program. It is important for data integrity and performance reasons to design transactions correctly. Note that if an error is encountered while processing an SQL statement, the transaction is rolled back. The details of transaction management are discussed in Chapter 6.

Error Processing

After every executable SQL statement or database call in an application program, Oracle returns status information indicating whether or not the statement was successful and, if successful, if there are any exceptions. Three general statuses can result from an SQL statement:

- **Success** The SQL statement was completely successful, and the expected result occurred in the database.

- **Warning** The statement was successful, but an exception occurred in the result. For instance, a SELECT statement may not find any rows, or a DELETE statement may not delete any rows. Also, the value of a database column may be "truncated" when it is assigned to a host variable.

- **Error** The statement failed completely. An error can result from a problem with the SQL statement itself, an error in the database system, or an error in the computer system (hardware, operating system, or network).

If an SQL statement is successful, the status information can be ignored and the result can be processed in the application program. If a warning occurs, the status information tells what the exception is, what processing may need to be performed (if any), and what to report to the user (if necessary). If an error occurs, the status information tells what the error is, allows for recovery processing, and allows error reporting.

Any errors and warnings that result from a call to an Oracle database can be processed using one of the following methods:

- **Explicit handling** After each database call, an explicit check for an error or warning can exist and, if necessary, can be processed at that point. Although effective, this method can clutter the application program with error-and-warning processing; the application will grow with each new call to the database. Also, this method is non-ANSI-compliant and will differ in other database systems.

- **Implicit handling** After each database call, Oracle implicitly checks for an error or warning and processes the error based on a method specified in the application program. An error-handling function can "goto" another section of the program to process the error, or processing can simply continue. This method is ANSI-compliant, so it is portable to other database systems that support SQL.

■ **Diagnostic handling**   After each database call, additional diagnostic information can be obtained from Oracle to diagnose a problem. Oracle provides additional information on CURSOR and system statistics, the SQL statement, and option settings.

Explicit handling requires error processing following each SQL statement; the status information returned by Oracle is checked and any errors or warnings processed. Oracle provides two mechanisms for reporting the status of an SQL statement:

■ **SQLCA**   The *SQLCA* (or SQL Communications Area) is a data structure that is INCLUDEd in an application program and in which Oracle returns the status information resulting from an SQL statement. This status information includes

– Error codes

– Warning flags

– The count of rows processed

– SQL statement errors

– Error message text

■ **SQLCODE**   The *SQLCODE* (or SQL Status Code) is a variable declared in the application program and in which Oracle sets only a status code, stating the error or warning, resulting from an SQL statement.

The following example from the Main Window listing shows how to declare the SQLCA and access the structure to check for errors after SQL statements execute (the SQLCODE is not used in the sample program):

```
EXEC SQL INCLUDE SQLCA.H;
    ...
if (sqlca.sqlcode < 0)
      {
      MessageBox(hWnd, sqlca.sqlerrm.sqlerrmc,
          "Database Error", MB_OK);
      return(FALSE);
      }
```

Note how the SQLCA data structure can be used to check the status of an SQL statement error. In practice, you would use the SQLCA rather than the SQLCODE because more information is available. Don't use both methods in the same program.

Implicit handling lets Oracle implicitly check for errors and warnings after each SQL statement. Also, how and where errors are processed can be defined in the program. Implicit handling is ANSI-compliant and lets Oracle do much of the work in checking for errors. The mechanism provided by the ANSI standard (and Oracle) to perform implicit error handling is the WHENEVER statement.

The WHENEVER statement specifies that Oracle implicitly checks for one or all of the following conditions:

- Error
- Warning
- Data not found

When the WHENEVER statement encounters one of these conditions, one of the following methods for handling the condition in your program can be defined:

- Continue processing, ignore the error, and continue.
- Call a function.
- Break out of a control loop.
- Go to another location in your program.
- Stop processing altogether.

This method is not used in our sample program, but it will be discussed in depth later in the book. It doesn't matter which method you select to process errors in your applications, so pick the one that best meets your needs. Just don't use more than one; design a consistent error-handling method and use it throughout your program.

Summary

This chapter showed you how to create an application program that accesses and manipulates data in an Oracle database. This program introduces the basic elements of the Oracle development tools used to access an Oracle database. The key sections of the program are:

- Program variables
- Include files
- Connecting to the database
- Embedded SQL
- Transaction processing
- Error processing

The following chapters discuss these elements in detail, along with more advanced topics. With this information, you can build application programs that can be embellished as additional details are presented in the following chapters.

CHAPTER 4

The Application Datatypes

This chapter discusses the datatypes you'll need to understand and use in your application program. Your application will *input* data to Oracle, and Oracle will *output* data to your application. Oracle will store the input data in tables in the database and store the output data in your program's host variables. You must be aware of the datatype of each data item: The datatype determines the storage form of the data item and the valid ranges of values for each item.

Oracle recognizes two kinds of datatypes: internal and external. We will discuss in detail the internal datatypes supported by Oracle and the external datatypes supported by the C language. We will cover what is and is not supported automatically by the system and reveal how you can use datatype equivalencing to process user-defined datatypes in your application program. When you've finished this chapter, you'll know the answers to the following questions:

■ What are the internal datatypes?

■ What are the external datatypes?

■ What are the ANSI standard datatypes?

■ What are host and indicator variables?

■ What are host and indicator arrays?

■ What is datatype conversion?

■ What is datatype equivalencing?

■ How can I use these tools in my application?

Internal Datatypes

Internal datatypes are native to the Oracle system. Oracle uses them to determine how data is stored in the columns of database tables. The internal datatypes were designed to allow accurate, efficient data storage across various platforms. Oracle also uses the internal datatypes to represent database *pseudocolumns*. Pseudocolumns are not really columns in a table, but are used to return certain types of data values from the database.

When your application program is executing, Oracle automatically converts the datatype of each input host variable referenced in an SQL statement to an appropriate internal datatype that the database can understand. Likewise, after processing the SQL statement and determining the result, Oracle automatically determines the datatype of each output host variable, converts the internal datatype to the external datatype, and returns the value.

Table 4-1 briefly summarizes each internal datatype supported by Oracle. Associated with each datatype is a code that is used for communication purposes throughout the Oracle system. As you can see, the Oracle internal datatypes are very different from the datatypes available in C. For example, the NUMBER datatype is designed to provide portability, high precision, and correct collation. C does not support a datatype with these features.

In this section we will discuss each internal datatype, where it is used, and any associated restrictions.

Code	Internal Datatype	Description
1	VARCHAR2	Variable-length character string having a maximum length of 2,000 bytes.
2	NUMBER	Number having precision p and scale s. The precision p can range from 1 to 38. The scale s can range from -84 to 127.
8	LONG	Variable-length character data having a maximum length in bytes. The maximum length allowed is 2 gigabytes (Gb), or 2^{31} −1.
13	DATE	A valid date and time that can range from January 1, 4712 B.C. to A.D. December 31, 4712.
23	RAW	Fixed-length raw binary data having a maximum length of 255 bytes.
24	LONG RAW	Variable-length raw binary data having a maximum length of 2Gb.
69	ROWID	Binary number representing the unique database address of a row in a database table. This datatype is primarily used for values returned by the ROWID pseudocolumn.
96	CHAR	Fixed-length character data having a maximum length of 255 bytes. Default length is one byte.
106	MLSLABEL	Binary format of an operating system label. This datatype is used primarily with Trusted Oracle.

TABLE 4-1.   *The Oracle internal datatypes*

Character Datatypes

The character datatypes in Oracle are used to store and manipulate words, strings, and free-form text. Character datatypes are alphanumeric data strings stored as byte values in the database based on the assigned *character set*. A character set defines the code used to store the characters of a particular language, such as seven-bit ASCII English characters or multibyte Japanese Kanji characters.

The internal character-string datatypes that Oracle provides are CHAR, VARCHAR2, and LONG; each has its own special properties.

CHAR Datatype

The CHAR datatype is used to store a relatively short *fixed-length character string.* A fixed-length character string always stores the same number of characters. If you assign a character string to a column that is shorter than the column's fixed length, the character string is padded with blanks up to the maximum length of the column. The maximum length of a CHAR datatype is 255. If a length is not specified, the default is 1. The syntax for the CHAR datatype is

```
CHAR(maximum_width)
```

where $1 \leq$ maximum_width ≤ 255.

VARCHAR2 Datatype

The VARCHAR2 datatype is used to store a *variable-length character string,* which can hold alphanumeric characters up to a maximum length. The maximum length that can be assigned to a VARCHAR2 database column is 2,000 bytes. (Note that the length is determined by the number of bytes rather than the number of characters.) The syntax for the VARCHAR2 datatype is

```
VARCHAR2(maximum_width)
```

where $1 \leq$ maximum_width $\leq 2,000$.

> **NOTE**
> There is no default length for VARCHAR2; you must specify a length.

The actual number of characters allowed in a VARCHAR2 column depends on the character set used to store the data. For example, seven-bit ASCII or multibyte Japanese Kanji will use a different number of bytes with the same number of characters. When a VARCHAR2 character string is stored in a database column, Oracle terminates it at the end of the string; it is not blank-filled to the maximum length assigned to the column. Thus, you don't need to be concerned that the maximum length allocated to the column will be used for each string.

NOTE
While the datatype VARCHAR is allowed in Oracle, it is strongly
advised that you use the VARCHAR2 datatype. Oracle has stated that
the behavior of VARCHAR may change in a future release because it
is an ANSI datatype. Currently, VARCHAR and VARCHAR2 are
identical.

LONG Datatype

The LONG datatype is used to store a very long, variable-length character string
(such as a document). A LONG has all the characteristics of a VARCHAR2 except
that it has a maximum length of 2Gb (2^{31}). The syntax for the LONG datatype is

LONG

LONG columns can be used in the following SQL statements:

- SELECT lists

- SET clauses of UPDATE statements

- VALUES clauses of INSERT statements

However, the LONG datatype does have some restrictions:

- The length of a LONG datatype may be restricted by the amount of
  memory in your computer system.

- A table cannot contain more than one LONG column.

- LONG columns cannot appear in integrity constraints (except for NOT
  NULL constraints).

- LONG columns cannot be indexed.

- You cannot pass a LONG to a procedure or stored function if the length is
  greater than 32K.

- A stored function cannot return a LONG value (unless the length is less
  than 32K).

- Within a single SQL statement, all LONG columns, updated tables, and
  locked tables must be located in the same database.

- LONG columns cannot appear in the following parts of SQL statements:

- WHERE, GROUP BY, ORDER BY, or CONNECT BY clauses or with the DISTINCT operator in SELECT statements
- SQL functions (such as **substr** or **instr**)
- Expressions or conditions
- Select lists of queries containing GROUP BY clauses
- Select lists of subqueries or queries combined by set operators
- Select lists of CREATE TABLE AS SELECT statements

■ LONG columns cannot appear in triggers.

Character Comparison Rules

Character-string values are compared based on a set of rules that determine whether the compared character strings are equal to, less than, or greater than each other in the character set collating sequence. The results of comparing two character strings using different comparison rules can be different. The rules of comparison are *blank-padded comparison rules* and *nonpadded comparison rules.*

Blank-Padded Comparison Rules   If two character strings being compared have different lengths, Oracle first adds blanks to the end of the shorter string so that the lengths are equal. It then compares the strings, character by character, up to the first character that differs. The string with the greater character in the first differing position is considered greater in the collating sequence. If two strings have no differing characters, they are considered equal. This rule means that the two strings are equal if they differ only in the number of trailing blanks. Oracle uses blank-padded comparison rules only when both values in the comparison are of fixed-length types.

Nonpadded Comparison Rules   Using nonpadded comparison rules, the two character strings are compared character by character up to the first character that differs. The string with the greater character in the first differing position is considered greater in the collating sequence. If two strings with different lengths are identical up to the end of the shorter string, the longer string is considered greater in the collating sequence. If two strings of equal length have no differing characters, they are considered equal. Oracle uses nonpadded comparison semantics whenever one or both strings in the comparison have a variable-length datatype. (Remember that the LONG datatype cannot be used in comparisons.)

Each character string is compared character by character based on the *collating sequence* of the character set assigned to the database. The collating sequence is a numeric value assigned to each character in a character set. One character is greater than another if it has a greater numeric value in the collating sequence of the character set. The collating sequence for a character set is defined in documented standards. Some of the more common standardized character sets are:

- Seven-bit ASCII (American Standard Code for Information Interchange)
- EBCDIC (Extended Binary Coded Decimal Interchange Code) Code Page
- ISO 8859/1 (International Standards Organization)
- JEUC (Japan Extended UNIX Code)
- SJIS (Shift Japan JIS)

NUMBER Datatype

The NUMBER datatype is used to store fixed-size or floating-point numbers (no alpha characters allowed!). This datatype is designed to provide portability, high precision, and consistent collating results. To get those benefits, you assign a precision and scale to each NUMBER datatype.

Precision

The precision of a NUMBER determines the maximum number of digits in the value assigned to it. The maximum number of digits is the total of the digits on both sides of a number's decimal point (the decimal point is not included). For example, a precision of 3 would allow the number 101 but not 1001 or 100.1. In Oracle, the maximum precision of a NUMBER is 38. If a data value exceeds the assigned precision of a NUMBER, Oracle returns an error. If no precision is specified, 38 is the default.

Scale

The scale of a NUMBER determines the number of digits allowed to the right of the decimal point and where rounding occurs in an assigned data value when it is stored in a database column. The scale can be zero, positive, or negative:

- A **zero** scale value means the data value is treated as an integer. The scale value determines the maximum number of digits allowed in the data value. Also, the data value is rounded to the next integer value; for example, 10.1 becomes 10 and 10.6 becomes 11.

- A **positive** scale value determines the number of digits allowed to the right of the decimal point and where the assigned data value is rounded to the next number. A scale of 1 rounds to tenths (0.11 becomes 0.1), a scale of 2 rounds to hundredths (0.0156 becomes 0.02), and so on.

- A **negative** scale value means the data value is treated as an integer. However, in this case the data value is rounded to the next number at the digit to the left of the decimal place based on the scale value. For example, a scale of –1 rounds to tens (12.5 becomes 10) and a scale of –2 rounds to hundreds (156.55 becomes 200).

In Oracle, the scale can range from –84 to 127. If no scale is assigned, the default is 10. If a data value exceeds the scale, the number is rounded and no error results. A NUMBER can have a data value in the range 1.0E–129 to 9.99E125. If you specify a data value whose magnitude is greater than or equal to these values, Oracle will return an error.

The syntax for the NUMBER datatype is

```
NUMBER(p,s)
```

where:

p is the precision, or the total number of digits, and $1 \leq p \leq 38$.

s is the scale, or the number of digits to the right of the decimal point, and $-84 \leq s \leq 127$.

Alternate forms are

```
NUMBER(p)
```

where NUMBER is an integer with precision p and scale 0, and

```
NUMBER
```

where NUMBER is a floating-point number with precision 38 and scale 10.

Table 4-2 shows how Oracle processes NUMBERs of varying precision and scale.

Actual Data	Specified As	Stored As
7456123.89	NUMBER	7456123.89
7456123.89	NUMBER (9)	7456124
7456123.89	NUMBER (9,2)	7456123.89
7456123.89	NUMBER (9,1)	7456123.9
7456123.8	NUMBER (6)	Exceeds precision
7456123.8	NUMBER (15,1)	7456123.8
7456123.89	NUMBER (7,–2)	7456100
7456123.89	NUMBER (–7,2)	Exceeds precision; the minus sign is ignored

TABLE 4-2. *Effects of precision and scale*

Although this is uncommon, you can specify a scale that is greater than its precision. In this case, the precision specifies the maximum number of digits to the right of the decimal point. For example, a column defined as NUMBER(4,5) requires a zero for the first digit to the right of the decimal point and rounds all values past the fifth digit to the right of the decimal point. Table 4-3 shows the effects of a scale greater than precision.

Binary Datatypes (RAW and LONG RAW)

The binary datatypes are used to store raw *byte-oriented binary data*. Byte-oriented binary data is data that has no structure or meaning to Oracle. These datatypes are typically used to store graphic images and digitized video or sound. Oracle processes binary data values as hexadecimal character strings. Binary data can only be stored and retrieved; you cannot perform string manipulation or other operations on binary data.

The internal binary datatypes in Oracle are RAW and LONG RAW. The RAW datatype is analogous to the CHAR datatype. The LONG RAW datatype is analogous to the LONG datatype, with one exception: VARCHAR2 and LONG data is automatically converted between the stored database format and the session character set. There is no such conversion for RAW and LONG RAW data. LONG RAW data is subject to the same restrictions as LONG data.

The syntax for the RAW datatype is

```
RAW(maximum_width)
```

where $1 \leq maximum\_width \leq 255$.

The syntax for the LONG RAW datatype is

```
LONG RAW
```

Actual Data	Specified As	Stored As
0.01234	NUMBER(4,5)	0.01234
0.00012	NUMBER(4,5)	0.00012
0.000127	NUMBER(4,5)	0.00013
0.0000012	NUMBER(2,7)	0.0000012
0.00000123	NUMBER(2,7)	0.0000012

TABLE 4-3.   *Effects of precision less than scale*

ROWID Datatype

Each table in an Oracle database has a pseudocolumn, called ROWID, that stores the *database address* for each row in the table. The database address is the unique identifier for a row in the database and is called its rowid. The rowid is what is used in an index to find a row in a table quickly. Although database columns can be assigned the ROWID datatype, Oracle does not guarantee that the data value is a valid rowid in the database.

The value of the pseudocolumn ROWID is a binary number whose length is platform-dependent. When you select ROWID into a character type, it is converted into an 18-character hexadecimal string with the format

```
block.row.file
```

where:

> **block** is a hexadecimal string identifying the data block of the operating system's data file containing the row. The length of this string is eight characters.
>
> **row** is a four-digit hexadecimal string identifying the row in the data block. The first row in the data block has the number 0.
>
> **file** is a hexadecimal string identifying the database file containing the row. The first data file has the number 1. The length of this string is four characters.
>
> Examine the following ROWID:

```
0000000A.0008.0005
```

This address points to the eighth row (0008) in the tenth data block (0000000A) of the fifth data file (0005).

DATE Datatype

The DATE datatype is used to store the date and time (calendar and clock) information. Because date and time information are considered inseparable in Oracle, they are referred to together as *date information*. Although a date can be represented by other datatypes (NUMBER and CHAR), the DATE datatype is designed to process the unique properties of date information.

Each DATE stored in the database is a fixed-length, seven-byte value containing the following information:

byte 1	**byte 2**	**byte 3**	**byte 4**	**byte 5**	**byte 6**	**byte 7**
century	year	month	day	hours	minutes	seconds

DATE Formatting

You can process a date value as a character string in the default date format when it is used in a *date expression*. A date expression is any operation that "expects" a DATE datatype. The default date format is determined by the Oracle session parameter NLS_DATE_FORMAT, which is by default DD-MON-YY. This format is interpreted as:

- **DD**   The day of the month.

- **MON**   The month of the year (for example, JAN for January).

- **YY**   The last two digits of the year in the current century.

If you need to process a date value in any format other than the default or you need to specify a date with a time, you must process the date value indirectly as a character string or a number. The character string or number is converted to a DATE datatype using special functions supplied by Oracle. The function to convert a DATE datatype to a character string is

```
TO_CHAR(date[,'format'])
```

where:

> **date** is a DATE datatype column.

> **format** is a character string used to describe the character-string output. If the format is left off, the default format is output.

For example:

```
TO_CHAR(PURCHASE_DATE, 'MM-DD-YYYY')
```

produces "2-15-1995" and

```
TO_CHAR(PURCHASE_DATE, 'MM-DD-YYYY HH:MI:SS')
```

produces "2-15-1995 1:35:30".

The function to convert a character string or number to a DATE datatype is

```
TO_DATE(input[,'format'])
```

where:

> **input** is a character-string literal, number literal, or database column containing a string or number.

> **format** is a character string used to describe the input. If the format is not specified, the input must be in the default format.

For example:

```
TO_DATE('2-15-1995', 'MM-DD-YYYY')
```

produces the date "15-FEB-1995 00:00:00" and

```
TO_DATE('2-15'1995  1:35:30', 'MM-DD-YYYY HH:MI:SS')
```

produces the date "15-FEB-1995 1:35:30".

These examples show the default behavior of the DATE conversion functions. If you don't specify a time with a date, the default time is 12:00:00 midnight. If you don't specify a date with a time, the default date is the first day of the current month (and current year).

The date-formatting functions are very powerful. You can format dates almost infinitely. Table 4-4 summarizes the options available for date formatting; these options are listed in detail in Appendix C.

Date Format	Description
CC	Number of the century
SCC	Signed century (B.C. is negative)
YYYY	Four-digit year (e.g., 1995)
SYYYY	Signed four-digit year (e.g., 4000 B.C. is -4000)
YYY	Last three digits of the year, current century (e.g., 995)
YY	Last two digits of the year, current century (e.g., 95)
Y	Last single digit of the year, current century (e.g., 5)
IYYY	Four-digit year, ISO standard
IYY	Last three digits of the year, current century, ISO standard
IY	Last two digits of the year, current century, ISO standard
I	Last single digit of the year, current century, ISO standard

TABLE 4-4.   *Date-formatting controls*

Date Format	Description
RR	Last two digits of the year relative to the current year
YEAR	Year spelled out (e.g., NINETEEN NINETY-FIVE)
B.C. or A.D.	Displays B.C. or A.D., depending on the year
BC or AD	Same as B.C. or A.D. minus the periods
Q	Number of the quarter (1 to 4)
MM	Number of the month (01 to 12)
RM	Roman numeral of the month (I to XII)
MON	Three-letter abbreviation of the month (JAN to DEC)
MONTH	Full name of the month (JANUARY to DECEMBER), padded to nine characters
WW	Number of the week in the year (1 to 52)
IW	Number of the week in the year, ISO standard
W	Number of the week in the month (1 to 5)
DDD	Number of the day in the year (1 to 365)
DD	Number of the day in the month (1 to 31)
D	Number of the day in the week (1 to 7)
DY	Three-letter abbreviation of the day (MON to SUN)
DAY	Full name of the day (MONDAY to SUNDAY), padded to nine characters
J	"Julian" days (the number of days since December 31, 4713 B.C.)
HH	Number of hours in a day (1 to 12)
HH12	Same as HH
HH24	Number of hours in a day (1 to 24)
MI	Number of minutes in an hour (1 to 60)
SS	Number of seconds in a minute (1 to 60)
SSSS	Number of seconds since midnight (0 to 86399)
A.M. or P.M.	Displays A.M. or P.M., depending on the time of day
AM or PM	Same as A.M. or P.M. minus the periods
- / , . ; :	Punctuation is produced in the result
"...text..."	Quoted string is produced in the result

TABLE 4-4.   *Date-formatting controls* (continued)

When you specify a date format, you can embed punctuation to create full sentences. The format is delimited by single quotes, and the literal strings are delimited by double quotes. For example:

```
TO_CHAR(DATE_PURCHASED, '"Purchased on:" Day, Month DD,
   "Year:" YYYY')
```

produces "Purchased on: Mon, February 15, Year: 1995".

NOTE
If the first letter of the format is capitalized and the rest of the format is not capitalized, the first letter of the result will be capitalized (for example, Mon or Гebruary). If the entire format is capitalized, the result is capitalized (as in MON).

Table 4-5 describes prefix and suffix formats that can be used to enhance the output of **to_char** (they cannot be used with **to_date**).

The power of the **to_char** function is enhanced by a feature that allows you to pass numeric values to the format argument of the function and format the numeric output. Table 4-6 summarizes the numeric formatting controls for the **to_char** function.

Date Format	Description
fm	Fill mode. Used as a prefix to Month or Day: *fmMonth* or *fmDay*. Normally Oracle pads Month and Day with blanks up to nine characters to align multiple dates correctly. The *fm* prefix suppresses this padding.
fx	Format exact. Specifies exact matching for the character argument and date format model of the **to_date** function.
TH	Used as a suffix to any number format to produce its ordinal value (23rd, 25th, and so on).
SP	Used as a suffix to any number format, forcing the number to be spelled out (*DDSP*, *DdSP*, and *ddsp* produce *FOUR*, *Four*, and *four*).
SPTH or THSP	A combination suffix of SP and TH to produce the spelled-out ordinal number (*DDSPTH* produces *FOURTH*).

TABLE 4-5. *Date-formatting prefixes and suffixes*

Format Control	Example	Function
9	9999	Number of 9's determines length of returned number.
0	0999	Prefixes value with leading zeros.
$	$9999	Prefixes value with dollar sign.
B	B9999	Returns zero value as blank instead of "0".
MI	9999MI	Returns "–" after negative values.
S	S9999	Returns "+" for positive values and "–" for negative values.
PR	9999PR	Returns negative values in angle brackets (<>).
D	99D99	Returns the decimal character.
G	9G999	Returns the group separator.
C	C999	Returns the international currency symbol.
L	L999	Returns the local currency symbol.
,	9,999	Returns a comma in this position.
.	99.99	Returns a period in this position.
V	999V99	Multiplies value by $10n$, where n is the number of 9's after the "V".
EEEE	9.999EEEE	Returns value in scientific notation. The format must contain a value for the exact number of E's.
RN or rn	RN	Upper- or lowercase Roman numerals (numbers in the range 1 to 3,999).
DATE	'DATE'	Returns value converted from Julian date to MM/DD/YY date format.

TABLE 4-6. *Numeric-formatting controls*

DATE Arithmetic

The special properties of the DATE datatype allow you to perform arithmetic operations with date values. This is called *date arithmetic*: Adding a number to a date produces a new date, and subtracting a number from a date produces a number. This seems very simple, but you can easily be tricked! Remember that all dates have hours, minutes, and seconds, which can produce fractional results. The difference between 4:00 P.M. today and 10:00 A.M. tomorrow is 0.667 days. (We'll discuss this in a moment.)

Oracle provides a function to give you the current system date and time. This function, SYSDATE, is useful in calculating date values relative to the current time. Table 4-7 summarizes the operators and functions that are specifically for performing date arithmetic.

Function or Operator	Description
+	Date addition: date + number = new date. The number is in days, so today + 1 = tomorrow; today + 7 = next week.
−	Date subtraction: date − date = number. The number is in days, so yesterday − today = 1.
*, /	Multiplication and division are not supported.
ADD_MONTHS(date, count)	Adds *count* months to *date*.
GREATEST(date1, date2, ...)	Finds the latest date of those listed. Warning: The dates must be DATE datatypes; otherwise, GREATEST will read the values as literal strings or numbers.
LEAST(date1, date2, ...)	The opposite of GREATEST.
LAST_DAY(date)	Produces the last day of the month the date is in.
MONTHS_BETWEEN(date2, date1)	Date subtraction with the result in months (can be fractional).
NEXT_DAY(date, 'day')	Produces the next 'day' after the date where *'day'* is Monday, Tuesday, etc.
NEW_TIME(date, 'tzone1', 'tzone2')	Replaces the date (and time) in time zone *tzone1* with the date (and time) in time zone *tzone2*.
ROUND(date, 'format')	Without a format, this rounds a date back to 12:00 midnight if the time is before noon; otherwise, it rounds up to the next day. With a format, the rounding is specific to the format.
TRUNC(date, 'format')	Without a format, this truncates a date back to 12:00 midnight of that date. With a format, the date is truncated based on that format.

TABLE 4-7. *Date arithmetic functions*

MLSLABEL Datatype

Trusted Oracle allows you to use the MLSLABEL datatype to store variable-length binary operating system labels. Trusted Oracle uses operating system labels to control access to data. For more information, see the Trusted Oracle 7 Server Administrator's Guide.

You can use the MLSLABEL datatype to define a database column. However, if you don't have Trusted Oracle, such columns will only store null values. With Trusted Oracle, you can insert any valid operating system label into a column of type MLSLABEL. If you pass the label as a character string, it is converted to a binary value automatically. Likewise, if you select an MLSLABEL from the database, Oracle automatically converts it to a character string. The text string can be up to 255 bytes long. However, the internal length of an MLSLABEL value is between two and five bytes.

External Datatypes

Oracle uses external datatypes to determine how data is stored in host variables. During execution of your application program, Oracle automatically converts the external datatype of each input host variable referenced in an SQL statement to the internal datatype of the corresponding database column. Likewise, after processing the SQL statement and determining the result, Oracle automatically determines the external datatype of each output host variable, converts the internal datatype to the external datatype, and returns the value.

Table 4-8 summarizes each Oracle-supported external datatype that is applicable to the C language. Other external datatypes (such as NUMBER, DECIMAL, and DISPLAY) exist, but they don't apply to C. Associated with each datatype is a code used for communication purposes throughout the Oracle system.

In this section we'll discuss each Oracle external datatype that is applicable to the C language, along with where it is used and any associated restrictions.

Character Datatypes

As we discussed earlier, the character datatypes in Oracle are used to store and manipulate words, strings, and free-form text. The internal character datatypes that are also external datatypes are CHAR, VARCHAR2, and LONG. In addition to these datatypes, Oracle supports the external character datatypes STRING, VARCHAR, LONG VARCHAR, and CHARZ.

Code	Name	Description
1	VARCHAR2	Variable-length character string
3	INTEGER	Signed integer
4	FLOAT	Floating-point number
5	STRING	Variable-length, null-terminated character string
6	VARNUM	Variable-length binary number
8	LONG	Long, fixed-length character string
9	VARCHAR	Variable-length character string with associated length
11	ROWID	Database address of a table row (binary value)
12	DATE	Fixed-length date/time value
15	VARRAW	Variable-length binary data with associated length
23	RAW	Fixed-length binary data
24	LONG RAW	Long, fixed-length binary data
68	UNSIGNED	Unsigned integer
94	LONG VARCHAR	Long, variable-length character string with associated length
95	LONG VARRAW	Long, variable-length binary data with associated length
96	CHAR	Short, fixed-length character string
97	CHARZ	Short, fixed-length, null-terminated character string
106	MLSLABEL	Variable-length binary data

TABLE 4-8. *Oracle external datatypes for C*

CHAR Datatype

The CHAR datatype is used to process relatively short (≤ 255), fixed-length character strings. The external CHAR datatype has all the characteristics of the internal CHAR datatype. A CHAR host variable is processed in the following manner.

On input, the assigned length of the host variable is used to determine the length of the string. If the length of the string value is shorter than the length of the target database column, the string value is padded with blanks up to the length of the column. If the string is longer than the database column, Oracle generates an error. If the input host variable is blank-filled, Oracle stores a string of blanks in the database rather than a null value (null values are discussed later).

On output, the string value returned from the database is assigned to the output host variable. If the string value is shorter than the host variable, the host variable is padded with blanks. If the string value is longer than the host variable, the string value is truncated and Oracle flags that it was truncated (we'll discuss this later as well).

CHARZ Datatype

The CHARZ datatype has all the characteristics of the CHAR datatype except that it is treated as a null-terminated string. A CHARZ host variable is processed in the following manner.

On input, you must null-terminate the input host variable string. Oracle scans the string value for a null terminator; if it is not found before the length of the column is reached, Oracle generates an error. If the first character in a string is a null terminator and the length of the host variable is 2, Oracle inserts a null in the database column. Unless the column is constrained not to contain null values (NOT NULL), Oracle generates an ORA-1400. On output, a CHARZ host variable behaves the same as a CHAR variable, with one exception: A null terminator is appended to the end of the string value after the blank-padding.

VARCHAR2 Datatype

The VARCHAR2 datatype is used to process variable-length character strings. The external VARCHAR2 datatype has all the characteristics of the internal VARCHAR2 datatype. A VARCHAR2 host variable is processed in the following manner.

On input, the length of the host variable is used to determine the maximum length of the string value. If the string value is shorter than the host variable length, blanks are stripped off the end before the value is stored in the database.

NOTE
Always blank-fill a variable-length host variable to its maximum length before using it. Oracle does not do this for you, and you may store uninitialized data fields in the database as a result.

If the input string value is longer than the host variable, Oracle generates an error. If the input value is blank-filled, Oracle assigns a null value to the database column unless it is constrained not to contain null values (NOT NULL), in which case Oracle generates an error (ORA-1400).

On output, Oracle assigns the string value from the database. No blank-padding or null-termination is done. If the database value is longer than the host variable, that value is truncated and Oracle flags that it was truncated.

STRING Datatype

The STRING datatype is used to process null-terminated, variable-length character strings. A STRING variable has the same properties as the VARCHAR2 datatype except that it is always null-terminated. If you don't specify a length when the variable is declared, the maximum length of 2,000 bytes is used by default. The minimum length of a STRING value is two bytes. The STRING datatype is processed in the following manner.

On input, Oracle uses the length of the STRING host variable to limit the search for the null terminator. If a null terminator is not found before the length of the host variable is reached, Oracle generates an error. If the first character in a string value is a null terminator and the host variable length is 2, Oracle inserts a null in the database column unless the column is constrained not to contain null values (NOT NULL), in which case Oracle generates an error (ORA-1400). STRING and CHARZ are identical on input.

On output, Oracle appends a null terminator to the end of the returned string value (with no blank-padding). If the returned string length exceeds the assigned length of the STRING host variable, Oracle truncates the output value and appends a null terminator. If a null value is returned from the database, a null terminator is assigned to the first character position of the STRING host variable.

VARCHAR Datatype

You use the VARCHAR datatype when you want to process a variable-length character string with its associated length. The VARCHAR datatype has a two-byte integer field followed by a variable-length string field. The two-byte integer field is used to store the length of the character string, and the string field stores the variable-length string. The maximum length of the string field is 65,533 bytes, although only 65,530 bytes are actually available for use. The syntax for the VARCHAR datatype is

```
VARCHAR variable_name[maximum_length];
```

where:

the maximum value is 65,530.

$1 \leq maximum\_length \leq 65,553$.

The VARCHAR datatype is actually defined as a data structure in C. Pro*C will comment out the VARCHAR declaration and replace it with the structure declaration. The VARCHAR data structure has the following definition:

```
struct
   {
   unsigned short len;
   unsigned char  arr[maximum_length];
   }   variable_name;
```

where:

len is the two-byte length field.

arr is the string field of maximum_length.

variable_name is the host variable name.

A VARCHAR host variable is processed in the following manner. On input, Oracle uses the assigned length to determine the string length that is stored in the database.

On output, Oracle assigns the returned string length to the length field and the string value to the string field. If the returned string value is shorter than the host variable, the string is not null-terminated or blank-filled. If it is longer than the host variable length, it is truncated as mentioned earlier. No null-termination or blank-padding is done.

LONG VARCHAR Datatype

You use the LONG VARCHAR datatype when you want to store a long, variable-length character string with its associated length. The LONG VARCHAR datatype has a four-byte integer field followed by a variable-length string field. The integer field is used to store the length of the character string, while the string field stores the variable-length string. The maximum length of the string field is approximately 2Gb ($2^{31} - 5$).

The syntax for the LONG VARCHAR datatype is

```
LONG VARCHAR(maximum_length)
```

where:

maximum value is 2,147,483,643.

$1 \leq maximum\_length \leq 2^{31} - 5$.

The LONG VARCHAR datatype is defined as a data structure, similar to VARCHAR. The data structure has the following definition:

```
struct
   {
   unsigned long len;
   unsigned char  arr[maximum_length];
   }   variable_name;
```

where:

len is the four-byte length field (note the difference).

arr is the string field of maximum_length.

variable_name is the host variable name.

The LONG VARCHAR datatype has the same input/output behavior as a VARCHAR datatype.

LONG Datatype

The LONG datatype is used to process a very long, fixed-length character string (such as a document). A LONG has all the characteristics of a VARCHAR2 except that a LONG datatype has a maximum length of 2Gb (2^{31}).

Numeric Datatypes

The *numeric datatypes* are external datatypes in Oracle that process numeric values in your application program. No internal numeric datatypes correspond to external datatypes. Oracle supports three external numeric datatypes: INTEGER, UNSIGNED, and FLOAT.

INTEGER Datatype   You use the INTEGER datatype to process numbers that have no fractional component (in other words, integers). An INTEGER is a signed, two- or four-byte binary number. A two-byte INTEGER number has a range of –32,768 to 32,767. A four-byte INTEGER has a range of –2,147,483,648 to 2,147,483,647. When you declare an INTEGER host variable, you must specify its size in bytes. The syntax for an INTEGER datatype is

```
INTEGER(size)
```

where **size** is 2 or 4, corresponding to two or four bytes.

This is valid only in EXEC SQL type or EXEC SQL variables. An INTEGER host variable is processed in the following manner. On input, the data value of an INTEGER host variable is compared with the precision and scale of the database column; if necessary, the data value is rounded before it is stored in the column. If the data value exceeds the column's precision, Oracle generates an error.

On output, the returned data value is compared with the size of the INTEGER host variable and assigned if it fits the size. Otherwise, Oracle generates an error.

UNSIGNED Datatype   You use the UNSIGNED datatype to process unsigned numbers that have no fractional component (integers). An UNSIGNED integer is a two-byte or four-byte binary number. A two-byte UNSIGNED number has a range of 0 to 65,535; a four-byte UNSIGNED datatype has a range of 0 to 4,294,967,295. When you declare an UNSIGNED host variable, you must specify its size in bytes. The syntax for an UNSIGNED datatype is

```
UNSIGNED(size)
```

where **size** is 2 or 4, corresponding to two or four bytes.

This is valid only in EXEC SQL type or EXEC SQL variables. An UNSIGNED host variable has the same behavior as an INTEGER host variable.

FLOAT Datatype   You use the FLOAT datatype to process numbers that have a fractional component or that exceed the size requirements for an INTEGER or UNSIGNED datatype (floating-point numbers). A FLOAT is a signed, floating-point, four- or eight-byte binary number. A four-byte FLOAT has a range of approximately 3.4E–38 to 3.4E+38. An eight-byte FLOAT has a range of approximately 1.7E–308 to 1.7E+308. You must specify the size of a FLOAT host variable. The syntax for a FLOAT datatype is

```
FLOAT(size)
```

where **size** is 4 or 8, corresponding to four or eight bytes.

This is valid only in EXEC SQL type or EXEC SQL variables. A FLOAT host variable is processed in the following manner. On input, the data value of a FLOAT host variable is compared with the precision and scale of the database column. If necessary, the data value is rounded and truncated before it is stored in the column. If the data value exceeds the column's precision, Oracle generates an error.

On output, the returned data value is compared with the size of the FLOAT host variable and assigned if it fits the size. Otherwise, Oracle generates an error.

CAUTION
It is possible to encounter rounding errors when you use FLOAT variables because FLOAT is binary and NUMBER is decimal.

VARNUM Datatype
You will not normally use the VARNUM datatype. It has the same characteristics as the internal NUMBER datatype, except that the first byte is used to store the length of the number.

On input, you must assign the length of the number to the first byte of the host variable; the second to *n* bytes contain the number value.

On output, Oracle assigns the length of the number to the first byte and the number value to the remaining byte fields. You must allocate 22 bytes for the host variable to accommodate the largest possible number that can be assigned to a VARNUM variable.

NOTE
You won't need to use this datatype. The INTEGER, UNSIGNED, and FLOAT datatypes are sufficient for almost every programming situation.

Binary Datatypes

As discussed earlier, binary datatypes are used to process raw binary data. These datatypes process graphic images and digitized video or sound. The internal binary datatypes that are also external datatypes are RAW and LONG RAW; the external datatypes have the same characteristics as their internal counterparts. In addition to these datatypes, Oracle supports the external character datatypes VARRAW and LONG VARRAW.

RAW Datatype
The RAW datatype is used to process relatively short (≤255), fixed-length binary data. The external RAW datatype has all the characteristics of the internal RAW datatype except that the internal RAW is variable and the external RAW is fixed. A RAW host variable is processed in the following manner.

On input, the assigned length of the host variable is used to determine the length of the binary data, which is stored in the database. If the binary data is longer than the database column, Oracle generates an error.

On output, the binary data value returned from the database is assigned to the output host variable. If the binary data is longer than the host variable, it is truncated and Oracle flags that it is truncated (this will be discussed in more detail later).

LONG RAW Datatype
The LONG RAW datatype is used to process very long, variable-length binary data. LONG RAW has all the characteristics of the RAW datatype except that it has a maximum length of 2Gb (2^{31}).

VARRAW Datatype
You use the VARRAW datatype when you want to process a variable-length binary data value with its associated length. The VARRAW datatype has a two-byte integer field followed by a variable-length binary data field. The two-byte integer field is

used to store the length of the binary data. The binary data field stores the variable-length binary data. The maximum length of the binary data field is 65,533 bytes, although only 65,530 bytes are actually available for use. The syntax for the VARRAW datatype is

```
VARRAW(2)
```

where:

> 2 is the two-byte integer field for the length.

> $1 \leq$ maximum_length $\leq 65,553$.

> The VARRAW datatype is actually defined as a data structure in C. The VARRAW data structure has the following definition:

```
struct
   {
   unsigned short len;
   unsigned char   arr[maximum_length];
   }   variable_name;
```

where:

> **len** is the two-byte length field.

> **arr** is the binary data field of **maximum_length**.

> **variable_name** is the host variable name.

> A VARRAW host variable is processed in the following manner. On input, Oracle uses the assigned length to determine the binary data length that is stored in the database.
> On output, Oracle assigns the returned binary data length to the length field and the binary data value to the binary data field. If the returned binary data value is shorter than the host variable, the binary data value is not null-terminated or blank-filled. If it is longer than the host variable length, it is truncated and flagged as having been truncated.

LONG VARRAW Datatype
You use the LONG VARRAW datatype when you want to store a long, variable-length binary data value with its associated length. The LONG VARRAW datatype has a four-byte integer field followed by a variable-length binary data

field. The four-byte integer field is used to store the length of the binary data. The binary data field stores the variable-length binary data. The maximum length of the binary data field is approximately 2Gb ($2^{31}-5$). The syntax for the LONG VARRAW datatype is

```
LONG VARRAW(4)
```

where:

4 is the four-byte integer field for the length.

$1 \leq \text{maximum\_length} \leq 2^{31} - 5$.

The LONG VARRAW datatype is defined as a data structure, similar to VARRAW. The LONG VARRAW data structure has the following definition:

```
struct
    {
    unsigned long len;
    unsigned char  arr[maximum_length];
    }   variable_name;
```

where:

len is the four-byte length field (note the difference).

arr is the binary data field of **maximum_length**.

variable_name is the host variable name.

The LONG VARRAW datatype has the same input/output behavior as a VARRAW datatype.

ROWID Datatype

The ROWID datatype is used to process binary rowids in fixed-length variables. A rowid's length is system-specific; consult the Oracle installation or user's guide for your system. The ROWID datatype has all the characteristics of the internal datatype.

NOTE
This datatype is seldom used. Normally, you should use the VARCHAR2 or STRING datatype to process rowids as hexadecimal

strings. When processing rowids as VARCHAR2 variables, use the ROWID pseudocolumn to compare data values.

DATE Datatype

The DATE datatype is used to process date and time values in fixed-length, seven-byte host variables. The DATE datatype has all the characteristics of the internal datatype.

NOTE
This datatype is seldom used. Normally, you use a character-string datatype to process dates and times.

MLSLABEL Datatype

You use the MLSLABEL datatype to process variable-length, binary operating system labels. Trusted Oracle uses operating system labels to control access to data. For more information, see the Trusted Oracle 7 Server Administrator's Guide.

The external MLSLABEL has all the characteristics of the internal datatype. The MLSLABEL is processed in the following manner.

On input, Oracle converts the input host variable into an internal binary label—which must be a valid operating system label—and stores it in the database column. If the label is not valid, Oracle generates an error.

On output, Oracle converts the binary label to a character string and assigns it to the output host variable.

NOTE
This datatype is seldom used. Normally, you should use a character-string host variable to process MLSLABELs.

ANSI Standard Datatypes

The external datatypes supported by Oracle support the ANSI standard datatypes defined in the ANSI standard for SQL. Table 4-9 describes the compatible datatypes.

ANSI SQL Datatype	Oracle Datatype
CHARACTER(n), CHAR(n)	CHAR(n)
CHARACTER VARYING(n), CHAR VARYING(n), VARCHAR(n)	VARCHAR2(n)
NUMERIC(p,s), DECIMAL(p,s), DEC(p,s)[1]	NUMBER(p,s)
INTEGER, INT, SMALLINT	NUMBER(38)
FLOAT(b)[2], REAL[3], DOUBLE PRECISION[4]	NUMBER

Notes:

1. The NUMERIC, DECIMAL, and DEC datatypes are used to specify fixed-point numbers. For these datatypes, scale s defaults to 0.

2. The FLOAT datatype is a floating-point number with binary precision b. The default precision for this datatype is 126 binary, or 38 decimal.

3. The REAL datatype is a floating-point number with binary precision 63, or 18 decimal.

4. The DOUBLE PRECISION datatype is a floating-point number with binary precision 126.

TABLE 4-9. *ANSI vs. Oracle datatypes*

Host and Indicator Variables

In Chapter 3, you saw a practical example of how to declare and use host and indicator variables. In this section, we'll expand on our current knowledge by discussing some additional details of these variables and how they are employed in your application program, along with some advanced topics. At the end, we'll evaluate a sample program that will show you all you need to know to take full advantage of the tools provided by Oracle.

Host Variables

Host variables are the key to communication between your application program and the Oracle database. As we just discussed, the Oracle internal and external datatypes are inherently incompatible. Because of this incompatibility, you must "declare" to Oracle which variables you will use in your application program to communicate with the Oracle database. A host variable is declared in an application program so that it can be shared with Oracle, allowing both the database and your application program to access the value of the host variable.

Host variables are used for both input to and output from the database. An input host variable is used to pass a data value from your application program to the database; an output host variable is used to return a data value from the database to your application program. Therefore, you must declare in your application program each variable that you use in an embedded SQL statement as a host variable.

Declaring Host Variables

As we discussed in Chapter 3, you declare host variables in a special section of your program called the DECLARE section. Oracle treats any variable declared in this section as a host variable. The syntax to create a DECLARE section in your program is

```
EXEC SQL BEGIN DECLARE SECTION;
    .
    .
    .

EXEC SQL END DECLARE SECTION;
```

Like C language variables, you can use DECLARE sections in your program to declare host variables as local variables, static global variables (global to a source module), or global variables. You can define multiple DECLARE sections in a function or source module as long as there are no conflicting variable declarations.

You declare host variables according to the rules of C. Oracle supports all the basic C datatypes that we discussed in Chapter 3. In addition to the basic C datatypes, Oracle supports the external datatypes we discussed in the section on external datatypes. Let's review our example to refresh our memory on how host variables are declared:

```
EXEC SQL BEGIN DECLARE SECTION;
    /*
    ** host variables for logging into the Oracle database
    */
    VARCHAR vcConnect[21];
    VARCHAR vcPassword[21];
    VARCHAR vcUserId[41];
EXEC SQL END DECLARE SECTION;
```

The following general rules apply when declaring host variables:

■ You declare host variables according to C rules.

■ You can declare a one-dimensional array for any datatype and a two-dimensional array for character types only.

■ You can repeat variable declarations of the same datatype on the same line.

■ You can initialize host variables when they are declared. However, you cannot initialize arrays in the DECLARE section.

■ You can put comments in the DECLARE section.

Three storage class identifiers can be used to declare host variables as local variables, static local variables, static global variables, or global variables. They are **auto**, **static**, and **extern**.

As for C variables, the default for local host variables is the **auto** storage class identifier. For global variables declared outside a function, the **extern** or **static** global storage class identifier must be explicitly assigned.

You must observe a few additional rules when declaring host variables:

■ Host variable names can be any length, but only the first 31 characters are used. To be ANSI/ISO-compliant, host variable names can be no longer than 18 characters, must begin with a letter, and cannot contain consecutive or trailing underscores.

■ Host variables are case-sensitive; they must be declared and referenced in the same case (since C is case-sensitive).

■ You cannot use the **register** storage class identifier for host variables.

■ You cannot use any of the Oracle reserved words.

The important thing to remember is that host variables can be declared just like any C variable except for the restrictions we have discussed.

Using Host Variables

Host variables can be referenced in regular C language statements and in embedded data-manipulation SQL statements in your application program. You reference host variables in regular C language statements just like any other C variable. However, you must prefix host variables with a colon (:) when they are referenced in embedded SQL statements. To illustrate how you reference host variables, let's return to our previous example.

```
/*
** Set the length of the input strings.
*/

vcUserId.len = strlen(vcUserId.arr);
vcPassword.len = strlen(vcPassword.arr);
vcConnect.len = strlen(vcConnect.arr);
```

```
/*
** Execute the Pro*C CONNECT statement...
**     one of several possible forms.
*/

EXEC SQL CONNECT :vcUserId
    IDENTIFIED BY :vcPassword
    USING :vcConnect;
```

From this example we learn the following:

1. You use host variables in C statements just like C variables.

2. You must prefix host variables with a colon (:) in embedded SQL statements.

There are some additional restrictions that don't exist in this example. A host variable cannot be:

◼ Used to identify a column, table, or other Oracle object.

◼ Used in data-definition SQL statements (such as ALTER, CREATE, and DROP).

◼ An Oracle reserved keyword.

Pointer Host Variables

A pointer variable stores the address (storage location) of another variable and is used to "point" to that variable's *location*, not its value. A pointer is used as a mechanism to access the value of a variable indirectly. Except for character strings (discussed in the next section), the size of the pointer variable is determined by the size of its declared base type. For example, the size of an **int** pointer variable is the size of **int**.

A pointer variable is declared using C language format with other host variables in the DECLARE section. Let's look at another example to see how pointer variables are declared and referenced.

```
EXEC SQL BEGIN DECLARE SECTION;
    int   iLength, iElement;
    int   *piLength, aiArray[100];
EXEC END DECLARE SECTION;
```

```
piLength = &iLength;
iElement =  aiArray[0];
```

From this example we learn the following:

1. You declare host pointer variables according to the C rules.

2. You can declare host pointer variables for any datatype. Host pointer variables have the same restrictions as host variables. (Note that the use of pointer variables as host variables is an Oracle extension to the ANSI standard. You can use the FIPS flagger, which is used to identify extensions to the ANSI/ISO standards. See Chapter 12 for more information on using the precompiler options.)

3. You use host pointer variables in C statements just like C variables.

4. Pointer host variables are referenced with a colon (:) in embedded SQL statements, just like other host variables.

5. You can use host pointer variables to reference the elements of a user-defined data structure.

NOTE
The ANSI standard does not support pointers as host variables. However, Oracle provides an extension to the ANSI standard to allow pointer host variables, even when MODE=ANSI. In this mode, the FIPS flagger can warn you that you have violated the standard if you choose that option.

Character-String Host Variables

Character strings are unique in C because the native C language doesn't support a character-string datatype; it only supports a single-character datatype (**char**). C does support character strings through the use of character arrays and character pointers. Also, ANSI-compliant C compilers provide a standard library of character-string processing functions.

Your application program processes character arrays and character pointers using identical methods; the only difference between a character array and a character pointer is that a character array is assigned a maximum length when it is declared and always points to the same location in memory. A character pointer is given a length by assigning it the address of dynamically allocated memory or by assigning it the address of another character variable (a single-character variable, a character-array variable, or another character pointer).

Oracle supports processing of character strings as character arrays and character pointers. It also supports processing of character arrays with an associated length. Table 4-10 summarizes the character-string datatypes supported by Oracle.

Now that we know the character-string datatypes, let's discuss how you use them as character-string host variables in your application program.

The MODE Option   First, you must understand that Oracle processes character-string variables (**char**-based variables, not VARCHAR or LONG VARCHAR variables) differently based on the MODE option you specify when you precompile your program. The MODE option allows you to specify how you want Oracle to process character strings, either according to ANSI standard rules or to remain compatible with previous versions of Oracle.

Two MODE options affect character-string processing: MODE=Oracle (the default, equivalent to MODE={ANSI13 | ANSI14}), and MODE=ANSI.

NOTE
The MODE option is version-dependent. Check the details for your system.

The MODE option affects the processing of character-string data when you input host variables to Oracle and when Oracle outputs host variables to your application program. The differences the MODE option imposes will be pointed out as we discuss each datatype.

Declaration	Datatype	Description
char name[n]	Character array	*name* is the variable name. *n* is the maximum array length and is optional, which results in a single-character variable (but don't specify the brackets in this case).
char *name	Character pointer	*name* is the variable name. * indicates that this is a pointer variable.
VARCHAR name[n]	Character array with length	*name* is the variable name. *n* is required and specifies the maximum array length ($1 \leq n \leq 65{,}533$).
VARCHAR *name	Character pointer with length	*name* is the variable name. * indicates that this is a pointer variable.

TABLE 4-10.   *Character datatypes supported by Oracle*

Character Arrays   A character array is assigned a maximum length when it is declared as a host variable in the DECLARE section of your program. The MODE option determines how the character-array variable must be formatted on input and how it is formatted on output. The character-array format may be padded with blanks and may be null-terminated.

On input, when MODE=Oracle, the variable is assigned the VARCHAR2 external datatype. Therefore, trailing blanks are stripped from a character array before its character-string value is stored in the database. You must be careful to ensure that a character array is padded with blanks before its character-string value is assigned to a database column. A character array can be padded with blanks using one of two methods: blank-initialization or blank-padding.

With blank-initialization, you initialize a character array with blanks before assigning to it a character-string value. If a character-array variable is used only once in your program, you can initialize it with blanks when it is declared as follows:

```
EXEC SQL BEGIN DECLARE SECTION;
    int iItemId = 1000;
    char scItemName[20] = "                    ";
EXEC SQL END DECLARE SECTION;

/* Note the use of strncpy, so that a trailing 0 isn't placed */
/* in the array. */
strncpy (scItemName, "Computer Monitor", 16);

EXEC SQL UPDATE item
    SET (item_name = :scItemName)
    WHERE item_id = :iItemId;
```

If a character array is used more than once in your program (as is more often the case), you should initialize the array with blanks before each use:

```
EXEC SQL BEGIN DECLARE SECTION;
    int iItemId = 1000;
    char scItemName[20];
EXEC SQL END DECLARE SECTION;

memset (scItemName, ' ', 20);
strncpy (scItemName, "Computer Monitor", 16);

EXEC SQL UPDATE item
    SET (item_name = :scItemName)
    WHERE item_id = :iItemId;
```

```
memset (scItemName, ' ', 20);
strncpy (scItemName, "Computer Mouse", 14);

EXEC SQL UPDATE item
   SET (item_name = :scItemName)
   WHERE item_id = :iItemId;
```

The second method is blank-padding. After assigning a character-string value to a character-string array, you pad the array with blanks to its maximum length. The following method is much more generic but will cost more in performance:

```
int iStringLen;
EXEC SQL BEGIN DECLARE SECTION;
   INT iItemId = 1000;
   char scItemName[20];
EXEC SQL END DECLARE SECTION;

strcpy (scItemName, "Computer Monitor");
iStringLen = strlen (scItemName);
memset (&scItemName[iStringLen], ' ', sizeof (scItemName) -
   iStringLen);   /* sizeof operator gives size of array. */

EXEC SQL UPDATE item
   SET (item_name = :scItemName)
   WHERE item_id = :iItemId;
```

If you don't blank-pad a character array as the examples show, you risk assigning unwanted data to a database column. If, for example, you didn't blank-pad the character array as shown in the preceding example, you may end up with a database column assigned the string "Computer Monitor\0\0\0\0" (four null values assigned to the end of the string). This value would not match a database comparison like the following:

```
... WHERE item_name = 'Computer Monitor';
```

On input, when MODE=ANSI, a character array doesn't need to be blank-padded, but its character-string value must be null-terminated before it is assigned to the database. This is actually a more natural method for processing character strings in C, because most of the C-provided character-string functions create or expect a null-terminated string. However, you should always declare your character arrays with a length that includes one extra element to hold the null terminator:

```
EXEC SQL BEGIN DECLARE SECTION;
    int iItemId = 1000;
    char scItemName[21]; /* extra element for null terminator */
EXEC SQL END DECLARE SECTION;

strcpy (scItemName, "Computer Monitor");

EXEC SQL UPDATE item
    SET (item_name = :scItemName)
    WHERE item_id = :iItemId;
```

On output, when MODE=Oracle, a character-array variable is assigned a character-string value from the database. A null terminator is not assigned to the end of the character string or to the array. When MODE=ANSI, the array is blank-padded and then null-terminated. The following example illustrates the differences between the two MODEs:

```
EXEC SQL BEGIN DECLARE SECTION;
    int iItemId = 1000;
    char scItemName[20];
EXEC SQL END DECLARE SECTION;

EXEC SQL SELECT item_name INTO :scItemName
    FROM item
    WHERE item_id = :iItemId;
```

If MODE=Oracle, the result assigned to **scItemName** would be

```
"Computer Monitor      "
```

Remember to null-terminate these character arrays before passing them to a function (such as **strcpy** or **strcmp**) that expects a null-terminated string.
If MODE=ANSI, the result is

```
/* three padded blanks and a NULL terminator */
"Computer Monitor   \0"
```

Character Pointers   A character pointer is used to "point" to an address in memory or to the address of another variable. To use a character pointer, you must first assign to it the address of dynamically allocated memory to hold a character string or the address of a previously declared character variable or character array.
Character pointers are processed in the same manner, regardless of MODE. On input, a character-pointer variable must point to the address of a valid character-

string buffer (dynamic memory or character array). You assign a character-string value to the character-string buffer and terminate it with a null. You are responsible for ensuring that the character-string buffer is large enough to hold the character-string value plus the null terminator (string length + 1). (For the STRING external datatype, this is the same behavior as when MODE=ANSI.) The following example shows how you declare, allocate, and assign a character pointer for input:

```
EXEC SQL BEGIN DECLARE SECTION;
    int iItemId = 1000;
    /* Always initialize a pointer to NULL. */
    char *scItemName = NULL;
EXEC SQL END DECLARE SECTION;

/* one extra element for the NULL */
scItemName = (char *) malloc (21);
/* Check here to see if malloc was successful. */
strcpy (scItemName, "Computer Monitor");

EXEC SQL UPDATE item
    SET (item_name = :scItemName)
    WHERE item_id = :iItemId;
```

On output, as on input, a character-pointer variable must point to the address of a valid character-string buffer. You are responsible for ensuring that the character-string buffer is large enough to hold the character-string value plus the null terminator.

Before Oracle can assign a character-string value from the database to a character-pointer variable, it must first determine the maximum length of the buffer. It does this by calling the **strlen** function. Thus, to assign a character-string value from the database to a character pointer, you initialize the buffer with something other than nulls, then null-terminate the buffer before you get the data. After Oracle assigns the character-string value, the string is blank-padded to the maximum length of the buffer. The following example shows how you declare, allocate, and use a character pointer for output:

```
EXEC SQL BEGIN DECLARE SECTION;
    int iItemId = 1000;
    /* Always initialize a pointer to NULL. */
    char *scItemName = NULL;
EXEC SQL END DECLARE SECTION;

/* one extra element for the NULL */
```

```
/* Check here to see if malloc was successful. */
scItemName = (char *) malloc (21);
memset (scItemName, ' ', 21);
scItemName[20] = NULL;

EXEC SQL SELECT item_name INTO :scItemName
   FROM item;
   WHERE item_id = iItemId;
```

The result of the SELECT statement would be

```
"Computer Monitor      "
```

VARCHAR Variables   A VARCHAR variable is used to process variable-length character strings with an associated length. The VARCHAR datatype is referred to as a *pseudotype* because the datatype declaration is actually translated into a data structure containing an entry for the string length and another for the string value. (This was discussed in the previous section on external datatypes.) The following example illustrates how the VARCHAR datatype is translated into a data structure:

```
EXEC SQL BEGIN DECLARE SECTION;
   /*
   ** host variables for logging into the Oracle database
   */
   VARCHAR vcConnect[21];
   VARCHAR vcPassword[21];
   VARCHAR vcUserId[41];
EXEC SQL END DECLARE SECTION;
```

translates to

```
struct {
   unsigned short len;
   unsigned char arr[21];
} vcConnect;

struct {
  unsigned short len;
  unsigned char arr[21];
  } vcPassword;

struct {
   unsigned short len;
```

```
    unsigned char arr[41];
    } vcUserId;
```

NOTE
The processing of VARCHAR variables is not affected by the
MODE option.

On input, you simply assign a character-string value to the string field in the
VARCHAR structure and the character-string length (not including a null
terminator) to the length field. It is important that you assign the exact length of the
character string to the length field; Oracle doesn't look for trailing blanks or null
values to terminate the string, but stores the string value up to the length specified,
including any blanks and nulls (if present). The following example shows how a
VARCHAR variable is declared, assigned, and inserted into the database:

```
EXEC SQL BEGIN DECLARE SECTION;
    /*
    ** host variables for logging into the Oracle database
    */
    VARCHAR vcConnect[21];
    VARCHAR vcPassword[21];
    VARCHAR vcUserId[41];
EXEC SQL END DECLARE SECTION;

/*
** Set the length of the input strings.
*/
strcpy(vcUserId.arr, "Scott");  /* Assign password and connect. */
vcUserId.len = strlen(vcUserId.arr);
vcPassword.len = strlen(vcPassword.arr);
vcConnect.len = strlen(vcConnect.arr);

EXEC SQL CONNECT :vcUserId
    IDENTIFIED BY :vcPassword
    USING :vcConnect;
```

On output, Oracle assigns the character-string value length to the length field of
the VARCHAR structure and assigns the character-string value to the string field.
The string field is not blank-padded or null-terminated. Remember to null-terminate
the character string before passing it to a function (such as **strcpy** or **strcmp**) that
expects a null-terminated string. The following example shows how this is
accomplished:

```
EXEC SQL BEGIN DECLARE SECTION;
    int iItemId = 1000;
        VARCHAR vcItemName[21];
    char scItemName[20];
EXEC SQL END DECLARE SECTION;

EXEC SQL SELECT item_name INTO :vcItemname
    FROM item
    WHERE item_id = iItemId;

vcItemName.arr[vcItemName.len] = '\0';
strcpy (scItemName, vcItemName.arr);
```

The advantage of VARCHAR variables is that the string length is already computed when you get it from the database. With character arrays, you may need to strip blanks before the length can be computed.

VARCHAR Pointers   A VARCHAR pointer is used in the same way as a VARCHAR variable, with the added advantage of using dynamically allocated memory for the character-string buffer instead of a fixed-length character array.

NOTE
As with VARCHAR variables, the processing of VARCHAR pointers is not affected by the MODE option.

On input, you process a VARCHAR pointer the same way as a VARCHAR variable except that you are responsible for allocating enough memory to hold the expanded VARCHAR data structure (plus the desired character-string buffer length). This is done in the following manner:

```
EXEC SQL BEGIN DECLARE SECTION;
    int iItemId = 1000;
    VARCHAR *pcItemName = NULL;
EXEC SQL END DECLARE SECTION;

pcItemName = malloc(sizeof(short) + 20);   /* len + arr in bytes */

/* Check here to see if malloc was successful. */
strcpy (pcItemName.arr, "Computer monitor");
pcItemName.len = strlen (pcItemName.arr);
```

```
EXEC SQL UPDATE item
   SET (item_name = :pcItemname);
   WHERE item_id = iItemId;
```

On output, Oracle determines the maximum length of the string field by looking at the value assigned to the length field. Thus, before you obtain the character-string value from the database, you must set the maximum length of the string field to the length field. Oracle will then process the character string just like a VARCHAR variable. The following example shows how this is done:

```
EXEC SQL BEGIN DECLARE SECTION;
   int iItemId = 1000;
   VARCHAR *pcItemName = NULL;
EXEC SQL END DECLARE SECTION;

pcItemName = malloc(sizeof(short) + 20);  /* len + arr in bytes */

/* Check here to see if malloc was successful. */
pcItemNam->len = 20;

EXEC SQL SELECT item_name INTO :pcItemName
   FROM item
   WHERE item_id = iItemId;
```

Table 4-11 shows the effect of MODE on external datatypes.

Indicator Variables

When a host variable is either passed from your application program to the database or retrieved from the database into your application program, often there is a need to know the status of the value assigned to the host variable. As discussed in Chapter 3, indicator variables are two-byte integer variables used to indicate the status of an associated host variable on either input or output.

An indicator variable can optionally be associated with any host variable. Indicator variables are used in your application program to indicate that a null value is to be assigned to an input host variable; they're also used to detect a null or truncated value that is assigned by the database to an output host variable.

Declaring Indicator Variables

Indicator variables are declared in the DECLARE section of your program in the same manner and following the same rules as host variables. However, an

Variable Declared As	External Datatype (MODE=Oracle)	External Datatype (MODE=ANSI)
CHAR X[n];	VARCHAR2	CHARZ
CHAR *X;	STRING	STRING
VARCHAR X[n];	VARCHAR	VARCHAR
VARCHAR *X;	VARCHAR	VARCHAR

TABLE 4-11. *The effect of MODE on external datatypes*

indicator variable must be declared as a **short** integer. To illustrate how you declare indicator variables, let's return to our previous example:

```
EXEC SQL BEGIN DECLARE SECTION;
    .
    .
    .
    VARCHAR vcTermDate[11];

    /*
    ** indicator variables for the host variables defined above
    */

    short indEmpSSN;
    short indFName;
    short indLName;
    short indMiddleInit;
    short indAddress;
    short indCity;
    short indState;
    short indZipcode;
    short indWPhone;
    short indHPhone;
    short indPayRate;
    short indPayType;
    short indHireDate;
    short indTermDate;
EXEC SQL END DECLARE SECTION;
```

Note that indicator variables are declared as **short** integers, like host variables, and that they can be declared anywhere in the DECLARE section; they need not precede or directly follow the declaration of their associated host variables.

Using Indicator Variables

Indicator variables can be referenced in regular C statements just like any other C variable. They are directly associated with host variables in embedded data-manipulation SQL statements in your application program; however, you must prefix indicator variables with a colon (:), and the indicator variable must directly follow (no separation by a comma) its associated host variable in embedded SQL statements or have the keyword INDICATOR. To illustrate how you reference indicator variables, let's return to our previous example:

```
indEmpSSN = indFName = indMiddleInit = indLName = indAddress =
indCity = indState = indZipcode = indWPhone = indHPhone =
indPayRate = indPayType = indHireDate = indTermDate = 0;


/*
** Get the values from each field of the Employee window. If the
** length of the value returned is zero (0), set the indicator
** variable to -1 (NULL).
*/


if ((vcEmpSSN.len = GetDlgItemText(hWnd, ID_EMPLOYEE_FLD_EMPSSN,
    (LPSTR)vcEmpSSN.arr, 12)) == 0)
    indEmpSSN = -1;


/* Other similar code would follow here to assign all values. */


EXEC SQL INSERT INTO EMPLOYEE
            (EMPLOYEE.EMPLOYEE_SSN, EMPLOYEE.FIRST_NAME,
            EMPLOYEE.MIDDLE_INITIAL, EMPLOYEE.LAST_NAME,
            EMPLOYEE.ADDRESS, EMPLOYEE.CITY,
            EMPLOYEE.STATE, EMPLOYEE.ZIPCODE, EMPLOYEE.WORK_PHONE,
            EMPLOYEE.HOME_PHONE, EMPLOYEE.PAY_RATE,
            EMPLOYEE.PAY_TYPE,
            EMPLOYEE.HIRE_DATE, EMPLOYEE.TERMINATION_DATE)
        VALUES (:vcEmpSSN:indEmpSSN,
                :vcFName:indFName,
                :vcMiddleInit:indMiddleInit,
                :vcLName:indLName,
```

```
:vcAddress:indAddress,
:vcCity:indCity,
:vcState:indState,
:vcZipcode:indZipcode,
:vcWPhone:indWPhone,
:vcHPhone:indHPhone,
:vcPayRate:indPayRate,
:vcPayType:indPayType,
:vcHireDate:indHireDate,
:vcTermDate:indTermDate);
```

From this example we learn that:

1. You use indicator variables in C statements as you would use C variables.

2. You must prefix indicator variables with a colon (:) in embedded SQL statements.

3. An indicator variable must directly follow (no comma separator) its associated host variable in an embedded SQL statement.

The keyword INDICATOR can precede an indicator variable in an SQL statement to improve readability. The correct syntax is

```
:host_variable INDICATOR :indicator_variable
```

which is equivalent to

```
:host_variable:indicator_variable
```

Both forms are legal.

Two additional restrictions that don't exist in this example are that an indicator variable cannot be used in SQL data-definition statements (such as ALTER, CREATE, or DROP), and it cannot be an Oracle reserved keyword. Note also that indicator variables are generally not useful in the WHERE clause of an SQL statement.

When an indicator variable is associated with an input host variable, you can assign a value to the indicator variable to control the value assigned to the database column. The following are the values you can assign an indicator variable on input and their meanings:

–1 Oracle will assign a null to the database column, ignoring the value of the host variable. For each column you want to assign a null, set the appropriate indicator variable to –1. If the column is constrained not to contain null values (NOT NULL), the database will return an error (ORA-1400).

≥ 0   Oracle will assign the value of the host variable to the database column.

When an indicator variable is associated with an output host variable, Oracle assigns a value to the indicator variable based on the value it assigns to the output host variable. The following are the values Oracle assigns to an indicator variable on output and their meanings:

–1   The column value is null, so the value of the host variable is indeterminate.

 0   The column value is assigned to the host variable without a problem.

> 0   The column value is truncated when it is assigned to the host variable. The integer assigned to the indicator variable is the original length of the column value.

When processing null values, you can experience the following behavior:

- ■ When DBMS=V6, you can SELECT or FETCH nulls into a host variable not associated with an indicator variable. However, when DBMS=V7, if you SELECT or FETCH nulls into a host variable not associated with an indicator variable, Oracle will generate an error (ORA-1405).

- ■ When MODE=Oracle, if you SELECT or FETCH a truncated column value into a host variable not associated with an indicator variable, Oracle will generate an error. However, when MODE={ANSI | ANSI14 | ANSI13}, no error is generated.

Host Arrays

Host variables are useful when you need to pass a single data value to the database or retrieve a single data value from the database. However, Oracle is a set-oriented relational database, which means that the database is designed specifically to operate on sets of data.

How can you make your application program set-oriented by operating on sets of data? Oracle allows you to declare arrays of host variables, called *host arrays*, that are used to process sets of data. An array is a set of related data items, or *elements*, of the same datatype that are referenced by a single variable name. Just like host variables, a host array is declared in the DECLARE section of your application program.

Because you can operate on large sets of data in a single SQL statement, you get the added benefit of improved performance. This is possible because the array is processed with a single call to the database instead of a single call for each member of the array. For example, let's say you need to update the sale price of a selected set of 100 items in your database. With a host array, you can do this in a single SQL statement rather than 100 statements.

Declaring Host Arrays

A host array is declared in the DECLARE section of your application program just like any other host variable except that the variable is dimensioned to contain a set of array elements. The following example illustrates how host arrays are declared:

```
EXEC SQL BEGIN DECLARE SECTION;
    int aiItemId[100];
    float afRetailPrice[100];
    float afItemCost[100];
EXEC END DECLARE SECTION;
```

From this example we learn that:

1. You declare host arrays according to C rules in the DECLARE section by dimensioning a variable to have an array size.

2. You can declare a one-dimensional array for any datatype.

There are some additional restrictions that don't exist in this example. One is that host arrays cannot be initialized when they are declared. For example, the following statements would not be legal:

```
EXEC SQL BEGIN DECLARE SECTION;
    int aiItemNumber[3] = {1, 2, 3};
EXEC SQL END DECLARE SECTION;
```

Host arrays also cannot have more than one dimension. The only exception is arrays of character strings, which can be declared with the following syntax:

```
datatype variable_name[m][n]
```

where:

m is the number of character strings in the array.

n is the maximum length of each string (this is discussed later in the chapter).

For example,

```
char ascItemName[100][20];
```

declares an array of 100 character strings, each 20 characters long.
Host arrays also cannot:

- Be an array of pointers (this is not supported).

- Be dimensioned to contain more than 32,767 elements. If you use an array whose size exceeds this amount, Oracle generates a run-time error.

- Have (or should not have) a different number of elements from that of other host arrays that are used together in a single SQL statement. Oracle assumes that all host arrays referenced in a single SQL statement have the same number of elements. If you violate this rule, Oracle generates a warning and uses the size of the host array with the fewest number of elements to process the SQL statement.

Declaring Indicator Arrays

Just as with host variables, you need the ability to associate an indicator variable with each element of a host array. You do this by declaring an array of indicator variables and associating it with a host array in an SQL statement, the same way an indicator variable is associated with a host variable. An array of indicator variables is called an *indicator array*. An indicator array is declared just like any other array of the datatype **short** (just like an indicator variable).

An indicator array is used in conjunction with a host array for exactly the same reason an indicator variable is used with a host variable: to set or obtain the status of a host array element. You can use an indicator array to assign null values to the elements of an input host array and to detect null or truncated values in an output host array. An indicator array must follow all the same restrictions we discussed for host arrays. The following example shows how an indicator array is declared.

```
EXEC SQL BEGIN DECLARE SECTION;
    int aiItemId[100];
    float afRetailPrice[100];
    float afItemCost[100];

    short indItemId[100];
    short indRetailPrice[100];
    short indItemCost[100];
EXEC END DECLARE SECTION;
```

NOTE
An indicator array must be dimensioned to at least the same length as its associated host array; it can be longer.

Using Host and Indicator Arrays

Oracle allows you to use host and indicator arrays in most data-manipulation SQL statements. Specifically, you can use arrays as input to INSERT, UPDATE, and DELETE statements and as output from the INTO clause of SELECT and FETCH statements. You cannot use arrays with data-definition SQL statements (such as CREATE, ALTER, and DROP).

As you know from earlier examples, the syntax to declare host and indicator arrays is almost identical to simple host and indicator variables (except for the array dimension). Likewise, host and indicator arrays are used in SQL statements with exactly the same syntax as host and indicator variables. One additional operator is provided for processing arrays—the optional FOR clause—so that you can control the number of array elements processed in a single SQL statement. In the following sections we'll discuss the use of host and indicator arrays in the various data-manipulation SQL statements, along with any restrictions.

NOTE
Arrays are not supported in the ANSI standard. Therefore, when MODE=ANSI14, array operations are not allowed. In other words, you can use arrays only when MODE={ANSI | ANSI13 | Oracle}.

Using Arrays with SELECT
You can use host and indicator arrays to obtain output from a SELECT statement. This is only possible if you know beforehand (at program creation) the maximum number of rows the SELECT statement will return. You simply dimension the host (and indicator) arrays that you use in the SELECT statement with that number of elements:

```
EXEC SQL BEGIN DECLARE SECTION;
    int aiItemId[100];
    float afRetailPrice[100];
    float afItemCost[100];

    short indItemId[100];
    short indRetailPrice[100];
    short indItemCost[100];
EXEC END DECLARE SECTION;
```

```
EXEC SQL SELECT item_id, item_cost, retail_price
   INTO :aiItemId:indItemId,
        :afItemCost:indItemCost,
        :afRetailPrice:indRetailPrice
   FROM item
   WHERE item_id >= 100 AND item_id <= 200;
```

This example shows that the syntax for using host and indicator arrays is the same as that for host and indicator variables. The SELECT statement must return no more than 100 rows, though it may return fewer than 100. If the SELECT statement returns more than 100 rows, the first 100 rows found are returned and Oracle generates error ORA-1422 (if SELECT_ERROR=YES).

If the WHERE clause of the SELECT statement returns more values than the array allows, you cannot call the SELECT statement a second time to return all of the available rows. If you reexecute the SELECT statement, the same 100 rows are returned, even if more rows are available in the SELECT statement. You must either increase the array size or use a cursor, as discussed in the next section. Remember, to use arrays with the SELECT statement (without a cursor) you must know beforehand the maximum number of rows the SELECT statement will return.

Using Arrays with a CURSOR

If you don't know the maximum number of rows a SELECT statement will return, you can declare a CURSOR and FETCH the SELECT results as you need them. Also, a CURSOR can be used to process the SELECT results in sets of rows.

A CURSOR allows you to SELECT a set of rows from the database, hold the results in memory, and process the results with the FETCH statement. You can use host and indicator arrays with the FETCH statement to return the SELECT results in smaller, more manageable sets of rows, called *batches*. The first time a batch of rows is FETCHed into an array, the array is filled to its dimensioned length. Thereafter, each time you FETCH a batch from a CURSOR into an array, the next available batch of rows is returned. To illustrate the differences between using arrays with SELECT by itself and using them with SELECT in a CURSOR, we'll use our previous example to process the CURSOR in batches of 20 rows.

```
int iRowCount;
EXEC SQL BEGIN DECLARE SECTION;
   int aiItemId[20];
   float afRetailPrice[20];
   float afItemCost[20];

   short indItemId[20];
   short indRetailPrice[20];
   short indItemCost[20];
```

```
EXEC END DECLARE SECTION;

EXEC SQL DECLARE item_cursor CURSOR FOR
   SELECT item_id, item_cost, retail_price
   FROM item
   WHERE item_id >= 100 AND item_id <= 200;

EXEC SQL OPEN item_cursor;
iRowCount = 0;
for (;;)    /* Loop until the end of the data is reached. */
   {
   EXEC SQL WHENEVER NOT FOUND DO break;
   EXEC SQL FETCH item_cursor;
      INTO :aiItemId:indItemId,
           :afItemCost:indItemCost,
           :afRetailPrice:indRetailPrice;
   display_data(sqlca.sqlerrd[2] - iRowCount);
   iRowCount = sqlca.sqlerrd[2];
   }
   if ((sqlca.sqlerrd[2] - iRowCount) > 0
      display_data(sqlca.sqlerrd[2] - iRowCount);
EXEC SQL CLOSE item_cursor;
void display_data(n)
{
   short      iRowIndex;

   for (iRowIndex = 0; iRowIndex < n; ++iRowIndex)
      {
      if (indItemId[iRowIndex] != 0)
         sprintf (scOutput, "Item ID = NULL");
      else if (indItemCost[iRowIndex] != 0)
         sprintf (scOutput, "Item Cost = NULL");
      else if (indRetailCost[iRowIndex] != 0)
         sprintf (scOutput, "Retail Price = NULL");
      else
         sprintf (scOutput, "Item ID = ", %d,
            "Item Cost = ", %f,
            "Retail Price = ", %d, aiItemId[iRowIndex],
            afItemCost[iRowIndex], afRetailPrice[iRowIndex]);
   }
}
```

This example shows how you can check for a status returned in an indicator array and alter the path of your program accordingly. It also shows that with each

FETCH, at most, the number of rows equal to the array dimension is returned. But what happens when the FETCH returns fewer rows than the number of elements in the array, or an error occurs? Fewer rows return from a FETCH than the number of elements in an array in the following situations:

- The end of the active set of rows available in a CURSOR is reached on the first FETCH. This occurs when you attempt to FETCH into an array that is larger than the total number of rows available in a CURSOR. For example, this would occur if you tried to FETCH into an array with dimension 100 but there were only 20 rows in the active set for the CURSOR.

- The end of the active set of rows available in a CURSOR is reached after consecutive FETCHes, and fewer rows remain to be FETCHed from a CURSOR than the number of elements in an array. This occurs when you FETCH the last batch of rows from a CURSOR and the number of remaining rows is less than the size of the array. In our example, this would happen if 450 rows were available in the active set for the CURSOR and on the fifth FETCH only 50 rows remained to be FETCHed.

- An error is detected while processing a row before the last row in a batch is reached.

In any of these situations, Oracle keeps track of the cumulative total of all rows FETCHed from a CURSOR for all FETCHes. When the end of the CURSOR is reached, Oracle sets the total number of rows FETCHed and generates the error "data NOT FOUND." If an error occurs while it is processing a row, Oracle sets the total number of rows FETCHed (including the row in which the error occurred), sets the rowid in which the error occurred, and generates the appropriate error. (We'll discuss array diagnostics and error processing in Chapter 7.)

There are two restrictions on using arrays in SELECT and FETCH statements:

- You cannot use host arrays in the WHERE clause of a SELECT statement, except when using a subquery (see "The WHERE Clause" later in this chapter).

- You cannot mix the use of host variables with the use of host arrays in the INTO clause of a SELECT or FETCH statement. If you use any host arrays in an INTO clause, they must *all* be host arrays.

When DBMS=V7!, if you SELECT or FETCH null column values into a host array not associated with an indicator array, Oracle stops processing, sets the number of rows processed, and generates an error (ORA-1405). In the same situation, when DBMS=V6!, no error is generated. To maintain consistency in your program, when SELECTing and FETCHing into host arrays—regardless of the value assigned to DBMS—you should always associate them with indicator arrays. That way, you won't encounter an error when you find a null value; however, you are responsible for processing null values by checking the status in an indicator array after a SELECT or FETCH (the same as for scalar variables).

When MODE=Oracle, if you SELECT or FETCH truncated column values into a host array not associated with an indicator array, Oracle stops processing, sets the number of rows processed, and generates an error. In the same situation, when MODE=ANSI13, Oracle stops processing and sets the number of rows processed but does not generate an error. When MODE=ANSI, truncation isn't considered an error, so Oracle continues processing. When SELECTing and FETCHing into host arrays, always associate them with indicator arrays. That way, you won't encounter an error when you find a truncated value. You are responsible for processing truncated values by checking for the original length of the truncated value in an indicator array after a SELECT or FETCH (the same as for scalar variables).

Using Arrays with INSERT

You can use host arrays to add sets of data to a database table with the INSERT statement. This is only possible if you know beforehand (at program creation) the maximum number of rows you need to add to a table. You must be sure to populate the host arrays with the appropriate data before you INSERT the data into the database. The following example illustrates how this is done:

```
EXEC SQL BEGIN DECLARE SECTION;
    int aiItemId[100];
    float afRetailPrice[100];
    float afItemCost[100];

    short indItemId[100];
    short indRetailPrice[100];
    short indItemCost[100];
EXEC END DECLARE SECTION;

/* Populate arrays here. */

EXEC SQL INSERT INTO item (item_id, item_cost, retail_price)
    VALUES (:aiItemId:indItemId, :afItemCost:indItemCost,
        :afRetailPrice:indRetailPrice);
```

This example shows that the syntax for using host arrays is the same as that for host variables. The INSERT statement will add exactly 100 rows to the ITEM table (unless an error occurs), so it's important to populate each element of the arrays properly. Oracle sets the number of rows added successfully to the database, even if an error occurs, so that you know which row caused the error.

The advantage of using a host array with the INSERT statement is improved performance: Instead of having to make 100 INSERT statements, you only execute one, eliminating the overhead associated with making 99 unnecessary calls to the database.

The only restriction on using arrays in an INSERT statement is that you can't mix simple host variables and host arrays in the VALUES clause of an INSERT statement. If you use any host arrays in a VALUES clause, they must *all* be host arrays. They should all be the same dimension as well.

Using Arrays with UPDATE

You can use host arrays to modify sets of data in a database table using the UPDATE statement. As with SELECT and INSERT, this is only possible if you know beforehand (at program creation) the maximum number of rows you need to modify in a table. You must be sure to populate the host arrays with the appropriate data before you UPDATE the data in the database. The following example shows how this is done:

```
EXEC SQL BEGIN DECLARE SECTION;
    int aiItemId[100];
    float afRetailPrice[100];
    float afItemCost[100];

    short indItemId[100];
    short indRetailPrice[100];
    short indItemCost[100];
EXEC END DECLARE SECTION;

/* Populate arrays here. */

EXEC SQL UPDATE item
    SET (item_cost = :afItemCost :indItemCost,
         retail_price = :afRetailPrice :indItemPrice)
    WHERE item_id = :aiItemId;
```

This example shows that the syntax for using host arrays is the same as that for host variables. The UPDATE statement will modify exactly 100 rows in the ITEM table (unless an error occurs), so it's important to populate each element of the arrays properly.

Oracle sets the number of rows added successfully to the database, even if an error occurs, so you know which row caused the error. The cumulative number of rows does not include rows that are updated due to cascading.

Using host arrays with the UPDATE statement has the same performance advantage as with the INSERT statement. There are two restrictions:

■ You cannot mix host variables and host arrays in the SET or WHERE clause of an UPDATE statement. If you use any host arrays in a SET or WHERE clause, they must *all* be host arrays. Also, if you use a host array in a SET clause, you must use one in the WHERE clause.

■ You cannot use the CURRENT OF clause when processing a CURSOR with host arrays in an UPDATE statement.

Using Arrays with DELETE

You can use a host array to delete a set of data from a database table using the DELETE statement. This is only possible if you know beforehand (at program creation) the maximum number of rows you need to delete from a table. You must be sure to populate the host arrays with the appropriate data before you DELETE the data from the database:

```
EXEC SQL BEGIN DECLARE SECTION;
    int aiItemId[100];
EXEC END DECLARE SECTION;

/* Populate the item ID array here. */
EXEC SQL DELETE FROM item
    WHERE item_id = :aiItemId;
```

This example shows that the syntax for using a host array is the same as that for a host variable. The DELETE statement will attempt to remove 100 rows from the ITEM table (unless an error occurs, and assuming order number is the primary key for the order table). That's why it's important to populate each element of the array properly.

Oracle sets the number of rows removed successfully from the database, even if an error occurs, so you know which row caused the error. The cumulative number of rows does not include rows that are deleted due to cascading.

Our previous example showed that you can delete an entire set of rows based on a unique qualifier. Each element of the array used in the WHERE clause qualified exactly one row in the order table. You can also use a nonunique qualifier to delete multiple rows from a table. This is done in the same manner as with the UPDATE statement.

NOTE
The DELETE statement has the same restrictions as the UPDATE statement.

The FOR Clause

When using host arrays with most of the SQL statements we've discussed, you must know beforehand the number of rows the statement will process. Most often, this is not possible and makes your application program inflexible. The FOR clause is provided to avoid this limitation and still give you the power of using host arrays. This clause is most often used with the following SQL statements when processing host arrays:

- FETCH
- INSERT
- UPDATE
- DELETE

The FOR clause is used to specify the number of host-array elements you want to process in one of these SQL statements. The FOR clause must use an integer host variable to tell it the number of elements in a host array to process. Because it uses a host variable, you can control in your program the number of array elements processed in each statement. The following examples illustrate how you use the FOR clause with each of the SQL statements:

- Example 1: Using FOR with FETCH

```
short iRowCount;
EXEC SQL BEGIN DECLARE SECTION;
    int aiItemId[20];
    float afRetailPrice[20];
    float afItemCost[20];

    short indItemId[20];
    short indRetailPrice[20];
    short indItemCost[20];
EXEC END DECLARE SECTION;

EXEC SQL DECLARE item_cursor CURSOR FOR
    SELECT item_id, item_cost, retail_price
    FROM item
    WHERE item_id >= 100 AND item_id <= 200;

EXEC SQL OPEN item_cursor;
iRowCount = 0;
for (;;)    /* Loop until the end of the data is reached */
```

```
    {
    EXEC SQL WHENEVER NOT FOUND DO break;
    EXEC SQL FOR :iRowCount FETCH item_cursor;
        INTO :aiItemId:indItemId,
             :afItemCost:indItemCost,
             :afRetailPrice:indRetailPrice;
    display_data(sqlca.sqlerrd[2] - iRowCount);

    iRowCount = sqlca.sqlerrd[2];

    }

    if ((sqlca.sqlerrd[2] - iRowCount) > 0

        display_data(sqlca.sqlerrd[2] - iRowCount);

    }

if ((sqlca.sqlerrd[2] - iRowCount) > 0

        display_data(sqlca.sqlerrd[2] - iRowCount);
EXEC SQL CLOSE item_cursor;

void display_data(n)

{

    short      iRowIndex;

    for (iRowIndex = 0; iRowIndex < n; ++iRowIndex)
       {
       if (indItemId[iRowIndex] != 0)
          sprintf (scOutput, "Item ID = NULL");
       else if (indItemCost[iRowIndex] != 0)
          sprintf (scOutput, "Item Cost = NULL");
       else if (indRetailCost[iRowIndex] != 0)
          sprintf (scOutput, "Retail Price = NULL");
       else
          sprintf (scOutput, "Item ID = ", %d,
             "Item Cost = ", %f,
             "Retail Price = ", %d, aiItemId[iRowIndex],
                 afItemCost[iRowIndex], afRetailPrice[iRowIndex]);
       }
}
```

■ Example 2: Using FOR with INSERT

```
EXEC SQL BEGIN DECLARE SECTION;
    short iRowCount;
    int aiItemId[100];
    float afRetailPrice[100];
    float afItemCost[100];
EXEC END DECLARE SECTION;

/* Populate arrays here. */

iRowCount = 10;
EXEC SQL FOR :iRowCount
    INSERT INTO item (item_id, item_cost, retail_price)
    VALUES (:aiItemId, :afItemCost, :afRetailPrice);
```

■ Example 3: Using FOR with UPDATE

```
EXEC SQL BEGIN DECLARE SECTION;
    short iRowCount;
    int aiItemId[10];        /* Note the difference. */
    float afRetailPrice[100];
    float afItemCost[100];
EXEC END DECLARE SECTION;

/* Populate arrays here. */

iRowCount = 10;
EXEC SQL FOR :iRowCount UPDATE item
    SET (item_cost = :afItemCost,
         retail_price = :afRetailPrice)
    WHERE item_id = :aiItemId;
```

■ Example 4: Using FOR with DELETE

```
EXEC SQL BEGIN DECLARE SECTION;
    short iRowCount;
    int aiItemId[100];
EXEC END DECLARE SECTION;

/* Populate the item ID array here. */

iRowCount = 10;
```

```
EXEC SQL FOR :iRowCount DELETE FROM item
    WHERE item_id = :aiItemId;
```

As each example shows, the FOR clause variable specifies the number of elements in the host array that the SQL statement processes. This number must be a positive, nonzero integer (or **short**) no larger than the smallest array dimension used in the SQL statement. If any of these constraints are violated, Oracle does not process the statement and generates an error.

There are several restrictions when using the FOR clause:

- You cannot use the FOR clause in a SELECT statement. The correct use of FOR is in a FETCH statement.

- You cannot use the FOR clause with the CURRENT OF clause in an UPDATE or DELETE statement.

- Variables must be in a DECLARE section.

The WHERE Clause

You can use host arrays with the WHERE clause in SQL statements. However, Oracle processes an SQL statement containing host arrays of *n* dimension the same way as if the same SQL statement is processed *n* times for each element in the array. When an SQL statement containing host arrays becomes ambiguous for Oracle to interpret, an error is generated. Ambiguous SQL statements using host arrays most often occur when a WHERE clause is involved. Consider the following example:

```
EXEC SQL BEGIN DECLARE SECTION;
    int aiItemId[100];
    VARCHAR avcItemName[100][21];
EXEC SQL END DECLARE SECTION;

EXEC SQL SELECT item_name INTO :avcItemName
    WHERE item_id = :aiItemId;
```

This statement is ambiguous because the statement is processed like the following hypothetical statement:

```
for (iIndex = 0; iIndex <100; ++iIndex)
    EXEC SQL SELECT item_name INTO :avcItemName[iIndex]
        WHERE item_id = :aiItemId[iIndex];
```

This example shows that the WHERE clause might return multiple rows, but only one value can be assigned to the array element. This is ambiguous and cannot be processed. To remove such ambiguity, you should use subquery statements to reduce the WHERE clause search to a single result. Let's look at our previous example using a subquery:

```
EXEC SQL SELECT item_name INTO :avcItemName
    WHERE item_id IN (SELECT item_id FROM item
    WHERE item_id = :aiItemId);
```

The important thing to note is that any SQL statement that uses host arrays in a WHERE clause must not be ambiguous; it cannot result in multiple rows when a single row is expected.

Datatype Conversion

When you precompile a source module of your application program, each host variable and host array in the DECLARE section is automatically assigned an external datatype. Each external datatype is assigned a datatype code (see Table 4-8), which at run time is passed to Oracle through an SQL statement and used to convert between internal and external datatypes. This process is called *datatype conversion*. Datatype conversion is completely automated through the precompile process.

On input, before comparing or assigning a data value in a host variable, Oracle converts the external datatype of the variable to the internal datatype associated with the target database column. On output, the opposite occurs: Oracle converts the internal datatype of each database column referenced in an SQL statement to the external datatype of each output host variable.

This would work if all internal datatypes were compatible with all external datatypes, but that's not the case. It's up to you to make sure the external datatype of each host variable in an SQL statement is compatible with that of the target column's internal datatype. For example, if you try to insert the string '10A65B' into a NUMBER column, Oracle will generate an error. Oracle doesn't perform any magic here; the datatype conversions follow a simple set of rules. Table 4-12 defines the supported conversions between internal and external datatypes.

The C language provides a set of basic datatypes, the details of which were discussed in Chapter 4. In addition to these basic datatypes, Oracle supports the external datatypes just listed. These datatypes can be used to declare variables, arrays, pointers, and user-defined datatypes, which are used in your application program to store and manipulate data.

When you use the basic C datatypes to declare host variables, Oracle automatically assigns an external datatype to the host variable, which is used to perform datatype conversion. Although you can control which external datatypes are assigned to a C datatype (more on this later in the chapter), by default Oracle assigns a specific external datatype. Table 4-13 defines these default assignments.

Internal Datatype

External Datatype	VARCHAR2	NUMBER	LONG	ROWID	DATE	RAW	LONG RAW	CHAR	MLSLABEL
VARCHAR2	I/O	I/O[8]	I/O	I/O[1]	I/O[2]	I/O[3]	I[3]	I/O	I/O[7]
STRING	I/O	I/O[8]	I/O	I/O[1]	I/O[2]	I/O[3]	I[3,5]	I/O	I/O[7]
LONG	I/O	I/O[8]	I/O	I/O[1]	I/O[2]	I/O[3]	I[3,5]	I/O	I/O[7]
VARCHAR	I/O	I/O[8]	I/O	I/O[1]	I/O[2]	I/O[3]	I[3,5]	I/O	I/O[7]
LONG VARCHAR	I/O	I/O[8]	I/O	I/O[1]	I/O[2]	I/O[3]	I[3,5]	I/O	I/O[7]
CHAR	I/O	I/O[8]	I/O	I/O[1]	I/O[2]	I/O[3]	I[3,5]	I/O	I/O[7]
CHARZ	I/O	I/O[8]	I/O	I/O[1]	I/O[2]	I/O[3]	I[3,5]	I/O	I/O[7]
INTEGER	I/O[4]	I/O	I					I/O[4]	
UNSIGNED	I/O[4]	I/O	I					I/O[4]	
FLOAT	I/O[4]	I/O	I					I/O[4]	
VARNUM	I/O[4]	I/O	I					I/O[4]	
RAW	I/O[6]		I[5,6]			I/O	I/O	I/O[6]	
LONG RAW	O[6]		I[5,6]			I/O	I/O	O[6]	
VARRAW	I/O[6]		I[5,6]			I/O	I/O	I/O[6]	
LONG VARRAW	I/O[6]		I[5,6]			I/O	I/O	I/O[6]	
ROWID	I		I	I/O				I	
DATE	I/O		I		I/O			I/O	
MLSLABEL	I/O[7]		I/O[7]					I/O[7]	I/O

Legend:
I = Input only
O = Output only
I/O = Both input and output

Notes:

1. On input, the string value must be in ROWID format 'BBBBBBBB.RRRR.FFFF'. On output, the column value is returned in the same format.

TABLE 4-12. *Supported datatype conversions*

2. On input, Oracle implicitly calls the **to_date** function, which expects a string in the default DATE format ('DD-MON-YY'). You must explicitly call **to_date** to pass nondefault DATE formats. On output, Oracle implicitly calls the **to_char** function, which returns a string in the default DATE format. You must explicitly call **to_char** to return nondefault DATE strings.

3. On input, the string must be in hexadecimal format. Use the **rawtohex** function to convert binary data to a hexadecimal string. On output, the column value is returned in the same format.

4. On output, the column value must be a valid number.

5. Data value length must be ≤ 2,000 bytes.

6. On input, the binary data is converted to a hexadecimal string. On output, the column value must be in hexadecimal format.

7. On input, the string must be a valid operating system label in text format. On output, the column value is returned in the same format.

8. On input, the value must be a valid number.

TABLE 4-12.   *Supported datatype conversions* (continued)

Table 4-14 will help you understand the compatibility between the internal and C datatypes.

Datatype Equivalencing

The default assignment of external datatypes to C datatypes will meet many of your application requirements. However, you'll often need the flexibility to override the default behavior. Oracle provides a mechanism to do just that: *datatype equivalencing.*

Datatype equivalencing allows you to customize the way input host variables are converted by Oracle and to customize the way Oracle formats column data into output host variables. Each host variable you declare can be equivalenced to a compatible external datatype. User-defined datatypes can also be equivalenced to an external datatype (more on this later).

Datatype equivalencing can be used for many purposes. For example, in your application program you want to use null-terminated character strings for all character-string operations (standard in C library functions). You can declare your host character-string variables as **char**, **char[n]**, or **char *** C datatypes and then equivalence the host variables to CHARZ or STRING external datatypes.

External Datatype

C Language Datatype	VARCHAR2	VARCHAR	CHARZ[1]	INTEGER	UNSIGNED	FLOAT
char, char[n],	X		X[1]			
VARCHAR		X				
int, int *				X		
short, short *				X		
long, long *				X		
unsigned, unsigned *					X	
float, float *						X
double, double *						X
char*						X

Note:

1. CHARZ is used in place of VARCHAR2 when MODE=ANSI.

TABLE 4-13. *Default external datatype assignments*

You can use datatype equivalencing to store and retrieve raw binary data, such as graphic characters or digitized sound. This can be done by declaring a host variable as a binary array (such as **char[n]**, **char ***, or **int[n]**) and then equivalencing the host variable to a RAW or LONG RAW external datatype.

You can even define your own datatypes and then equivalence them to an external datatype so they can be used in SQL statements. For example, suppose you want to create your own data structure to process graphic pictures. The data structure is defined much like the VARRAW or LONG VARRAW datatype (length field and data field) and equivalenced to the external datatype. The data structure can then be used to process the graphic pictures in your application program using SQL statements.

Host Variable Equivalencing

Datatype equivalencing is performed in your program's DECLARE section. Equivalencing a host variable to an external datatype is called *host variable equivalencing.* You declare equivalent datatypes in the DECLARE section *after* you

Internal Datatype

C Language Datatype	VARCHAR2	NUMBER	LONG	ROWID	DATE	RAW	LONG RAW	CHAR	MI
char, char[n], char*	X	X	X	X	X	X	X	X	X
VARCHAR	X	X	X	X	X	X	X	X	X
int, int *	X	X						X	
short, short *	X	X						X	
long, long *	X	X						X	
unsigned, unsigned *	X	X						X	
float, float *	X	X						X	
double, double *	X	X						X	

TABLE 4-14.   *Internal and C datatype compatibility*

have declared the host variables you are equivalencing. The following is the syntax you use to equivalence datatypes:

```
EXEC SQL VAR host_variable IS type_name [ (length) ];
```

where:

host_variable is an input or output host variable (or host array) declared earlier in the DECLARE section. The host variable must be declared with a large enough length to accommodate the external datatype. For example, the VARCHAR external datatype has a two-byte field followed by a string field. The C datatype must be declared large enough to include the two-byte field *plus* the length of the string field, or a minimum of three bytes.

type_name is the name of a valid external datatype such as UNSIGNED or STRING.

length is an optional integer parameter that is used to specify a valid length in bytes (such as STRING(n) or FLOAT(n)). The length must be a large enough value to accommodate the external datatype. For VARCHAR, LONG VARCHAR, VARRAW, and LONG VARRAW, **length** is required and specifies the length of the string or data field. The length field is already included. If

length is not specified for other variables, it defaults to the length of the host variable.

In the following example, you want to declare a character-string host variable in which you always terminate with a null:

```
EXEC SQL BEGIN DECLARE SECTION;
    char   var_name[101];
    EXEC SQL VAR var_name IS STRING[101];
EXEC SQL END DECLARE SECTION;
```

The associated database column has 100 characters, but we add one character to the variable length to account for the null character.

Table 4-15 defines the optional and required parameters for declaring equivalent datatypes.

User-Defined Datatype Equivalencing

Oracle allows you to equivalence user-defined datatypes to external datatypes. This *user-defined datatype equivalencing* allows you to create customized datatypes that can be used instead of the external Oracle datatypes, then process these customized datatypes as host variables in SQL statements. The only limitation is that the user-defined datatype must have the same basic structure as the external datatype. We will discuss this as we look at some examples.

The following is the syntax to equivalence user-defined datatypes:

```
EXEC SQL TYPE user_type IS type_name [ (length) ] [REFERENCE];
```

where:

user_type is a user-defined datatype previously declared in the DECLARE section. The same rules hold as for host variables. The user-defined datatype must be declared with a large enough length to accommodate the external datatype. For example, the VARCHAR external datatype has a two-byte field followed by a string field. The user-defined datatype must be large enough to include the two-byte field *plus* the string field (minimum three bytes; five bytes for LONG VARCHAR).

type_name is the name of a valid external datatype such as VARCHAR or STRING.

length is an optional integer parameter used to specify a valid length in bytes (such as STRING(n) or FLOAT(n)). The length must be a large enough value to accommodate the external datatype. For VARCHAR, LONG VARCHAR, VARRAW, and LONG VARRAW, **length** is required and specifies the length of the string or data field. The length field is already included. If **length** is not specified for other variables, it defaults to the length of the host variable.

REFERENCE, an optional keyword, is used when **user_type** is defined as a pointer.

Although you equivalence user-defined datatypes in the DECLARE section of your program, this kind of equivalencing is quite different from host variable

External Datatype	Length	Range	Default
VARCHAR2	Optional	1 to 2000	Declared length of the host variable
STRING	Optional	1 to 65535	Declared length of the host variable
LONG	Optional	1 to 2^{31}	Declared length of the host variable
VARCHAR	Required	1 to 65533	
LONG VARCHAR	Required	1 to $2^{31} - 5$	
CHAR	Optional	1 to 255	Declared length of the host variable
CHARZ	Optional	1 to 255	Declared length of the host variable
INTEGER UNSIGNED	Optional	1, 2, or 4	Declared length of the host variable
FLOAT	Optional	4 or 8	Declared length of the host variable
VARNUM	N/A		Declared length of the host variable (must be 22 bytes)
RAW	Optional	1 to 255	Declared length of the host variable
LONG RAW	Optional	1 to 2^{31}	Declared length of the host variable
VARRAW	Required	1 to 65533	
LONG VARRAW	Optional	1 to $2^{31} - 5$	
ROWID	N/A		System specific (fixed-length)
DATE	N/A		Declared length of the host variable (must be at least seven bytes)
MLSLABEL	Required	1 to 255	

TABLE 4-15. *Parameters for external datatypes*

equivalencing. Host variables are equivalenced *after* they are declared; the user-defined datatype must be declared *before* it can be equivalenced to an external datatype. Also, the user-defined datatype must be equivalenced before it can be used to declare a host variable.

The following is the syntax to equivalence user-defined datatypes and declare host variables of that type:

```
typedef user_type;

EXEC SQL BEGIN DECLARE SECTION;
    EXEC SQL TYPE user_type IS type_name [ (length) ] [REFERENCE];
    user_type variable_name;
EXEC SQL END DECLARE SECTION;
```

where:

user_type is the user-defined datatype. This can be a structure, an array, a pointer, or any of the basic C datatypes. This declaration can be done inside or outside the DECLARE section, though it is typically done outside the DECLARE section in an include file or at the top of the source module or function.

type_name, **length**, and REFERENCE are as defined earlier.

variable_name is the name you give to the host variable that is equivalenced as a user-defined datatype.

NOTE
You must equivalence a user-defined datatype before it can be used to declare a host variable. Otherwise, the Oracle precompiler will issue an "invalid forward reference" error.

The following examples show the various aspects of used-defined datatype equivalencing. Any one of these equivalence datatypes can be used in a C language statement or SQL statement, just like any other host variable or host array.

Example 1: Processing Digitized Pictures

In this first example, you want to create a specific datatype to process digitized pictures. You create a user-defined data structure with a field to store the data length and one to store the data. In this example, the pictures can be up to 1 megabyte.

```
typedef struct picture
    {
```

```
    short iLength;
    char scPicture[1024]; -- up to 1 megabyte (1024 = 1 megabyte)
    } Picture;

EXEC SQL BEGIN DECLARE SECTION;
    EXEC SQL TYPE Picture IS VARRAW(1024);
    Picture zDisplay;
EXEC SQL END DECLARE SECTION;
```

Note the order of the elements in the **picture** data structure. The length field must be first because that is what the VARRAW datatype expects. Also note that the **char[n]** datatype is used to hold the data because it is byte-oriented. Finally, the length assigned to the data field in the data structure (1024) is the same as that declared in the TYPE equivalence statement. The length field is included in the variable declaration by Oracle.

Example 2: Processing Floating-Point Numbers

In the second example, you want to create a specific datatype to process floating-point numbers as pointers.

```
typedef float * Numbers;

EXEC SQL BEGIN DECLARE SECTION;
    EXEC SQL TYPE Numbers IS FLOAT REFERENCE;
    Numbers pfAccountTotal;
EXEC SQL END DECLARE SECTION;
```

Note the use of REFERENCE, which is required anytime a pointer is used in the declaration of a user-defined datatype.

Example 3: Processing a Two-Dimensional Array

Now you want to create a specific datatype to process a two-dimensional array of four-byte integers as raw data.

```
typedef long IntArray[2][100];

EXEC SQL BEGIN DECLARE SECTION;

/* 2*100*4 bytes = 8000*/
    EXEC SQL TYPE IntArray IS LONG RAW(8000);
    IntArray aiNumberColumns;
EXEC SQL END DECLARE SECTION;
```

Guidelines for Datatype Equivalencing

The following guidelines will help you avoid some of the pitfalls commonly encountered in datatype equivalencing.

When processing VARNUM and DATE datatypes in equivalencing, you must pass the data values in the internal Oracle format. When Oracle returns these datatypes, the internal format is assigned.

When you declare user-defined arrays, the external datatype length must exactly match the total size of the array declaration in bytes (in the last example we looked at, 2 * 100 * 4 bytes = 8,000 bytes).

For user-defined datatype equivalencing, you should place all of your EXEC SQL TYPE equivalence statements immediately after the BEGIN DECLARE SECTION statement (as in the examples). Also, placing these types of declarations in an include file and including that file at the beginning of each source module where the datatypes are needed will prevent you from making an illegal forward reference when defining host variables.

Oracle requires VARCHAR, LONG VARCHAR, VARRAW, and LONG VARRAW arrays to be *word-aligned*; that is, the extent of an array is aligned with the end of a word. This is determined as follows.

The array declaration must be divisible by the number of bytes in a word (a word is four bytes long on a 32-bit system, eight on a 64-bit system). When you equivalence an array to these external datatypes, make sure the array length in bytes is the total of the length field in bytes and the external datatype length in bytes. For example:

```
typedef char Array[100];
EXEC SQL BEGIN DECLARE SECTION;
    EXEC SQL TYPE Array IS VARCHAR(98); -- 2 + 98 = 100
    Array   scString;
EXEC SQL END DECLARE SECTION;
```

Summary

In this chapter we have discussed the datatypes you need to understand and use in your application program. You learned that Oracle recognizes two kinds of datatypes: Internal datatypes are those supported by Oracle to store data in the database; external datatypes are those that Oracle supports for automatic conversion between program variables and the internal datatypes. You learned what is and is not automatically supported by the system. We discussed host and indicator variables and arrays and how they are declared and used in an application program. We also discussed how you can use datatype equivalencing to process external datatypes and user-defined datatypes in your application program.

You can now answer the questions posed at the beginning of the chapter:

- What are the internal datatypes?
- What are the external datatypes?
- What are the ANSI standard datatypes?
- What are host and indicator variables?
- What are host and indicator arrays?
- What is datatype conversion?
- What is datatype equivalencing?
- How can I use these tools in my application?

CHAPTER 5

Oracle Database Access

Before your application can access the data in an Oracle database, you must first establish a *connection* to the database. A database context must be established before you can execute any database operations in your application program. After your application has connected to the database, the SQL statements or OCI calls can be executed.

A database context is established by creating a communication link between your application program and the target Oracle database. This is called *a database connection.* Through this connection all communication with the Oracle database takes place. For example, through this connection each SQL statement is packaged, sent to the database, and processed by the database and the results returned to your application program.

As discussed in Chapter 1, the Oracle database system is built on the client/server architecture. In this architecture, a *server* program or system services the requirements to access, manipulate, and process information from other programs, called *clients*. The Oracle database system acts as the database server to all clients that need to access an Oracle database. Your application program is an example of a client.

The series of events that occurs after the connection is established is called a *session*. The Oracle database system can process multiple, simultaneous sessions. When your application program establishes a session with an Oracle database, other applications may be using the same server. Figure 5-1 illustrates how a typical Oracle database system services multiple clients.

Oracle gives you many options for establishing a session with any database that you can access (locally or over a computer network). For example, you can:

- Establish a session with a single database on a local or remote computer

- Establish a session with multiple databases on local and/or remote computers

- Establish multiple sessions with a single database or multiple databases on local and/or remote computers

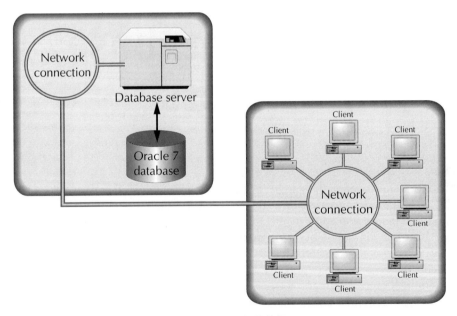

FIGURE 5-1. *The Oracle client/server architecture*

Once you have established a database session (or sessions), Oracle makes database access virtually transparent to your application program.

In this chapter you'll learn how to:

■ Connect to the Oracle database

■ Connect to a specific database

■ Connect to multiple databases

■ Connect to remote databases

■ Reference a database in an application

The next section discusses how you create database connections to establish sessions in your application program.

Connecting to Oracle

Before you can access a database, you must create a database connection to establish a session. This is done with the CONNECT statement. The basic syntax for the CONNECT statement is

```
EXEC SQL CONNECT :username IDENTIFIED BY :password;
```

where:

username must be a **char** or **varchar** host variable assigned a valid Oracle username. The username is a user that has been granted access to the database.

password must be a **char** or **varchar** host variable assigned the valid Oracle password associated with **username**.

Note that **username** and **password** must be declared as host variables. Character-string literals (like 'username') cannot be hard-coded into the CONNECT statement. For example, the following statements are invalid:

```
EXEC SQL CONNECT JSMITH IDENTIFIED BY SECRET;
```

and

```
EXEC SQL CONNECT 'JSMITH' IDENTIFIED BY 'SECRET';
```

You can also use the more concise syntax

```
EXEC SQL CONNECT :username_password;
```

where:

> **username_password** must be a **char** or **varchar** host variable assigned a valid Oracle username and password separated by the slash character (/)—for example, *"username/password"*. The username and password cannot have any embedded slash characters (/).

The CONNECT statement must be the first executable SQL statement in your program. Of course, the DECLARF section will precede this statement (in addition to other declarative SQL statements).

There are several ways to obtain the username and password information for the CONNECT statement. The three most common are:

- **User input** You prompt the user to input the username and password to your program.

- **Initialization file** You read the username and password from an initialization file. However, placing a password in an initialization file may violate security rules, so you may still need to prompt the user for a password. This can be avoided by encrypting the password.

- **Automatic** This method requires some synchronization between the operating system username and password and the database username and password. The username must have the following syntax:

  ```
  OPS$username
  ```

  where:

  > **OPS$** is the prefix of the username (set in INIT.ORA).

  > **username** is the operating system username of the user or task executing the program.

  > **OPS$username** must be a valid Oracle username, and the associated password must be the same as the operating system password associated with the operating system username.

To invoke an automatic connection, pass a slash (/) as the username password to the CONNECT statement as in the following example:

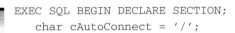

```
EXEC SQL BEGIN DECLARE SECTION;
   char cAutoConnect = '/';
```

```
EXEC SQL END DECLARE SECTION;

    . . .

EXEC SQL CONNECT :cAutoConnect;
```

This will automatically connect you to Oracle as OPS$username. For example, if your operating system username is JSMITH, and OPS$JSMITH is a valid Oracle username, you would be connected to Oracle as OPS$JSMITH.

A connection can be one of three types:

■ A default connection, using the environment to determine the database information.

```
EXEC SQL CONNECT :username IDENTIFIED BY :password;
```

■ A default connection to an explicit server, using a CONNECT string to reach a specific server.

```
EXEC SQL CONNECT :username IDENTIFIED BY :password
   USING :databasename;
```

■ A connection that uses an AT clause to provide the details.

```
EXEC SQL CONNECT :username IDENTIFIED BY :password
   AT databaseid USING :databasename;
```

More information on these types of connections follows in the next sections.

Default Connections

You may have observed that a particular database was not specified in the CONNECT statements in the examples. How does the CONNECT statement resolve to which database you connect and establish a session? If you don't specify a database name in your CONNECT statement, you are creating what is called a *default connection*. Every computer in an Oracle system is assigned a *default database*.

A default connection establishes a session with the default database assigned to the Oracle server that is running on the computer node to which your application is connected. The default database is assigned to an Oracle server by the Oracle administrator. You cannot control this in your application program.

If you create a default connection in your application program, any SQL statements are executed against the default connection and serviced by the default database. The following example illustrates how you create a default connection and how it is implicitly used in an SQL statement:

```
EXEC SQL BEGIN DECLARE SECTION;
    char    scUserName[21];
    char    scPassword[21];
    char    scItemName[41];
    int  iItemId;
EXEC SQL END DECLARE SECTION;

strcpy (scUserName, "JSMITH"); /* We could have prompted for */
strcpy (scPassword, "SECRET"); /* the username and password. */

EXEC SQL CONNECT :scUserName IDENTIFIED BY :scPassword;

iItemId = 1000;
EXEC SQL SELECT item_name -- implicit default reference
    INTO :scItemName
    FROM item
    WHERE item_id = :iItemId;
```

You can specify a specific database with the USING clause. The form of the CONNECT statement would then be

```
EXEC SQL CONNECT :username IDENTIFIED BY :password
    USING :databasename;
```

Concurrent Connections

Most application programs require access to a specific database or set of databases. These databases may be located on your local computer or distributed on other computers on your network. The computers may be PC servers, workstations, minicomputers, or mainframes of various makes and operating systems.

Oracle allows your application program to connect to any database on any computer that you can access over your network. You can establish multiple, concurrent sessions in your application program with any combination of local and remote databases. You can even establish multiple sessions with the same database.

Oracle provides computer-to-computer communications through an optional product called SQL*Net. SQL*Net transparently allows you to connect to a set of databases on your local computer or on any remote computer. It eliminates the boundaries in a computer network created by different makes of hardware and operating systems. SQL*Net also allows two or more servers to communicate, so that a server may become a client to another server. Figure 5-2 illustrates how SQL*Net allows you to connect to distributed databases on your computer network.

SQL*Net makes this possible by taking care of the network connections and *communication protocols* (rules) required to communicate over a computer network. You don't need to be concerned with how this happens; the details are handled by SQL*Net.

To establish a connection to a database other than the default on your local computer, you must identify to SQL*Net which database, on which computer, and with which network you're connecting. The syntax to identify a database to SQL*Net is system-specific, determined by the type of communication protocol (for example, TCP/IP, DECNet, SNA, or DCE) used on your computer. Regardless of the communication protocol, you must specify three pieces of information:

■   **Network identifier**   This is a unique identifier that indicates which network and communication protocol is used on your computer network.

■   **Node identifier**   This identifies a node on the network where a database is located. SQL*Net refers to a computer or communication point in a network as a *node.* You must specify a network identifier with a node identifier.

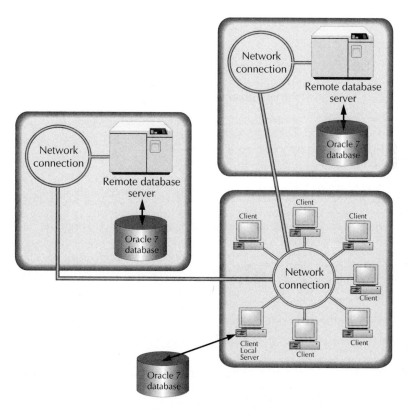

FIGURE 5-2.   *Distributed database connections using SQL*Net*

■ **Database name** This identifies the database to which you want to connect. This is the name assigned to the database when it was created.

If you specify a network and node identifier but do not specify a database name, you are connected to the default database assigned to that node. If you specify a database name but not a network and node identifier, you are connected to the specific database on your local computer. For consistency, the examples will use the SQL*Net Version 2 syntax to connect to an Oracle database on a Netware server and a Windows NT server. The SQL*Net Version 2 syntax is as follows:

```
database_identifier =
    (DESCRIPTION=
        (ADDRESS=
            (PROTOCOL=network_protocol)
            (HOST=host_node_name)
            (PORT=host_node_port))
        (CONNECT DATA=
            (SID=database_name)))
```

where:

database_identifier is the identifier used in SQL statements to identify the database connection.

network_protocol is the network protocol used to communicate over your computer network.

host_node_name is the name of the host computer (node) database server.

host_node_port is the port identifier on the host computer where the network connection is established.

database_name is the name of the Oracle database to which the connection is established.

Examine the following code:

```
store_database =
    (DESCRIPTION=
        (ADDRESS=
            (PROTOCOL=IPX)
```

```
      (HOST=STORE1)
      (PORT=1459))
  (CONNECT DATA=
      (SID=STORE_DATABASE)))
```

This example establishes the SQL*Net database connection for the STORE_DATABASE database on the STORE1 host at PORT 1459, using Netware IPX protocol. The SQL*Net Version 1 syntax for the same database is

```
I:STORE1:STORE_DATABASE
```

Explicit Connections

You can access a specific database by creating a connection to it using the CONNECT statement. When you create a connection to a specific database, you create what is called a *nondefault* or *explicit connection*. You create an explicit connection by specifying a *database name* in your CONNECT statement.

   After you have created an explicit connection to a database, you must reference that connection in each SQL statement intended to access that database. This is done by declaring a *database identifier* that can be referenced in your CONNECT statement and in subsequent SQL statements. You can declare a database identifier and specify a database name in your CONNECT statement with the following syntax:

```
EXEC SQL DECLARE databaseid DATABASE;

EXEC SQL CONNECT :username IDENTIFIED BY :password
   AT databaseid USING :databasename;
```

where:

> **databaseid** is a unique identifier (which can be alphanumeric) used in your application program to identify a specific database connection in all SQL statements. This is a precompiler identifier, like a cursor or statement name, used by Oracle; it is not a host variable.

> **username** and **password** are as defined earlier.

> **databasename** must be a **char** or **varchar** host variable that is assigned the name of a valid node and/or an Oracle database. The database name consists of the network identifier, node identifier, and database SID (system ID) and is optional.

NOTE
As stated earlier, **username**, **password**, and **databasename** must be declared as host variables. Character-string literals cannot be hard-coded into the CONNECT statement.

The following example illustrates how you create an explicit connection by using a database identifier:

```
EXEC SQL BEGIN DECLARE SECTION;
    char    scUserName[21];
    char    scPassword[21];
    char    scDatabaseName[41];
EXEC SQL END DECLARE SECTION;

strcpy (scUserName, "JSMITH");
strcpy (scPassword, "SECRET");
strcpy(scDatabaseName, "STORE_DATABASE");

EXEC SQL DECLARE store_database DATABASE;
EXEC SQL CONNECT :scUserName IDENTIFIED BY :scPassword
    AT store_database USING :scDatabaseName;
```

To make your program more flexible, you may want to use a host variable to identify a database connection. This is allowed. That way, you can pass the database identifier to an SQL statement as a variable that can be changed if necessary to process multiple databases. When you use a host variable to identify a database, you do not need to DECLARE it as an identifier. The following is the syntax to use a host variable as a database identifier. (Note that the DECLARE statement is gone.)

```
EXEC SQL CONNECT :username IDENTIFIED BY :password
    AT :databaseid USING :databasename;
```

where:

databaseid must be a **char** or **varchar** host variable that is assigned a unique identifier. This identifier is used in your application program to identify a specific database connection in SQL statements.

username, **password**, and **databasename** are as defined earlier.

Let's return to the previous example to illustrate how you create an explicit connection using a host variable as a database identifier:

```
EXEC SQL BEGIN DECLARE SECTION;
    char    scUserName[21];
    char    scPassword[21];
    char    scDatabaseName[41];
    char    scDatabaseId[21];
EXEC SQL END DECLARE SECTION;

strcpy (scUserName, "JSMITH");
strcpy (scPassword, "SECRET");
strcpy (scDatabaseId, "Local_Store");
strcpy (scDatabaseName, "STORE_DATABASE");

EXEC SQL CONNECT :scUserName IDENTIFIED BY :scPassword
    AT :scDatabaseId USING :scDatabaseName;
```

Multiple Connections

You can create connections to multiple databases or create multiple connections to the same database in your application program. Oracle allows you to have as many CONNECT statements in your program as the resources on your computer will allow. The following example shows how this can be done using multiple database identifiers:

```
EXEC SQL BEGIN DECLARE SECTION;
    char    scUserName[21];
    char    scPassword[21];
    char    scDatabaseName1[41];
    char    scDatabaseName2[41];
EXEC SQL END DECLARE SECTION;

strcpy (scUserName, "JSMITH");
strcpy (scPassword, "SECRET");
strcpy(scDatabaseName1, "STORE1_DATABASE");
strcpy(scDatabaseName2, "STORE2_DATABASE");

EXEC SQL DECLARE database_1 DATABASE;
EXEC SQL DECLARE database_2 DATABASE;

EXEC SQL CONNECT :scUserName IDENTIFIED BY :scPassword
    AT database_1 USING :scDatabaseName1;
```

```
EXEC SQL CONNECT :scUserName IDENTIFIED BY :scPassword
    AT database_2 USING :scDatabaseName2;
```

Just as with a single explicit connection, you can create multiple database connections using host variables as database identifiers. The following example shows how this is done:

```
EXEC SQL BEGIN DECLARE SECTION;
    char    scUserName[21];
    char    scPassword[21];
    char    scDatabaseName1[41];
    char    scDatabaseId1[41];
    char    scDatabaseNamc2[41];
    char    scDatabaseId2[41];
EXEC SQL END DECLARE SECTION;

strcpy (scUserName, "JSMITH");
strcpy (scPassword, "SECRET");
strcpy(scDatabaseName1, "STORE1_DATABASE");
strcpy(scDatabaseId1, "Store_1");
strcpy(scDatabaseName2, "STORE2_DATABASE");
strcpy(scDatabaseId2, "Store_2");

EXEC SQL CONNECT :scUserName IDENTIFIED BY :scPassword
    AT  :scDatabaseId1 USING :scDatabaseName1;

EXEC SQL CONNECT :scUserName IDENTIFIED BY :scPassword
    AT  :scDatabaseId2 USING :scDatabaseName2;
```

You can also create multiple connections to a single database using these methods. You don't need to see an example to do this; just use the same database name for each database identifier in the preceding examples. It's that simple.

Many more details are involved in creating distributed database applications; distributed database computing will be discussed in Chapter 13.

Using Database Connections in SQL Statements

If you create an explicit connection in your application program, SQL statements intended to access that connection must explicitly reference the database identifier

used in a CONNECT statement. A database identifier is referenced in an SQL
statement with the AT clause, using the following syntax:

```
EXEC SQL AT databaseid SQL Statement ...
```

or

```
EXEC SQL AT :databaseid SQL Statement ...
```

For example, you may use one of the following statements:

```
EXEC SQL AT databaseid SELECT ...
   ...
EXEC SQL AT databaseid INSERT ...
   ...
EXEC SQL AT databaseid UPDATE ...
```

or

```
EXEC SQL AT :databaseid SELECT ...
   ...
EXEC SQL AT :databaseid INSERT ...
   ...
EXEC SQL AT :databaseid UPDATE ...
```

The following example shows how you create an explicit connection and how
it is used explicitly in an SQL statement:

```
EXEC SQL BEGIN DECLARE SECTION;
    char    scUserName[21];
    char    scPassword[21];
    char    scDatabaseName[41];
    char    scDatabaseId[21];
    char    scItemName[81];
    int     iItemId;
EXEC SQL END DECLARE SECTION;

strcpy (scUserName, "JSMITH");
strcpy (scPassword, "SECRET");
strcpy (scDatabaseName, "STORE_DATABASE");
strcpy (scDatabaseId, "Local_Store");

iItemId = 1000;
EXEC SQL CONNECT :scUserName IDENTIFIED BY :scPassword
```

```
    AT :scDatabaseId USING :scDatabaseName;

EXEC SQL AT :scDatabaseId SELECT item_name
    INTO :scItemName
    FROM item
    WHERE item_id = :iItemId;
```

This example shows just how easy it is to reference a database connection in an SQL statement. This syntax applies to most, but not all, SQL statements you will use in your application program. The syntax is slightly different when using CURSORs.

NOTE
The variable used in the SQL statement may be different from that in the CONNECT, but it must contain the same string (database identifier).

The CURSOR control statements need a slightly different syntax to use a database connection explicitly, as discussed in the preceding section. You don't need to use an AT clause with the OPEN, FETCH, and CLOSE statements; you only need it when you DECLARE a CURSOR. This is allowed because the CURSOR declaration is valid until it is redeclared. Therefore, the database identifier or host variable identifier used when the CURSOR is DECLAREd is valid until the CURSOR is redeclared. The syntax to DECLARE, OPEN, FETCH, and CLOSE a CURSOR using an explicit database connection is as follows:

```
EXEC SQL AT databaseid (or :databaseid) DECLARE cursorname
    CURSOR FOR ...
    . . .
EXEC SQL OPEN cursorname ...
    . . .
EXEC SQL FETCH cursorname ...
    . . .
EXEC SQL CLOSE cursorname ...
```

The database connection used when the CURSOR is DECLAREd applies to the OPEN, FETCH, and CLOSE statements.

If you use a host variable to identify a database in the AT clause of a DECLARE CURSOR statement, that host variable declaration must be valid within the scope of all SQL statements that reference the declared CURSOR. In other words, if you OPEN, FETCH, or CLOSE a CURSOR in a different function from that in which the CURSOR is declared, the host variable must be valid in both functions. You can either declare the host variable to be global to the functions or pass it through function parameters.

Also, a host variable used for the database identifier allows you to change the database connection associated with the declared CURSOR. However, this is not allowed while the CURSOR is open. You must CLOSE the CURSOR before you change the database identifier.

Summary

This chapter discussed the need to establish a database connection with your application program before any SQL statements can be executed. This is done with the CONNECT statement. You can create a single database connection to a local database, or you can establish multiple database connections to remote databases. In Chapter 13, you will learn more about how to access and process data in remote databases. Database links and synonyms will be discussed.

CHAPTER 6

Data Consistency and Concurrency

This chapter examines the mechanisms available in Oracle for ensuring data consistency and concurrency in your application program.

Each application that issues a request to an Oracle database must be managed individually as a session by the Oracle database system. Oracle is designed to process multiple sessions simultaneously while allowing sessions to share database resources. In a multisession information processing environment, there are two primary requirements. First, data must be read and modified in a consistent, predictable manner without risk of loss or corruption. Second, concurrent data access by multiple users must be maximized with the highest possible performance to provide maximum productivity for all users of the system.

In a single-user environment, only the first requirement is a concern. A single user performs a series of database operations sequentially. Each subsequent operation is affected by and sees the results of all the previous operations. As long as each operation provides a consistent, predictable result, the first requirement is fulfilled.

However, the second requirement seems to conflict with the first. How do you manage multiple, concurrent operations without seriously affecting performance or risking inconsistent results, data loss, or corruption? The answer is one of the primary features of any multiuser database system like Oracle: Provide mechanisms to ensure data consistency and data concurrency in the face of the volatility of computer system environments and the need to process multiple, simultaneous sessions. Now let's define some terms.

- **Data consistency** Ensures that a user always sees a consistent, predictable view of the data. Data consists of all information modified and committed by other users as of a particular time and all changes made by the user up to that time. Even if a problem occurs during the operation, the view of the data will remain consistent. All the data in the database is correct and complete at any point in time.

- **Data concurrency** Simultaneous access to and modification of the same data by multiple users must be consistent and coordinated. Data concurrency must be guaranteed to be correct, or the data consistency of the database can be jeopardized.

If data consistency is compromised, the data in the database is said to be *corrupted*—no longer correct and no longer reliable. For example, you may move money from a savings account to a checking account (say, $100) by updating the balance of each account. If the system only updated one of the accounts, the data would be incorrect. For example, if the system subtracted $100 from the savings account and did not add that to the checking account, the data would be incorrect.

A multiuser DBMS must prevent the following problems, which can occur because of the inherent complexities of providing data consistency and data concurrency:

- **Inconsistent reads** Changes to data in one user's session, whether committed or uncommitted to the database, are visible during the execution of a single query in other users' sessions. Therefore, the set of data returned for a query is not guaranteed to be consistent with respect to any single point in time.

- **Nonrepeatable reads (phantoms)** Two or more identical queries (queries for the same data) in a single operation or unit of work do not return the same result. This occurs because the changes from other committed users' transactions are detected by one but not all of the queries. (Transactions will be discussed in more detail in a moment.)

- **Dirty reads**   A query issued by one user's session reads data that is modified but is not yet committed to the database by another user's session. Therefore, the first user's operation has read data that effectively does not yet exist in the database.

- **Lost updates**   An update to data in one user's session overwrites a simultaneous update to the same data before the second user's operation commits to the database.

- **Destructive data definition language (DDL) operations**   While one user updates data in a table, another user simultaneously modifies or drops the table from the database.

- **Inconsistent cursors**   When data is FETCHed from a cursor, locks are released so that other users can update the data associated with the cursor. Therefore, if the query revisits the unlocked data in the cursor, different data may be returned if other users have changed that data between the original and subsequent fetch.

Oracle maintains data consistency and concurrency by providing various features that are inherent to the Oracle system and by providing tools you can use in your application program. Data consistency, and the tools used to maintain it, will be discussed in a later section. These issues are common to all relational database systems, not just to Oracle.

An Introduction to Transactions

Transactions safeguard the consistency of your database and control when changes to Oracle data are made permanent or undone.

A *transaction* is an atomic unit of work that consists of one or more logically related SQL statements. A transaction is called an atomic unit of work because the changes brought about by the SQL statements that constitute a transaction can collectively be either *committed* (made permanent) to the database or *rolled back* (undone) from the database.

Oracle uses transactions to ensure data integrity. In fact, Oracle is classified as a transaction-oriented system. If the SQL statements in a transaction perform the task successfully, all the changes made by that unit of work are committed to the database at the same time. If any SQL statement in a transaction fails, or something occurs to interrupt the transaction (a software, computer system, or network failure), the changes made by the transaction are rolled back. If a transaction is rolled back, the database is restored to its state prior to the transaction (as if the transaction never occurred).

All transaction-oriented systems should pass the ACID test (as proposed in *Transaction Processing: Concepts and Techniques* by Jim Gray and Andreas Reuter, Kaufmann Publishers, 1993). ACID stands for:

- **Atomic** A transaction is a collection of operations in an atomic unit of work. All the operations complete successfully or none occur, and they are committed or rolled back at the same time.

- **Consistent** Transactions must consistently and correctly perform transformations of the system state. The transaction system allows the application developer to define the points at which these transformations occur. The system is allowed to validate the correctness of the transformation through application-supplied checks.

- **Isolated** When a transaction updates data shared by multiple sessions, the data may temporarily exist in an inconsistent state. That state must not be exposed to other sessions with open transactions until the updating transaction is complete. Thus, each session with an open transaction exists in isolation; all other transactions appear to process either before the beginning of a single session's transaction or after it is complete.

- **Durable** When a committed transaction is complete, the updates that occur as a result of that transaction must be permanent, even if the software, computer system, or network fails.

Because Oracle provides all of these characteristics, you can be confident that your data is safe. To illustrate the concept of a transaction, suppose a credit purchase occurs in the database. When a customer purchases an item using a credit account, the transaction might consist of three operations: decrement the credit account, record the item invoice, and decrement the item inventory.

Oracle must provide for two outcomes. First, it must guarantee that all three operations are performed correctly and are committed at the same time to maintain the data in proper balance. Second, if something prevents one of the statements in the transaction from executing (such as insufficient credit, an invalid item number, or a hardware failure), the other statements in the transaction must be undone or rolled back.

Briefly, let's discuss the basics of the mechanisms used to control and manage transactions before getting into the details.

Committing and Rolling Back Transactions

An SQL statement that "executes successfully" is different from a "committed" transaction. Executing successfully means that a single SQL statement is parsed and found to be valid. The entire statement executes without error as an atomic unit (for example, all rows of a multirow update are updated). However, until the transaction that contains the statement is committed, the transaction can be rolled back and all the changes of the statement can be undone. A statement, rather than a transaction, executes successfully.

Committing a transaction makes permanent the changes resulting from all successful SQL statements in a transaction. *Committing* means that a user has either explicitly or implicitly said, "Make the changes in this transaction permanent." You explicitly commit an entire transaction, which can consist of one or many SQL statements; you do not explicitly commit every single statement. An implicit commit occurs at the beginning of a DDL SQL statement because DDL statements always change data and must be committed to be successful. The changes made by the SQL statement(s) of your transaction only become permanent and visible to other users' transactions that start *after* your transaction has been committed.

Before Oracle commits a transaction that modifies data, the following takes place:

1. Oracle records the original data (modified as a result of the SQL statements in the transaction) in a rollback segment.

2. Oracle generates redo log changes in the *redo log buffers,* which allow for recovery if a failure occurs. The changes to the redo log buffers may be stored on disk before a transaction is committed.

3. The modified data is stored in the database memory buffers. Changes to the database buffers may be stored on disk before a transaction is committed.

After Oracle commits a transaction to the database, the following takes place:

1. An internal transaction table associated with the rollback segment records that the transaction is committed. A unique system control number, designated for the transaction, is assigned and recorded in the table.

2. The redo log entries in the redo log buffers are written to the online redo log file. The transaction's system control number is also written to the online redo log file; this is the atomic event that commits the transaction.

3. The data changes in the database memory buffers are made visible to other users.

4. All savepoints are erased (see the next section, "Savepoints").

5. All open cursors referenced in a CURRENT OF clause are closed, or, when MODE={ANSI | ANSI14}, all explicitly opened cursors are closed. When MODE={Oracle | ANSI13}, explicitly open cursors remain open, which can boost performance.

6. Locks held on rows and tables are released.

7. The transaction is marked "complete."

NOTE
The data changes for a committed transaction, which are stored in the database buffers, are not necessarily written immediately to the database files. The data changes are written when it is most efficient to do so; as mentioned earlier, this may happen before the transaction is committed, or it may happen sometime after the transaction commits.

If at any time during execution an SQL statement causes an error, all effects of the statement are rolled back. The effect of the rollback is as if that statement never executed (but the remaining statements in the transaction may still be completed).

Before executing an SQL statement, Oracle must *parse* it (examine it) to make sure it follows syntax rules and refers to valid database objects. Errors that cause statement rollbacks are those that are discovered during the execution stage of the SQL statement processing (such as attempting to insert a duplicate value in a primary key or an invalid number into a numeric column), not the parsing stage (such as syntax errors in an SQL statement). Single SQL statements can also be rolled back to resolve deadlocks. A *deadlock* (discussed later in this chapter) results from competition among multiple sessions for the same data. Therefore, an SQL statement that fails only causes the loss of any work it would have performed itself; it does not cause the loss of any work that preceded it in the current transaction. If a DDL statement fails, the implicit commit that immediately precedes it is not undone. This is a statement-level rollback.

Rolling back a transaction throws away any changes resulting from the SQL statements in a transaction. It means that a user has either explicitly or implicitly said "throw away the changes in this transaction." You explicitly roll back a transaction, which can consist of one or many SQL statements; you do not explicitly roll back each individual statement. An implicit rollback occurs for a single statement if an error is encountered while the statement is being processed. A complete transaction can be rolled back explicitly if necessary. When a transaction is rolled back, it is as if the transaction never occurred.

When an entire transaction is rolled back, the following actions take place:

1. All the original data stored in the rollback segments is restored to the database buffers.

2. All savepoints are erased (see the next section, "Savepoints").

3. All open cursors referenced in a CURRENT OF clause are closed, or, when MODE={ANSI | ANSI14}, all explicitly opened cursors are closed. When MODE={Oracle | ANSI13}, explicitly open cursors remain open, which can boost performance.

4. Locks held on rows and tables are released.

5. The transaction is ended.

Savepoints

For long transactions that contain many SQL statements, you may want to break the transaction into smaller units. You can do this by declaring intermediate markers, or *savepoints*. Using savepoints, you can arbitrarily place a marker at any point in a long transaction. This allows you later to roll back all work performed from the current point in the transaction to the savepoint. For example, you can use savepoints throughout a long, complex series of updates to prevent having to resubmit all updates if you make an error.

When Oracle encounters a savepoint in your program, the following takes place:

1. Oracle records all the changes that have occurred in the transaction up to that point and marks them as permanent relative to the declared savepoint.

2. Any subsequent changes are recorded as pertaining to that savepoint.

When you partially roll back a transaction to a savepoint, Oracle causes the following to take place:

1. Only the statements executed after the savepoint is declared are rolled back.

2. The specified savepoint is preserved, but all savepoints that were established after the specified savepoint are lost.

3. Locks acquired on rows and tables since the specified savepoint are released, but all locks acquired before that savepoint are retained.

4. The transaction is still active; it can be continued.

Data Consistency Using Transactions

Transactions allow the database user or application developer to guarantee consistent changes to data, as long as the SQL statements within a transaction are grouped logically. A transaction should consist of all the necessary parts for one logical unit of work—no more and no less. Data in all referenced tables is in a consistent state before the transaction begins and after it ends. Transactions should consist of only the SQL statements that make up one consistent change to the data.

For example, recall the credit purchase example. A credit purchase requires the adjustment of data in multiple tables (the transaction), which should include the adjustment to the credit account, the adjustment to the inventory level, and the record of the item invoice. All actions should either fail or succeed together. Other unrelated actions, such as an increment to the customer's credit level, should not be included in the credit purchase transaction; such statements should be in other transactions.

Data Consistency

Data consistency means giving the user a consistent, predictable view of all data at any point in time; no failed operation, regardless of the cause, can allow data to be corrupted or lost.

If a user issues a query to the database, for example, and the table or tables being queried are being updated by another user at the same time, Oracle maintains a consistent view of the data for the query. Once a query begins, the data read by the query does not change. As the update progresses, Oracle maintains a record of the modified data separately from the "real" data. It does that so the query is not affected by the updates, the updated data does not corrupt the "real" data, and the data modifications can be discarded if a problem occurs.

This section discusses Oracle's mechanisms for maintaining data consistency and how you use these mechanisms to ensure data consistency in your application program.

Read Consistency

When a user issues a query to the database, a consistent result is returned relative to the beginning of the statement, regardless of any changes to the database made by other simultaneous users. This is called *read consistency.* Oracle guarantees read consistency through the following features:

■   The set of data accessed by an SQL statement is guaranteed to be consistent with respect to a single point in time (the beginning of the statement) and does not change during statement execution.

■   A user who is reading data from the database does not wait for other users who may be simultaneously adding to, modifying, or reading the same data.

■   A user who is adding data to or modifying data in the database does not wait for other users who may be reading the same data simultaneously.

■   A user who is adding data to or modifying data in the database waits only for others who are simultaneously attempting to add or modify the same data.

The easiest way to visualize read consistency is to imagine that each user is operating on his or her private copy of the database. This is called the *multiversion consistency model*. Oracle provides for multiversion read consistency at the statement level and the transaction level.

Statement-Level Read Consistency

Statement-level read consistency guarantees that the data returned by a single query is consistent with respect to the time the query begins. Oracle always enforces statement-level read consistency. Therefore, a query never sees any of the changes committed by statements from other sessions that occur during query execution.

Oracle enforces statement-level read consistency by observing the state of the data in the database as the query begins and executing queries only on data that is committed as of that moment. Oracle tracks the state of the data in the database with a mechanism called the *system control number* (SCN), which tracks every change committed to the database. Because each committed change increases the SCN, it can be used to determine the state of the database. To produce statement-level read consistency, Oracle observes the current SCN as a query enters the execution phase of an SQL statement (after the statement is parsed). As the query progresses, data that is committed as of the observed SCN is available for the query; the query does not see changes from other sessions that are committed after the query begins execution.

Oracle guarantees a consistent result set for every query. This guarantees data consistency without requiring any action on your part. All the SQL statements—SELECT, INSERT (with a query), UPDATE, and DELETE—query data, either explicitly or implicitly, and return a consistent set of data. Each of these statements uses a query to determine which data will be affected by the statement. A SELECT statement is an explicit query and may have nested queries or a join operation. An

INSERT statement can be used in nested queries. UPDATE and DELETE statements can use WHERE clauses or subqueries to affect only some rows in a table rather than all rows. While queries used in INSERT, UPDATE, and DELETE statements are guaranteed a consistent set of results, they do not see the changes made by the statement itself.

Transaction-Level Read Consistency

Transaction-level read consistency guarantees that the data returned by a group of query statements is consistent with respect to the time that the group of statements begins. Any grouped set of SQL statements is called a *transaction* (transactions are discussed later in this chapter). Oracle gives you the option of enforcing transaction-level read consistency. A transaction does not see any of the changes committed by statements in other sessions that occur while the statements in the transaction are executing.

Oracle assures transaction-level read consistency by using read-only transactions and table and row locks. *Read-only transactions* are groups of SQL statements that contain only query statements; they cannot contain data manipulation statements. To provide consistent query results within a read-only transaction, Oracle observes the start of the transaction. For the duration of the transaction, only data committed *before* the transaction started is available for the set of query statements. You can execute as many queries as you like against any table, knowing that the results of each query are consistent with respect to the same point in time (the beginning of the transaction). You have a "snapshot" of the database at that point in time.

If a consistent set of data is required in a transaction that contains data manipulation statements, you can explicitly acquire *share locks* on the tables involved in the transaction or *exclusive locks* on the rows involved (table and row locks will be discussed later in this chapter). The tables or rows involved in the transaction must return a consistent result. This solution provides transaction-level read consistency, but the drawback is that the level of data concurrency is reduced.

Consider the following example. When transaction A issues the query (three seconds into the example), that query will see the result of the INSERT and UPDATE 1 but not the result of UPDATE 2:

Time	Transaction A	Transaction B
1	INSERT	UPDATE 1
2		COMMIT
3	SELECT (begin query)	
4		UPDATE 2
5	END SELECT	

In summary, Oracle provides both statement-level and transaction-level read consistency by giving each statement or transaction its own "version" of data as of a specific point in time (the start of a statement execution or a transaction).

Rollback Segments and Transactions

This multiversion consistency model is possible because Oracle creates a read-consistent set of data when a table is queried while simultaneously being updated. When data is updated in the database, the original data values (which are modified by the update operation) are recorded in special locations in the database called *rollback segments.* As long as the modified data remains uncommitted to the database, all other users who query the database view the original data values. Oracle does this by combining the data stored in the database with the data stored in the rollback segments. The combination of this data results in a read-consistent view of a table's data for a query. After the modified data is committed to the database, the rollback segments are cleared and the data changes are made permanent so they can be viewed by other users.

A transaction provides transaction-level read consistency by using rollback segments. A transaction is a unit of SQL statements that dictates the start point (the SCN) for read-consistent views generated for queries; it controls when modified data can be seen by other database users for querying or updating.

When a transaction begins execution, the current SCN is determined. As data is read in database blocks, only blocks modified before or within the observed SCN are used. Database blocks with changed data (more recent SCNs) are reconstructed using the data in the rollback segments, and the reconstructed data is returned. Therefore, each transaction returns all committed data with respect to the SCN recorded at the time transaction execution begins. Committed or uncommitted changes from other transactions that occur during a query's execution are not observed, guaranteeing that a consistent set of data is returned for each statement in the transaction.

In rare situations, Oracle cannot return a consistent set of results (often called a *snapshot*) for a long-running query. This happens because not enough of the original information remains in the rollback segments to reconstruct the original data values. This problem is usually encountered when a lot of update activity occurs during a long-running query and the rollback segment is not large enough to hold all the changes. This causes the rollback segment to overflow, wrap around, and overwrite data needed to reconstruct the original data needed by the query. In this event, Oracle will generate an error (ORA-1555).

You can avoid this error condition by creating more or larger rollback segments. You can explicitly assign a transaction to specific rollback segments. Alternatively, long-running queries can be issued when the volume of update transactions is at a minimum. This is a good idea in general for RDBMS applications. You can also obtain a lock (discussed later in this chapter) on the table you are querying, prohibiting any other updates during the query.

Generally, the Oracle server automatically assigns a rollback segment to a transaction. However, you can explicitly assign a transaction to an appropriately sized rollback segment. Transactions are explicitly assigned to rollback segments for two reasons. First, the anticipated amount of rollback information generated by a transaction can fit in the current extents of the assigned rollback segment. Second, additional extents don't have to be allocated (and subsequently truncated) dynamically for rollback segments, which would reduce overall system performance.

You assign a rollback segment to a transaction with the SET TRANSACTION command. The syntax for using a specific rollback segment is

```
EXEC SQL SET TRANSACTION USE ROLLBACK SEGMENT  segment_name;
```

The designated rollback segment must be available on the computer system, and the SET TRANSACTION USE ROLLBACK SEGMENT statement must be the first statement of the transaction. If either requirement is not met, an error is generated.

After a transaction that is assigned to a specific rollback segment is committed, the Oracle server automatically assigns the next transaction to a rollback segment. Inform your database administrator that your application requires a large rollback segment and find out its name so you can use it for your large transactions. The segment name cannot be in a host variable.

Transaction Management

As the application developer, you control and manage transactions in your application program. You determine the SQL statements that constitute transactions, so it's important to get it right! To help you do this, this section discusses the mechanisms you'll use in your application program to manage and control transactions, including how to:

- Begin and end transactions.
- Use the COMMIT statement to make transactions permanent.
- Use the SAVEPOINT statement with the ROLLBACK TO statement to undo parts of transactions.
- Use the ROLLBACK statement to undo whole transactions.
- Specify the RELEASE option to free resources and log off the database.
- Use the SET TRANSACTION statement to set read-only transactions.

You don't need any specific Oracle database privileges to control your own transactions. Any user can issue a COMMIT, ROLLBACK, or SAVEPOINT statement for a transaction; you only need the appropriate access to the data your application is processing.

Beginning and Ending Transactions

According to the ANSI/ISO SQL standard, a transaction begins the first time an executable SQL statement (other than CONNECT) is issued to the database. An executable SQL statement can be any SQL statement that generates a call to the database to perform data manipulation or definition. Any subsequent executable SQL statements are executed in the context of that transaction.

A transaction terminates when any of the following occurs:

- An explicit statement is issued to commit or roll back (without a SAVEPOINT) the changes made during the transaction.

- A DDL statement (such as CREATE, DROP, RENAME, or ALTER) executes. If the currently open transaction contains any data manipulation language (DML) statements, the open transaction is committed; the DDL statement is then executed and committed as a new, single-statement transaction.

- A user disconnects from Oracle. (Any open transaction is committed.)

- There is a system failure or your user session stops unexpectedly because of software problems, hardware problems, or a forced interrupt (any open transaction is rolled back).

If your program fails in the middle of a transaction, Oracle detects the error and rolls back the transaction. If your operating system fails, Oracle restores the database to its former (pretransaction) state. The next transaction begins when the next executable SQL statement is issued. Thus, you are in complete control of when transactions are processed in your application program.

NOTE
You should always explicitly commit or roll back transactions before program termination.

Committing Transactions

Committing a transaction means making permanent the changes caused by the SQL statements that constitute the transaction. To commit a transaction in your application program, use the COMMIT command. It has the following syntax:

```
EXEC SQL COMMIT [WORK] [COMMENT comment] [RELEASE];
```

where:

WORK is an optional keyword that is needed to comply with the ANSI standard. It has no effect on the execution of the COMMIT command.

COMMENT is an optional keyword that allows you to record, along with the committed transaction, a *comment* (of less than 50 characters). This comment is a character-string literal or host variable that provides information about a transaction being committed. This comment is useful for including information about the origin of a distributed transaction:

```
EXEC SQL COMMIT COMMENT 'Store 1/Order/Trans_type  Order Item';
```

This comment can also be used to identify interrupted or in-doubt transactions. See your Oracle documentation to learn how to commit or roll back in-doubt transactions.

RELEASE is an optional keyword that is used to commit a transaction and disconnect a session from the Oracle server. The program can continue, but to perform more database work it has to reconnect.

If you do not create transactions in your application program by placing explicit calls to the COMMIT statement, Oracle will treat your entire program as a single transaction (unless the program contains data definition statements, which issue implicit COMMIT).

The COMMIT statement has no effect on the values of host variables or on the flow of control in your program. Therefore, you should insert COMMIT statements in logical places throughout your program to group logical operations into units of work.

Before your program terminates, you must explicitly COMMIT pending changes. Otherwise, Oracle will implicitly roll them back. This is done with the RELEASE option, as illustrated in the following statement:

```
EXEC SQL COMMIT WORK RELEASE;
```

The RELEASE option frees all Oracle resources (locks and cursors) held by your program and logs off the database.

You need not follow a data definition statement with a COMMIT statement because data definition statements issue an implicit COMMIT before and after statement execution. Whether the statement succeeds or fails, the prior transaction is implicitly committed.

Rolling Back Transactions

Rolling back a transaction means throwing away all changes caused by the SQL statements that constitute the uncommitted transaction. When a transaction is rolled back, it is as if the transaction never occurred. To roll back an entire transaction in your application program, use the ROLLBACK command. It has the following syntax:

```
EXEC SQL ROLLBACK [WORK] [RELEASE];
```

where:

> WORK is an optional keyword that is needed to comply with the ANSI standard. It has no effect on the execution of the ROLLBACK command.

> RELEASE is an optional keyword that is used to roll back a transaction and disconnect a session from the Oracle server. This can be done as a precautionary measure as the last action before you terminate execution of your program.

The ROLLBACK statement has no effect on the values of host variables or on the flow of control in your program. However, before your program terminates, you can explicitly RELEASE pending changes as a precautionary measure; otherwise, Oracle will implicitly roll them back. This is done with the RELEASE option:

```
EXEC SQL ROLLBACK WORK RELEASE;
```

The RELEASE option frees all Oracle resources (locks and cursors) held by your program and logs off the database. Oracle implicitly rolls back transactions if your program terminates abnormally. Abnormal termination occurs when your program does not explicitly commit or roll back work and disconnect from Oracle using the RELEASE option.

Normal termination occurs when your program runs its course, closes open cursors, explicitly commits or rolls back work, disconnects from Oracle, and returns control to the user. This is all accomplished using the RELEASE option. Otherwise, locks and cursors acquired by your user session are held after program termination until Oracle recognizes that the user session is no longer active. This might cause other users in a multiuser environment to wait longer than necessary for the locked resources.

You need not follow a data definition statement with a RELEASE statement because data definition statements issue an implicit COMMIT before statement execution. If an error is encountered during processing of the statement, an implicit ROLLBACK occurs. Whether the statement succeeds or fails, the prior transaction is implicitly committed.

The ROLLBACK statement should be an integral part of error processing in your program. ROLLBACK statements should be used in your error processing routines, off the main control path of your program. This will ensure that ROLLBACK statements execute anytime you encounter an error.

If you have a WHENEVER SQLERROR GOTO statement branch to an error handling routine that includes a ROLLBACK statement, your program might enter an infinite loop if the ROLLBACK fails with an error. You can avoid this by coding WHENEVER SQLERROR CONTINUE before the ROLLBACK statement:

```
...
EXEC SQL WHENEVER SQLERROR GOTO sql_error;
...
sql_error:
    EXEC SQL WHENEVER SQLERROR CONTINUE;
    EXEC SQL ROLLBACK WORK RELEASE;
...
```

Transaction Savepoints

You can break down large transactions into smaller, more manageable units by creating savepoints in the context of transactions. Using savepoints, you can arbitrarily mark any point in your program to which you would want to roll back changes in a transaction should an error occur. Changes that occur before the savepoints are preserved.

Savepoints are useful in application programs. If a transaction consists of several functions in your application program, a savepoint can be created before each function begins. Then, if a function fails, it's easy to return the data to its original state (before the function began) and then reexecute the function with revised parameters or perform a recovery action.

You create a savepoint in your application program by declaring its name and location with the SAVEPOINT command, which has the following syntax:

```
EXEC SQL SAVEPOINT savepoint_name;
```

where:

The location of the SAVEPOINT command in your program marks the location of the savepoint.

savepoint_name is an alphanumeric identifier used to refer to the savepoint when it is rolled back. This identifier is not a character-string literal or host variable and is not declared in the DECLARE section of your program. It is used by Oracle to identify the savepoint. If you declare a second savepoint with the same identifier as an earlier savepoint, the earlier savepoint is erased.

The upper limit on the number of active savepoints allowed per user session is 255. An active savepoint is one that has been specified since the last commit or rollback. However, by default, the number of active savepoints per user session is limited to five. Your database administrator can raise this limit by increasing the value of the Oracle initialization parameter savepoints.

You partially roll back a transaction to a savepoint with the TO SAVEPOINT clause of the ROLLBACK command. The syntax to do this is

```
EXEC SQL ROLLBACK TO SAVEPOINT savepoint_name;
```

where:

> **savepoint_name** is the savepoint identifier assigned when the savepoint is created.

NOTE
You cannot specify the RELEASE option in a ROLLBACK TO SAVEPOINT statement.

Rolling back to a savepoint erases any savepoints marked after that savepoint. The savepoint to which you roll back, however, is not erased. For example, if you mark five savepoints, then roll back to the third, only the fourth and fifth are erased. Again, the savepoint name cannot be a host variable.

Read-Only Transactions
By default, the multiversion consistency model provided by Oracle always guarantees statement-level read consistency but does not guarantee transaction-level read consistency. One way to guarantee transaction-level read consistency is to create a read-only transaction. As the name suggests, the transaction cannot contain any data manipulation or definition SQL statements that will cause changes to data.

A read-only transaction allows you to execute as many queries as are necessary against any set of database tables. You can be confident that the results of each query statement in the transaction are consistent with respect to a single point in time (the beginning of the transaction).

A read-only transaction does not acquire any additional data locks to provide transaction-level read consistency. The multiversion consistency model used for statement-level read consistency also provides transaction-level read consistency. In other words, all queries return information with respect to the SCN determined when the read-only transaction begins. Because no data locks are acquired, other transactions can query and update data that is concurrently being queried by a read-only transaction.

A read-only transaction is started with the SET TRANSACTION statement. The syntax to create a read-only transaction is

```
EXEC SQL SET TRANSACTION READ ONLY;
```

The SET TRANSACTION statement must be the first statement of a new transaction and can only be executed once per transaction. If any other executable SQL statements precede a SET TRANSACTION READ ONLY statement in a transaction, an error is returned. After you successfully execute a SET TRANSACTION READ ONLY statement, you can only execute the following SQL statements in the transaction:

- SELECT (without a FOR UPDATE clause)
- OPEN, FETCH, and CLOSE cursor commands
- COMMIT
- ROLLBACK
- DDL statements (such as SET ROLE, ALTER SYSTEM, or LOCK TABLE)

If any other SQL statement is executed, an error is returned. A COMMIT, ROLLBACK, or DDL statement terminates the read-only transaction (a DDL statement causes an implicit commit of the read-only transaction and commits in its own transaction).

Discrete Transactions

You can improve the performance of short, nondistributed transactions by using the Oracle-supplied procedure BEGIN_DISCRETE_TRANSACTION, which is only available with the Oracle Server procedural option. This procedure streamlines transaction processing so that short transactions can execute more rapidly.

Discrete transactions can only be used and have benefits when:

- Only a few database blocks are modified.
- An individual database block is seldom changed more than once per transaction.
- Data likely to be requested by long-running queries is not modified.
- You do not need to see the new value of the modified data in the same transaction.
- No tables containing LONG values are modified.

Given these restrictions, you need to consider two questions: Can the transaction be designed to work within the constraints placed on discrete transactions? And does using discrete transactions result in a significant performance improvement under normal usage conditions?

Discrete transactions can be used concurrently with standard transactions. Choosing whether to use discrete transactions should be a part of your normal performance tuning procedures. Although discrete transactions can only be used for a subset of all transactions, the performance improvements can make working within the design constraints worthwhile.

During a discrete transaction, all changes made to the data are deferred until the transaction commits. Other concurrent transactions are unable to see the uncommitted changes of a transaction during normal transaction processing or during the processing of discrete transactions.

The rollback segment information is generated, but it is stored in a separate location in memory. When you end the transaction with a commit request, the redo log information is written to the redo log file (along with other group commits). The changes to the database block are applied directly to the block. Control is returned to your application program once the commit completes. This eliminates the need to generate undo information because the block is not actually modified until the transaction is committed, and the redo information is stored in the redo log buffers.

As with other transactions, the uncommitted changes of a discrete transaction are not visible to concurrent transactions. For regular transactions, rollback segment information is used to re-create old versions of data for queries that require a consistent view of the data. Because no rollback segment information is generated for discrete transactions, a discrete transaction that starts and completes during a long query can cause the query (if it queries the data modified by the discrete transaction) to receive the error caused when the rollback segment overflows. For this reason, you might want to avoid performing queries that access a large subset of a table that is modified by frequent discrete transactions.

To use the BEGIN_DISCRETE_TRANSACTION procedure, the DISCRETE_TRANSACTIONS_ENABLED initialization parameter must be set to TRUE. If this parameter is set to FALSE, all calls to BEGIN_DISCRETE_TRANSACTION are ignored, and transactions requesting this service are handled as standard transactions.

To use the BEGIN_DISCRETE_TRANSACTION procedure, you must follow these guidelines:

- The procedure must be called before the first statement in a transaction. The call to this procedure is effective only for the duration of the transaction (that is, once the transaction is committed or rolled back, the next transaction is processed as a standard transaction).

■   Transactions that use this procedure cannot participate in distributed
    transactions.

If these guidelines are not observed, any error encountered during processing of a
discrete transaction generates the predefined error code DISCRETE_TRANSAC-
TION_FAILED. For example, this error is generated by calling BEGIN_DISCRETE_
TRANSACTION after a transaction has begun or by attempting to modify a
database block more than once during a transaction.

Discrete transactions cannot see their own changes. However, you can obtain
an old value and lock the row that contains it (using the FOR UPDATE clause of
the SELECT statement) before updating the value.

Because discrete transactions cannot see their own changes, a discrete
transaction cannot perform inserts or updates on both tables involved in a
referential integrity constraint.

Since discrete transactions can change each database block only once, certain
combinations of data manipulation statements are better suited for discrete
transactions than others. For example:

■   One INSERT statement and one UPDATE statement used together are the
    least likely to affect the same block.

■   Multiple UPDATE statements are also unlikely to affect the same block,
    depending on the size of the affected tables.

■   Multiple INSERT statements (or INSERT statements that use queries to
    specify values), however, are likely to affect the same database block.

■   Multiple DML operations performed on separate tables do not affect the
    same database blocks unless the tables are clustered.

NOTE
When processing a discrete transaction in a loop structure, beware of
the following scenario: The DISCRETE_TRANSACTION_FAILED error
occurs while processing in a loop, and as a result of the error you roll
back the transaction. Because the rollback terminates the transaction,
the next iteration of the loop is executed as a standard transaction
(remember that after a discrete transaction terminates, the next
transaction is a standard one).

Distributed Transactions
A *distributed database* is a single, logical database comprising multiple physical
databases that are on different, remote computers in a network. A *distributed SQL
statement* is any statement that accesses a remote database. A *distributed
transaction* includes at least one distributed SQL statement that updates data at

multiple locations of a distributed database. If the update affects only one node, the transaction is nondistributed.

When you issue a COMMIT, changes to all locations of the distributed database affected by the distributed transaction are made permanent. If you issue a ROLLBACK instead, all the changes in all the database locations are undone. Oracle ensures that all changes are committed to all remote databases before changes to the local database are committed. This is called *two-phase commit.* If any distributed statement fails, all of the distributed transactions are rolled back. However, if a network or machine fails during the commit or rollback, the state of the distributed transaction might be unknown or in doubt. In such a case, you can commit or roll back the transaction manually at your local database by using the FORCE clause. (Consult the Oracle Server documentation to find out how to use this clause.) To allow for manual commits or rollbacks, you must supply a COMMENT clause in the COMMIT statement of the transaction.

An Example

The SQL statements in Table 6-1 illustrate how the COMMIT, SAVEPOINT, and ROLLBACK statements are used in a transaction.

Data Concurrency

Earlier in this chapter, data concurrency was defined as allowing multiple users to access and modify the same data concurrently in a consistent and coordinated manner. Data concurrency must be guaranteed to be correct, or the data consistency of the database can be jeopardized.

A primary concern of a multiuser DBMS is how to control data concurrency. Without adequate controls, data could be updated or changed improperly, compromising data integrity. In a multiuser database environment, one way to control data concurrency is to make users wait their turn to access the database. For adequate system performance and user throughput, the DBMS has to reduce that wait so it is nonexistent or negligible for each user. Each SQL statement should proceed with as little interference as possible while preventing destructive interactions between concurrent user sessions. Neither performance nor data integrity can be sacrificed.

Oracle uses various locking mechanisms to control concurrent access to data. Locks give you temporary ownership of a database resource such as a table or row of data. Thus, data cannot be changed by other users until you finish with it.

The magic of data locking is that the Oracle system, by default, does it automatically. You don't need to be concerned with how this is accomplished or when; you only need to know that it occurs. However, Oracle's default database

SQL Statement	Results
SAVEPOINT A;	First savepoint of this transaction
DELETE . . . ;	First DML statement of this transaction
SAVEPOINT B;	Second savepoint of this transaction
INSERT INTO . . . ;	Second DML statement of this transaction
SAVEPOINT C;	Third savepoint of this transaction
UPDATE . . . ;	Third DML statement of this transaction
ROLLBACK TO C;	UPDATE statement is rolled back; all savepoints remain defined
ROLLBACK TO B;	INSERT statement is rolled back; savepoint C is erased; savepoints A and B remain defined
ROLLBACK TO C;	Error—savepoint C no longer defined
INSERT INTO . . . ;	New DML statement in this transaction
COMMIT;	Commits all actions performed by the first DML statement (the DELETE statement) and the last DML statement (the second INSERT statement). All other statements (the second and third statements) of the transaction are rolled back before the COMMIT.

TABLE 6-1. *A sample transaction*

locking may not always be sufficient for your needs. For example, you may want to lock an entire table during a transaction to get exclusive access to its contents. Maybe you want to lock multiple tables to perform a large query operation so that you get consistent results. You can choose from several modes of locking that allow you to share a resource or acquire exclusive access.

This section discusses how Oracle maintains data concurrency using lock mechanisms. First, let's discuss the concepts involved in data locking.

Data Locking Concepts

Data locking allows database resources to be "locked" by a single session while the data is accessed or updated. Other sessions cannot access or update that resource until the updating transaction is completed. Database resources can be of two general types: user objects, such as tables and rows (structures and data), and system objects not visible to users, such as shared data structures in memory and data dictionary rows.

Data locks are used to prevent destructive interaction between users accessing the same database resource. A destructive interaction is any interaction that updates data or alters underlying data structures, such as tables, column definitions, or indexes. Lost updates and destructive DDL operations are two examples.

Queries and Data Locking

Queries are statements that read data from the database according to a specified set of search criteria. Queries include or are part of the following SQL statements:

```
SELECT ... FROM ...;
INSERT ... SELECT ...;
UPDATE ...;
DELETE ...;
```

The following statement is not a query, as you might expect:

```
SELECT ... FOR UPDATE OF ...;
```

Note that INSERT, UPDATE, and DELETE can have implicit queries as part of the statement.

Queries are SQL statements that create the transactions least likely to interfere with concurrent transactions on the same data. Queries that don't use the FOR UPDATE clause acquire no data locks. Therefore, other transactions can query and update a table being queried, including the specific rows being queried. Because they don't acquire any data locks to block other operations, queries in Oracle are often referred to as *nonblocking*.

In addition, queries that don't use the FOR UPDATE clause don't have to wait for data locks to be released; they can always proceed. (Queries may have to wait for data locks in some very specific cases of pending distributed transactions.)

Restrictiveness of Locks

Locks place a range of restrictiveness on database resources. This allows Oracle to provide varying levels of data concurrency, from high to low, depending on the needs of the operation. The levels of data concurrency have an impact on the following situations:

- A user who is reading data from the database doesn't wait for other users who may be adding to, modifying, or reading the same data simultaneously.

- A user who is adding data to or modifying data in the database doesn't wait for other users who may be reading the same data simultaneously.

- A user who is adding data to or modifying data in the database only waits for others who are attempting to add or modify the same data simultaneously.

For each situation, Oracle automatically acquires the necessary locks to provide the lowest level of lock restrictiveness, which in turn provides the highest degree of data concurrency possible. You don't need to be concerned with what locks are set or the level of restrictiveness used; if Oracle doesn't use a lock with enough restrictiveness, you can set your own locks as your needs dictate.

Oracle provides two levels of lock restrictiveness: exclusive and share.

An *exclusive* lock prohibits sharing of the designated database resource. The first transaction to lock a database resource exclusively is the only one that can change that resource until the lock is released.

A *share* lock allows the designated resource to be shared, depending on the operations involved (several users can read the same data at the same time). Several transactions can acquire share locks on the same resource. Share locks can prevent exclusive locks from being set on a database resource, and they allow a higher degree of data concurrency than exclusive locks.

Deadlocks

When two or more users attempt to access a database resource while holding locks on the resources requested by the other(s), a deadlock results. For example, two users who simultaneously update the same table might have to wait if each tries to update a row currently locked by the other. Because each user is waiting for database resources locked by another user, neither can continue and Oracle must break the deadlock. When Oracle detects a deadlock condition, it returns an error to the participating transaction that has completed the least amount of work.

Data Lock Escalation

When numerous locks exist at one level (share) and the database automatically changes the locks to different locks at a higher level (exclusive), this is called *lock escalation*. For example, if a single user locks many rows in a table, the database might automatically escalate the user's row locks to a single table lock. With this plan, the number of locks has been reduced, but the restrictiveness of what is being locked has increased.

Lock escalation greatly increases the likelihood of deadlocks. For example, the system attempts to escalate locks on behalf of a transaction accessing a database resource but cannot because of the locks held by another transaction on the same resource. A deadlock occurs if the second transaction requires a lock escalation before it can proceed.

NOTE
Oracle does not support lock escalation because of the increased opportunity for deadlocks.

Data Lock Conversion

In certain situations, a transaction may re-request a lock on a database resource on which it already holds a lock. When that happens, the lock restrictiveness may need to be converted to a higher level depending on the later request.

For example, if the most recently requested lock is of a restrictiveness lower than or equivalent to the previously acquired lock, the previously acquired lock is sufficient, and the user's transaction can continue without delay. However, if the most recently requested lock is of higher restrictiveness than the previously acquired lock, the previously acquired lock must be converted to the more restrictive lock. The user's transaction must wait until the lock conversion is accomplished.

Data Locks and Transactions

Oracle must use a combination of locking mechanisms and transactions to provide complete data concurrency and consistency. However, locks are subordinate to transactions. All locks acquired by statements within a transaction exist for the duration of the transaction, preventing destructive interference (including dirty reads, lost updates, and destructive DDL operations) from concurrent transactions. All locks acquired by the SQL statements within a transaction are released when the transaction is either committed or rolled back. Because the locking mechanisms that Oracle provides are tied closely to transaction control, you are responsible for assuring that transactions are defined properly.

Implicit (Automatic) Data Locking

Oracle automatically performs all the necessary data locking to provide the highest level of data concurrency without compromising data integrity; no explicit or manual user action is required. Implicit locking occurs for SQL statements as necessary, depending on the action requested.

Oracle's sophisticated lock manager automatically locks table data at the row level, minimizing contention for the same data. Oracle's lock manager maintains several types of row locks, depending on what type of operation established the lock. The types of locks set for each operation will be discussed later in this chapter.

Explicit (Manual) Data Locking

In all cases, Oracle automatically performs data locking to ensure data concurrency, integrity, and statement-level read consistency. However, you can explicitly override the default locking mechanisms.

Applications require transaction-level read consistency, or "repeatable reads." Transactions must query a consistent set of data for the duration of the transaction, knowing that the data is not changed by any other concurrent transactions in the system. Transaction-level read consistency can only be achieved by using explicit locking, by read-only transactions, or by overriding default locking.

Applications require that a transaction have exclusive access to a database resource. To proceed with its statements, the transaction with exclusive access does not have to wait for other transactions to complete.

Locking Mechanisms

To control concurrent data access and prevent destructive actions by multiple users, Oracle uses different types of locking mechanisms. While reading this section, keep in mind that Oracle automatically performs implicit locking for all SQL statements so that you never need to lock any database resource explicitly. Oracle's default locking mechanisms lock data at the lowest level of restrictiveness to allow the highest degree of data concurrency while guaranteeing data integrity. Some situations may require that you override the default behavior of the automatic Oracle locking mechanisms. Oracle provides a set of explicit locking mechanisms to allow you to do just that.

Oracle's lock mechanisms fall into the following general categories: data, dictionary, internal, distributed, and parallel cache management.

- Data locks (DML locks) protect the data content of data objects, such as all the rows in a table or selected rows in a table.

- Dictionary locks (DDL locks) protect the structure of data objects, such as table definitions, view definitions, and index definitions (also known as *parse locks*).

- Internal locks and latches protect internal database structures, such as database files and memory structures. Internal locks and latches are entirely automatic. These mechanisms are not discussed in this book; see your Oracle Server documentation for more information.

- Distributed locks ensure that the data and other resources distributed among the various locations of a distributed database remain consistent. Distributed locks are held by database instances rather than transactions; they communicate the current status of a resource among the locations of a distributed database. These mechanisms are discussed later in the chapter on distributed processing.

- Parallel cache management (PCM) locks are the distributed locks that cover one or more data blocks (table and index blocks) in the database buffer cache. PCM locks do not lock any rows on behalf of transactions. These mechanisms are not discussed in this book; see your Oracle Server documentation for more information.

The following sections discuss in detail the lock mechanisms that are within the scope of this book.

Data Locks

The purpose of a data lock is to protect the data stored in a database table, guaranteeing data integrity when data in that table is being accessed concurrently by multiple users. Also, data locks prevent destructive interference of multiple, simultaneous, conflicting DML and DDL statements. For example, Oracle data locks guarantee that a specific row in a table can be updated by only one transaction at any time and that a table cannot be dropped if an uncommitted transaction contains an insert into the table.

Explicit (Manual) Data Locks   Earlier you learned that Oracle provides the option to override Oracle's implicit lock management. You can do this by explicitly acquiring a lock on a database table for a transaction. You can explicitly override Oracle's automatic data locking at two levels: transaction and system.

You can override automatic locking at the transaction level by using the following SQL statements: LOCK TABLE; SELECT, including the FOR UPDATE clause; and SET TRANSACTION READ ONLY.

At the system level, a database session can be started with nondefault locking by adjusting the initialization parameters SERIALIZABLE and ROW_LOCKING.

Explicit transaction-level locking is discussed later in the chapter, when the SQL commands used to invoke it are discussed.

Explicit System-Level Data Locks   When a session is connected to a database, the two system-level initialization parameters just mentioned determine how the system handles data locking for the session. To provide the highest level of data concurrency automatically, Oracle assumes these parameters are set to the default values of SERIALIZABLE = FALSE and ROW_LOCKING = ALWAYS.

> *WARNING*
> In almost all situations, **these parameters should not be altered**. They are provided for sites that must run in ANSI/ISO-compliant mode or that want to use applications written to run with earlier versions of Oracle. These are the only cases where these parameters should be altered—significant performance degradation results if you use parameters other than the defaults.
>
> If you decide you must change the default settings of these parameters, you should do so only after all sessions have disconnected from a single database. It is essential that all sessions connected to a single database run with the same settings for these parameters.

Three global settings are available for these parameters other than the defaults. Table 6-2 summarizes the nondefault settings.

For more information on how these settings affect automatic data locking, see your Oracle Server documentation.

NOTE
If you override Oracle's implicit locking at any level, you are responsible for ensuring that the explicit locking procedures operate correctly. They must satisfy the same criteria as the implicit locking—data integrity is guaranteed, data concurrency is acceptable, and deadlocks are not possible or are handled appropriately.

Let's explore each data lock in the context of which SQL commands cause it to be acquired, whether that command acquires the lock implicitly or explicitly. Regardless of whether you use Oracle's automatic lock mechanisms or the explicit lock mechanisms, all transactions that execute DML statements can acquire data locks at two levels: the row level (for specific rows in a table) and the table level (for the table itself and all rows in the table).

Row-Level Locks

A row-level lock is used to protect individual rows in a table while they are being modified in the context of a transaction. Because Oracle can lock individual rows of a table, a high degree of data concurrency can be maintained. Instead of locking an entire table when modifying a set of rows in that table, Oracle can lock only the

Case	Description	SERIALIZABLE	ROW_LOCKING
default	Oracle Version 7	FALSE	ALWAYS
1	Equivalent to Oracle Version 5 and earlier (no concurrent inserts, updates, or deletes in a table)	FALSE	INTENT
2	ANSI-compatible	TRUE	ALWAYS
3	ANSI-compatible, with table-level locking (no concurrent inserts, updates, or deletes in a table)	TRUE	INTENT

TABLE 6-2. *Summary of system-level locking options*

rows that are involved in the operation, leaving the remaining rows for access by other users.

Row-level locks are implicitly acquired by Oracle when certain SQL statements are issued. If necessary, you can override such locks by acquiring them explicitly.

Implicit Row Locks   Oracle implicitly acquires an exclusive data lock on each row in a table that is modified in the context of a transaction by an INSERT, UPDATE, or DELETE statement.

Each individually modified row is locked exclusively to prevent other transactions from simultaneously modifying it. Other transactions must wait to update or delete the locked rows until the locking transaction either commits or rolls back.

If a transaction obtains an exclusive row lock for a modified row in a transaction, a table lock is automatically acquired for the corresponding table. This is done to prevent a conflicting DDL operation that would override data modifications in an ongoing transaction.

Explicit Row Locks   You can override Oracle's implicit row-locking behavior by using a SELECT statement that includes the FOR UPDATE clause. The SELECT ... FOR UPDATE statement is used to acquire exclusive row locks for selected rows before they are updated.

The SELECT ... FOR UPDATE statement exclusively locks rows without actually modifying them; it only reserves the rows for later modification. It is typically used in an application program in conjunction with a CURSOR. The CURSOR is used to process UPDATE or DELETE statements that use the CURRENT OF clause.

If you use a SELECT ... FOR UPDATE statement to define a CURSOR, the rows that meet the SELECT statement search criteria are locked exclusively for modification (FOR UPDATE) when the cursor is opened. Because the rows are not individually locked as they are FETCHed from the cursor, you can exclusively lock the rows in the CURSOR so that you can UPDATE or DELETE them as needed. You can be confident that another user cannot UPDATE or DELETE those rows before you process them in your cursor.

The exclusive row locks are held until the transaction that opened the cursor is committed or rolled back. Locks are not released when a cursor is closed.

NOTE
Each row in the CURSOR is exclusively locked individually. The SELECT ... FOR UPDATE statement must wait until other conflicting transactions release the rows for UPDATE. Therefore, if a SELECT ... FOR UPDATE statement locks many rows in a table that experiences reasonable update activity, you can improve performance by acquiring an exclusive table lock.

The FOR UPDATE OF clause is optional in a CURSOR declaration whenever you use the CURRENT OF clause when processing the rows in a CURSOR. For example, instead of creating the following CURSOR declaration:

```
EXEC SQL DECLARE cursor_name CURSOR FOR
    SELECT ... FROM ... WHERE ...
    FOR UPDATE OF ...;

EXEC SQL UPDATE ... CURRENT OF cursor_name;
```

you can drop the FOR UPDATE OF clause and simply write

```
EXEC SQL DECLARE cursor_name CURSOR FOR
    SELECT ... FROM   ... WHERE ...

EXEC SQL UPDATE ... CURRENT OF cursor_name;
```

The precompiler detects the CURRENT OF clause and inserts the FOR UPDATE OF clause for you.

NOTE
If you use the FOR UPDATE OF clause, you cannot reference multiple tables. Also, you cannot FETCH from a FOR UPDATE OF cursor after a COMMIT (the row locks are released after the COMMIT). If you do this, you will get an ORA-1001 error (fetch out of sequence).

When issuing a SELECT ... FOR UPDATE statement, you can indicate whether you want to wait to acquire the row locks. If you don't want to wait to acquire the locks, you can specify the NOWAIT option at the end of the statement. With the NOWAIT option, you only acquire the row lock if it is immediately possible. Otherwise, an error (ORA-54) is returned to notify you that the lock is not available. You can retry the statement later.

If you don't specify the NOWAIT option (the default), the transaction will wait until the row locks can be obtained. If the wait is excessive, you may want to provide a way for the user to cancel the transaction. However, a distributed transaction can time out while it waits to acquire row locks if the elapsed time reaches the interval set by the DISTRIBUTED_LOCK_TIMEOUT initialization parameter.

Table-Level Locks
A table-level lock is used to protect some or all of the rows in a table, as well as the table itself, while it is being modified in the context of a transaction. Because

table-level locks can lock an entire table, data concurrency can be at a lower level than for row-level locks.

Table-level locks are implicitly acquired by Oracle when certain SQL statements are issued. If necessary, you can override these implicit table-level locks by acquiring them explicitly.

Implicit Table Locks   Oracle implicitly acquires a data lock on a table that is modified in the context of a transaction by an INSERT, UPDATE, or DELETE statement. Each table is locked at a level of restrictiveness required by the SQL statement to maintain data integrity while providing maximum data concurrency. Locks are acquired on tables to reserve a level of access to the table on behalf of a transaction and to prevent conflicting DDL statements that would override data modifications in an ongoing transaction.

When a table lock is acquired, all attempts to acquire an exclusive DDL lock on that table are prevented. This restricts any DDL operations that require an exclusive DDL lock on the table. For example, a table must not be altered or dropped if an uncommitted transaction holds a table lock.

Later in this section, the types of table locks that can be implicitly obtained on tables and the operations that acquire them will be discussed.

Explicit Table Locks   You can override Oracle's implicit table-locking behavior with the LOCK TABLE command and the SET TRANSACTION READ ONLY statement. (The latter was discussed earlier in this chapter.)

The LOCK TABLE statement explicitly locks a table; it lets you manually override Oracle's default locking mechanisms. When a LOCK TABLE statement is issued on a view, the underlying base tables are locked. You can specify several tables or views in the same LOCK TABLE statement; however, only a single lock type can be specified per LOCK TABLE statement. The LOCK TABLE statement has the following syntax:

```
EXEC SQL LOCK TABLE table1, table2,... IN lock_type MODE [NOWAIT];
```

where:

table1, **table2**,... is a list of table names and/or view names that are to be locked.

lock_type is the type of lock to set on the list of tables and/or views. Lock types will be discussed in detail later in this section.

NOWAIT is an optional parameter that specifies whether you want to wait to acquire the lock. If you specify the NOWAIT option, you only acquire the table lock if it is immediately available. Otherwise, an error (ORA-54) is returned to notify you that the lock is not available at this time. In this case, you can reattempt to lock the resource later.

If the NOWAIT option is not specified (the default), the transaction does not proceed until the requested table lock is acquired. There is no time limit for waiting to acquire a lock on a table. If the wait for a table lock is excessive, you might want to provide a way in your application program to cancel the operation and retry later.

NOTE
A distributed transaction can time out while waiting for a requested table lock if the elapsed time reaches the interval set by the DISTRIBUTED_LOCK_TIMEOUT initialization parameter.

Now that you understand that tables can be locked implicitly by Oracle or explicitly by you, let's look at the types of locks available and how they are used in your application program.

Types of Table Locks   Depending on the types of SQL statements that constitute a transaction, the tables modified by the transaction are locked by one of the following: row share, row exclusive, share, share row exclusive, or exclusive locks.

The type of table lock obtained on a table determines the level of lock restrictiveness on that table. The restrictiveness of the table lock determines the types of locks that can be obtained and held on that table by other simultaneous transactions. Table 6-3 summarizes the types of table locks acquired implicitly and explicitly by various SQL statements and the types of table locks that are permitted once those locks are obtained.

This table gives an overview of the table lock types, but you need to understand what SQL operations are permitted and prevented for each. This section describes each table lock type, from least restrictive to most restrictive; the actions that cause a transaction to acquire a table lock of that type; and which actions are permitted and which are prohibited in other transactions when your transaction acquires a lock.

SQL Statement	Table Lock Obtained	Row Exclusive	Row	Share Exclusive	Row Share	Share Row Exclusive
SELECT ... FROM ...	None	X	X	X	X	X
INSERT INTO ...	Row exclusive	X	X			

TABLE 6-3.   *Summary of table locks*

SQL Statement	Table Lock Obtained	Row Exclusive	Row	Share Exclusive	Row Share	Share Row Exclusive
UPDATE ...	Row exclusive	X*	X*			
DELETE FROM ...	Row exclusive	X*	X*			
SELECT ... FROM ... FOR UPDATE OF ...	Row share	X*	X*	X*	X*	
LOCK TABLE table IN ROW SHARE MODE	Row share	X	X	X	X	
LOCK TABLE table IN ROW EXCLUSIVE MODE	Row exclusive	X	X			
LOCK TABLE table IN SHARE MODE	Share	X		X		
LOCK TABLE table IN SHARE ROW EXCLUSIVE MODE	Share row exclusive	X				
LOCK TABLE table IN EXCLUSIVE MODE	Exclusive					

* Permitted if no conflicting row locks are held by another transaction; otherwise, you wait.

TABLE 6-3. *Summary of table locks* (continued)

Row Share Table Lock   A row share table lock indicates that the transaction holding the lock on the table has exclusively locked rows in that table and intends to update them. A row share table lock is implicitly acquired on a table using the following statement:

```
EXEC SQL SELECT ... FROM table ... FOR UPDATE OF ... ;
```

You explicitly acquire this lock using the following statement:

```
EXEC SQL LOCK TABLE table IN ROW SHARE MODE;
```

A row share table lock is the least restrictive type of table lock, offering the highest degree of concurrency on a table.

Permitted Operations: A row share table lock held by a transaction allows other transactions to query, insert, update, delete, or lock rows in that table concurrently. Therefore, other transactions can obtain simultaneous row share, row exclusive, share, and share row exclusive locks for the same table.

Prohibited Operations: A row share table lock held by a transaction prevents other transactions from explicitly acquiring exclusive write access to that table using the following statement:

```
EXEC SQL LOCK TABLE table IN EXCLUSIVE MODE;
```

Row Exclusive Table Lock   A row exclusive table lock generally indicates that the transaction holding the lock has made one or more updates to rows in the table. A row exclusive table lock is implicitly acquired for a table modified by the following statements:

```
EXEC SQL INSERT INTO table ... ;
```

or

```
EXEC SQL UPDATE table ... ;
```

or

```
EXEC SQL DELETE FROM table ... ;
```

A row exclusive table lock is explicitly acquired on a table by the following statement:

```
EXEC SQL LOCK TABLE table IN ROW EXCLUSIVE MODE;
```

A row exclusive table lock is slightly more restrictive than a row share table lock.

Permitted Operations: A row exclusive table lock held by a transaction allows other transactions to query, insert, update, delete, or lock rows concurrently in the same table. Therefore, row exclusive table locks allow multiple transactions to obtain simultaneous row exclusive and row share locks for the same table.

Prohibited Operations: A row exclusive table lock held by a transaction prevents other transactions from explicitly locking the table for exclusive reading or writing; therefore, other transactions cannot explicitly lock the table using the following statements:

```
EXEC SQL LOCK TABLE table IN SHARE MODE;
```

or

```
EXEC SQL LOCK TABLE table IN SHARE EXCLUSIVE MODE;
```

or

```
EXEC SQL LOCK TABLE table IN EXCLUSIVE MODE;
```

Row share and row exclusive table locks offer the highest degree of data concurrency. The explicit acquisition of a row share or row exclusive table lock could be warranted if your transaction needed to prevent another transaction from acquiring an intervening share, share row, or exclusive table lock before the table could be updated in your transaction. It could also be warranted if another transaction acquired an intervening share, share row, or exclusive table lock and no other transactions could update the table until the locking transaction committed or rolled back.

Your transaction needs to prevent a table from being altered or dropped before the table can be modified later in your transaction.

Share Table Lock   A share table lock is an explicit lock that indicates that the transaction holding the lock wants to prevent any simultaneous updates on the locked table. This lock is explicitly acquired using the following statement:

```
EXEC SQL LOCK TABLE table IN SHARE MODE;
```

Permitted Operations: A share table lock held by a transaction allows other transactions to query, lock specific rows with SELECT ... FOR UPDATE OF, or successfully execute LOCK TABLE ... IN SHARE MODE statements. No updates are allowed by other transactions. Multiple transactions can concurrently hold share table locks for the same table; in this case, no transaction can update the table (even if a transaction holds row locks as the result of a SELECT ... FOR UPDATE statement). Therefore, a transaction that has a share table lock can only update the table if no other transactions also have a share table lock for that table.

Prohibited Operations: A share table lock held by a transaction prevents other transactions from modifying the same table. A transaction cannot insert, update, or delete rows in a table when a share table lock is held by another transaction. A share table lock held by a transaction also prohibits other transactions from successfully executing the following explicit lock statements:

```
EXEC SQL LOCK TABLE table IN SHARE ROW EXCLUSIVE MODE;
```

or

```
EXEC SQL LOCK TABLE table IN EXCLUSIVE MODE;
```

or

```
EXEC SQL LOCK TABLE table IN ROW EXCLUSIVE MODE;
```

Share table locks are relatively restrictive. Conditions that could warrant the explicit acquisition of a share table lock include:

■ Your transaction only queries the table and requires a consistent set of the table's data for the duration of the transaction (that is, requires transaction-level read consistency for the locked table). This is effectively equivalent to setting a read-only transaction, but you are allowed to update the table.

■ It is acceptable if other transactions that attempt to update the locked table concurrently wait until all transactions with share table locks commit or roll back.

■ It is acceptable to allow other transactions to acquire concurrent share table locks on the same table, also allowing them the option of transaction-level read consistency.

WARNING
Your transaction may or may not update the table later in the same transaction. However, if multiple transactions concurrently hold share table locks for the same table, no transaction can update the table (even if row locks are held as the result of a SELECT . . . FOR UPDATE statement). Therefore, if concurrent share table locks on the same table are common, updates cannot proceed and deadlocks will be common. (Use share row exclusive or exclusive table locks instead.)

Share Row Exclusive Table Lock   A share row exclusive table lock is an explicit lock indicating that the transaction holding the lock wants to prevent any simultaneous updates on the locked table. The share row exclusive lock is more restrictive than a share table lock. A share row exclusive table lock is explicitly acquired using the following statement:

```
EXEC SQL LOCK TABLE table IN SHARE ROW EXCLUSIVE MODE;
```

Permitted Operations: Only one transaction can acquire a share row exclusive table lock. When held by a transaction, this lock allows other transactions to query or lock specific rows with the SELECT ... FOR UPDATE command, but they cannot update the table.

Prohibited Operations: A share row exclusive table lock held by a transaction prevents other transactions from obtaining row exclusive table locks and prevents them from modifying the same table. A transaction cannot insert, update, or delete rows in a table when a share row exclusive table lock is held by another transaction. When held by a transaction, this lock also prohibits other transactions from successfully executing the following explicit lock statements:

```
EXEC SQL LOCK TABLE table IN SHARE MODE;
```

or

```
EXEC SQL LOCK TABLE table IN SHARE ROW EXCLUSIVE MODE;
```

or

```
EXEC SQL LOCK TABLE table IN ROW EXCLUSIVE MODE;
```

or

```
EXEC SQL LOCK TABLE table IN EXCLUSIVE MODE;
```

Conditions that warrant the explicit acquisition of a share row exclusive table lock include:

- Your transaction requires both transaction-level read consistency for the specified table and the ability to update the locked table.

- You are not concerned about explicit row locks being obtained (that is, via SELECT ... FOR UPDATE) by other transactions. These other transactions may or may not cause UPDATE and INSERT statements in the locking transaction to wait to update the table (in other words, deadlocks may occur). You only want a single transaction to have this behavior.

Exclusive Table Lock   An exclusive table lock is the most restrictive type of table lock, giving the transaction that holds it exclusive write access to the table. An exclusive table lock is explicitly acquired with the following statement:

```
LOCK TABLE table IN EXCLUSIVE MODE;
```

Permitted Operations: Only one transaction can obtain an exclusive lock for a table. This lock permits other transactions to query the same table.

Prohibited Operations: An exclusive table lock held by a transaction prohibits other transactions from performing any type of DML statement on the same table. Other transactions cannot insert, update, or delete rows in the same table, lock rows in the same table, or lock the table in any mode.

Conditions that warrant the explicit acquisition of an exclusive table lock include:

- Your transaction requires immediate update access to the locked table. Therefore, if your transaction holds an exclusive table lock, other transactions cannot lock specific rows in the locked table.

- Your transaction also observes transaction-level read consistency for the locked table until the transaction is committed or rolled back.

- You are not concerned about low levels of data concurrency, making transactions that request exclusive table locks wait in line to update the table sequentially.

Privileges Required to Lock Data

You can acquire any type of table lock on tables in any schema that you own. However, to acquire a table lock on a table in a schema owned by another user, you must have the LOCK ANY TABLE system privilege or any object privilege required for the table—for example, SELECT or UPDATE.

Duration of Data Locks

All data locks acquired by a transaction, including row and table locks, are released when the transaction commits or rolls back. Data locks acquired after a savepoint are released if the transaction is rolled back to the savepoint. However, transactions not waiting for the previously locked resources can acquire locks on them when they become available. Waiting transactions will continue to wait until the original transaction commits or rolls back completely.

Data Lock Conversion

A transaction holds exclusive row locks for all rows inserted, updated, or deleted within the transaction. Because row locks are automatically acquired at the highest degree of restrictiveness, no lock conversion is required or performed.

Oracle automatically converts a table lock of lower restrictiveness to one of higher restrictiveness as appropriate. For example, assume that a transaction uses a SELECT statement with the FOR UPDATE clause to lock rows of a table. As a result, it acquires the exclusive row locks and a row share table lock for the table. If the transaction later updates one or more of the locked rows, the row share table lock is automatically converted to a row exclusive table lock.

Deadlock Detection

Oracle automatically detects deadlock situations. When a deadlock is detected, Oracle automatically resolves it by rolling back the statement involved in the deadlock that had performed the least amount of work up to that point, thereby releasing one set of the conflicting row locks. An error is returned to the transaction that issued the rolled-back transaction.

NOTE
In distributed transactions, local deadlocks are detected by analyzing a "waits for" graph, and global deadlocks are detected by a timeout. Once detected, nondistributed and distributed deadlocks are handled by the database and application in the same way.

Deadlocks most often occur when transactions explicitly override the default locking provided by the Oracle server. Because Oracle itself performs no lock escalation, does not use read locks for queries, and uses row-level (rather than page-level) locking, deadlocks occur infrequently when the Oracle's implicit locking mechanisms are used and not explicitly overridden in your application program.

DDL Locks

A DDL lock protects the definition of a schema object (a table, a view, or an index, for example) while that object is acted upon by an ongoing DDL operation in a transaction. Recall that a DDL statement implicitly commits the previous transaction. A DDL lock is acquired automatically by Oracle on behalf of any DDL transaction requiring it. Users cannot explicitly request DDL locks. Only individual schema objects that are modified or referenced are locked during DDL operations; the data dictionary is never locked in its entirety.

DDL locks fall into three categories: exclusive DDL, share DDL, and breakable parse locks.

Exclusive DDL Locks   Certain DDL statements require exclusive DDL locks for a resource to prevent destructive interference with other DDL operations that might modify or reference the same object. For example, a DROP TABLE operation is not allowed to drop a table while an ALTER TABLE operation is adding a column to the table, and vice versa.

In addition to DDL locks, DDL operations also acquire data locks on the object to be modified. Most DDL operations acquire exclusive DDL locks on the object to be modified (except for those listed in the next section, "Share DDL Locks").

While an exclusive DDL lock is being acquired, if another DDL lock is already held on the object by another operation, the acquisition waits until the previous DDL lock is released.

Share DDL Locks   Certain DDL operations require share DDL locks on a resource to prevent destructive interference with conflicting DDL operations, but allow data concurrency for similar DDL operations. For example, when a CREATE PROCEDURE statement is executed, the transaction acquires share DDL locks for all referenced tables. Other transactions can concurrently create procedures that reference the same tables and therefore acquire concurrent share DDL locks on those tables. However, no transaction can acquire an exclusive DDL lock on any referenced table. No transaction can alter or drop a referenced table. As a result, a transaction that holds a share DDL lock is guaranteed that the definition of the referenced object will remain constant for the duration of the transaction.

A share DDL lock is acquired on an object for DDL statements that include the following commands: AUDIT, NOAUDIT, GRANT, REVOKE, COMMENT, CREATE [or REPLACE] VIEW/PROCEDURE/PACKAGE/PACKAGE BODY/FUNCTION/ TRIGGER, CREATE SYNONYM, and CREATE TABLE (when the CLUSTER parameter is not included).

Breakable Parse Locks   Each SQL statement (or PL/SQL program unit) stored in the shared SQL pool holds a parse lock for each object referenced by the SQL statement. Parse locks are acquired so that the associated shared SQL area can be invalidated if a referenced object is altered or dropped. A parse lock does not prevent any DDL operation and can be broken to allow conflicting DDL operations—hence the name "breakable parse lock."

A parse lock is acquired during the parse phase of SQL statement execution and is held as long as the shared SQL area remains in the shared pool.

Duration of DDL Locks   The duration of a DDL lock varies depending on the type of DDL lock. Exclusive and share DDL locks last for the duration of DDL statement execution and the ensuing implicit transaction commit. A parse lock persists as long as the associated SQL statement remains in the shared pool.

A DDL operation on a cluster acquires exclusive DDL locks on the cluster and also on all tables and snapshots in the cluster. A DDL operation on a table or snapshot in a cluster acquires a share lock on the cluster, in addition to a share or exclusive DDL lock on the table or snapshot. The share DDL lock on the cluster prevents another operation from dropping the cluster while the first operation proceeds.

Guidelines for Data Locking

Observe the following guidelines when considering data locking in your application program. This will help you avoid some common pitfalls.

- If you explicitly override Oracle's default locking in your application program with the methods discussed in this chapter, make sure the Oracle users requesting locks have the privileges needed to obtain the locks. The DBA has the privilege to lock any table or row. Common users can lock any table they own as part of their schema or any table for which they have proper privilege, such as ALTER, SELECT, INSERT, UPDATE, or DELETE.

- If a PL/SQL block is part of a transaction, COMMITs and ROLLBACKs inside the block affect the whole transaction.

- You can usually avoid multitable deadlocks if you always lock the tables involved in the transactions in the same order for all transactions that lock those tables, either through implicit or explicit locks. For example, all application developers might follow the rule that when both master and detail tables are updated, the master table is locked first, then the detail table. If such rules are properly designed and followed in all applications, deadlocks are very unlikely to occur.

- When you know you will require a sequence of locks for one transaction, you should consider acquiring the most exclusive lock first.

Summary

This chapter defined the concepts of data consistency and data concurrency, along with the mechanisms (transactions and data locking) Oracle uses to address these problems. It also discussed in detail the mechanisms available in Oracle to ensure data consistency and data concurrency in your application program.

CHAPTER 7

Errors, Warnings, and Diagnostics

This chapter will introduce you to the tools and techniques available in Oracle to process errors and warnings in your application program. It will also discuss the tools available in Oracle for performing program diagnostics to determine run-time problems.

First, we'll discuss the importance of processing errors and warnings; second, we'll look at the kinds of errors and warnings you can expect from Oracle and discuss the tools used to process errors, warnings, and diagnostics.

Why Do I Need to Process Errors and Warnings?

Errors occur in every application program. The purpose of processing errors and warnings in your program is to make it "bulletproof." Nonexistent, improper, or insufficient error processing causes most of the software failures in systems today. As Winston Churchill once said, "There is nothing more exhilarating than to be shot at without result." Thus, the goal is to create a robust application that—when confronted with anything that the user, the database, the operating system, the computer hardware, or the computer network can shoot at it—will recover, report what happened, and continue executing.

When processing information in a database, you must also keep in mind the prime directive: "Do not corrupt the data!!!" Chapter 6 discussed some tools (transactions and database locking) Oracle provides to protect the integrity of the database. However, you are still responsible for meeting the prime directive in your application program.

A robust application requires correct and efficient error and warning processing. In fact, from a user's perspective, one of the major differences between a robust program and a poor-quality program is how well it responds to and reports errors and warnings. You cannot plan for every error your application might encounter; however, you can design robust error and warning processing into your application for those errors that you expect to occur and design contingencies for those that you do not expect.

It is particularly important to process errors and warnings that occur as a result of an SQL statement. This is because you must determine whether the database operation is successful before proceeding with your application. Oracle provides a set of tools to handle any error or warning that might occur while you're communicating with the Oracle system. These tools and techniques will be discussed in detail in the following sections, but first let's discuss what errors and warnings you can expect to be returned from a call to the Oracle database.

Errors and Warnings

Oracle returns status information after every executable SQL statement or database call in your application program. This status information tells you whether the statement is successful and, if it was, if there are any exceptions. Three general states can result from an SQL statement:

■ **Success** The SQL statement was completely successful, and the expected result occurred in the database.

■ **Warning** The SQL statement was successful, but an exception occurred in the result. For instance, a SELECT statement may not have found any rows, or a DELETE statement may not have deleted any rows. Also, the value of a database column may have been truncated when it was assigned to a host variable.

■ **Error** The SQL statement failed completely. An error can result from a problem with the SQL statement itself, the database system, or the computer system (hardware, operating system, or network).

If an SQL statement is successful, you can ignore the status information and process the result in your application program. If a warning occurs, the status information describes the exception, what processing you may need to perform (if any), and what to report to the user (if necessary). If an error occurs, the status information tells what error occurred, allows you to perform recovery processing, and allows you to report it to the user.

You can process any errors and warnings that may result from a call to an Oracle database with a combination of three methods:

■ **Explicit handling** After each database call, you can explicitly check for an error or warning and, if necessary, process it at that point. Although effective, this method can cause your application program to become cluttered with error and warning processing and grow with each new call to the database.

■ **Implicit handling** After each database call, Oracle implicitly checks for an error or warning and will process the error based on a method that you specify. You can call an error-handling function, "goto" another section of your program to process the error, or simply continue processing. This method is more efficient, easier to program, and ANSI-compliant, so it is portable to other database systems that support SQL.

■ **Diagnostic handling** After each database call, you can obtain additional diagnostic information from Oracle to diagnose a problem. Oracle provides additional information on CURSOR statistics, the SQL statement, option settings, and system statistics.

The following sections discuss in detail each of these methods and how to use them in your program.

Explicit Handling

After each executable SQL statement in your application program, you need to determine its success or failure. You can do this by explicitly checking the status information returned from Oracle following each SQL statement. This is called explicit handling.

Explicit handling requires that you insert code following each SQL statement to check the Oracle status information and process any errors or warnings. Explicit handling is best used in situations where you must do very specific processing if an error or warning occurs after an SQL statement—for example, if you need to COMMIT or ROLLBACK a transaction after the last SQL statement in a transaction. This method of handling errors and warnings is effective, but it can become problematic for the following reasons:

- You may overlook a problem if you forget to check for an error following a database operation.

- It is difficult to enforce consistent error handling throughout a program if multiple developers are involved.

- The program can become cluttered with error-checking and error-processing statements.

- This is not an ANSI/ISO-supported method for processing errors and warnings.

Oracle has two mechanisms for informing you of the status of an SQL statement: SQLCA and SQLCODE.

The SQLCA

The SQLCA (or SQL Communications Area) is an Oracle data structure that you include in your application program. Oracle uses the SQLCA to return the status information resulting from each SQL statement. This status information includes error codes, warning flags, the count of rows processed, SQL statement errors, and error-message text.

The following listing shows the definition of the SQLCA data structure:

```
struct sqlca
  {
  char        sqlcaid[8];
  long        sqlabc;
  long        sqlcode;
  struct
    {
```

```
        unsigned short    sqlerrml;
        char        sqlerrmc[70];
    }   sqlerrm;
char          sqlerrp[8];
long          sqlerrd[6];
char          sqlwarn[8];
char          sqlext[8];
};
struct sqlca sqlca;
```

The SQLCA fields and the values they can store are as follows:

■ **sqlcaid** A character string containing the value "SQLCA" to identify the SQL Communications Area. It is referenced as **sqlca.sqlcaid**.

■ **sqlcabc** An integer field that holds the length, in bytes, of the SQLCA data structure. It is referenced as **sqlca.sqlcabc**.

■ **sqlcode** An integer field that holds the status code resulting from the most recent SQL statement. It is referenced as **sqlca.sqlcode**. The **sqlcode** value can be zero, positive, or negative, depending on the status of the SQL operation.

A **sqlcode** value of 0 means the SQL statement was completely successful, with no errors or warnings. You can continue processing the result of the statement and COMMIT the transaction, if necessary.

A positive (> 0) **sqlcode** value means the SQL statement was successful but encountered an exception. An exception occurs whenever no data is found as a result of a SELECT or FETCH statement or a WHERE clause. Another exception occurs when no rows are inserted as a result of an INSERT statement. This can occur when you use a subquery that results in no rows.

NOTE
This is an error only when MODE={ANSI | ANSI14 | ANSI13}. The value of this number may be different based on the exception and the MODE setting. You must determine in your program how to handle a "no data found" situation. In some instances (CURSOR and array processing) it is necessary and very useful to know this information. In other instances it can be ignored or just reported to the user.

A negative (< 0) **sqlcode** value means the SQL statement did not complete successfully as a result of an error in the SQL statement, a database error, or a system error (hardware, operating system, network, and so on). In all instances you should react to and recover from any error with a negative value. Most errors will require you to ROLLBACK a transaction, perform cleanup (close cursors, free allocated memory, and so on), and report to the user. Some errors will require you to abort processing. Some errors can be ignored.

For more information on the Oracle run-time errors, see Appendix E.

■ **sqlerrm**   A substructure containing the error message associated with the error code assigned to **sqlca.sqlcode**. You must be sure to check the value of **sqlcode** and make sure it is negative before you reference **sqlerrmc**. Otherwise, you will get the error message associated with a previous error condition. The contents of this substructure are **sqlerrml** and **sqlerrmc**.

– **sqlerrml** is an integer field containing the length of the error-message text stored in **sqlerrmc**. It is referenced as **sqlca.sqlerrm.sqlerrml**.

– **sqlerrmc** is a character string that holds the error-message text. It is referenced as **sqlca.sqlerrm.sqlerrmc**. The maximum length of the error-message text is 70 characters; if it exceeds 70 characters, you must call the function **sqlglm**. If the message is exactly 70 characters long, Oracle may truncate the last character.

NOTE
The error-message text is not null-terminated. Therefore, before you use the error-message text in any functions that expect a null-terminated string, you must null-terminate it with the following syntax:

```
sqlca.sqlerrm.sqlerrmc[sqlca.sqlerrm.sqlerrml] = '\0'
```

■ **sqlerrp**   A character-string field reserved for future use.

■ **sqlerrd**   An array of six integers that are used to assign diagnostic information. It is referenced as **sqlca.sqlerrd[n]**, where $0 \leq n \leq 5$. The fields 0, 1, 3, and 5 are not currently used and are reserved for futue use. Fields 2 and 4 can be assigned the following values:

– The **sqlerrd[2]** field is assigned the number of rows processed successfully by the SQL statement. If the SQL statement fails, the value is undefined except when processing arrays. If an error occurs while processing arrays, this field is assigned the number of rows processed successfully.

– For the EXECUTE, SELECT, INSERT, UPDATE, and DELETE statements, this value is assigned the total number of rows processed successfully. However, for CURSOR processing, this value is assigned zero (0) after the OPEN statement and incremented after each FETCH statement. Therefore, for CURSORs this value holds the total number of rows processed, not the   total for an individual FETCH. The row count does not include rows processed in an UPDATE or DELETE cascade.

– The **sqlerrd[4]** field is assigned what is called the parse error offset. Before executing an SQL statement, Oracle must parse it—in other words, examine it to make sure it follows syntax rules and refers to valid database objects. If Oracle finds an error in the statement, an error is assigned to sqlcode, and the offset position in the character string where the parse error begins is assigned to this field.

The first character in the SQL statement occupies position 0. For example, if the offset is 9, the parse error begins at the 10th character. If no parse error occurs, Oracle sets the parse error offset to 0. Also, if a parse error occurs at position 0, the field is assigned 0. How do you know which it is? You should only check for a parse error if **sqlcode** is negative.

By default, static SQL statements are checked for syntactic errors at precompile time. Therefore, this field is mostly useful for debugging dynamic SQL statements, which your program accepts or builds at run time.

■ **sqlwarn** An array of eight single characters (not a character string) that are used as warning flags. It is referenced as **sqlca.sqlwarn[n]**, where $0 \leq n \leq 7$. The fields 2, 6, and 7 are currently not used. Fields 0, 1, and 3-5 can be assigned the following values.

– The **sqlwarn[0]** field is assigned a W if one of the other flags is set.

– The **sqlwarn[1]** field is assigned a nonzero value if a character column value is truncated when it is assigned to an output host variable. This does not apply to numeric data. This field should not be used to detect that a column value is truncated. You should use an indicator variable to detect this condition and determine how much of the string is truncated.

– The **sqlwarn[3]** field is assigned a nonzero value if in a SELECT or FETCH statement the number of columns in a query select list does not equal the number of host variables in the INTO clause. The value assigned to this field is the lesser of the two.

– The **sqlwarn[4]** field is assigned a nonzero value if every row in a table is processed by an UPDATE or DELETE statement. This typically occurs when the statement contains no WHERE clause. This is called an unconditional operation. Oracle considers this an unusual situation, so it sets a warning. That way you can ROLLBACK the transaction if this is not the intent.

– The **sqlwarn[5]** field is assigned a nonzero value when an EXEC SQL CREATE {PROCEDURE | FUNCTION | PACKAGE | PACKAGE BODY} statement fails because of a PL/SQL compilation error.

– The **sqlext** character-string field is reserved for future use.

Now that you understand the contents of the SQLCA data structure, let's discuss how you declare it in your program and use it for processing errors and warnings.

Declaring the SQLCA　　The SQLCA is a data structure and must be declared as such in your application program. You can declare the SQLCA explicitly, as shown in the preceding SQLCA data structure listing, or you can copy it into your program by using the INCLUDE statement, as follows:

```
EXEC SQL INCLUDE sqlca;
```

When you precompile your program, the INCLUDE statement is replaced by the data structure declaration shown in the preceding SQLCA data structure listing.

The SQLCA can be declared anywhere a C variable can be declared, with one exception: It must be declared outside the DECLARE section. The SQLCA must be declared before any call to an executable SQL statement or before being initialized or referenced. It is suggested that you declare and initialize the SQLCA before you connect to Oracle or call any SQL statements.

You can declare more than one SQLCA in your program. You can declare it globally to your entire program, statically in your source modules, or in any of your functions. Access to a particular SQLCA is limited by its scope within your program, just like any other variable. Oracle returns information only to the "active" SQLCA.

You can assign any valid C storage class (Pro*C does not support **register**) to the SQLCA. This is done by defining the symbol SQLCA_STORAGE_CLASS. If, for example, you wanted to declare a global SQLCA, you would declare it in one module and then use the following symbol definition in all other modules:

```
#define SQLCA_STORAGE_CLASS extern
EXEC SQL INCLUDE SQLCA;
```

NOTE
If you are concurrently performing distributed processing on a combination of local and remote databases, all the databases write to one SQLCA; there is not a different SQLCA for each database.

You should initialize the SQLCA before using it (it's always good programming practice to initialize a variable before it is used). You do that by defining the symbol SQLCA_INIT, as follows:

```
#define SQLCA_INIT
```

However, if you declare the SQLCA in a function with a storage class of **auto** (the default), your compiler may not allow this type of initialization. Check your compiler user guide.

The declaration of SQLCA is required or optional, depending on the MODE setting. The rules are as follows:

- When MODE={ORACLE | ANSI13}, the SQLCA must be declared; otherwise, compile-time errors will result.

- When MODE={ANSI | ANSI14}, the SQLCA declaration is optional. You must declare the status variable SQLCODE (to be discussed in the next section). If you declare them both, Oracle returns the same status code to both after every SQL operation.

Using the SQLCA   From the sample application program on the disk available for this book, you can see how the SQLCA is used in a program. As is shown in the example, a single error-processing function is created to process all errors. In this function, the SQLCA is checked for errors or warnings and, if necessary, the result is reported to the user.

```
BOOL ProcErrorCode(HWND hWnd)
{
    /*
    ** Check the SQLCA structure for a database error.
    ** Database errors are less than zero.
    */

    if (sqlca.sqlcode < 0)
        {
```

```
    MessageBox(hWnd, sqlca.sqlerrm.sqlerrmc,
        "Database Error", MB_OK);
    return(FALSE);
    }
    return(TRUE);
}
```

Using sqlglm   The SQLCA can accommodate error messages up to 70 characters long. To get the complete text of longer (or nested) error messages, you need to use the function **sqlglm**. After you have encountered an error as a result of an SQL statement, you can call the **sqlglm** function with the following syntax:

```
char    scMessageBuffer[m];
long    iBufferSize = m;
long    iMessageLength = 0;

sqlglm(scMessageBuffer, &iBufferSize, &iMessageLength);
```

where:

> **scMessageBuffer** is the text buffer in which you want Oracle to store the error-message text. On output, Oracle blank-pads to the end of the buffer (**iBufferSize**).

> **iBufferSize** (assigned *m*) specifies the maximum length of the buffer in bytes.

> **iMessageLength** is assigned the length of the error-message text returned in **scMessageBuffer**. The maximum length of an Oracle error message is 512 characters, including the error code, nested messages, and message inserts, such as table and column names. The maximum length of an error message returned by **sqlglm** depends on the value you specify for **iBufferSize**.

> *NOTE*
> You should only call **sqlglm** when an SQL statement results in an error (SQLCODE or **sqlca.sqlcode** is negative). Otherwise, **sqlglm** returns the message text associated with an error from a prior SQL statement.

Diagnostics for Arrays   For INSERT, UPDATE, DELETE, and SELECT INTO statements, **sqlca.sqlerrd[2]** records the number of rows processed. For FETCH statements, it records the cumulative sum of rows processed.

When you use host arrays with FETCH, to find the number of rows returned by the most recent iteration, subtract the current value of **sqlca.sqlerrd[2]** from its previous value (stored in another variable). In the following example, you determine the number of rows returned by the most recent FETCH:

```
int nRows;
int nRowsBefore;
int nCurrentRows;

EXEC SQL BEGIN DECLARE SECTION;
    int aiItemNumber[100];
    char ascItemName[20][100];
EXEC SQL END DECLARE SECTION;

EXEC SQL DECLARE item_cursor CURSOR FOR
    SELECT item_id, item_name
        FROM INVENTORY
        WHERE category = "Monitor";

EXEC SQL OPEN item_cursor;
EXEC SQL WHENEVER NOT FOUND CONTINUE;

-- initialize loop variables
nRows = 20;        -- number of rows in each array "batch"
nRowsBefore = 0;   -- previous value of sqlerrd[2]
nCurrentRows = 20;

WHILE nCurrentRows = nRows
    {
    EXEC SQL FOR :nRows
        FETCH item_cursor
        INTO :aiItemId, :ascItemName;

    nCurrentRows = sqlca.sqlerrd[2] - nRowsBefore;
    nRowsBefore = sqlca.sqlerrd[2];

  /* Process data here. */
    }
...
```

The number of rows processed in **sqlca.sqlerrd[2]** is also useful when an error occurs during an array operation. Processing stops at the row that caused the error, so **sqlca.sqlerrd[2]** stores the number of rows processed successfully.

The SQLCODE

An alternative to using the SQLCA is the SQLCODE (or SQL Status Code). The SQLCODE is a four-byte-long integer variable, declared in your application program, to which Oracle assigns the status code resulting from an SQL statement. The SQLCODE is used in exactly the same manner as the **sqlcode** field of the SQLCA (**sqlca.sqlcode**).

The SQLCODE is provided by Oracle for ANSI compliance. If you use the SQLCODE in your program and do not declare an SQLCA, Oracle implicitly declares an SQLCA that is used to assign the value of SQLCODE. Thus, no overhead is eliminated by using only the SQLCODE.

Declaring the SQLCODE   The SQLCODE is declared as a **long** integer in your application program. Therefore, the SQLCODE variable can be declared in your program anywhere a C variable can be declared, including inside the DECLARE section. If you do not declare an SQLCA, the SQLCODE must be declared before any call to an executable SQL statement or before being initialized or referenced. It is suggested that you declare and initialize the SQLCODE before you connect to Oracle or call any SQL statements. The SQLCODE variable is declared with the following syntax:

```
long SQLCODE;
```

> **NOTE**
> SQLCODE must be declared in uppercase.

The scope rules for the SQLCODE variable are the same as those for the SQLCA. You can declare more than one SQLCODE in your program. You can declare it globally to your entire program, statically in your source modules, or in any function definition. Access to a particular SQLCODE is limited by its scope within your program, just like any other variable. Oracle returns information only to the active SQLCODE. You can assign any valid C storage class (Pro*C does not support registers) to the SQLCODE.

The declaration of SQLCODE is required or optional, depending on the MODE setting. The rules are as follows:

■   When MODE={ANSI | ANSI14}, the SQLCODE must be declared; otherwise, compile-time errors will result. The SQLCA is optional in this mode. If you declare them both, Oracle returns the same status code to both after every SQL operation. When you declare a SQLCODE instead of the SQLCA in a particular source module, the precompiler allocates an internal SQLCA for that module. Your program cannot access the internal SQLCA.

■ When MODE={Oracle | ANSI13}, the SQLCODE declaration is optional and goes unused. The SQLCA is required in this mode.

Using the SQLCODE   The SQLCODE is used in exactly the same manner as the **sqlca.sqlcode**. However, only the error status is available; the function **sqlglm** must be called to report an error message to the user.

Implicit Handling

When explicit handling of errors and warnings was discussed earlier in this chapter, the need to insert code that explicitly checks for and processes errors and warnings after each executable SQL statement was mentioned. The ANSI standard defines a method, supported by Oracle, to implicitly check for and process each error and warning for each SQL statement. This is called *implicit handling*. You can define how and where you want to process the problem in your program. Implicit handling is ANSI-compliant, is easy to program and maintain, and lets Oracle do much of the work for you.

The mechanism provided by the ANSI standard (and Oracle) to implicitly handle errors and warnings is the WHENEVER clause.

The WHENEVER Clause

If an error occurs when an executable SQL statement is processed, it is returned to the SQLCA (or SQLCODE). You must explicitly check for the error or tell Oracle to implicitly check it for you. By default, the error is ignored and processing will continue, if possible, as if nothing happened. The WHENEVER statement allows you to tell Oracle to implicitly check for any returned errors or warnings. Also, the WHENEVER statement lets you define how to process the error in your program.

You can specify in a WHENEVER statement to have Oracle implicitly check for any one or all of the following conditions: error, warning, and data not found. When the WHENEVER statement encounters one of these conditions, it allows you to specify how you want to handle the condition in your program. You have the option to process the condition with one of the following programming constructs:

■ Continue processing, ignore the error, and continue.

■ Call a function.

■ Break out of a control loop.

■ Go to another location in your program.

■ Stop processing altogether.

You define a WHENEVER statement with the following syntax:

```
EXEC SQL WHENEVER condition action;
```

where:

condition is one of the following:

■ **SQLERROR** You want Oracle to detect WHENEVER an error occurs as the result of an SQL statement. This means the **sqlca.sqlcode** (and SQLCODE) has a negative value.

■ **SQLWARNING** You want Oracle to detect WHENEVER a warning occurs as the result of an SQL statement. This means the **sqlca.sqlcode** (and SQLCODE) has a positive value. Also, **sqlca.sqlwarn[0]** and one of the warning flags (**sqlca.sqlwarn[1-7]**) are set.

NOTE
You must declare the SQLCA to use WHENEVER SQLWARNING. In MODE={ANSI | ANSI14}, declaring the SQLCA is optional.

■ **NOT FOUND**   You want Oracle to detect WHENEVER a "data not found" condition occurs as the result of an SQL statement. This means the **sqlca.sqlcode** (and SQLCODE) is assigned a positive value.

action is one of the following actions you can direct your program to take when one of the preceding conditions occurs:

■ **CONTINUE** Your program continues to execute the next statement if possible. This is the default action, equivalent to not using the WHENEVER statement. You can use it to "turn off" condition checking.

■ **DO function** Your program calls a specified function. When the end of that function routine is reached, control transfers to the statement that follows the failed SQL statement. A *function* is any functional program unit that can be invoked, such as a C function.

NOTE
You cannot pass or return any parameters in the function parameter list (notice the empty parameter list), and it cannot return any values (a **void** function). The usual rules for entering and exiting a function apply.

■ **DO break**   Your program breaks out of a control structure such as an IF, FOR, WHILE, **do...while**, or **switch** statement.

■ **DO return**   Your program returns program control to the previous calling function.

■ **goto label_name**   Your program branches to a labeled statement.

■ **STOP**   Your program stops processing, and uncommitted work is rolled back.

NOTE
The STOP action displays no messages before disconnecting from Oracle and is therefore not recommended.

Using WHENEVER   You can declare multiple WHENEVER statements, each to process one of the conditions just discussed. Simply insert the following WHENEVER statements into your program before the first executable SQL statement if you want your program to go to a **close_cursor** label if a NOT FOUND condition occurs, CONTINUE with the next statement if an SQLWARNING occurs, and go to an **error_handler** label if an SQLERROR occurs:

```
EXEC SQL WHENEVER NOT FOUND goto close_cursor;
EXEC SQL WHENEVER SQLWARNING CONTINUE;
EXEC SQL WHENEVER SQLERROR goto error_handler;
...
EXEC SQL DECLARE CURSOR ...
EXEC SQL OPEN ...
...
close_cursor:
   EXEC SQL CLOSE ...
   return;
error_handler:
   ...
```

In the following example, you use WHENEVER...DO statements to handle specific errors:

```
...
EXEC SQL WHENEVER SQLERROR DO handle_insert_error();
EXEC SQL INSERT INTO item (item_id, item_name, category)
   VALUES (:iItemId, :scItemName, :scCategory);
```

```
EXEC SQL WHENEVER SQLERROR DO handle_delete_error;
EXEC SQL DELETE FROM employee WHERE employee_ssn = :scEmpSSN;
...

void handle_insert_error();
   {
   if (sqlca.sqlcode == -1) then          -- duplicate key value
      ...
   elseif (sqlca.sqlcode == -1401) then   -- value too large
      ...
 ...
   }

void handle_delete_error();
   {
   if (sqlca.sqlerrd[2] == 0) then    -- no rows deleted
      ...
   else
      ...
   }
...
```

Notice how the procedures check variables in the SQLCA to determine a course of action.

Scope of WHENEVER   Because WHENEVER is a declarative statement, its scope in a source module is positional, not logical. In other words, it tests all executable SQL statements that physically follow it in the source file, not in the logical flow of your program. Therefore, you insert the WHENEVER statement in your source module before the first executable SQL statement you want to test.

A WHENEVER statement stays in effect until it is positionally superseded by another WHENEVER statement checking for the same condition. In other words, a WHENEVER statement that checks for a specific condition is in effect in a source module from where it is declared until the next WHENEVER statement for the same condition is encountered in the same source module.

Guidelines for Using WHENEVER   Using the WHENEVER statement in your program can be somewhat tricky. Because the placement of a WHENEVER clause is positional in a file and not logical in your program, it may not always be clear how its placement will affect the control of your program. You should observe the following guidelines to avoid some common mistakes.

In general, place a WHENEVER SQLERROR statement before the first executable SQL statement in your program source file, preferably at the top of the file. This ensures that all ensuing errors are trapped in your program, since WHENEVER statements stay in effect to the end of a file (unless another WHENEVER statement for the same condition is encountered).

Your program should be prepared to handle a NOT FOUND condition when using a CURSOR to FETCH rows. If a FETCH returns no data, the program should branch to a labeled section of code where a CLOSE command is issued on the OPEN CURSOR.

If a WHENEVER SQLERROR goto statement branches to an error-handling function that includes an executable SQL statement, your program might enter an infinite loop if the SQL statement fails with an error. You can avoid this by coding WHENEVER SQLERROR CONTINUE before the SQL statement in the error-handling function, as shown in the following example:

```
EXEC SQL WHENEVER SQLERROR goto sql_error;
    ...
sql_error:
    EXEC SQL WHENEVER SQLERROR CONTINUE;
    EXEC SQL ROLLBACK WORK RELEASE;
```

Without the WHENEVER SQLERROR CONTINUE statement, a ROLLBACK error would invoke the routine again, starting an infinite loop.

Careless use of WHENEVER can cause problems. For example, the following code enters an infinite loop if the DELETE statement sets NOT FOUND because no rows meet the search condition:

```
EXEC SQL WHENEVER NOT FOUND goto no_more;
for (;;)
    {
    EXEC SQL FETCH emp_cursor INTO :scEmpName,  :dPayRate;
        ...
    };

no_more:
    EXEC SQL DELETE FROM employee WHERE employee_ssn = :scEmpSSN;
        ...
```

In the next example, you handle the NOT FOUND condition properly by resetting the goto target:

```
EXEC SQL WHENEVER NOT FOUND goto no_more;
for (;;)
    {
    EXEC SQL FETCH emp_cursor INTO :scEmpName, :dPayRate;
```

```
        . . .
    };

no_more:
    EXEC SQL WHENEVER NOT FOUND goto no_match;
    EXEC SQL DELETE FROM employee WHERE employee_ssn = :scEmpSSN;
        . . .
no_match:
    . . .
```

In C, you can define local as well as global identifiers. Make sure all SQL statements governed by a WHENEVER goto statement can branch to the **goto** label. The label to which a WHENEVER goto statement branches must be in the same precompilation file as the WHENEVER statement and must be reachable by all SQL statements.

If your program must return after handling an error, use DO return:

```
EXEC SQL WHENEVER SQLERROR return;
EXEC SQL UPDATE employee SET pay_rate = pay_rate * 1.10;
EXEC SQL DROP INDEX EMP_INDEX;
```

Alternatively, you can test the value of SQLCODE:

```
EXEC SQL UPDATE employee SET pay_rate = pay_rate * 1.10;
if (sqlca.sqlcode < 0)
    return;
EXEC SQL DROP INDEX EMP_INDEX;
```

Just make sure no WHENEVER goto or WHENEVER STOP statement is active. It is considered good style to have WHENEVER statements in each function and WHENEVER CONTINUE at the end of each function. The drawback of WHENEVER is that if you do the same thing for all errors, it can mask which SQL statement actually caused the error. The ORACA, described in the next section, can give you this information.

Program Diagnostics

The SQLCA supplies you with information about standard SQL communications. Typically, it will supply you with enough information to process errors and warnings. However, sometimes you need more information to diagnose a run-time problem or analyze your program's use of Oracle resources. Oracle provides a similar mechanism to do that: the Oracle Communications Area (or ORACA).

The ORACA operates in the same manner as the SQLCA. Following each SQL statement in your application program, Oracle assigns a set of extended diagnostic information to the ORACA. The following sections discuss the details of the ORACA—what it contains and how to use it.

The ORACA

The ORACA gives you an extended set of information that you can use to diagnose, analyze, and troubleshoot run-time problems in your program. Use the ORACA only when absolutely necessary, however, because it adds program overhead that affects run-time performance. With the ORACA you can monitor and analyze your program's use of Oracle system resources, such as the SQL statement executor and the cursor cache (the cursor cache is an area of memory reserved for CURSOR processing).

The ORACA is a data structure (like the SQLCA) that you include in your application program and in which Oracle returns option settings, system statistics, and extended diagnostics such as:

- SQL statement text
- The name of the source file in which an error occurs
- The location in a source file where an error occurs
- Cursor cache errors and statistics

The following listing shows how the ORACA data structure is defined:

```
struct oraca
   {
   char          oracaid[8];
   long          oracabc;
   long          oracchf;
   long          oradbgf;
   long          orahchf;
   long          orastxtf;
   struct
      {
         unsigned short    orastxtl;
         char        orastxtc[70];
      }   orastxt;
   struct
      {
```

```
        unsigned short    orasfnml;
        char        orasfnmc[70];
    }    orasfnm;
long            oraslnr;
long            orahoc;
long            oramoc
long            oracoc;
long            oranor;
long            oranpr'
long            oranex;
};
struct oraca oraca;
```

The ORACA data structure contains many fields that you can set to turn on the ORACA diagnostic options. Setting these diagnostic options allows you to gather information such as:

■ SQL statement text

■ DEBUG operations

■ Cursor cache usage

■ Heap usage (the *heap* is an area of memory reserved for dynamic variables)

■ Cursor statistics

Let's discuss the definition of each ORACA field and the values they can store. This will help you decide which options will be useful to you.

■ **oracaid** A character string that is assigned the value "ORACA" to identify the Oracle Communications Area. It is referenced as **oraca.oracaid**.

■ **oracabc** An integer field that is assigned the length of the ORACA data structure in bytes. It is referenced as **oraca.oracabc**.

■ **oradbgf** An integer field that is used to set the master DEBUG option, which allows you to control the setting of all the other DEBUG operations. It is referenced as **oraca.oradbgf**. If this field is disabled, all the other DEBUG operations are effectively turned off regardless of their settings. You can set this field to 0 (the default) to disable all DEBUG operations or to 1 to enable the control of all DEBUG operations.

■ **oracchf** An integer field used to set the option to gather cursor cache statistics and consistency checks. It is referenced as **oraca.oracchf**. If the master DEBUG option (**oraca.oradbgf**) is set on (= 1), this field is used to enable the gathering of cursor cache statistics. It allows you to turn on cursor cache consistency checks before every CURSOR operation. This is useful for checking when memory overwrites affect the cursor cache. Cursor cache consistency checks occur in the Oracle run-time library, which might generate errors. These errors are returned to the SQLCA just like normal errors. The Oracle run-time errors are documented in Appendix E.

You can set this field to 0 (the default) to disable cursor cache statistics and consistency checking or to 1 to enable cursor cache statistics and consistency checking.

■ **orahchf** An integer field used to set the option to check the heap for consistency. It is referenced as **oraca.orahchf**. If the master DEBUG option (**oraca.oradbgf**) is set on (= 1), this field is used to enable heap consistency checks in the Oracle run-time library each time heap memory is dynamically allocated or deallocated. This is useful for checking to see if memory overwrites affect the heap. This field must be enabled before you CONNECT to a database. Once it is enabled, it cannot be turned off.

You can set this field to 0 (the default) to disable heap consistency checking or to 1 to enable heap consistency checking.

■ **orastxtf** An integer field used to tell Oracle when to save the text of an SQL statement. It is referenced as **orca.orastxtf**. Saving the SQL statement text allows you to diagnose the statement. This is most useful for diagnosing dynamic SQL problems. The SQL statement text is saved in the ORACA field **orastxt**.

You can set this field to 0 (the default) to never save the SQL statement text, to 1 to save the SQL statement text on SQLERROR only, to 2 to save the SQL statement text on SQLERROR or SQLWARNING, or to 3 to save the SQL statement text after each SQL statement.

■ **orastxt** A substructure containing the SQL statement text controlled by the ORACA field **oraca.orastxtf**. This substructure allows you to save the text of an SQL statement parsed by Oracle. You must be sure to set the value of **oraca.orastxtf** before you reference **orastxtc**. Otherwise, you will get the text associated with an unknown SQL statement. This substructure contains the **orastxtl** and **orastxtc** fields.

– **orastxtl** is an integer field that is assigned the length of the saved SQL statement text stored in **orastxtc**. It is referenced as **oraca.orastxt.orastxtl**.

– **orastxtc** is a character string that is assigned the saved SQL statement text. It is referenced as **oraca.orastxt.orastxtc**. The maximum length of the SQL statement text is 70 characters. SQL statements parsed by the Pro*C precompiler (CONNECT, FETCH, and COMMIT) cannot be saved.

NOTE
The SQL statement text is not null-terminated. Before you use the text in any functions that expect a null-terminated string, you must null-terminate it with the following syntax:

```
oraca.orastxt.orastxtc[oraca.orastxt.orastxtl] = '\0';
```

NOTE
The last character of the text may be truncated if the text is exactly 70 characters long.

■ **orasfnm** A substructure containing the name of the source file where the last saved SQL statement occurs in your program. This substructure contains the **orasfnml** and **orasfnmc** fields. **orasfnml** is an integer field that is assigned the length of the source file name stored in **orasfnmc**. It is referenced as **oraca.orastxt.orasfnml**. **orasfnmc** is a character string that is assigned the name of the source file where the last saved SQL statement occurs in your program. It is referenced as **oraca.orastxt.orasfnmc**. The maximum length of the source file name is 70 characters.

NOTE
The source file name is not null-terminated. Before you use the text in any functions that expect a null-terminated string, you **must** null-terminate it with the following syntax:

```
oraca.orastxt.orasfnmc[oraca.orastxt.orasfnml] = '\0';
```

NOTE
The last character of the text may be truncated if the text is exactly 70 characters long.

■ **oraslnr** An integer field that is assigned the line number in the source file that contains (or is nearest) the last saved SQL statement in your program. It is referenced as **oraca.oraslnr**.

When the cursor cache statistics option is enabled (and the master DEBUG option is on), the next ORACA fields are assigned the values of the cursor cache statistics. Those statistics are gathered at every COMMIT or ROLLBACK statement. Internally, Oracle maintains a set of cursor cache statistics for each CONNECTed database. The statistics assigned to the current ORACA pertain to the database against which the last COMMIT or ROLLBACK is executed.

- **orahoc** An integer field that is assigned the highest value assigned to MAXOPENCURSORS during program execution. It is referenced as **oraca.orahoc**.

- **oramoc** An integer field that is assigned the maximum number of simultaneously open CURSORs required by your program. It is referenced as **oraca.oramoc**. This value may be higher than the value assigned to **orahoc** if MAXOPENCURSORS is set too low, in which case Oracle is forced to extend the cursor cache dynamically.

- **oracoc** An integer field that is assigned the current number of open CURSORs in your program. It is referenced as **oraca.oracoc**.

- **oranor** An integer field that is assigned the number of cursor cache reassignments in your program. It is referenced as **oraca.oracoc**. This number shows the degree of memory "thrashing" in the cursor cache of your program. You should optimize this number to its lowest possible value.

- **oranpr** An integer field that is assigned the number of SQL statement parses in your program. It is referenced as **oraca.oracoc**.

- **oranex** An integer field that is assigned the number of SQL statement executions in your program. It is referenced as **oraca.oracex**. The ratio of this number to that assigned to **oranpr** should be kept as high as possible. In other words, the number of parses and executions should be equal. You want to eliminate reparsing, if possible.

Now that you understand the contents of the ORACA data structure, let's discuss how you declare it in your program and use it to handle program diagnostics.

Declaring the ORACA

The ORACA is a data structure just like the SQLCA and is declared in exactly the same manner. You can declare the ORACA explicitly, as shown in the preceding ORACA data structure listing, or you can copy it into your program by using the INCLUDE statement:

```
EXEC SQL INCLUDE oraca;
```

When you precompile your program, the INCLUDE statement is replaced by the data structure declaration shown in the preceding ORACA data structure listing.

The ORACA has the same declaration rules as the SQLCA, with three exceptions. First, because of the overhead associated with the ORACA, you must enable its use in your program. This is done either on the Pro*C command line with (ORACA=YES) or in your program with the following declarative statement:

```
EXEC SQL OPTION (ORACA=YES);
```

Second, the MODE setting does not affect the ORACA. Finally, you must set the desired option fields in the ORACA before it begins to gather information.

Using the ORACA

The ORACA is used in exactly the same manner as the SQLCA. You must determine which aspects of the ORACA are useful for diagnosing problems with your application program. In general, the ORACA is used to debug memory overwrite problems, to improve performance, to evaluate dynamic SQL statements, and to determine memory usage.

Summary

This chapter discussed the importance of processing errors and warnings and described the types of errors and warnings you can expect from Oracle. It also discussed the specific tools used to process errors, warnings, and diagnostics.

CHAPTER 8

The Pro*C
Precompiler

You've learned about the basic features of Oracle that allow you to create a full-featured application program. They include host and identifier variables, host arrays, datatype conversion, datatype equivalencing, static embedded SQL, and the ability to connect with, transact with, and process errors from the Oracle database. The primary Oracle tool you will leverage to take advantage of these features is the Oracle precompiler, called *Pro*C.

In Chapter 2, the Pro*C precompiler was introduced from a conceptual point of view. This chapter will discuss how you actually use the Pro*C precompiler to produce source modules for your application program and the features of Pro*C that allow you to build your application.

What Is Pro*C?

The Oracle Pro*C precompiler is a programming tool that allows you to define host and indicator variables and host arrays and to embed SQL statements in your application program. Host variables and arrays are declared like C variables in your application program. SQL statements are defined just like the C statements, and the two can be intermixed.

Typically, after you have finished editing a source module (or compilation unit) of your application program, the module is ready to be compiled and run. However, when embedding SQL for use with Oracle, Pro*C introduces an extra step into the process. After the module is edited, it is passed to the Pro*C precompiler, which converts the host variables and arrays to the correct datatypes in the SQL statements inserted in your program. The SQL statements are converted to call standard Oracle run-time library subroutines. This step generates a modified source module that can then be compiled, linked, and executed like a C source module. Figure 8 -1 depicts the process of developing a Pro*C application program.

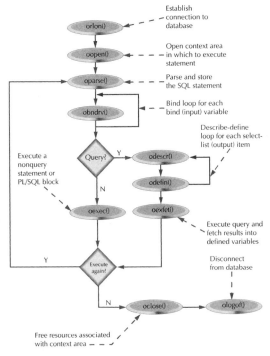

FIGURE 8-1. *Pro*C application program development*

Why Use Pro*C?

The Pro*C precompiler lets you combine the power, flexibility, and standardization of both C and SQL into a single full-featured application program. Because Pro*C automatically converts datatypes and SQL statements, the application developer is free to create a highly customized application without being burdened with these details. The extra step introduced into the implementation process—precompilation—is a minor inconvenience.

In addition to saving time, the Pro*C precompiler provides a set of tools that let you monitor the performance of your application. With the information from these tools, you can optimize your application for better performance. With Pro*C, you can:

- Create your application program with the power and flexibility of C

- Embed ANSI-standard SQL statements into your application program

- Create highly flexible dynamic SQL applications

- Automatically convert between Oracle internal datatypes and C language datatypes

- Use arrays as input and output program variables in SQL statements

- Use datatype equivalencing to control the way Oracle interprets input data and formats output data

- Embed PL/SQL blocks, procedures, and functions in your application program to improve performance

- Specify precompiler options on the command line and in your program, allowing you to change their values during precompilation

- Separately precompile several program source modules, then link them into one executable program

- Completely check the syntax and semantics of embedded SQL statements and PL/SQL blocks

- Connect to Oracle databases and concurrently access databases on multiple computer nodes using SQL*Net

- Conditionally precompile sections of code in your host program so the program can run in different environments

- Handle errors and warnings with the SQL Communications Area (SQLCA) and the WHENEVER statement

■   Use an enhanced set of diagnostics provided by the Oracle Communications Area (ORACA)

In essence, the Pro*C precompiler gives you all the tools you need to be productive while creating full-featured, highly flexible application programs that connect to the Oracle database system.

Pro*C does have its limitations, however. Local parsing of PL/SQL is not supported. All PL/SQL must be in anonymous PL/SQL blocks and is processed by the Oracle 7 Server. Also, + syntax is only supported with Pro*C 2.1 (or later).

Introduction to Pro*C

Now that you know what Pro*C has to offer, you need to know how to use it. This section discusses how you invoke the precompiler command, specify precompiler options, conditionally precompile sections of code, and precompile separate source modules. It also tells you what occurs during precompilation and what the precompiler outputs.

The first step in using the Pro*C precompiler is to create your application program (or a single source module) using an editor. Normally, when programming in C, you create each source module filename using the standard C (*.c) filename extension. Since you process each Pro*C source module through the precompiler before you compile it, Pro*C expects a different filename extension (*.pc). Therefore, each of your Pro*C source modules should include the filename extension *.pc. If you choose not to use the standard extension, you must explicitly include it in the filename when you invoke the Pro*C precompiler. Otherwise, Pro*C will look for the *.pc extension.

Invoking the Pro*C Precompiler

After you have edited your Pro*C source module, you run the Pro*C precompiler by issuing the following command at the operating system prompt:

```
PROC INAME=filename[.ext] [option=value, ...]
```

where:

INAME is the command-line option to specify the Pro*C source module you intend to precompile. This is the only command-line option that is required.

filename is the name of the source module file you intend to precompile.

.ext is the optional source module filename extension. The Pro*C precompiler expects the extension *.pc. If you use this extension, you don't need to specify it with the filename. If you use a different extension, you must specify it.

option is the name of any optional command-line argument you want to specify. The number of command-line arguments you can specify is only limited by the number of characters your operating system will allow on a single command line.

value is the value of the associated command-line option. Do not allow any spaces between the option name, the equal sign (=), and the value. Otherwise, the precompiler will interpret this as another command-line option.

Using the Precompiler Options

As you can see from the Pro*C command syntax, you can specify any number of command-line arguments when you invoke the precompiler. These options give you control over how the precompiler interprets your source module, how system resources are used, how errors are reported, how input and output are formatted, and how cursors are managed. Table 8-1 summarizes the precompiler options that you can specify on the command line and that are applicable to Pro*C. A detailed explanation of each of these options is included in Chapter 12; you can also get online help for the precompiler options.

You can display the precompiler options simply by entering the PROC compiler command without any options at the operating system prompt. The display gives the name, syntax, default value, and purpose of each option. Options marked with an asterisk (*) can be specified as precompile directives in your program as well as on the command line.

If you specify a set of command-line options when you precompile a source module, those options affect only that source module; you must respecify the options for other source modules when they are precompiled.

You can enter a precompiler option in the command line when a source module is precompiled. You can also specify precompiler options in each source module using the following syntax:

```
EXEC ORACLE OPTION (option=value);
```

For example, you might include the following option in a source module:

```
EXEC ORACLE OPTION (RELEASE_CURSOR=YES);
```

Option	Valid Values	Default	Description
ASACC	YES | NO	NO	Specifies carriage control for the listing file
CODE	ANSI_C | KR_C	KR_C	Specifies how C function prototypes are generated
DBMS	NATIVE | V6 | V7	NATIVE	Specifies to use version-specific behavior of Oracle
DEFINE	Symbol		Defines a symbol used in conditional precompilation
ERRORS	YES | NO*	YES	Specifies to send errors to the terminal
FIPS	YES | NO	NO	Specifies whether extensions to ANSI/ISO are flagged
HOLD_CURSOR	YES | NO*	NO	Specifies how the cursor cache handles SQL statements
HOST	C | COB74 | COBOL | FORTRAN | PASCAL | PLI	C	Host language of input
INAME	Path name and filename		Specifies name of input file
INCLUDE	Path*	Current directory	Specifies directory path for INCLUDEd files
IRECLEN	Integer	80	Specifies record length of input file
LINES	YES | NO	NO	Specifies whether C #line directives are generated
LNAME	Path name and filename		Specifies name of listing file
LRECLEN	Integer	132	Specifies record length of listing file

TABLE 8-1.   *Pro*C precompiler options*

Option	Valid Values	Default	Description
LTYPE	LONG | SHORT | NONE	LONG	Specifies type of listing
MAXLITERAL	Integer*	Platform-dependent	Specifies maximum length of strings
MAXOPENCURSORS	Integer*	10	Specifies the maximum number of cursors cached in memory
MODE	ANSI | ISO | ANSI14 | ISO14 | ANSI13 | ISO13 | Oracle	Oracle	Specifies compliance with ANSI/ISO standards
ONAME	Path name and filename	Same as input file with *c extension	Specifies name of output file
ORACA	YES | NO*	NO	Specifies whether the ORACA is used
ORECLEN	Integer	80	Specifies record length of output file
PAGELEN	Integer	66	Specifies lines per page in listing file
RELEASE_CURSOR	YES | NO*	NO	Specifies how cursor cache handles SQL statements
SELECT_ERROR	YES | NO*	YES	Specifies how SELECT errors are handled
SQLCHECK	SEMATICS | FULL | SYNTAX | LIMITED | NONE*	SYNTAX	Specifies extent of syntactic and/or semantic checking
USERID	Username/password		Specifies a valid Oracle username and password
XREF	YES | NO*	YES	Specifies cross-reference section in listing file

*Can be specified as a precompile option in a source module.

TABLE 8-1.   *Pro*C precompiler options* (continued)

When you specify a precompiler option in a source module, it overrides the same option specified as a command-line option for that module. Also, the option remains in effect until the end of the source module is reached or until you specify the same option later in that module. Thus, the placement of options in a source module is positional rather than logical.

You specify precompiler options with the EXEC ORACLE statement when you need to change the value of an option during precompilation. For example, you might want to change the values of HOLD_CURSOR and RELEASE_CURSOR on a statement-by-statement basis.

You can specify precompiler options in a source module to avoid operating system limitations on the number of characters allowed in a command line. It is useful to specify precompiler options in a separate file and then use the INCLUDE statement to place the options in your program where they are needed.

Conditional Precompilations

You can conditionally include or exclude sections of source code in a source module based on a specified set of conditions. These sections of code are included (or excluded) during precompilation; it is as if that source code doesn't exist when the specified conditions are met. For example, you might want to include one section of code when precompiling under DOS or Windows and another section when precompiling under UNIX. That would allow you to write your application program so that it can easily be ported to run in different operating system environments.

You specify sections of source code that you want to include (or exclude) during precompilation by marking them with statements that specify the conditions under which they should be included and the actions that should be taken. You can place any C statements and SQL statements inside these sections of code. The following statements allow you to exercise control over precompilation:

```
EXEC ORACLE DEFINE symbol;    -- Define a symbol.
   ...
EXEC ORACLE IFDEF symbol;     -- If symbol is defined,
   ...                        -- include subsequent code.
EXEC ORACLE IFNDEF symbol;    -- If symbol not defined, include...
   ...
EXEC ORACLE ELSE;             -- Otherwise, include...
   ...
EXEC ORACLE ENDIF;            -- End this control block.
```

In the following example, the SELECT statement is precompiled only when the symbol UNIX is defined:

```
EXEC ORACLE DEFINE UNIX;
    . . .
EXEC ORACLE IFDEF UNIX;
    EXEC SQL SELECT ...
        INTO ...
        FROM ...
        WHERE ...;
EXEC ORACLE ENDIF;
```

Conditional blocks can be nested, as shown in the following example:

```
EXEC ORACLE IFDEF outer;
    EXEC ORACLE IFDEF inner;
    . . .
    EXEC ORACLE ENDIF;
EXEC ORACLE ENDIF;
```

As you can see, you can "comment out" any source code by placing it between an IFDEF and ENDIF control block and then not defining the symbol. You should also note that these statements work exactly like the **#define**, **#ifdef**, **#ifndef**, **#else**, and **#endif** statements for the C compiler. However, the EXEC ORACLE statements only affect precompilation, while the C **#define** (and other) statements only affect compilation.

Because DEFINE is a precompiler option, it can be specified either as a command-line option or in your program with the EXEC ORACLE DEFINE statement. You can specify any number of uniquely named symbols with either method.

Oracle provides some predefined, system-specific symbols. They include operating system-specific symbols (CMS, MVS, MSDOS, UNIX, and VMS) and hardware-specific symbols (IBM and DEC). For example, on a VMS-based system, the symbols DEC and VMS are predefined.

Separate Precompilations

As with most compilers, the Pro*C compiler allows you to precompile many source modules separately, compile them separately, and then link them into a single executable application program. In fact, it is much more productive to break an application into separate source modules so you don't need to re-precompile and recompile your entire program each time you make a change.

What Occurs During Precompilation?

During precompilation, the Pro*C precompiler does the following:

- It processes any conditional EXEC ORACLE statements.

- It determines the datatype of all host variables, indicator variables, host arrays, and indicator arrays and decides how to perform datatype conversion during program execution.

- It checks for correct syntax in your SQL statements.

- It replaces all SQL statements with Oracle run-time library calls.

- It processes all WHENEVER statements.

This is not an inclusive list, but it gives you an idea what goes on during precompilation. Essentially, the precompiler performs the source-code conversion that you would need to do manually to compile a source module directly. To see what happens during precompilation, let's examine the following portion of the precompiler output example from Chapter 3.

```
/*
*****************************************************************
** EmployeeWndProc - Process the command dialog for the Employee
**                   window.
**
** Description:
**
**     This function is used to process the command dialog
**     for the Employee window.
**
** Parameters:
**
**     hWnd        INPUT
**         Window handle
**
**     uiMessage   INPUT
**         Window dialog command message
**
**     wParam      INPUT
**         Window parameter
**
**     lParam      INPUT
```

```
**        Window parameter
**
** Return:
**
**      bDialogStatus
**        Dialog status.  Possible values:
**
**            TRUE  - A command was processed.
**            FALSE - The default was processed.
**
*******************************************************************
*/
#ifdef __BORLANDC__
BOOL CALLBACK EmployeeWndProc(HWND hWnd, UINT uiMessage,
    WPARAM wParam, LPARAM lParam)
#else
BOOL FAR PASCAL EmployeeWndProc(HWND hWnd, unsigned uiMessage,
    WORD wParam, LONG lParam)
#endif
{
    BOOL bReturn = TRUE;
    /*
    ** Process the event message from the Employeee window.
    */
    switch (uiMessage)
        {
        /* Process the command from the window event. */
        case WM_COMMAND :
            switch (wParam)
                {
                /* Process the Close command button. */
                case ID_EMPLOYEE_CLOSE :
                    EndDialog(hWnd, 1);
                    break;

                /* Process the Select command button. */
                case ID_EMPLOYEE_SELECT :
                    /*
                    ** Check the cursor open status.
                    ** If it is open, close it, then reopen.
                    */
                    if (zDbStatus.bOpened)
```

```
/* SQL stmt #6
                EXEC SQL CLOSE employee_cursor;
*/
{
                sqlstm.iters = (unsigned long  )1;
                sqlstm.offset = (unsigned short)2;
                sqlstm.cud = sqlcud0;
                sqlstm.sqlest = (unsigned char  *)&sqlca;
                sqlstm.sqlety = (unsigned short)0;
                sqlcex(&sqlctx, &sqlstm, &sqlfpn);
}


/* SQL stmt #7
                EXEC SQL OPEN employee_cursor;
*/
{
                sqlstm.stmt = sq0001;
                sqlstm.iters = (unsigned long  )1;
                sqlstm.offset = (unsigned short)21;
                sqlstm.cud = sqlcud0;
                sqlstm.sqlest = (unsigned char  *)&sqlca;
                sqlstm.sqlety = (unsigned short)0;
                sqlcex(&sqlctx, &sqlstm, &sqlfpn);
}


                /*
                ** Process the error from the OPEN command.
                ** On error, skip the following processing.
                ** Otherwise, drop into the FETCH processing to
                ** retrieve the data.
                */
                if (!ProcErrorCode(hWnd))
                   break;

                zDbStatus.bOpened = TRUE;
            case ID_EMPLOYEE_FETCH :
                /*
                ** Check the cursor open status.
                ** If it is not open, report an error.
                */
                if (!zDbStatus.bOpened)
                   {
                   MessageBox(hWnd,
```

```
                          "Cursor not open, no active set!",
                           "ORACLE", MB_OK);
                      break;
                      }

             /*
             ** FETCH the data from the cursor into the host
             ** variables.
             */

/* SQL stmt #8
             EXEC SQL FETCH employee_cursor
                 INTO :vcEmpSSN:indEmpSSN,
                      :vcFName:indFName,
                      :vcMiddleInit:indMiddleInit,
                      :vcLName:indLName,
                      :vcAddress:indAddress,
                      :vcCity:indCity,
                      :vcState:indState,
                      :vcZipcode:indZipcode,
                      :vcWPhone:indWPhone,
                      :vcHPhone:indHPhone,
                      :vcPayRate:indPayRate,
                      :vcPayType:indPayType,
                      :vcHireDate:indHireDate,
                      :vcTermDate:indTermDate;
*/
{

             sqlstm.iters = (unsigned long  )1;
             sqlstm.offset = (unsigned short)40;
             sqlstm.cud = sqlcud0;
             sqlstm.sqlest = (unsigned char  *)&sqlca;
             sqlstm.sqlety = (unsigned short)0;
             sqlstm.sqhstv[0] = (unsigned char  *)&vcEmpSSN;
             sqlstm.sqhstl[0] = (unsigned long  )14;
             sqlstm.sqindv[0] = (          short *)&indEmpSSN;
             sqlstm.sqharm[0] = (unsigned long  )0;
             sqlstm.sqhstv[1] = (unsigned char  *)&vcFName;
             sqlstm.sqhstl[1] = (unsigned long  )43;
             sqlstm.sqindv[1] = (          short *)&indFName;
             sqlstm.sqharm[1] = (unsigned long  )0;
             sqlstm.sqhstv[2] = (unsigned char  *)&vcMiddleInit;
             sqlstm.sqhstl[2] = (unsigned long  )4;
```

```
sqlstm.sqindv[2]  = (short *)&indMiddleInit;
sqlstm.sqharm[2]  = (unsigned long )0;
sqlstm.sqhstv[3]  = (unsigned char  *)&vcLName;
sqlstm.sqhstl[3]  = (unsigned long )43;
sqlstm.sqindv[3]  = (          short *)&indLName;
sqlstm.sqharm[3]  = (unsigned long )0;
sqlstm.sqhstv[4]  = (unsigned char  *)&vcAddress;
sqlstm.sqhstl[4]  = (unsigned long )43;
sqlstm.sqindv[4]  = (          short *)&indAddress;
sqlstm.sqharm[4]  = (unsigned long )0;
sqlstm.sqhstv[5]  = (unsigned char  *)&vcCity;
sqlstm.sqhstl[5]  = (unsigned long )43;
sqlstm.sqindv[5]  = (          short *)&indCity;
sqlstm.sqharm[5]  = (unsigned long )0;
sqlstm.sqhstv[6]  = (unsigned char  *)&vcState;
sqlstm.sqhstl[6]  = (unsigned long )5;
sqlstm.sqindv[6]  = (          short *)&indState;
sqlstm.sqharm[6]  = (unsigned long )0;
sqlstm.sqhstv[7]  = (unsigned char  *)&vcZipcode;
sqlstm.sqhstl[7]  = (unsigned long )13;
sqlstm.sqindv[7]  = (          short *)&indZipcode;
sqlstm.sqharm[7]  = (unsigned long )0;
sqlstm.sqhstv[8]  = (unsigned char  *)&vcWPhone;
sqlstm.sqhstl[8]  = (unsigned long )15;
sqlstm.sqindv[8]  = (          short *)&indWPhone;
sqlstm.sqharm[8]  = (unsigned long )0;
sqlstm.sqhstv[9]  = (unsigned char  *)&vcHPhone;
sqlstm.sqhstl[9]  = (unsigned long )15;
sqlstm.sqindv[9]  = (          short *)&indHPhone;
sqlstm.sqharm[9]  = (unsigned long )0;
sqlstm.sqhstv[10] = (unsigned char  *)&vcPayRate;
sqlstm.sqhstl[10] = (unsigned long )12;
sqlstm.sqindv[10] = (          short *)&indPayRate;
sqlstm.sqharm[10] = (unsigned long )0;
sqlstm.sqhstv[11] = (unsigned char  *)&vcPayType;
sqlstm.sqhstl[11] = (unsigned long )5;
sqlstm.sqindv[11] = (          short *)&indPayType;
sqlstm.sqharm[11] = (unsigned long )0;
sqlstm.sqhstv[12] = (unsigned char  *)&vcHireDate;
sqlstm.sqhstl[12] = (unsigned long )13;
sqlstm.sqindv[12] = (          short *)&indHireDate;
sqlstm.sqharm[12] = (unsigned long )0;
```

```
                sqlstm.sqhstv[13] = (unsigned char  *)&vcTermDate;
                sqlstm.sqhstl[13] = (unsigned long  )13;
                sqlstm.sqindv[13] = (           short *)&indTermDate;
                sqlstm.sqharm[13] = (unsigned long )0;
                sqlstm.sqphsv = sqlstm.sqhstv;
                sqlstm.sqphsl = sqlstm.sqhstl;
                sqlstm.sqpind = sqlstm.sqindv;
                sqlstm.sqparm = sqlstm.sqharm;
                sqlstm.sqparc = sqlstm.sqharc;
                sqlcex(&sqlctx, &sqlstm, &sqlfpn);
}

            /*
            ** Check the SQLCA for no more data in the set.
            */
            if (sqlca.sqlcode == 1403)
                {
                MessageBox(hWnd, "No data left in the set!",
                    "ORACLE", MB_OK);
                break;
                }

            /*
            ** Process the error code. If there is no error,
            ** set the values in the employee window.
            */
            if (ProcErrorCode (hWnd))
                EmployeeWndSet(hWnd);
            break;

        /* Process the Insert command button. */
        case ID_EMPLOYEE_INSERT :
            /*
            ** Get the values from the employee window.
            */
            EmployeeWndGet(hWnd);

            /*
            ** Insert the values from the employee window
            ** into the database.
            */
/* SQL stmt #9
            EXEC SQL INSERT INTO EMPLOYEE
```

```
                    (EMPLOYEE.EMPLOYEE_SSN, EMPLOYEE.FIRST_NAME,
                     EMPLOYEE.MIDDLE_INITIAL, EMPLOYEE.LAST_NAME,
                     EMPLOYEE.ADDRESS, EMPLOYEE.CITY,
                     EMPLOYEE.STATE, EMPLOYEE.ZIPCODE,

                    EMPLOYEE.WORK_PHONE,
                     EMPLOYEE.HOME_PHONE, EMPLOYEE.PAY_RATE,
                     EMPLOYEE.PAY_TYPE,
                     EMPLOYEE.HIRE_DATE, EMPLOYEE.TERMINATION_DATE)
                VALUES (:vcEmpSSN:indEmpSSN,
                        :vcFName:indFName,
                        :vcMiddleInit:indMiddleInit,
                        :vcLName:indLName,
                        :vcAddress:indAddress,
                        :vcCity:indCity,
                        :vcState:indState,
                        :vcZipcode:indZipcode,
                        :vcWPhone:indWPhone,
                        :vcHPhone:indHPhone,
                        :vcPayRate:indPayRate,
                        :vcPayType:indPayType,
                        :vcHireDate:indHireDate,
                        :vcTermDate:indTermDate);
*/
{
            sqlstm.stmt = "INSERT INTO \

EMPLOYEE(EMPLOYEE.EMPLOYEE_SSN,\

EMPLOYEE.FIRST_NAME,EMPLOYEE.MIDDLE_INITIAL,EMPLOYEE.LAST_NAME,\

EMPLOYEE.ADDRESS,EMPLOYEE.CITY,EMPLOYEE.STATE,EMPLOYEE.ZIPCODE,\

EMPLOYEE.WORK_PHONE,EMPLOYEEHOME_PHONE,EMPLOYEE.PAY_RATE,\

EMPLOYEE.PAY_TYPE,EMPLOYEE.HIRE_DATE,EMPLOYEE.TEMINATION_DATE)

VALUES(:b1:i1,:b2:i2,:b3:i3,:b4:i4,:b5:i5,:b6:i6,:b7:i7,:b8:i8,\

b9:i9,:b10:i10,:b11:i11,:b12:i12,:b13:i13,:b14:i14)";
            sqlstm.iters = (unsigned long  )1;
            sqlstm.offset = (unsigned short)115;
```

```
sqlstm.cud = sqlcud0;
sqlstm.sqlest = (unsigned char  *)&sqlca;
sqlstm.sqlety = (unsigned short)0;
sqlstm.sqhstv[0] = (unsigned char  *)&vcEmpSSN;
sqlstm.sqhstl[0] = (unsigned long  )14;
sqlstm.sqindv[0] = (          short *)&indEmpSSN;
sqlstm.sqharm[0] = (unsigned long  )0;
sqlstm.sqhstv[1] = (unsigned char  *)&vcFName;
sqlstm.sqhstl[1] = (unsigned long  )43;
sqlstm.sqindv[1] = (          short *)&indFName;
sqlstm.sqharm[1] = (unsigned long  )0;
sqlstm.sqhstv[2] = (unsigned char  *)&vcMiddleInit;
sqlstm.sqhstl[2] = (unsigned long  )4;
sqlstm.sqindv[2] = (          short *)&indMiddleInit;
sqlstm.sqharm[2] = (unsigned long  )0;
sqlstm.sqhstv[3] = (unsigned char  *)&vcLName;
sqlstm.sqhstl[3] = (unsigned long  )43;
sqlstm.sqindv[3] = (          short *)&indLName;
sqlstm.sqharm[3] = (unsigned long  )0;
sqlstm.sqhstv[4] = (unsigned char  *)&vcAddress;
sqlstm.sqhstl[4] = (unsigned long  )43;
sqlstm.sqindv[4] = (          short *)&indAddress;
sqlstm.sqharm[4] = (unsigned long  )0;
sqlstm.sqhstv[5] = (unsigned char  *)&vcCity;
sqlstm.sqhstl[5] = (unsigned long  )43;
sqlstm.sqindv[5] = (          short *)&indCity;
sqlstm.sqharm[5] = (unsigned long  )0;
sqlstm.sqhstv[6] = (unsigned char  *)&vcState;
sqlstm.sqhstl[6] = (unsigned long  )5;
sqlstm.sqindv[6] = (          short *)&indState;
sqlstm.sqharm[6] = (unsigned long  )0;
sqlstm.sqhstv[7] = (unsigned char  *)&vcZipcode;
sqlstm.sqhstl[7] = (unsigned long  )13;
sqlstm.sqindv[7] = (          short *)&indZipcode;
sqlstm.sqharm[7] = (unsigned long  )0;
sqlstm.sqhstv[8] = (unsigned char  *)&vcWPhone;
sqlstm.sqhstl[8] = (unsigned long  )15;
sqlstm.sqindv[8] = (          short *)&indWPhone;
sqlstm.sqharm[8] = (unsigned long  )0;
sqlstm.sqhstv[9] = (unsigned char  *)&vcHPhone;
sqlstm.sqhstl[9] = (unsigned long  )15;
sqlstm.sqindv[9] = (          short *)&indHPhone;
```

```
        sqlstm.sqharm[9] = (unsigned long )0;
        sqlstm.sqhstv[10] = (unsigned char  *)&vcPayRate;
        sqlstm.sqhstl[10] = (unsigned long )12;
        sqlstm.sqindv[10] = (         short *)&indPayRate;
        sqlstm.sqharm[10] = (unsigned long )0;
        sqlstm.sqhstv[11] = (unsigned char  *)&vcPayType;
        sqlstm.sqhstl[11] = (unsigned long )5;
        sqlstm.sqindv[11] = (         short *)&indPayType;
        sqlstm.sqharm[11] = (unsigned long )0;
        sqlstm.sqhstv[12] = (unsigned char  *)&vcHireDate;
        sqlstm.sqhstl[12] = (unsigned long )13;
        sqlstm.sqindv[12] = (         short *)&indHireDate;
        sqlstm.sqharm[12] = (unsigned long )0;
        sqlstm.sqhstv[13] = (unsigned char  *)&vcTermDate;
        sqlstm.sqhstl[13] = (unsigned long )13;
        sqlstm.sqindv[13] = (         short *)&indTermDate;
        sqlstm.sqharm[13] = (unsigned long )0;
        sqlstm.sqphsv = sqlstm.sqhstv;
        sqlstm.sqphsl = sqlstm.sqhstl;
        sqlstm.sqpind = sqlstm.sqindv;
        sqlstm.sqparm = sqlstm.sqharm;
        sqlstm.sqparc = sqlstm.sqharc;
        sqlcex(&sqlctx, &sqlstm, &sqlfpn);
    }


        /*
        ** Process the error code.
        */
        ProcErrorCode(hWnd);
        break;

    /* Process the Update command button. */
    case ID_EMPLOYEE_UPDATE :
        /*
        ** Check the cursor open status.
        ** If it is not open, report an error.
        */
        if (!zDbStatus.bOpened)
            {
            MessageBox(hWnd,
```

```
                              "Cursor not open, no active set!",
                              "ORACLE", MB_OK);
                       break;
                       }

                /*
                ** Get the values from the employee window.
                */
                EmployeeWndGet(hWnd);

                /*
                ** Update the values from the employee window
                ** in the database.
                */
/* SQL stmt #10
                EXEC SQL UPDATE EMPLOYEE
                    SET EMPLOYEE_SSN = :vcEmpSSN:indEmpSSN,
                        FIRST_NAME = :vcFName:indFName,
                        MIDDLE_INITIAL = :vcMiddleInit:indMiddleInit,
                        LAST_NAME = :vcLName:indLName,
                        ADDRESS = :vcAddress:indAddress,
                        CITY = :vcCity:indCity,
                        STATE = :vcState:indState,
                        ZIPCODE = :vcZipcode:indZipcode,
                        WORK_PHONE = :vcWPhone:indWPhone,
                        HOME_PHONE = :vcHPhone:indHPhone,
                        PAY_RATE = :vcPayRate:indPayRate,
                        PAY_TYPE = :vcPayType:indPayType,
                        HIRE_DATE = :vcHireDate:indHireDate,
                        TERMINATION_DATE = :vcTermDate:indTermDate
                    WHERE CURRENT OF employee_cursor;
*/
{
                sqlstm.stmt = "UPDATE EMPLOYEE SET
EMPLOYEE_SSN=:b1:i1,FIRST_NAME=:b2:i2,MIDDLE_INITIAL=:b3:i3,\
LAST_NAME=:b4:i4,ADDRESS=:b5:i5,CITY=:b:I6,STATE=:b7:i7,\
ZIPCODE=:b8:i8,WORK_PHONE=:b9:i9,HOME_PHONE=:b10:i10,\
PAY_RAT=:b11:i11,PAY_TYPE=:b12:i12,HIRE_DATE=:b13:i13,\
TERMINATION_DATE=:b14:i14 WHERE ROWID=:b15";
                sqlstm.iters = (unsigned long  )1;
                sqlstm.offset = (unsigned short)190;
                sqlstm.cud = sqlcud0;
```

```
sqlstm.sqlest = (unsigned char  *)&sqlca;
sqlstm.sqlety = (unsigned short)0;
sqlstm.sqhstv[0] = (unsigned char  *)&vcEmpSSN;
sqlstm.sqhstl[0] = (unsigned long )14;
sqlstm.sqindv[0] = (         short *)&indEmpSSN;
sqlstm.sqharm[0] = (unsigned long )0;
sqlstm.sqhstv[1] = (unsigned char  *)&vcFName;
sqlstm.sqhstl[1] = (unsigned long )43;
sqlstm.sqindv[1] = (         short *)&indFName;
sqlstm.sqharm[1] = (unsigned long )0;
sqlstm.sqhstv[2] = (unsigned char  *)&vcMiddleInit;
sqlstm.sqhstl[2] = (unsigned long )4;
sqlstm.sqindv[2] = (         short *)&indMiddleInit;
sqlstm.sqharm[2] = (unsigned long )0;
sqlstm.sqhstv[3] = (unsigned char  *)&vcLName;
sqlstm.sqhstl[3] = (unsigned long )43;
sqlstm.sqindv[3] = (         short *)&indLName;
sqlstm.sqharm[3] = (unsigned long )0;
sqlstm.sqhstv[4] = (unsigned char  *)&vcAddress;
sqlstm.sqhstl[4] = (unsigned long )43;
sqlstm.sqindv[4] = (         short *)&indAddress;
sqlstm.sqharm[4] = (unsigned long )0;
sqlstm.sqhstv[5] = (unsigned char  *)&vcCity;
sqlstm.sqhstl[5] = (unsigned long )43;
sqlstm.sqindv[5] = (         short *)&indCity;
sqlstm.sqharm[5] = (unsigned long )0;
sqlstm.sqhstv[6] = (unsigned char  *)&vcState;
sqlstm.sqhstl[6] = (unsigned long )5;
sqlstm.sqindv[6] = (         short *)&indState;
sqlstm.sqharm[6] = (unsigned long )0;
sqlstm.sqhstv[7] = (unsigned char  *)&vcZipcode;
sqlstm.sqhstl[7] = (unsigned long )13;
sqlstm.sqindv[7] = (         short *)&indZipcode;
sqlstm.sqharm[7] = (unsigned long )0;
sqlstm.sqhstv[8] = (unsigned char  *)&vcWPhone;
sqlstm.sqhstl[8] = (unsigned long )15;
sqlstm.sqindv[8] = (         short *)&indWPhone;
sqlstm.sqharm[8] = (unsigned long )0;
sqlstm.sqhstv[9] = (unsigned char  *)&vcHPhone;
sqlstm.sqhstl[9] = (unsigned long )15;
sqlstm.sqindv[9] = (         short *)&indHPhone;
sqlstm.sqharm[9] = (unsigned long )0;
```

```
        sqlstm.sqhstv[10] = (unsigned char  *)&vcPayRate;
        sqlstm.sqhstl[10] = (unsigned long  )12;
        sqlstm.sqindv[10] = (         short *)&indPayRate;
        sqlstm.sqharm[10] = (unsigned long  )0;
        sqlstm.sqhstv[11] = (unsigned char  *)&vcPayType;
        sqlstm.sqhstl[11] = (unsigned long  )5;
        sqlstm.sqindv[11] = (         short *)&indPayType;
        sqlstm.sqharm[11] = (unsigned long  )0;
        sqlstm.sqhstv[12] = (unsigned char  *)&vcHireDate;
        sqlstm.sqhstl[12] = (unsigned long  )13;
        sqlstm.sqindv[12] = (         short *)&indHireDate;
        sqlstm.sqharm[12] = (unsigned long  )0;
        sqlstm.sqhstv[13] = (unsigned char  *)&vcTermDate;
        sqlstm.sqhstl[13] = (unsigned long  )13;
        sqlstm.sqindv[13] = (         short *)&indTermDate;
        sqlstm.sqharm[13] = (unsigned long  )0;
        sqlstm.sqphsv = sqlstm.sqhstv;
        sqlstm.sqphsl = sqlstm.sqhstl;
        sqlstm.sqpind = sqlstm.sqindv;
        sqlstm.sqparm = sqlstm.sqharm;
        sqlstm.sqparc = sqlstm.sqharc;
        sqlcex(&sqlctx, &sqlstm, &sqlfpn);
}


        /*
        ** Process the error code.
        */
        ProcErrorCode(hWnd);
        break;

/* Process the Delete command button. */
case ID_EMPLOYEE_DELETE :
    /*
    ** Check the cursor open status.
    ** If it is not open, report an error.
    */
    if (!zDbStatus.bOpened)
        {
        MessageBox(hWnd, "Cursor not open, no active set!",
            "ORACLE", MB_OK);
        break;
        }
```

```
            /*
            ** Delete current record from the employee cursor.
            */

/* SQL stmt #11
                 EXEC SQL DELETE FROM EMPLOYEE
                    WHERE CURRENT OF employee_cursor;
*/
{

                 sqlstm.stmt =

                   "DELETE FROM EMPLOYEE WHERE ROWID=:b1";
                 sqlstm.iters = (unsigned long   )1;
                 sqlstm.offset = (unsigned short)265;
                 sqlstm.cud = sqlcud0;
                 sqlstm.sqlest = (unsigned char   *)&sqlca;
                 sqlstm.sqlety = (unsigned short)0;
                 sqlcex(&sqlctx, &sqlstm, &sqlfpn);
}


            /*
            ** Process the error code.
            */
            if (ProcErrorCode(hWnd))
               EmployeeWndClear(hWnd);
            break;

         /* Process the Clear command button. */
         case ID_EMPLOYEE_CLEAR :
            EmployeeWndClear(hWnd);
            break;

         /* Process the Commit and Rollback command button. */
         case ID_EMPLOYEE_COMMIT :
         case ID_EMPLOYEE_ROLLBACK :
             if (wParam = ID_EMPLOYEE_COMMIT)
/* SQL stmt #12
                 EXEC SQL COMMIT WORK;
*/
{

                 sqlstm.iters = (unsigned long   )1;
```

```
                    sqlstm.offset = (unsigned short)284;
                    sqlstm.cud = sqlcud0;
                    sqlstm.sqlest = (unsigned char  *)&sqlca;
                    sqlstm.sqlety = (unsigned short)0;
                    sqlcex(&sqlctx, &sqlstm, &sqlfpn);
    }
                else
/* SQL stmt #13
                EXEC SQL ROLLBACK WORK;
*/
{
                    sqlstm.iters = (unsigned long  )1;
                    sqlstm.offset = (unsigned short)303;
                    sqlstm.cud = sqlcud0;
                    sqlstm.sqlest = (unsigned char  *)&sqlca;
                    sqlstm.sqlety = (unsigned short)0;
                    sqlcex(&sqlctx, &sqlstm, &sqlfpn);
    }
                /*
                ** The COMMIT and ROLLBACK operations release all
                ** locks, so the employee cursor should be closed.
                */
/* SQL stmt #14
                EXEC SQL CLOSE employee_cursor;
*/
{
                sqlstm.iters = (unsigned long  )1;
                sqlstm.offset = (unsigned short)322;
                sqlstm.cud = sqlcud0;
                sqlstm.sqlest = (unsigned char  *)&sqlca;
                sqlstm.sqlety = (unsigned short)0;
                sqlcex(&sqlctx, &sqlstm, &sqlfpn);
    }
                zDbStatus.bOpened = FALSE;
                /*
                ** Process the error code.
                */
                ProcErrorCode(hWnd);
                break;
            default :
                bReturn = FALSE;
                break;
```

```
        }
        break;
    case WM_INITDIALOG :
        break;
    default :
        bReturn = FALSE;
        break;
    }
    return(bReturn);
}
```

You can see from this example that the Pro*C precompiler saves much of the tedious work necessary to communicate with the Oracle database.

Compiling and Linking

Now that the Pro*C source module is precompiled, you can compile it and link it to create your example program. To produce an executable program, you must compile the precompiled (modified by the precompiler) source module (or modules), then link the resulting object module (or modules) with the Oracle run-time libraries.

The link process resolves all symbolic references in the object modules with the objects in the run-time libraries. If these references conflict, the link fails. This can happen when you try to link third-party software into a precompiled program. Not all third-party software is compatible with Oracle. This can be resolved by linking in stand-alone mode or in two-task mode.

Compiling and linking an executable program is specific to each compiler and operating system. Many commercial development environments integrate Pro*C into themselves very nicely and make this process relatively painless. As a practical example, Chapter 12 will discuss how to precompile, compile, and link an executable program using the Oracle Pro*C precompiler with the Microsoft Visual C++ development environment.

Summary

This chapter discussed the Pro*C precompiler's features and benefits. The Pro*C precompiler allows you to perform complex programming tasks with relatively simple syntax, as demonstrated in the example from the Pro*C precompiler output.

CHAPTER 9

PL/SQL: The Procedural Data Language

PL/SQL incorporates many of the features of modern third-generation languages like C and C++. It is designed to enhance SQL's features and integrate tightly with Oracle. Along with Chapter 10, this chapter will introduce you to the concepts behind PL/SQL and point out its basic features, then explore the specifics of PL/SQL. You'll come away with a clear understanding of how, where, and when PL/SQL should be used in your application program and in your database. You'll also learn in these chapters how PL/SQL can bridge the gap between your application program, the Oracle database system, and the databases you are accessing.

This chapter presents the following topics:

- The main features of PL/SQL
- The basic constructs of this language
- PL/SQL control structures
- PL/SQL language details

What is PL/SQL?

SQL is the international data language that provides both power and flexibility to create, manipulate, and manage data. However, it is a nonprocedural language, meaning you can state what you want done without stating how to do it—Oracle determines the best way to carry out your request. Moreover, there is no connection between consecutive statements because Oracle executes SQL statements one at a time. PL/SQL lets you use the power of SQL while providing procedural extensions that let you create full-featured programs.

Oracle created PL/SQL to overcome the limitations that exist in SQL because it is a nonprocedural language. PL/SQL supports embedded SQL statements and provides all the features of a modern structured and procedural language, including:

- Datatypes
- Variables
- Subroutines
- Modules
- Procedural constructs

Thus, PL/SQL combines the data-processing features of SQL with the programming features of a procedural language.

PL/SQL is a *block-structured language*, the blocks being the logical sections of your program that perform a specific service. In PL/SQL, these are called *anonymous* blocks, procedures, and functions. PL/SQL procedures and functions can be organized into modules called *packages*. Packages are used to organize logically related procedures or functions into packaged units. This feature allows you to decompose a problem easily into its logical components

PL/SQL lets you store common procedures in the database so that you can share application processing with many applications. Without PL/SQL, Oracle must process SQL statements one at a time. Each SQL statement results in another call to Oracle and higher performance overhead. In a networked environment, the overhead can become significant. Every time an SQL statement is issued, it must be sent over the network, creating more traffic. With PL/SQL, however, an entire block of statements can be sent to Oracle at one time. This can drastically reduce communication between your application and Oracle. If your application is database-intensive, you can use control structures to group SQL statements before sending them to Oracle for execution. Also, you can call procedures and functions to reduce calls from your application to Oracle.

Applications written in PL/SQL are portable to any operating system and platform on which Oracle runs. In other words, these programs can run anywhere Oracle can run; you need not tailor them to each new environment. That means you can write portable program libraries, which can be reused in different environments.

Both PL/SQL and Oracle are SQL-based. Moreover, PL/SQL supports all the Oracle datatypes. Combined with the direct access SQL provides, these shared datatypes integrate PL/SQL with the Oracle data dictionary. The %TYPE and %ROWTYPE attributes further integrate PL/SQL with the data dictionary.

Why Use PL/SQL?

You're probably wondering why you would use PL/SQL instead of C. There are some drawbacks to using embedded SQL in your application program; most of them are related to performance.

First, PL/SQL is designed to integrate closely with the Oracle database system and with SQL. Therefore, it supports all the internal datatypes native to the Oracle database and SQL. You can declare PL/SQL variables that are directly compatible with SQL and the Oracle internal datatypes. Although supported, datatype conversion is seldom needed to process data in a PL/SQL procedure or function.

Second, if your application program is written in C, the Oracle database must process each embedded SQL statement individually. If your application program and the Oracle database are running on the same computer, this may not be an issue. However, if your application is running in a client/server environment connected to the Oracle database over a computer network, you may encounter a significant performance problem. In this environment, each SQL statement is sent over the computer network and processed by the Oracle database, and the results are sent back to your application before the operation is complete. This can produce significant overhead if your program has many SQL statements to process. PL/SQL overcomes this drawback by allowing you to send a group or block of SQL statements to the database to be processed in one call.

PL/SQL can be embedded in your application program using two methods. You can explicitly create anonymous PL/SQL blocks of SQL statements, which are then processed together in one call to the database. Alternately, you can create procedures and functions in PL/SQL that combine multiple SQL statements with procedural processing. You can create entire transactions or combine multiple transactions and process them in procedures and functions. A call to a procedure or function is treated as a single call to the database. Your application program can call these procedures and functions directly. If you use either of these methods, you will reduce the number of calls in your application program to the Oracle database.

A third drawback is that you can combine PL/SQL procedures and functions into packages, which in turn can be stored in the Oracle database as database objects. When you use these packages in your program, Oracle stores them in memory so that subsequent calls to the package only need to access memory, not the disk. As database objects, PL/SQL packages can be reused by multiple application programs. These stored packages—or, better yet, their contents (data, procedures, and functions)—can be standardized for reuse throughout your business. Also, stored procedures and functions are used in database triggers to enforce data integrity for all applications that access the same database. This releases the application developer from the need to build data integrity processing into each application program that accesses the database.

PL/SQL provides for data encapsulation and information hiding. You can encapsulate data by creating a set of procedures to access and process data in a package. You can declare package contents to be private, rather than giving direct access to the contents. This isolates the details of how the data is stored, accessed, and processed in a package from higher-level application processing. If the data processing inside a package needs to be changed (as is often the case) to fix problems or add enhancements, the higher-level application processing is not affected. It also prevents inadvertent modification of variables, which can cause undesired side effects.

PL/SQL allows information hiding in two ways. First, you can hide information by isolating processing into logical procedures. Higher-level areas of a program need not know how a procedure performs a task or how it processes data; they only need to know the status of the task when it is complete. Second, information can be explicitly hidden by declaring variables, data structures, and procedures as public or private within a package. If something is declared to be private within a package, it can only be processed inside that package and is inaccessible outside the package. If something is declared public, it is accessible by the entire program.

Basics of PL/SQL

In this chapter we'll look at a simple PL/SQL program example that illustrates the basic tenets of a real PL/SQL program. The key sections of the sample program to be discussed are:

- PL/SQL variables and constants
- Connecting to the database
- Embedded SQL
- Transactions
- Error processing

Subsequent sections will provide detailed explanations (with practical examples) of each of these key program elements. Before looking at the sample program, let's look at the general outline of a PL/SQL procedure:

```
CONNECT to the database
DECLARE variables and constants
BEGIN procedure
        Process SQL statements
        Process procedural statements
        COMMIT transaction
        Process errors (ROLLBACK transaction)
END procedure
```

It's that simple. Now let's look at a real example. The following listing shows an example of a PL/SQL procedure that is used to process a reorder transaction.

```
PROCEDURE reorder_item (iItemId IN INTEGER, nPurchased IN INTEGER,
    iError OUT INTEGER) IS
    cReorderFlag CHAR;
    nQtyOnHand INTEGER;
    iReorderLimit INTEGER;
    nReorderQty INTEGER;
    iReqDelivery INTEGER;
```

```
    iSupplierId INTEGER;
BEGIN
    /*
    ** First see if the item can be automatically reordered.
    */
    SELECT inventory.reorderable INTO cReorderFLag
        FROM inventory
        WHERE inventory.item_id = iItemId;

    IF cReorderFlag = 'Y' THEN
        /*
        ** Check the item's reorder limit to see if a reorder entry
        ** should be created.  In the same process, get the item's
        ** preferred supplier.
        */
        SELECT inventory.quantity_on_hand, inventory.reorder_limit,
            inventory.reorder_quantity, inventory.required_delivery
            item_supplier.supplier_id
          INTO nQtyOnHand, iReorderLimit, nReorderQty,
            iReqDelivery, iSupplierId
          FROM inventory, item_supplier
          WHERE inventory.item_id = iItemId AND
            inventory.item_id = item_supplier.item_id AND
            item_supplier.preferred_list = 1;

    IF (iQtyOnHand - nPurchased) <= iReorderLimit THEN
            /*
            ** Enter a reorder record into the reorder table.
            */
            INSERT INTO reorder (item_id, supplier_id,
                reorder_quantity,reorder_date, required_date)
              VALUES (iItemId, iSupplierId, nReorderQty, SYSDATE(),
                ADD_MONTHS (SYSDATE(),
                iReqDelivery / LAST_DAY(SYSDATE()))));

            /*
            ** Commit the reorder transaction.
            */
            COMMIT WORK;
        END IF; -- Reorder Limit Check
    END IF; -- reorderable flag check
```

```
EXCEPTION
    WHEN OTHERS THEN
        ROLLBACK;

END reorder_item;
```

This example shows some of the basic features of PL/SQL. As you can see, you can declare variables, embed SQL statements to access and manipulate data, and use logic control statements to process the data, manage transactions, and process run-time errors.

Program Variables and Constants

You can declare variables and constants in your PL/SQL program and use them in SQL statements and procedural statements. PL/SQL variables and constants can be used in any statement where you can specify an expression. The only restriction is that the variable or constant must be explicitly declared before you reference it or use it in any other statement.

PL/SQL variables can be declared as any Oracle internal datatype, such as CHAR, DATE, or NUMBER, or as any PL/SQL datatype, such as BOOLEAN or BINARY_INTEGER. Also, PL/SQL allows you to declare composite datatypes called RECORD and TABLE (to be discussed later in this chapter).

The syntax to declare a variable with a basic datatype is

```
<variable_name> <datatype>;
```

For example:

```
tax REAL;
```

You can assign a value to a PL/SQL variable in two ways. First, you can explicitly assign a value to a variable in an assignment expression. To do this, place a variable to the left of the assignment operator, := (a colon followed by an equal sign), and an expression to the right. The syntax of an assignment operation is

```
<variable> := <expression>;
```

For example:

```
sales_tax_rate := 0.06;
```

or

```
tax := price * sales_tax_rate;
```

The second way to assign a value to a variable is to SELECT or FETCH values from the database INTO the variable. This process is similar to that discussed earlier for assigning values to host variables when creating programs in C, by using the Pro*C precompiler. However, PL/SQL variables do not require the colon (:) as a prefix when referenced in SQL statements.

The essential difference between a variable and a constant is that you can assign a data value to a variable and change it anywhere in your program after it is declared. A constant is assigned a value when it is declared, after which its value cannot be changed.

You declare a constant much as you declare a variable, except that you precede the datatype in the constant declaration with the keyword CONSTANT and immediately assign a value to it. Following the constant declaration, you cannot assign any more values to the constant; its value remains the same. The syntax to declare a constant is

```
<variable_name> CONSTANT <datatype> := value;
```

For example:

```
sales_tax_rate CONSTANT REAL := 0.06;
```

Attributes

PL/SQL provides attributes for variables, constants, and database objects, such as tables, cursors, and columns. Attributes are properties that describe the definition of any of these entities. Attributes can give you run-time access to the datatype and structure definition of variables, constants, and database objects. The attributes that are available for you to access are:

- **%TYPE**   This attribute provides access to the datatype of a declared variable, constant, or database column. It is used to declare one identifier to have the same datatype as another.

- **%ROWTYPE**   This attribute allows you to declare a record variable that represents a row in a table, view, or cursor. It is used when you SELECT or FETCH a row to be processed in your program.

- **Cursor attributes**   The cursor attributes provide access to the status of a declared cursor. Available cursor attributes are:

  - **%FOUND**   If true, this attribute tells you the last row fetched from a cursor returned data. If false, there are no more rows in the cursor.

  - **%NOTFOUND**   If true, there are no more rows in the cursor. If false, there are remaining rows in the cursor.

  - **%ISOPEN**   If true, the cursor is open. If false, the cursor is closed.

  - **%ROWCOUNT**   Tells you the number of rows already processed in the cursor.

These attributes can help you more easily process data and maintain your PL/SQL programs.

Control Structures

PL/SQL provides control structures that let you dynamically control the flow of processing in your PL/SQL program. These structures are very similar to those available in C. For example, you can process information based on conditional, iterative, and sequential control statements (for example, IF-THEN-ELSIF-ELSE, FOR-LOOP, WHILE-LOOP, EXIT-WHEN, and GOTO). Control structures are the most important PL/SQL extension to SQL. Collectively, these statements give you the control you need to meet virtually any processing requirements.

You'll often need to process information based on a conditional situation. The IF-THEN-ELSIF-ELSE statement lets you execute a sequence of statements based on a set of specified conditions. The IF clause checks the truth of a condition. The THEN clause defines what to do if the condition is true. If necessary, the ELSIF clause checks the truth of another condition. If the previous condition is false, the ELSE clause defines what to do if all the IF or ELSIF conditions are false or null.

When you need to process sets of information or use sections of your program repeatedly, you can use various forms of the LOOP control statement. This statement allows you to process a section of your program repeatedly, even infinitely. The FOR-LOOP statement allows you to specify a range of integers, then execute a section of your program once for each integer in the range. The WHILE-LOOP statement allows you to process a section of your program repeatedly until a condition is true.

The EXIT-WHEN statement is used with the LOOP control statements to allow you to exit a LOOP structure based on a condition. When the EXIT statement is encountered in a LOOP structure, the condition specified in the WHEN clause is checked for truth. If the condition is TRUE, the loop completes and control passes to the next statement following the LOOP structure.

If you need to branch unconditionally to a different section of your program, you can use the GOTO statement. This statement allows you to branch unconditionally to a declared label in your program.

As you can see, the procedural control structures provided by PL/SQL give you the control you need to handle any processing requirements in your application program.

Cursor Processing

Cursors have been discussed throughout this book. They are an inherent structure in PL/SQL that let you store and process sets of information easily in your PL/SQL program.

In PL/SQL, the two kinds of cursors are *implicit* and *explicit.* A cursor is implicitly declared for each data manipulation SQL statement, including queries that return only one row. You can explicitly declare a cursor when you want to process the individual rows of a query that returns more than one row. The set of rows returned by a multirow query is called the *active set.* The size of the active set is the number of rows that meet your search criteria. An explicit cursor "points" to the current row in the active set, allowing your program to process the rows one at a time.

As discussed in previous chapters, you must DECLARE and OPEN a cursor before you can use it. You can FETCH, UPDATE, or DELETE the current row in the active set, then CLOSE the cursor when you are finished. The CLOSE statement disables the cursor and frees up any allocated system resources.

A useful feature of PL/SQL is the ability to use a FOR loop when processing a cursor instead of the OPEN, FETCH, and CLOSE statements. A cursor FOR loop implicitly declares its loop index as a RECORD datatype based on the %ROWTYPE of the cursor. It then automatically opens the cursor, repeatedly fetches a row of values from the active set into the fields in the record, and closes the cursor when all rows have been processed. This is useful when you intend to perform similar operations on all the rows in a cursor.

Error Handling

PL/SQL provides features for easily detecting and processing predefined and user-defined error conditions. In PL/SQL, error conditions are called *exceptions.* When an error occurs, an exception is implicitly raised; normal execution stops, and control transfers to an exception-handling section of your PL/SQL program.

You must define a specific section in your program to handle these exceptions. It is best to create separate subroutines, called *exception handlers,* to perform all exception processing.

PL/SQL provides a predefined set of exceptions that are implicitly raised by the system at run time. For example, if you try to divide a number by zero, the predefined exception ZERO_DIVIDE is raised automatically. Control is automatically transferred to a specified exception handler in your program.

You can define your own set of exceptions and explicitly raise them when you encounter an error condition. You define your own set of exceptions in any DECLARE section of a PL/SQL program. While processing your program, you check for the error conditions you defined as exceptions in the DECLARE section. If you encounter these conditions, you explicitly raise one of your defined exceptions by calling the RAISE statement. When the RAISE statement is called with a defined exception, program control is passed to the exception handler defined to process that exception. Thus, you can create a standard set of error-processing routines to be used throughout your program simply by raising the appropriate exceptions.

Procedures and Functions

As mentioned earlier, PL/SQL is a block-structured language. You can design your program so that logical sets of processing can be divided into blocks of statements. These blocks can be reused repeatedly throughout your program. In fact, a block can consist of many subblocks, each block and subblock providing a separate service. When the services of these blocks are combined, they provide the overall services of your program.

A block-structured language allows you to isolate the details of data and processing into the individual blocks of your program so that higher-level program structures are not affected by changes in a lower-level block. The blocks in PL/SQL are called anonymous blocks, procedures, and functions.

Anonymous blocks are sets of PL/SQL statements that you can embed in your Pro*C (or OCI) source modules or in other PL/SQL programs. Anonymous blocks are processed in a single call to the database, regardless of the number of SQL statements it contains.

Procedures and functions can be defined to have parameters through which data can be passed from and returned to your program. Procedures and functions can be called from your Pro*C application program; from other PL/SQL blocks, procedures, and functions; and from database triggers (to be discussed in a moment). A procedure or function is a subprogram that provides a specific service that can be reused throughout your application and, ideally, in other application programs. The only difference between a procedure and a function is that a procedure can accept multiple input parameters and return multiple output parameters. A function can accept multiple input parameters but can only return a single value.

As shown in the program example, a PL/SQL block has three parts: a declarative part, an executable part, and an optional exception-handling part. Only the executable part is required. The order of the parts is logical: First, variables, constants, and exceptions are declared in the declarative part. Once declared, variables can be manipulated and constants can be referenced in the executable part. Exceptions raised during execution can be resolved in the exception-handling part.

You can define local subblocks in the declarative part of any block. However, you can call local subblocks only from the block in which they are defined. You can call procedures and functions from the executable and exception-handling parts of a PL/SQL block or program but not from the declarative part. The rules of block declaration and definition will be discussed later in this chapter.

Procedure and Function Overloading

PL/SQL allows you to overload the definition of procedure and function names. Overloading occurs when you create two or more procedures or functions with the same name but different parameter lists. This allows you to create procedures or functions that perform essentially the same service but use different input or output parameters based on the datatypes of the parameters. Overloading is useful when you want to create a common interface for a service that can accept different variables or constants of varying datatypes.

Packages

The block-structured aspects of PL/SQL allow you to break down your problem into manageable, well-defined blocks. Through successive refinement, you can reduce a complex problem to a set of simple problems that have easy-to-implement solutions. A set of solutions, represented by a set of data, procedures, and functions, can be grouped together into a unit called a package. Packages provide a similar function in PL/SQL as source modules provide in C: They allow you to group logically related sets of data, procedures, and functions into a packaged unit for reuse in other applications.

Packages are organized into two sections: a specification and a body. The *specification* is where you declare the interface to access the contents of your package from outside the package. In the specification you declare the datatypes, constants, variables, exceptions, cursors, procedures, and functions you want to make available outside your package. Anything not explicitly declared in the package specification is not accessible from outside the package.

The *body* is where you actually define the cursors, procedures, and functions that make up your package. Implementation details in the package body are hidden and inaccessible from outside your package.

In PL/SQL packages, you can explicitly specify whether any of the package contents are public or private. This allows you to specify only the package contents that you want to make available outside the package. By hiding information and information-processing details from higher-level program structures, you can concentrate on high-level design decisions rather than low-level implementation details. You should only be concerned that the contents of a package perform a task and return a result, not how they perform the task or how they might affect your program. Once you define the purpose and interface specifications of a low-level procedure, you can ignore the implementation details.

Also, you can implement information hiding for data structures through data encapsulation techniques. You do this by developing a set of utility procedures to access and manipulate the fields in a data structure that is defined in a package. This way, you insulate the data-structure details from higher-level program structures and other applications that might inadvertently modify the data structure, causing undesired side effects. Also, you isolate them from any changes you may need to make later.

Stored Packages, Procedures, and Functions

Oracle's Procedural Database Extension allows you to compile procedures, functions, and packages separately and store them permanently in an Oracle database as database objects. Once one of these objects is stored in a database, it becomes a part of that database's data dictionary. The stored object is then available to be called by any application that has access and can connect to that database.

Stored packages, procedures, and functions use Oracle's shared-memory capability. When you call a stored procedure, function, or package from your application for the first time, the whole object is loaded into memory. Therefore, subsequent calls to that object eliminate the need to read the object from the database; the object is already in memory. If other applications make calls to the object, they reference the object in memory. Thus, only one copy of the stored object is used by many applications simultaneously. If you group a logical set of procedures and/or functions together in a package, subsequent calls to any of the package contents eliminate disk access. Thus, packages can enhance productivity and improve the performance of your application program.

Database Triggers

A database *trigger* is another kind of stored procedure that can be associated with a specific database table. The purpose of a database trigger is to perform a service when a specified operation occurs on a table. You create a database trigger by specifying a database table and a database operation (INSERT, UPDATE, or DELETE) on that table for which a stored procedure should be invoked. When the specified operation occurs on the table, Oracle automatically pulls the database trigger and invokes the associated stored procedure.

Database triggers have many uses, as you can imagine. They are most often used to verify data when it is inserted or updated. Also, database triggers are often used to initiate downstream business processes. Our sample procedure could be called from a database trigger to create a reorder entry when an item is purchased.

The PL/SQL Engine

The PL/SQL run-time system is a technology with an architecture, not an independent product like a compiler. Think of this technology as an engine that executes PL/SQL blocks and subprograms. The PL/SQL engine can be installed in an Oracle Server or in one of Oracle's application development tools such as SQL*Forms, SQL*Menu, or SQL*ReportWriter. Thus, PL/SQL can reside in two environments: the Oracle Server and the Oracle tools.

When the PL/SQL engine is installed in either of these environments, the environments are independent. PL/SQL can be installed in either one or both; the engine processes PL/SQL blocks, procedures, and functions no matter where it is installed. Figure 9-1 illustrates how the PL/SQL engine accepts input and processes it.

Stored packages, procedures, and functions are stored in parsed and compiled form. When called, they are loaded and passed to the PL/SQL engine immediately. The PL/SQL engine can execute procedural statements, but SQL statements are passed to the SQL Statement Executor in the Oracle Server.

If the PL/SQL engine is loaded in an Oracle development tool, then the PL/SQL procedural statements are executed there. SQL statements are still passed to the Oracle server. When Oracle development tools lack a local PL/SQL engine, they must rely on the PL/SQL engine in the Oracle Server to process PL/SQL procedural statements.

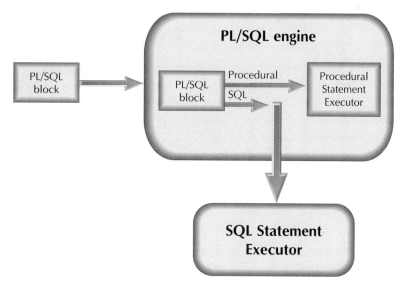

FIGURE 9-1. *The PL/SQL engine*

There are three environments in which PL/SQL programs can be executed: the application program, stored procedures and functions, and database triggers.

Anonymous blocks with calls to stored procedures or functions can be embedded in your application program. When one of these PL/SQL blocks is encountered at run time, your program, lacking a local PL/SQL engine, sends it to the Oracle Server. There the blocks are compiled and executed by the PL/SQL engine in the server (see Figure 9-2). The same process occurs in an Oracle development tool lacking a local PL/SQL engine.

Stored procedures and functions can be called from your application program. At run time, when your program calls a stored procedure or function, your program sends a request to the database to execute it. Oracle loads the stored object into memory (if it is not already there) and executes the procedure with the PL/SQL

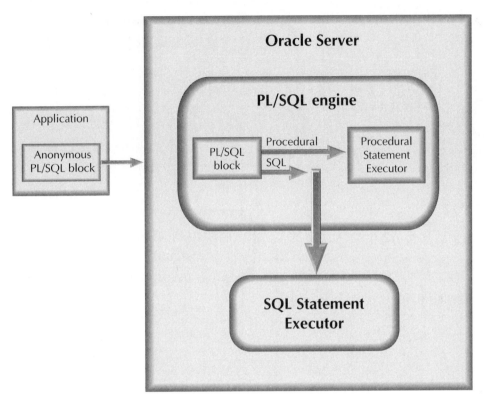

FIGURE 9-2. *PL/SQL engine in Oracle Server*

engine in the server. The same process occurs in an Oracle development tool lacking a local PL/SQL engine. Figure 9-3 illustrates how stored procedures are invoked in the Oracle Server.

When database triggers are automatically invoked by the Oracle Server as a result of an operation on a table, they may also call a stored procedure. Oracle loads the stored object into memory, if it is not already there, and the PL/SQL engine in the server executes the procedure. This process works much like the process shown in Figure 9-3.

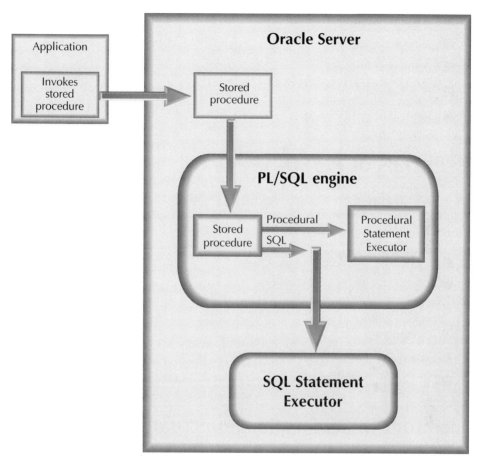

FIGURE 9-3. *Stored procedure in Oracle Server*

Advantages of Using PL/SQL

In summary, there are several advantages to using PL/SQL as a development tool for your application. This completely portable, high-performance information processing language offers:

- Support for SQL
- Higher productivity
- Better performance
- Portability
- Integration with Oracle

Essentials of PL/SQL

The previous section gave you an overview of PL/SQL and the features it offers. The rest of this chapter will explore the details of the PL/SQL language. This section discusses the following essential language elements and the rules that govern them:

- Operators, symbols, and punctuation
- Identifiers
- Literals
- Comments
- Datatypes and declarations
- Expressions and comparisons

Operators, Indicators, and Punctuation

As with any language, the first things you need to become familiar with are the symbols used to construct the language. In a computer language, these symbols are used as operators, indicators, and punctuation to build language statements. In PL/SQL, these symbols are divided into a few groups:

- Arithmetic operators and symbols
- Expression operators
- Relational operators
- Indicators
- Punctuation

The following tables describe the symbols in each of these groups. Table 9-1 summarizes the arithmetic operators used in PL/SQL to create arithmetic operations or expressions.

Table 9-2 summarizes the operators used in PL/SQL to create expressions, such as assignment, range, and string concatenation expressions.

Table 9-3 summarizes the relational operators used in PL/SQL to create comparison operations.

Table 9-4 summarizes the special symbols used in PL/SQL to indicate special language operations, such as attributes, remote database instances, and host variable references.

Table 9-5 summarizes the symbols used in PL/SQL to specify language punctuation. Punctuation is used to separate language constructs and to define language statements.

These symbols are used throughout PL/SQL. The following sections discuss where they are used and how to use them.

Identifiers

In PL/SQL, identifiers are used to name objects, such as constants, variables, exceptions, cursors, procedures, functions, and packages. PL/SQL identifiers follow many of the same rules as C. An identifier can consist of alphanumeric characters, dollar signs, underscores, and number signs. No other characters are legal, including hyphens, slashes, and spaces. An identifier must begin with a letter of the alphabet.

Operator	Examples	Description
+	1 + 2; a + b; sales + tax	Adds two operands.
–	3 – 1; c – a; total – discount	Subtracts the second operand from the first.
*	5 * 9; d * e; count * items	Multiplies two operands.
/	10 / 2; g / h; total / count	Divides the first operand by the second.
**	2**3; a**2; base**10	Raises the first operand to the exponent of the second.

TABLE 9-1. *Arithmetic operators and symbols*

Operator	Examples	Description
:=	a := b; total := count * price	Assigns the value of the operand or expression on the right to the operand on the left.
..	1..3; 0..d; 1..count −1	Defines an integer range from the first operand to the second.
||	'con' || 'cat'; a || b	Concatenates two or more strings.

TABLE 9-2. *Expression operators*

You can use upper- and lowercase characters to specify PL/SQL identifiers. However, PL/SQL is not case-sensitive; lowercase letters are treated the same as the corresponding uppercase letters, except within string and character literals. If the only difference between two identifiers is the case of corresponding letters, as in the following example, PL/SQL considers the identifiers to be the same:

```
lastname
LastName
LASTNAME
```

Operator	Example	Description
=	a = b	Checks for equality of two operands.
<	a < b	Checks to see if the first operand is less than the second.
>	c > b	Checks to see if the first operand is greater than the second.
<>	d <> e	Checks for inequality of two operands.
!=	d != e	Same as <>.
<=	f <= g	Checks to see if the first operand is less than or equal to the second.
>=	i >= j	Checks to see if the first operand is greater than or equal to the second.

TABLE 9-3. *Relational operators*

Indicator	Example	Description
%	column_name%TYPE	Indicates an attribute of an object.
@	table_name@database_name	Indicates a remote access database.
:	:total	Indicates that the identifier is a host variable.

TABLE 9-4.   *Indicators*

You can specify descriptive identifier names of up to 30 characters. After that, the characters are ignored. You can use just about any name you want for an identifier except a PL/SQL reserved word. Reserved words have a special syntactic meaning to PL/SQL, so you cannot redefine their meaning. For example, the words BEGIN and END, which bracket the executable part of a block or subprogram, are reserved.

Punctuation	Examples	Description
( )	(a + b); (sales / 2)	Combines operations in an expression or specifies a list.
;	a := b + c;	Specifies the end of a complete statement.
,	a, b, c	Separates items in a list.
.	schema.table.column record.field	Separates components in a database object specification or accesses fields of a RECORD.
' '	'one'	Specifies a character-string literal.
" "	"Table"	Specifies an exact named identifier.
<< >>	<<label_name>>	Specifies a named label.
--	-- Single-line comment	Specifies a single-line comment (ANSI SQL-compliant).
/* */	/* Multiline comment */	Specifies a multiline comment.

TABLE 9-5.   *Punctuation*

You cannot use either word as an identifier. Although you can embed reserved words in an identifier name, such as **end_of_sale**, this practice is not recommended; you should normally write reserved words in all uppercase to promote readability. However, like other PL/SQL identifiers, reserved words *can* be written in lowercase or mixed case. For a list of PL/SQL reserved words, see Appendix E.

Oracle supplies a library of predefined variables, exceptions, procedures, and functions. The identifiers for these standard objects are not reserved. Although you can override these identifiers in your programs, this practice will cause you many headaches and should be avoided.

To provide flexibility, PL/SQL allows you to override some of these identifier naming rules by enclosing the identifier names in double quotation marks. Quoted identifiers are seldom needed, but occasionally they can be useful. They can contain any sequence of printable characters, including spaces but excluding double quotes (double quotes are the delimiters). The maximum length of a quoted identifier is 30 characters, not counting the double quotations.

Using PL/SQL reserved words as quoted identifiers is allowed but not recommended. In general, it is poor programming practice to reuse reserved words for any reason. However, some PL/SQL reserved words are not reserved by SQL, so you may run across some conflicts between the names of some database objects and PL/SQL reserved words. For example, the PL/SQL reserved word TYPE can be used to create a database column name. If an SQL statement in your program refers to that column, you get a compilation error. To prevent the error, enclose the column name (all uppercase) in double quotes (a quoted identifier). This way, you have explicitly told PL/SQL that "TYPE" is the name of the column, not the reserved word TYPE.

Literals

A literal is an explicitly specified number, character, string, or Boolean value. Literals specify an exact value in your program. They are used to initialize constants, variables, and other data values.

Numeric Literals

Two types of numeric literals can be specified in arithmetic expressions: integers and reals. An *integer literal* is a whole number without a decimal point. You can optionally specify a signed value (+ or –). For example:

```
021
7
-21
```

```
0
+512
```

A *real literal* is a whole number or fractional number with a decimal point. You can optionally specify a signed value (+ or –). For example:

```
3.3333
0.0
-21.0
2.50
+100.00
.25
50.
```

Even though a number, such as 10.0 or –5.0, has an integer value, PL/SQL considers the number to be real. Numeric literals cannot contain dollar signs or commas but can be written using scientific notation. This is done by simply specifying an *E* (or *e*) suffix on the number followed by an optionally signed integer. For example:

```
3E4
1.0E-21
3.14159e0
-1E27
-2.5e-3
```

E stands for "times 10 to the power of." The number after the *E* corresponds to the number of places the decimal point shifts.

Character Literals

A *character literal* is an individual character enclosed by single quotation marks (apostrophes). For example:

```
'A'
'a'
'4'
'%'
'\'
'('
```

Character literals include all the printable characters in the PL/SQL character set, which includes upper- and lowercase letters, numerals, spaces, and special symbols. Character literals are case-sensitive. From the previous example, PL/SQL considers the literals 'A' and 'a' to be different.

NOTE
Do not confuse the character literals '0' through '9' with integer literals. Character literals cannot be used in arithmetic expressions.

String Literals

A *string literal* is a sequence of two or more characters enclosed by single quotation marks. For example:

```
'Hello, world!'
'ABC School'
'25-MAR-95'
'He said "You look marvelous."'
'$1,000,000,000'
'1024'
```

If apostrophes (single quotes) delimit string literals, how do you represent an apostrophe within a string? You specify two apostrophes together, which is not the same as a double quote. For example:

```
'Don''t leave home without it.'
```

String literals are case-sensitive. PL/SQL considers all strings to be unique as long as the characters do not match exactly by character and by case.

Boolean Literals

Boolean literals are the predefined values TRUE and FALSE and the nonvalue NULL. NULL represents a missing, unknown, or inapplicable value. Boolean literals can be used in expressions that test for truth. You don't have to use them, but they do promote readability. For example, in the truth test in the following statement:

```
IF first_pass THEN
   ...
END IF;
```

you can do the following:

```
IF (first_pass = TRUE) THEN
   ...
END IF;
```

Comments

The PL/SQL compiler allows you to embellish your program with descriptive comments. You should take advantage of this feature. It is good programming practice to describe the purpose of each section of your program, including what it does, why it does it, and the expected result.

The two types of comments in PL/SQL are single-line, like in Pro*C, and multiline, like in C. Single-line comments begin with a double hyphen (--) anywhere on a line and extend to the end of the line. For example:

```
-- Declare variables.
```

or

```
SELECT item_id INTO identifier   -- Get item identifier.
   FROM item
   WHERE item_id = 1000;
```

Notice that single-line comments can appear within a statement at the end of a line.

During testing or debugging, you may want to "comment out" a line of troublesome code. To do this, just place a double hyphen (--) at the beginning of the line you want to comment out. For example, the following statement does not compile:

```
-- DELETE item_num FROM item WHERE item_id = 1000;
```

Be careful! If the statement spans multiple lines, this method will not comment out the entire statement. You must place a double hyphen at the beginning of each line in the statement. For example:

```
-- SELECT item_num INTO item_number   -- Get item number.
--          FROM item
--          WHERE item_num = 1000;
```

A better method is to use a multiline comment. Multiline comments begin with a slash-asterisk (/*) and end with an asterisk-slash (*/), just like C language comments. You can span multiple lines of code between the delimiters. For example:

```
/*
** Select all the reorder entries from the reorder table for the
** specified item identifier.
*/

SELECT * FROM reorder
    WHERE item_id = iItemId;
```

You can comment out entire sections of code with multiline comments. From the previous example:

```
/*
SELECT item_num INTO item_number   -- Get item number.
    FROM item
    WHERE item_num = 1000;
*/
```

There are a few restrictions you should keep in mind. First, you cannot nest comments. Also, you cannot use single-line comments in a PL/SQL block that will be processed dynamically by Pro*C. This is because end-of-line characters are ignored in dynamically processed PL/SQL blocks. As a result, single-line comments extend to the end of the block, not just to the end of a line. Use multiline comments instead.

Datatypes, Declarations, and Assignments

In PL/SQL, as in C, a variable or constant is used to store data values in your program. Each variable or constant is assigned a datatype. The datatype specifies a storage format, constraints, and a valid range of values. PL/SQL provides support for most of the Oracle internal datatypes that were discussed in Chapter 2. In addition, PL/SQL provides support for additional datatypes, including composite datatypes (similar to data structures).

PL/SQL datatypes are grouped into eight categories: numeric, character, Boolean, date/time, raw, rowid, MLSLABEL, and composite. Table 9-6 summarizes the datatypes provided by PL/SQL.

This section describes each PL/SQL datatype in detail and gives the basic syntax of how it is declared, where it is used, and any associated restrictions. At the end of this section, the general rules that govern the declaration, initialization, and assignment of variables and constants are discussed.

Category	Name	Description
Numeric	BINARY_INTEGER	Integer of any size ranging from $-2^{31}-1$ to $2^{31}-1$
	NUMBER	Same as the NUMBER internal datatype
Character	CHAR	Short, fixed-length character string
	VARCHAR2	Variable-length character string
	LONG	Long, variable-length character string
Boolean	BOOLEAN	TRUE, FALSE, or NULL
Date/Time	DATE	Fixed-length date/time value (same as internal)
Raw	RAW	Variable-length binary data
	LONG RAW	Variable-length binary data
RowID	ROWID	Database address of a table row; binary value
MLSLABEL	MLSLABEL	Trusted Oracle address; variable-length binary data
Composite	RECORD	The composite data type for sets of column data
	TABLE	The composite data type that operates like an array

TABLE 9-6. *PL/SQL datatypes*

Numeric Datatypes

The numeric datatypes are used to process numeric values in your PL/SQL program. PL/SQL provides two basic numeric datatypes: BINARY_INTEGER and NUMBER. All other numeric datatypes are derived from (are *subtypes* of) these basic datatypes. A subtype is created by placing a constraint on a basic datatype, such as a restricted range.

BINARY_INTEGER Datatype   You use the BINARY_INTEGER datatype to process signed integers. The magnitude range of a BINARY_INTEGER value is $-2^{31}-1$ to $2^{31}-1$ (-2147483647 to 2147483647). PL/SQL stores BINARY_INTEGER values as signed binary numbers, which, unlike NUMBER values, are used in calculations without data conversion. Therefore, BINARY_INTEGER variables can provide better performance when processing integer values.

For convenience, PL/SQL redefines the following BINARY_INTEGER subtypes with restricted ranges:

NATURAL (range 0 to $2^{31} - 1$)
POSITIVE (1 to $2^{31} - 1$)

You use the NATURAL or POSITIVE subtype when you want to restrict an integer variable to nonnegative values. The basic syntax to declare a BINARY_INTEGER variable (or any of its subtypes, NATURAL and POSITIVE) is

```
<variable_name> BINARY_INTEGER;
```

or

```
<variable_name> NATURAL;
```

or

```
<variable_name> POSITIVE;
```

NUMBER Datatype   You use the NUMBER datatype to process fixed- or floating-point numbers of virtually any size. The NUMBER datatype has all the characteristics of the Oracle internal NUMBER datatype. You can specify precision, which is the total number of digits, and scale, which determines where rounding occurs. You must use integer literals to specify precision and scale. The basic syntax to declare a NUMBER variable is

```
<variable_name> NUMBER[(precision[, scale])];
```

where:

precision is the largest number of digits the number can be assigned.

scale determines where rounding occurs.

The maximum precision of a NUMBER value is 38; the magnitude range is 1.0E–129 to 9.99E125. Precision is optional. If you do not specify precision, it defaults to the maximum value supported by your system.

Scale can range from –84 to 127. It can be negative, which causes rounding to the left of the decimal point. A scale of zero rounds to the nearest whole number. Scale is also optional. If you do not specify the scale, it defaults to zero.

To help you meet the varying requirements to process numeric values, PL/SQL provides the following predefined NUMBER subtypes:

- DECIMAL
- FLOAT
- INTEGER
- REAL
- SMALLINT

These NUMBER subtypes have the same range of values as the NUMBER base type. For example, FLOAT is just another name for NUMBER. You can use these subtypes for compatibility with ANSI/ISO datatypes or when you want a more descriptive identifier than NUMBER.

Character Datatypes

The character datatypes in PL/SQL are used to store and manipulate words, strings, and free-form text. The character datatypes are CHAR, VARCHAR2, VARCHAR, and LONG.

CHAR Datatype   You use the CHAR datatype to process fixed-length character strings. This datatype accepts an optional parameter that lets you specify a maximum length up to 32,767 bytes. The syntax to specify a CHAR variable is

```
<variable_name> CHAR[(maximum_length)];
```

where:

   maximum_length is the maximum length of an assigned string value.

   maximum_length is optional. If you do not specify the maximum length, it defaults to 1. You must use an integer literal to specify the maximum length. Remember, you specify the maximum length of a CHAR variable in bytes, not characters. Therefore, if a CHAR variable stores multibyte characters, it will store fewer characters than the specified maximum length.

   CHAR variables are blank-padded. Although the maximum length of these variables is 32,767 bytes, the maximum width of a CHAR database column is 255 bytes. Therefore, you cannot insert CHAR variable values longer than 255 bytes into a CHAR column. You can insert any CHAR variable value into a LONG database column of sufficient size because the maximum width of a LONG column is $2^{31} - 1$ (2,147,483,647) bytes, or 2 gigabytes. However, you cannot select a value longer than 32,767 bytes from a LONG column into a CHAR variable.

   CHARACTER and STRING are subtypes, provided by PL/SQL for convenience. The CHAR subtypes that follow have the same range of values as the CHAR base type. In other words, using them is the same as specifying CHAR.

You can use these subtypes for compatibility with ANSI/ISO or when you want a more descriptive identifier than CHAR.

VARCHAR2 Datatype   You use the VARCHAR2 datatype to process variable-length character strings. The VARCHAR2 datatype stores a string variable up to the length of the string. The CHAR datatype stores a string variable up to the maximum length of the variable, even if it is longer than the string value. It will be blank-padded if necessary. The VARCHAR2 datatype is more efficient than CHAR from a storage basis. The VARCHAR2 datatype accepts a parameter that lets you specify a maximum length up to 32,767 bytes. The syntax to declare a VARCHAR2 variable is

```
<variable_name> VARCHAR2(maximum_length);
```

where:

maximum_length is the maximum length of an assigned string value.

maximum_length is required. You must specify an integer literal to specify the maximum length. Remember, you specify the maximum length of a VARCHAR2 variable in bytes, not characters. Therefore, if a VARCHAR2 variable stores multibyte characters, it will store fewer characters than the specified maximum length.

Although the maximum length of a VARCHAR2 variable is 32,767 bytes, the maximum width of a VARCHAR2 database column is 2,000 bytes. Therefore, you cannot insert VARCHAR2 variable values longer than 2,000 bytes into a VARCHAR2 column. You can insert any VARCHAR2 variable value into a LONG database column of sufficient size because the maximum width of a LONG column is $2^{31} - 1$ (2,147,483,647) bytes. However, you cannot select a value longer than 32,767 bytes from a LONG column into a VARCHAR2 variable.

NOTE
VARCHAR is a subtype of VARCHAR2 and has the same range of values as its base type. In other words, VARCHAR is just another name for VARCHAR2. You can use this subtype for compatibility with ANSI/ISO. However, because the VARCHAR datatype might change to accommodate emerging SQL standards, it is a good idea to use VARCHAR2 rather than VARCHAR.

Chapter 2 discussed the semantic differences between CHAR and VARCHAR2. Review the section on character-string semantics in that chapter if necessary.

LONG Datatype You use the LONG datatype to process long, variable-length character data. The LONG datatype has the same properties as the VARCHAR2 datatype except that it has a maximum length of 32,767 bytes. The syntax to declare a LONG variable is

```
<variable_name> LONG(maximum_length);
```

where:

maximum_length is the maximum length of an assigned string value.

maximum_length is required. You must use an integer literal to specify the maximum length. Remember, you specify the maximum length of a LONG variable in bytes, not characters. Therefore, if a LONG variable stores multibyte characters, it will store fewer characters than the specified maximum length.

Although the maximum length of a LONG variable is 32,767 bytes, the maximum width of a LONG database column is $2^{31} - 1$ (2,147,483,647) bytes. You can insert a LONG variable value up to 32,767 bytes into a LONG column. However, you cannot select a value longer than 32,767 bytes from a LONG column into a LONG variable.

BOOLEAN Datatype

You use the BOOLEAN datatype to process the values TRUE and FALSE and the nonvalue NULL. You cannot insert the value TRUE or FALSE into a database column. Also, you cannot SELECT or FETCH column values into a BOOLEAN variable.

DATE Datatype

You use the DATE datatype to process fixed-length date/time values. The DATE datatype has all the properties of the Oracle internal DATE datatype. The same rules and restrictions apply, including the data conversion rules mentioned in Chapter 2.

Binary Datatypes

Binary datatypes are used to process raw binary data. Binary datatypes are used to process character strings, graphic images, and digitized video or sound. PL/SQL supports the datatypes RAW and LONG RAW. The binary datatypes in PL/SQL have the same characteristics as the Oracle internal binary datatypes, including the data conversion rules mentioned in Chapter 2.

RAW Datatype You use the RAW datatype to process variable-length binary data or byte strings. The RAW datatype accepts a required parameter that allows you to specify a maximum length up to 32,767 bytes. The syntax to specify a RAW variable is

```
<variable_name> RAW(maximum_length);
```

where:

> **maximum_length** is the maximum length of an assigned binary value.

> **maximum_length** is required. You must use an integer literal to specify the maximum length. Although the maximum length of a RAW variable is 32,767 bytes, the maximum width of a RAW database column is 255 bytes. Therefore, you cannot insert RAW variable values longer than 255 bytes into a RAW column. You can insert a RAW variable value into a LONG RAW.

LONG RAW Datatype   You use the LONG RAW datatype to process large, variable-length binary data or byte strings. The LONG RAW datatype accepts a required parameter that allows you to specify a maximum length up to 32,767 bytes. The syntax to specify a RAW variable is

```
<variable_name> LONG RAW(maximum_length);
```

where:

> **maximum_length** is the maximum length of an assigned binary value.

> The maximum width of a LONG RAW column is $2^{31} - 1$ (2,147,483,647) bytes. However, you cannot select a value longer than 32,767 bytes from a LONG RAW column into a RAW variable.

ROWID Datatype

The ROWID datatype is used to process binary rowids in fixed-length variables. A *rowid* represents the database address of a specific row in a database table; each rowid is unique. Rowids are stored internally in binary format. You use the ROWID datatype to store rowids in a readable hexadecimal format. The length of a rowid is system-specific; consult your Oracle installation or user's guide for your system.

ROWID can be converted into a CHAR type. Therefore, when you SELECT or FETCH a rowid into a CHAR variable, you can use the function ROWIDTOCHAR. This function converts the binary value to an 18-byte character string and returns it in the following format:

```
BBBBBBBB.RRRR.FFFF
```

where:

BBBBBBBB is the block in the database file.

RRRR is the row in the block (the first row is 0).

FFFF is the database file.

These numbers are in hexadecimal format.

Typically, ROWID variables are compared to the ROWID pseudocolumn in the WHERE clause of an UPDATE or DELETE statement to identify the latest row fetched by a cursor. This is done instead of using the CURRENT OF clause.

MLSLABEL Datatype

If you have the Trusted Oracle security option, use the MLSLABEL datatype to process variable-length, binary operating system labels. Trusted Oracle uses labels to control access to database data.

With Trusted Oracle, you can insert any valid operating system label into an MLSLABEL column. If the label is in text format, Trusted Oracle converts it to a binary value automatically. The text string can be up to 255 bytes long. However, the internal length of an MLSLABEL value is between two and five bytes.

With Trusted Oracle, you can also select values from an MLSLABEL column into a character variable. Trusted Oracle converts the internal binary value to a VARCHAR2 value automatically.

Composite Datatypes

With the RECORD and TABLE composite datatypes, you can create composite variables much like data structures and arrays in C. These composite datatypes are designed to let you process rows of data from database tables very easily. For example, you can FETCH an entire row of data into a RECORD variable and access the fields of the record as if you were accessing the columns of the cursor.

RECORD Datatype   The RECORD datatype is used to create data structures that group variables into a named unit. There are two ways to create RECORD variables. First, you can use the %ROWTYPE attribute to declare a RECORD variable that represents the row in a table, view, or cursor. Second, you can explicitly declare a RECORD data structure that contains variables of your own definition, then use this user-defined RECORD type to declare RECORD variables. Let's discuss the use of the %ROWTYPE attribute first.

The %ROWTYPE attribute lets you declare RECORD variables that represent a row in a table, view, or cursor. The RECORD variable can store an entire row of data selected from the table (or view) or fetched by a cursor. The syntax to declare a RECORD variable for a table or view with the %ROWTYPE attribute is

```
<variable_name> table_name%ROWTYPE;
```

or

```
<variable_name> view_name%ROWTYPE;
```

where:

> **variable_name** is the name of the RECORD variable.
>
> **table_name** or **view_name** is the name of the table or view used to define the RECORD variable.

For example:

```
DECLARE
    item_rec item%ROWTYPE;
    reorder_rec reorder%ROWTYPE;
BEGIN
...
END;
```

> The syntax to declare a RECORD variable for a cursor with the %ROWTYPE attribute is

```
CURSOR <cursor_name> IS SELECT ...
<variable_name> <cursor_name>%ROWTYPE;
```

where:

> **cursor_name** is the name of the declared cursor.
>
> **variable_name** is the name of the RECORD variable.

For example:

```
DECLARE
    CURSOR item_cursor IS SELECT item_id, item_name, category
        FROM item
        WHERE item_id < 10000;
    item_cur_rec item_cursor%ROWTYPE;
```

```
BEGIN
...
END;
```

When you declare a RECORD variable with either of these methods, the variable contains a field for each column in the table, view, or cursor referenced in the SQL statement. Each field in the variable is assigned the same name and datatype as the corresponding column in the table, view, or cursor. To reference a field or assign a value to a field, you use dot notation with the following syntax:

```
<record_name>.<field_name>
```

where:

record_name is the name of the record variable previously declared.

field_name is the name of the field you are referencing or to which you are assigning a value.

For example, you would reference the fields in the **item_rec** variable as follows:

```
IF item_rec.item_id = 1000 THEN
    item_rec.item_name = new_name;
END IF;
```

The %ROWTYPE attribute is very useful when you need to process rows of database objects, as just demonstrated. You cannot create your own fields in a RECORD variable using these methods, but PL/SQL does allow you to create your own data structures explicitly with the RECORD datatype. These structures are called *user-defined* records.

User-defined records have uniquely named fields that can belong to different datatypes. Like user-defined data structures in C, you declare them in two steps. First, you declare the fields in your user-defined RECORD datatype. Second, you declare RECORD variables of that datatype. You can declare user-defined RECORD datatypes and RECORD variables in the declarative part of any block, subprogram, or package using the following syntax:

```
TYPE <type_name> IS RECORD
    (<field_name1> {<datatype> | <variable>%TYPE |
    <table>.<column>%TYPE | <table>%ROWTYPE} [NOT NULL],
    <field_name2> {<datatype> | <variable>%TYPE |
```

```
     <table>.<column>%TYPE | <table>%ROWTYPE} [NOT NULL],
     ...);
```

```
<variable_name> <type_name>;
```

where:

> **type_name** is the identifier you assign to the user-defined RECORD datatype. You use this identifier in subsequent declarations of record variables of this type.

> **datatype** is any datatype including RECORD and TABLE. User-defined datatypes can have nested composite datatype fields. You can use the %TYPE attribute for any variable or database column to create a field of a user-defined record. You can use the %ROWTYPE attribute for a table to specify a nested RECORD variable in a user-defined record.

> **variable_name** is the name you assign to the user-defined RECORD variable.

After you have declared the user-defined record datatype, you can declare a RECORD variable of that type. For example:

```
TYPE item_reorder IS RECORD
    (iItemId INTEGER,
    iSupplierId INTEGER,
    nReorderQty INTEGER,
    dtReorderDate DATE);


recItemReorder item_reorder;
```

Notice that the field declarations for a RECORD use the same syntax as variable declarations. You can use the %TYPE or %ROWTYPE attribute to specify a field datatype. Also, you can initialize the fields of the datatype when it is declared. Each field in the RECORD has a unique name and specific datatype. You reference user-defined record fields in the same manner as discussed for records defined by the %ROWTYPE attribute.

You can add the NOT NULL constraint to any field declaration to prevent the assignment of nulls to that field. Fields declared as NOT NULL must be initialized (the NOT NULL constraint will be discussed later in this section).

TABLE Datatype   PL/SQL gives you the ability to create arraylike structures, called *tables*, using the TABLE datatype. This datatype is modeled after (but not the same as) database tables. Thus, a TABLE variable uses a primary key to give you arraylike access to rows in the TABLE variable.

Like a database table, the size of a TABLE variable is unconstrained. In other words, the number of rows in a TABLE variable can increase dynamically as new rows are added.

Currently, a TABLE variable can have a primary key index and one column, to which you can assign values. Neither the primary key nor the column can be assigned names. The primary key must be assigned the BINARY_INTEGER datatype; the column can be assigned any of the PL/SQL datatypes except RECORD and TABLE.

In PL/SQL version 2.3, Oracle adds support for multiple, named columns and composite primary keys of any datatype. In earlier versions, you use the TABLE datatype, much as you would an array in C.

Like user-defined RECORD datatypes, TABLE variables must be declared in two steps. You define a user-defined TABLE datatype, then declare TABLE variables of that type. You can declare user-defined TABLE datatypes and TABLE variables in the declarative part of any block, subprogram, or package by using the following syntax:

```
TYPE <type_name> IS TABLE OF
    {<datatype> | <variable>%TYPE | <table>.<column>%TYPE }
        [NOT NULL]
    INDEX BY BINARY_INTEGER;

variable_name type_name;
```

where:

type_name is the identifier you assign to the user-defined TABLE datatype. You use this identifier in subsequent declarations of table variables of this type.

datatype is any datatype except RECORD or TABLE. You can use the %TYPE attribute for any variable or database column to create the column of a user-defined table. You declare the INDEX to be BINARY_INTEGER.

After you have declared the user-defined table datatype, you can declare a TABLE variable of that type. For example:

```
TYPE inventory_table IS TABLE OF
    INTEGER
    INDEX BY BINARY_INTEGER;

tabQtyOnHand inventory_table;
```

You can add the NOT NULL constraint to the column declaration to prevent the assignment of nulls to that column. The size of a TABLE variable is only constrained by the range of a BINARY_INTEGER. As a result, you cannot initialize a TABLE variable in its declaration (you would have to initialize all entries in the table). To reference rows in a PL/SQL table, you specify a primary key value using the following arraylike syntax:

```
<table_name>(primary_key_value)
```

where:

>   **table_name** is the name of the TABLE variable declared previously.

>   **primary_key_value** is the primary key index into the TABLE variable (you can think of it as the array index). The primary key value must be a numeric integer literal or a variable of datatype BINARY_INTEGER (or type-compatible with BINARY_INTEGER).

For example, you would reference the column in the **tabQtyOnHand** variable as follows:

```
IF tabQtyOnHand(index) < 0 THEN
    tabQtyOnHand(index) = 0;
END IF;
```

The magnitude range of a BINARY_INTEGER value is $-2^{31}-1$ to $2^{31}-1$. The primary key value can be negative. However, this is not allowed when using host arrays and table variables together. Host arrays cannot be indexed by a negative value. If you reference a table element before assigning it, you get a "no data found" error.

Declaring and Using Variables and Constants

The previous section discussed the PL/SQL datatypes and how you declare them in your program. This section will discuss some general rules, restrictions, and guidelines for declaring and using variables in your PL/SQL programs.

First, all variables and constants must be declared in the DECLARE section of your PL/SQL program. This section must come before the BEGIN statement in any block, subprogram, or package. In the DECLARE section you can define datatypes, declare variables and constants, declare cursors, and insert comments. You cannot make any calls to subprograms or error-handling routines in this section.

When you declare a variable or constant, the PL/SQL engine allocates storage space for a value, specifies a datatype, and names the storage location so that the value can be referenced. The difference between a variable and a constant is that a variable can be assigned a value anytime in your program, as long as the variable was previously declared. A constant is assigned a value when it is declared, after which the value cannot change. When you declare a variable, you can optionally assign it a value to initialize it. To initialize a constant, you must assign it a value when it is declared. Otherwise, you get a compilation error. To declare a constant, you simply place the reserved word CONSTANT before the datatype when it is declared. The syntax to declare a variable or a constant is

```
<variable_name> <datatype> [NOT NULL] [:= <expression> | <value>];
```

or

```
<constant_name> CONSTANT <datatype> [NOT NULL] := <expression> | <value>;
```

where:

variable_name or **constant_name** is the name you assign to the variable or constant.

datatype is any of the valid PL/SQL datatypes or user-defined datatypes (RECORD or TABLE).

expression is a valid assignment expression that contains references to literals or previously declared variables or constants with assigned values.

value is a valid literal value.

NOT NULL constrains the variable so that NULL values are not assigned to it. If you try to assign a NULL, the predefined exception VALUE_ERROR is raised. A variable or constant assigned the NOT NULL constraint must be initialized when it is declared; otherwise, you get a compilation error. For example, the following declaration is illegal:

```
iItemIdMax BINARY_INTEGER NOT NULL;
```

The following are a few examples of variable declarations, with and without NOT NULL constraints:

```
DECLARE
    nItemCount BINARY_INTEGER;
    numSaleTotal NUMBER(10,2) NOT NULL := 100.50;
```

```
   numSalesTaxRate CONSTANT NUMBER(4,2) := 0.06;
BEGIN
...
END;
```

When you declare a variable or constant, you can use assignment expressions to initialize the value. These expressions can reference previously declared variables or constants that are initialized with valid values. For example:

```
DECLARE
   nItemCount BINARY_INTEGER := 5;
   numItemCost NUMBER(10,2) := 100.50;
   numSalesTaxRate NUMBER (4,2) NOT NULL := 0. 07;
   numTotalSale NUMBER(10,2) NOT NULL := nItemCount *
      numItemCost * numSalesTaxRate;
BEGIN
...
END;
```

To promote readability, PL/SQL provides an alternative to the assignment operator (:=) when a variable or constant is declared. You can use the reserved word DEFAULT instead of the assignment operator. For example, the declarations from the previous example could be rewritten as:

```
DECLARE
   nItemCount BINARY_INTEGER DEFAULT 5;
   numItemCost NUMBER(10,2) DEFAULT 100.50;
   numSalesTaxRate NUMBER (4,2) NOT NULL DEFAULT 0. 07;
   numTotalSale NUMBER(10,2) NOT NULL DEFAULT nItemCount *
      numItemCost * numSalesTaxRate;
BEGIN
...
END;
```

You can also use the DEFAULT reserved word to initialize subprogram parameters, cursor parameters, and fields in a user-defined record.

Using the %TYPE Attribute The %TYPE attribute returns the datatype of a variable, constant, or database column. This is particularly useful when you want to declare a variable or constant to have the same datatype as a database column and maintain the same datatypes throughout the life of your program. The syntax to declare a variable using the %TYPE attribute of a database column is

```
<variable_name> <table_name>.<column_name>%TYPE;
```

For example, you can see how the datatype of the **item_cost** column is assigned to the corresponding variable :

```
ItemCost item.item_cost%TYPE;
```

You can declare variables and constants similarly, using the %TYPE attribute of any other previously defined variable, constant, or database column. Declaring a variable or constant with the %TYPE attribute has two advantages. First, you need not know the exact datatype of the variable or constant; it is derived from the associated object. Second, if you change the datatype of the associated variable, constant, or database column, the datatype of the declared entity changes accordingly at run time. The syntax to declare a variable using the %TYPE attribute of another variable or constant is

```
<variable_name1> <variable_name2>%TYPE;
```

When you use the %TYPE attribute, all the normal rules of variable or constant declaration apply, including initialization and scoping. Note that a NOT NULL column constraint does not apply to variables declared using %TYPE. In the next example, even though the **item_id** database column is defined as NOT NULL, you can assign a null to the variable **iCurItemId**:

```
DECLARE
    iCurItemId item.item_id%TYPE;
BEGIN
    iCurItemId := NULL; -- this is legal
END;
```

Naming Variables and Constants   Variables and constants follow all the naming rules for identifiers described previously in this chapter. Like other identifiers, the names of variables and constants are not case-sensitive. For example, the following variable names are considered to be the same:

```
item_id INTEGER;
Item_ID INTEGER;
ITEM_ID INTEGER;
```

You should be careful to name your PL/SQL variables and constants uniquely so they don't collide with the names of database objects. In potentially ambiguous SQL statements, the names of local variables and constants take precedence over the names of database objects, such as tables, views, and cursors. You usually get run-time SQL errors if this occurs.

Unlike other database objects, the names of database columns take precedence over the names of local variables and constants. In this case, if the name of a column and a variable collide, you could get undefined results. This is because the reference to the PL/SQL variable in the SQL statement is treated as if the column were referenced multiple times.

To avoid these situations, you should devise a set of naming conventions for the variables and constants (and, for that matter, all your PL/SQL identifiers) in your PL/SQL programs that is different from that used to name the objects in your databases. You can also avoid problems by using fully qualified database object names when referencing them in SQL statements. However, this can become tedious, unreadable, and cumbersome. It is better programming practice simply to rename the variable or constant.

Another method to avoid name collisions is to use dot notation to reference variables or constants in the scope of the block or subprogram in which they are declared. See the next section to understand the rules of scope and visibility of variables and constants.

For example, you can use a label to name a PL/SQL block:

```
<<main>>
DECLARE
    item_name CHAR(20) := 'Computer Cover';
BEGIN
    DELETE FROM item WHERE item_name = main.item_name;
END;
```

In the next example, let's assume you perform the same operation in a subprogram, where you can use the subprogram name to qualify the variables and constants:

```
PROCEDURE del_item (item_name CHAR(20)) IS
BEGIN
    DELETE FROM item WHERE item_name = del_item.item_name;
END;
```

Scope and Visibility   When you reference a variable or constant, the reference is resolved according to its scope and visibility within your program. The scope of a variable or constant is determined by the portion of your program (block, subprogram, or package) from which the variable or constant can be referenced, whether or not the name is qualified. The visibility of a variable or constant is determined by the portion of your program from which the variable or constant can be referenced without a qualified name.

For example, variables and constants declared in a PL/SQL block are considered local to that block and global to all its subblocks. If a variable or constant is declared in a block (making it global to its subblocks) and it is redeclared in a subblock, both declarations are considered to be within the scope of the program block. Within the subblock, however, only the locally declared variable or constant is visible because you must use a qualified name to reference the globally declared identifier. The following example illustrates the scope and visibility of a variable named **iItemId**, which is declared in an enclosing block, then redeclared in a subblock.

```
DECLARE
   iItemId INTEGER;
BEGIN
   DECLARE
     iItemId INTEGER;
   BEGIN
     . . .
   END;
   . . .
END;
```

All declared variables or constants within the same block must be unique, even if their datatypes differ. Variables, constants, and parameters cannot have the same name. For example, the second declaration is illegal:

```
DECLARE
   ItemId INTEGER;
   ItemId CHAR(20);   -- Illegal declaration
   . . .
```

Although you cannot declare same-named variables and constants more than once in the same block, you can declare same-named variables and constants in two different blocks. Identifiers declared in this manner are distinct; a change in one does not affect the other.

A variable or constant declared in one block cannot reference identifiers declared in other blocks nested at the same level because those identifiers are neither local nor global to that block. The following example illustrates these scoping rules:

```
DECLARE
   var1 INTEGER;
   var2 REAL;
BEGIN
```

```
/*
** var1 (INTEGER) and var2 are available here.
*/
DECLARE
 var1 VARCHAR2(20);
 var3 CHAR;
 var4 REAL;
BEGIN
 /*
 ** var1 (VARCHAR2), var2, var3, and var4 are available here.
 */
END;

DECLARE
 var2 CHAR;
 var3 REAL;
 var5 DATE;
BEGIN
 /*
 ** var1 (INTEGER), var2 (CHAR), var3 (REAL), and var5
 ** are available here.
 */
END;
 /*
 ** var1 (INTEGER) and var2 are available here (same as at the
 ** beginning).
 */
END;
```

As mentioned earlier, global identifiers can be redeclared in a subblock. In this case, the local declaration prevails, and the subblock cannot reference the global identifier unless you use a qualified name with dot notation. This method can also be used to avoid collisions between the variable and constant names and database objects. For example, you can use a label to name a PL/SQL block:

```
<<main>>
DECLARE
  cItemName CHAR(20) := 'Computer Cover';
BEGIN
  DELETE FROM item WHERE item_name = main.cItemName;
  DECLARE
  cItemName CHAR(20) := 'Computer Case';
  BEGIN
```

```
      IF item_name = main.cItemName THEN
         ...
      END IF;
    END;
END;
```

In the next example, let's assume you perform the same operation in a subprogram, where you can use the subprogram name to qualify the variables and constants:

```
PROCEDURE del_item (cItemName CHAR(20)) IS
BEGIN
  DELETE FROM item WHERE item_name = del_item.cItemName;
  DECLARE
    cItemName CHAR(20) := 'Computer Case';
  BEGIN
    IF item_name = del_item.cItemName THEN
       ...
    END IF;
  END;
END;
```

Declaration Restrictions   PL/SQL does not allow forward references to variables or constants. You must declare a variable or constant before you reference it in any other statements, including other declarative statements.

C allows you to declare a list of variables belonging to the same datatype in the same statement. PL/SQL does not allow this. For example, the following declaration is illegal:

```
iItemId, iInvoiceId, iCustomerId INTEGER; -- Illegal declaration
```

The legal declaration is

```
iItemId    INTEGER;
iInvoiceId INTEGER;
iCustomerId INTEGER;
```

Assigning Values
Each time you enter a block, subblock, or subprogram, the locally declared variables and constants are allocated and initialized. Constants are required to be initialized with a value when they are declared. By default, variables are initialized to NULL. Unless you explicitly initialize a variable, its value is undefined. Therefore, you should never reference a variable before you assign it a value.

You can assign values to variables in a variety of ways. You can use assignment statements to assign simple literals or the results of complex expressions to a variable. The expression following the assignment operator can be arbitrarily complex, but it must result in a datatype that is the same as or convertible to the datatype of the assigned variable. For example:

```
DECLARE
   iItemCount INTEGER;
   numItemCost NUMBER(10,2);
   numSaleTotal NUMBER(10,2);
   numSalesTaxRate CONSTANT NUMBER(6,2) := 0.06;
BEGIN
   iItemCount := 10;
   numItemCost := 100.50;
   numSaleTotal := (iItemCount * numItemCost) * numSalesTaxRate;
END;
```

Alternately, you can use the SELECT or FETCH statement to have Oracle assign values to variables. This is as discussed for any embedded SQL operation, but the colon prefix (:) is not used to delineate a PL/SQL variable as it is in Pro*C. For example:

```
DECLARE
   iItemId INTEGER;
   cItemName VARCHAR(20);
BEGIN
   iItemId := 1000;
   SELECT item_name INTO cItemName
     FROM item
     WHERE item_id = iItemId;
END;
```

For each column in the SELECT list, there must be a corresponding variable in the INTO list. Also, each item must return a value that is implicitly convertible to the datatype of its corresponding variable.

For Boolean variables, only the values TRUE, FALSE, and NULL can be assigned. You cannot SELECT or FETCH Boolean values from the database into Boolean variables. However, PL/SQL returns these values from comparison operations, as illustrated in the next example:

```
DECLARE
   bSaleComplete BOOLEAN := FALSE;
   nItemCount INTEGER;
```

```
    numItemCost NUMBER(10,2);
    numSaleTotal NUMBER(10,2);
    numSalesTaxRate CONSTANT NUMBER(6,2) := 0.06;
BEGIN
  nItemCount := 0;
  WHILE NOT bSaleComplete LOOP
   nItemCount := nItemCount + 1;
   bSaleComplete := (nItemCount >= 10);
  END LOOP;

  IF bSaleComplete THEN
   numItemCost := 100.50;
   numSaleTotal := (nItemCount * iItemCost) * numSalesTaxRate;
  END IF;
END;
```

Notice that the variable **bSaleComplete** can be explicitly assigned a Boolean value, or it can be a result of a comparison operation.

Using the %ROWTYPE Attribute   The %ROWTYPE attribute allows you to use the definition of a row in a database table, view, or cursor to create a RECORD variable. A RECORD variable defined in this manner contains fields with the same definition as all the columns of the associated database object (including the datatype and column name). Thus, you can store an entire row of data in a RECORD variable when you SELECT from a table (or view) or FETCH from a cursor.

A %ROWTYPE declaration does not allow you to initialize the record in any way. However, there are two ways to assign values to all fields in a record at once. First, PL/SQL lets you assign the value of one record to another if the two records are defined by the same table, view, or cursor. For example:

```
DECLARE
   item_rec1 item%ROWTYPE;
   item_rec2 item%ROWTYPE;
   CURSOR item_cursor IS SELECT item_id, item_name
    FROM item;
   item_rec3 item_cursor%ROWTYPE;
   item_rec4 item_cursor%ROWTYPE;
BEGIN
   item_rec1 := item_rec2;
   item_rec4 := item_rec3;
   ...
END;
```

Because **item_rec2** is based on a table and **item_rec3** is based on a cursor, the following assignment is illegal:

```
item_rec2 := item_rec3; -- illegal assignment
```

Second, you can assign a list of column values to a record by using the SELECT or FETCH statement. The column names must appear in the order in which they are defined by the CREATE TABLE, CREATE VIEW, or CURSOR declaration statement.

```
DECLARE
   item_rec item%ROWTYPE;
BEGIN
   SELECT item_id, item_name, item_desc INTO item_rec FROM item
     WHERE item_id = 1000;
END;
```

You cannot assign a list of column values to a record by using an assignment statement. For example, the following statement is illegal:

```
item_rec := (val1, val2, val3, ...); -- illegal assignment
```

Also, records cannot be tested for equality or inequality. For instance, the following statement is illegal:

```
IF item_rec1 = item_rec2 THEN -- illegal statement
   ...
END IF;
```

Additionally, although you can retrieve entire records from a table, you cannot insert them into a table.

The items specified in the select-list of a cursor associated with %ROWTYPE must have simple names or, if they are expressions, aliases. Let's look at an example:

```
/*
** The following example calculates a reduction in the retail
** price of an item by 10% if the profit on the item is greater
** than 10% of the current retail price.
*/
DECLARE
  CURSOR item_cursor IS SELECT retail_price,
    retail_price - NVL(item_cost, 0) profit, item_id
    FROM item;
```

```
    item_rec item_cursor%ROWTYPE;
BEGIN
  OPEN item_cursor;
  LOOP
   FETCH item_cursor INTO item_rec;
   EXIT WHEN item_cursor%NOTFOUND;

   IF item_rec.profit > (item_rec.retail_price * 0.10) THEN
      item_rec.retail_price := item_rec.retail_price -
      (item_rec.retail_price * 0.10);
   END IF;
  END LOOP;
  CLOSE item_cursor;
END;
```

Using RECORD Variables   User-defined records follow all the declaration and scoping rules that apply to other variables. They are allocated when you first enter a block or subprogram where they are declared, and they are deallocated when you leave. When you first access a package, the tables are allocated where they are declared and deallocated when you exit the application or end the database session.

As discussed earlier, you reference individual fields in a record by using dot notation with the following syntax:

```
<record_name>.<field_name>
```

Instead of assigning values individually to each field in a record, you can assign values to all fields at once. This is done using the same two methods discussed for the %ROWTYPE attribute. Remember, a variable declared with this attribute has the characteristics of a RECORD.

Even if the field declarations of different record types match exactly (in name and datatype), you cannot assign them to each other. The records must be declared as the same record type. Also, a user-defined record and a %ROWTYPE record are considered different datatypes, even if the fields match.

All the restrictions that were discussed for %ROWTYPE records also apply to user-defined records. However, with user-defined records you can declare and reference nested records. In other words, you can create user-defined records that contain other %ROWTYPE or user-defined records as a component of the record definition.

Using TABLE Variables   Like user-defined records, tables follow all the declaration and scoping rules that apply to other variables. They are allocated when you first enter a block or subprogram where they are declared and are deallocated when you leave. When you first access a package, the records are allocated where they are declared and deallocated when you exit the application or end the database session.

As discussed earlier, you reference individual entries in a table by using arraylike syntax:

```
<table_name>(primary_index_value)
```

You can assign the value of an expression to a specific entry in a table by using the following syntax:

```
<table_name>(primary_index_value) := <expression>;
```

For example:

```
item_total(item_index) := retail_price * sales_tax_rate;
```

You must be careful when processing tables because the entries in a table do not exist until a value is assigned to the entry. If you try to reference an unassigned entry, the predefined exception NO_DATA_FOUND is raised.

The size of a TABLE variable is only constrained by the range of a BINARY_INTEGER variable. No implicit row count is maintained by the system; if you want to maintain a row count, you must declare a variable for that purpose. What happens if you allow a TABLE variable to grow too large? Look at the following example:

```
DECLARE
   TYPE ItemTableType IS TABLE OF REAL
   INDEX BY BINARY_INTEGER;
   item_cost_table ItemTableType;
   item_index BINARY_INTEGER := 1;
BEGIN
   /*
   ** Assign default values to the item_cost_table.
   */
   LOOP
     item_cost_table(item_index) := 10.00;
     -- EXIT WHEN statement omitted for debugging
     item_index := item_index + 1;
   END LOOP;
END;
```

Each iteration of the loop causes another row to be added to **item_cost_table**. This is an infinite loop because there is no EXIT WHEN statement. When the system runs out of memory, the predefined exception STORAGE_ERROR is raised.

You must use a loop structure to INSERT values from a TABLE variable into a database column and to FETCH values from a database column into the same. PL/SQL does not support the features of host arrays available with Pro*C. For example:

```
DECLARE
  TYPE ItemIdTableType IS TABLE OF BINARY_INTEGER
    INDEX BY BINARY_INTEGER;
  TYPE ItemCostTableType IS TABLE OF REAL
    INDEX BY BINARY_INTEGER;
  TYPE ItemPriceTableType IS TABLE OF REAL
    INDEX BY BINARY_INTEGER;

  item_id_table  ItemIdTableType;
  item_cost_table ItemCostTableType;
  item_price_table ItemPriceTableType;
BEGIN
  /*
  ** Assign default values to the item_id_table, item_cost_table,
  ** and item_price_table and insert them into the item table.
  */
  FOR item_index IN 1..1000 LOOP
    item_id_table(item_index) := item_index;
    item_cost_table(item_index) := 10.00;
    item_price_table(item_index) := 11.00;
  END LOOP;

  FOR item_index IN 1..1000 LOOP
    INSERT INTO item (item_id, item_cost, item_price)
      VALUES (item_id_table(item_index),
        item_cost_table(item_index),
        item_price_table(item_index));
  END LOOP;
END;
```

Also, you can use a loop structure to FETCH the rows from a table into TABLE variables. A cursor FOR loop (discussed later in the chapter) is convenient for this purpose. For example:

```
DECLARE
  TYPE ItemIdTableType IS TABLE OF BINARY_INTEGER
   INDEX BY BINARY_INTEGER;
  TYPE ItemCostTableType IS TABLE OF REAL
   INDEX BY BINARY_INTEGER;
  TYPE ItemPriceTableType IS TABLE OF REAL
   INDEX BY BINARY_INTEGER;

  item_id_table ItemIdTableType;
  item_cost_table ItemCostTableType;
  item_price_table ItemPriceTableType;
  item_index BINARY_INTEGER := 0;
BEGIN
  /*
  ** FETCH the values into the item_rec record and assign them to
  ** the item_id_table, item_cost_table, and item_price_table.
  */
  FOR item_rec IN (SELECT item_id, item_cost, item_price
   FROM item) LOOP
     item_index := item_index + 1;
     item_id_table(item_index) := item_rec.item_id;
     item_cost_table(item_index) := item_rec.item_cost;
     item_price_table(item_index) := item_rec.item_price;
  END LOOP;
END;
```

However, you cannot reference TABLE variables in the INTO clause of a SELECT statement.

PL/SQL does not provide a way to delete the entries from a TABLE variable. Once you assign a value to a table entry, the entry is allocated and remains until the TABLE is deallocated. Even if you assign a NULL value, the entry remains allocated. Although you cannot explicitly delete individual rows from a TABLE variable, you can use a simple workaround to delete the entire table. First, declare another TABLE variable of the same type and leave it empty. Later, when you want to delete the original TABLE variable of the same type, simply assign the empty table to it, or assign NULL to the table variable.

Datatype Conversion

Because of the variety of datatypes supported by SQL and PL/SQL, it is sometimes necessary to convert a value from one datatype to another. For example, if you need to examine a ROWID variable, you must convert it to a character string. PL/SQL allows you to convert datatypes both explicitly and implicitly.

Explicit Conversion   PL/SQL supplies a set of standard functions that you can use to convert variable values explicitly from one datatype to another. Table 9-7 shows you which function to use given a specific conversion need.

Implicit Conversion   When feasible, PL/SQL can implicitly convert the datatype of a value for you. This allows you to specify constants, literals, variables, and parameters of one datatype where another datatype is expected. Implicit conversion rules are not magic. You must be careful not to specify a variable that would not logically be convertible to the datatype of the target object.

When you SELECT a column from a table, PL/SQL will, if needed, implicitly convert the column value to the datatype of the target variable. The most common example is when you SELECT a DATE column value into a CHAR or VARCHAR2 variable. Also, when you assign or compare the value of a variable to a database column, PL/SQL converts the datatype of the variable to the internal datatype of the column if necessary.

If the implicit data conversion is not supported by PL/SQL, you will receive a compilation error. You must then use the explicit datatype conversion functions instead. Table 9-8 shows which implicit data conversions are supported by PL/SQL.

Although PL/SQL handles many of your data conversion requirements, you are responsible for ensuring that data values are convertible. The data values must be in a format that PL/SQL can convert. For example, PL/SQL can convert the string '25-MAR-95' to a DATE value, but it cannot convert 'TODAY' to a DATE value. Along the same lines, PL/SQL cannot convert a CHAR value containing alphabetic characters to a NUMBER value.

Avoid relying on implicit datatype conversion to process information in your program. Such conversions impede performance and may not be supported in the same manner in a future release of Oracle. Additionally, implicit data conversions are context-sensitive and therefore not always predictable. If at all possible, use variables that are of the same datatype as the database columns being processed in your program. If you need to use datatype conversion, use the explicit conversion functions instead. That way, your applications will be more reliable and easier to maintain.

To/From	CHAR	DATE	NUMBER	RAW	ROWID
CHAR	—	TO_DATE	TO_NUMBER	HEXTORAW	CHARTOROWID
DATE	TO_CHAR	—			
NUMBER	TO_CHAR	TO_DATE	—		
RAW	RAWTOHEX			—	
ROWID	ROWIDTOCHAR				—

TABLE 9-7.   *Explicit conversion functions*

Convert From:	Convert To: BINARY INTEGER	CHAR	DATE	LONG	NUMBER	RAW	ROWID	VARCHAR2
BINARY INTEGER	—	Yes		Yes	Yes			Yes
CHAR	Yes	—	Yes	Yes	Yes	Yes	Yes	Yes
DATE		Yes	—	Yes				Yes
LONG		Yes		—		Yes		Yes
NUMBER	Yes	Yes		Yes	—			Yes
RAW		Yes		Yes				Yes
ROWID		Yes					—	Yes

TABLE 9-8. *Implicit conversions*

Expressions and Comparisons

Expressions are used to construct or calculate a value that you assign to a variable. Expressions are constructed with operands and operators. An operand can be a literal, variable, constant, or function return value.

PL/SQL has unary operators such as the negation operator (–) that operate on one operand. Other binary operators, such as the multiplication operator (*), take two operands.

The simplest expressions consist of a single variable or constant that provides a direct value. An expression is evaluated by (in other words, its value is determined by) combining the values of the operands in the ways specified by the operators. An expression always produces a single value of a specific datatype. The datatype is determined by examining the expression, its operands, its operators, and the context in which the expression is used.

Operator Precedence

The operations within an expression are evaluated in a specific order based on the precedence of the operators specified. Table 9-9 shows the PL/SQL default order of first to last (top to bottom).

Operators with higher precedence are applied first, and those with the same precedence are applied in no particular order. You can use parentheses to control the order of evaluation. Parentheses override the default operator precedence. In

Operator	Operation
**, NOT	Exponentiation, logical negation
+, –	Identity, negation
*, /	Multiplication, division
+, –, ||	Addition, subtraction, concatenation
=, !=, <, >, <=, >=, IS NULL,LIKE, BETWEEN, IN	Comparison
AND	Conjunction
OR	Inclusion

TABLE 9-9.   *Operator precedence*

the following example, the subtraction is done before the division because the most deeply nested subexpression is always evaluated first:

```
1250 + (300 / 20 + (17 - 8))
```

It is good programming practice to use parentheses in expressions; doing so improves readability and ensures that the expression is evaluated in the order you intended.

The PL/SQL operators are grouped into four categories:

- Arithmetic operators
- Logical operators
- Comparison operators
- String operators

Let's discuss each of these categories.

Arithmetic Operators

The arithmetic operators allow you to create arbitrarily complex arithmetic expressions that produce a numeric result. The sign operators (–, +) are unary operators that are used to apply a negative or positive value to an operand. The other arithmetic operators are binary operators used to calculate an arithmetic result. Table 9-10 lists the arithmetic operators available in PL/SQL in the order of precedence.

Operator	Operation
**	Exponentiation
+, −	Sign operators: positive and negative
*, /	Multiplication, division
+, −	Addition, subtraction

TABLE 9-10. *Arithmetic operators*

Logical Operators

The logical operators are AND, OR, and NOT. NOT is a unary operator used to negate the Boolean value of a Boolean operand. OR and AND are binary operators that combine the Boolean value of two operands to produce a Boolean result. These operators operate according to the logic illustrated by Table 9-11.

As shown in the truth tables, NOT returns the opposite value (logical negation) of its operand. For example, NOT TRUE returns FALSE. NOT NULL returns NULL, because nulls are indeterminate. It makes sense that if you apply an operator to an indeterminate value, the result is also indeterminate. However, nulls can cause unexpected results (nulls are discussed later in this section).

NOT	TRUE	**FALSE**	**NULL**
	FALSE	TRUE	NULL
AND	TRUE	**FALSE**	**NULL**
TRUE	TRUE	FALSE	NULL
FALSE	FALSE	FALSE	FALSE
NULL	NULL	FALSE	NULL
OR	TRUE	**FALSE**	**NULL**
TRUE	TRUE	TRUE	TRUE
FALSE	TRUE	FALSE	NULL
NULL	TRUE	NULL	NULL

TABLE 9-11. *Truth tables*

AND returns a TRUE value only if both its operands are true. OR returns a TRUE value if either of its operands is true.

Comparison Operators

Comparison operators are used to compare the value of one expression to another. The result is always TRUE, FALSE, or NULL. Comparison operators are used in conditional control statements and in the WHERE clause of data manipulation SQL statements. You can use the comparison operators to compare the value of arithmetic, character, and date expressions.

The comparison operators consist of relational operators, which allow you to compare the value of two or more expressions. Table 9-12 lists the relational operators available in PL/SQL.

PL/SQL also provides the comparison operators IS NULL, LIKE, BETWEEN, and IN.

IS NULL Operator   The IS NULL operator is used to test for null values. If an operand is null, the IS NULL operator returns the Boolean value TRUE. It returns FALSE if the operand is not null. This operator is necessary because comparisons involving nulls always produce a NULL result. If you use the following statement to test for a null value, for example, when you encounter a null value the result is NULL, not TRUE as you might expect.

```
IF value = NULL THEN ...
```

Instead, the correct use is as follows:

```
IF value IS NULL THEN ...
```

Operator	Description
=	Is equal to
!=	Is not equal to
<	Is less than
>	Is greater than
<=	Is less than or equal to
>=	Is greater than or equal to

TABLE 9-12.   *Relational operators*

LIKE Operator　The LIKE operator is used to compare a character string to a specified pattern. The LIKE operator returns the Boolean value TRUE if the operand matches the specified character-string pattern and FALSE if it does not match. The LIKE operator is case-sensitive.

The patterns specified for the LIKE operator can use literal character strings and two wildcard characters. You use an underscore (_) to match exactly one printable character. You use a percent sign (%) to match zero or more printable characters in a string. For example, the pattern 'S%d_y' would evaluate to true if the variable **day_of_the_week** were Saturday or Sunday.

```
day_of_the_week LIKE 'S%d_y'
```

BETWEEN Operator　The BETWEEN operator is used to test whether a value lies within a range of values. This is equivalent to saying: (a <= value) AND (value <= b). If the operand lies within the specified range of values, the expression evaluates to the Boolean value TRUE. Otherwise, it is FALSE (or NULL).

For example, the following expression evaluates to FALSE if value = 55:

```
value BETWEEN 75 AND 100
```

IN Operator　The IN operator is used to test that an operand exists in a specified set of values. It is equivalent to saying

(value = a) OR (value = b) OR (value = c) OR ...

You can specify a NULL value in a set, but it is ignored. For example, the following statement will delete all rows that have an item name equal to 'Floppy Drive' or 'Tape Drive' but will not delete rows where the item name is null.

```
DELETE FROM item WHERE item_name IN (NULL, 'Floppy Drive', 'Tape Drive');
```

Also, any statement with the following syntax will always evaluate to NULL if the set contains a null.

```
value NOT IN set
```

This is because NOT IN a null set is equivalent to saying

(value = NULL) OR (value = val1) OR ...

which results in a null value (see the truth tables, Table 9-11).

Concatenation Operator

The concatenation operator (||) is used to append multiple strings. The operands of the concatenation operator can be character literals, string literals, variables, or constants. For example, the expression

```
'half' || 'price'
```

returns the value

```
'halfprice'
```

If both operands are of the datatype CHAR, the concatenation operator returns a CHAR value. Otherwise, it returns a VARCHAR2 value.

Expression Guidelines

As a rule, you should not compare real numbers for exact equality or inequality. Real numbers are stored as approximate values. You should use an approximation of precision (say within three or five decimal places) to compare for equality or inequality.

It is good programming practice to use parentheses when creating any kind of expression. It promotes readability and ensures that the expression is evaluated as you intend, not based on the default order of precedence.

The value associated with a Boolean variable is itself either true or false. Therefore, comparisons with the Boolean values TRUE and FALSE are redundant.

When processing operands that can contain null values, you can avoid some common mistakes by observing two rules: Comparisons involving nulls always result in NULL, and applying the logical operator NOT to a null results in NULL. In conditional control statements, if the condition evaluates to NULL, its associated sequence of statements is not executed; it is treated as an indeterminate value.

PL/SQL treats any zero-length string as a null. This includes values returned by character functions and Boolean expressions. Therefore, use the IS NULL operator to test for null strings. The concatenation operator ignores null operands. For example, the expression

```
'char' || NULL || NULL || 'acter'
```

returns the value

```
'character'
```

Normally, if you pass a null argument to a standard function, a null is returned except for three functions:

■ **DECODE** The function DECODE compares its first argument to one or more search expressions, which are paired with result expressions. Any search or result expression can be null. If a search expression is matched, the corresponding result expression is returned.

■ **NVL** The NVL function tests its first parameter for a null value. If it is null, the value of its second parameter is returned.

■ **REPLACE** The REPLACE function returns the value of its first parameter if its second parameter is null, whether or not the optional third parameter is present. If the third parameter is null, REPLACE returns its first parameter with every occurrence of its second parameter removed. If the second and third parameters are null, REPLACE simply returns its first argument.

Standard Functions

PL/SQL supplies a standard library of powerful functions to help you process and manipulate data. Each function provides a specific service and optionally returns a value based on one of the valid PL/SQL datatypes. The standard PL/SQL functions fall into the following categories:

■ Error-handling functions

■ Number functions

■ String functions

■ Conversion functions

■ Date functions

■ Miscellaneous functions

The following tables summarize the standard functions supplied by PL/SQL: error-handling functions (Table 9-13), number functions (Table 9-14), string functions (Table 9-15), conversion functions (Table 9-16), date functions (Table 9-17), and miscellaneous functions (Table 9-18). For a more detailed explanation of these functions and their usage, see Appendix B.

You can use these functions in any expression or statement where expressions of the same datatype are allowed. Also, you can nest these functions by calling one or more of them as input parameters of another function.

Function Name	Description
SQLCODE	Returns the number associated with the most recently raised exception.
SQLERRM	Returns the error message associated with the current value of SQLCODE.

TABLE 9-13. *Error-handling functions*

Function Name	Description
ABS	Returns the absolute value of a number.
CEIL	Returns the smallest integer greater than or equal to a number.
COS	Returns the cosine of an angle, which must be expressed in radians.
COSH	Returns the hyperbolic cosine of a number.
EXP	Returns a number raised to the nth power.
FLOOR	Returns the largest integer equal to or less than a number.
LN	Returns the natural logarithm of a number, where the number is greater than 0.
LOG	Returns the base logarithm of a number, where the base is greater than 1 and the number is greater than 0.
MOD	Returns the remainder of a number when divided by another number.
POWER	Returns the number m raised to the nth power.
ROUND	Returns a number rounded to a specified number of decimal places.
SIGN	Returns -1 if a number is less than 0, 0 if the number equals 0, or 1 if the number is greater than 0.
SIN	Returns the sine of an angle, which must be expressed in radians.
SINH	Returns the hyperbolic sine of a number.
SQRT	Returns the square root of a number, which cannot be negative.
TAN	Returns the tangent of an angle, which must be expressed in radians.
TANH	Returns the hyperbolic tangent of a number.
TRUNC	Returns a number truncated to a specified number of decimal places.

TABLE 9-14. *Number functions*

Function Name	Description
ASCII	Returns the collating code that represents a character in the database character set.
CHR	Returns the character in the database character set that a collating code number represents.
CONCAT	Concatenates a string to a second string, then returns the combined string.
INITCAP	Returns the string, with the first letter of each word in uppercase and all other letters in lowercase. Words are delimited by spaces or nonalphanumeric characters.
INSTR	Searches a string starting at a specified character position for the nth occurrence of a second string and returns the position of the first character of that occurrence.
INSTRB	Searches a string starting at a specified byte position for the nth occurrence of a second string and returns the position of the first byte of that occurrence.
LENGTH	Returns the number of characters in a string.
LENGTHB	Returns the number of bytes in a string.
LOWER	Returns a string, with all letters in lowercase.
LPAD	Returns a string left-padded to a specified length, with a specified sequence of characters replicated as many times as necessary.
LTRIM	Returns a string, with the initial characters removed up to the first character not in a specified character set.
NLS_INITCAP	Returns a string, with the first letter of each word in uppercase and all other letters in lowercase.
NLS_LOWER	Returns a string, with all letters in lowercase.
NLS_UPPER	Returns a string, with all letters in uppercase.
NLSSORT	Returns the value of a string in the linguistic sort sequence specified by a second parameter.
REPLACE	Returns a string, with every occurrence of a specified substring replaced by another string.
RPAD	Returns a string right-padded to a specified length, with the specified sequence of characters replicated as many times as necessary.

TABLE 9-15. *String functions*

Function Name	Description
RTRIM	Returns a string, with the final characters removed after the last character not in a specified character set.
SOUNDEX	Returns a character string containing the phonetic representation of a specified string.
SUBSTR	Returns a substring from a specified string, starting at a specified character position, including the first number of characters or, if you omit the number of characters, all characters to the end of the string.
SUBSTRB	Returns a substring from a specified string starting at a specified byte position, including the first number of bytes or, if you omit the number of bytes, all bytes to the end of the string.
TRANSLATE	Returns a string after replacing all occurrences of a specified set of characters with the corresponding characters in another set of characters.
UPPER	Returns a string with all letters in uppercase.

TABLE 9-15.   *String functions* (continued)

Function Name	Description
CHARTOROWID	Converts a string from type CHAR or VARCHAR2 to type ROWID.
CONVERT	Converts a string from one character set to another.
HEXTORAW	Converts a hexadecimal string from type CHAR or VARCHAR2 to type RAW.
RAWTOHEX	Converts a binary value from type RAW to a hexadecimal string of type VARCHAR2.
ROWIDTOCHAR	Converts a binary value from type ROWID to an 18-byte hexadecimal string of type VARCHAR2.
TO_CHAR for Dates	Converts a date to a character string of type VARCHAR2 in the format specified by a format model.

TABLE 9-16.   *Conversion functions*

Function Name	Description
TO_CHAR for Numbers	Converts a number to a character string of type VARCHAR2 in the format specified by a format model.
TO_CHAR for Labels	Converts a label of type MLSLABEL to a value of type VARCHAR2 in a format specified by a format model.
TO_DATE	Converts a string or a number to a value of type DATE in the format specified by a format model.
TO_LABEL	Converts a string, which contains a label in the format specified by a format model, to a value of type MLSLABEL.
TO_MULTI_BYTE	Returns a string, with all its single-byte characters converted to their multibyte equivalents.
TO_NUMBER	Converts a string from a value of type CHAR or VARCHAR2 to a value of type NUMBER in the format specified by a format model.
TO_SINGLE_BYTE	Returns a string, with all its multibyte characters converted to their single-byte equivalents.

TABLE 9-16.   *Conversion functions (continued)*

Function Name	Description
ADD_MONTHS	Returns a date plus or minus a specified number of months.
LAST_DAY	Returns the date of the last day of the month containing a specified date.
MONTHS_BETWEEN	Returns the number of months between two specified dates.
NEW_TIME	Given a date and time in a specified time zone, returns the corresponding date and time in a different specified time zone.
NEXT_DAY	Returns the date of the first day of the week named by day that is later than a specified date.
ROUND	Returns a specified date rounded to the unit specified by a format model.
SYSDATE	Returns the current system date and time.
TRUNC	Returns a date with the time portion of the day truncated as specified by a format model.

TABLE 9-17.   *Date functions*

Function Name	Description
DECODE	An expression is compared to a specified set of search values. If the expression equals a search value, the corresponding result is returned. If no match is found, DECODE returns the default value, or a null if a default value was not supplied.
DUMP	Returns the internal representation of an expression.
GREATEST	Returns the greatest value in a list of values.
GREATEST_LB	Returns the greatest lower bound of the list of labels.
LEAST	Returns the least value in a list of values.
LEAST_UB	Returns the least upper bound of the list of labels.
NVL	Takes two arguments of the same type and returns a value of that type.
UID	Returns the unique identification number assigned to the current Oracle user.
USER	Returns the username of the current Oracle user.
USERENV	Returns information about the current session.
VSIZE	Returns the number of bytes in the internal representation of an expression.

TABLE 9-18. *Miscellaneous functions*

You can use all the standard functions in SQL statements except the error-reporting functions SQLCODE and SQLERRM. In addition, you can use all the functions in procedural statements except the miscellaneous function DECODE.

The SQL group functions AVG, MIN, MAX, COUNT, SUM, STDDEV, and VARIANCE are not standard in PL/SQL. You cannot use these functions in PL/SQL procedural statements, but you can use them in SQL statements.

Control Structures

The most important enhancements to basic SQL that PL/SQL provides are the control structures that let you order the logic and flow of your PL/SQL programs. Combined with SQL, these control structures allow you to tackle any situation. Use of these structures promotes a well-architected application program.

According to structured programming theory, three classes of control structures are required to solve any programming problem:

- Conditional control
- Iterative control
- Sequential control

You can combine these control structures to address any problem at hand.

Conditional control allows you to test the truth of a condition, then executes one section of your program if the condition is true or another if it is false. A condition can be a variable or an expression that results in a Boolean value of TRUE, FALSE, or NULL. Conditional control statements can be combined to test multiple conditions and select multiple program paths. Conditional control is used to make decisions on which program paths are appropriate for a given situation.

Iterative control allows you to execute a section of your program repeatedly as long as a specified condition remains true. This allows you to process the same section of your program with potentially different data until there is no more data to process.

Sequential control allows you to order the sequence of processing sections of your program. This lets you change the order in which your program executes, if necessary.

Let's discuss each of these control structures in detail and see how they are implemented in PL/SQL.

Conditional Control

Often you'll need to make decisions in your programs about the appropriate operation to execute in a given situation. Typically, you can test a set of conditions to determine what the situation is and what operation you should execute. PL/SQL provides a set of IF statements that allows you to test these conditions and decide which path you should take in your program.

PL/SQL provides three forms of IF statements, each an expansion of a more basic form, to handle any decision you may need to make in your program:

- **IF-THEN**   If a condition is true, execute a section of your program.
- **IF-THEN-ELSE**   If a condition is true, execute a section of your program; otherwise, execute a different section of your program.
- **IF-THEN-ELSIF**   If a condition is true, execute a section of your program; otherwise, if another condition is true, execute a different section of your program; and so on.

Let's discuss how you use each of these forms in your program.

IF-THEN Statement

The most basic form of the IF statement allows you to test the truth of a condition and execute a section of your program if the condition is true. This is called an IF-THEN statement. The syntax of an IF-THEN statement is

```
IF condition THEN
    statement1;
    statement2;
    ...
END IF;
```

where:

> **condition** is any variable or expression that results in a Boolean value of TRUE, FALSE, or NULL.

> **statement1**... is any sequence of statements you want to process if the condition is true.

NOTE
You must specify the END IF (not ENDIF) keyword to end the IF-THEN statement. Otherwise, the compiler will return an error.

The sequence of statements is executed only if the condition results in a TRUE value. If the condition results in a FALSE or NULL value, the sequence of statements is skipped, and processing continues with the statement that follows the END IF statement. For example:

```
IF item_rec.profit  > (item_rec.retail_price * 0.10) THEN
    item_rec.retail_price := item_rec.retail_price -
        (item_rec.retail_price * 0.10);
END IF;
```

For simple conditions, you can place the entire statement on one line. For example:

```
IF profit  > retail_price THEN retail_price := profit END IF;
```

However, this practice is discouraged because it makes the statement more difficult to read.

IF-THEN-ELSE Statement

The second form of the IF statement allows you to test the truth of a condition and execute a section of your program if the condition is true. Otherwise, if the condition is false, you can execute a different section of your program. This is called an IF-THEN-ELSE statement. The syntax of an IF-THEN-ELSE statement is

```
IF condition THEN
    statement1;
    statement2;
    . . .
ELSE
    statementa;
    statementb;
    . . .
END IF;
```

where:

condition is any variable or expression that results in a Boolean value of TRUE, FALSE, or NULL.

statement1... is any sequence of statements you want to process if the condition is true.

statementa... is any sequence of statements you want to process if the condition is false or null.

Note that you must specify the END IF (not ENDIF) keyword to end the IF-THEN-ELSE statement.

The first sequence of statements is executed only if the condition results in a TRUE value. The second sequence of statements is executed if the condition results in a FALSE or NULL value. Thus, the ELSE ensures that one or the other is executed. For example:

```
IF item_rec.profit  > (item_rec.retail_price * 0.10) THEN
    item_rec.retail_price := item_rec.retail_price -
        (item_rec.retail_price * 0.10);
ELSE
    item_rec.retail_price := item_rec.retail_price +
        (item_rec.retail_price * 0.10);
END IF;
```

You can nest IF-THEN and IF-THEN-ELSE statements inside other IF statements. However, this is not recommended because it makes your program harder to read and hides the flow of logic. You should use the third form of the IF statement: IF-THEN-ELSIF.

IF-THEN-ELSIF Statement

Often you will encounter situations where you need to make multiple, mutually exclusive decisions based on a set of multiple conditions. PL/SQL allows you to do this with the IF-THEN-ELSIF statement (not ELSEIF or ELSE IF). The syntax of an IF-THEN-ELSIF statement is

```
IF condition1 THEN
    statement1;
    statement2;
    ...
ELSE IF condition2 THEN
    statementa;
    statementb;
    ...
ELSE IF ... THEN
    ...
ELSE
    statementx;
    statementy;
    ...
END IF;
```

where:

condition1 is any variable or expression that results in a Boolean value of TRUE, FALSE, or NULL.

statement1... is any sequence of statements you want to process if **condition1** is true.

condition2 is any variable or expression that results in a Boolean value of TRUE, FALSE, or NULL. **condition2** is only evaluated if **condition1** is false.

statementa... is any sequence of statements you want to process if **condition2** is true.

statementx... is any sequence of statements you want to process if all other conditions are false or null.

NOTE
You must specify the END IF (not ENDIF) keyword to end the
IF-THEN-ELSIF statement. You can have any number of ELSIF
conditions specified in the IF-THEN-ELSIF statement; the final ELSE
clause is optional.

The conditions in the IF and ELSIF clauses are evaluated from top to bottom. If
any of them evaluates to true, the sequence of statements following the condition is
executed; no other sequence of statements in the IF-THEN-ELSIF statement is
executed. If none of the conditions is true and an ELSE clause is specified, the
sequence of statements following the ELSE clause is executed. For example:

```
IF item_rec.profit  > (item_rec.retail_price * 0.10) THEN
    item_rec.retail_price := item_rec.retail_price -
        (item_rec.retail_price * 0.10);
ELSE IF item_rec.profit  < (item_rec.retail_price * 0.10) THEN
    item_rec.retail_price := item_rec.retail_price +
        (item_rec.retail_price * 0.10);
ELSE
    item_rec.retail_price := item_rec.profit;
END IF;
```

In this example, **item_rec.retail_price** will always be assigned a value because of
the ELSE clause.

You can nest IF-THEN and IF-THEN-ELSE statements inside other IF statements.
However, this is not a recommended practice because it makes your program
harder to read and hides the flow of logic. You should use the IF-THEN-ELSIF
statement.

Be careful not to overuse IF statements if it can be avoided. Remember that you
can directly test the result of an expression in an IF condition. Consider the
following example:

```
DECLARE
    bCreditPurchase BOOLEAN;
    bOverLimit  BOOLEAN := FALSE;
    fCreditLimit NUMBER(10,2);
    fTotalSale NUMBER(10,2);
BEGIN
    IF bCreditPurchase = TRUE THEN
        IF fTotalSale > fCreditLimit THEN
            bOverLimit := TRUE;
        ELSE
            bOverLimit := FALSE;
```

```
        END IF;
    END IF;

    IF bOverLimit = TRUE THEN
        RAISE over_credit_limit;
    END IF;

EXCEPTION
    WHEN over_credit_limit THEN
        --handle error
END;
```

You could reduce the preceding example to a few statements:

```
DECLARE
    bCreditPurchase BOOLEAN;
    fCreditLimit NUMBER(10,2);
    fTotalSale NUMBER(10,2);
BEGIN
    IF bCreditPurchase AND (fTotalSale > fCreditLimit) THEN
        RAISE over_credit_limit;
    END IF;

EXCEPTION
    WHEN over_credit_limit THEN
        --handle error
END;
```

Iterative Control

You will encounter situations in your program where you need to execute an operation multiple times. This is often the case when you're processing multiple rows of data in database tables. PL/SQL provides a set of three iterative control statements that allow you to process sections of your program repeatedly:

- ■ LOOP iteratively processes a section of your program either infinitely or until you exit the loop.

- ■ WHILE-LOOP iteratively processes a section of your program while a condition remains true.

- ■ FOR-LOOP iteratively processes a section of your program for a range of iterations.

Let's discuss how you employ each of these forms of iterative control statements in your program.

LOOP Statement

The most basic form of iterative control statement in PL/SQL allows you to simply execute a section of your program either infinitely or until you force the loop to exit. The LOOP statement actually has three forms. The first is the basic LOOP statement, which lets you process a section of your program infinitely. The syntax of a LOOP statement is

```
LOOP
    statement1;
    statement2;
    . . .
END LOOP;
```

where:

> **statement1**... is any sequence of statements you want to process in each iteration of the loop.

NOTE
You must specify the END LOOP keyword to end the LOOP statement. Otherwise, the compiler will return an error. The LOOP statement has limited value in practice unless you provide a way to exit the statement in your program.

The second form of the LOOP statement is LOOP-EXIT. This statement lets you process a section of your program iteratively until you force the loop to exit. The syntax of a LOOP-EXIT statement is

```
LOOP
    statement1;
    statement2;
    . . .
    EXIT;
END LOOP;
```

where:

> **statement1**... is any sequence of statements you want to process in each iteration of the loop.

You can place any number of EXIT statements in a loop to cause the loop to end immediately when an EXIT statement is encountered. However, you cannot use the EXIT statement anywhere outside a LOOP structure. You can use the EXIT statement inside an IF statement to conditionally exit a loop, using the following syntax:

```
LOOP
    statement1;
    statement2;
    . . .
    IF condition THEN
        EXIT;
    END IF;
END LOOP;
```

The loop exits when the condition in the IF-THEN statement evaluates to true. However, a better way to construct a loop of this type is to use the third form of the LOOP structure: LOOP-EXIT WHEN. The syntax of this statement is

```
LOOP
    statement1;
    statement2;
    . . .
    EXIT WHEN condition;
END LOOP;
```

where:

statement1... is any sequence of statements you want to process in each iteration of the loop.

condition is a Boolean variable or expression that will force the loop to exit when the condition evaluates to true.

The LOOP continues to execute iteratively until the WHEN condition is true. Therefore, you must change the value of the condition inside the loop structure. When the condition is true, the loop exits and passes control to the next statement following the END LOOP statement. The EXIT WHEN statement replaces the IF statement in the LOOP-EXIT statement shown earlier.

The C language provides a DO-UNTIL structure that allows you to execute a loop at least once before a condition is tested. PL/SQL does not directly support this structure, but you can create a functionally equivalent structure with the LOOP-EXIT WHEN statement.

You can assign a label to a LOOP structure. For loops with large numbers of statements, you can label the END LOOP statement to improve readability. The label must be declared immediately before the LOOP begins, using the following syntax:

```
<<label_name>>
LOOP
    statement1;
    statement2;
    . . .
    EXIT WHEN condition;
END LOOP label_name;
```

You can nest LOOP structures to perform multiple looping operations. You can reference a loop label in an EXIT statement to exit all the nested loops up to and including the labeled loop structure. For example:

```
<<label_name>>
LOOP
    statement1;
    statement2;
    . . .
    LOOP
        . . .
        EXIT label_name WHEN condition;
    END LOOP;
END LOOP label_name;
```

In this example, when the condition in the EXIT WHEN statement in the nested loop structure is true, both loops exit completely.

WHILE-LOOP Statement

The second form of iterative statement in PL/SQL allows you to execute a section of your program iteratively while a condition remains true. This is called the WHILE-LOOP statement. The syntax of a WHILE-LOOP statement is

```
WHILE condition LOOP
    statement1;
    statement2;
    . . .
END LOOP;
```

where:

> **condition** is a Boolean variable or expression that is evaluated before each iteration of the loop structure. The sequence of statements in the loop structure is executed if the condition evaluates to true.

> **statement1**... is any sequence of statements you want to process in each iteration of the loop.

You must specify the END LOOP keyword to end the WHILE-LOOP statement. Before the loop structure is entered the first time and for each subsequent iteration, the condition in the WHILE statement is evaluated. If the condition evaluates to TRUE, the sequence of statements is executed and the condition is evaluated again. If the condition evaluates to FALSE or NULL, the loop is skipped and control is passed to the statement following the END-LOOP statement.

The number of loop iterations depends on the condition in the WHILE statement and is unknown until the condition becomes false or null and the loop completes. You must change the value of the condition at some point inside the loop structure for the condition to become false or null. Otherwise, you have an infinite loop.

Since the condition is tested at the top of the loop, the sequence of statements may never be executed. To ensure that a WHILE loop executes at least once, use a Boolean variable in the condition that is initialized to produce a true value.

FOR-LOOP Statement

The third form of iterative statement in PL/SQL allows you to execute a section of your program over a range of integer values. This is called the FOR-LOOP statement. The range of integer values in a FOR-LOOP statement can take many forms as long as it increments or decrements by 1 for each iteration. The syntax of a FOR-LOOP statement is

```
FOR counter IN [REVERSE] lower..upper LOOP
    statement1;
    statement2;
    ...
END LOOP;
```

where:

> **counter** is a BINARY-INTEGER variable used as the range counter for the loop structure. Each iteration of the loop increments or decrements the counter by 1.

lower is the lower bound of the specified range of values. The lower bound can be a positive or negative literal, variable, or expression.

upper is the upper bound of the specified range of values. The upper bound can be a positive or negative literal, variable, or expression. It must be greater than or equal to the lower bound.

statement1... is any sequence of statements you want to process in each iteration of the loop.

Note that you must specify the END LOOP keyword to end the FOR-LOOP statement. The lower and upper range values are evaluated the first time the FOR loop is entered and are never reevaluated. This prevents any side effects if you were to inadvertently modify one of the variables used to determine the lower and upper range values.

You can optionally specify the keyword REVERSE in the range declaration. If you do not specify the REVERSE keyword, when you enter the FOR-LOOP the first time, the counter is initialized to the lower range value and incremented by 1 for each subsequent iteration of the loop. The loop terminates when the counter is greater than the upper range value. For example:

```
FOR count IN 1..3 LOOP
    statement1;
    statement2;
    ...
END LOOP;
```

This loop will execute three times with the variable count starting at 1 and ending at 3.

Alternatively, if you specify the REVERSE keyword, when you enter the FOR-LOOP the first time, the counter is initialized to the upper range value and decremented by 1 for each subsequent iteration of the loop. The loop terminates when the counter is less than the lower range value. For example:

```
FOR count IN REVERSE 1..3 LOOP
    statement1;
    statement2;
    ...
END LOOP;
```

This loop will execute three times with the count starting at 3 and ending at 1. Nevertheless, you must still specify the lower and upper range values with the lower (or lesser) value on the left and the upper (or higher) value on the right. If the lower and upper range values are equal, the loop will only execute once.

The lower and upper range values can be literals, variables, constants, or expressions but must always evaluate to integers. This gives you a variety of options for determining ranges in a FOR loop. For example, the following ranges are legal:

```
count IN -5..5
count IN REVERSE first..last
count IN 0..TRUNC(first/last) * 2
count IN ASCII('A')..ASCII('J')
```

As these examples show, the lower range value does not need to begin at 1 and can be negative. The upper range value can also be negative as long as it is always greater than or equal to the lower range value. Also, the loop counter must always be allowed to increment or decrement by 1. Other languages support a loop counter that can increment or decrement by more than 1; PL/SQL does not. To overcome this limitation, an intermediate variable would have to be provided. For example:

```
DECLARE
    count INTEGER;
    ...
BEGIN
    FOR index IN 1..10 LOOP
        /*
        ** The variable count becomes the counter in the
        ** FOR-LOOP, incremented by 5 for each iteration.
        */
        count := index * 5;
        ...
    END LOOP;
END;
```

Because a range value can be a variable or expression, the range of a FOR-LOOP can be determined at run time. If the run-time variable or expression results in a lower range value that is greater than the upper range value, the loop does not execute, and control passes to the next statement following the END-LOOP statement.

You need not explicitly declare the FOR-LOOP counter in your program. It is declared as a local constant INTEGER within the scope of the loop structure. You can reference its value inside the loop, but it cannot be modified. This protects you from inadvertently modifying the loop counter inside the loop, which can have disastrous side effects. Also, you cannot reference the counter outside the loop. After the loop is exited, the loop counter is undefined and cannot be referenced.

If you explicitly declare a counter variable in your program, the implicit local counter declaration overrides the global declaration. For example:

```
DECLARE
    count   INTEGER;
BEGIN
    FOR count IN 1..50 LOOP -- Local overrides global declaration.
        IF count > 10 THEN ...  -- Refers to loop counter.
    END LOOP;
END;
```

To reference the global variable in this example, you must use a label and dot notation, as follows:

```
<<main>>
DECLARE
    count   INTEGER;
BEGIN
    FOR count IN 1..50 LOOP  -- Local overrides global declaration.
        IF main.count > 10 THEN ... -- Refers to global declaration.
    END LOOP;
END;
```

The same scope rules apply to nested FOR loops. To reference an outer loop counter from a nested loop, you must use a label and dot notation.

If you need to exit a FOR-LOOP before it reaches the end of its range of values, you can use the EXIT or EXIT WHEN statement. For example, the following loop would normally execute 50 times, but as soon as the FETCH fails to return a row, the loop exits whether or not it has iterated 50 times.

```
FOR count IN 1..50 LOOP
    FETCH item_cursor INTO item_rec;
    EXIT WHEN item_cursor%NOTFOUND;
END LOOP;
```

Just as with other LOOP statements, you can use labels to identify loops and refer to them in EXIT statements to exit FOR-LOOP structures and nested loops.

Sequential Control

The conditional and iterative control statements just discussed provide most of the control you will need in your programs. You will seldom need the sequential control statements presented here. Occasionally, however, you may need sequential control to simplify logic or improve readability. Two sequential control statements are provided by PL/SQL: GOTO and NULL.

GOTO Statement

As in C, the GOTO statement allows you to branch unconditionally to another section of your program. You branch to a declared label that is within the scope of the GOTO statement. The label must precede an executable statement or a PL/SQL block. The GOTO statement is used as shown here:

```
BEGIN
   ...
   GOTO label_name;
   ...
   <<label_name>>
   SELECT ...
END;
```

The label does not need to be positioned after the GOTO statement in your program. For example:

```
BEGIN
   ...
   <<label_name>>
   SELECT ...
   ...
   GOTO label_name;
   ...
END;
```

Also, a GOTO statement can branch to a block that encloses the block containing the GOTO because it is within the scope of the GOTO. For example:

```
BEGIN
   ...
   <<label_name>>
   SELECT ...
   ...
   BEGIN
```

```
   . . .
      GOTO label_name;
   END;
   . . .
END;
```

The GOTO statement branches to the first enclosing block in which the referenced label appears.

A GOTO statement does have some restrictions. It cannot:

■ Branch into an IF statement, a LOOP statement, or a subblock

■ Branch from one IF statement clause to another

■ Branch out of a subprogram

■ Branch from an exception handler into the current block

Despite the availability of the GOTO statement, its existence should be ignored if at all possible. Overuse of GOTO statements can result in complex, unstructured code that is hard to understand and maintain. Use GOTOs sparingly.

NULL Statement
The NULL statement is like the CONTINUE statement available in C. This statement specifies no action or a no-operation. It does nothing more than pass control to the next statement.

The NULL statement can be used to improve readability in your programs. For example, you can use the NULL in an IF-THEN-ELSIF statement to specify that no action is to occur for a certain condition but that you have considered that condition in your program. Also, the NULL statement can be used in an exception handler to process unnamed exceptions.

Generally, you can use the NULL statement anywhere you want no action to take place in your program but need a placeholder to satisfy the compiler.

Summary

This chapter discussed PL/SQL, Oracle's procedural language extension to the SQL data language. PL/SQL incorporates many of the features of a modern third-generation language like C or C++. It greatly enhances the power of SQL and is integrated closely with Oracle.

PL/SQL can be used in your application program; it can also be used to create procedures that are then stored in the database. PL/SQL bridges the gap between the application program, the Oracle Server, and the databases you are accessing.

This chapter also covered the basic constructs of this language and the PL/SQL control structures.

CHAPTER 10

Database Access with PL/SQL

This chapter will continue to explore the depths of PL/SQL. It will present the following topics:

- Using cursors with PL/SQL
- Error handling with PL/SQL
- PL/SQL procedures and functions
- Calling stored procedures and functions
- Database triggers
- Packages

Database Access

PL/SQL is specifically designed to integrate closely with the Oracle database system. This chapter will discuss the tools that PL/SQL provides to access the database and process information in your PL/SQL program. It will discuss the SQL commands, functions, and operators that allow your program to manipulate data in the Oracle database. Also, this chapter will discuss database connection, how to manage cursors and transactions, and how to safeguard the consistency of your database.

Support for SQL

In PL/SQL, you can manipulate data in the Oracle database flexibly and safely because PL/SQL supports all SQL data manipulation commands (except EXPLAIN PLAN), transaction management commands, database locking commands, functions, pseudocolumns, and operators. Also, PL/SQL allows you to take advantage of optimizer hints and national language support. However, PL/SQL does not support data definition commands such as CREATE; session control commands such as SET ROLE; or the system control command ALTER SYSTEM.

Data Manipulation SQL

PL/SQL supports all of the data manipulation SQL commands including SELECT, INSERT, UPDATE, and DELETE.

However, PL/SQL does not support the EXPLAIN PLAN command. In PL/SQL, it is not necessary to prefix the SQL statements with the EXEC SQL clause as in Pro*C. Also, it is not necessary to prefix PL/SQL variables with the colon (:) in SQL statements as in Pro*C. You will get compile errors if you do either.

SQL Functions

PL/SQL does not directly support the standard SQL functions. In other words, you cannot use the SQL functions in PL/SQL procedural statements. However, you can use the SQL functions in SQL statements in your PL/SQL programs. The SQL functions include the following group functions: AVG, COUNT, MAX, MIN, STDDEV, SUM, and VARIANCE.

There are two additional group functions, GLB and LUB, that are available only with Trusted Oracle.

SQL Pseudocolumns

As with SQL functions, you can reference the SQL pseudocolumns in SQL statements in your PL/SQL program. However, you cannot reference them in PL/SQL procedural statements. The SQL pseudocolumns return specific data items. The SQL pseudocolumns include CURRVAL, LEVEL, NEXTVAL, ROWID, and ROWNUM.

SQL Operators

PL/SQL allows you to use all the SQL comparison, set, and row operators in SQL statements. Typically, you use comparison operators in the WHERE clause of a data manipulation SQL statement to form selection criteria, which compare one expression to another and always evaluate to TRUE, FALSE, or null. The SQL comparison operators are

- ALL
- ANY
- SOME
- BETWEEN
- EXISTS
- IN
- IS null
- LIKE

You can combine your selection criteria in statements by using the logical operators AND, OR, and NOT to create complex expressions.

Set operators are used to combine the results of two queries into one result. You can use all the set operators in SELECT statements, including INTERSECT, MINUS, UNION, and UNION ALL. Row operators are used to return or reference specific rows in a query or an aggregate operation. You can use all the row operators, including ALL, DISTINCT, and PRIOR.

Database Connection

There is no explicit CONNECT statement in PL/SQL. You can access single or multiple databases on your local or remote computers. You can use database links and synonyms to create location transparency and easy access to remote databases.

Transaction Management

PL/SQL supports all of the transaction management commands including COMMIT, SAVEPOINT, and ROLLBACK.

As in Pro*C, you are still responsible to ensure that the transaction boundaries are correct in your PL/SQL programs. This is the primary way that you can protect the integrity of the database.

The first SQL statement in your program begins a transaction. When one transaction ends, the next SQL statement automatically begins another transaction. Thus, every SQL statement is part of a transaction.

NOTE
A block does not start a transaction, and a transaction does not support a block.

Database Locking

The default implicit Oracle database locking mechanisms work as usual in your PL/SQL program. Also, PL/SQL supports all the explicit database locking mechanisms discussed in Chapter 6, which includes SET TRANSACTION, FOR UPDATE OF, and LOCK TABLE.

As in Pro*C, if you override the default locking mechanisms, you are still responsible to ensure that the mechanisms are employed correctly in your programs.

Cursor Management

Earlier in this chapter you learned about the features of PL/SQL, where the features and advantages of cursors were discussed. Cursors are an inherent structure in PL/SQL. Cursors allow you to easily store and process sets of information in your PL/SQL program.

Remember, in PL/SQL there are two kinds of cursors: implicit and explicit. An implicit cursor is created for each data manipulation SQL statement in your PL/SQL program, including query statements that return only one row. You can create an explicit cursor when you want to process the individual rows of a query that returns more than one row. Remember, the set of rows that result from the query statement associated to a cursor is called the *active set*. An explicit cursor points to the current row in the active set. After you declare and open a cursor, you can FETCH, UPDATE, or DELETE the current row in the active set. Then, you CLOSE the cursor to disable it and free up any allocated system resources.

PL/SQL enhances the management of cursors by providing the cursor FOR loop. A cursor FOR loop replaces the cursor declaration, OPEN, and CLOSE statements. A cursor FOR loop implicitly declares its loop index as a RECORD datatype based on the %ROWTYPE of the cursor. Then, it automatically opens the cursor, repeatedly fetches a row of values from the active set into the fields in the record, and closes the cursor when all rows have been processed. This is useful when you intend to perform similar operations on all the rows in a cursor.

Implicit Cursors

In PL/SQL, an implicit cursor is automatically created for each data manipulation SQL statement not associated with an explicit cursor, even if the statement processes a single row. PL/SQL allows you to reference the implicit cursor associated to the most recently executed SQL statement as the "SQL" cursor. Although the OPEN, FETCH, and CLOSE statements are not used to control the "SQL" cursor, you can still access information about the cursor by referencing attributes, called *cursor attributes,* associated with the cursor.

Implicit Cursor Attributes

In PL/SQL, every cursor (implicit and explicit) has four associated cursor attributes. They are %NOTFOUND, %FOUND, %ROWCOUNT, and %ISOPEN.

These attributes, associated with the implicit "SQL" cursor, can be accessed by appending the attribute name to the implicit cursor name (SQL). The syntax to do this is

```
SQL%<attribute_name>
```

where:

> **SQL** is how the "SQL" cursor is referenced.
>
> **attribute_name** is the name of one of the cursor attributes listed previously.

For example, the %NOTFOUND cursor attribute for the SQL cursor is referenced in the following manner:

```
SQL%NOTFOUND
```

The SQL cursor attributes provide access to information about the execution of SELECT, INSERT, UPDATE, and DELETE statements. These attributes can only be referenced in PL/SQL procedural statements, not in SQL statements.

The value of a cursor attribute always refers to the most recently executed SQL statement, wherever that statement appears in your program. For instance, the last SQL statement may have been executed in a different subblock or subprogram. So, you must be careful when referencing the SQL cursor attributes; they may not reflect the value that you might expect. If you need to access the value of an SQL cursor attribute and use it later in your program, assign its value to a Boolean variable that you can access later in your program. For example:

```
UPDATE item SET item_cost = item_cost - 1.00
    WHERE item_id < 10000;
IF SQL%NOTFOUND THEN   -- reference to SQL cursor attribute
    ...
END IF;
check_item;   -- procedure call
```

In this example, if you had called the **check_item** procedure before the cursor attribute is referenced, the attribute value might be changed due to a different SQL statement in the **check_item** procedure. It is dangerous to assume that no SQL statement occurs between the attribute reference and the procedure call. You should always reference SQL cursor attributes immediately following the intended SQL statement, or assign the SQL cursor attribute to a variable for later reference. For example:

```
UPDATE item SET item_cost = item_cost - 1.00
    WHERE item_id < 10000;
item_not_found := SQL%NOTFOUND; -- assign SQL cursor attribute to
    --variable
check_item;   -- procedure call
IF item_not_found THEN   -- reference Boolean variable
    ...
END IF;
```

NOTE
Before the SQL cursor is created for the first time (after the first SQL statement), the cursor attributes evaluate to null.

Using %NOTFOUND

The SQL cursor attribute %NOTFOUND is used to determine that no rows are processed in an SQL statement. The %NOTFOUND attribute returns the Boolean value TRUE if an INSERT, UPDATE, or DELETE statement affected no rows, or if a SELECT statement returned no rows. Otherwise, %NOTFOUND returns the value FALSE.

The %NOTFOUND attribute can be useful in any situation where you want to report or process a "no data affected" condition. For example, it may be necessary to alter the path of your program if no data is processed in an INSERT, UPDATE, or DELETE operation, or you may want to report this condition to the user.

Be careful when using the %NOTFOUND cursor attribute with the SELECT statement. If a SELECT statement does not return any data, the predefined exception NO_DATA_FOUND is automatically raised, and program control is sent to an exception handler, if an exception handler is present in your program. If you try to check the %NOTFOUND attribute after a SELECT statement, it will be completely skipped when the SELECT statement returns no data. Consider the following example:

```
DECLARE
    cItemName   CHAR(40);
    iItemId   INTEGER := 1000;
BEGIN
    SELECT item_name INTO cItemName    -- might raise NO_DATA_FOUND
        FROM item
        WHERE item_id = iItemId;
    IF SQL%NOTFOUND THEN  -- condition tested only when false
        /*
        ** The statements here are never executed because the IF
        ** statement is never TRUE.
        */
    END IF;

EXCEPTION
    WHEN NO_DATA_FOUND THEN
        ...
END;
```

The %NOTFOUND check is useless because it will always be FALSE when it is checked, or it will be completely skipped. Instead, you should check for the NO_DATA_FOUND exception in the exception handler (exception handlers will be discussed later in this chapter).

If you use an SQL group function in a SELECT statement, the NO_DATA _FOUND exception is never raised. That is because group functions such as AVG and SUM always return a value or a null. Also, in this case, the %NOTFOUND attribute is always FALSE.

Using %FOUND

The %FOUND cursor attribute is the logical opposite of %NOTFOUND. The %FOUND attribute is used to determine if rows are processed in an SQL statement. The %FOUND attribute returns TRUE if an INSERT, UPDATE, or DELETE statement affects one or more rows, or if a SELECT statement returns one row. Otherwise, the %FOUND attribute returns FALSE. If a SELECT statement returns more than one row, the predefined exception TOO_MANY_ROWS is automatically raised, and the %FOUND attribute is set to FALSE.

Using %ROWCOUNT

The %ROWCOUNT attribute is used to determine the number of rows that are processed by an SQL statement. The %ROWCOUNT attribute returns the number of rows affected by an INSERT, UPDATE, or DELETE statement or returned by a SELECT statement. If no rows are affected or returned by an SQL statement, the %ROWCOUNT returns a zero.

If a SELECT statement returns more than one row, the predefined exception TOO_MANY_ROWS is automatically raised and the %ROWCOUNT attribute is set to 1; not the actual number of rows that satisfies the query. In this situation, you should process the TOO_MANY_ROWS exception in an exception handler.

Using %ISOPEN

The %ISOPEN is not applicable to the SQL cursor, because Oracle closes the SQL cursor automatically after executing its associated SQL statement. As a result, %ISOPEN always returns FALSE.

Explicit Cursors

Explicit cursors are used to process individual rows that result from SELECT statements. The results of a cursor SELECT statement can consist of zero, one, or multiple rows, depending upon the query criteria associated with the SELECT statement.

In PL/SQL, a cursor is declared, like a variable, in the DECLARE section of a PL/SQL block, subprogram, or package. When a cursor is declared, you assign it a unique name and specify a SELECT statement. Then you can use commands to open, process, and close the cursor.

After a cursor is declared, it is opened with the OPEN statement. You must OPEN the cursor before the rows in the cursor can be processed. The SELECT statement associated with the cursor is executed when the cursor is opened, which defines the active set associated with the cursor. After a cursor has been opened, you can FETCH rows individually from the cursor, UPDATE rows in the cursor, or DELETE rows from the cursor. After you have processed the rows in the cursor, you release the cursor with the CLOSE statement.

Several cursors can be declared and opened simultaneously (up to a system-defined limit), as long as they are uniquely named. Let's discuss how you process cursors in your PL/SQL programs.

Declaring a Cursor

In PL/SQL, you must declare a cursor in the DECLARE section of any PL/SQL block, subprogram, or package. Forward references are not allowed, so, you must declare a cursor before it can be referenced in a program. When a cursor is declared, it is assigned a unique name and assigned a SELECT statement to define the active set. The active set is not created when the cursor is declared, it is only defined by the SELECT statement.

When the SELECT statement is defined, the table(s) and column(s) that are referenced in the query identify the column(s) that can be referenced in the cursor. The basic syntax to declare a cursor is

```
CURSOR <cursor_name> IS
    SELECT ...
```

where:

> **cursor_name** is a unique identifier used to name and reference the cursor in your program.

> **SELECT**... is any valid SELECT statement used to define the active set.

For example:

```
DECLARE
    CURSOR item_cursor IS
        SELECT retail_price, item_cost, item_id FROM item;
BEGIN
    ...
END;
```

Note that there is no INTO clause in the cursor definition. This is used later on the FETCH statement. In this example, the **retail_price**, **item_cost**, and **item_id** columns from the item table become the columns that can be referenced when the cursor is accessed.

The cursor name is an undeclared identifier, not a PL/SQL variable. The cursor name is used only to name and reference the cursor in your program. Thus, the cursor name cannot be assigned a value or used in any expression. The cursor name can only be used in cursor control statements. Cursor names follow the same scope rules as variables.

The SELECT statement associated to a cursor declaration can reference previously declared variables. For example:

```
DECLARE
    iItemId INTEGER := 10000;
    iFactor  INTEGER := 2;
    CURSOR item_cursor IS
```

```
        SELECT iFactor * retail_price total FROM item
            WHERE item_id = identifier;
BEGIN
   iFactor := iFactor + 1;
   ...
END;
```

In this example, the specified item **retail_price** is multiplied by a factor of 3. Variables are referenced at OPEN time.

Declaring Parameterized Cursors

In PL/SQL, you can declare cursors that can accept input parameters. The input parameters are used to pass values to the WHERE clause of the SELECT statement associated with the cursor, when the cursor is opened. A cursor parameter can be used in the SELECT statement wherever a constant can appear. The syntax to declare a parameterized cursor is

```
CURSOR <cursor_name> [(parameter [,parameter, ...])] IS
   SELECT ...
       WHERE <column_name> = parameter[,...];
```

where:

> **cursor_name** is a unique identifier used to name and reference the cursor in your program.
>
> **column_name** is a reference to a valid column name that is used in the WHERE clause and compared to the cursor parameter value.
>
> **parameter** is an input parameter to the cursor SELECT statement WHERE clause and is compared to a column. A parameter is defined with the syntax

```
<variable_name> [IN] <datatype> [{:= | DEFAULT} value]
```

where:

> **variable_name** is the name given to the input variable. This variable name is used to reference the variable in the SELECT statement WHERE clause.
>
> **IN** is an optional parameter mode designator indicating that the parameter is an input parameter. By default, all cursor parameters are input parameters, so the IN clause is redundant but can improve readability.
>
> **datatype** is any valid PL/SQL datatype that is compatible with the cursor parameter's usage in the SELECT statement.
>
> **value** is an assigned default value for the parameter. The default value can be a literal, a previously declared and initialized variable or constant, or an expression that references previously defined and initialized variables or constants.

For example:

```
DECLARE
    CURSOR item_cursor (
        iItemId INTEGER := 1000,
        cItemName IN CHAR(40)) IS
        SELECT retail_price, item_cost, item_id
            FROM item
            WHERE item_id = iItemId AND item_name = cItemName;
BEGIN
    ...
END;
```

In this example, the parameters **iItemId** and **cItemName** can be used to pass values to the cursor SELECT statement WHERE clause when the cursor is opened (to be discussed in a moment). As the example shows, you can initialize cursor parameters to default values. That way, you can pass some value to the actual cursor parameters, without being required to pass values to all of the parameters. If you pass a value to an actual cursor parameter, it overrides the default value assigned to that parameter. If you do not pass a value to an actual cursor parameter, you accept the default value associated to that parameter.

The scope of a cursor parameter is local only to the cursor, meaning that a cursor parameter can be referenced only within the SELECT statement associated to the cursor declaration. The values passed to the cursor parameters are used by the associated SELECT statement when the cursor is OPENed.

Opening a Cursor

After a cursor has been declared, it must be opened before it can be referenced in your program. A cursor is opened with the OPEN statement. When a cursor is opened, the SELECT statement associated with the cursor is executed, and the cursor's active set is created. Remember, the active set consists of all rows that meet the SELECT statement criteria. The basic syntax to OPEN a cursor is

```
OPEN <cursor_name>;
```

where:

> **cursor_name** is the name of the cursor that was previously declared in the
> DECLARE section of the PL/SQL block, subprogram, or package.

For example:

```
DECLARE
    CURSOR item_cursor IS
        SELECT retail_price, item_cost, item_id FROM item;
BEGIN
    OPEN item_cursor;
```

```
    . . .
END;
```

The active set is defined when the cursor is declared, and it is created when the cursor is opened. The rows in the active set are not retrieved until the FETCH statement is executed. Any variables referenced in the cursor are evaluated now.

Passing Cursor Parameters   If a cursor is declared with defined parameters, you can pass values for those parameters to the cursor SELECT statement when the cursor is opened. The syntax to pass parameters when a cursor is opened is

```
OPEN <cursor_name> [(value, [value, ...])];
```

where:

> **cursor_name** is the name of the parameterized cursor that was previously declared in the DECLARE section of the PL/SQL block, subprogram, or package.
>
> **value** is the parameter value that is used in the cursor SELECT statement when the cursor is opened. **value** can be a literal, constant, variable, or expression, all of which must result in a value that is compatible with the declared parameter datatype.

For example:

```
DECLARE
    iInputItemId INTEGER;
    cInputItemName CHAR(40);
    CURSOR item_cursor (
        iItemId IN INTEGER := 1000,
        cItemName IN CHAR(40)) IS
        SELECT retail_price, item_cost, item_id
        FROM item
        WHERE item_id <= iItemId AND item_name LIKE cItemName;
BEGIN
    iInputItemId := 10000;
    cInputItemName := 'Computer%';
    OPEN item_cursor (iInputItemId, cInputItemName);
    . . .
END;
```

Remember that the cursor parameters are local only to the cursor SELECT statement. To avoid confusion, use unique names that are different from the formal cursor parameter declarations, for the variables that are used to pass values to the cursor parameters. Also, unless the intent is to accept a default value assigned when a cursor parameter is declared, a value should be passed to each corresponding cursor parameter in the OPEN statement.

If a cursor parameter is declared with a default value, a value need not be passed to that parameter when the cursor is opened. However, if the cursor parameter is not declared with a default value, a value is required to be passed when the cursor is opened.

The rules to pass values to cursor parameters are the same as those for procedures and functions (see the "Procedures and Functions" section later in this chapter).

Fetching with a Cursor

When a cursor is opened, the SELECT statement associated with the cursor is executed, and the active set is created. However, to get access to the rows in the active set, they must first be retrieved. The FETCH statement is used to retrieve a row in the active set one at a time. Each time the FETCH statement is executed, the cursor advances to the next row in the active set and retrieves it. The syntax to retrieve a row with the FETCH statement is

```
FETCH <cursor_name> INTO <variable_name1>, <variable_name2>[, ...];
```

where:

> **cursor_name** is the name of the cursor that is previously declared in the DECLARE section of the PL/SQL block, subprogram, or package and opened by an OPEN statement.

> **variable_name** is the name of a variable to which a column value is assigned. This value corresponds to a column, pseudocolumn, or column expression identified in the SELECT statement associated to the cursor declaration. The variable datatype must be compatible with the corresponding database column, pseudocolumn, or column expression.

There must be a variable specified in the INTO list of the FETCH statement for each corresponding column value declared in the SELECT statement associated with the cursor declaration. For example, a typical use of a cursor with the FETCH statement is

```
DECLARE
    iItemId INTEGER;
    fPrice NUMBER(10,2);
    fCost NUMBER(10,2);
    CURSOR item_cursor IS
        SELECT retail_price, item_cost, item_id FROM item;
BEGIN
    OPEN item_cursor;
```

```
   LOOP
       FETCH item_cursor INTO fPrice, fCost, iItemId;
       EXIT WHEN item_cursor%NOTFOUND;

       ...
   END LOOP;
END;
```

Notice the use of **fPrice**, **fCost**, and **iItemId** in the FETCH statement, which corresponds to the **retail_price**, **item_cost**, and **item_id** columns referenced in the cursor SELECT statement.

To change the active set in a cursor or the values of the variables referenced in the cursor SELECT statement, you must release the cursor with the CLOSE statement and reOPEN the cursor (with the cursor parameters set to their new values, if applicable).

Explicit Cursor Attributes

As we discussed previously regarding the implicit cursor, explicit cursors have the same set of cursor attributes: %NOTFOUND, %FOUND, %ROWCOUNT, and %ISOPEN.

However, the explicit cursor attributes are used in a different manner and for somewhat different purposes than the implicit cursor attributes. The explicit cursor attributes let you access useful information about the status of an explicit cursor. You can reference the explicit cursor attributes in PL/SQL procedural statements but not in SQL statements. The syntax to access an explicit cursor attribute is

```
<cursor_name>%<attribute_name>
```

where:

> **cursor_name** is the name of a declared and opened cursor.

> **attribute_name** is the name of one of the explicit cursor attributes.

Let's discuss how you can use these attributes in your programs.

Using %NOTFOUND   The %NOTFOUND cursor attribute is used to determine whether a row is retrieved after a FETCH statement is executed on a cursor. If a row is retrieved when the FETCH statement is executed, the %NOTFOUND attribute is set to the Boolean value FALSE. If no rows are left in the cursor and the FETCH statement does not retrieve a row, the %NOTFOUND attribute is set to TRUE. The FETCH statement is expected to eventually reach the end of the active set, so no exception is raised when no more rows are retrieved (the active set is empty).

From a previous example, you can see that the %NOTFOUND attribute is useful to determine when the active set is empty and the cursor is finished processing.

```
DECLARE
    iItemId INTEGER;
    fPrice NUMBER(10,2);
    fCost NUMBER(10,2);
    CURSOR item_cursor IS
        SELECT retail_price, item_cost, item_id FROM item;
BEGIN
    OPEN item_cursor;
    LOOP
        FETCH item_cursor INTO fPrice, fCost, iItemId;
        EXIT WHEN item_cursor%NOTFOUND;
        ...
    END LOOP;
END;
```

Before the first FETCH statement is executed, the %NOTFOUND attribute is assigned null. If the FETCH statement encounters an error, this will raise an exception and end the loop. This is because the EXIT WHEN condition will be null (not TRUE or FALSE) until the FETCH statement is executed successfully the first time. It is much safer to use the following statement when checking for the end of the active set when using a loop structure as shown in the previous example:

```
EXIT WHEN item_cursor%NOTFOUND OR item_cursor%NOTFOUND IS null;
```

Multiple cursors can be opened simultaneously, and the %NOTFOUND attribute can be used for each cursor individually. Also, if the %NOTFOUND attribute is referenced for a cursor that is not open, the predefined exception INVALID_CURSOR is raised.

Using %FOUND   As with the implicit cursor, the %FOUND attribute is the logical opposite of the %NOTFOUND attribute. After an explicit cursor is OPEN but before the first FETCH statement, the %FOUND attribute is assigned null. After the first FETCH statement, the %FOUND attribute is assigned TRUE if a row is retrieved and FALSE if no row is retrieved.

Multiple cursors can be opened simultaneously, and the %FOUND attribute can be used for each cursor individually. Also, if the %FOUND attribute is referenced for a cursor that is not open, the predefined exception INVALID_ CURSOR is raised.

Using %ROWCOUNT   The %ROWCOUNT attribute is used to determine the number of rows that have been FETCHed from a cursor's active set. It is not the number of rows that are in the active set. When you open a cursor, the %ROWCOUNT attribute is assigned zero, because no rows have been FETCHed from the active set. Therefore, before the first FETCH statement is executed, the %ROWCOUNT attribute returns a zero. After each successful FETCH statement that retrieves a row from the active set, the %ROWCOUNT attribute is incremented by 1. Thus, the %ROWCOUNT attribute returns the number of rows FETCHed from a cursor to that point in time.

Multiple cursors can be opened simultaneously, and the %ROWCOUNT attribute can be used for each cursor individually. Also, if the %ROWCOUNT attribute is referenced for a cursor that is not open, the predefined exception INVALID_CURSOR is raised.

Using %ISOPEN   The %ISOPEN attribute is used to determine whether a declared cursor is open. If a cursor is open, the %ISOPEN attribute is assigned TRUE. Otherwise, it is assigned FALSE. The %ISOPEN attribute is useful in situations where a cursor may have been closed in a previous operation, for example:

```
IF item_cursor%ISOPEN THEN    -- cursor is open
   ...
ELSE    -- cursor is closed, so open it
   OPEN item_cursor;
END IF;
```

Closing a Cursor

When the rows of a cursor have been processed, the cursor must be released to free up system resources used by the cursor. The CLOSE statement is used to release a cursor. The CLOSE statement disables the cursor, and frees up system resources; the active set associated to the cursor becomes undefined. The syntax to close a cursor is simply:

```
CLOSE <cursor_name>;
```

where:

        cursor_name is the name of a previously declared and opened cursor.

After a cursor has been closed, it can be reOPENed. Any other operation on a closed cursor raises the predefined exception INVALID_CURSOR. The following is a complete example of processing a cursor:

```
DECLARE
    iItemId INTEGER;
    fPrice NUMBER(10,2);
    fCost NUMBER(10,2);
    CURSOR item_cursor IS
        SELECT retail_price, item_cost, item_id FROM item;
```

```
BEGIN
   OPEN item_cursor;
   LOOP
      FETCH item_cursor INTO fPrice, fCost, iItemId;
      EXIT WHEN item_cursor%NOTFOUND;
      ...
   END LOOP;
   CLOSE item_cursor;
END;
```

Using FOR UPDATE OF and CURRENT

If your intent is to update or delete the rows in a cursor, you must first exclusively lock all the rows in the active set to allow the rows to be exclusively modified by your program. This protects you from simultaneous modifications by other users and protects other users from your modifications until they are complete. The FOR UPDATE clause is used to specify that the rows in the active set of a cursor are to be locked for modification. This is done with the following syntax:

```
CURSOR <cursor_name> IS
   SELECT <column_name>[, ...] FROM ...
      FOR UPDATE [OF <column_name>[, ...]];
```

where:

cursor_name is a unique identifier used to name and reference the cursor in your program.

SELECT... is any valid SELECT statement used to define the active set.

column_name is a list of valid column names selected from a single table (only single tables can be referenced in a SELECT statement using FOR UPDATE OF).

FOR UPDATE OF specifies that the rows of the active set are to be exclusively locked when the cursor is opened and specifies the column names that can be updated.

The FOR UPDATE OF clause must be used in the cursor declaration statement whenever UPDATE or DELETE are to be used after rows are FETCHed from a cursor. The syntax to use the CURRENT OF clause with the UPDATE statement is

```
UPDATE <table_name> SET <column_name> = expression[, ...]
   WHERE CURRENT OF <cursor_name>;
```

where:

table_name is the table referenced in the cursor SELECT statement and in which the columns are to be modified by the UPDATE statement.

column_name is a valid column name that is to be modified by the UPDATE statement.

expression is any valid assignment expression used to assign a value to the referenced column.

cursor_name is a unique identifier from which the row being updated was previously fetched.

The syntax to use the CURRENT OF clause with the DELETE statement is

```
DELETE table_name WHERE CURRENT OF cursor_name;
```

where:

table_name is the table referenced in the cursor SELECT statement and from which the columns are to be deleted by the DELETE statement.

cursor_name is a unique identifier from which the row being deleted was previously fetched.

In the following example, a row is fetched from a cursor and updated or deleted depending upon the value of the retail price in the table:

```
DECLARE
    iItemId INTEGER;
    fPrice NUMBER(10,2);
    fCost NUMBER(10,2);
    CURSOR item_cursor IS
        SELECT retail_price, item_cost, item_id FROM item
            FOR UPDATE OF retail_price, item_cost;
BEGIN
    OPEN item_cursor;
    LOOP
        FETCH item_cursor INTO fPrice, fCost, iItemId;
        EXIT WHEN item_cursor%NOTFOUND or
            item_cursor%NOTFOUND IS null;

        /*
        ** If the profit on an item is greater than 10% of the
        ** retail price, reduce the retail price by 10%.
        */
        IF (fPrice - fCost) > (fPrice * 0.10) THEN
            UPDATE item SET retail_price = fPrice - fPrice * 0.10
                WHERE CURRENT OF item_cursor;

        /*
        ** If the profit on an item is less than or equal to 10%
        ** but is still greater than zero, set the retail price
        ** equal to the item cost plus 5%.
        */
```

```
    ELSIF ((fPrice - fCost) <= (fPrice * 0.10)) AND
        ((fPrice - fCost) > 0) THEN
        UPDATE item SET retail_price = fCost + fCost * 0.05
            WHERE CURRENT OF item_cursor;

    /*
    ** If there is no profit on an item, delete it from the
    ** database.
    */
    ELSE
        DELETE item WHERE CURRENT OF item_cursor;
    END IF;
END LOOP;

COMMIT;    -- Commit the transaction
CLOSE item_cursor;    -- Close the cursor

EXCEPTION    -- Exception handling will be discussed later in the
    -- chapter.


    WHEN OTHERS THEN
        ROLLBACK;
END;
```

Notice the use of the COMMIT statement to complete the transaction. The modifications to the active set in a cursor are not permanent in the database until a COMMIT statement is executed.

Another item to note is that the locks on the rows in the active set (as a result of the FOR UPDATE OF clause) are active when a cursor is opened, not when each row is fetched. The row locks are held until the transaction is committed or rolled back. Note that the COMMIT is after the loop.

Cursor FOR Loops

PL/SQL provides an effective feature to help simplify the management of cursors. This feature is the cursor FOR loop. The cursor FOR loop can be used in any situation where the rows in the active set of a cursor are to be repeatedly processed in a looping manner. A cursor FOR loop simplifies all aspects of processing a cursor in this manner.

The syntax to declare and process a cursor in a cursor FOR loop is

```
DECLARE
    CURSOR <cursor_name> IS
        SELECT ... FROM ...;
BEGIN
    FOR <record_name> IN <cursor_name> LOOP
        ...
    END LOOP;
    ...
END;
```

where:

> **cursor_name** is a unique identifier used to name and reference the cursor in your program.
>
> **SELECT**... is any valid SELECT statement used to define the active set.
>
> **record_name** is the cursor FOR loop index implicitly declared as a record type of %ROWTYPE.

First, the cursor is declared just like any other explicit cursor in the DECLARE section. Second, in the FOR loop declaration, the FOR loop index is uniquely named and implicitly declared as a record of type %ROWTYPE. This index RECORD variable consists of the columns referenced in the cursor select statement. Third, also in the FOR loop declaration, the cursor is implicitly opened for processing. No explicit OPEN statement is required.

Fourth, inside the FOR loop, the column values for each row in the active set can be referenced by the FOR loop index with dot notation in any procedural statement or SQL statement. The sequence of statements inside the loop is executed once for each row that satisfies the cursor select statement.

Fifth, when the end of the active set is reached, the FOR loop implicitly closes the cursor and exits the FOR loop. No explicit CLOSE statement is required. This is true even if you use an EXIT or GOTO statement to leave the loop prematurely, or if an exception is raised inside the loop. A COMMIT statement is still required to complete the operation.

From the previous example, you can see how the cursor FOR loop can be used to simplify processing:

```
DECLARE
    iItemId INTEGER;
    fPrice NUMBER(10,2);
    fCost NUMBER(10,2);
    CURSOR item_cursor IS
        SELECT retail_price, item_cost, item_id FROM item
            FOR UPDATE OF retail_price, item_cost;
BEGIN
    FOR item_rec IN item_cursor LOOP
```

```
     /*
     ** If the profit on an item is greater than 10% of the
     ** retail price, reduce the retail price by 10%.
     */
   IF (item_rec.retail_price - item_rec.item_cost) >
         (item_rec.retail_price * 0.10) THEN
         UPDATE item SET retail_price =
             item_rec.retail_price -
             item_rec.retail_price * 0.10
     WHERE CURRENT OF item_cursor;

     /*
     ** If the profit on an item is less than or equal to 10%
     ** but is still greater than zero, set the retail price
     ** equal to the item cost plus 5%.
     */
     ELSIF ((item_rec.retail_price - item_rec.item_cost) <=
         (item_rec.retail_price * 0.10)) AND
         ((item_rec.retail_price - item_rec.item_cost) > 0) THEN
         UPDATE item SET retail_price =
             item_rec.item_cost + item_rec.item_cost * 0.05
             WHERE CURRENT OF item_cursor;

     /*
     ** If there is no profit on an item, delete it from the
     ** database.
     */
     ELSE
         DELETE item WHERE CURRENT OF item_cursor;
     END IF;
   END LOOP;

   COMMIT;    -- Commit the transaction

EXCEPTION    -- Exception handling will be discussed later in the
   -- chapter.
   WHEN OTHERS THEN
       ROLLBACK;
END;
```

Note that before each iteration of the cursor FOR loop, the column values from the current row of the cursor's active set are fetched into the implicitly declared record **item_rec**. Then, the column values are referenced with dot notation inside the cursor FOR loop. The **item_rec** record is defined only inside the FOR loop. You cannot refer to its fields outside the loop. As this example illustrates, the cursor FOR loop clearly simplifies the processing of a cursor processed in this manner.

Using Aliases   The fields in the implicitly declared FOR loop record index hold column values from the most recently fetched row. These fields are assigned the same names as the corresponding columns referenced in the cursor select list. What happens if a select list item is defined as a column expression? For example:

```
DECLARE
   CURSOR item_cursor IS
      SELECT retail_price, item_cost, retail_price - item_cost
         FROM item;
BEGIN
   FOR item_rec IN item_cursor LOOP
      ...
   END LOOP;
END;
```

In this example, you could not reference the select list expression for **retail_price - item_cost**. In fact, you would receive an error. In this case, you must define an alias for the select list expression. The following example corrects this:

```
DECLARE CURSOR item_cursor IS
   SELECT retail_price, item_cost, retail_price - item_cost profit
      FROM item;
BEGIN
   FOR item_rec IN item_cursor LOOP
      IF item_rec.profit > (item_rec.retail_price * 0.10) THEN
         ...
      END IF;
      ...
   END LOOP;
END;
```

Passing Parameters   PL/SQL allows you to pass parameters to a cursor used in a cursor FOR loop. This is done in much the same manner as any other explicit cursor. Observe the following example:

```
DECLARE
   iInputItemId INTEGER;
   cInputItemName CHAR(40);
   CURSOR item_cursor (
```

```
        iItemId INTEGER := 1000,
        cItemName IN CHAR(40)) IS
        SELECT retail_price, item_cost, item_id
            FROM item
            WHERE item_id <= iItemId AND item_name = cItemName;
BEGIN
    iInputItemId := 10000;
    cInputItemName := 'Computer%';
    FOR item_rec IN item_cursor(iInputItemId, cInputItemName) LOOP
        ...
    END LOOP;
    ...
END;
```

Error Handling

Chapter 7 discussed the reasons to robustly handle errors in an application program. You saw that proper error handling can bullet-proof a program, which provides the look and feel of robustness and quality. Also, you learned about the mechanisms available in embedded SQL to help process errors. PL/SQL provides a similar set of tools to aid the handling of errors encountered in your PL/SQL programs.

PL/SQL provides features to easily detect and handle two kinds of error conditions: predefined system errors and user-defined application program errors. In PL/SQL, error conditions are called exceptions. Exceptions are processed in a specific section of a program designated to handle these exceptions, called exception handlers. When an error is encountered in a program, an exception is raised, which means normal execution stops, and control is transferred to an exception handler, where the exception can be processed.

Why Exceptions?

PL/SQL exceptions provide many advantages. If you do not use exceptions, after each SQL command you must check for error conditions. For example, when using the SELECT statement, the "no data found" error may occur:

```
BEGIN
    SELECT ...
    IF SQLCODE = 100 THEN    -- check for "no data found" error
        ...
    END IF
```

```
    SELECT ...
    IF SQLCODE = 100 THEN      -- check for "no data found" error
      ...
    END IF

    SELECT ...
    IF SQLCODE = 100 THEN      -- check for "no data found" error
      ...
    END IF
    ...
END;
```

Notice how an error check must follow each SQL statement; error processing is intermixed with normal processing. Also, this manner of error checking is not robust, because it is difficult and clumsy to check for and process all errors that might result from the select statement. What if an error condition is missed? If you neglect to check for an error condition, the error goes undetected and is likely to cause other, seemingly unrelated errors.

Exceptions provide the mechanism to handle multiple errors conveniently, without the need to intermix the error checks with normal code and to process errors in a designated area in a program. Observe the previous example using exceptions:

```
BEGIN
    SELECT ...
    SELECT ...
    SELECT ...
    ...
EXCEPTION
    WHEN NO_DATA_FOUND THEN    -- "no data found" exception handler
      ...
    WHEN OTHERS THEN
      ...
END;
```

Notice how the use of exceptions can improve the readability of a program and how you can capture all error conditions with the OTHERS clause in the exception handler. This provides a mechanism to process all expected errors as well as those that are unforeseen.

In PL/SQL, a set of exceptions are predefined for the common Oracle system errors that can occur at run time. When an Oracle system error occurs at run time, the corresponding predefined exception is implicitly raised, which means normal execution stops and control is automatically transferred to a specified exception handler in the program. For example, if you try to divide a number by zero, the predefined exception ZERO_DIVIDE is implicitly raised, and program control is transferred to the exception handler designated to process that exception.

In PL/SQL, you can declare a set of user-defined exceptions that can be customized to handle error conditions that are specific to your application program. When one of these error conditions occurs at run time, the appropriate user-defined exception can be explicitly raised. Then, just as with predefined exceptions, normal execution stops and control is transferred to the exception handler designated to process that user-defined exception. Thus, you can create a standard set of exception handlers that can be used throughout your program. Let's discuss predefined exceptions and user-defined exceptions and determine how they are handled in a PL/SQL program.

Predefined Exceptions

PL/SQL provides a set of predefined exceptions that can be used to process internal Oracle system errors. Every Oracle system error has an associated number. However, exceptions must be handled by name. Therefore, predefined exceptions are used to detect and handle Oracle system errors that occur internally at program run time.

Oracle system errors occur when an Oracle system rule is violated, such as when there's a duplicate index value, an invalid cursor, and so on. Oracle system errors also occur when a system resource is exceeded, as with an out of memory error, a resource time-out, and so on. Only the most common Oracle system errors are predefined as exceptions. Table 10-1 is a list of the predefined exceptions.

Appendix E contains a description of all the Oracle system errors and the conditions under which they occur. This appendix will help you determine where you need to provide specific processing for any of these predefined exceptions—for example, processing "no data found" conditions.

This list only contains predefined exceptions for the most common Oracle system errors. How do you handle other system errors? PL/SQL provides the predefined exception called OTHERS. The OTHERS exception is used to capture all the exceptions not explicitly processed in an exception handler. The use of the OTHERS exception will be discussed later in this section.

User-Defined Exceptions

In many situations, error conditions exist that are unique to a specific application program. These error conditions are not covered by the internal Oracle system errors or the predefined exceptions. Also, it may be necessary to process an internal

Exception Name	Oracle Error	SQLCODE Value
CURSOR_ALREADY_OPEN	ORA-06511	−6511
DUP_VAL_ON_INDEX	ORA-00001	−1
INVALID_CURSOR	ORA-01001	−1001
INVALID_NUMBER	ORA-01722	−1722
LOGIN_DENIED	ORA-01017	−1017
NO_DATA_FOUND	ORA-01403	+100
NOT_LOGGED_ON	ORA-01012	−1012
PROGRAM_ERROR	ORA-06501	−6501
STORAGE_ERROR	ORA-06500	−6500
TIMEOUT_ON_RESOURCE	ORA-00051	−51
TOO_MANY_ROWS	ORA-01422	−1422
TRANSACTION_BACKED_OUT	ORA-00061	−61
VALUE_ERROR	ORA-06502	−6502
ZERO_DIVIDE	ORA-01476	−1476

TABLE 10-1. *Predefined exceptions*

Oracle system error that is not a predefined exception. In either case, PL/SQL provides the mechanisms to declare user-defined exceptions and process them in a PL/SQL program. Predefined exceptions are declared and raised implicitly as part of the Oracle system. User-defined exceptions must be explicitly declared and explicitly raised to be processed in a PL/SQL program.

Declaring User-Defined Exceptions
User-defined exceptions are declared much like variables, in the DECLARE section of any PL/SQL anonymous block, subprogram, or package. When a user-defined exception is declared, it is assigned a unique name, which is used to reference the exception in a program. The syntax to declare a user-defined exception is

```
<exception_name> EXCEPTION;
```

where:

> **exception_name** is a unique name used to identify the user-defined exception throughout an anonymous block, subprogram, subblock, or package.

In the following example, a user-defined exception is defined to report when a customer exceeds a credit limit.

```
DECLARE
    over_credit_limit EXCEPTION;
    fTotalSale NUMBER(10,2);
    fSalesTaxRate CONSTANT := 0.06;
    nItemCount INTEGER := 10;
    iItemId INTEGER := 10000;
    fCost NUMBER (10,2);
    fCreditLimit NUMBER (10,2);
    fCreditBalance NUMBER (10,2);
    iCustId INTEGER := 100;
BEGIN
    SELECT item_cost INTO fCost FROM item
        WHERE item_id = iItemId;
    SELECT limit, balance INTO fCreditLimit, fCreditBalance

        FROM credit
        WHERE customer_id = iCustId;

    fTotalSale := fCost * nItemCount * fSalesTaxRate;
    IF fTotalSale + fCreditBalance > fCreditLimit THEN
        RAISE over_credit_limit;
    END IF;

EXCEPTION
    WHEN over_credit_limit THEN
        -- Process credit limit exceeded for customer
    WHEN NO_DATA_FOUND THEN
        -- Process invalid item identifier or customer identifier
    WHEN OTHERS THEN
        -- Process all other exceptions
END;
```

Although user-defined exceptions are declared in the same manner as variables, exceptions can only be used to handle error conditions, not to process data. Exceptions cannot be assigned data values and cannot be used in SQL statements. However, the same scope rules apply to exceptions that apply to variables.

Exceptions cannot be declared twice in the same block, but they can be declared in separate blocks. Exceptions declared in a block are considered local to that block and global to all its subblocks. An enclosing block can reference only local or global exceptions, not exceptions declared in a subblock. If an exception is declared globally and it is redeclared locally in a subblock, the local exception declaration overrides the global declaration. Therefore, a global exception that is redeclared in a subblock can only be referenced in the subblock if the global exception is declared in a labeled block or subprogram.

Unless it is absolutely necessary, it is always best to uniquely declare user-defined exceptions throughout a program to improve readability, avoid confusion, and prevent unhandled exceptions.

PL/SQL declares the predefined exceptions globally in the Oracle provided package called STANDARD. This is why you do not need to declare them in your program. A predefined exception can be redeclared by simply redeclaring a predefined exception as a local exception. However, this practice is error prone and is strongly discouraged. If a predefined exception is locally redeclared, the global declaration is overridden, which causes the internal error condition for the predefined exception to be missed.

Declaring User-Defined System Exceptions

Because PL/SQL only supplies a limited set of predefined exceptions for the internal Oracle system errors, PL/SQL provides a mechanism to declare user-defined exceptions to handle the other unnamed Oracle system errors.

As discussed previously, the OTHERS exception can be used to capture all exceptions that are not explicitly handled. However, the OTHERS exception does not allow you to handle specific Oracle system errors of interest in your programs. For this reason, PL/SQL has provided what is called a *pragma statement* to declare a name for any unnamed Oracle system error.

A *pragma statement* is a compiler directive (or instruction) that is processed at compile time, not at run time. This statement directs the compiler to perform a special action. Pragma statements do not alter the meaning of a program, they provide information to the compiler. In this case, the pragma statement EXCEPTION_INIT tells the compiler to associate an exception name with an Oracle system error number. When that Oracle system error occurs, you can provide an exception handler to process that specific exception in a program.

Just like user-defined exceptions, the pragma statement EXCEPTION_INIT is declared in any PL/SQL anonymous block, subprogram, or package by use of the following syntax:

```
PRAGMA EXCEPTION_INIT(exception_name, error_number);
```

where:

> **exception_name** is the name of a previously declared user-defined exception used to identify the exception in a program.

> **error_number** is any valid Oracle system error defined in Appendix E.

The pragma statement must appear somewhere after the **user_defined** exception declaration in the same declarative part of a block, subprogram, or package. For example, to declare a user-defined exception for the Oracle system error for privilege violations:

```
DECLARE
   insufficient_privileges  EXCEPTION;
   PRAGMA EXCEPTION_INIT(insufficient_privileges, -1031);
BEGIN
   ...
EXCEPTION
   WHEN insufficient_privileges THEN
      -- handle the error
END;
```

User-defined exceptions defined for internal Oracle system errors are raised implicitly by the system when that error is encountered. It is not necessary to explicitly raise such an exception (though you can if you like).

Raising User-Defined Exceptions

All predefined exceptions and user-defined exceptions that are associated with an Oracle system error with the EXCEPTION_INIT statement are implicitly raised at run time when the system encounters one of these system error conditions. However, other application specific user-defined exceptions must be explicitly raised when the associated error condition is detected. Such a user-defined exception is raised by calling the RAISE statement. The syntax to RAISE a user-defined exception is simply:

```
RAISE <exception_name>;
```

where:

> **exception_name** is any previously declared user-defined exception, not used in an EXCEPTION_INIT statement.

The RAISE statement is used after an error condition has been detected. You stop the program's normal processing and transfer control to an exception handler. Therefore, explicit checks for the error condition associated with a user-defined exception must exist in a program. When the error condition is detected, the user-defined exception is raised, and program control is sent to an exception handler. Thus, user-defined exceptions should be used only for error conditions that make it undesirable or impossible to continue normal processing. The RAISE

statement can be used for a user-defined exception anywhere within the scope of
that exception. The following example shows how a user-defined exception is
raised:

```
DECLARE
    over_credit_limit EXCEPTION;
    fTotalSale NUMBER(10,2);
    fSalesTaxRate CONSTANT := 0.06;
    nItemCount INTEGER := 10;
    iItemId INTEGER := 10000;
    fCost NUMBER (10,2);
    fCreditLimit NUMBER (10,2);
    fCreditBalance NUMBER (10,2);
    iCustId INTEGER := 100;
BEGIN
    SELECT item_cost INTO fCost FROM item
        WHERE item_id = iItemId;
    SELECT limit, balance INTO fCreditLimit, fCreditBalance
        FROM credit
        WHERE customer_id = iCustId;

    fTotalSale := fCost * nItemCount * fSalesTaxRate;
    IF fTotalSale + fCreditBalance > fCreditLimit THEN
        RAISE over_credit_limit;
    END IF;

EXCEPTION
    WHEN over_credit_limit THEN
        -- Process credit limit exceeded for customer
    WHEN NO_DATA_FOUND THEN
        -- Process invalid item identifier or customer identifier
    WHEN OTHERS THEN
        -- Process all other exceptions
END;
```

Handling Exceptions

Whether a predefined exception is implicitly raised by the system or a user-defined
exception is explicitly raised in a program, they are handled in exactly the same
manner. When an exception is raised, either implicitly or explicitly, normal
program execution stops, and control is transferred to the exception part of the
program. You've seen the basic usage of the exception part of a program through

previous examples. Here is a formal discussion of how the exception part of a program is used. The syntax for the exception part of a program is

```
EXCEPTION
    WHEN exception_name1 THEN    -- first exception handler
        statement_sequence1
    WHEN exception_name2 THEN    -- second exception handler
        statement_sequence2
    ...
    WHEN exception_namen THEN    -- nth exception handler
        statement_sequencen
    WHEN OTHERS THEN             -- optional exception handler
        catch_all_statement_sequence
END;
```

where:

> **exception_name** is the name of a predefined exception or previously declared and raised user-defined exception. Multiple exceptions can be handled in multiple successive WHEN statements. An exception name can appear only once in the exception part of a program.

> **statement_sequence** is a sequence of statements used to process the exception and perform any operations in reaction to the error condition, such as free memory, close cursors, and roll back transactions.

> **OTHERS** is an optional exception handler used to catch all exceptions not explicitly handled previously.

The previous example shows how exceptions can be easily handled in PL/SQL.

A block can have only one OTHERS exception handler. Use of the OTHERS exception handler guarantees that no exception will go unhandled. The error reporting functions SQLCODE and SQLERRM are especially useful in the OTHERS handler because they return the Oracle error code and message text. Alternately, you can use the pragma statement EXCEPTION_INIT to associate user-defined exceptions with Oracle system errors.

NOTE
The EXCEPTION part of the block is optional.

When an exception is raised and control is transferred to the exception part of a program, control cannot return to the execution part of the program. Multiple exceptions can be handled with the same sequence of statements by simply separating the exception names in the WHEN statement with the keyword OR.

For example:

```
EXCEPTION
    WHEN over_credit_limit OR no_credit THEN
        -- Process credit limit exceeded for customer
    WHEN NO_DATA_FOUND THEN
        -- Process invalid item identifier or customer identifier
    WHEN OTHERS THEN
        ...
```

If any of the exceptions in the WHEN statement are raised, the same sequence of statements is executed. The OTHERS exception handler cannot appear in the WHEN statement if the keyword OR is used.

The normal scope rules for PL/SQL variables apply to the exception part of a program. Only local and global variables can be referenced in an exception handler. However, when an exception is raised inside a cursor FOR loop, the cursor is closed implicitly before the exception handler is invoked. The values of explicit cursor attributes and the cursor record index are not available in the exception handler.

Reraising Exceptions

The most effective method to decompose a program into its logical parts is to use modular techniques. With modular techniques, the program is organized into higher-level user interface programs and lower-level subprograms that provide services for the user. In this environment, when errors are encountered in a lower-level subprogram, it is necessary to pass an error condition up through the program hierarchy until the point is reached where the error can be reported to the user or logged for troubleshooting.

PL/SQL allows exceptions to be reraised in a lower-level subprogram so that the exception can be passed to a higher-level program. Reraising an exception allows the exception to be handled in the subprogram where the error condition occurs, and then allows the exception to be passed to the next higher-level program. For example, when an exception occurs in a low-level subprogram, it may be necessary to roll back a transaction and close a cursor, and then report the error to the user at the user-interface level several levels higher in the program.

An exception is reraised by simply placing the RAISE statement by itself (with no reference to any exception name) in the exception handler where the exception is to be passed to the next higher level. For example:

```
EXCEPTION
    WHEN over_credit_limit THEN
        -- Process credit limit exceeded for customer
        RAISE;   -- Pass the exception to the next higher level
    END;
    ...
```

```
EXCEPTION        -- Next higher-level procedure
   WHEN over_credit_limit THEN
      -- Report credit limit exceeded for customer
   WHEN NO_DATA_FOUND THEN
      -- Report invalid item identifier or customer identifier
   WHEN OTHERS THEN
      -- Report generic errors
END;
```

Exception Propagation

In PL/SQL, it is assumed that all exceptions will be handled at some level of a program by an exception handler, either explicitly in a WHEN statement or implicitly with the OTHERS exception handler. When an exception is raised, if PL/SQL cannot find an exception handler for that exception in the local program, the exception is propagated to the next higher level. In other words, the exception implicitly reproduces itself at each higher level in a program until an exception handler is found (in a WHEN statement or with an OTHERS exception), or there are no more levels of the program to search for an exception handler. In the latter case, PL/SQL returns an unhandled exception error to the host environment.

According to the exception scope rules, higher-level programs cannot reference exceptions declared in a subblock. If an exception propagates outside its scope (beyond the block in which it is declared), the exception can only be handled by the OTHERS handler at higher levels of the program.

Only one exception at a time can be active in the exception part of a program. An exception raised inside an exception handler immediately propagates to the next higher level in a program, which is searched to find an exception handler for the newly raised exception. From there on, the exception propagates normally.

In cases where a constant or variable is improperly initialized in the DECLARE section of a program, an exception is raised in the DECLARE section. However, the exception cannot be handled by the exception part of that program because the exception part does not become active until the program BEGINs. In this case, the exception is propagated to the next higher-level program or the host environment. For example, the following declaration implicitly raises the predefined exception VALUE_ERROR because the variable cannot store numbers larger than 9999:

```
DECLARE
   count NUMBER(4) := 10000;        -- raises VALUE_ERROR
BEGIN
   ...
EXCEPTION
   WHEN VALUE_ERROR THEN       -- Exception not handled here
      ...
END;
```

The exception handler in this program cannot handle the exception because an exception raised in the DECLARE part of a program propagates immediately to the next higher-level program.

Unhandled Exceptions

Remember, if an error handler cannot be found for a raised exception anywhere in a program, PL/SQL returns an unhandled exception error to the host environment. The host environment then determines the outcome of the error condition. For example, if you call a PL/SQL program from a Pro*C application program and an unhandled exception error is returned, any database changes made to that point are rolled back.

Unhandled exceptions can affect transactions. Before a PL/SQL block or subprogram is executed, Oracle implicitly sets a *savepoint.* If the block or subprogram fails with an unhandled exception, Oracle rolls back the transaction to the savepoint. Thus, any database work done by the block or subprogram is undone.

Unhandled exceptions can also affect subprograms. If you exit a subprogram successfully, PL/SQL assigns values to the output parameters of the subprogram. However, if you exit with an unhandled exception, PL/SQL does not assign values to the output parameters, thus leaving the values indeterminate. Also, if a stored subprogram fails with an unhandled exception, Oracle implicitly rolls back all database work done by the subprogram. However, if the subprogram issues a COMMIT before the unhandled exception is raised, only the uncommitted work is rolled back.

The effects of unhandled exception errors may not be surprising but may not be what you expect. It is best to avoid unhandled exceptions by placing an OTHERS exception handler at the topmost level of every PL/SQL block and subprogram.

Branching from Exception Handlers

A GOTO statement cannot branch to an exception handler; nor can a GOTO statement branch from an exception handler into the execution part (BEGIN...END) of the current program. However, a GOTO statement can branch from an exception handler of a subprogram into the execution part of an enclosing program.

Error Reporting

You can use SQLCODE and SQLERRM in an exception handler to retrieve the Oracle error code and standard message associated to an Oracle system error.

For internal Oracle system errors, handled either by predefined exceptions or user-defined exceptions defined by an EXCEPTION_INIT statement, the error code and error message can be retrieved using SQLCODE and SQLERRM, respectively. All Oracle error codes are negative except for NO_DATA_FOUND, which returns +100.

The Oracle system error message returned by SQLERRM begins with the error code. The length of the error message cannot exceed 512 characters including the error code, nested error messages, and inserted objects such as table names and column names. For all other user-defined exceptions, SQLCODE returns +1 and SQLERRM returns the message

```
User-Defined Exception
```

If no exception has been raised and SQLCODE is accessed, it returns zero. In this case SQLERRM returns the message

```
ORA-0000: normal, successful completion
```

You can pass an error number to SQLERRM, in which case SQLERRM returns the message associated with that error number. Remember, the error number passed to SQLERRM should be negative (except +100). Passing a zero to SQLERRM always returns the "successful completion" message. If you pass a positive number (except +100) to SQLERRM, it always returns the "user-defined exception" message.

You cannot use SQLCODE or SQLERRM directly in an SQL statement. Instead, you must assign their values to local variables, and then use the variables in the SQL statement.

Error Handling Guidelines

Here are some general guidelines to help you avoid some common pitfalls encountered when handling errors in PL/SQL.

- Define a set of common user-defined exceptions for application-specific error conditions and some common Oracle system errors that are not handled by the predefined exceptions. Declare these as global exceptions throughout your program so that the exceptions are within scope regardless of the program level.

- Define a set of common exception-handling functions to process the common set of defined exceptions. Define these exception-handling functions globally so that they can be used throughout a program at all levels. Use specific exception handlers only when necessary to close cursors or free memory.

■ Do not override the predefined exceptions with user-defined exception names.

■ Always place an OTHERS exception handler at each level of a program so that all exceptions will be processed and to avoid the unhandled exception error in a host environment.

When an exception is raised, program control is sent to the exception part of the program, where the exceptions are handled and program control returns to the next higher level. If the intent is to handle an exception, perform corrective action, and continue processing the next statement with the correct results, you must place a statement or statement sequence in a subblock with its own exception handlers. If an error occurs in the subblock, the local exception handler can process the error condition and perform corrective action. When the subblock terminates, the enclosing block continues to execute at the point where the subblock ends.

If you encounter an error condition and an exception is raised, you can retry a transaction with corrective action rather than abandoning it. This can be very simple. Just place the transaction in a subblock with an exception handler to provide corrective action. Then encase the subblock in a loop structure with a limit on the number of retries that are performed. That way, with each loop iteration the transaction will be retried with corrective action.

Procedures and Functions

In PL/SQL, there are two types of subprograms called procedures and functions. Subprograms allow you to decompose a program into logical units that provide specific services or perform specific operations. These logical units can be used as building blocks to create complete application programs. If you create subprograms in a general manner, they can be reused in many application programs that access a database.

Previous discussions briefly covered various parts of anonymous blocks, procedures, and functions including the declaration (DECLARE) part, the executable (BEGIN...END) part, and the error-handling (EXCEPTION) part. Each part is common among blocks, procedures, and functions.

Anonymous blocks are intended to be embedded in a Pro*C application or as subblocks in other blocks, procedures, or functions. Anonymous blocks can provide specific operations, but cannot accept parameters or return values.

Procedures and functions are different because they can be called from any block, procedure, or function at any level of a program, and they can accept parameters and return values. This section will discuss the details of procedures and functions and demonstrate how they should be used in an application program.

What Are Procedures and Functions?

Procedures and functions can be thought of as named anonymous blocks that can accept parameters, return values, and be called from other blocks, procedures, and functions. The basic difference between a procedure and a function is that a procedure is used to accept and return parameters and perform an action. A function is intended to accept parameters, compute a value, and return that value to the caller.

Procedures and functions have a declarative part, an executable part, and an optional exception-handling part. The declarative part contains declarations of types, cursors, constants, variables, exceptions, and nested procedures and functions. Objects declared in a procedure or function are local to that subprogram and global to any subblocks. When a procedure or function is entered, these objects come into scope and become active. When the procedure or function is exited, these objects cease to exist.

Where to Use Procedures and Functions?

Procedures and functions can be created using any Oracle tool that supports PL/SQL. Procedures and functions can be declared as part of any anonymous block, procedure, function, or package. A procedure or function must be declared at the end of a declarative section after all other objects are declared.

Procedures and functions that are declared locally in other blocks, procedures, or functions are only accessible from that program. However, procedures and functions can be created and stored in an Oracle database, where they can be generally accessed from multiple programs. Local declarations and stored subprograms will be discussed later in this chapter.

Advantages of Procedures and Functions

Procedures and functions are subprograms in PL/SQL and, as in other programming languages, provide all the advantages of modular programming techniques, including modularity, extensibility, reusability, maintainability, and abstraction.

Procedures and functions provide *modularity* because they allow you to break a problem into logical, manageable units which provide specific services in a program. This allows for the top-down decomposition of problems into logical program modules.

Procedures and functions provide for *extensibility* by allowing for the creation of new program services in new modules without affecting existing program modules.

Procedures and functions can promote *reusability* by allowing you to create subprograms that can be used not only throughout an application, but also in many applications. Also, *maintainability* is promoted when a subprogram is reused because only the subprogram is affected if the subprogram code changes or is enhanced.

Finally, procedures and functions allow for *abstraction* of data and program internals. It is only necessary to understand what a subprogram does, not what data it contains or how it processes that data. The application developer is isolated from the internal details of the subprogram.

Procedures

A *procedure* is a subprogram that can accept parameters, perform an action, and return values. A procedure can be called from anonymous blocks, other procedures, and functions. The syntax to define a procedure is

```
PROCEDURE <name> [(parameter [, parameter, ...])] IS
    [declarations]
BEGIN
    statements
[EXCEPTION
    exception handlers]
END [name];
```

where:

name is the procedure name used to identify the procedure when it is called in a program. The name can optionally be added to the END of the procedure to improve readability.

declarations is the optional declaration section where local variable, constant, exception, or cursor declarations are placed.

EXCEPTION... is the optional exception-handling section for a procedure.

parameter is a procedure parameter that has the following syntax:

```
<var_name> [IN | OUT | IN OUT] datatype [{:= | DEFAULT} value]
```

where:

var_name is a unique name for a parameter variable. Each variable can be assigned one of the optional parameter modes IN, OUT, or IN OUT (these parameter modes will be discussed later in this chapter).

datatype is any valid PL/SQL datatype. The datatype is assigned to the variable. Unlike the datatype assignment in a variable declaration, the datatype assignment in a parameter declaration cannot be constrained. For example, the following declaration of the parameter name is illegal:

```
PROCEDURE ... (name CHAR(20)) IS...
```

The declaration of CHAR(20) is illegal; it should be CHAR.

Each procedure has two main parts: the procedure *specification* and the procedure *body*. The procedure specification is where the procedure name and all the procedure parameters are declared. The procedure specification begins with the keyword PROCEDURE and ends with the procedure name or the parameter list. The procedure name is an identifier that follows all the normal rules associated with identifiers.

Each parameter is declared as a variable of a valid PL/SQL datatype. The parameter declarations are optional. A procedure is not required to have a parameter list. A procedure declared with no parameters has the following procedure specification:

```
PROCEDURE name IS...
```

The procedure body contains three subparts: the declaration part, the executable (BEGIN...END) part, and the optional exception-handling part. The procedure body begins with the keyword IS and ends with the keyword END. As mentioned previously, the procedure name can be appended to the END of the procedure to improve readability.

The declarative part of the procedure body contains local declarations of variables, constants, exceptions, cursors, or other procedures or functions. These local declarations are placed between the keywords IS and BEGIN. The keyword DECLARE, which introduces object declarations in an anonymous block, is not used.

The executable part contains procedural statements and SQL statements, which are placed between the keywords BEGIN and EXCEPTION, or END if no exception-handling part exists. At least one statement must appear in the executable part of a procedure. The null statement meets this requirement and is useful when creating stubs during early program development.

The exception-handling part contains the exception handlers, which are placed between the keywords EXCEPTION and END.

Consider the following example:

```
PROCEDURE update_item_cost (iItemId INTEGER, fNewCost NUMBER) IS
    fCurCost NUMBER(10,2);
    missing_cost EXCEPTION;
BEGIN
    SELECT item_cost INTO fCurCost FROM item
```

```
      WHERE item_id = iItemId;
   IF fCurCost IS null THEN
      RAISE missing_cost;
   ELSE
      UPDATE item SET item_cost = fNewCost
         WHERE item_id = iItemId;
   END IF;

COMMIT;

EXCEPTION
   WHEN NO_DATA_FOUND THEN
      INSERT INTO item_audit

         VALUES (iItemId, 'Invalid Item identifier.');
      COMMIT;
   WHEN missing_cost THEN
      INSERT INTO item_audit

         VALUES (iItemId, 'Item Cost is null.');
      COMMIT;
   WHEN OTHERS THEN

      ROLLBACK;
      INSERT INTO item_audit

         VALUES (iItemId, 'Miscellaneous error.');
      COMMIT;

END update_item_cost;
```

When this procedure is called, the item cost is updated to reflect the input parameter of **fNewCost**. If an error occurs, the item identifier and an error message are logged to the **item_audit** table. This example shows all the parts of a procedure.

A procedure can be called from any anonymous block, procedure, or function as a PL/SQL statement. For example, the previous procedure could be called as follows:

```
update_item_cost (item_identifier, discounted_cost);
```

Notice that the parameter names passed to the procedure do not need to match the names of the declared parameter names. The parameter variables passed to a procedure must be of a compatible PL/SQL datatype.

Although a procedure can return values through its parameters, the procedure
cannot return a value as a direct output of the procedure call itself. For example, a
procedure cannot be called as part of an expression or procedural statement. The
procedure call must be a single procedural statement as shown in the previous example.

Functions

A function is a subprogram like a procedure that can accept parameters, perform
an action, and return values. However, unlike a procedure, a function can return a
value as a direct output of the function call itself. Typically, a function is used to
compute a value or perform an operation that returns a specific value. A function
can, but should not, return more than one value. A function can be called from
anonymous blocks, procedures, and other functions. The syntax to define a
function is

```
FUNCTION <name> [(parameter [, parm2, ...])]
    RETURN datatype IS
    [declarations]
BEGIN
    statements
[EXCEPTION
    exception handlers]
END [name];
```

where:

> **name** is the function name used to identify the function when it is called in
> a program. The name can optionally be added to the END of the function
> to improve readability.
>
> **RETURN datatype** is used to declare the datatype of the return value of the
> function. The datatype must be a valid PL/SQL datatype.
>
> **declarations** is the optional declaration section where local variable,
> constant, exception, or cursor declarations are placed.
>
> **EXCEPTION...** is the optional exception-handling section for a procedure.
>
> **parameter** is a function parameter that has the following syntax:

```
<var_name> [IN | OUT | IN OUT] datatype [{:= | DEFAULT} value]
```

where:

> **variable_name** is a unique name for a parameter variable. Each variable
> can be assigned one of the optional parameter modes IN, OUT, or IN OUT
> (these parameter modes will be discussed later in this chapter).

datatype is any valid PL/SQL datatype. The datatype is assigned to the variable. Unlike the datatype assignment in a variable declaration, the datatype assignment in a parameter declaration cannot be constrained. For example, the following declaration of the parameter name is illegal:

```
FUNCTION ... (name CHAR(20)) IS...
```

The declaration of CHAR(20) is illegal, it should be CHAR.

Like a procedure, a function has the same two main parts: the function specification and the function body. The function specification has all the same characteristics as a procedure specification. However, a function includes a RETURN clause, which is used to declare the datatype of the function return value. Like other function parameters, the datatype in the RETURN clause cannot be constrained. The function specification begins with the keyword FUNCTION and ends with the RETURN clause. Like a procedure, the function parameter declarations are optional. A function declared with no parameters has the following function specification:

```
FUNCTION name RETURN datatype IS...
```

The function body contains the same three subparts as a procedure: the declaration part, the executable (BEGIN...END) part, and the optional exception-handling part. Each of these parts is used in the same manner as a procedure.

Consider the following example:

```
FUNCTION subtotal (iItemId INTEGER, nItemCount INTEGER)

   RETURN NUMBER IS
   fPrice NUMBER(10,2);
   missing_price EXCEPTION;
BEGIN
   SELECT retail_price INTO fPrice FROM item
      WHERE item_id = iItemId;
   IF fPrice IS null THEN
      RAISE missing_price;
   ELSE
      RETURN (fPrice * nItemCount);
   END IF;

EXCEPTION
```

```
    WHEN NO_DATA_FOUND THEN
        INSERT INTO item_audit
            VALUES (iItemId, 'Invalid Item identifier.');
        COMMIT;
    WHEN missing_price THEN
        INSERT INTO item_audit
            VALUES (iItemId, 'Item Price is null.');
        COMMIT;
END subtotal;
```

When this function is called, the item subtotal is calculated from the item's retail price and the input parameter **nItemCount**. This value is calculated and assigned to the function RETURN statement (not to be confused with the function RETURN clause). The function RETURN statement is used to assign the function return value and return control to the caller of the function. The RETURN statement must contain an expression that results in a value that is compatible with the datatype declared in the function RETURN clause. At least one RETURN statement is required in a function. Multiple RETURN statements are allowed in a function, none of which must be the last statement in the function. However, it is poor programming practice to have multiple exit points in a subprogram.

RETURN statements can be placed in procedures, which immediately return control to the caller of the procedure. In this case, an expression cannot be specified in the procedure RETURN statement.

A function can be called from any anonymous block, procedure, or function as an expression. For example:

```
total := subtotal(item_id1, 10) + subtotal (item_id2, 20);
```

Also, unlike a procedure, a function can be called as any part of a procedural statement or as a parameter to another procedure or function. However, a function cannot be called as part of an SQL statement.

Forward Declarations

PL/SQL requires that a procedure or function must be declared before it can be called. This is not possible or convenient in all cases. Thus, PL/SQL provides a method to declare a procedure or function specification before it is actually defined with its body. This is much like function prototypes in the C language.

A forward declaration is done simply by adding a semicolon (;) to the end of a procedure or function declaration just before the IS clause. Later in the program the complete specification is declared with its body. For example:

```
DECLARE
    ...
    PROCEDURE update_item_cost (iItemId INTEGER, fNewCost NUMBER);
    ...
    PROCEDURE update_item_cost (iItemId INTEGER, fNewCost NUMBER)

        IS
        fCurCost NUMBER(10,2);
    missing_cost EXCEPTION;
    BEGIN
        SELECT item_cost INTO current_cost FROM item
            WHERE item_id = iItemId;
        ...
    END update_item_cost;
    ...
BEGIN
    update_item_cost(...);
    ...
END;
```

Although the formal parameter list appears in the forward declaration, it must also appear in the body. You can place the body anywhere after the forward declaration, but they must appear in the same block, procedure, function, or package.

Parameters

Procedures and functions pass information by using parameters. The parameters declared in the parameter list of a procedure or a function definition are called *formal parameters.* The parameters referenced in a procedure or function call are called *actual parameters.* Actual parameters can be literals, constants, variables, or expressions.

When a procedure or function is called, the actual parameter values are evaluated and assigned to the formal parameters of the procedure or function. When the actual parameter values are evaluated, PL/SQL converts the values to compatible datatypes in the formal procedure or function parameters. The actual parameter values must be compatible with the formal parameter datatypes.

Parameter Modes

Parameter modes are the optional qualifiers IN, OUT, and IN OUT that can be assigned to any procedure or function formal parameter. The parameter modes indicate whether a parameter is used for input, output, or for both input and output, respectively. If one of these parameter modes is not specified, IN is the default.

The IN parameter mode forces a parameter to be considered for input only and is treated like a constant variable; its value cannot be changed inside the procedure. The actual parameter associated with an input formal parameter can be a constant, literal, initialized variable, or expression. An input formal parameter can be initialized with a default value (see the next section on parameter default values).

The OUT parameter mode forces a parameter to be considered for output only. An output parameter is treated as an uninitialized variable. Its input value is ignored and a value must be assigned to the parameter inside the procedure or function. Otherwise, its value will be indeterminate when the procedure or function exits. Also, an output parameter cannot be assigned to another variable or to itself, even after it has been assigned a value. An output formal parameter cannot be initialized with a default value. When a procedure or function exits, the value assigned to an output parameter is returned to the calling statement. However, if a procedure or function exits with an unhandled exception, values are not assigned to the output parameters, and the actual parameters become indeterminate. The actual parameter associated with an output formal parameter must be a variable. The actual parameter in this case cannot be a literal, constant, or expression.

The IN OUT parameter mode allows a parameter to be considered for input and output. An IN OUT parameter is treated like an initialized variable. Its value on input can be used in the body of the procedure, in expressions much as any other variable. Also, a value can be assigned to the parameter for output. However, an output formal parameter cannot be initialized with a default value in the procedure or function definition. The actual parameter associated with an IN OUT formal parameter must be a variable. The actual parameter in this case cannot be a literal, constant, or expression.

Table 10-2 summarizes the parameter mode rules.

Parameter Default Values

As mentioned in the previous section, an input (IN) parameter can be initialized with a default value in the procedure or function definition. This allows the caller of a procedure or function to accept the default parameter by not passing an actual input parameter to a formal input parameter, or to override the default value by passing an actual parameter. Also, this feature allows the addition of new formal input parameters to a procedure or function, without the need to change every call

In	Out	In Out
The default if no parameter mode is specified	Must be explicitly specified	Must be explicitly specified
Used to pass actual parameter values	Used to return values to actual parameters	Used to pass actual parameter values and return updated values to actual parameters
Can be initialized with a default value	Cannot be initialized with a default value	Cannot be initialized with a default value
Treated like a constant	Treated like an uninitialized variable	Treated like an initialized variable
Can access its value, but cannot be assigned a value	Cannot be used in an expression; must be assigned a value	Can be used in an expression; should be assigned a value
Actual parameter can be a literal, constant, initialized variable, or expression	Actual parameter must be a variable	Actual parameter must be a variable

TABLE 10-2. *Parameter mode rules*

to that subprogram. The following example illustrates how a formal input parameter is assigned a default value.

```
PROCEDURE update_item_cost (iItemId INTEGER := 1000,
   fNewCost NUMBER := 100.00) IS
   fCurCost NUMBER(10,2);
   missing_cost EXCEPTION;
BEGIN
   ...
END;
```

Alternately, the keyword DEFAULT can be used in place of the assignment operator (:=). This promotes readability. For example:

```
PROCEDURE update_item_cost (iItemId INTEGER DEFAULT 1000,
   fNewCost NUMBER DEFAULT 100.00) IS
   fCurCost NUMBER(10,2);
   missing_cost EXCEPTION;
```

B

```
BEGIN
   ...
END;
```

When a procedure or function is called, if an actual parameter is not passed for a formal input parameter, the default value assigned to the formal parameter is used. The following calls to the procedure declared previously are all legitimate, because a default value is assigned to each of the formal input parameters.

```
update_item_cost (item_ident, discounted_cost);
update_item_cost (item_ident);
update_item_cost;
```

If the intent is to not pass an actual input parameter and accept the default value for a formal parameter, you must use positional or named notation.

Positional and Named Notation

When a procedure or function is called, the actual parameters can be specified with two methods: *positional notation* or *named notation.* This means that actual parameters can be associated to formal parameters by position or by name.

Positional notation is used when the actual parameters in a procedure or function call are associated by position to the declared formal parameters. In other words, the first actual parameter is associated with the first formal parameter; the second actual parameter is associated with the second formal parameter; and so on. With positional notation, the default value associated with a formal parameter can be accepted by not specifying an actual parameter in that position. As shown in the following example, an actual parameter can be eliminated for the trailing parameters:

```
update_item_cost (item_ident, discounted_cost);
update_item_cost (item_ident);
update_item_cost;
```

The first actual parameter must be specified, unless all the actual parameters are eliminated. For example, the following call is illegal:

```
update_item_cost (, discounted_cost);   -- Illegal syntax
```

Named notation is used when the actual parameters in a procedure or function call are associated by name to the declared formal parameters. In other words, each actual parameter is specified by assigning it to each formal parameter by the name of the formal parameter. Named notation allows the specification of actual parameters in any order, and any of the parameters can be eliminated. The following example shows how actual parameters are specified, and how named actual parameters can be ordered as desired.

```
update_item_cost (iItemId => item_ident,

   fNewCost => discounted_cost);
update_item_cost (fNewCost => discounted_cost,

   iItemId => item_ident);
update_item_cost (iItemId => item_ident);
update_item_cost (fNewCost => discounted_cost);
```

Positional and named notation can be mixed. In this case, positional notation must precede named notation; the reverse is not allowed. The following example shows how positional and named notation can be mixed.

```
update_item_cost (item_ident, fNewCost => discounted_cost);
```

Parameter Aliasing

Parameter aliasing occurs when the same variable is used as an actual parameter multiple times in a procedure or function call. Unless each formal parameter is an IN parameter, the result of the call is indeterminate. This is because the result of the actual parameter value depends upon the method that the compiler chooses to pass the parameter, either by copy or by reference. Consider the following example:

```
DECLARE
   nItemCount INTEGER;
   iItemId INTEGER;

   PROCEDURE update_inventory (iItemId INTEGER,
      nPurchased IN INTEGER,
      nQtyOnHand OUT INTEGER) IS
   BEGIN
      UPDATE inventory SET quantity_on_hand =
         quantity_on_hand - nPurchased
         WHERE item_id = iItemId;

      SELECT quantity_on_hand INTO nQtyOnHand
         FROM inventory
         WHERE item_id = iItemId;
   END update_inventory;

BEGIN
   nItemCount := 10;
   iItemId := 1000;
```

```
    update_inventory (iItemId, nItemCount, nItemCount);
                    -- nItemCount indeterminate
END;
```

In this example, the variable **nItemCount** is indeterminate because the compiler may choose to pass the value by copy or by reference, because it is used both as input and output.

Parameter aliasing also occurs when a global variable is used in the body of a procedure or function and as an actual parameter of the procedure or function call.

```
DECLARE
    nItemCount INTEGER;
    iItemId INTEGER;

    PROCEDURE update_inventory (iItemId INTEGER,
        nPurchased IN INTEGER,
        nQtyOnHand OUT INTEGER) IS
    BEGIN
        nItemCount := nPurchased;
        UPDATE inventory SET quantity_on_hand =
            quantity_on_hand - nItemCount
            WHERE item_id = iItemId;

        SELECT quantity_on_hand INTO nQtyOnHand
            FROM inventory
            WHERE item_id = iItemId;
    END update_inventory;

BEGIN
    nItemCount := 10;
    iItemId := 1000;
    update_inventory (iItemId, nItemCount, nItemCount);
                    -- nItemCount indeterminate
END;
```

Again, the result of **nItemCount** is indeterminate. This example and the previous example are simply poor programming practice and should be avoided.

Procedure and Function Overloading

PL/SQL provides the feature of procedure and function *overloading*. Procedure and function overloading allows for the creation of multiple procedures or functions with identical names, but different parameter lists. In other words, procedures or functions can be created with the same names, but their formal parameters must differ in number, order, or datatype family (for example, NUMBER, CHARACTER, DATE, and so on; not NUMBER, INTEGER, and so on). Thus, it is not a requirement that procedures or functions be uniquely named, only that the entire specification be unique.

Overloading is useful when multiple procedures or functions perform the same operation on parameters of different datatypes. Multiple overloaded procedures or functions can only be placed in the same block, procedure, function, or package. In other words, you cannot overload stand-alone procedures or functions. PL/SQL determines which one to use by checking the parameter lists. However, you cannot overload multiple functions that differ only in the datatype of the function return value, even if the datatypes are in different families.

Be careful not to declare global procedures or functions and then redeclare them locally. This is not overloading, because the local declaration overrides the global declaration. This can be error prone and may not result in what you expect, or may return incorrect results.

Recursion

PL/SQL allows for recursion of procedure and function calls. Recursion is a powerful tool to simplify the design of algorithms. Essentially, *recursion* means self-reference. A recursive procedure or function is one that calls itself. Each time a recursive call occurs, a new instance is created of any objects declared in the procedure or function, including parameters, variables, cursors, and exceptions. Likewise, new instances of SQL statements are created.

There must be at least two paths through a recursive procedure or function: one path must lead to the recursive call, and one path must lead to a terminating condition. Otherwise, the recursion creates an infinite series of calls. In practice, if an infinite recursion occurs, PL/SQL eventually runs out of memory and raises the predefined exception STORAGE_ERROR.

To solve some problems, an operation must be repeated until a condition is met. You can use iteration or recursion to solve such problems. Recursion is appropriate when the problem can be broken down into simpler versions of itself. Unlike iteration, recursion is not essential to PL/SQL programming. Any problem that can be solved by using recursion can be solved using iteration. Also, the iterative version of a subprogram is usually easier to design than the recursive version. However, the recursive version is usually simpler, smaller, and therefore easier to debug.

Typically, the iterative version of a program is more efficient, runs faster, and uses less storage. That is because each recursive call requires additional time and memory. As the number of recursive calls gets larger, so does the difference in efficiency. Still, if the number of recursive calls is manageable, you might choose the recursive version for its elegance and maintainability.

Be careful where a recursive call is placed. With each recursive call a new instance of all subprogram objects is created, including cursors. If too many recursive calls occur, the system can easily exceed the system limits on open cursors or memory limitations.

Stored Procedures and Functions

If the Oracle Procedural Database Extension is available in your environment, then you have the option to compile and store procedures and functions separately in a database as database objects, ready to be executed. As database objects, stored procedures and functions become accessible to multiple application programs and are easily maintainable in a central repository.

Advantages of Stored Procedures and Functions

Stored procedures and functions provide the following advantages: higher productivity, better performance, memory savings, application integrity, and tighter security.

Stored procedures and functions provide higher productivity because applications can be designed by use of a central repository of standardized stored subprograms. Redundant effort can be avoided, and knowledge can be captured and shared. Business rules can be encapsulated and stored in procedures and functions for consistent access and implementation throughout an organization. For example, suppose multiple applications use stored procedures that standardize the management of supplier information in an organization. If the management method changes or supplier information changes, only the stored procedures must be revised, not the applications.

Stored procedures and functions provide better performance because they can reduce the number of calls to an Oracle database in an application. For example, to execute ten individual SQL statements, ten database calls are required, but to execute a stored procedure containing ten SQL statements, only one database call is required. Reducing the number of database calls in an application can significantly boost performance, particularly in a networked environment.

Stored procedures and functions conserve memory because they take advantage of the Oracle shared memory capability. The shared memory capability allows for only one copy of a stored procedure or function to be loaded into memory for all applications that access it. As a result, your applications require less memory.

Stored procedures and functions can provide improved integrity and consistency of a database and of the applications that access it. If applications are designed using standardized stored procedures and functions, the occurrence of errors is reduced and maintenance is centralized. For example, a procedure can be created and tested once, then it can be used with confidence throughout many applications. Also, stored procedures and functions can be used to implement business rules consistently throughout an organization.

Stored procedures and functions can be used to enforce consistent data security for a database. A database administrator (DBA) can restrict users to specific database operations by granting access only through stored procedures and functions. For example, a DBA might grant users EXECUTE access to a stored procedure that updates the supplier table, but not grant them access to the table itself. That way, users can call the procedure, but cannot arbitrarily manipulate table data.

Creating Stored Procedures and Functions

The Procedural Database Extension allows you to create procedures and functions and store them permanently as database objects in an Oracle database. The CREATE PROCEDURE and CREATE FUNCTION statements are used to compile and store procedures and functions in a database. The syntax for the CREATE PROCEDURE and CREATE FUNCTION statements are

```
CREATE PROCEDURE ... AS
    ...
BEGIN
...
END;
```

or

```
CREATE FUNCTION ... RETURN ... AS
    ...
BEGIN
...
END;
```

Notice that the CREATE statement can use the IS clause and the AS clause interchangeably. For example, the **update_item_cost** procedure would be created as a stored procedure as follows:

```
CREATE PROCEDURE update_item_cost (iItemId INTEGER,

        fNewCost NUMBER) AS
    fCurCost NUMBER(10,2);
    missing_cost EXCEPTION;
BEGIN
    SELECT item_cost INTO fCurCost FROM item
        WHERE item_id = iItemId;
    IF fCurCost IS null THEN
        RAISE missing_cost;
    ELSE
        UPDATE item SET item_cost = fNewCost
            WHERE item_id = iItemId;
    END IF;

COMMIT;

EXCEPTION
    WHEN NO_DATA_FOUND THEN
        INSERT INTO item_audit

        VALUES (iItemId, 'Invalid Item identifier.');
        COMMIT;
    WHEN missing_cost THEN
        INSERT INTO item_audit

        VALUES (iItemId, 'Item Cost is null.');
        COMMIT;
    WHEN OTHERS THEN

        ROLLBACK;
        INSERT INTO item_audit

        VALUES (iItemId, 'Miscellaneous error.');
        COMMIT;

END update_item_cost;
```

The CREATE PROCEDURE and CREATE FUNCTION statements can be issued interactively in the SQL*Plus or SQL*DBA Oracle tools. The CREATE statement and source code for a stored procedure or function should be created in a separate text file. That way, the text file can be interactively submitted as an SQL script. If any errors occur during compilation, they can be easily fixed in the source code text file and resubmitted for recompilation.

When a procedure or function is created for storage in a database, Oracle automatically compiles the source code, caches the object code in a shared SQL memory area, and stores the source code and object code in the data dictionary. The object code stays cached in the shared SQL area, where it can be executed quickly. When Oracle begins to run out of shared SQL memory area, a least recently used algorithm is applied to select the shared SQL areas to be flushed to make room for other shared objects.

When a stored procedure or function is executed, Oracle checks to see if an existing shared SQL area holds the object code for that subprogram. If not, Oracle allocates a shared SQL area and loads the object code into it. Then, Oracle allocates a private SQL area, which holds session-specific procedure or function values and objects, such as variables, cursors, and so on. If multiple sessions execute a stored procedure or function simultaneously, only one shared SQL area is used, but multiple private SQL areas are maintained, one for each session.

SQL statements within a stored procedure or function are processed in the same manner as the subprogram itself. SQL statements use shared SQL areas to hold their parsed representations and use private SQL areas to hold session-specific information. The shared SQL area used by a procedure or function is called a *parent cursor;* the shared SQL area used by an SQL statement within the procedure or function are called *child cursors.*

Calling Stored Procedures and Functions

You can call a stored procedure or function from the following constructs:

- Anonymous block, procedure, or function
- Stored procedure or function
- Database trigger
- Precompiler application (Pro*C)
- OCI application
- Oracle tool (SQL*Forms)

A stored procedure or function can be called from an anonymous block, procedure, or function, or from another stored procedure or function. As long as the stored procedure or function is stored in the local database, the stored subprogram can be called directly by name as previously discussed in the section

on calling procedures and functions in this chapter. For example, a call to the
update_item_cost procedure would be as follows:

```
update_item_cost (item_ident, cost);
```

A stored procedure or function can be called from an Oracle precompiler
application like Pro*C or an OCI application. This is done by use of anonymous
blocks inside the application program. For example, the **update_item_cost** function
would be called from a Pro*C application program as follows:

```
EXEC SQL EXECUTE
    BEGIN
        update_item_cost(:item_ident, :cost);
    END;
END-EXEC;
```

Notice the actual parameters passed to the procedure call are host variables. They
could also be local variables declared in the embedded block.

Stored procedures and functions can be called from Oracle tools such as
SQL*Plus, SQL*Forms, and SQL*DBA. That way, stored subprograms can be
included in SQL scripts for maintenance operations. For example, the
update_item_cost procedure would be called from SQL*Plus as follows:

```
SQL> EXECUTE update_item_cost('1000', '100.50');
```

Remote Access

A stored procedure or function can be accessed from remote database locations.
The following syntax is used to access a stored subprogram remotely:

```
<subprogram_name>@<database_link>(param1, param2, ...);
```

where:

> **subprogram_name** is the name of a stored procedure or function in the
> remote database.
>
> **database_link** is the defined link to the remote database. A synonym can
> be created to provide location transparency for remote procedures and
> functions. For example:

```
CREATE SYNONYM update_item_list FOR update_item_list@denver;
```

Oracle assumes that all calls to remote procedures or functions do an update,
which requires a two-phase commit of the transaction. As a result, if the local
transaction is rolled back, so is the database work done by the remote subprogram.

If the remote subprogram fails, an error might be returned that requires the local PL/SQL program to roll back the local transaction.

Stored procedures or functions that participate in a distributed transaction, database trigger, or SQL*Forms application cannot call remote or local stored procedures or functions that contain a COMMIT, ROLLBACK, or SAVEPOINT statement.

Stored Procedure and Function Maintenance

A stored procedure or function always exists in one of the following states: valid or invalid. A *valid* stored procedure or function is one that has been compiled without error, and neither its source code nor any object that it references (for example, table, column, or other stored procedure or function) has been DROPped, REPLACEd, or ALTERed since the stored procedure or function was last compiled. When a valid stored procedure or function is called, it operates normally as discussed previously in this section.

Alternately, an *invalid* stored procedure or function is one where its source code or any object that it references has been DROPped, REPLACEd, or ALTERed since the last compilation. Thus, the stored procedure or function is said to be dependent upon the objects which it references.

If a stored procedure or function is invalid, the next time it is executed Oracle will automatically recompile it. Recompilation occurs in two phases.

First, Oracle determines if any referenced stored procedures, functions, or packages are themselves invalid; if so, they must be recompiled first, and so on. This can lead to a cascade of recompilations, all of which must succeed. Otherwise, Oracle returns a run time error, and the stored procedure or function remains invalid.

Second, the invalid stored procedure or function is recompiled, after which it can be executed. This does not guarantee that the change to a related object that caused the invalid status won't affect the execution of the subprogram; it only ensures correct recompilation.

Automatic recompilation of stored procedures and functions should be avoided. It can reduce performance, it will stop the execution of an application if recompilation fails, and it can be problematic if no testing is done to verify the effects of the related object change. To avoid automatic recompilation, invalid stored procedures and functions should be manually recompiled. The ALTER PROCEDURE or ALTER FUNCTION commands are used to recompile a procedure or function. The syntax to recompile a procedure or function is

```
ALTER PROCEDURE procedure_name COMPILE
```

or

```
ALTER FUNCTION function_name COMPILE
```

The ALTER PROCEDURE and ALTER FUNCTION statements can also be issued interactively in the SQL*Plus or SQL*DBA Oracle tools.

Complete validation testing should occur on any stored procedure or function that has been invalidated due to a change in a referenced object and recompiled. This will ensure proper execution of the stored procedure or function in a production environment.

Database Triggers

A database trigger is a PL/SQL block that can be associated to a specific database table. The purpose of a database trigger is to perform a service when a specified operation occurs on a table. You create a database trigger by specifying a database table and by specifying that before or after a database operation (INSERT, UPDATE, or DELETE) on that table, a procedure should be invoked. When the specified operation occurs on the table, Oracle automatically "fires" the database trigger.

Database triggers have many uses, as you can imagine. They are most often used to verify data when it is inserted or updated. Also, database triggers are often used to initiate downstream business processes. For example, database triggers can be used to start the following operations:

- Verify data integrity on insertion or update
- Implement delete cascades
- Log events transparently
- Enforce complex business rules
- Initiate business processes
- Derive column values automatically
- Enforce complex security rules
- Maintain replicated data

Database Trigger Options

Up to 12 database triggers can be associated with a specific table in version 7.0. Version 7.1 (and after) allow more than 12 multiple triggers of the same type per table. Each database trigger has three primary options: when to fire, for which operation, and for the statement or each row affected by the statement.

The first option is to specify when the database trigger is initiated (BEFORE or AFTER) for a specific operation. The second option is to specify for which operation should the database trigger execute (INSERT, UPDATE, or DELETE). The third option is to specify whether the database trigger should be executed once when the trigger is initiated or for each row affected by the trigger (FOR EACH ROW). Table 10-3 contains all the possible database trigger combinations for these three options.

The CREATE TRIGGER command is used to create and maintain a database trigger. This command has the following syntax:

```
CREATE [OR REPLACE] TRIGGER <trigger_name> {BEFORE | AFTER}
   {DELETE | INSERT | UPDATE [OF column_name1 [, column_name2] ...]}
   [OR {DELETE | INSERT | UPDATE [OF column [, column] ...]}] ...
   ON <table_name>
   [[REFERENCING {OLD [AS] old [NEW [AS] new]
   | NEW [AS] new [OLD [AS] old]}]
   [FOR EACH ROW
   [WHEN (condition)]]
[DECLARE]
...
BEGIN
...
[EXCEPTION
...]
END;
```

where:

> **trigger_name** is the name of the database trigger used to identify it in the database. This name must be unique in any database schema.
>
> **ta**ble_name is the name of the database table to which the database trigger applies.

The OR REPLACE option is used when an existing database trigger needs to be recompiled. This syntax looks rather complex, so let's break this command into manageable parts.

BEFORE or AFTER Option

There are two options, BEFORE or AFTER, that can be specified to indicate when a database trigger should be fired when the trigger operation occurs on a table. One of these options must be specified. The BEFORE option specifies that the database trigger is to be fired before the table operation. The AFTER option specifies that the database trigger is to be fired after the table operation.

Before or After	Insert, Update, or Delete	For Each Row
BEFORE	INSERT	
BEFORE	UPDATE	
BEFORE	DELETE	
BEFORE	INSERT	FOR EACH ROW
BEFORE	UPDATE	FOR EACH ROW
BEFORE	DELETE	FOR EACH ROW
AFTER	INSERT	
AFTER	UPDATE	
AFTER	DELETE	
AFTER	INSERT	FOR EACH ROW
AFTER	UPDATE	FOR EACH ROW
AFTER	DELETE	FOR EACH ROW

TABLE 10-3.   *Database trigger options*

Table Operations

There are three database table operations for which a database trigger can be
created: INSERT, UPDATE, and DELETE. One of these operations must be
specified. These operations can be specified individually, or they can be specified
in any combination, including all at the same time. To specify the operations in
combinations, the OR clause is used to separate the operations. For example, any
of the following is legal:

```
INSERT OR DELETE
DELETE OR UPDATE
INSERT OR UPDATE
DELETE OR UPDATE OR INSERT
```

Notice that the order of the operations is not important.

The UPDATE operation can be optionally accompanied with a list of database
columns. The column list constrains the database trigger to fire only when the list

of columns is updated. When a column list is specified, the optional OF clause must also be specified. For example:

```
UPDATE OF item_cost, item_name...
```

FOR EACH ROW Option
By default, when a database trigger is initiated for the specified table operation(s), the database trigger executes once per table operation. Optionally, the FOR EACH ROW option can be specified which, when initiated, causes a database trigger to execute for the specified operation(s) once per row affected by the table operation. A database trigger that is specified with the FOR EACH ROW option is called a *row trigger.*

WHEN Option
Optionally, a Boolean condition can be specified for a row trigger. A row trigger condition is specified with the WHEN clause. If specified, the WHEN condition is evaluated for each row affected by the table operation. If the WHEN condition evaluates to TRUE for a row affected by the table operation, the trigger is fired on behalf of that row. However, if the WHEN condition evaluates to FALSE or null for a row affected by the table operation, the trigger does not fire for that row. In this case, the trigger simply does not fire for that row; it does not mean that the entire trigger statement fails.

The condition in a WHEN clause must be an SQL expression (not a PL/SQL expression) and cannot include a subquery.

REFERENCING Option
Within a database trigger, the "old" and "new" values associated with the columns of the current row affected by the database trigger statement can be referenced. By default, the old and new column values can be referenced with the following syntax:

```
:old.column_name
```

or

```
:new.column_name
```

Do not confuse this syntax with the use of colons for host variables in Pro*C. This syntax can be used in the trigger body (BEGIN...END) and in the trigger WHEN condition. However, the colon is not used in the WHEN condition.

Depending on the operation associated with a database trigger statement, the old or new column values may not have any meaning. For instance:

■   A database trigger fired by an INSERT statement can access only the new column values for an AFTER trigger. The row is created by the INSERT, therefore, the old values are null. The new values are null for a BEFORE INSERT trigger.

■   A database trigger fired by an UPDATE statement can access both old and new column values for both BEFORE and AFTER row triggers.

■   A trigger fired by a DELETE statement can access only old column values for both a BEFORE and AFTER trigger. Because the row will no longer exist after the row is deleted, the new values are null.

The REFERENCING clause of the database trigger statement is used in a database trigger definition to replace the **:old** and **:new** names with other unique names. This is typically done to remove conflicts with database tables named OLD or NEW. Since this is rare, this option is infrequently used.

Conditional Options

Because a database trigger can be created for multiple table operations (for example, "INSERT OR DELETE OR UPDATE OF..."), conditional options or predicates can be used in the trigger body to distinguish between which operation has caused the trigger to be fired. These conditional predicates are INSERTING, DELETING, and UPDATING. They are used to execute specific sections of a database trigger body based upon the operation that fired the database trigger. For example, assume the following database trigger operation:

```
INSERT OR UPDATE ON item ...
```

Within the body of the database trigger, the following conditions could be specified:

```
IF INSERTING THEN
   ...
END IF;
```

```
IF UPDATING THEN
   ...
END IF;
```

The first condition evaluates to TRUE only if the database trigger is fired due to an INSERT operation; the second condition evaluates to TRUE only if the database trigger is fired due to an UPDATE operation.

In an UPDATE trigger, a column name can be specified in an UPDATING condition to determine if the named column is being updated. For example, assume the following database trigger operation definition:

```
CREATE TRIGGER ...
... UPDATE OF item_cost, item_name ON item ...
BEGIN
    IF UPDATING ('ITEM_COST') THEN
        ...
    END IF;
END;
```

The statements in the IF...END IF condition execute only if the UPDATE statement updates the **item_cost** or **item_name** columns.

The Database Trigger Body

The database trigger body is simply a PL/SQL block, including the DECLARE part, BEGIN...END part, and an optional EXCEPTION part. Except for transaction control statements such as COMMIT and ROLLBACK, any SQL or procedural statement, including subprogram calls, can appear in the BEGIN ... END block. A database trigger must be included inside a database transaction, it cannot contain or end a transaction in the trigger body.

Database Trigger Privileges

When a database trigger is fired, the privileges of the user who owns the database trigger are used during execution, not the privileges of the current user. So, the database trigger owner must have appropriate privileges to access to all the objects referenced in the database trigger body.

To create a database trigger, the user must have CREATE TRIGGER privileges and either own the associated table, have ALTER privileges for the associated table, or have ALTER ANY TABLE privileges.

An Example

The following example illustrates a typical use of a database trigger. The database trigger ensures that an item is reordered when its inventory quantity on hand drops below the reorder point.

```
CREATE TRIGGER item_reorder
   AFTER UPDATE OF quantity_on_hand    -- Trigger operation
   ON reorder   -- Table
   FOR EACH ROW    -- Row trigger
   WHEN (new.reorderable = 'T')    -- Row trigger; T = TRUE
BEGIN
   IF :new.quantity_on_hand < :new.reorder_limit THEN
      INSERT INTO item_reorder
         VALUES (:new.item_id, :new.reorder_quantity, SYSDATE,
         SYSDATE + :new.required_delivery);
   END IF;
END;
```

Packages

As with stored procedures and functions, if you have the Oracle Procedural Database Extension, PL/SQL allows related program objects to be collected together into a unit called a package.

What Is a Package?

A package is like a source module in the C language. A package may collect a set of related procedures and functions that serve as a subsystem to enforce specific business rules. For example, a package can contain all the procedures and functions used to enforce inventory management rules. In essence, a package serves as the mechanism to store logically related procedures and functions as a single database object, instead of storing them separately as database objects. Also, a package may contain a set of standardized datatypes, exceptions, variables, or cursors declared for use throughout many PL/SQL applications in a business operation.

Once a package is created, it is compiled and stored, like stored procedures and functions, in an Oracle database as a database object. The stored package acts as a software library or repository, where its contents can be shared in many applications.

Packages are typically constructed of two main parts: the package specification and the package body. Sometimes the package body is unnecessary. The package specification defines the interface from applications outside the package to the package contents. The package specification declares the datatypes, variables, constants, exceptions, cursors, procedures, and functions available for use outside the package. The package body fully defines the cursors, procedures, and functions in the package. Thus, the package body implements the package specification. If the package specification only contains the declaration of datatypes, constants, variables, or exceptions, the package body is not necessary.

Although a package specification looks much like a procedure or function declaration, it is not directly called like a procedure or function. The package is the container of the program objects, which are accessed through the package name.

Advantages of Packages

Packages offer many of the same advantages of stored procedures and functions, because, in essence, packages collect a group of logically related procedures and functions into a single stored database object. In addition, packages offer the following advantages:

- Easier application development

- Encapsulation and information hiding

- Better performance

- Easier maintenance

Packages allow for the grouping of logically related datatypes, program objects, procedures, and functions into a single named module. Each package has a clearly defined specification that is easy to understand and provides an interface that is simple, clear, and well-defined. This makes application development easier.

During initial application development, the package specification can be defined and communicated to other application developers. The package specification can be compiled separately, without its package body. Thus, after the specification is defined and compiled, other applications that reference the package contents can also be compiled. It is not necessary to define the complete package body until it is necessary.

Packages allow for the encapsulation of access to package contents and the hiding of information that should not be accessed outside the package boundaries. The package specification defines all the program objects that are *public* (visible and accessible outside the package). All other program objects defined inside the package body are *private* (hidden and inaccessible outside the package).

The package body hides the details of the package contents and the definition of private program objects so that only the package contents (not other applications) are affected if the package body changes. This simplifies maintenance and enhancement. Also, by hiding implementation details, the integrity of the package itself is protected from inadvertent modification at run time.

Packages provide better performance than stored procedures and functions because public package variables and cursors persist in memory for the duration of a session. So, they can be shared by all procedures and functions that access them during that session. They do not need to be reinstantiated in memory with each access. Also, they allow you to maintain data across transactions without the need to store the data in the database.

When a packaged procedure or function is called in a session for the first time, the subprogram and the whole package is loaded into memory. Therefore, subsequent calls to other procedures or functions in that package are already in memory and avoid any more disk access.

Packages provide easier application maintenance because they stop cascading dependencies that often occur in stored procedures and functions. By avoiding cascading dependencies, unnecessary recompilations are avoided. For example, if you change a stored procedure or function and recompile it, Oracle must recompile all dependent stored procedures or functions that call the changed subprogram. However, if you change a packaged procedure or function, as long as the package specification remains unchanged, Oracle need not recompile the dependent calling subprograms. Dependent subprograms depend upon the state of the package specification, not the package body.

Creating a Package

A package is simply a named module that contains program objects. The general format of a package is as follows:

```
PACKAGE <package_name> IS
   /*
   ** Public datatype, variable, constant, exception, and cursor
   ** declarations.
   ** Public procedure and function specifications (forward
   ** declarations).
   */
END [package_name];

PACKAGE BODY <pacakage_name> IS
   /*
   ** Private datatype, variable, constant, exception, and cursor
```

```
    ** declarations.
    ** Public and private procedure and function bodies.
    */
[BEGIN
    -- initialization statements]
END [package_name];
```

where:

> **package_name** is a unique name within the scope of a database schema that is used to identify the package when accessing the package contents.

The package specification and package body are created interactively with the SQL*Plus or SQL*DBA tools, or with OCI or Pro*C. The CREATE PACKAGE statement is used to create a package specification and has the following syntax:

```
CREATE PACKAGE <package_name> AS
    ...
END;
```

The CREATE PACKAGE BODY statement is used to create a package body and has the following syntax:

```
CREATE PACKAGE BODY <package_name> AS
    ...
END;
```

Notice the use of AS when issuing these commands. Like stored procedures and functions, the source module for the package should be created in a separate text file. That way, the package can be easily submitted for compilation and storage in the database with a separate SQL script.

The Package Specification

The package specification declares the public package objects, which are visible and accessible outside the package. The scope of the objects in a package specification is within the current database schema in which the specification is defined and global to the package itself. Thus, the package objects declared in the package specification are visible and accessible to any application that can access the containing database schema and from anywhere inside the package. The syntax to declare a package specification is

```
CREATE PACKAGE <package_name> AS
    -- Datatype, constant, variable, expression declarations.
    [CURSOR <cursor_name> RETURN <datatype>;]
```

```
    [PROCEDURE <procedure_name> [(formal_parameters)];]
    [FUNCTION <function_name> [(formal_parameters)]

      RETURN <datatype>;]
END;
```

Notice that the procedure and function declarations are forward declarations as discussed in the previous section on procedures and functions. The following example illustrates how a package specification is defined:

```
CREATE PACKAGE item_operations AS
    PROCEDURE update_item_cost (iItemId INTEGER, fNewCost NUMBER);
    FUNCTION subtotal (iItemId INTEGER, nItemCount INTEGER)

      RETURN NUMBER;
END;
```

The package specification only declares the existence of package objects, such as cursors, procedures, and functions; it does not implement the details. After one of these objects is declared, applications outside the package need not be concerned with the implementation details, as long as the specification stays constant.

If a package specification declares only datatypes, constants, variables, and exceptions, the package body is unnecessary. This allows for the definition of global datatypes, constants, variables, and exceptions that persist in memory throughout a session and are accessible by other procedures and functions.

The WITH INTERFACE Clause

The WITH INTERFACE clause allows for the creation of a direct interface between a packaged procedure in a package specification and a C language program. Normally, a call from a Pro*C (or other precompiler) or OCI application to a packaged procedure would need to be encapsulated in an anonymous PL/SQL block. The WITH INTERFACE clause allows a packaged procedure to be directly called from a Pro*C or OCI application. The WITH INTERFACE clause cannot be specified for a packaged function. The WITH INTERFACE clause is specified in a package specification using the following syntax:

```
PACKAGE <package_name> IS
    ...
    PROCEDURE <procedure_name> [(formal_parameters)]
      [WITH INTERFACE PROCEDURE <interface_name>
      [(interface_parameters)]];
```

```
...
END;
```

where:

> **interface_parameters** are the parameters that can be used in a direct call to the procedure from a Pro*C or OCI application. The parameters have the following syntax:

```
<parameter_name> <datatype> [INDICATOR indicator_name], ...
```

where:

> **parameter_name** is the name of each interface parameter that corresponds to each formal parameter in the procedure.
>
> **datatype** is a valid ANSI/ISO datatype, compatible with the formal parameter of the procedure.
>
> **indicator_name** is an optional indicator variable that can be associated with an interface parameter. The indicator variable does not have a corresponding formal parameter.

The following rules apply:

- The procedure name and interface name should be the same, but can be different.

- Each formal parameter and indicator parameter of the procedure must appear as an interface parameter.

- One of the interface parameters can be a variable named **sqlcode** of datatype INTEGER with no indicator variable.

- All datatypes must be ANSI/ISO SQL datatypes.

The WITH INTERFACE clause creates a mapping between each formal parameter of the procedure to an interface parameter. Also, an optional indicator variable can be specified with each interface parameter (indicator variables were discussed in Chapter 4). The following example illustrates how the WITH INTERFACE clause is specified:

```
CREATE PACKAGE item_operations AS
    PROCEDURE update_item_cost (iItemId INTEGER, fNewCost NUMBER)
        WITH INTERFACE PROCEDURE update_item_cost
            (iItemId INTEGER, fNewCost NUMBER, sqlcode INTEGER);
    FUNCTION subtotal (iItemId INTEGER, nItemCount INTEGER) RETURN NUMBER;
END;
```

NOTE
A variable named **sqlcode** of type INTEGER must be included in the
WITH INTERFACE declaration.

The Oracle tool SQL*Module processes the WITH INTERFACE clause and
actually produces a Pro*C source module. This module contains a C program with
the interface name and with the interface parameters as specified. This program
calls the packaged procedure from an anonymous block using host variables.

The C program can then be called directly from within a C, C++, Pro*C, or OCI
application. The WITH INTERFACE clause makes it possible to call packaged
procedures directly from C or C++ applications.

The Package Body

The package specification defines the interface to the public package contents, the
package body is the implementation of that interface. Keep in mind that cursors,
procedures, or functions defined in a package body are accessible outside the
package only if their specifications also appear in the package specification.

The package body defines the implementation details of all cursor, procedure,
and function bodies. Also, the package body contains the declaration of private
package objects, such as datatypes, constants, variables, expressions, and cursors.
The scope of these declarations is local to the package body. Therefore, the private
package objects are only accessible from within the package body. The syntax to
define a package body is

```
PACKAGE BODY <package_name> IS
   /*
   ** datatype, variable, constant, and exception declarations.
   */
   [CURSOR <cursor_name> RETURN <datatype>
      SELECT ...;]

   [PROCEDURE <procedure_name> [(parameter_list)] IS
      -- Local procedure object declarations
   BEGIN
      ...
   [EXCEPTION
      -- exception handlers]
      ...
   END;]

   [FUNCTION <function_name> [(parameter_list)] RETURN <datatype>
```

```
      IS
        -- Local function object declarations
      BEGIN
        ...
      [EXCEPTION
        -- exception handlers]
        ...
      END;]
[BEGIN
    -- initialization statements]
END [package_name];
```

Unlike a package specification, the declarative part of a package body can contain procedure or function bodies. This is where the details of all package contents are defined. The package body can be thought of as a "black box"; it can be debugged, enhanced, or completely replaced without changing or affecting the package specification.

Following the declarative part of a package body, an optional initialization part can be specified. The initialization part of a package typically contains statements that initialize variables previously declared in the package or performs certain initialization actions. The initialization part of a package cannot be passed parameters, so it must be self-contained. Also, the initialization part is executed only once; the first time the package is accessed in a session.

The following example illustrates how a package body is defined:

```
CREATE PACKAGE BODY item_operations AS
    PROCEDURE update_item_cost (iItemId INTEGER, fNewCost NUMBER);
        fCurCost NUMBER(10,2);
        missing_cost EXCEPTION;
    BEGIN
        SELECT item_cost INTO fCurCost FROM item
            WHERE item_id = iItemId;
        IF fCurCost IS null THEN
            RAISE missing_cost;
        ELSE
            UPDATE item SET item_cost = fNewCost
                WHERE item_id = iItemId;
        END IF;

    COMMIT;

    EXCEPTION
        WHEN NO_DATA_FOUND THEN
```

```
            INSERT INTO item_audit VALUES (iItemId, 'Invalid Item
                identifier.');
            COMMIT;
        WHEN missing_cost THEN
            INSERT INTO item_audit

                VALUES (iItemId, 'Item Cost is null.');
            COMMIT;
        WHEN OTHERS THEN

            ROLLBACK;
            INSERT INTO item_audit

                VALUES (iItemId, 'Miscellaneous error.');
            COMMIT;
END update_item_cost;

FUNCTION subtotal (iItemId INTEGER, nItemCount INTEGER)
    RETURN NUMBER IS
    fPrice NUMBER(10,2);
    missing_price EXCEPTION;
BEGIN
    SELECT retail_price INTO fPrice FROM item
        WHERE item_id = iItemId;
    IF fPrice IS null THEN
        RAISE missing_price;
    ELSE
        RETURN (fPrice * nItemCount);
    END IF;

EXCEPTION
    WHEN NO_DATA_FOUND THEN
        INSERT INTO item_audit VALUES (iItemId, 'Invalid Item
            identifier.');
        COMMIT;
    WHEN missing_price THEN
        INSERT INTO item_audit
            VALUES (iItemId, 'Item Price is null.');
        COMMIT;
END subtotal;
```

Packaged Cursors

A packaged public cursor is declared in a package specification and is defined separately in the package body. The public cursor declaration defines the cursor name and the datatype of the result returned when a row is fetched from the cursor. The datatype can be any PL/SQL datatype including a %TYPE or %ROWTYPE attribute. The RETURN clause is used to define the datatype of the cursor result value. The syntax to declare a public cursor in a package specification with the RETURN clause is

```
CURSOR <cursor_name> RETURN <datatype>;
```

where:

> **cursor_name** is the unique name of the public cursor.
>
> **datatype** is a valid PL/SQL datatype. This datatype can be a %TYPE or %ROWTYPE attribute of a previously declared variable or row.

A cursor specification has no SELECT statement because the RETURN clause defines the datatype of the result value. You can use the %ROWTYPE attribute in a RETURN clause to define a record type that represents a row in a database table or the cursor itself. You can also use the %TYPE attribute in a RETURN clause to provide the datatype of a previously declared variable, constant, or database column.

The syntax to define a public cursor in the package body with the RETURN clause is

```
CURSOR <cursor_name> RETURN <datatype>
   SELECT ...;
```

The cursor definition in the package body must have the same cursor name and RETURN datatype as the cursor declaration in the package specification. Also, the cursor definition must include a SELECT statement to define the active set associated with the cursor. In addition, the number and datatypes of the items in the SELECT statement select list must match the datatype of the RETURN clause.

The cursor definition in the package body can be changed at will without changing the cursor specification.

Referencing Package Contents

Public package contents are referenced from outside a package using dot notation. This is done by prefixing the package object (datatype, variable, procedure, and so on) with the package name. For example:

```
package_name.datatype_name
```

or

```
package_name.variable_name
```

or

```
package_name.procedure_name(...);
```

or

```
package_name.function_name(...)
```

Package contents can be referenced from database triggers, stored procedures or functions, embedded PL/SQL blocks, and anonymous PL/SQL blocks sent to Oracle interactively by SQL*Plus or SQL*DBA.

Public package contents can be accessed remotely by use of the notation shown previously with database links, as was discussed for stored procedures and functions. The following syntax is used to remotely access public package contents:

```
package_name.object_name@db_link(...);
```

Package Maintenance

A package specification can have the same states as a stored procedure or function: valid or invalid. A package specification is valid if neither the package specification nor any object it references has been DROPped, REPLACEd, or ALTERed since the package specification was last compiled.

Alternatively, if any of these conditions exist, the package specification is invalid. When a package specification is invalid and recompiled, Oracle invalidates dependent objects. Dependent objects include stored or packaged procedures, or functions that call or reference objects declared in the recompiled package specification. If an invalid dependent object is called or referenced before it is recompiled, Oracle automatically recompiles it at run time. This can have the same problems associated with invalidated stored procedures and functions.

A package body is subject to the same rules as a package specification, except that Oracle can recompile a package body without invalidating the corresponding package specification. This allows for a package body to be debugged, enhanced, and maintained without causing cascading invalidations for all objects that reference the package contents. Any object that references the package contents is only dependent on the package specification, not the package body.

When a package body is recompiled, Oracle determines if objects on which the package body depends are valid. These dependent objects can be stored procedures or functions or any packaged objects in any package specification that are called or referenced in the recompiled package body. If any of these objects are invalid, Oracle recompiles them before recompiling the package body. If all of these objects can be recompiled successfully, the package body becomes valid. Otherwise, Oracle returns a run time error, and the package body remains invalid.

Oracle stores the package specification and body separately in the data dictionary. Compilation errors are stored in the data dictionary with the package specification or the package body, to whichever they pertain.

The commands to recompile a package specification and package body are

```
ALTER PACKAGE <package_name> COMPILE PACKAGE;
```

or

```
ALTER PACKAGE <package_name> COMPILE BODY;
```

Supplied Packages

Various standardized packages are supplied with the Oracle environment and with Oracle development tools, such as SQL*Forms, SQL*ReportWriter, and so on. Some packages are supplied with third-party tools.

The STANDARD Package

The Oracle PL/SQL environment is defined by a package called STANDARD. The STANDARD package specification globally declares standard PL/SQL datatypes, exceptions, procedures, and functions, which are directly accessible to any PL/SQL program. For example, the predefined exceptions and standard PL/SQL functions are declared in the STANDARD package.

The contents of the STANDARD package are directly visible to any application, including a database trigger, a stored or packaged procedure or function, a Pro*C application, an OCI application, and a variety of Oracle tools.

Product-Specific Packages

The Oracle Server and several Oracle tools supply packages containing product-specific procedures and functions, which aid in the development of PL/SQL-based applications. For instance, SQL*Forms supplies a package named SQLFORMS. The Oracle Server provides a package named DBMS_STANDARD, which provides facilities that help develop customized applications. For example, this package provides a procedure named **raise_application_error**, which lets you issue user-defined error messages. That way, you can report errors to an application and avoid returning unhandled exceptions. Package DBMS_STANDARD is an extension of package STANDARD, so you need not qualify references to it.

Package Guidelines

Packages will provide many advantages and help avoid common pitfalls if you observe the following guidelines:

- When a package is designed and created in a database, it should be generalized for reuse in many applications. This improves productivity and eases maintenance.

- Avoid recreating packages that duplicate the features of other existing packages or the Oracle system packages (STANDARD or DBMS_ STANDARD).

- Early in the development process, define package specifications so that they can be compiled into other packages. This speeds application development and forces the design of specifications to be completed before the package bodies are developed.

- Use packages to encapsulate implementation details and data into the package body, and hide information and processing details. This is done by placing only the necessary objects in the package specification. This reduces the need to repeatedly recompile the package specification.

Embedding PL/SQL in a Pro*C Application

Throughout this chapter, the features of PL/SQL have been discussed to show how they can be used to create PL/SQL blocks, subblocks, procedures, and functions. This section will show how these PL/SQL features can be embedded in a Pro*C application.

Remember, in a Pro*C application, each SQL statement requires a single call to the Oracle Server. This can create a significant amount of overhead. PL/SQL allows multiple SQL statements, even complete transactions, to be combined into blocks, procedures, or functions that only require one call to the Oracle Server—thus, eliminating the overhead.

Embedding a PL/SQL Anonymous Block

When an anonymous PL/SQL block is encountered in a Pro*C application program, the entire block is treated like a single embedded SQL statement. Therefore, an anonymous block can be placed anywhere in a Pro*C program where a SQL statement can be placed.

An anonymous PL/SQL block is embedded in a Pro*C program by simply encasing the block between the keywords EXEC SQL EXECUTE and END-EXEC as follows:

```
EXEC SQL EXECUTE
    DECLARE
        . . .
    BEGIN
        . . .
    END;
END-EXEC;
```

Of course, the PL/SQL block follows all the rules that have been discussed throughout this chapter. The block's DECLARE section is optional. After a Pro*C program is created that includes anonymous blocks, it is precompiled as normal. The syntax and semantics of the embedded PL/SQL blocks can be checked by specifying the SQLCHECK precompiler option.

Using Host Variables

As in any Pro*C application program, host variables are used as the primary communication mechanism between the application program and the Oracle Server. There is no difference when embedding PL/SQL blocks in a Pro*C program.

Host variables are used as the mechanism to pass data to and receive data from an anonymous block. In a PL/SQL block, host variables can be referenced and their values can be set. For example, the user can be prompted for information that is then stored in host variables. The values of those host variables can then be passed to a PL/SQL block to perform an operation. Then the PL/SQL can access the database and use host variables to pass the results back to the Pro*C program.

Inside a PL/SQL block, host variables are global to the entire block and can be used anywhere a PL/SQL variable is allowed. Like host variables in an SQL statement, host variables in a PL/SQL block must be prefixed with a colon (:). The colon distinguishes the host variables from PL/SQL variables and database objects.

Host variables can be used in a PL/SQL block just like any PL/SQL variable. One exception is the use of a VARCHAR host variable. Recall from Chapter 4 where the VARCHAR datatype is discussed, the length field must be initialized to its maximum length before it can be used. Oracle sets the length field to the length of the string returned from an SQL statement. When using a VARCHAR variable in a PL/SQL block, the length field must be initialized to its maximum length before the PL/SQL block is entered; it cannot be initialized inside the PL/SQL block.

Using Indicator Variables

PL/SQL handles null values inherently; it can test for null values with the IS null operator and can directly assign null values to variables with the assignment operator (:=).

Pro*C must use indicator variables to handle null values. So, PL/SQL has provided a method to use indicator variables to accept null values as input from a Pro*C program and output null values to a Pro*C program.

Indicator variables are declared as normal in the DECLARE section of a Pro*C program. However, when used in a PL/SQL block, an indicator variable must be appended to its associated host variable. The syntax to use an indicator variable in a PL/SQL block is

```
:host_variable:indicator_variable
```

The following example illustrates this syntax, the indicator variable **indCost** is appended to cost.

```
EXEC SQL EXECUTE
    BEGIN
        SELECT item_name, item_cost

          INTO :scItemName, :fItemCost:indCost
          FROM item
          WHERE item_id = :iItemId;
        IF :fItemCost:indCost IS null THEN
          ...
        END IF;
    END;
END-EXEC;
```

Notice that the indicator variables are handled just like any other variable.

Although you cannot refer directly to an indicator variable inside a PL/SQL block, when a PL/SQL block is entered, if an indicator variable is assigned a value of –1, PL/SQL automatically assigns a null to the associated host variable. When the block is exited, if a host variable is null, PL/SQL automatically assigns a value of –1 to the indicator variable.

Similarly, PL/SQL does not raise an exception when a truncated string value is assigned to a host variable. If you use an indicator variable, PL/SQL sets its value to the original length of the string. Otherwise, the indicator variable is set to zero (0). That way, the Pro*C program can tell if the string is truncated upon return from the PL/SQL block.

Using Host Arrays

Host arrays and indicator arrays can be passed to a PL/SQL block. They can be indexed by a PL/SQL variable of datatype BINARY_INTEGER or by a host variable compatible with that datatype.

Furthermore, you can assign all the values in a host array to rows in a PL/SQL table. Given that the host array subscript range is m .. n, the corresponding PL/SQL table index range is always 1 .. n − m + 1. For example, if the host array subscript range is 5 .. 10, the corresponding PL/SQL table index range is 1 .. (10 − 5 + 1) or 1 .. 6. Pro*C does not check the usage of indexes in host arrays. In other words, if an index exceeds the range of a host array, no error is returned.

Table 10-4 shows the legal datatype conversions between row values in a PL/SQL table and elements in a host array.

Calling Stored and Packaged Procedures and Functions

A stored or packaged procedure or function can be called from a Pro*C application program, but generally it must be embedded in an anonymous PL/SQL block. For example:

```
EXEC SQL EXECUTE
    BEGIN
        update_item_cost(:item_ident, :cost);
    END;
END-EXEC;
```

If this were a packaged procedure or function, it would need to be prefixed with the package name. Also, notice that a stored procedure or function can accept host variables as parameters.

An IN parameter can be a literal, host variable, host array, PL/SQL constant or variable, PL/SQL table, PL/SQL user-defined record, function call, or expression. However, an OUT parameter cannot be a literal, function call, or expression.

Remember, the datatype of each actual parameter must be convertible to the datatype of its corresponding formal parameter. Also, before a stored procedure is exited, all OUT formal parameters must be assigned values. Otherwise, the values of corresponding actual parameters are indeterminate.

Calling a WITH INTERFACE Packaged Procedure

Recall that previously in this chapter the WITH INTERFACE clause is described as a method to allow a packaged procedure to be directly called from a Pro*C or OCI application. If a packaged procedure is defined with the WITH INTERFACE clause,

PL/SQL Datatype	NUMBER	CHAR	VARCHAR2	LONG	RAW	DATE	ROWID
NUMBER	X						
CHAR		X					
VARCHAR2			X		X	X	X
LONG			X		X	X	X
RAW			X		X	X	X
LONG RAW			X		X	X	X
DATE							
ROWID							

TABLE 10-4. *Legal datatype conversions*

a packaged procedure need not be embedded in an anonymous PL/SQL block. The only restriction is that one of the interface parameters must be named **sqlcode**.

The SQL*Module tool uses the contents of the WITH INTERFACE clause to generate a C program, which links the PL/SQL procedure specification to the calling Pro*C program. In effect, the WITH INTERFACE clause provides a C language prototype so that the associated PL/SQL procedure can be called just like any other C language subprogram. To execute this procedure from a Pro*C, C++, or OCI application program, simply invoke the program just as any other C program.

CHAPTER 11

Oracle Call Interface (OCI)

The Oracle Call Interface (OCI) is a set of functions that you can call from a C program to access the database. In this chapter, we'll discuss:

- What OCI is and how it compares with Pro*C
- Basic OCI routines
- Array handling with OCI

This chapter and Appendix C, which lists the OCI calls, complement each other.

What Is OCI?

OCI is an example of an application program interface (API). An API is a library of functions that you can call from your program. Other APIs include the C I/O library, the DBMS_OUTPUT package in PL/SQL, and the Windows API. Using an API such as OCI doesn't require a special precompiler or compiler—you can use the regular compiler for your language. All that is required is that you link with the library containing the definitions for the functions.

OCI can be called from COBOL and FORTRAN, but it is used primarily in C programs.

OCI Versus Pro*C

Like Pro*C, OCI enables you to access the database from a C program and to use cursor control, array processing, and dynamic SQL. Since OCI is an API, the Pro*C precompiler is unnecessary. This results in some significant differences between Pro*C and OCI, as described in the following paragraphs.

Context-Sensitive Debuggers and Editors   The Pro*C precompiler adds an extra step to the development process as a result of the code it generates for you. Because Pro*C source code isn't understood by most context-sensitive debuggers and editors, you may have to debug the generated code rather than your original source, and context-sensitive editors won't necessarily work as you expect.

Learning Curve   As you have seen, learning to use Pro*C is straightforward due to the simplicity of embedded SQL. OCI is generally considered to be harder to learn.

ANSI Standards   There are no ANSI standards for APIs such as OCI. Thus, OCI is specific to Oracle and won't work with other relational databases. On the other hand, the FIPS flagger and ANSI mode of Pro*C can let you write more portable code.

Host Variables   Pro*C requires that variables to be used for communication with the database (host variables) be declared in a DECLARE section. This is not required in OCI; any C variable can be used as a bind variable in an SQL statement.

Performance   The OCI library is simpler than the precompiler run-time library, so the code path is shorter. This means OCI programs will generally run somewhat faster than equivalent Pro*C programs. The performance is on the same level in OCI programs and Pro*C programs, however. Depending on your application requirements, either Pro*C or OCI might be appropriate.

Necessary Control Structures

With Pro*C, communication between your program and the database takes place via the SQL Communications Area (SQLCA) and host variables. OCI programs also use variables, but instead of the SQLCA, they use the *logon data area* and *cursor data area*. The LDA and CDA also contain information about errors.

Standard OCI Types

Each OCI call expects its arguments to be a certain size. For example, the **obndrv** and **odefin** calls take indicator variables as arguments. Indicator variables need to be exactly two bytes long and are treated as signed integers. Normally, you could declare these variables as the C type **short**. However, on some platforms a **short** may not be two bytes, causing very subtle problems that are difficult to debug.

To fix this, Oracle provides a port-specific header file that defines common types. Each platform will have a different version of this file. These types are either signed or unsigned integers, with lengths ranging from one to four bytes. Their definitions are shown in Table 11-1.

The file that defines these types is called ORATYPES.H. Its location varies according to platform; consult your Oracle system-specific documentation for the exact location. ORATYPES.H also defines the type **sword**, which is a signed word. This is usually defined as **int** and thus takes the size of an integer on your platform.

Name	Description
ub1	Unsigned 1-byte integer
ub2	Unsigned 2-byte integer
ub4	Unsigned 4-byte integer
sb1	Signed 1-byte integer
sb2	Signed 2-byte integer
sb4	Signed 4-byte integer

TABLE 11-1. *Platform-dependent definition file*

LDA and CDA Structures

The LDA and CDA are the primary means of communication between your program and the database. Between them, they incorporate much of the information stored in the SQLCA in Pro*C programs. The LDA and CDA are of the same type, which is included in the following listing. Note that they are defined in terms of the common types in ORATYPES.H.

```c
struct cda_def {

    sb2             v2_rc;    /* V2 return code */
    ub2             ft;       /* SQL function type */
    ub4             rpc;      /* rows processed count */
    ub2             peo;      /* parse error offset */
    ub1             fc;       /* OCI function code */
    ub1             rcs1;     /* filler area */
    ub2             rc;       /* V7 return code */
    ub1             wrn;      /* warning flags */
    ub1             rcs2;     /* reserved */
    sword           rcs3;     /* reserved */
    struct {                  /* ROWID structure */
        struct {
            ub4     rcs4;
            ub2     rcs5;
            ub1     rcs6;
        } rd;
        ub4     rcs7;
        ub2     rcs8;
    } rid;
    sword           ose;  /* OSD-dependent error */
    dvoid          *rcsp;     /* pointer to reserved area */
    ub1             rcs9[64 - sizeof (struct cda_head)]; /*filler*/
};

typedef struct cda_def Cda_Def;

/* The LDA is the same shape as the CDA. */
typedef struct cda_def Lda_Def;
```

Note that both the CDA and LDA are exactly 64 bytes long. The **rcs9** field is included to pad the structure to 64 bytes. Table 11-2 describes each of the fields in the LDA and CDA.

Structure Field	Description
sb2 v2_rc;	Version 2 return code
ub2 ft;	SQL function type
ub4 rpc;	Rows processed count
ub2 peo;	Parse Error Offset
ub1 fc;	OCI function code
ub1 rcs1;	Reserved area
ub2 rc;	Return code
ub1 wrn;	Warning flags
ub1 rcs2;	Reserved area
ub1 rcs3;	Reserved area
struct rid;	ROWID structure
sword ose;	Operating System Error
dvoid *rcsp;	Pointer to reserved area
ub1 rcs9;	Filler to 64 bytes

TABLE 11-2. *LDA and CDA fields*

Using the types defined in the previous listing, you can declare an LDA and a CDA as follows:

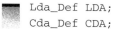

```
Lda_Def LDA;
Cda_Def CDA;
```

Version 2 Return Code

This field contains the return code from Oracle version 2. It is included only for backward compatibility and shouldn't be used for new programs.

SQL Function Type

This field contains a code for the current SQL statement being executed in the CDA. It is valid after the **oparse** call until the next statement is parsed. This field can be useful for error handling. The values for this table are described in Table 11-3. These values are subject to change from one version to the next; consult the *Programmer's Guide to the Oracle Call Interfaces* for the version appropriate for your system.

Code	SQL Function	Code	SQL Function	Code	SQL Function
01	Create table	26	Alter table	51	Drop table space
02	Set role	27	Explain	52	Alter session
03	Insert	28	Grant	53	Alter user
04	Select	29	Revoke	54	Commit
05	Update	30	Create synonym	55	Roll back
06	Drop role	31	Drop synonym	56	Savepoint
07	Drop view	32	Alter system switch log	57	Create control file
08	Drop table	33	Set transaction	58	Alter tracing
09	Delete	34	PL/SQL execute	59	Create trigger
10	Create view	35	Lock table	60	Alter trigger
11	Drop user	36	(Not used)	61	Drop trigger
12	Create role	37	Rename	62	Analyze table
13	Create sequence	38	Comment	63	Analyze index
14	Alter sequence	39	Audit	64	Analyze cluster
15	(Not used)	40	No audit	65	Create profile
16	Drop sequence	41	Alter index	66	Drop profile
17	Create schema	42	Create external datatype	67	Alter profile
18	Create cluster	43	Drop external datatype	68	Drop procedure
19	Create user	44	Create database	69	Drop procedure
20	Create index	45	Alter database	70	Alter resource cost
21	Drop index	46	Create rollback segment	71	Create snapshot log
22	Drop cluster	47	Alter rollback segment	72	Alter snapshot log
23	Validate index	48	Drop rollback segment	73	Drop snapshot log
24	Create procedure	49	Create table space	74	Create snapshot
25	Alter procedure	50	Alter table space	75	Alter snapshot
				76	Drop snapshot

TABLE 11-3. *SQL function codes*

Rows Processed Count

This field contains the current number of rows processed by this cursor. It is valid after the **oexec** or **oexfet** call and is incremented by **ofetch** or **ofen** (query only).

Parse Error Offset

This field contains the 0-based offset into the SQL statement where any parse error occurred. It is equivalent to the **sqlerrd[4]** field in the SQLCA. It is valid after the **oparse** call and is also useful for error handling.

OCI Function Code

Similar to the SQL function code, this field contains a code for the OCI function that was used most recently for this CDA. It is useful for error handling, and the valid values are described in Table 11-4. These values are subject to change from one version to the next; consult the *Programmer's Guide to the Oracle Call Interfaces* for the version appropriate for your system.

Return Code

This field contains the return code for the SQL statement being executed. It is valid after the **oexec** call and is used extensively for error handling.

Warning Flags

Similar to the **sqlwarn** array in the SQLCA, this field contains information about warnings that could occur during execution of the SQL statement. Each bit within this field signifies a different warning, as shown in Table 11-5.

Code	OCI Routine	Code	OCI Routine	Code	OCI Routine
04	oexec, oexn	24	oname	54	oparse
08	odefin	26	osql3	56	oexfet
12	ofetch, ofen	28	obndrv	58	oflng
14	oopen	30	obndrn	60	odescr
16	oclose	34	oopt	62	obndra
22	odsc	52	ocan		

TABLE 11-4. *SQL function codes*

Bit Value	Description	Equivalent Field in SQLCA
1	Set when any other bit is set	sqlwarn[0]
2	Set if any column is truncated during a SELECT statement	sqlwarn[1]
4	Set if a null is encountered during evaluation of an SQL group function such as AVG or MAX	sqlwarn[2]
8	Not used	N/A
16	Set if an UPDATE or DELETE statement affected all rows in a table (no WHERE clause)	sqlwarn[4]
32	Set when a PL/SQL CREATE statement (CREATE PROCEDURE/FUNCTION/ PACKAGE/TRIGGER) failed due to PL/SQL compilation errors	sqlwarn[5]
64	No longer in use	sqlwarn[6]
128	No longer in use	sqlwarn[7]

TABLE 11-5. *OCI warning flags*

ROWID Structure

This field contains the binary version of an Oracle ROWID. This is the same format as the ROWID internal datatype (type 11). It is usually 13 bytes long, although this length is system-dependent. ROWID is valid after an INSERT, UPDATE, DELETE, or SELECT FOR UPDATE statement.

Operating System-Dependent Error

If an SQL statement fails due to an operating system error (such as "out of disk space"), the error code is indicated in this field.

Error Handling

Error handling is as important for OCI programs as it is for Pro*C programs. Unlike Pro*C, OCI has no implicit checking for errors (the WHENEVER statement). After each OCI call, you should check for errors. In general, OCI functions will return a nonzero value in case of an error and zero if successful. Therefore, a good way to check for errors is with the following syntax:

```
if (<OCI call with arguments>)
  handle_error();
```

The **.rc** field in the CDA and LDA will hold the actual error code returned. Given this value, the **oerhms** function will return the error message text (similar to **sqlca.sqlerrm.sqlerrmc** in the SQLCA). Since **oerhms** also requires a database context to determine this error (given by the LDA structure), the **handle_error** function could be written as follows:

```
void handle_error(Lda_Def *lda, Cda_Def *cda, char *cMessageTxt) {
  char cMessageBuffer[512];
  oerhms(lda, cda->rc, cMessageBuffer,
      (sword) sizeof(MessageBuffer));
/* Output error message here. */
```

The **oerhms** function is described in more detail in Appendix C.

Program Flow

Figure 11-1 illustrates the typical sequence of calls in an OCI program. Each of these calls will be described in detail in this chapter.

Many OCI functions take strings as arguments. These strings are usually passed with two parameters: one for the string itself, the other for the length of the string. For example, *uid* and *uidl,* part of the **orlon** call, are two such parameters. In these cases, the length parameter can be passed as –1 if the string parameter is null-terminated. If the length parameter isn't –1, it should contain the number of characters in the string.

A number of OCI routines (**oopen**, for example) contain parameters that are optional or unused. These may be retained for backward compatibility; otherwise, the parameters may not make sense for C.

The following sections describe in more detail each of the components of an OCI program. The format of each section is similar to Appendix C. Each OCI call is introduced, followed by a parameter description, usage notes, and an example. Each section continues the example begun in the first listing in this chapter.

Similar to a PL/SQL stored procedure, each parameter for an OCI call is classified as IN, OUT, or IN/OUT (see Table 11-6).

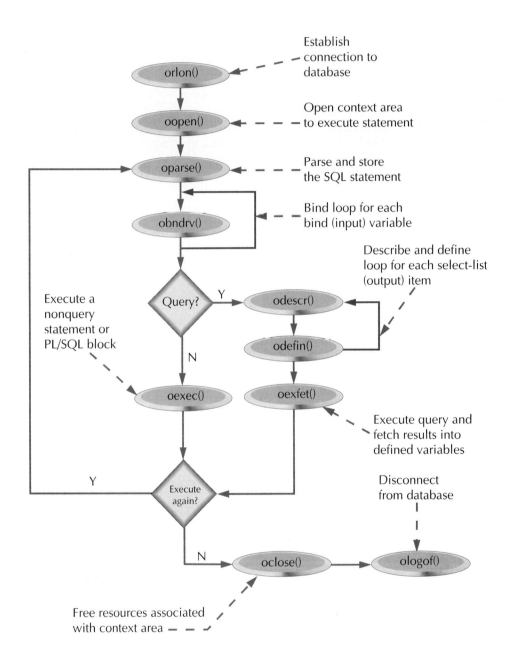

FIGURE 11-1. *OCI program flow*

Parameter Mode	Description
IN	Parameter's value is read by the function but not changed. May be passed either by value or by reference.
OUT	After the function call, this parameter will have a new value, set by the function. Must be passed by reference.
IN/OUT	Parameter's value is read by the function and may also be changed by the function. Must be passed by reference.

TABLE 11-6. *Parameter modes for OCI calls*

Connecting to the Database

Just like Pro*C, before your program can do any useful work, it must connect to the database. It connects via the **orlon** call:

```
sword  orlon (Lda_Def *lda,
              ub1 *hda,
              text *uid,
              sword uidl,
              text *pswd,
              sword pswdl,
              sword audit);
```

orlon Parameter Descriptions
Table 11-7 shows the **orlon** parameters.

Use of the orlon Function
orlon should be the first OCI call executed by your program—none of the other OCI calls will return successfully until you have established a valid connection to the database.

Each LDA/HDA pair indicates a separate connection, or database context, similar to the AT clause in Pro*C. If you want your OCI program to have more than one simultaneous connection, you need to allocate an LDA and an HDA for each connection and make an **orlon** call for each one.

You can specify the password as part of the *uid* parameter. If you do this, pass NULL for *pswd* and 0 for *pswdl*. For example, a valid *uid* would be

```
scott/tiger
```

Parameter	Type	Mode	Description
lda	Lda_Def *	IN/OUT	Address of an LDA structure
hda	ub1 *	IN/OUT	Address of a previously allocated area of memory[1]
uid	text *	IN	Oracle userid to be used for the connection
uidl	sword	IN	Length of uid[2]
pswd	text *	IN	Password for the Oracle userid
pswdl	sword	IN	Length of pswd[2]
audit	sword	IN	No longer used

Notes:

1. The HDA must be allocated by your program before **orlon** is called. On most systems, it should be 256 bytes long. However, on 64-bit systems the HDA needs to be 512 bytes. For portability, use 512 for the HDA size unless memory requirements prevent it.

2. This parameter can be passed as –1 if its associated string is null-terminated.

TABLE 11-7. *The orlon parameters*

If you want to establish a connection via SQL*Net, include the SQL*Net connect string as part of *uid*:

```
scott/tiger@newyork
```

The **orlon** call is equivalent to EXEC SQL CONNECT in Pro*C.

Example
Using the preceding declarations, a valid **orlon** call would be

```
ub1 HDA[512];
if (orlon(&LDA, HDA, (text *) "scott", (sword) -1,
      (text *) "tiger", (sword) -1, -1))
  handle_error(&LDA, &LDA, "orlon - connecting to the database");
```

Opening a Cursor

Each SQL statement in OCI is executed within a *context area*. The context area is an area of memory in which Oracle stores information relevant to the SQL statement processing. This information includes a pointer to the parsed representation of the statement in the shared pool portion of the SGA and the active set of a query. The context area is allocated on the client in a client-server program.

The CDA structure serves as a handle into the context area. The context area is allocated and initialized by the **oopen** call and is freed by the **oclose** call. The syntax of **oopen** is

```
sword   oopen (Cda_Def *cursor,
               Lda_Def *lda,
               text *dbn,
               sword dbnl,
               sword arsize,
               text *uid,
               sword uidl);
```

oopen Parameter Descriptions
Table 11-8 lists the **oopen** parameters.

Parameter	Type	Mode	Description
cursor	Cda_Def *	OUT	Address of a cursor data area in the program
lda	Lda_Def *	IN/OUT	Address of a logon data area, previously initialized by orlon
dbn	text *	IN	Included for V2 compatibility; pass as NULL
dbnl	sword	IN	Included for V2 compatibility; pass as –1
arsize	arsize	IN	Not used by Oracle 7—cursors will dynamically adjust their array size, pass as –1
uid	text *	IN	Not used by Oracle 7; pass as NULL
uidl	sword	IN	Not used by Oracle 7; pass as –1

TABLE 11-8.   *oopen parameters*

Use of the oopen Function

Since the CDA used by **oopen** will be used for subsequent calls, it is important that its storage remain visible until the cursor is closed with **oclose**.

Subsequent OCI calls will use the CDA but will not need to reference the LDA. **oopen** stores a pointer to the database context in the context area.

Example

```
if (oopen(&CDA, &LDA, (text *) NULL, -1, -1, (text *) NULL, -1))
    handle_error(&CDA, &LDA, "oopen - opening CDA");
```

Parsing the SQL Statement

The OCI routine used to parse the SQL statement is **oparse**. During the parse, the following things happen:

- The text of the SQL statement is sent to the server.

- The server examines the statement for any syntactic or semantic errors and reports them to the user.

- If the statement is correct, the execution plan for the statement is determined. The execution plan is Oracle's "method of attack" for the statemen—what indexes will be used, whether a sort will be necessary, and so on.

- The parsed form of the statement and the execution plan are stored in the shared pool, if they aren't there already. If they are in the shared pool, the execution plan is not determined again.

The syntax of the **oparse** call is

```
sword  oparse(Cda_Def *cursor,
              text *sqlstm,
              sb4 sqllen,
              sword defflg,
              ub4 lngflg);
```

oparse Parameter Descriptions

Table 11-9 lists the **oparse** parameters.

Parameter	Type	Mode	Description
cursor	Cda_Def *	IN/OUT	Address of a cursor data area in your program
sqlstm	text *	IN	String containing the SQL statement to be parsed
sqllen	sb4	IN	Length of sqlstm[1]
defflg	sword	IN	Deferred parse flag[2]
lngflg	ub4	IN	Database version flag[2]

Notes:

1. If sqlstm is null-terminated, pass as –1.

2. See the usage notes for the values of this parameter.

TABLE 11-9. *oparse parameters*

Use of the oparse Function

After **oparse**, the CDA contains the parsed representation of the statement. The string containing the SQL statement should remain valid (the memory not freed) until the statement is executed. Once an SQL statement is parsed for a particular CDA, it will remain until either the cursor is closed with **oclose** or another statement is parsed in the same CDA. This enables you to parse an SQL statement once and execute it multiple times, possibly with different values for the bind variables. The ability to avoid reparsing is one of the main features of tuning OCI programs for performance.

Deferring the Parse   The *defflg* parameter indicates whether the parse should be deferred. If *defflg* is nonzero and the program was linked with the deferred libraries, then the parse is deferred. This means that the parse is not actually done at the time of the **oparse** call itself; rather, it is done when the statement is executed (**oexec**) or described (**odescr**), whichever comes first.

Whenever possible, you should defer the parse. To do this, you need to set *defflg* to a nonzero value and link with the necessary libraries. On most platforms, the default OCI libraries will allow you to defer the parse. Check your system-specific Oracle documentation for more information on these libraries.

What does deferring the parse mean? If the parse is deferred, the SQL statement is stored at the time of the parse, but the parse itself isn't actually done. Completing the parse involves communication with the database, and in a client-server environment this can be an expensive operation. Instead, the parse is done when the statement is described or executed. By deferring the parse and using the array interface, you can complete an entire SQL statement (query or nonquery) in a single network round trip.

This means that if an error occurs during the parse (such as ORA-942: table or view does not exist), it won't be reported until the statement is executed. If you defer the parse, your error handling needs to be robust enough to handle this situation.

V6 Versus V7 Behavior   The *lngflg* parameter indicates how a statement should be treated. This flag controls whether the SQL statement should be processed like version 7 of Oracle or version 6. The precompilers require you to have either V6 or V7 behavior for every SQL statement in the file, while OCI allows you to specify this behavior for individual SQL statements. Valid values for this parameter are shown in Table 11-10.

For new applications, you should specify version 7 behavior. Version 6 behavior should only be used for porting existing OCI applications to Oracle 7.

oparse and DDL Statements   If you pass a DDL statement to **oparse** and you are not deferring the parse, the statement is executed immediately; no execute call is needed. If you are deferring the parse, then the execute is still necessary. For example:

```
#define PARSE_NONDEFERRED 0
#define V7_BEHAVIOR 2
text *tDropStmt = "drop table employee"
/* No execute necessary - upon successful completion of this
 * call, the EMPLOYEE table will be dropped! */
if (oparse(&CDA, tDropStmt, (sb4) -1,
       (sword) PARSE_NONDEFERRED, (ub4) V7_BEHAVIOR))
   handle_error(&LDA, &CDA, "oparse - tDropStmt");
```

Value of lngflg	Description
0	Version 6 behavior. You must be connected to a database at version 6 or higher.
1	Version 6 or 7, depending on the database you are connected to.
2	Version 7 behavior. If you are connected to a version 6 database, Oracle will return an error.

TABLE 11-10.   *lngflg parameter values*

Example

```
#define PARSE_DEFERRED 1
#define V7_BEHAVIOR 2
/* Note that there is no semicolon in the SQL statement. */
text *tEmployeeStmt = (text *)
    "select employee_ssn, pay_rate, first_name,
        last_name, hire_date\
        from employee \
        where state = :b_state \
        and pay_rate >= :b_pay_rate";
if (oparse(&CDA, tEmployeeStmt, (sb4) -1, (sword) PARSE_DEFERRED,
        (ub4) V7_BEHAVIOR))
    handle_error(&LDA, &CDA, "oparse - parsing SQL query");
```

Binding Input Variables

As in Pro*C, SQL statements can use host variables. This process in OCI is known as *binding,* and the **obndrv** function is the primary function used. During the bind, information about host variables is passed to the database. The values of these host variables (or *bind variables*) will be used as placeholders in the SQL statement.

For each bind variable, four pieces of information need to be passed to the database:

- Address of the variable
- External datatype associated with the variable
- Length of the data
- Address of an associated indicator variable (if any)

These are passed via the **obndrv** function:

```
sword   obndrv(Cda_Def *cursor,
            text *sqlvar,
            sword sqlvl,
            ub1 *progv,
            sword progvl,
            sword ftype,
            sword scale,
            sb2 *indp,
            text *fmt,
            sword fmtl,
            sword fmtt);
```

Each call to **obndrv** passes these four pieces of information about one bind variable. The same information is passed to the database in Pro*C for each host variable.

obndrv Parameter Descriptions
Table 11-11 lists the **obndrv** parameters.

Parameter	Type	Mode	Description
cursor	Cda_Def *	IN/OUT	Address of a cursor data area in your program
sqlvar	text *	IN	String containing the name of a placeholder in the SQL statement[1]
sqlvl	sword	IN	Length of sqlvar[2]
progv	ub1 *	IN/OUT	Address of the bind variable to be substituted for the placeholder[3,4]
progvl	sword	IN	Length of the bind variable
ftype	sword	IN	External datatype for the bind variable
scale	sword	IN	Not normally used for C types; pass as −1
indp	sb2 *	IN/OUT	Address of indicator variable associated with bind variable[3,4]
fmt	text *	IN	Not normally used for C types; pass as NULL
fmtl	sword	IN	Not normally used for C types; pass as −1
fmtt	sword	IN	Not normally used for C types; pass as −1

Notes:

1. **progv** should include the colon.

2. If **sqlvar** is null-terminated, you can pass −1.

3. The address of this parameter must remain valid until the **oexec** call.

4. This parameter will be written to after the **oexec** call for PL/SQL blocks.

TABLE 11-11.   *obndrv parameters*

Use of the obndrv Function

Two additional bind functions are **obndrn** and **obndra**. **obndrn** is used to bind by number rather than by name—the placeholders would be *:1*, *:2*, and so on, rather than *:b_pay_rate*. **obndra** is used to bind PL/SQL tables to C arrays. **obndrn** and **obndra** are discussed in Appendix C.

   If the statement being executed is a PL/SQL block, all placeholders are bound. This is true even if a placeholder is used in a call to a stored procedure and is an OUT parameter. In this case, the bound variable will be written into rather than read from. No define call is necessary, and attempting to define a statement that is not a query will result in an error.

Example

```
#define STRING_TYPE 5
#define FLOAT_TYPE 3
/* Bind variables. They are being assigned constants here, but
** you may prompt the user for their values or read them
** from a file. */
char cBindState[3] = "CA";
float fBindPayRate = 1000.00;
sb2 indBindState = 0, indBindPayRate = 0;
char cState[3] = "CA";
if (obndrv(&CDA, (text *) ":b_state",
      (sword) -1, (ub1 *) cBindState,
      (sword) strlen(cBindState) + 1,
      (sword) STRING_TYPE, (sword) -1,
       &indBindState, (text *) NULL, (sword) -1, (sword) -1))
   handle_error(&LDA, &CDA, "obndrv - b_state");

  /* Note that we are passing the address of fPayRate. */
  if (obndrv(&CDA, (text *) ":b_pay_rate", (sword) -1,
     (ub1 *) &fBindPayRate,
     (sword) sizeof (fBindPayRate), (sword) FLOAT_TYPE,
     (sword) -1, &indBindPayRate, (text *) NULL,
     (sword) -1, (sword) -1))
   handle_error(&LDA, &CDA, "obndrv - b_pay_rate");
```

Describing the Select List

In many cases, the exact SQL statement may not be known until run time. For example, you may prompt the user to enter an SQL statement, and your program will then need to execute it. If the statement is a query, your program will need to allocate space for the active set. To do this, you will need to know the datatypes and lengths of the select list items being returned so you can allocate enough memory for them. This operation is known as a *describe* and is the same as the EXEC SQL DESCRIBE SELECT LIST command.

The OCI function that does the describe is **odescr**:

```
sword   odescr(Cda_Def *cursor,
               sword pos,
               sb4 *dbsize,
               sb2 *dbtype,
               sb1 *cbuf,
               sb4 *cbufl,
               sb4 *dsize,
               sb2 *prec,
               sb2 *scale,
               sb2 *nullok);
```

odescr Parameter Descriptions
Table 11-12 lists the **odescr** parameters.

Use of the odescr Function
You don't need to describe the select list if you know its structure at compile time. In many cases, this will be true. **odescr** can't be deferred—it will always require a call to the database. If the parse was deferred, it is done before the results of the describe.

Each call to **odescr** will return information about one select list item, so in most cases it will be called in a loop, with the value of *pos* incremented by 1 each time. The loop will end when **odescr** returns ORA-1007: variable not in select list, as the following example shows. (Note that *cbufl* must be initialized to the maximum size of *cbuf* before the call.)

Parameter	Type	Mode	Description
cursor	Cda_Def *	IN/OUT	Address of a cursor data area in your program
pos	sword	IN	Position within select list to describe[1]
dbsize	sb4 *	OUT	Size of the select list item
dbtype	sb2 *	OUT	Internal datatype of the select list item
cbuf	sb1 *	OUT	Buffer to store the name of the select list item[2]
cbufl	sb4 *	IN/OUT	Length of cbuf[3]
dsize	sb4 *	OUT	Display size of the select list item[4,5]
prec	sb2 *	OUT	Precision of the select list item[4,5]
scale	sb2 *	OUT	Scale of the select list item[4,5]
nullok	sb2 *	OUT	Nonzero if the select list item can contain null, otherwise zero[5]

Notes:

1. The first select list item is position 1.

2. If the select list item is an expression, you can use an alias in the select statement to get a useful name.

3. Before the call to **odescr**, *cbufl* should contain the size of *cbuf*. After the call, *cbufl* will contain the actual length of the string in *cbuf*, which won't be null-terminated.

4. As stored in the data dictionary.

5. Pass NULL for this parameter if you are not interested in its value.

TABLE 11-12.   *odescr parameters*

Example

```
sb4 iDbSize;
sb2 iDbType;
text tSelectName[25];
sb4 iSelectNameLength = sizeof(tSelectName);
sb4 iDisplaySize;
sb2 iPrecision;
```

```
sb2 iScale;
sb2 iNullok;
for (i = 1; ;i++ ) { /* Loop until you get the ORA-1007 error. */
  /* Reset size of cbufl before the call. */
  iSelectNameLength = sizeof(tSelectName);
  odescr(&CDA, (sword) i, &iDbSize, &iDbType, (sb1 *) tSelectName,
         &iSelectNameLength, &iDisplaySize, &iPrecision,
         &iScale, &iNullok);

  /* Check for any errors. */
  if (CDA.rc == 1007)
    /* End of select list reached. */
    break;
  else if (CDA.rc != 0)
    handle_error(&LDA, &CDA, "odescr - describing select list");

  /* Describe successful - print out results. */
  printf("Column %d, %*.*s,  has type %d, precision %d, \
         scale %d, length %d.",
         i, iSelectNameLength, iSelectNameLength, tSelectName,
         iDbType, iPrecision, iScale, iDisplaySize);
  if (iNullok)
    printf("This column allows nulls.\n");
  else
    printf("This column does not allow nulls.\n");
}
```

Defining Output Variables

Binding is used for input variables to replace placeholders in the SQL statement. *Defining* is similar to binding in that the same four pieces of information are passed to the database. The difference is that each define call provides information for output variables; each fetch will put values into these variables. If the statement isn't a query, it is an error to attempt to define it. The define operation is done via the **odescr** call:

```
sword  odefin(Cda_Def *cursor,
              sword pos,
              ub1 *buf,
              sword bufl,
              sword ftype,
              sword scale,
              sb2 *indp,
              text *fmt,
```

```
sword fmtl,
sword fmtt,
ub2 *rlen,
ub2 *rcode);
```

odefin Parameter Descriptions

Table 11-13 lists the **odefin** parameters.

Parameter	Type	Mode	Description
cursor	Cda_Def *	IN/OUT	Address of a cursor data area within your program
pos	sword	IN	Position within select list for this output variable[1]
buf	ub1 *	IN/OUT[2]	Address of the buffer that will receive the fetched data
bufl	sword	IN	Length of buf
ftype	sword	IN	External datatype associated with this output variable
scale	sword	IN	Not normally used in C; pass as –1
indp	ub2 *	IN/OUT[2]	Address of an associated indicator variable[3]
fmt	text *	IN	Not normally used in C; pass as NULL
fmtl	sword	IN	Not normally used in C; pass as –1
fmtt	sword	IN	Not normally used in C; pass as –1
rlen	ub2 *	IN/OUT[2]	Column-level return length[3,4]
rcode	ub2 *	IN/OUT[2]	Column-level return code[3,5]

Notes:

1. The first select list item is at position 1.

2. This parameter is written to by the **ofetch** or **oexfet** call.

3. Pass NULL for this parameter if you are not interested in its value.

4. *rlen* will contain the actual length of the fetched data.

5. *rcode* indicates that the variable was NULL or truncated (ORA-1405 or ORA-1406).

TABLE 11-13. *odefin parameters*

Use of the odefin Function

Often, **odefin** is called from the same loop as **odescr**. That way, as the internal datatype for each select list item is determined, the external datatype can be determined as well. For more information, see CDEMO2.C, one of the Oracle sample OCI programs, for an example of this method.

Example

```c
char cEmployeeSSN[12];
float fPayRate;
char cFirstName[41];
char cLastName[41];
char cHireDate[10];
sb2 indEmployeeSSN, indPayRate, indFirstName, indLastName
sb2 indHireDate;
ub2 LengthSSN, LengthPayRate, LengthFirstName;
ub2 LengthLastName, LengthHireDate;
ub2 CodeSSN, CodePayRate, CodeFirstName;
ub2 CodeLastName, CodeHireDate;
if (odefin(&CDA, (sword ) 1, (ub1 *) cEmployeeSSN,
         (sword) sizeof(cEmployeeSSN),
         (sword) STRING_TYPE, (sword) -1, &indEmployeeSSN,
         (text *) NULL, (sword) -1, (sword) -1, &LengthSSN,
         &CodeSSN))
   handle_error(&LDA, &CDA, "odefin - SSN");

if (odefin(&CDA, (sword ) 2, (ub1 *) &fPayRate,
         (sword) sizeof(fPayRate),
         (sword) FLOAT_TYPE, (sword) -1, &indPayRate,
         (text *) NULL, (sword) -1, (sword) -1, &LengthPayRate,
         &CodePayRate))
   handle_error(&LDA, &CDA, "odefin - PayRate");

if (odefin(&CDA, (sword ) 3, (ub1 *) cFirstName,
         (sword) sizeof(cFirstName),
         (sword) STRING_TYPE, (sword) -1, &indFirstName,
         (text *) NULL, (sword) -1, (sword) -1,
         &LengthFirstName,
         &CodeFirstName))
   handle_error(&LDA, &CDA, "odefin - FirstName");
```

```
if (odefin(&CDA, (sword ) 4, (ub1 *) cLastName,
          (sword) sizeof(cLastName),
          (sword) STRING_TYPE, (sword) -1, &indLastName,
          (text *) NULL, (sword) -1, (sword) -1,
          &LengthLastName, &CodeLastName))
  handle_error(&LDA, &CDA, "odefin - LastName");

if (odefin(&CDA, (sword ) 5, (ub1 *) cHireDate,
          (sword) sizeof(cHireDate),
          (sword) STRING_TYPE, (sword) -1, &indHireDate,
          (text *) NULL, (sword) -1, (sword) -1,
          &LengthHireDate, &CodeHireDate))
  handle_error(&LDA, &CDA, "odefin - HireDate");
```

Executing and Fetching

The statement is executed using the **oexec** function:

```
sword  oexec (Cda_Def *cursor);
```

Note that the only parameter is the CDA. In the case of a nonquery SQL statement, after the **oexec** call, processing of this statement is complete. However, in the case of a query, you still need to fetch the data. **oexec** will evaluate the value of the bind variables and determine the active set, similar to EXEC SQL OPEN. To fetch the data, you need the **ofetch** routine:

```
sword  ofetch(Cda_Def *cursor);
```

Again, the only parameter is the CDA. Each call to **ofetch** will return one more row of data, similar to EXEC SQL FETCH. The data will be stored in the variables specified by **odefin**.

These calls can be combined in one call to **oexfet**:

```
sword  oexfet(Cda_Def *cursor,
              ub4 nrows,
              sword cancel,
              sword exact);
```

oexfet Parameter Descriptions
Table 11-14 lists the **oexfet** parameters.

Parameter	Type	Mode	Description
cursor	Cda_Def *	IN/OUT	Address of a cursor data area in your program
nrows	sword	IN	Number of rows to fetch[1]
cancel	sword	IN	If nonzero, **ocan** is called after the rows are fetched
exact	sword	IN	If nonzero, an error is raised if the number of rows in the active set does not match nrows

Notes:

1. If nrows > 1, this is an array fetch and the parameters to **odefin** should have been arrays.

TABLE 11-14. *oexfet parameters*

Use of the oexfet Function

oexfet is called once. If there are more rows to fetch, **ofetch** can be called in a loop to return the rest of the rows, as the following example shows. If no rows match the query, **oexfet** will return ORA-1403: no data found.

Example

```
if (oexfet(&CDA, (ub4) 1, (sword) 0, (sword) 0))
   handle_error(&LDA, &CDA, "oexec - executing and fetching");

for (;;) {
/* Process fetched data here. */

  iReturnCode = ofetch(&CDA);
  if (CDA.rc == 1403)
    break;
  else if (iReturnCode != 0)
    handle_error(&LDA, &CDA, "ofetch - fetch the next row");
}
```

Committing or Rolling Back the Transaction

Just like Pro*C, SQL statements executed via OCI are in the context of a transaction, which needs to be committed or rolled back. To commit a transaction, use the **ocom** function:

```
sword   ocom  (Lda_Def *lda);
```

To roll back a transaction, use the **orol** function:

```
sword   orol  (Lda_Def *lda);
```

ocom and orol Parameter Descriptions
Table 11-15 describes the **ocom** and **orol** parameter.

Use of the ocom Function
Note that both **ocom** and **orol** take only the LDA as an argument—not a CDA. This is because both functions affect all SQL statements in the transaction, not just a particular statement.

Example

```
if (ocom(&LDA))
    handle_error(&LDA, &LDA, "ocom - committing transaction");
```

Closing the Cursor

Closing the cursor frees all resources acquired by that cursor. These include the context area itself and any resources acquired by the execution of the SQL statement, such as database locks and sort space. You can free just the SQL resources via the **ocan** function. Cursors are closed via the **oclose** function:

```
sword  oclose(struct cda_def *cursor);
```

Parameter	Type	Mode	Description
lda	Lda_Def *	IN/OUT	Address of a logon data area within your program

TABLE 11-15. *ocom and orol parameter*

oclose Parameter Descriptions

Table 11-16 describes the **oclose** parameter.

Use of the oclose Function

After you call **oclose**, the cursor is no longer available for use. It can be opened again by calling **oopen**. Normally, this is not done; if the same cursor is to be used by more than one SQL statement, the second statement can be reparsed in the CDA without closing and reopening.

Example

```
if (oclose(&CDA))
  handle_error(&LDA, &CDA, "oclose - CDA");
```

Logging Off the Database

When your program is finished with database work, it should disconnect from the database. Similar to the RELEASE parameter of EXEC SQL COMMIT or EXEC SQL ROLLBACK, in OCI the function to use is **ologof**:

```
sword  ologof(Lda_Def *lda);
```

ologof Parameter Descriptions

Table 11-17 describes the **ologof** parameter.

Use of the ologof Function

This should be the last OCI statement executed by your program. If you haven't committed the transaction prior to **ologof** with **ocom**, the transaction is rolled back. Like **ocom** and **orlo**, **ologof** takes an LDA as an argument, not a CDA.

Parameter	Type	Mode	Description
cursor	Cda_Def *	IN/OUT	Address of a cursor data area within your program

TABLE 11-16. *oclose parameter*

Parameter	Type	Mode	Description
lda	Lda_Def *	IN/OUT	Address of a logon data area in your program

TABLE 11-17. *ologof parameter*

Example

```
if (ologof(&LDA))
    handle_error(&LDA, &LDA, "ologof - disconnecting from db");
```

Mixing Pro*C and OCI Programs

Depending on your application, you may find it necessary to combine Pro*C and OCI in the same program. This is perfectly legal. You can have separate connections with Pro*C and OCI (in which case each would be in a different transaction), or both Pro*C and OCI can have the same database context. The latter is done via the **sqllda** function:

```
void sqllda(Lda_Def *lda);
```

Note that **sqllda** is a void function: If the call fails, it will be indicated in the *rc* field of the LDA. **sqllda** should be called after an EXEC SQL CONNECT statement. It will modify its argument to point to the Pro*C connection. For example:

```
VARCHAR vUserName[20];
VARCHAR vPassword[20];
Lda_Def LDA;
strcpy((char *)vUserName.arr, "scott");
vUserName.len = strlen((char *)vUserName.arr);
strcpy((char *)vPassword.arr, "tiger");
vPassword.len = strlen((char *)vPassword.arr);
EXEC SQL CONNECT :vUserName IDENTIFIED BY :vPassword;
sqllda(&LDA);
if (LDA.rc != 0)
  handle_error(&LDA, &LDA, "sqllda");
```

Note that the connection must be made with Pro*C, and then you get a valid HDA for it. You can't connect in OCI and use that connection in Pro*C. Also note that no HDA is necessary.

The Future of OCI

A number of new features will be available for OCI in the 7.2 and 7.3 releases.

Nonblocking Calls (OCI 7.2)

With this version, you can establish a nonblocking connection to the database. This means that you submit an OCI call, and control returns immediately to your program while the server processes the request. Your program then periodically polls the database to see if the call is finished. You could use this feature to allow the user to cancel a long-running query.

Cursor Variables (OCI 7.2)

PL/SQL 2.2 has a feature known as *cursor variables*. These are similar to PL/SQL cursors, but they can be opened for different queries over their lifetime. This allows you to open a cursor for a particular query on the server (perhaps in a stored procedure) and fetch from the query directly into C variables on the client using **ofen** or **ofetch**.

Thread Safety (OCI 7.3)

Currently, neither the precompiler library nor the OCI library is thread-safe. Starting with version 7.3, they will be; this feature will allow you to write multithreaded OCI programs, with multiple connections per thread and multiple threads per connection.

Piecewise Insert, Update, and Fetch of LONG Data (OCI 7.3)

OCI 7.3 will allow you to modify LONG and LONG RAW data piecewise; you won't have to allocate space for all the data (up to 2Gb) on the client. The pieces will also be transmitted efficiently via SQL*Net.

Addresses and How They Are Handled

Many OCI programs take addresses as parameters. These addresses must remain valid after the call, a requirement that can cause some subtle problems. Consider the following code:

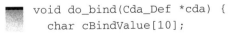

```
void do_bind(Cda_Def *cda) {
   char cBindValue[10];
```

```
    /* Fill in cBindValue, possibly by prompting the user. */
    if (obndrv(cda, ..., cBindValue, ...)) ...
}
```

At first glance, this procedure may seem fine. But note that the value of a local variable is passed to **obndrv** for the *prov* parameter. Storage for local variables can be reclaimed by the system after the call returns, so upon return from **do_bind**, the address passed to **obndrv** will no longer be valid. Depending on whether the storage was actually reused, this code may work. More likely, however, the **oexec** call will fail. Essentially, you need to make sure all addresses you pass to OCI calls are valid until the statement is executed. For defined variables, the address needs to be valid until the last row is fetched. You can do this by:

- Allocating space on the heap rather than the stack (using the **malloc** system call instead of a declared variable).

- Making sure the declared variable is in scope throughout execution.

- Declaring the variable as global to the entire program.

Examples

This section presents a complete OCI program containing the program fragments used for examples for the preceding individual routines. This example is written for a UNIX system.

```c
#include <stdio.h>
#include <stdlib.h>
#include <ctype.h>
#include <string.h>
#include <oratypes.h>
#include <ociapr.h>
#include <ocidem.h>

#define PARSE_DEFERRED 1
#define V7_BEHAVIOR 2

#define STRING_TYPE 5
#define FLOAT_TYPE 4

void handle_error(Lda_Def *lda, Cda_Def *cda, char *message);

int main() {
```

```
ub1 HDA[512];
Lda_Def LDA;
Cda_Def CDA;
sword iReturnCode;
int i;

/* variables to hold the result of the describe */
sb4 iDbSize;
sb2 iDbType;
text tSelectName[25];
sb4 iSelectNameLength = sizeof(tSelectName);
sb4 iDisplaySize;
sb2 iPrecision;
sb2 iScale;
sb2 iNullok;

/* Variable to hold the SQL query that will be executed.
   Note that there is no semicolon in the SQL statement. */
text *tEmployeeStmt = (text *)
  "select employee_ssn, pay_rate, first_name, last_name, \
     hire_date from employee \
     where state = :b_state \
     and pay_rate >= :b_pay_rate";

/* bind variables */
char cBindState[3];
float fBindPayRate;
sb2 indBindState = 0, indBindPayRate = 0;

/* output variables */
char cEmployeeSSN[12];
float fPayRate;
char cFirstName[41];
char cLastName[41];
char cHireDate[10];
sb2 indEmployeeSSN, indPayRate, indFirstName, indLastName;
sb2 indHireDate;
ub2 LengthSSN, LengthPayRate, LengthFirstName;
ub2 LengthLastName, LengthHireDate;
ub2 CodeSSN, CodePayRate, CodeFirstName, CodeLastName;
ub2 CodeHireDate;
```

```
/* Connect to the database. */
if (orlon(&LDA, HDA, (text *) "scott", (sword) -1,
          (text *) "tiger",
          (sword) -1, -1))
  handle_error(&LDA, &LDA, "orlon connecting to the database");

/* Open a cursor. */
if (oopen(&CDA, &LDA, (text *) NULL, -1, -1, (text *) NULL, -1))
  handle_error(&LDA, &CDA, "oopen - opening the cursor");

/* Parse the query. The parse will be deferred for
   performance. */
if (oparse(&CDA, tEmployeeStmt, (sb4) -1,
   (sword) PARSE_DEFERRED, (ub4) V7_BEHAVIOR))
  handle_error(&LDA, &CDA, "oparse - parsing SQL query");

strcpy(cBindState, "CA");
fBindPayRate = 1000;

/* Bind the two input variables. */
if (obndrv(&CDA, (text *) ":b_state", (sword) -1,
          (ub1 *) cBindState,
          (sword) strlen(cBindState) + 1, (sword) STRING_TYPE,
          (sword) -1,
          &indBindState, (text *) NULL, (sword) -1, (sword) -1))
  handle_error(&LDA, &CDA, "obndrv - b_state");

/* Note that the address of fPayRate is being passed. */
if (obndrv(&CDA, (text *) ":b_pay_rate",
          (sword) -1, (ub1 *) &fBindPayRate,
          (sword) sizeof (fBindPayRate),
          (sword) FLOAT_TYPE, (sword) -1,
          &indBindPayRate, (text *) NULL, (sword) -1,
          (sword) -1))
  handle_error(&LDA, &CDA, "obndrv - b_pay_rate");

/* Describe the select list. */
for (i = 1; ;i++ ) { /* Loop until we get the ORA-1007. */
  iSelectNameLength = sizeof(tSelectName);
  odescr(&CDA, (sword) i, &iDbSize, &iDbType,
          (sb1 *) tSelectName,
```

```
            &iSelectNameLength, &iDisplaySize, &iPrecision,
            &iScale, &iNullok);

   /* Check for any errors. */
   if (CDA.rc == 1007)
     /* end of select list reached */
     break;
   else if (CDA.rc != 0)
     handle_error(&LDA, &CDA, "odescr - describing select list");

   /* Describe successful - print out results. */
   printf("Column %d, %*.*s,  has type %d, precision %d, \
          scale %d, and length %d.  ",
          i, iSelectNameLength, iSelectNameLength, tSelectName,
          iDbType,iPrecision, iScale, iDisplaySize);
   if (iNullok)
     printf("This column allows nulls.\n");
   else
     printf("This column does not allow nulls.\n");
}


/* Define the output variables. */
if (odefin(&CDA, (sword ) 1, (ub1 *) cEmployeeSSN,
          (sword) sizeof(cEmployeeSSN),
          (sword) STRING_TYPE, (sword) -1, &indEmployeeSSN,
          (text *) NULL, (sword) -1, (sword) -1,
          &LengthSSN, &CodeSSN))
   handle_error(&LDA, &CDA, "odefin - SSN");

if (odefin(&CDA, (sword ) 2, (ub1 *) &fPayRate,
          (sword) sizeof(fPayRate),
          (sword) FLOAT_TYPE, (sword) -1, &indPayRate,
          (text *) NULL, (sword) -1, (sword) -1, &LengthPayRate,
          &CodePayRate))
   handle_error(&LDA, &CDA, "odefin - PayRate");

if (odefin(&CDA, (sword ) 3, (ub1 *) cFirstName,
          (sword) sizeof(cFirstName),
          (sword) STRING_TYPE, (sword) -1, &indFirstName,
          (text *) NULL, (sword) -1, (sword) -1,
          &LengthFirstName, &CodeFirstName))
   handle_error(&LDA, &CDA, "odefin - FirstName");
```

```
if (odefin(&CDA, (sword ) 4, (ub1 *) cLastName,
           (sword) sizeof(cLastName),
           (sword) STRING_TYPE, (sword) -1, &indLastName,
           (text *) NULL, (sword) -1, (sword) -1,
           &LengthLastName, &CodeLastName))
  handle_error(&LDA, &CDA, "odefin - LastName");

if (odefin(&CDA, (sword ) 5, (ub1 *) cHireDate,
           (sword) sizeof(cHireDate),
           (sword) STRING_TYPE, (sword) -1, &indHireDate,
           (text *) NULL, (sword) -1, (sword) -1,
           &LengthHireDate, &CodeHireDate))
  handle_error(&LDA, &CDA, "odefin - HireDate");

/* Execute the query and fetch the first row. */
if (oexfet(&CDA, (ub4) 1, (sword) 0, (sword) 0))
  handle_error(&LDA, &CDA, "oexec - executing and fetching");

for (;;) {
  printf("SSN: %s Pay Rate: %f First Name: %s Last Name: \
          %s Hire Date: %s\n",
          cEmployeeSSN, fPayRate, cFirstName, cLastName,
          cHireDate);

  iReturnCode = ofetch(&CDA);
  if (CDA.rc == 1403)
    break;
  else if (iReturnCode != 0)
    handle_error(&LDA, &CDA, "ofetch - fetch the next row");
}

printf("Done!\n");

/* Commit the transaction. */
if (ocom(&LDA))
  handle_error(&LDA, &CDA, "ocom - committing transaction");

/* Close the cursor. */
if (oclose(&CDA))
  handle_error(&LDA, &CDA, "oclose - close CDA");
```

```
    /* Disconnect from the database. */
    if (ologof(&LDA))
      handle_error(&LDA, &CDA, "ologof - disconnecting from DB");

}

void handle_error(Lda_Def *lda, Cda_Def *cda, char *message) {

    /* Buffer to hold error - maximum length is 512 characters. */
    text ErrorBuffer[512];

    oerhms(lda, cda->rc, ErrorBuffer, (sword) sizeof(ErrorBuffer));
    printf("Oracle error: %s\n", message);
    printf("%s\n", ErrorBuffer);

    exit(1);;}
```

■ Arrays and OCI

There are two ways of using arrays with OCI: the Oracle array interface and
binding arrays to PL/SQL tables.

The Oracle Array Interface

One of the main things you can do to increase performance is to take advantage of
the array interface. The same rationale applies to OCI as to the precompilers—by
using arrays, you minimize the amount of traffic over the network between the
client and the server. Arrays can be used both in DML statements (INSERT,
UPDATE, and DELETE) and for queries. Wherever you can use an array in Pro*C,
you can use an array in OCI.

Arrays in DML Statements
To use an array for a DML statement, you need to bind the address of the array
using **obndrv** and use **oexn** to indicate the number of rows. During the bind, you
pass the same four pieces of information as before. The only difference is that they
apply to an individual array element rather than a scalar.

It is important that the arrays be contiguous in memory; although C doesn't
distinguish between the following declarations, Oracle does:

```
char **contiguous_array;   /* This is legal as a host array. */
contiguous_array = (char **) malloc(<number of rows> *
```

```
   <size of each element>);
char ** non_contiguous_array /* not legal as a host array */
non_contiguous_array = (char **) malloc(<number of rows>);
for (i = 0; i < <number of rows>; I++)
  non_contiguous_array[i] =
      (char *)malloc(<size of each element>);
```

For this reason, arrays of pointers aren't supported as host arrays.

Array Fetches

Array fetches are similar to arrays in DML statements. For the **odefin** call, you pass information about each array element and specify the number of rows in the **oexfet** or **ofen** routine.

Binding Arrays to PL/SQL Tables

Arrays can also be used as bind variables to replace PL/SQL tables. For example, a stored procedure can take a PL/SQL table as an argument. Using OCI, you can bind this parameter with a C array. The main difference here is that you use the **obndra** routine instead of **obndrv**. **obndra** allows you to specify the number of rows in the array bind variable. This is different from the *nrows* parameter in **oexn**: When a stored procedure is called, **oexec** is used. A good example of this is CDEMO4.C in the *Programmer's Guide to the Oracle Call Interfaces*.

Summary

This chapter has covered all the details of the Oracle Call Interface, a set of functions in a C program that let you access a database. You should now understand OCI and how it compares with Pro*C. We also covered the basic OCI routines and array handling with OCI. For more information, see Appendix C.

CHAPTER 12

Using the Pro*C Precompiler

Chapter 8 intoduced you to the Pro*C precompiler. However, this chapter explains all of the Pro*C precompiler options available and shows a practical example of how to use Pro*C to build application programs. Use this chapter as a guide and reference in your day-to-day use of the Pro*C precompiler and all of its options.

Each precompiler option is defined here in detail; you will learn its purpose, syntax, default, and usage. In this chapter, you will see practical examples of using Pro*C. The error messages that can be generated by the precompiler are documented in Appendix E.

Using the Pro*C Precompiler Options

As discussed in Chapter 8, you can specify the precompiler options as command-line arguments when you invoke the precompiler command:

PROC INAME=filename [option=value] [option=value]...

Some options can be specified in any source module with the following statement:

EXEC ORACLE OPTION (option=value);

These options give you control over how the precompiler interprets your source module, how system resources are used, how errors are reported, how input and output are formatted, and how cursors are managed. Table 12-1 summarizes the precompiler options you can specify.

Option	Valid Values	Default	Description
ASACC	YES | NO	NO	Specifies carriage control for the listing file
CODE	ANSI_C | KR_C	KR_C	Specifies how C function prototypes are generated; either ANSI C format or the Kernighan/Ritchie format
DBMS	NATIVE | V6 | V7	NATIVE	Specifies to use version-specific behavior of Oracle
DEFINE	Symbol		Defines a symbol used in conditional precompilation
ERRORS	YES | NO*	YES	Specifies to send errors to the terminal
FIPS	YES | NO	NO	Specifies whether extensions to ANSI/ISO are flagged
HOLD_CURSOR	YES | NO*	NO	Specifies how the cursor cache handles SQL statements

TABLE 12-1. *Pro*C precompiler options*

Option	Valid Values	Default	Description
HOST	C | COB74 | COBOL | FORTRAN | PASCAL | PLI	C	Host language of input
INAME	Path and filename		Specifies name of the input file
INCLUDE	Path*	Current directory	Specifies directory path for INCLUDEd files
IRECLEN	Integer	80	Specifies record length of input file
LINES	YES | NO	NO	Specifies whether C #line directives are generated
LNAME	Path and filename		Specifies name of listing file
LRECLEN	Integer	132	Specifies record length of listing file
LTYPE	LONG | SHORT | NONE	LONG	Specifies type of listing
MAXLITERAL	Integer*	1000	Specifies a maximum length of strings
MAXOPENCURSORS	Integer*	10	Specifies the maximum number of cursors cached in memory
MODE	ANSI | ISO | ANSI14 | ISO14 | ANSI13 | ISO13 | ORACLE	ORACLE	Specifies compliance with ANSI/ISO standards
ONAME	Path and filename	Same as input file with *.c extension	Specifies name of output file
ORACA	YES | NO*	NO	Specifies whether the Oracle Communications Area (ORACA) is used
ORECLEN	Integer	80	Specifies record length of output file

TABLE 12-1. *Pro*C precompiler options* (continued)

Option	Valid Values	Default	Description
PAGELEN	Integer	66	Specifies lines per page in listing file
RELEASE_CURSOR	YES | NO*	NO	Specifies how cursor cache handles SQL statements
SELECT_ERROR	YES | NO*	YES	Specifies how select errors are handled
SQLCHECK	SEMATICS | FULL | SYNTAX | LIMITED | NONE*	SYNTAX	Specifies extent of syntactic and/or semantic checking
USERID	Username/password		Specifies a valid Oracle username and password
XREF	YES | NO*	YES	Specifies cross-reference section in listing file

* Can be specified as options in your source module

TABLE 12-1. *Pro*C precompiler options* (continued)

Pro*C Precompiler Options

This section serves as a reference to help you understand each precompiler option and how to use it. It describes each option's purpose, syntax, default value, and usage.

ASACC

Purpose:
     This option specifies whether the output listing file follows the ASA convention of using the first column in each line for carriage control.

Syntax:

```
ASACC=YES|NO
```

Default:
NO

Usage Notes:
This option can be entered only on the command line.

CODE

Purpose:
This option specifies the format of C function prototypes generated by the
Pro*C precompiler. The precompiler generates function prototypes for SQL library
routines so that your C compiler can resolve external references. The CODE option
lets you control the prototype formats. The prototypes can be in either ANSI Standard
C or the Kernighan/Ritchie de facto standard format (described in a moment).

Syntax:

```
CODE=ANSI_C|KR_C
```

Default:
KR_C

Usage Notes:
This option can be entered inline or on the command line.
ANSI C standard X3.159-1989 provides for function prototyping. When
CODE=ANSI_C, the Pro*C precompiler generates full-function prototypes that
conform to the ANSI C standard. For example:

```
extern void sqlora(long *, void *);
```

The precompiler can also generate other ANSI-approved constructs, such as the
const type qualifier. Before specifying CODE=ANSI_C, make sure you understand
all the ANSI requirements, including the rules for argument promotion. Also be
sure to invoke an ANSI-compliant C compiler by using the appropriate
command-line switches, which are compiler-specific.
When CODE=KR_C (the default), the precompiler generates code compatible
with the earlier C specification documented in Kernighan and Ritchie's book, *The
C Programming Language*. Consequently, the precompiler comments out the
argument lists of generated function prototypes, as shown in the following example:

```
extern void sqlora(/*_ long *, void * _*/);
```

Therefore, you should specify CODE=KR_C only if your C compiler is not ANSI-compliant.

DBMS

Purpose:

This option specifies whether Oracle follows the semantic and syntactic rules of Oracle version 6, Oracle 7, or the native version of Oracle (that is, the version resident on your system, which must be version 6 or later).

Syntax:

```
DBMS=NATIVE|V6|V7
```

Default:

NATIVE

Usage Notes:

This option can be entered only on the command line.

The DBMS option lets you control the version-specific behavior of Oracle. When DBMS=NATIVE (the default), Oracle follows the semantic and syntactic rules of the native version of Oracle. However, not knowing the version, the precompiler cannot check for compatibility errors (such as specifying DBMS=V6 with MODE=ANSI).

When DBMS={V6 | V7}, Oracle follows the rules of Oracle version 6 or Oracle 7, respectively. DBMS=V6 and DBMS=V7 differ in several ways:

- When DBMS=V6, Oracle treats string literals like variable-length character values. When DBMS=V7, however, Oracle treats string literals like fixed-length character values, and CHAR semantics change slightly to comply with the current ANSI/ISO SQL standard. For more information, see Chapter 4, which discusses the handling of character values.

- When DBMS=V6, Oracle treats local CHAR variables in a PL/SQL block like variable-length character values. When DBMS=V7, however, Oracle treats the CHAR variables like ANSI-compliant, fixed-length character values.

- When DBMS=V6, Oracle treats the return value of the function USER like a variable-length character value. However, when DBMS=V7, Oracle treats the return value of USER like an ANSI-compliant, fixed-length character value.

- When DBMS=V6, if you process a multirow query that calls an SQL group function such as AVG or COUNT, the function is called when the CURSOR is OPEN. When DBMS=V7, however, the function is called when you FETCH the rows from the CURSOR. At OPEN or FETCH time, if the function call fails, Oracle immediately issues an error message. Thus, the DBMS value affects error reporting slightly.

- When DBMS=V6 and RELEASE_CURSOR=YES, after Oracle executes an SQL statement and its cursor is closed, its parsed representation is lost. Before the SQL statement can be reexecuted, therefore, it must be reparsed. However, when DBMS=V7 and RELEASE_CURSOR=YES, the reparse might not require processing because Oracle 7 caches the parsed representations of SQL statements and PL/SQL blocks in its Shared SQL Cache. Even if its cursor is closed, the parsed representation remains available until the cache runs out of room to store it.

- When DBMS=V6, RELEASE_CURSOR=NO, and HOLD_CURSOR=YES, after Oracle executes an SQL statement, its parsed representation remains available. However, when DBMS=V7, RELEASE_CURSOR=NO, and HOLD_CURSOR=YES, the parsed representation remains available only until the Shared SQL Cache runs out of room to store it. Normally this is not a problem, but you might get unexpected results if the definition of a referenced object changes before the SQL statement is reparsed.

As Table 12-2 shows, some DBMS and MODE option values are incompatible or not recommended.

DEFINE

Purpose:

This option specifies a user-defined symbol that is used to include or exclude portions of source code during a conditional precompilation.

DBMS	MODE	Compatible?	Recommended?
V6	ANSI	No	—
V6	ANSI14	Yes	No
V6	ANSI13	Yes	No
V6	Oracle	Yes	Yes
V7	ANSI	Yes	Yes
V7	ANSI14	No	—
V7	ANSI13	No	—
V7	Oracle	Yes	Yes

TABLE 12-2. *DBMS and MODE options*

Syntax:

```
DEFINE=symbol
```

Default:
> None

Usage Notes:
> This option can be entered inline or on the command line.
> If you enter DEFINE inline, the EXEC ORACLE statement takes the following form:

```
EXEC Oracle DEFINE symbol;
```

ERRORS

Purpose:
> This option specifies whether precompiler error messages are sent to the terminal and output listing file or only to the output listing file.

Syntax:

```
ERRORS=YES|NO
```

Default:
> YES

Usage Notes:
> This option can be entered inline or on the command line.
> When ERRORS=YES, error messages are sent to the terminal and output listing file. When ERRORS=NO, error messages are sent only to the output listing file.

FIPS

Purpose:
> This option specifies whether Oracle extensions to ANSI SQL are flagged (by the FIPS flagger). An extension is any SQL element that violates ANSI format or syntax rules, except privilege enforcement rules.

Syntax:

```
FIPS=YES|NO
```

Default:
> NO

Usage Notes:
> This option can be entered inline or on the command line.

When FIPS=YES, the FIPS flagger issues warning (not error) messages if you use an Oracle extension to ANSI SQL or use a nonconforming ANSI SQL feature. The following extensions to ANSI SQL are flagged at precompile time:

- An array interface including the FOR clause
- SQL Communications Area (SQLCA), ORACA, and SQLDA data structures
- Dynamic SQL including the DESCRIBE statement
- Embedded PL/SQL blocks
- Automatic datatype conversion
- DATE, NUMBER, RAW, LONGRAW, VARRAW, ROWID, and VARCHAR datatypes
- Pointer host variables
- EXEC ORACLE statement for specifying run-time options
- IAF statements in user exits
- CONNECT statement
- TYPE and VAR datatype equivalencing statements
- AT database_name clause
- DECLARE...DATABASE, ...STATEMENT, and ...TABLE statements
- SQLWARNING condition in the WHENEVER statement
- DO, DO BREAK, and STOP actions in the WHENEVER statement
- COMMENT and FORCE TRANSACTION clauses in a COMMIT statement
- FORCE TRANSACTION and TO SAVEPOINT clauses in a ROLLBACK statement
- RELEASE parameter in COMMIT and ROLLBACK statements
- Optional colon-prefixing of WHENEVER...GOTO labels and of host variables in the INTO clause

HOLD_CURSOR

Purpose:
This option specifies how the cursors for SQL statements and PL/SQL blocks are handled in the cursor cache.

Syntax:

```
HOLD_CURSOR=YES|NO
```

Default:
    NO

Usage Notes:
    This option can be entered inline or on the command line.
    You can use HOLD_CURSOR to improve the performance of your program. When an SQL data manipulation statement is executed, its associated cursor is linked to an entry in the cursor cache. The cursor cache entry is in turn linked to an Oracle private SQL area, which stores information needed to process the statement. HOLD_CURSOR controls what happens to the link between the cursor and the cursor cache.
    When HOLD_CURSOR=NO, after Oracle executes the SQL statement and the cursor is closed, the precompiler marks the link as reusable. The link is reused when the cursor cache entry to which it points is needed for another SQL statement. This frees memory allocated to the private SQL area and releases parse locks.
    When HOLD_CURSOR=YES, the link is maintained; the precompiler does not reuse it. This is useful for SQL statements that are executed often because it speeds up subsequent executions. There is no need to reparse the statement or allocate memory for an Oracle private SQL area.
    When you specify this option in a source module for use with implicit cursors, set HOLD_CURSOR before executing the SQL statement. When you specify this option in a source module for use with explicit cursors, set HOLD_CURSOR before you CLOSE the cursor.

> **NOTE**
> RELEASE_CURSOR=YES overrides HOLD_CURSOR=YES, and HOLD_CURSOR=NO overrides RELEASE_CURSOR=NO.

HOST

Purpose:
    This option specifies the host language of the input file.

Syntax:

```
HOST=C|COB74|COBOL|FORTRAN|PASCAL|PLI
```

Default:
    C

Usage Notes:
This option can be entered only on the command line. This option is obsolete and is typically not necessary.

INAME

Purpose:
This option specifies the name of the input file to be precompiled.

Syntax:

```
INAME=path and filename
```

Default:
N/A

Usage Notes:
The INAME option is the only required command-line option. This option must be specified when you invoke the precompiler command.

INCLUDE

Purpose:
This option specifies a directory path for EXEC SQL INCLUDE files. It only applies to operating systems that use directories.

Syntax:

```
INCLUDE=path
```

Default:
Current directory

Usage Notes:
This option can be entered inline or on the command line.
Typically, you use the INCLUDE option to specify a directory path for the SQLCA and ORACA files. The precompiler searches first in the current directory, then in the directory specified by INCLUDE, and finally in a directory for standard include files. Hence, you need not specify a directory path for standard files such as the SQLCA and ORACA.
You must still use the INCLUDE option to specify a directory path for nonstandard files, unless they are stored in the current directory. You can specify more than one path on the command line, as follows:

```
EXEC SQL INCLUDE=path1 INCLUDE=path2 ...
```

The precompiler searches first in the current directory, then in the directory named by *path1*, then in the directory named by *path2*, and finally in the directory for standard include files.

Remember, the precompiler looks for a file in the current directory first, even if you specify a directory path; if the file you want to INCLUDE resides in another directory, make sure no file with the same name resides in the current directory.

The syntax for specifying a directory path is system-specific. Check the Oracle installation or user's guide for your system.

IRECLEN

Purpose:
This option specifies the record length of the input file.

Syntax:

```
IRECLEN=integer
```

Default:
80

Usage Notes:
This option can be entered only on the command line.

The value you specify for IRECLEN should not exceed the value of ORECLEN. The maximum value allowed is system-dependent.

LINES

Purpose:
This option specifies whether the Pro*C precompiler adds **#line** preprocessor directives to its output C source file.

Syntax:

```
LINES=YES|NO
```

Default:
NO

Usage Notes:
This option can be entered only on the command line.

The LINES option helps with debugging. When LINES=YES, the Pro*C precompiler adds **#line** preprocessor directives to its output C source file.

Normally, your C compiler increments its line count after each input line is processed. The **#line** directives force the compiler to reset its input line counter so that lines of precompiler-generated code are not counted. Moreover, when the name of the input file changes, the next **#line** directive specifies the new filename.

The C compiler uses the line numbers and filenames to show the location of errors. Thus, error messages issued by the compiler always refer to your original source files, not the modified source file.

When LINES=NO (the default), the precompiler adds no **#line** directives to its output C source file.

LNAME

Purpose:

This option specifies a nondefault name for the output listing file.

Syntax:

```
LNAME=path and filename
```

Default:

FILENAME.LIS, where **filename** is the base name of the input file specified by INAME.

Usage Notes:

This option can be entered only on the command line. By default, the output listing file is written to the current directory.

LRECLEN

Purpose:

This option specifies the record length of the output listing file.

Syntax:

```
LRECLEN=integer
```

Default:

132

Usage Notes:

This option can be entered only on the command line.

The value of LRECLEN can range from 80 through 255. If you specify a value below this range, 80 is used as the default. If you specify a value above the range, 255 is used. LRECLEN should exceed IRECLEN by at least 8 to allow for the insertion of line numbers.

LTYPE

Purpose:
This option specifies the output listing file type.

Syntax:

```
LTYPE=LONG|SHORT|NONE
```

Default:
LONG

Usage Notes:
This option can be entered only on the command line.
When LTYPE=LONG, input lines appear in the listing file. When LTYPE=SHORT, input lines do not appear in the listing file; only output lines are included. When LTYPE=NONE, no listing file is created.

MAXLITERAL

Purpose:
This option specifies the maximum length of string literals generated by the precompiler so that compiler limits are not exceeded. For example, if your compiler cannot handle string literals longer than 256 characters, you can specify MAXLITERAL=256 as an option.

Syntax:

```
MAXLITERAL=integer
```

Default:
1000

Usage Notes:
This option can be entered inline or on the command line.
The maximum value of MAXLITERAL is compiler-dependent. The default value for C is 1000. However, if your C compiler cannot handle string literals longer than 512 characters, you would specify MAXLITERAL=512.
Strings that exceed the length specified by MAXLITERAL are divided during precompilation, then recombined (concatenated) at run time. You can enter MAXLITERAL inline, as the following example shows:

```
EXEC Oracle OPTION (MAXLITERAL=512);
```

Your program can set MAXLITERAL just once, and the EXEC ORACLE statement must precede the first EXEC SQL statement. Otherwise, the precompiler issues a warning message, ignores the extra or misplaced EXEC ORACLE statement, and continues processing.

MAXOPENCURSORS

Purpose:
This option specifies the number of concurrently open cursors that the precompiler tries to keep cached.

Syntax:

```
MAXOPENCURSORS=integer
```

Default:
10

Usage Notes:
This option can be entered inline or on the command line.

You can use MAXOPENCURSORS to improve the performance of your program. The maximum number of open cursors per user process is set by the Oracle initialization parameter OPEN_CURSORS. The range is from 5 to 255, with 50 as the default. You can override this parameter by using MAXOPENCURSORS to specify a lower (but not higher) value. To avoid a "maximum open cursors exceeded" Oracle error, you must set MAXOPENCURSORS lower than OPEN_CURSORS by at least 6.

MAXOPENCURSORS specifies the initial size of the cursor cache. If a new cursor is needed and there are no free cache entries, Oracle tries to reuse an entry. Its success depends on the values of HOLD_CURSOR and RELEASE_CURSOR and, for explicit cursors, on the status of the cursor itself. Oracle allocates an additional cache entry if it cannot find one to reuse. If necessary, Oracle keeps allocating additional cache entries until it runs out of memory or reaches the limit set by OPEN_CURSORS.

As your program's need for concurrently open cursors grows, you might want to respecify MAXOPENCURSORS to match the need. A value of 45 to 50 is not uncommon, but remember that each cursor requires another private SQL area in the user process memory space. This can require a significant amount of local memory. The default value of 10 is adequate for most programs. Only the value in effect at connect time is used.

MODE

Purpose:
This option specifies whether your program observes Oracle practices or complies with the current ANSI SQL standard.

Syntax:

```
MODE=ANSI|ISO|ANSI14|ISO14|ANSI13|ISO13|Oracle
```

Default:
Oracle

Usage Notes:
This option can be entered only on the command line.

The following pairs of MODE values are equivalent: ANSI and ISO, ANSI14 and ISO14, and ANSI13 and ISO13.

When MODE=Oracle (the default), your embedded SQL program observes Oracle practices. When MODE={ANSI14 | ANSI13}, your program complies closely with the current ANSI SQL standard. When MODE=ANSI, your program complies fully with the ANSI standard and the following changes go into effect:

- CHAR column values, USER pseudocolumn values, character host values, and quoted literals are treated like ANSI fixed-length character strings. Also, ANSI-compliant blank-padding semantics are used when you assign, compare, INSERT, UPDATE, SELECT, or FETCH such values. When MODE={ANSI14 | ANSI13 | Oracle}, such values are treated like VARCHAR2 variable-length character strings, and non-blank-padding semantics are used.

- Issuing a COMMIT or ROLLBACK closes all explicit cursors. When MODE={ANSI13 | Oracle}, COMMIT or ROLLBACK only closes cursors referenced in a CURRENT OF clause.

- You cannot OPEN an already open cursor or CLOSE an already closed cursor. When MODE=Oracle, you can reOPEN an open cursor to avoid reparsing.

- You cannot SELECT or FETCH nulls into a host variable not associated with an indicator variable. When DBMS=V7, you need not supply an indicator variable.

- You must declare a four-byte integer variable named SQLCODE inside or outside the DECLARE section.

- Declaring the SQLCA is optional. You need not declare the SQLCA or copy it into your program with the INCLUDE statement. When MODE={ANSI13 | Oracle}, the SQLCA must be declared.

- No error message is issued if Oracle assigns a truncated column value to an output host variable.

- The "no data found" Oracle error code returned to SQLCODE becomes +100 instead of +1403. The error-message text does not change.

- In SQL data manipulation statements, every host variable must be prefixed with a colon. When MODE={ANSI13 | Oracle}, the colon prefix is optional in the INTO clause of a SELECT or FETCH statement.

As Table 12-3 shows, some of these changes were not in effect under versions 1.3 and 1.4 of Pro*C. If you want to trade some ANSI compatibility for more flexibility, specify MODE={ANSI14 | ANSI13}. Note, however, that when MODE=ANSI14, array operations are not allowed. You can reference host arrays in a data manipulation statement only when MODE={ANSI | ANSI13 | Oracle}.

To ensure downward compatibility with applications written for Pro*C versions 1.3 and 1.4, specify MODE=ANSI13 and MODE=ANSI14, respectively.

Some MODE and DBMS option values are incompatible or not recommended. For more information, see Table 12-2.

Change	V1.3	V1.4	V1.5
CHAR values treated like ANSI strings	No	No	Yes
Array operations allowed	Yes	No	Yes
COMMIT and ROLLBACK close explicit cursors	No	Yes	Yes
Illegal to OPEN an already open cursor	Yes	Yes	Yes
Must declare SQLCODE	No	Yes	Yes
Declaring the SQLCA is optional	No	Yes	Yes
No error message if output value is truncated	Yes	Yes	Yes
"No data found" Oracle error code is +100	Yes	Yes	Yes
Colon prefix required in the INTO clause	No	Yes	Yes

TABLE 12-3. *Changes implemented in versions 1.3, 1.4, and 1.5*

ONAME

Purpose:
This option specifies the name of the output C source file.

Syntax:

```
ONAME=path and filename
```

Default:
FILENAME.C, where **filename** is the base name of the input filename.

Usage Notes:
This option can be entered only on the command line. By default, the output file is written to the current directory.

ORACA

Purpose:
This option specifies whether a program can use the ORACA.

Syntax:

```
ORACA=YES|NO
```

Default:
NO

Usage Notes:
This option can be entered inline or on the command line.
When ORACA=YES, you must place the INCLUDE ORACA statement in your program.

ORECLEN

Purpose:
This option specifies the record length of the output file.

Syntax:

```
ORECLEN=integer
```

Default:
80

Usage Notes:

This option can be entered only on the command line. The value you specify for ORECLEN should equal or exceed the value of IRECLEN. The maximum value allowed is system-dependent.

PAGELEN

Purpose:

This option specifies the number of lines per physical page of the listing file.

Syntax:

```
PAGELEN=integer
```

Default:

66

Usage Notes:

This option can be entered only on the command line. The maximum value allowed is system-dependent.

RELEASE_CURSOR

Purpose:

This option specifies how the cursors for SQL statements and PL/SQL blocks are handled in the cursor cache.

Syntax:

```
RELEASE_CURSOR=YES|NO
```

Default:

NO

Usage Notes:

This option can be entered inline or on the command line.

You can use RELEASE_CURSOR to improve the performance of your program.

When an SQL data manipulation statement is executed, its associated cursor is linked to an entry in the cursor cache. The cursor cache entry is in turn linked to an Oracle private SQL area, which stores information needed to process the statement. RELEASE_CURSOR controls what happens to the link between the cursor cache and the private SQL area.

When RELEASE_CURSOR=YES, after Oracle executes the SQL statement and the cursor is closed, the precompiler immediately removes the link. This frees memory allocated to the private SQL area and releases parse locks. To make sure the associated resources are freed when you CLOSE a cursor, you must specify RELEASE_CURSOR=YES.

When RELEASE_CURSOR=NO and HOLD_CURSOR=YES, the link is maintained. The precompiler does not reuse the link unless the number of open cursors exceeds the value of MAXOPENCURSORS. This is useful for SQL statements that are executed often because it speeds up subsequent executions. There is no need to reparse the statement or allocate memory for an Oracle private SQL area.

When you specify this option in a source module for use with implicit cursors, set RELEASE_CURSOR before executing the SQL statement. When you specify this option in a source module for use with explicit cursors, set RELEASE_CURSOR before you CLOSE the cursor.

NOTE
RELEASE_CURSOR=YES overrides HOLD_CURSOR=YES, and HOLD_CURSOR=NO overrides RELEASE_CURSOR=NO.

SELECT_ERROR

Purpose:
This option specifies whether your program generates an error when a single-row SELECT statement returns more than one row or when a SELECT returns more rows than a host array can accommodate.

Syntax:

```
SELECT_ERROR=YES|NO
```

Default:
YES

Usage Notes:
This option can be entered inline or on the command line.

When SELECT_ERROR=YES, an error (ORA-1422) is generated when a single-row SELECT returns more than one row or when a SELECT returns more rows than the host array can accommodate. The result of the SELECT is indeterminate.

When SELECT_ERROR=NO, no error is generated for either of these situations.

Whether you specify YES or NO, multiple rows are selected from a table at random. The only way to ensure a specific ordering of rows is to use the ORDER BY clause in your SELECT statement. When SELECT_ERROR=NO and you use ORDER BY, Oracle returns the first row, or the first *n* rows when you are

SELECTing into an array. When SELECT_ERROR=YES, whether or not you use ORDER BY, an error is generated when too many rows are returned.

SQLCHECK

Purpose:

This option specifies the type and extent of syntactic and semantic checking.

Syntax:

```
SQLCHECK=SEMANTICS|FULL|SYNTAX|LIMITED|NONE
```

Default:

SYNTAX

Usage Notes:

This option can be entered inline or on the command line.

Pro*C can help you debug a program by checking the syntax and semantics of embedded SQL statements and PL/SQL blocks. You control the level of checking by specifying the SQLCHECK option inline and/or on the command line. However, the level of checking you specify inline cannot be higher than the level you specify (or accept by default) on the command line. For example, if you specify SQLCHECK={SYNTAX | LIMITED} on the command line, you cannot specify SQLCHECK={SEMANTICS | FULL} inline.

When SQLCHECK={SEMANTICS | FULL}, the precompiler checks the syntax and semantics of the following:

■ Data manipulation statements such as INSERT and UPDATE

■ PL/SQL blocks

■ Host variable datatypes

■ The syntax of data definition statements such as CREATE and ALTER. However, only syntactic checking is done on data manipulation statements that use the AT **database_name** clause.

When SQLCHECK={SEMANTICS | FULL}, the precompiler gets information needed for a semantic check either by using embedded DECLARE TABLE statements in your source module or (if you specify the USERID option on the command line) by connecting to the Oracle database and accessing the data dictionary. You need not connect to Oracle if every table referenced in a data manipulation statement or PL/SQL block is defined in a DECLARE TABLE statement.

If you connect to Oracle but some needed information cannot be found in the data dictionary, you must use DECLARE TABLE statements to supply the missing information. A DECLARE TABLE definition overrides a data dictionary definition if they conflict.

If you embed PL/SQL blocks in a host program, you must specify SQLCHECK={SEMANTICS | FULL}. When SQLCHECK={SYNTAX | LIMITED}, the precompiler checks the syntax of the following:

- Data manipulation statements

- Data definition statements

- Host variable datatypes

No semantic check is done. DECLARE TABLE statements are ignored, and PL/SQL blocks are not allowed.

NOTE
The option values LIMITED and SYNTAX are equivalent. In other words, they specify the same action. However, in Pro*C version 1.3, the value LIMITED specifies a different action: When SQLCHECK=LIMITED, the precompiler checks the syntax and semantics of data manipulation statements and PL/SQL blocks. Also, to do the semantic check, the precompiler connects to Oracle, so you must specify the USERID option.

When SQLCHECK=NONE, the precompiler does no semantic checking and minimal syntactic checking, DECLARE TABLE statements are ignored, and PL/SQL blocks are not allowed.

Specify SQLCHECK=NONE only when your program reference's table is not yet created and is missing DECLARE TABLE statements for those tables, or when stricter datatype checking is undesirable.

For more information on the SQLCHECK option, see the section "Syntactic and Semantic Checking" later in this chapter.

USERID

Purpose:
This option specifies an Oracle username and password.

Syntax:

```
USERID=username/password
```

Default:
N/A

Usage Notes:
This option can be entered only on the command line.

When SQLCHECK=SEMANTICS, if you want the precompiler to get needed information by connecting to Oracle and accessing the data dictionary, you must also specify USERID.

XREF

Purpose:
This option specifies whether a cross-reference section is included in the output listing file.

Syntax:

```
XREF=YES|NO
```

Default:
YES

Usage Notes:
This option can be entered inline or on the command line.

When XREF=YES, cross-references are included for host variables, cursor names, and statement names. The cross-references show where each object is defined and referenced in your program.

When XREF=NO, the cross-reference section is not included.

Obsolete Options

The following options are no longer supported or available in the current version of the Pro*C precompiler.

In earlier versions of Pro*C, the AREASIZE option specified the size of the initial private SQL area opened for Oracle cursors. You could respecify AREASIZE for each cursor or set of cursors your program used.

The REBIND option specified how often host variables in SQL statements were bound. You could respecify REBIND for each SQL statement or set of SQL statements in your program.

The REENTRANT option specified whether reentrant code was generated. (A reentrant program or subroutine can be reentered before it has finished executing. Thus, it can be used simultaneously by two or more processes.) On some systems, you had to specify REENTRANT=YES.

In Pro*C version 1.5, private SQL areas are automatically resized, host variables are rebound only when necessary, and reentrant code is generated automatically for systems that require it. These advances make the AREASIZE, REBIND, and REENTRANT options obsolete.

WARNING
You should no longer specify AREASIZE, REBIND, and REENTRANT when precompiling. In fact, if you specify these obsolete options, Oracle generates an error.

Syntactic and Semantic Checking

You can have the Pro*C precompiler find SQL programming errors quickly and easily using syntactic and semantic checking. If you specify this option, the precompiler checks for syntax and semantic errors in the SQL statements embedded in your application program.

This section shows you how to use the SQLCHECK precompiler option to control the type and extent of checking.

The rules of syntax specify how language elements are combined to form valid statements. Thus, syntactic checking verifies that keywords, object names, operators, delimiters, and so on are combined and placed correctly in an SQL statement.

Rules of semantics determine how valid external references are specified. Thus, semantic checking verifies that references to database objects and host variables are valid and that host variable datatypes are correct.

Controlling Syntactic and Semantic Checking

You control the type and extent of checking by specifying the SQLCHECK option on the Pro*C precompiler command line. The type of checking can be syntactic, semantic, or both. The extent of checking can include data definition statements (for example, CREATE and GRANT), data manipulation statements (such as SELECT and INSERT), and PL/SQL blocks.

The SQLCHECK option only allows you to check static embedded SQL statements; you cannot check dynamic SQL statements because they are not fully defined until run time. You can specify the following values for the SQLCHECK option: SEMANTICS | FULL (the values are equivalent—they mean the same thing), SYNTAX | LIMITED (the values are equivalent), and NONE (checking is turned off). The default value is SYNTAX.

SEMANTICS (FULL) Checking
If you specify SQLCHECK={SEMANTICS | FULL}, the precompiler checks both the syntax and semantics of data manipulation statements, PL/SQL blocks, and host variable datatypes.

With this option, the precompiler checks only the syntax of the data definition statements. However, only syntactic checking is done on data manipulation statements that use the AT **database_name** clause.

When you specify SQLCHECK={SEMANTICS | FULL}, the precompiler gets information needed for a semantic check by using DECLARE TABLE statements embedded in your program or (if you specify the USERID option on the command line) by connecting to the Oracle database and accessing the data dictionary. You need not connect to Oracle if every table referenced in a data manipulation statement or PL/SQL block is defined in a DECLARE TABLE statement.

If you connect to Oracle but some needed information cannot be found in the data dictionary, you must use DECLARE TABLE statements to supply the missing information. A DECLARE TABLE definition overrides a data dictionary definition if they conflict. If you embed PL/SQL blocks in a host program, you must specify SQLCHECK={SEMANTICS | FULL}.

When the precompiler checks the syntax of data manipulation statements, the Oracle 7 set of syntax rules is used (see the SQL language reference in your Oracle documentation). However, the precompiler uses a stricter set of semantic rules. In particular, stricter datatype checking is performed. As a result, existing applications written for earlier versions of Oracle might not precompile successfully when SQLCHECK={SEMANTICS | FULL}. You should always specify this option when you precompile new programs or want stricter datatype checking.

As discussed earlier, the precompiler obtains information needed to perform a semantic check by connecting to the Oracle database and accessing the data dictionary or by using embedded DECLARE TABLE statements. Let's discuss how you use each of these methods.

Connecting to Oracle   You can connect to an Oracle database to perform a semantic check on the database objects (tables, views, columns, rows, and so on) referenced in the SQL statements embedded in your application program. You must connect to the database because the precompiler needs to access the data dictionary to obtain the data definition for the referenced objects. The data dictionary stores table and column names, table and column constraints, column lengths, column datatypes, and so on.

If some of the needed information cannot be found in the data dictionary (for example, your program refers to a table that is not yet created), you must supply the missing information using the DECLARE TABLE statement (discussed in the next section).

You connect to an Oracle database by specifying the username and password on the precompiler command line. The option to do this is USERID, using the following syntax:

```
USERID=username/password
```

where **username** and **password** form a valid Oracle userid. If you omit the password, the precompiler will prompt you for it.

Alternatively, you can specify USERID with the following syntax:

```
USERID=/
```

where the slash (/) causes the precompiler to connect automatically to Oracle using the implicit username and password prefixed by OPS$.

If you try connecting to Oracle but cannot (for example, the database is unavailable), an error message is issued and your program is not precompiled.

If you omit the USERID option, the precompiler must get needed information from embedded DECLARE TABLE statements.

Using DECLARE TABLE Statements   If you choose (or out of necessity), you can have the precompiler perform semantic checks without connecting to Oracle. To do this, you must first define the needed information about the tables and views you reference in your embedded SQL statements by using the DECLARE TABLE statement. Thus, every table referenced in a data manipulation statement or PL/SQL block must be defined in a DECLARE TABLE statement.

The DECLARE TABLE statement has the following syntax:

```
EXEC SQL DECLARE table_name TABLE
    (column_name column_datatype
        [DEFAULT expr] [NULL|NOT NULL], ...);
```

where:

> **table_name** is the name of the table you are defining.
> **column_name** is the name of each column in the table.
> **column_datatype** is the datatype assigned to each column.
> **expr** is any expression that can be used as a default column value in the CREATE TABLE statement.

The DEFAULT and NOT NULL information is currently ignored. It serves only as documentation.

If you use DECLARE TABLE to define a database table that already exists, the precompiler uses your definition, ignoring the one in the data dictionary.

SYNTAX (LIMITED) Checking

Although it's not obvious from the name, SYNTAX checking is a subset of SEMANTICS checking. If you specify SQLCHECK={SYNTAX | LIMITED}, the precompiler checks the syntax of the data manipulation statements, data definition statements, and host variable datatypes.

No semantic checking is performed, which imposes the following restrictions:

■ No attempt to connect to Oracle is made, and USERID becomes an invalid option. If you specify USERID, a warning message is issued.

■ DECLARE TABLE statements are ignored; they serve only as documentation.

■ PL/SQL blocks are not allowed. If the precompiler finds a PL/SQL block, an error message is issued.

In Pro*C version 1.5, the option values LIMITED and SYNTAX are equivalent. In other words, they specify the same action. However, in Pro*C version 1.3, the value LIMITED specifies that the precompiler is to check the syntax and semantics of data manipulation statements and PL/SQL blocks. Also, because a semantic check is performed, the precompiler connects to Oracle, so you must specify the USERID option.

When checking data manipulation statements, the precompiler uses Oracle 7 syntax rules. These rules are downward-compatible, so specify SQLCHECK= {SYNTAX | LIMITED} when migrating your precompiled programs.

No (**NONE**) Checking

If you specify SQLCHECK=NONE (the default), no semantic checking is performed, a minimal amount of syntactic checking is performed, and the same restrictions apply as for SQLCHECK={SYNTAX | LIMITED}.

You should specify SQLCHECK=NONE if the SQL statements in your program reference tables that are not yet created and you have not defined them using DECLARE TABLE statements. Also, you should specify NONE if stricter datatype checking is not desired.

You can enter the SQLCHECK option on the command line or in your program by using the EXEC ORACLE OPTION statement. However, the level of checking you specify inline cannot be higher than the level you specify (or accept by default) on the command line. For example, if you specify SQLCHECK={SYNTAX | LIMITED} on the command line, you cannot specify SQLCHECK={SEMANTICS | FULL} in your program.

Using Pro*C for Windows

This section shows you a practical example of how you can use the Pro*C precompiler as an integrated tool with the Microsoft Visual C++ development environment to produce a running application program. These tools run under the Windows operating system.

If you have Microsoft Visual C++ and Pro*C for Windows, it is assumed that you have already integrated Pro*C as a development tool into the Visual C++ development environment. If you have not done this, consult your Pro*C for Windows installation and user's guide for instructions.

The Pro*C for Windows application is a *single-document interface*, which means that only one document (in this case, a project) can be open at one time. A project consists of a list of one or more source modules that can be precompiled separately or as a batch.

You can easily add, delete, or change the source modules on this list. For most of the functions of the Pro*C application, you can use the menu bar, the toolbar, or keyboard commands.

The following sections explain the steps to enter Pro*C from Visual C++, create and precompile a project, exit Pro*C, and compile and link your modules in Visual C++.

Accessing the Visual C++ Environment

To begin using Visual C++, select the Visual C++ icon from the Visual C++ program group in the Windows Program Manager. The Visual C++ Main screen appears, as shown in Figure 12-1.

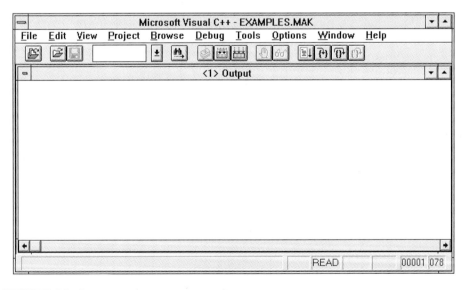

FIGURE 12-1. *Visual C++ main application screen*

To work in Visual C++, you must define a project for your application program. A project consists of the program source modules, include and definition files, a *.mak file to compile and link your program, and the executable program.

If you are just beginning to create your application program, you want to create a new project. If you are editing your program, you want to select an existing project, or it is automatically selected for you if it was the project in use when you last exited Visual C++.

Creating a New Project

To create a new project, select the Project|New menu option from the menu bar. Enter a project name and select the type of project you are creating from the Project Type menu. In this case, select Windows Application, as shown in Figure 12-2. Click OK. You now have a new project.

Opening an Existing Project

To open an existing project, select the Project|Open menu option from the menu bar. Select an existing project file from the Directories list, as shown in Figure 12-3. Click OK. You now have an active project.

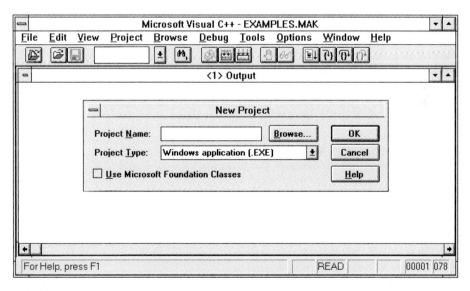

FIGURE 12-2.   *New Project screen*

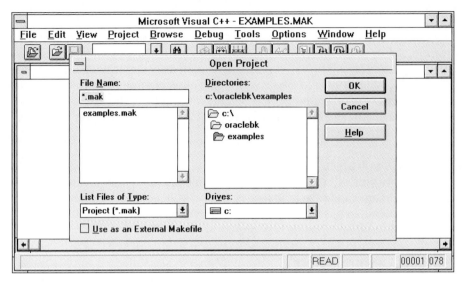

FIGURE 12-3. *Open Project screen*

Accessing the Pro*C Application

To precompile your source modules using Pro*C, select the Tools|Oracle Pro*C menu option from the menu bar (assuming you have already created this menu option), as shown in Figure 12-4. This will start the Pro*C application.

Your project file name is passed to Pro*C, but with the extension *.pre rather than *.mak. The Pro*C main screen appears, as shown in Figure 12-5.

Creating a Precompile File List

The first step is to create or modify a list of files to be precompiled. To do this, either choose the Add icon button on the toolbar or select the Edit|Add menu option from the menu bar. The Input File dialog box appears (see Figure 12-6).

You can select one or more files from the list that appears. If the file you want to select is on a different drive or directory, you can either enter the full path name in the File Name box or use the drives and directory list boxes to locate your file. When you are finished selecting files, click the OK button.

Specifying the Default Output File Name

Once you have selected or entered your files, what happens next depends on the Default Output File Name setting. Under the Preferences menu item is the toggle item Default Output File Name. If you select that item (this is the default), the files you enter or select are placed in the Input File and Output File lists on the main screen, as shown in Figure 12-5.

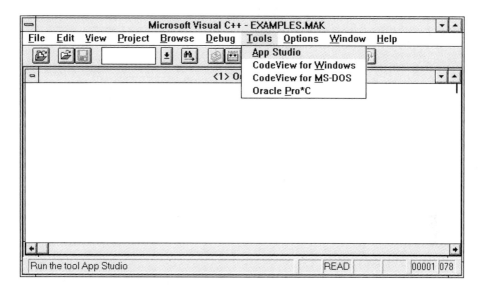

FIGURE 12-4. *Pro*C option in the Tools menu*

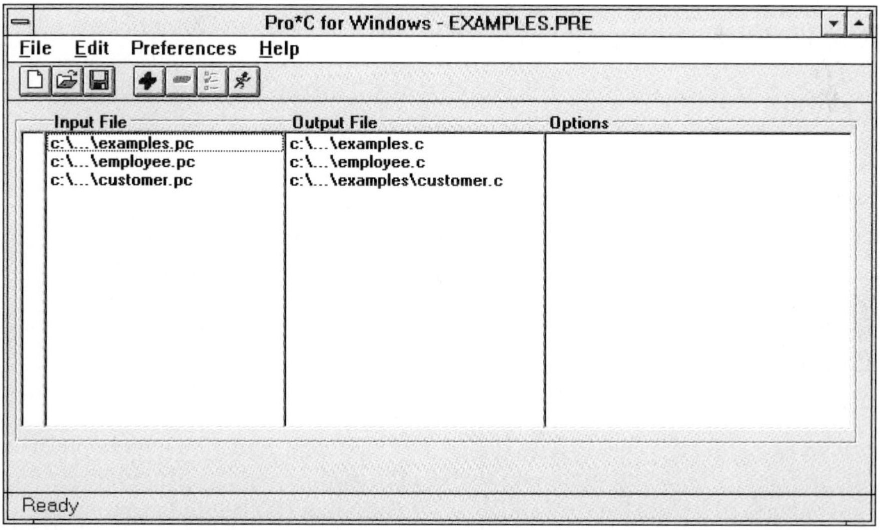

FIGURE 12-5. *Pro*C main application screen*

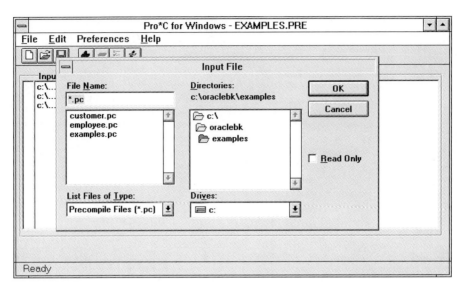

FIGURE 12-6. *Input File dialog box*

The output file has the same name as the input file, except it has a .c extension. If you deselect the Default Output File Name menu option, an Output File dialog box appears. You must enter an output name for each file selected in the File Name field. Once you select or enter a filename, it is placed in the Output File list on the main screen.

NOTE
If you want to change the name of an input or output file, double-click on the filename in the Input File or Output File list on the main screen. The appropriate dialog box appears, and you can change the filename.

Deleting a Filename (Optional)

To delete files from the list, select a file by clicking on the filename. Once you have selected a file, the Delete icon button in the toolbar and the Delete option under the Edit menu bar item are enabled. Choose either one. The highlighted file disappears from the list. You can select and delete many files at the same time.

Specifying Precompile Options (Optional)

To select precompile options, you must access the Options dialog box. You can do this in two ways:

■ Highlight one or more files in the Input File list. This enables the Options icon button in the toolbar and the Edit|Options menu option. Choose either one. The Options dialog box shown in Figure 12-7 appears.

■ Double-click in the option area of the precompile list in the main screen. The Options dialog box appears.

The Options dialog box allows you to deviate from the default options when a file is precompiled. Also, if you select the Listing/Errors button, another dialog box appears that allows you to change the settings that affect the format of the output list file written to disk by the precompiler. Any changes you make here to the default options are applied to the files you highlighted in the main screen.

Let's discuss some of the features of the Options dialog box.

Selecting or Changing a Precompile Option

To turn on an option or change it, do one of the following:

■ Click on a check box

■ Pull down a list box and select an item

■ Enter text into an edit field

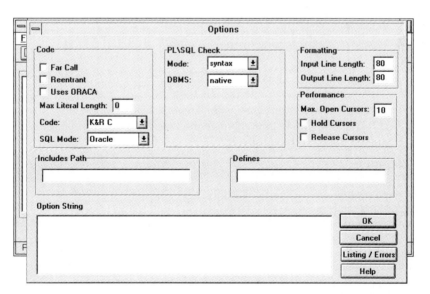

FIGURE 12-7. *Options dialog box*

The default options settings are in effect for all newly added files. When you change an option's default setting, text that describes the change appears in the Option String box at the bottom of this screen and in the Options list on the main screen.

When you have chosen all of the desired options in the Options dialog box, click OK to return to the main screen. Any option you changed from its default value appears as a command-line string in the Options section of the main screen.

Option Settings   The following suggestions will help you avoid some common pitfalls:

- **Numeric Fields**   You can enter integers from 0 through 999. When you change an option using valid values, text relating to that option appears in the Option String box. If you enter invalid characters (that is, letters in a numeric field), nothing appears in the Option String box because the program cannot translate these characters into an integer. If you leave nonnumeric characters or nothing when you tab out of the field, the contents are restored to their default settings, causing the text to disappear from the Option String box.

- **Mode**   If you select semantic checking, you must specify a database connect string before precompiling. For information on how to do this, see the next section.

- **Includes Path**   Use this field to enter include path directories. If you want to enter more than one, separate them with a semicolon. This causes a separate "includes=" string to appear in front of each directory.

Formatting the List File   If you want to change the settings that affect the format of the output list file written to disk by the precompiler after precompilation, click on the Listing/Errors button. The Listing/Errors dialog box appears, as shown in Figure 12-8. This dialog box lets you change the type of error information generated and the name of the errors file.

Using the Connect Dialog (Optional)

If you select semantic checking in the Options dialog box, you must specify a database connect string. To do this, when you are in the main screen, select the File|Connect menu option from the menu bar. The Connect dialog box appears, as shown in Figure 12-9. Enter the username, password, and connect information, then select OK.

A database connect is not performed at this time; the information is used when you run a precompile. If you want to save this information between Pro*C sessions, select the check box for Save Connect String To Disk. Otherwise, none of the fields are stored, and you will need to enter this information each time you start Pro*C.

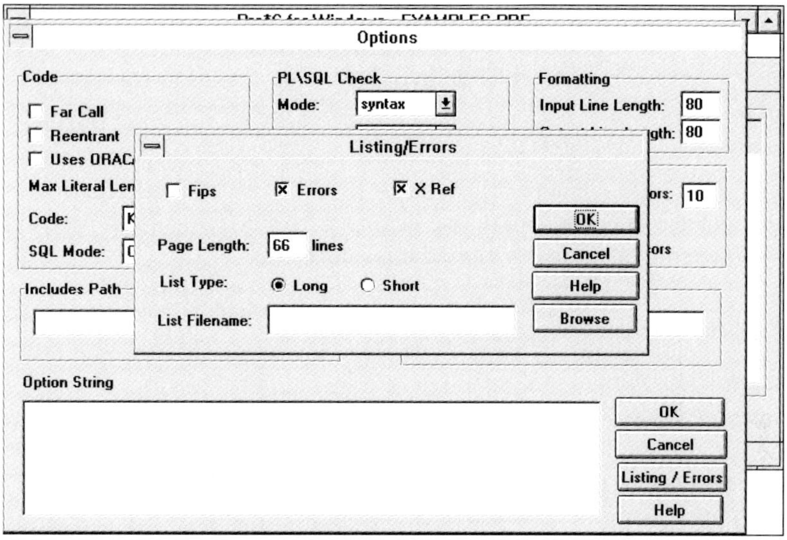

FIGURE 12-8. *Listing/Errors dialog box*

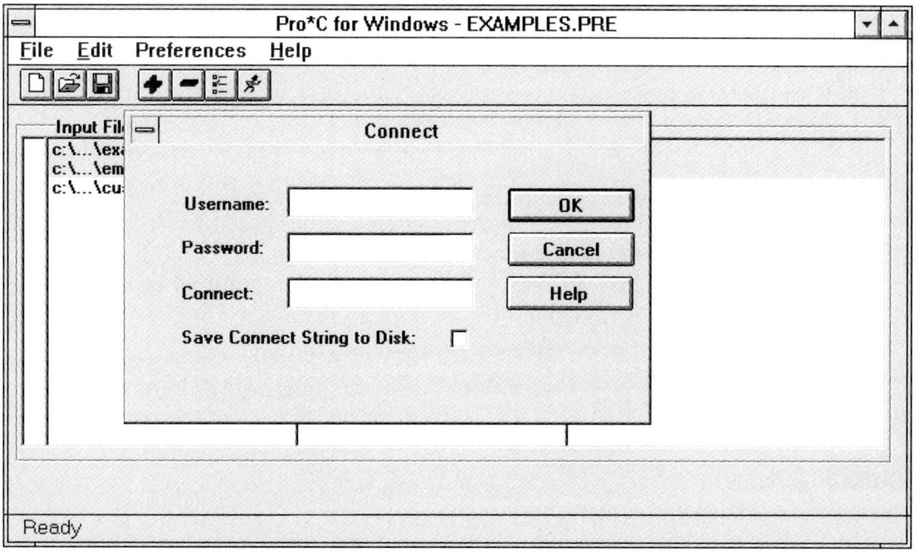

FIGURE 12-9. *Connect dialog box*

NOTE
If you do store this information, note that your password is saved as well and is available to anyone who has access to your PC.

Only one database connect string can be specified for all files requiring semantic checking. The Connect dialog box appears automatically at precompile time if you have not previously supplied this information.

Running the Precompiler

You can precompile all files in the project list or just a few. To precompile all files, select the Run icon button on the toolbar or select the File|Run menu option from the menu bar. To precompile one or more files, select the appropriate files from the list and select Run. A dialog box appears informing you of the progress of the precompile process for each selected file.

You can press the Cancel button in the dialog box at any time to cancel the precompile process. However, this will not affect the file being precompiled—just the remaining files. When the precompile process is complete, the message in the dialog box says "Precompiling Finished," and the Cancel button changes to OK. Click OK to continue.

After the desired files are precompiled, icons appear next to each precompiled file. A green check mark indicates that the precompile was successful. A yellow check mark indicates that the precompile process was successful but that certain warnings are issued (for example, a line is too long). A red cross indicates that the precompile was unsuccessful. See Figure 12-10 for an example.

If all your files precompiled successfully or contained acceptable warnings, skip the following. If, however, you receive a red cross or a yellow check mark, double-click on this icon to display the Precompiler Errors list box (shown in Figure 12-11). This shows you why the precompile failed, or, in the case of a yellow check mark, provides a list of warnings. Switch back either to your development environment or to your own editor to fix the problems associated with the file.

If the list file is not created due to a failure before the precompile process begins, the message "Unable to open list file" appears. This error might occur if you try to precompile a file that does not exist or if the precompile is not able to find or open the message file. In the case of these errors, a message box appears to alert you to these problems.

Exiting Pro*C

When you have finished all precompile operations, exit Pro*C for Windows by selecting the File|Exit menu option from the menu bar. You will be prompted to save your project file if you have changed it in any way. You will return to Visual C++, and the project you originally selected will be active.

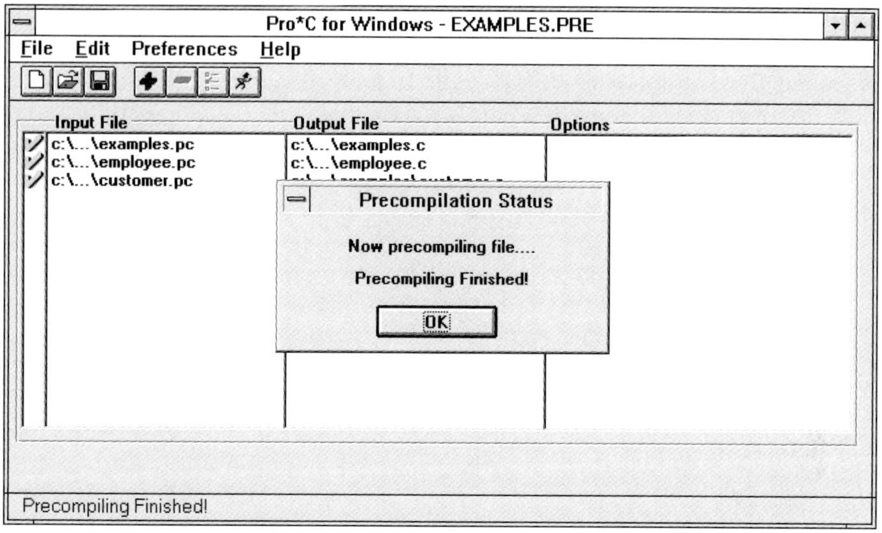

FIGURE 12-10.   *Precompiled files*

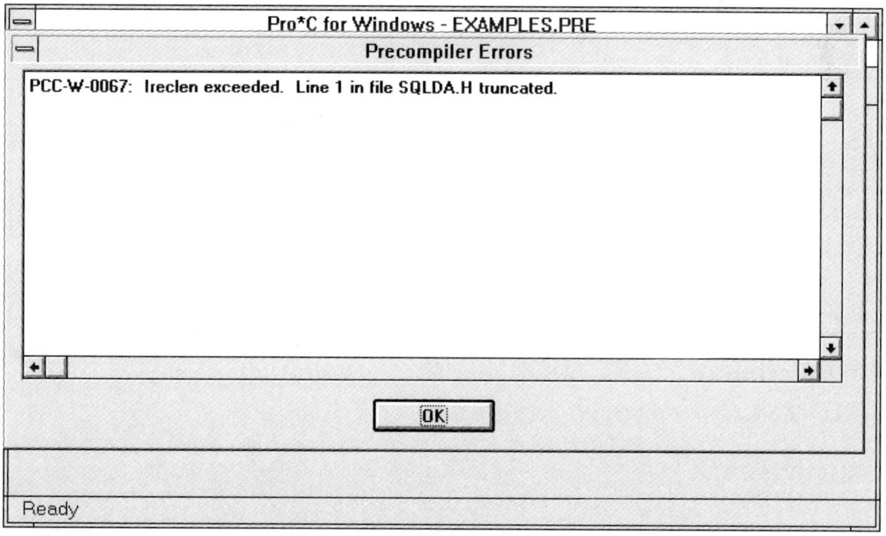

FIGURE 12-11.   *Precompiler Errors list box*

Adding Source Modules to Your Project

After you have precompiled the files in your project, you need to add your source modules generated in Pro*C to the project. To do this, select the Project|Edit menu option from the menu bar. This displays the Edit Project dialog box shown in Figure 12-12. In this dialog box you can select the files you want to add to the project. When you have finished adding files, select OK.

Building Your Application Program

You are now ready to build (compile and link) your application program. Select the Project|Build or Project|Rebuild menu option from the menu. Select the Build menu option if you are building your application or you want to recompile all source modules. Select the Rebuild option if you have just modified and precompiled a few source modules.

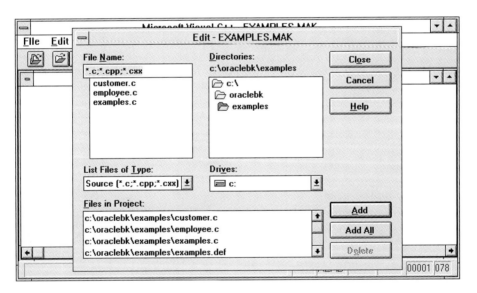

FIGURE 12-12.   *Edit Project dialog box*

Running Your Application Program

If your application program builds successfully without any errors, you can now run your program. To do this, select the Project|Execute menu option from the menu bar. Your program will then be executed.

Summary

This chapter discussed in detail the options available for the Pro*C precompiler, including the purpose, syntax, default, and usage notes for each option. With this information you can use the precompiler options with confidence to generate and troubleshoot your application program.

This chapter also showed you how to precompile and troubleshoot your source modules and how to build and execute your application program.

CHAPTER 13

An Introduction to Distributed Databases

This chapter will introduce you to distributed databases and give you a basic understanding of how distributed database applications are developed. We'll discuss the following topics:

■ Basic concepts of distributed databases

■ Oracle SQL*Net

■ Database links

Distributed Databases

Oracle 7 provides support for distributed databases. A distributed database system creates one logical database from two or more physically separate databases (this chapter refers to the separate databases as *nodes,* though multiple databases could actually reside on the same machine). Each node database is managed separately by a local Oracle server. A distributed database system makes the data located on remote nodes available as easily as if the data were on the local database, allowing enterprisewide sharing of data in a client-server architecture. From an office in Cincinnati, for example, you can query or update tables across the databases at the New York and Los Angeles offices.

User access data in any of the node databases that participate in the distributed system via a connection to a local Oracle 7 server, which can be on any node on the network. In this networked system of databases, the servers communicate with each other using SQL*Net to create the distributed database system. Data access on remote systems is relatively transparent. In a banking system, for example, a transaction may move $500 from a savings account stored in a table in Atlanta to a checking account in a table in Cincinnati. The following SQL statements would do that task for us:

```
UPDATE checking@Cinti SET balance = balance + 500
   WHERE account = 123;
UPDATE savings@Atlanta SET balance = balance - 500
   WHERE account = 456;
COMMIT;
```

In this example, "@Cinti" and "@Atlanta" are links (discussed in a moment) that refer to the databases where the tables to be updated reside. In effect, these statements represent a path to the table similar to the one in the following statement:

```
UPDATE company.checking@t:PROD.SUNIS01.NATIONAL.COM:accounts
```

Even though this transaction bridges two different and autonomous databases, you are guaranteed data integrity for the transaction. The Oracle DBMS ensures, via a *two-phase commit*, that either both update statements complete successfully or neither is applied to the database (the return code would signal a failure). The two-phase commit mechanism guarantees data consistency by making sure all elements of a transaction either succeed or are rolled back on all nodes involved in the transaction. You do nothing special to invoke the two-phase commit in a distributed transaction; just use the COMMIT or ROLLBACK statement to control your transactions as usual.

Oracle 7 allows users to insert, update, delete, and select across the distributed network (including SELECT .. FOR UPDATE and LOCK TABLE). The tables on the remote (nonlocal) databases are qualified by a global object name such as:

```
"human_resources.emp@hq.us.americas.big_blue.com"
```

A distributed query retrieves data from two or more nodes. For example:

```
SELECT a.inv_no, a.rep_id, b.line_no, b.line_item
    FROM invoice@Cinti a, inv_line@Atlanta b
    WHERE  a.inv_no = b.inv_no AND a.rep_id = 100;
```

Next, we'll look at how communications are set up and implemented in the Oracle 7 system.

SQL*Net

Communication between each node is provided by SQL*Net, an Oracle communications product that provides hardware- and OS-independent communications between Oracle clients and servers (including server to server). SQL*Net eliminates the boundaries in a computer network created by different makes of hardware and operating systems. It also allows two or more servers to communicate, so that a server may become a client to another server. Figure 13-1 shows how SQL*Net lets you connect to distributed databases on your computer network.

Two versions of SQL*Net are available. The distributed database functionality works with either Version 1 or Version 2 of SQL*Net. Oracle developed Version 2 as the basis for its next generation of products. In general, Version 2 simplifies the configuration of the system and is the version of choice, especially when communicating with Version 7 databases.

To establish a connection to a database other than the default on your local computer, you must identify to SQL*Net which database, on which computer, and with which network you will connect. The syntax to identify a database to SQL*Net is system-specific and determined by the type of communication protocol—TCP/IP, DECNet, SNA, DCE, and so on—used on your computer.

Using SQL*NET Version 1

Your system administrator will start up SQL*Net V1 using the Oracle TCPCTL program. You can check to see if SQL*Net V1 is running by listing the active

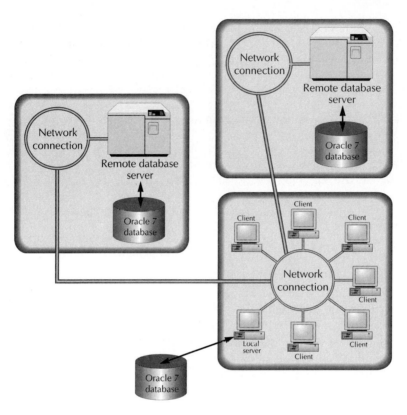

FIGURE 13-1. *Distributed database connections using SQL*Net*

processes owned by the Oracle account; you should see the entry "orasrv" if SQL*Net is up. On UNIX systems, you enter the command

```
>ps -ef | grep oracle
```

and receive the following type of response:

```
oracle    250      1  0   Jan 17 ?        0:00 orasrv
oracle 23757 23738   3 11:04:02 pts/3     0:01 -csh
oracle 23769 23757 12 11:04:11 pts/3      0:00 ps -ef
oracle    581      1  0   Jan 13 ?        3:17 ora_pmon_dev2
oracle    582      1  1   Jan 13 ?        6:43 ora_dbwr_dev2
oracle    583      1  0   Jan 13 ?        3:24 ora_lgwr_dev2
oracle    584      1  0   Jan 13 ?        3:05 ora_smon_dev2
oracle    585      1  0   Jan 13 ?        0:04 ora_reco_dev2
```

You use a connect string to specify the path to a remote database; an example in Version 1 would be "t:sunes2.bank1.com:dev2". In this example, the "t" represents the protocol (TCP/IP), "sunes2.bank1.com" is the address of the network node running the Oracle database, and "dev2" is the SID (system ID) of the Oracle instance to which we wish to connect.

If you are running SQL Plus and are connected to a server on another node, you can connect to the remote database as follows:

```
SQL> CONNECT system/manager@t:sunes2.bank1.com:dev2
```

To use the distributed database functionality, you must use a database link. This is, in effect, a logical name for each remote database you wish to access. The following statement creates a database link:

```
SQL>CREATE DATABASE LINK sales USING 't:sunes2.bank1.com:dev2'
```

This example creates a private database link that will be known only for the user who defined it. Another example is:

```
SQL> CREATE PUBLIC DATABASE LINK sales
SQL> CONNECT TO scott IDENTIFIED BY tiger
     USING 't:sunes2.bank1.com:dev2'
```

This code creates a public database link that will be in effect for all users. The link is used as follows:

```
SELECT * FROM order@sales
```

The link also provides the schema name (user ID) and login password for the remote database. If these are not specified, the connection is made with the current user ID and password.

When you use a database link in an SQL statement, Oracle looks first for a privately defined database link. If one is not found, it checks for a global link to resolve the reference. You can query the **user_db_links** data dictionary view for the privately defined links and **dba_db_links** for the public ones. For example, to see the private link that was just defined, use the following code:

```
SQL> SELECT * FROM user_db_links;

DB_LINK                      HOST                    CREATED
-----------------------------------------------------------

SALES.HPES12.BANK1.COM    t:sunes2.bank1.com:dev2    11-JAN-94
```

Using SQL*NET Version 2

With SQL*Net Version 2 you have several additional components to deal with, but a new configuration tool (net_conf) simplifies the configuration process greatly. The new components we're interested in are the TNS Listener process and the configuration files LISTENER.ORA and TNSNAMES.ORA.

The TNS Listener on the Server

Each Oracle instance (server) must have a listener process running on its node to use SQL*Net V2. This process "listens" to the network and receives incoming connection requests from SQL*Net V2 clients, which may also be other servers. The clients don't need to run a listener, but if a server exists on the client's node, a listener will be running for it. The new files are used to configure the listener and to allow clients to reach the listener. The LISTENER.ORA file contains parameters for the listener process on the server machine. The TNSNAMES.ORA file defines the connection details necessary for the client machines that will be accessing the server.

The listener uses on its machine a specific port address; this address must also be known to any machine running a client application that needs to contact the server. This port address and other configuration data (such as type of protocol) is found in the LISTENER.ORA file. The following shows what an excerpt from this file might look like:

```
LISTENER_SUNES2 =
    (PROTOCOL = TCP)
    (HOST = sunes2)
    (PORT = 1523)
```

Here the listener is named "LISTENER_SUNES2" and the protocol is TCP/IP. The listener will be listening at port 1523 on the sunes2 machine. The TNSNAMES.ORA file on any client machine (such as hpes12) wishing to access this sever will reference LISTENER_SUNES2 with the parameters HOST = sunes2, PORT = 1523, and PROTOCOL = TCP.

The database administrator will start up the listener process for your installation. To list the active processes and check to see, if the listener is up type the following (on Unix systems):

```
%ps -ef | grep ora
```

The screen should display something like the following:

```
    oracle 23757 23738  3 11:04:02 pts/3    0:01 -csh
    oracle 23769 23757 12 11:04:11 pts/3    0:00 ps -ef
```

```
oracle   581    1  0   Jan 13  ?        3:17 ora_pmon_mtisgi2
oracle   582    1  1   Jan 13  ?        6:43 ora_dbwr_mtisgi2
oracle   583    1  0   Jan 13  ?        3:24 ora_lgwr_mtisgi2
oracle   584    1  0   Jan 13  ?        3:05 ora_smon_mtisgi2
oracle   585    1  0   Jan 13  ?        0:04 ora_reco_mtisgi2
oracle   595    1  0   Jan 13  ?
              0:01 /u/oracle/bin/tnslsnr LISTENER_SUNES2 -
```

LISTENER.ORA

The listener's name and port address are also entered into the TNSNAMES.ORA file, which must be placed on each client and server machine. This file contains the information SQL*Net needs to identify and connect to other machines. Each entry contains a database name and a connect descriptor telling where the TNS listener is located. An example is:

```
###########
# FILENAME: tnsnames.ora
# TIME....: 93-11-18 10:18:18
# NETWORK.: CINTI
# NODE....: HPES12
# SERVICE.: C_TCP.CLASS
###########
dev2_tcp =
  (DESCRIPTION =
    (ADDRESS_LIST =
       (ADDRESS =
          (COMMUNITY = TCP.CLASS)
          (PROTOCOL = TCP)
          (HOST = hpes2)
          (PORT = 1521)
       )
    )
    (CONNECT_DATA =
      (SID = dev2)
    )
  )

prod2_tcp =
  (DESCRIPTION =
    (ADDRESS_LIST =
       (ADDRESS =
          (COMMUNITY = TCP.CLASS)
```

```
        (PROTOCOL = TCP)
        (HOST = sgipd2)
        (PORT = 1523)
      )
  )
  (CONNECT_DATA =
    (SID = prod2)
  )
)
```

Note that the SIDs of the Oracle instances are also specified. The new net_conf utility will create the configuration files automatically. The same TNSNAMES.ORA file can be copied to each node of the system. The same files will work on various platforms.

For SQL*Net V2, the database links refer to the TNSNAMES.ORA label instead of the Version 1 connect string. For example,

```
SQL>CREATE DATABASE LINK sales USING 'dev2_tcp'
```

would be used as follows:

```
SQL>select * from orders@sales
```

You can simplify this even more by defining an alias:

```
CREATE SYNONYM new_orders FOR orders@sales;
```

That would reduce the SELECT statement to:

```
SELECT * FROM new_orders;
```

Summary

This chapter introduced you to distributed databases. The distributed functionality of Oracle 7 allows you to access data in remote databases. To access objects in a remote database, you must define database links, which are logical labels for each database. The links refer to the entries in the TNSNAMES.ORA file to find the connect information. The LISTENER.ORA file configures the listener and ties the listener to a port and an Oracle instance.

APPENDIX A

Datatype Reference

This appendix contains the datatypes for Pro*C and PL/SQL.

C Datatypes

Table A-1 summarizes the basic C language datatypes with the valid datatype modifiers. The size is platform-specific; this table is for Windows.

Oracle Datatypes

Table A-2 summarizes each internal datatype supported by the Oracle system. Associated with each datatype is a code, which is used for communication purposes throughout the Oracle system.

C Datatype	Valid Modifier(s)	Size in Bits	Description
char, char(n)	unsigned, signed	8	Character or character-string data
int, short int	unsigned, signed	16	Integer data, 2 bytes long
long int	unsigned, signed	32	Integer data, 4 bytes long
float	—	32	Floating-point data, 4 bytes long, 6 digits of precision
double	—	64	Floating-point data, 8 bytes long, 10 digits of precision
long double	—	128	Floating-point data, 16 bytes long, 20 digits of precision

TABLE A-1. *The C datatypes*

Code	Internal Datatype	Description
1	VARCHAR2(length)	Variable-length character string having a maximum length in bytes. The maximum length allowed is 2,000 bytes.
2	NUMBER(p,s)	Number having precision **p** and scale **s**. Precision **p** can range from 1 to 38. Scale **s** can range from –84 to 127.
8	LONG	Variable-length character data. The maximum length allowed is 2Gb, or $2^{31} - 1$.
13	DATE	A valid date and time that can range from January 1, 4712 B.C. to A.D. December 31, 4712.

TABLE A-2. *The Oracle internal datatypes*

Code	Internal Datatype	Description
23	RAW(length)	Variable-length raw binary data having a maximum length in bytes. The maximum length allowed is 255 bytes.
24	LONG RAW	Variable-length raw binary data. The maximum length allowed is 2Gb.
69	ROWID	Hexadecimal string representing the unique database address of a row in a database table. This datatype is primarily used for values returned by the ROWID pseudocolumn.
96	CHAR(length)	Fixed-length character data. The maximum length allowed is 255 bytes. Default length is 1 byte.
106	MLSLABEL	Binary format of an operating system label. This datatype is used primarily with Trusted Oracle.

TABLE A-2.   *The Oracle internal datatypes* (continued)

Table A-3 summarizes each external datatype supported by the Oracle system that is applicable to the C language. There are other external datatypes—such as NUMBER, DECIMAL, and DISPLAY—but they are not applicable to C. Associated with each datatype is a code, which is used for communication purposes throughout the Oracle system.

PL/SQL Datatypes

PL/SQL datatypes are grouped into eight categories: numeric, character, Boolean, date/time, raw, rowid, MLSLABEL, and composite. Table A-4 summarizes the datatypes provided by PL/SQL.

Code	Name	Description
1	VARCHAR2	Variable-length character string
3	INTEGER	Signed integer
4	FLOAT	Floating-point number
5	STRING	Variable-length, null-terminated character string
6	VARNUM	Variable-length binary number
8	LONG	Long, fixed-length character string
9	VARCHAR	Variable-length character string with associated length
11	ROWID	Database address of a table row, binary value
12	DATE	Fixed-length date/time value
15	VARRAW	Variable-length binary data with associated length
23	RAW	Fixed-length binary data
24	LONG RAW	Fixed-length binary data
68	UNSIGNED	Unsigned integer
94	LONG VARCHAR	Long, variable-length character string with associated length
95	LONG VARRAW	Long, variable-length binary data with associated length
96	CHAR	Short, fixed-length character string
97	CHARZ	Short, fixed-length, null-terminated character string
106	MLSLABEL	Variable-length binary data

TABLE A-3. *Oracle external datatypes for C*

Category	Name	Description
Numeric	BINARY_INTEGER	Integer of any size from $-2^{31} - 1$ to $2^{31} - 1$
	NUMBER	Same as the NUMBER internal datatype
Character	CHAR	Short, fixed-length character string
	VARCHAR2	Variable-length character string
	LONG	Long, variable-length character string
Boolean	BOOLEAN	TRUE, FALSE, or NULL
Date/Time	DATE	Fixed-length date/time value
Raw	RAW	Variable-length binary data
	LONG RAW	Variable-length binary data
Rowid	ROWID	Database address of a table row; binary value
MLSLABEL	MLSLABEL	Trusted Oracle address; variable-length binary data
Composite	RECORD	A set of named fields that form a logical unit
	TABLE	A single-column array of rows

TABLE A-4. *PL/SQL datatypes*

APPENDIX B

PL/SQL Quick Reference

This appendix is a quick reference for the PL/SQL application developer or database administrator. It includes detailed descriptions and usage notes for the PL/SQL standard functions and language constructs.

Standard Functions

For each built-in function, the arguments, the datatypes of the arguments, and the datatype of the returned value are given. The following example shows that the function LENGTH takes an argument of type VARCHAR2 and returns a value of type NUMBER:

```
function LENGTH (str VARCHAR2) return NUMBER
```

Error-Reporting Functions

Two functions, SQLCODE and SQLERRM, give you information about PL/SQL execution errors. These functions are not allowed in SQL statements.

SQLCODE

```
function SQLCODE return NUMBER
```

Returns the number associated with the most recently raised exception. This function is meaningful only in an exception handler. Outside a handler, SQLCODE always returns zero.

For internal exceptions, SQLCODE returns the number of the associated Oracle error. The number SQLCODE returns is negative unless the Oracle error is "no data found," in which case SQLCODE returns +100. For user-defined exceptions, SQLCODE + returns +1 unless you used the pragma EXCEPTION_INIT to associate the exception with an Oracle error number, in which case SQLCODE returns that error number.

SQLERRM

```
function SQLERRM [(error_number NUMBER)] return CHAR
```

Returns the error message associated with the current value of SQLCODE. Without an argument, SQLERRM is meaningful only in an exception handler. Outside a handler, SQLERRM with no argument always returns the message "ORA-0000: normal, successful completion."

For internal exceptions, SQLERRM returns the message associated with the Oracle error that occurred. The message begins with the Oracle error code.

For user-defined exceptions, SQLERRM returns the message "User-Defined Exception," unless you used the pragma EXCEPTION_INIT to associate the exception with an Oracle error number, in which case SQLERRM returns the corresponding error message.

You can pass the argument error_number to SQLERRM, in which case SQLERRM returns the message associated with **error_number**.

Number Functions

Number functions take numeric arguments and return numeric values. The transcendental functions include trigonometric, logarithmic, and exponential functions.

The ordinary trigonometric functions (SIN, COS, and TAN) and the hyperbolic trigonometric functions (SINH, COSH, and TANH) are closely related. If n is a real number and $i = -1$ (the imaginary square root of -1), then $SIN(i*n) = i*SINH(n)$, $COS(i*n) = COSH(n)$, and $TAN(i*n) = i*TANH(n)$.

ABS

```
function ABS (n NUMBER) return NUMBER
```

Returns the absolute value of the number n.

CEIL

```
function CEIL (n NUMBER) return NUMBER
```

Returns the smallest integer greater than or equal to the number n.

COS

```
function COS (a NUMBER) return NUMBER
```

Returns the cosine of the angle a, which must be expressed in radians. A radian is 57.29578 (180/p) degrees. If a is in degrees, simply take COS(a/57.29578).

COSH

```
function COSH (n NUMBER) return NUMBER
```

Returns the hyperbolic cosine of the number n.

EXP

```
function EXP (n NUMBER) return NUMBER
```

Returns e raised to the nth power. The number e (<155> 2.71828) is the base of the system of natural logarithms.

FLOOR

```
function FLOOR (n NUMBER) return NUMBER
```

Returns the largest integer equal to or less than the number *n*.

LN

```
function LN (n NUMBER) return NUMBER
```

Returns the natural logarithm of the number *n*, where n is greater than 0.

LOG

```
function LOG (m NUMBER, n NUMBER) return NUMBER
```

Returns the base-*m* logarithm of the number *n*, where *m* is greater than 1 and *n* is greater than 0.

MOD

```
function MOD (m NUMBER, n NUMBER) return NUMBER
```

Returns the remainder of the number *m* when divided by *n*. If *n* is 0, *m* is returned.

POWER

```
function POWER (m NUMBER, n NUMBER) return NUMBER
```

Returns the number *m* raised to the *n*th power. The base *m* and the exponent *n* can be any numbers, but if *m* is negative, *n* must be an integer.

ROUND

```
function ROUND (m NUMBER [, n NUMBER]) return NUMBER
```

Returns the number *m* rounded to *n* decimal places. If you omit *n*, *m* is rounded to zero decimal places. The number *n* can be negative, in which case ROUND rounds digits to the left of the decimal point.

SIGN

```
function SIGN (n NUMBER) return NUMBER
```

Returns –1 if the number *n* is less than 0, 0 if *n* equals 0, or 1 if *n* is greater than 0.

SIN

```
function SIN (a NUMBER) return NUMBER
```

Returns the sine of the angle *a*, which must be expressed in radians.

SINH

```
function SINH (n NUMBER) return NUMBER
```

Returns the hyperbolic sine of the number *n*.

SQRT

```
function SQRT (n NUMBER) return NUMBER
```

Returns the square root of the number *n*, which cannot be negative.

TAN

```
function TAN (a NUMBER) return NUMBER
```

Returns the tangent of the angle *a*, which must be expressed in radians.

TANH

```
function TANH (n NUMBER) return NUMBER
```

Returns the hyperbolic tangent of the number *n*.

TRUNC

```
function TRUNC (m NUMBER [, n NUMBER]) returns NUMBER
```

Returns the number *m* truncated to *n* decimal places. If you omit *n*, *m* is truncated to zero decimal places. The number *n* can be negative, in which case TRUNC truncates (zeros) digits to the left of the decimal point.

Character Functions

Character functions take character arguments. Some functions return character values; others return numeric values. Those functions that return a character value always return a VARCHAR2 value, with two exceptions. If passed a CHAR argument, the functions UPPER and LOWER return a CHAR value. Otherwise, they return a VARCHAR2 value.

ASCII

```
function ASCII (char VARCHAR2) return NUMBER
```

Returns the collating code that represents the character **char** in the database character set. Whether the character set is (for example) 7-bit ASCII or EBCDIC Code Page 500, ASCII returns the appropriate collating code. ASCII is the inverse of the function CHR.

CHR

```
function CHR (num NUMBER) return VARCHAR2
```

Returns the character in the database character set that the collating code **num** represents. Whether the character set is (for example) 7-bit ASCII or EBCDIC Code Page 500, CHR returns the appropriate character. CHR is the inverse of the function ASCII.

CONCAT

```
function CONCAT (str1 VARCHAR2, str2 VARCHAR2) return VARCHAR2
```

Appends string **str2** to string **str1**, then returns the combined string. If either argument is NULL, CONCAT returns the other argument. If both arguments are NULL, CONCAT returns a NULL.

INITCAP

```
function INITCAP (str VARCHAR2) return VARCHAR2
```

Returns the string **str**, with the first letter of each word in uppercase and all other letters in lowercase. Words are delimited by spaces or nonalphanumeric characters.

INSTR

```
function INSTR (str1 VARCHAR2, str2 VARCHAR2
   [, pos NUMBER[,n NUMBER]]) return NUMBER
```

Searches string **str1** starting at character position **pos** for the *n*th occurrence of string **str2** and returns the position of the first character of that occurrence. If **pos** is negative, INSTR counts and searches backward from the end of **str1**. The arguments **pos** and *n* default to 1. The return value is relative to the beginning of **str1** regardless of the value of **pos** and is expressed in characters. If the search fails, INSTR returns 0.

INSTRB

```
function INSTRB (str1 VARCHAR2, str2 VARCHAR2
   [, pos NUMBER[,n NUMBER]]) return NUMBER
```

Searches string **str1** starting at byte position **pos** for the *n*th occurrence of string **str2**, and returns the position of the first byte of that occurrence. If **pos** is negative, INSTRB counts and searches backward from the end of **str1**. The arguments **pos** and *n* default to 1. The return value is relative to the beginning of **str1** regardless of the value of **pos** and is expressed in bytes. If the search fails, INSTRB returns 0. For single-byte character sets, INSTRB is equivalent to INSTR.

LENGTH

```
function LENGTH (str CHAR) return NUMBER
```

```
function LENGTH (str VARCHAR2) return NUMBER
```

Returns the number of characters in string **str**. If **str** belongs to datatype CHAR, the length includes trailing blanks. If **str** is NULL, LENGTH returns a NULL.

LENGTHB

```
function LENGTHB (str CHAR) return NUMBER
```

```
function LENGTHB (str VARCHAR2) return NUMBER
```

Returns the number of bytes in string **str**. If **str** belongs to datatype CHAR, the length includes any trailing blanks. If **str** is NULL, LENGTHB returns a NULL. For single-byte character sets, LENGTHB is equivalent to LENGTH.

LOWER

```
function LOWER (str CHAR) return CHAR

function LOWER (str VARCHAR2) return VARCHAR2
```

Returns the string **str** with all letters in lowercase.

LPAD

```
function LPAD (str VARCHAR2, len NUMBER [, pad VARCHAR2]) return VARCHAR2
```

Returns the string **str** left-padded to length **len**, with the sequence of characters in **pad** replicated as many times as necessary. If you do not specify **pad**, it defaults to a single blank. If **str** is longer than **len** characters, LPAD returns the first **len** characters in **str**.

LTRIM

```
function LTRIM (str VARCHAR2 [, set VARCHAR2]) return VARCHAR2
```

Returns the string **str**, with the initial characters removed up to the first character not in **set**. If you do not specify **set**, it defaults to a single blank.

NLS_INITCAP

```
function NLS_INITCAP (str VARCHAR2 [, nlsparms VARCHAR2])
    return VARCHAR2
```

Returns the string **str**, with the first letter of each word in uppercase and all other letters in lowercase. Words are delimited by spaces or nonalphanumeric characters. The value of **nlsparms** has the form 'NLS_SORT = <sort>,' where **sort** is either a linguistic sort sequence or the keyword BINARY. The sort sequence handles special linguistic requirements for case conversion. To meet these requirements, NLS_INITCAP might return a value of different length than **str**. If you omit **nlsparms**, NLS_INITCAP uses the default sort sequence for your session.

NLS_LOWER

```
function NLS_LOWER (str VARCHAR2 [, nlsparms VARCHAR2]) return VARCHAR2
```

Returns the string **str**, with all letters in lowercase. The value of **nlsparms** has the form 'NLS_SORT = <sort>,' where **sort** is either a linguistic sort sequence or the keyword BINARY. The sort sequence handles special linguistic requirements for case conversion. To meet these requirements, NLS_LOWER might return a value of different length than **str**. If you omit **nlsparms**, NLS_LOWER uses the default sort sequence for your session.

NLS_UPPER

```
function NLS_UPPER (str VARCHAR2 [, nlsparms VARCHAR2])
   return VARCHAR2
```

Returns the string **str**, with all letters in uppercase. The value of **nlsparms** has the form 'NLS_SORT = <sort>,' where **sort** is either a linguistic sort sequence or the keyword BINARY. The sort sequence handles special linguistic requirements for case conversion. To meet these requirements, NLS_UPPER might return a value of different length than **str**. If you omit **nlsparms**, NLS_UPPER uses the default sort sequence for your session.

NLSSORT

```
function NLSSORT (str VARCHAR2 [, nlsparms VARCHAR2]) return RAW
```

Returns the value of string **str** in the linguistic sort sequence specified by **nlsparms**. If you omit **nlsparms**, NLSSORT uses the default sort sequence for your session. The value of **nlsparms** has the form 'NLS_SORT = <sort>,' where **sort** is either a linguistic sort sequence or the keyword BINARY. If you specify BINARY, NLSSORT returns **str**.

In the WHERE clause, NLSSORT lets you specify comparisons based on linguistic rather than binary ordering. NLSSORT also lets you control the behavior of an ORDER BY clause independently of the NLS_SORT parameter.

REPLACE

```
function REPLACE (str1 VARCHAR2, str2 VARCHAR2[, str3 VARCHAR2])
   return VARCHAR2
```

Returns the string **str1**, with every occurrence of substring **str2** replaced by string **str3**. If you do not specify **str3**, all occurrences of **str2** are removed. If you specify neither **str2** nor **str3**, REPLACE returns a NULL.

RPAD

```
function RPAD (str VARCHAR2, len NUMBER [, pad VARCHAR2])
   return VARCHAR2
```

Returns the string **str** right-padded to length **len**, with the sequence of characters in **pad** replicated as many times as necessary. If you do not specify **pad**, it defaults to a single blank. If **str** is longer than **len** characters, RPAD returns the first **len** characters in **str**.

RTRIM

```
function RTRIM (str VARCHAR2 [, set VARCHAR2]) return VARCHAR2
```

Returns the string **str**, with the final characters removed after the last character not in **set**. If you do not specify **set**, it defaults to a single blank.

SOUNDEX

```
function SOUNDEX (str VARCHAR2) return VARCHAR2
```

Returns a character string containing the phonetic representation of string **str**. SOUNDEX allows you to compare English words that are spelled differently but sound alike.

SUBSTR

```
function SUBSTR (str VARCHAR2, pos NUMBER [, len NUMBER])
    return VARCHAR2
```

Returns a substring of string **str**, starting at character position pos and including **len** characters or, if you omit **len**, all characters to the end of **str**. The number pos cannot be zero. If pos is negative, SUBSTR counts backward from the end of **str**. The number **len** must be positive.

SUBSTRB

```
function SUBSTRB (str VARCHAR2, pos NUMBER [, len NUMBER])
    return VARCHAR2
```

Returns a substring of string **str**, starting at byte position pos and including **len** bytes or, if you omit **len**, all bytes to the end of **str**. The number pos cannot be zero. If pos is negative, SUBSTR counts backward from the end of **str**. The number **len** must be positive. For single-byte character sets, SUBSTRB is equivalent to SUBSTR.

TRANSLATE

```
function TRANSLATE (str VARCHAR2, set1 VARCHAR2, set2 CHAR)
    return VARCHAR2
```

Returns the string **str** after replacing all occurrences of **set1** with the corresponding characters in **set2**. Characters that appear in **str** but not in **set1** are unaffected. If **set1** contains more characters than **set2**, the extra characters at the end of **set1** have no corresponding characters in **set2**. Therefore, if these extra characters appear in **str**, TRANSLATE removes them from the result value.

UPPER

```
function UPPER (str CHAR) return CHAR
function UPPER (str VARCHAR2) return VARCHAR2
```

Returns the string **str**, with all letters in uppercase.

Conversion Functions

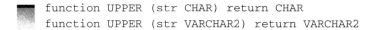

The following conversion functions convert a value from one datatype to another.

CHARTOROWID

```
function CHARTOROWID (str CHAR) return ROWID
function CHARTOROWID (str VARCHAR2) return ROWID
```

Converts the string **str** from type CHAR or VARCHAR2 to type ROWID.

CONVERT

```
function CONVERT (str VARCHAR2, set1 VARCHAR2,
    [, set2 VARCHAR2]) return VARCHAR2
```

Converts the string **str** from one character set (**set2**) to another (**set1**). Like **set1**, **set2** can be a database column or a literal representing the name of a character set. Table B-1 lists some common character sets.

For complete conversion, the destination character set (**set1**) must contain representations of all characters in the source character set (**set2**). Otherwise, replacement characters, which you can specify when defining a character set, are used.

Character Set	Description
US7ASCII	U.S. 7-bit ASCII character set
WE8DEC	DEC West European 8-bit character set
WE8HP	HP West European Laserjet 8-bit character set
F7DEC	DEC French 7-bit character set
WE8EBCDIC500	IBM West European EBCDIC Code Page 500
WE8PC850	IBM PC Code Page 850
WE8ISO8859P1	ISO 8859-1 West European 8-bit character set

TABLE B-1. *Character sets*

HEXTORAW

```
function HEXTORAW (str CHAR) return RAW
function HEXTORAW (str VARCHAR2) return RAW
```

Converts the hexadecimal string **str** from type CHAR or VARCHAR2 to type RAW.

RAWTOHEX

```
function RAWTOHEX (bin RAW) return VARCHAR2
```

Converts the binary value **bin** from type RAW to a hexadecimal string of type VARCHAR2.

ROWIDTOCHAR

```
function ROWIDTOCHAR (bin ROWID) return VARCHAR2
```

Converts the binary value **bin** from type ROWID to an 18-byte hexadecimal string of type VARCHAR2.

TO_CHAR

```
function TO_CHAR (dte DATE [, fmt VARCHAR2 [, nlsparms] ])
   return VARCHAR2
```

Converts the date **dte** to a character string of type VARCHAR2 in the format specified by format model **fmt**. (For a list of available format models, see the function TO_DATE.) If you omit **fmt**, **dte** is converted to a character string in the default date format.

The argument **nlsparms** specifies the language in which the names and abbreviations of months and days are returned. It has the following form:

```
'NLS_DATE_LANGUAGE = <language>'
```

If you omit **nlsparms**, TO_CHAR uses the default language for your session.

TO_CHAR

```
function TO_CHAR (num NUMBER [, fmt VARCHAR2 [, nlsparms]]) return VARCHAR2
```

Converts the number **num** to a character string of type VARCHAR2 in the format specified by format model **fmt**. (For a list of available format elements, see the function TO_NUMBER.) If you omit **fmt**, **num** is converted to a character string exactly long enough to hold the significant digits.

The argument **nlsparms** specifies the following characters, which are returned by the number format elements:

- Decimal character
- Group separator
- Local currency symbol
- International currency symbol

This argument has the following form:

```
'NLS_NUMERIC_CHARACTERS = ''dg'',
NLS_CURRENCY = ''text'',
NLS_ISO_CURRENCY = ''text'' '
```

The characters *d* and *g* represent the decimal character and group separator, respectively. Notice that within the quoted string, you must use two single quotes to represent one. If you omit **nlsparms**, TO_CHAR uses the default parameter values for your session.

TO_CHAR

```
function TO_CHAR (label [, fmt VARCHAR2]) return VARCHAR2
```

Converts a label of type MLSLABEL to a value of type VARCHAR2 in the format specified by **fmt**. If you omit **fmt**, the label is converted to a VARCHAR2 value in the default label format. Use TO_CHAR for label conversion only with Trusted Oracle.

TO_DATE

```
function TO_DATE (str VARCHAR2 [, fmt VARCHAR2 [, nlsparms]])
    return DATE
function TO_DATE (num NUMBER, fmt VARCHAR2 [, nlsparms]])
    return DATE
```

Converts the string **str** or the number **num** to a value of type DATE in the format specified by format model **fmt**. Table B-2 lists the available format models.

If you omit fmt, **str** must be in the default date format. If **fmt** is 'J' (for Julian day, the number of days since January 1, 4712 B.C.), **num** must be an integer.

The argument **nlsparms** specifies the language in which the names and abbreviations of months and days are returned. It has the following form:

```
'NLS_DATE_LANGUAGE = <language>'
```

If you omit **nlsparms**, TO_DATE uses the default language for your session.

TO_LABEL

```
function TO_LABEL (str CHAR [, fmt VARCHAR2]) return MLSLABEL
function TO_LABEL (str VARCHAR2 [, fmt VARCHAR2]) return MLSLABEL
```

Converts the string **str**, which contains a label in the format specified by **fmt**, to a value of type MLSLABEL. If you omit **fmt**, **str** must be in the default label format.

TO_MULTI_BYTE

```
function TO_MULTI_BYTE (str CHAR) return CHAR
function TO_MULTI_BYTE (str VARCHAR2) return VARCHAR2
```

Returns the string **str**, with all its single-byte characters converted to their multibyte equivalents. Single-byte characters in **str** that have no multibyte equivalents are returned unconverted. TO_MULTI_BYTE is useful only if your database character set contains single-byte and multibyte characters.

Format Model	Description
CC, SCC	Century (S prefixes B.C. dates with a minus sign)
YYYY, SYYYY	Year (S prefixes B.C. dates with minus sign)
IYYY	Year based on ISO standard
YYY, YY, Y	Last three, two, or one digit(s) of year
IYY, IY, I	Last three, two, or one digit(s) of ISO year
Y,YYY	Year with comma
YEAR, SYEAR	Year spelled out (S prefixes B.C. dates with a minus sign)
RR	Last two digits of year in another century
BC, AD	B.C. or A.D. indicator
B.C., A.D.	B.C. or A.D. indicator with periods
Q	Quarter of year (1-4; JAN-MAR = 1)
MM	Month (01-12; JAN = 01)
RM	Roman numeral month (I-XII; JAN=I0)
MONTH	Name of month (this is case-sensitive; i.e., MONTH = AUGUST, Month = August, month = august)
MON	Abbreviated name of month
WW	Week of year (1-53)
IW	Week of year (1-52 or 1-53) based on ISO standard
W	Week of month (1-5)
DDD	Day of year (1-366)
DD	Day of month (1-31)
D	Day of week (1-7)
DAY	Name of day
DY	Abbreviated name of day
J	Julian day (number of days since January 1, 4712 B.C.)
AM, PM	Meridian indicator
A.M., P.M.	Meridian indicator with periods
HH, HH12	Hour of day (1-12)
HH24	Hour of day (0-23)
MI	Minute (0-59)
SS	Second (0-59)
SSSSS	Seconds past midnight (0-86399)

TABLE B-2. *Date format models*

TO_NUMBER

```
function TO_NUMBER (str CHAR [, fmt VARCHAR2 [, nlsparms]])
   return NUMBER
function TO_NUMBER (str VARCHAR2 [, fmt VARCHAR2 [, nlsparms]])
   return NUMBER
```

Converts the string **str** from a value of type CHAR or VARCHAR2 to a value of type NUMBER in the format specified by format model **fmt**. A number format model consists of the format elements listed in Table B-3.

The string **str** must represent a valid number. The argument **nlsparms** specifies the following characters, which are returned by the number format model:

- Decimal character

- Group separator

- Local currency symbol

- International currency symbol

Element	Example	Description
9	9999	Significant digit
0	0999	Leading zero (instead of a blank)
$	$999	Leading dollar sign
B	B999	Leading blank (instead of a zero)
MI	999MI	Trailing minus sign
S	S999	Leading plus or minus sign
PR	999PR	Angle brackets for negative values
D	99D99	Decimal character
G	9G99	Group separator
C	C999	ISO currency symbol
L	L999	Local currency symbol
,	9,999	Comma
.	99.99	Period
V	999V99	10n multiplier; n is the number of 9's after V
EEEE	9.99EEEE	Scientific notation
RN, rn	RN	Upper- or lowercase Roman numeral

TABLE B-3. *Number format model*

This argument has the following form:

```
'NLS_NUMERIC_CHARACTERS = ''dg'',
NLS_CURRENCY = ''text'',
NLS_ISO_CURRENCY = ''text'' '
```

The characters *d* and *g* represent the decimal character and group separator, respectively. Notice that within the quoted string, you must use two single quotes to represent one. If you omit **nlsparms**, TO_NUMBER uses the default parameter values for your session.

TO_SINGLE_BYTE

```
function TO_SINGLE_BYTE (str CHAR) return CHAR
function TO_SINGLE_BYTE (str VARCHAR2) return VARCHAR2
```

Returns the string **str**, with all its multibyte characters converted to their single-byte equivalents. Multibyte characters in **str** that have no single-byte equivalents are returned unconverted. TO_SINGLE_BYTE is useful only if your database character set contains single-byte and multibyte characters.

Date Functions

Date functions take date arguments and return date values, except MONTHS_BETWEEN, which returns a numeric value.

ADD_MONTHS

```
function ADD_MONTHS (dte DATE, num NUMBER) return DATE
function ADD_MONTHS (num NUMBER, dte DATE) return DATE
```

Returns the date **dte** plus or minus **num** months. The number **num** must be an integer. If **dte** is the last day of the month or if the resulting month has fewer days than the day component of **dte**, ADD_MONTHS returns the last day of the resulting month. Otherwise, ADD_MONTHS returns the day component of **dte**.

LAST_DAY

```
function LAST_DAY (dte DATE) return DATE
```

Returns the date of the last day of the month containing date **dte**.

MONTHS_BETWEEN

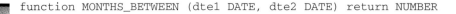

```
function MONTHS_BETWEEN (dte1 DATE, dte2 DATE) return NUMBER
```

Returns the number of months between date **dte1** and date **dte2**. If **dte1** is later than **dte2**, the result is positive. If **dte1** is earlier than **dte2**, the result is negative. If **dte1** and **dte2** fall on the same (or the last) days of their respective months, MONTHS_BETWEEN returns an integer. Otherwise, MONTHS_BETWEEN returns a fractional number, which is based on a 31-day month and reflects any difference in the time components of **dte1** and **dte2**.

NEW_TIME

```
function NEW_TIME (dte DATE, zon1 VARCHAR2, zon2 VARCHAR2)
    return DATE
```

Given a date and time **dte** in time zone **zon1**, returns the corresponding date and time in **zon2**. Table B-4 lists the possible values of **zon1** and **zon2**.

Value	Description
AST	Atlantic Standard Time
ADT	Atlantic Daylight Time
BST	Bering Standard Time
BDT	Bering Daylight Time
CST	Central Standard Time
CDT	Central Daylight Time
EST	Eastern Standard Time
EDT	Eastern Daylight Time
GMT	Greenwich Mean Time
HST	Alaska-Hawaii Standard Time
HDT	Alaska-Hawaii Daylight Time
MST	Mountain Standard Time
MDT	Mountain Daylight Time
NST	Newfoundland Standard Time
PST	Pacific Standard Time
PDT	Pacific Daylight Time
YST	Yukon Standard Time
YDT	Yukon Daylight Time

TABLE B-4. *Time zones*

NEXT_DAY

```
function NEXT_DAY (dte DATE, day VARCHAR2) return DATE
```

Returns the date of the first day of the week named by **day** that is later than date **dte**. The argument **day** must be one of the seven days of a week.

ROUND

```
function ROUND (dte DATE [, fmt VARCHAR2]) return DATE
```

Returns **dte** rounded to the unit specified by format model **fmt**. If you omit **fmt**, **dte** is rounded to the nearest day. Table B-5 lists the available format models.

SYSDATE

```
function SYSDATE return DATE
```

Returns the current system date and time. SYSDATE takes no arguments.

TRUNC

```
function TRUNC (dte DATE [, fmt VARCHAR2]) return DATE
```

Format Model	Description
CC, SCC	Century
SYYY, YYYY, YEAR, SYEAR, YYY, YY, Y	Year (rounds up on July 1)
Q	Quarter (rounds up on 16th day of 2nd month)
MONTH, MON, MM	Month (rounds up on 16th day)
WW	First day of the week in year
W	First day of the week in month
DDD, DD, J	Day
DAY, DY, D	Nearest Sunday
HH, HH12, HH24	Hour
MI	Minute

TABLE B-5. *Date rounding format models*

Returns date **dte** with the time portion of the day truncated as specified by format model **fmt**. (For a list of available format models, see the function ROUND.) If you omit **fmt**, **dte** is truncated to the nearest day.

Miscellaneous Functions

All the miscellaneous functions are allowed in SQL statements and, except for DECODE, in procedural statements.

DECODE

```
function DECODE (expr, search1, result1 [,search2, result2]
    ...[default])
```

The expression **expr** is compared to each search value. If **expr** equals a search value, the corresponding result is returned. If no match is found, DECODE returns the default value, or a NULL if a default value was not supplied.

The expression **expr** can be any datatype, but the search value should be the same datatype as **expr**. The value returned is forced to the same datatype as **result1**. DECODE is allowed only in SQL statements.

DUMP

```
function DUMP (expr DATE [, fmt BINARY_INTEGER
    [, pos BINARY_INTEGER [, len BINARY_INTEGER]]])
    return VARCHAR2

function DUMP (expr NUMBER [, fmt BINARY_INTEGER
    [, pos BINARY_INTEGER [, len BINARY_INTEGER]]])
    return VARCHAR2

function DUMP (expr VARCHAR2 [, fmt BINARY_INTEGER
    [, pos BINARY_INTEGER [, len BINARY_INTEGER]]])
    return VARCHAR2
```

Returns the internal representation of expression **expr**. The argument **fmt** determines the format of the return value (8=octal, 10=decimal, 16=hexadecimal, and 17=single characters). The arguments **pos** and **len** specify which part of the representation is returned. The default is to return the entire representation in decimal.

GREATEST

```
function GREATEST (expr1, expr2, expr3, ...)
```

Returns the greatest value in a list of values. The values of expressions **expr2**, **expr3**, and so on are converted to the datatype of expression **expr1**. Therefore, all datatypes must be compatible with that of **expr1**. GREATEST compares the expressions using nonblank-padding semantics.

GREATEST_LB

```
function GREATEST_LB (label [,label] ...) return MLSLABEL
```

Returns the greatest lower bound of the list of labels. Each label must belong to datatype MLSLABEL or be a quoted literal in the default label format.

LEAST

```
function LEAST (expr1, expr2, expr3, ...)
```

Returns the least value in a list of values. The values of expressions **expr2**, **expr3**, and so on are converted to the datatype of expression **expr1**. Therefore, all datatypes must be compatible with that of **expr1**. LEAST compares the expressions using nonblank-padding semantics.

LEAST_UB

```
function LEAST_UB (label [,label] ...) return MLSLABEL
```

Returns the least upper bound of the list of labels. Each label must belong to datatype MLSLABEL or be a quoted literal in the default label format.

NVL

```
function NVL (str1 CHAR, str2 CHAR) return CHAR
function NVL (dte1 DATE, dte2 DATE) return DATE
function NVL (bool1 BOOLEAN, bool2 BOOLEAN) return BOOLEAN
function NVL (num1 NUMBER, num2 NUMBER) return NUMBER
function NVL (str1 VARCHAR2, str2 VARCHAR2) return VARCHAR2
function NVL (lbl1 MLSLABEL, lbl2 MLSLABEL) return MLSLABEL
```

Takes two arguments of the same type and returns a value of that type. If the first argument is not NULL, its value is returned. If the first argument is NULL, the value of the second argument is returned.

UID

```
function UID return NUMBER
```

Returns the unique identification number assigned to the current Oracle user. UID takes no arguments.

USER

```
function USER return VARCHAR2
```

Returns the username of the current Oracle user. USER takes no arguments.

USERENV

```
function USERENV (str VARCHAR2) return VARCHAR2
```

Returns information about the current session. You can use the information to write an application audit trail table or to determine which language and character set are in use.

The string **str** can have any of the following values:

- **ENTRYID** Returns an auditing entry identifier.
- **LABEL** Returns the session label.
- **LANGUAGE** Returns the language, territory, and database character set in use.
- **SESSIONID** Returns the auditing session identifier.
- **TERMINAL** Returns the operating system identifier for the session terminal.

You cannot specify the ENTRYID or SESSIONID option in SQL statements that access a remote database.

VSIZE

```
function VSIZE (expr DATE) return NUMBER
function VSIZE (expr NUMBER) return NUMBER
function VSIZE (expr VARCHAR2) return NUMBER
```

Returns the number of bytes in the internal representation of expression **expr**. If **expr** is NULL, VSIZE returns a NULL.

PL/SQL Language Constructs

This section uses syntax notation to show how commands, parameters, and other language elements are constructed to form PL/SQL statements. It serves as a quick reference guide to PL/SQL syntax and coding conventions. In addition, it provides usage notes to save you time and trouble.

Each command has some or all of the following subsections:

- Description
- Syntax
- Keyword and Parameter Description
- Usage Notes
- Related Topics

Easy-to-understand syntax notation is used to illustrate PL/SQL syntax. This is the same syntax notation that has been used throughout the book. See the introduction to the book for an explanation of this notation.

Assignment Statement

An assignment statement sets the current value of a variable, formal parameter, field in a record, or row in a PL/SQL table.

Alternatively, you can use the SELECT or FETCH statement to have Oracle assign values to a variable.

Syntax

```
assignment_statement ::=
    object_name := <plsql_expression>????;
object ::=
    {plsql_variable | record.field | plsql_table(subscript)
        | :host_variable}
```

Keyword and Parameter Description

Keyword or Parameter	Description
object_name	This is the name of a previously declared object to which you want to assign a value.
plsql_expression	This is an arbitrarily complex expression. The value of plsql_expression is assigned to the object identified by object_name. The datatype of plsql_expression must be the same as or convertible to the datatype of object.
plsql_variable	This refers to a PL/SQL variable previously declared within the current scope.
record.field	This refers to a field in a user-defined or %ROWTYPE record previously declared within the current scope.
plsql_table(subscript)	This refers to a row in a PL/SQL table previously declared within the current scope.
host_variable	This refers to a host variable previously declared within the current scope.

Usage Notes

By default, unless an object is initialized in its declaration, it is initialized to NULL every time a block or subprogram is entered. Therefore, you should never reference an object before you assign it a value.

You cannot assign NULLs to an object defined as NOT NULL. If you try, the predefined exception VALUE_ERROR is raised.

Only the values TRUE and FALSE and the nonvalue NULL can be assigned to a Boolean variable. When applied to PL/SQL expressions, the relational operators return a Boolean value.

Related Topics

Expressions, FETCH, SELECT INTO, Variables and Constants

PL/SQL Blocks

The basic program unit in PL/SQL is the block. A PL/SQL block is defined by the following keywords:

- **DECLARE** Declarative part
- **BEGIN** Execution part
- **EXCEPTION** Exception-handler part
- **END**

Only the executable part is required. You can nest a block within another block wherever you can place an executable statement.

Syntax

```
plsql_block ::=
[<<label_name>>]
[DECLARE {variable_declaration; | cursor_declaration; |
exception_declaration; | record_declaration; |
   plsql_table_declaration; |
procedure_declaration; | function_declaration;}]
BEGIN seq_of_statements [EXCEPTION exception_handler;,...] END
   [label_name] ;
seq_of_statements ::=
statement; ,...
statement ::=
[<<label_name>>] {assignment_statement | exit_statement
   | goto_statement |
if_statement | loop_statement | null_statement
   | raise_statement |
return_statement | sql_statement | plsql_block}
sql_statement ::=
{close_statement | commit_statement | delete_statement
   | fetch_statement |
insert_statement | lock_table_statement | open_statement |
rollback_statement | savepoint_statement | select_statement |
update_statement}
```

Keyword and Parameter Description

Keyword or Parameter	Description
label_name	This is an undeclared identifier, which optionally labels a PL/SQL block. If used, label_name must be enclosed by double angle brackets and must appear at the beginning of the block. (However, in the SQL*Plus environment, the first line you input cannot start with label_name.) Optionally, label_name can also appear at the end of the block.
DECLARE	This keyword signals the start of the optional declarative part of a PL/SQL block, which contains local declarations. Objects declared locally exist only within the current block and all its subblocks and are not visible to enclosing blocks. The declarative part of a PL/SQL block is optional. It is terminated implicitly by the keyword BEGIN, which introduces the executable part of the block.
variable_declaration	This construct declares variables and constants.
cursor_declaration	This construct declares an explicit cursor.
exception_declaration	This construct declares exceptions.
record_declaration	This construct declares user-defined records.
plsql_table_declaration	This construct declares PL/SQL tables.
procedure_declaration	This construct declares a procedure.
function_declaration	This construct declares a function.
BEGIN	This keyword signals the start of the executable part of a PL/SQL block, which contains executable statements. The executable part of a PL/SQL block or subprogram is required. That is, a block or subprogram must contain at least one executable statement. The NULL statement does meet this requirement.
seq_of_statements	This represents a sequence of statements.

Keyword or Parameter	Description
statement	Any legal PL/SQL statement, including another plsql_block. You use this construct to create algorithms. There are PL/SQL statements for conditional, iterative, and sequential control as well as for error handling. PL/SQL statements are free-format; that is, they can continue from line to line, provided you do not split keywords, delimiters, or literals across lines. A semicolon (;) must terminate every PL/SQL statement.
EXCEPTION	This keyword signals the start of the exception-handling part of a PL/SQL block. When an exception is raised, normal execution of the block stops and control transfers to the appropriate exception handler. After the exception handler completes, execution proceeds with the statement following the block. This is optional.
exception_handler	An exception handler associates an exception with a sequence of statements, which is executed when that exception is raised.
END	The keyword END signals the end of a PL/SQL block. It must be the last keyword in a block. Neither the END IF in an IF statement nor the END LOOP in a LOOP statement can substitute for the keyword END.

Related Topics

Exceptions, Cursors, Variables and Constants, Procedures

CLOSE Statement

The CLOSE statement allows resources held by an opened cursor to be reused. No more rows can be fetched from a closed cursor. Parameter information and the parsed representation of the associated query are marked as reusable.

Syntax

```
close_cursor_statement ::=
CLOSE <cursor_name> ;
```

Keyword and Parameter Description

Keyword or Parameter	Description
cursor_name	This must be the name of a previously declared and currently open cursor.

Usage Notes

Once a cursor is closed, you can reopen it either by issuing the OPEN command to reevaluate parameters and reinitialize the active set or by using a cursor FOR loop to implicitly open the cursor. An attempt to execute any other operation on a closed cursor raises the predefined exception INVALID_CURSOR. You must CLOSE a cursor before reOPENing it.

Related Topics

DECLARE, FETCH, OPEN

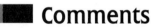

Comments

Comments describe the purpose and use of code segments and so promote readability. PL/SQL supports two comment styles: single-line and multiline. Single-line comments begin with a double hyphen (--) anywhere on a line and extend to the end of the line. Multiline comments begin with a slash-asterisk (/*) and end with an asterisk-slash (*/) and can span multiple lines.

Syntax

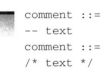

```
comment ::=
-- text
comment ::=
/* text */
```

Usage Notes

Comments can appear within a statement at the end of a line. However, you cannot nest comments. Also, you cannot use single-line comments in a PL/SQL block that will be processed dynamically by an Oracle precompiler program because end-of-line characters are ignored. As a result, single-line comments extend to the end of the block, not just to the end of a line. Instead, use multiline comments.

 ## COMMIT Statement

The COMMIT statement explicitly makes permanent any changes made to the database during the current transaction. Changes made to the database are not considered permanent until they are committed. COMMIT also makes the changes visible to other users.

Syntax

```
commit_statement ::=
COMMIT [WORK] [COMMENT 'text'] ;
```

Keyword and Parameter Description

Keyword or Parameter	Description
COMMIT and COMMIT WORK	Both COMMIT and COMMIT WORK make any changes to the database permanent. The keyword WORK is optional and has no effect except to improve readability.
COMMENT	COMMENT specifies a comment to be associated with the current transaction and is most often used with distributed transactions. The text must be a quoted literal <50 characters long.

Usage Notes

The COMMIT statement releases all row and table locks. It also erases any savepoints you marked since the last commit or rollback. Until your changes are committed, the following conditions hold:

■ You can see the changes when you query the tables you modified, but other users cannot see the changes when they query those tables.

■ If you change your mind or need to correct a mistake, you can use the ROLLBACK statement to roll back (discard) the changes.

If COMMIT is executed while a cursor that was declared using FOR UPDATE is open, a subsequent FETCH on that cursor raises an exception. The cursor remains open, however, so you should CLOSE it.

With embedded SQL, the optional RELEASE parameter is allowed after COMMIT WORK. Serving the purpose of a "disconnect" statement, RELEASE signifies that you want to log off the database once your transaction is committed. Since PL/SQL does not allow data control statements such as CONNECT, GRANT, and REVOKE, it does not allow the RELEASE parameter.

Related Topics

ROLLBACK, SAVEPOINT

Conditions

PL/SQL conditions are the basis for conditional control. Like Boolean expressions, PL/SQL conditions always evaluate to TRUE, FALSE, or NULL. Moreover, a PL/SQL condition is allowed wherever a Boolean expression is allowed.

In conditional control statements, if a PL/SQL condition evaluates to TRUE, its associated sequence of statements is executed. If a PL/SQL condition evaluates to FALSE or NULL, its associated sequence of statements is not executed.

Syntax

```
plsql_condition ::=
boolean_expression
boolean_expression ::=
[NOT] {boolean_literal | boolean_variable
    | boolean_function_call |
other_boolean_ forms | (boolean_expression)}
{AND | OR} ,...
other_boolean_ forms ::=
plsql_expression {relational_operator plsql_expression
    | IS [NOT] NULL |
```

```
[NOT] LIKE pattern |
[NOT] BETWEEN plsql_expression AND plsql_expression |
[NOT] IN (plsql_expression, ...) |
{cursor_name | SQL} {%NOTFOUND | %FOUND | %ISOPEN}}
```

Keyword and Parameter Description

Keyword or Parameter	Description
AND, OR, NOT	AND returns the value TRUE only if both its operands are true. OR returns the value TRUE if either of its operands is true. NOT returns the opposite value (logical negation) of its operand. NOT NULL returns NULL because NULLs are indeterminate.
boolean_literal	This is the predefined value TRUE or FALSE or the nonvalue NULL, which stands for a missing, unknown, or inapplicable value. You cannot insert the values TRUE and FALSE into a database column.
boolean_variable	In a variable_declaration, this parameter is any variable or constant that belongs to type BOOLEAN. Only the values TRUE and FALSE and the nonvalue NULL can be assigned to a Boolean variable. However, you cannot select or fetch column values into a Boolean variable. Also, arithmetic operations on Boolean variables are illegal.
boolean_function_call	This is any function call that returns a value of type BOOLEAN.
boolean_expression	When parentheses enclose a boolean_expression that is part of a larger boolean_expression, PL/SQL evaluates the innermost expression first. The result value is then used in the larger expression.
plsql_expression	This is an arbitrarily complex expression.
relational_operator	The relational operators allow you to you compare arbitrarily complex expressions.
IS [NOT] NULL	The IS NULL operator returns the Boolean value TRUE if its operand is NULL or FALSE if it is not NULL.

Keyword or Parameter	Description
[NOT] LIKE	The LIKE operator compares a character value to a pattern. Case is significant. LIKE returns the Boolean value TRUE if the character patterns match or FALSE if they do not match.
pattern	This is a character string compared by the LIKE operator to a specified string value. It can include two special-purpose characters called wildcards. An underscore (_) matches exactly one character; a percent sign (%) matches zero or more characters.
[NOT] BETWEEN	The BETWEEN operator tests whether a value lies in a specified range. It means "greater than or equal to <low value> and less than or equal to <high value>."
[NOT] IN	The IN operator tests set membership. It means "equal to any member of." The set can contain NULLs, but they are ignored.
cursor_name	This is the name of a previously declared cursor.
%NOTFOUND, %FOUND, %ISOPEN	These parameters are cursor attributes. Each cursor that you explicitly define has these attributes. When appended to the cursor name, they let you access useful information about the execution of a multirow query. You can also use them to access the SQL cursor's private SQL area, in which case their values always refer to the most recently executed SQL statement.

Usage Notes

In a plsql_condition, you can only compare values that belong to (or are convertible to) the same datatype. When PL/SQL evaluates a Boolean_expression, NOT has the highest precedence, AND has the next-highest precedence, and OR has the lowest precedence. However, you can use parentheses to override the default operator precedence. AND and OR are short-circuit operators. If the first operand of OR evaluates to TRUE, its second operand is not evaluated. Similarly, if the first operand of AND evaluates to FALSE, its second operand is not evaluated.

The relational operators can be applied to operands of type BOOLEAN. By definition, TRUE is greater than FALSE. Comparisons involving NULLs always result in a NULL.

The value of a Boolean expression can be assigned only to Boolean variables, not to host variables or database columns. Furthermore, no implicit or explicit datatype conversion to (or from) type BOOLEAN is supported.

Related Topics

Assignment Statement, EXIT, Expressions, IF, LOOP

Cursors

For queries that return more than one row, a cursor lets you name the query and process the rows individually.

Syntax

```
cursor_specification ::=
CURSOR <cursor_name> [(parameter_name parameter_type, ...)] ;
cursor_declaration ::=
cursor_body
cursor_body ::=
CURSOR <cursor_name> [(parameter_name parameter_type, ...)]
IS select_statement
```

Keyword and Parameter Description

Keyword or Parameter	Description
cursor_name	This identifier names a cursor. The cursor name is like a function name and follows the usual scope rules.
parameter_name	This identifier names a cursor formal parameter.
parameter_type	This specifies the datatype of a cursor parameter. The datatype of the corresponding actual parameter must be the same as or convertible to parameter_type.
select_statement	A query associated with cursor_name, which returns a set of values. If the cursor defines parameters, each parameter must be used in the select_statement.

Usage Notes

You must declare a cursor before referencing it in an OPEN, FETCH, or CLOSE statement. You must also declare a variable before referencing it in a cursor declaration. You cannot assign values to a cursor name or use it in an expression. However, cursors and variables follow the same scoping rules.

You retrieve data from a cursor by OPENing it, then FETCHing from it. Since the FETCH statement specifies the target variables, using an INTO clause in the SELECT statement of a cursor_declaration is redundant and invalid.

Related Topics

CLOSE, FETCH, OPEN, SELECT INTO

DELETE Statement

The DELETE statement removes entire rows of data from a specified table or view.

Syntax

```
delete_statement ::=
DELETE [FROM] table_reference [alias]
[WHERE {search_condition | CURRENT OF cursor_name}] ;
table_reference::=
[schema.] {table | view} [@dblink]
```

Keyword and Parameter Description

Keyword or Parameter	Description
table_reference	The table or view specified by table_reference must be accessible when you execute the DELETE statement, and you must have DELETE privileges.
alias	This is another (usually short) name for the referenced table or view and is typically used in the WHERE clause.

Keyword or Parameter	Description
WHERE search_condition	This clause conditionally chooses rows to be deleted from the referenced table or view. Only rows that meet the search_condition are deleted. If you omit the WHERE clause, all rows in the table or view are deleted.
WHERE CURRENT OF cursor_name	This refers to the latest row processed by the FETCH statement associated with cursor_name. The named cursor must have been declared using the FOR UPDATE clause and must be open and positioned on a row. If the cursor is not open, the CURRENT OF clause results in an error.

Usage Notes

A plsql_expression (except one of type BOOLEAN) can be used in a DELETE statement wherever a literal can be used.

The DELETE ... WHERE CURRENT OF statement can be used after a FETCH is executed on an open cursor (this includes implicit FETCHes executed in a cursor FOR loop), provided the associated query was declared with a FOR UPDATE clause. The DELETE ... WHERE CURRENT OF cursor_name deletes the current row—that is, the one just FETCHed.

EXCEPTION_INIT Pragma

EXCEPTION_INIT associates an exception name with an Oracle error number. That allows you to refer to any internal exception by name and write a specific handler for it instead of using the OTHERS handler.

Syntax

```
exception_init_pragma ::=
PRAGMA EXCEPTION_INIT (exception_name, error_number);
```

Keyword and Parameter Description

Keyword or Parameter	Description
PRAGMA	This signifies that the statement is a pragma (compiler directive). Pragmas are processed at compile time, not at run time. They do not affect the meaning of a program; they simply convey information to the compiler.
exception_name	This is the name of an exception previously declared using an exception_declaration.
error_number	The error_number can be any valid Oracle error number. These are the same error numbers that the function SQLCODE returns.

Usage Notes

The pragma EXCEPTION_INIT must appear in the same declarative section as its associated exception, somewhere after the exception declaration. Thus, EXCEPTION_INIT can be used only in the declarative part of a PL/SQL block, subprogram, or package.

Related Topics

Exceptions, EXCEPTION_INIT, SQLCODE

Exceptions

An exception declaration names a user-defined exception. You raise an exception using the RAISE statement, then process it in an exception handler. An exception handler executes statements in response to a raised exception. When an exception is raised, normal execution of the PL/SQL block stops, and the statements in the appropriate exception handler are executed. After the exception handler completes, processing of the block stops, and control returns to the calling environment.

Syntax

```
exception_declaration ::=
<exception_name> EXCEPTION;
exception_handler ::=
WHEN {exception_name | OTHERS} [OR] ,... THEN seq_of_statements
```

Keyword and Parameter Description

Keyword or Parameter	Description
exception_name	This identifier names a predefined or user-defined exception.
WHEN	You can have multiple exceptions execute the same sequence of statements by following the keyword WHEN with a list of the exceptions, separating them by the keyword OR. If any exception in the list is raised, the associated statements are executed.
OTHERS	OTHERS stands for all the other exceptions not explicitly named in the exception-handling part of the block. The use of OTHERS is optional and is allowed only as the last exception handler. You cannot include OTHERS in a list of exceptions following the keyword WHEN.
seq_of_statements	This represents a sequence of statements.

Usage Notes

An exception declaration can appear only in the declarative part of a block, subprogram, or package. The scope rules for exceptions and variables are the same. However, unlike variables and constants, exceptions cannot be passed as parameters to subprograms.

The exception-handling part of a PL/SQL block is optional. Exception handlers must come at the end of the block. They are introduced by the keyword EXCEPTION. The exception-handling part of the block is terminated by the same keyword, END, that terminates the entire block.

An exception should be raised only when an error occurs that makes it impossible or undesirable to finish processing. If there is no exception handler in the current block for a raised exception, the exception propagates according to the following rules:

- If there is an enclosing block for the current block, the exception is passed on to that block. The enclosing block then becomes the current block. If a handler for the raised exception is not found, the process repeats.

- If there is no enclosing block for the current block, an "unhandled exception" error is passed back to the host environment.

Only one exception at a time can be active in the exception-handling part of a block. Therefore, if an exception is raised inside a handler, the block that encloses the current block is the first block searched to find a handler for the newly raised exception. From there on, the exception propagates normally.

An exception handler can reference only those variables that the current block can reference.

Related Topics

Blocks, EXCEPTION_INIT, RAISE

EXIT Statement

You use the EXIT statement to exit a loop. The EXIT statement has two forms: the unconditional EXIT and the conditional EXIT WHEN. With either form, you can name the loop to be exited.

Syntax

```
exit_statement ::=
EXIT [label_name] [WHEN plsql_condition] ;
```

Keyword and Parameter Description

Keyword or Parameter	Description
EXIT	When the EXIT statement is processed and there is no label_name and no WHEN clause in the statement, PL/SQL exits the current loop immediately. Execution resumes with the statement following the loop.
label_name	This identifies the loop you want to exit. By using label_name, you can exit not only the current loop, but any outer loop that encloses the current loop, provided the outer loop has been named in an enclosing loop_statement.
plsql_condition	This is a condition to be evaluated each time PL/SQL encounters the EXIT statement during normal execution of the sequence of statements in a loop. If plsql_condition evaluates to TRUE, PL/SQL exits the current loop.

Usage Notes

An exit_statement can be used only within the seq_of_statements contained within loop_statement. If you use exit_statement to leave a cursor FOR loop prematurely, the cursor is closed automatically. The cursor is also closed automatically if an exception is raised inside the loop.

Related Topics

Conditions, LOOP

Expressions

An expression is a combination of variables, constants, literals, and operators. The PL/SQL compiler determines the datatype of an expression from the types of the variables, constants, literals, and operators that make up the expression. Every time the expression is evaluated, a value of that type results.

Syntax

```
plsql_expression ::=
[num_expression | char_expression | date_expression
    | boolean_expression]
num_expression ::=
[{+ | -}]
[numeric_literal | numeric_variable | host_object_reference
    | numeric_function_call | NULL | (num_expression) |
{cursor_name | SQL} %ROWCOUNT}
[**integer_expr] {/ | * / - / +} ,...
char_expression ::=
{char_literal | char_variable | host_object_reference
    | char_function_call | NULL | (char_expression)} || ,...
date_expression ::=
{date_literal | date_variable | host_object_reference
    | date_function_call | NULL | (date_expression)}
host_object_reference ::=
{:num_host_object | :char_host_object | :date_host_object}
    [:indicator]
```

Keyword and Parameter Description

Keyword or Parameter	Description
boolean_expression	This is an expression that evaluates to TRUE, FALSE, or NULL.

Keyword and Parameter Description for Numeric Expression

Keyword or Parameter	Description
numeric_literal	This is a numeric literal, or a literal that can be implicitly converted to a numeric value.
numeric_variable	This is the name of a previously declared variable or constant of type NUMBER or a type that can be implicitly converted to type NUMBER.

Keyword or Parameter	Description
numeric_function_call	This is a function call that returns a value of type NUMBER or of a type that can be implicitly converted to type NUMBER.
:num_host_object	This is the name of a previously declared object of type NUMBER or of a type that can be implicitly converted to type NUMBER.
NULL	This represents a NULL. When used in a num_expression, the result is always a NULL.
integer_expr	This is a numeric expression with an integer value.
+, −	The symbols plus (+) and minus (−) are unary operators when used as the first characters in num_expression. The + has no effect. The − negates the value of num_expression. When used in num_expression, + and − are the addition and subtraction operators, respectively.
/, *, **	The symbols /, *, and ** are the division, multiplication, and exponentiation operators, respectively.

Keyword and Parameter Description for Character Expression

Keyword or Parameter	Description
char_literal	This is any valid string literal.
char_variable	This is the name of a previously declared string variable or constant.
char_function_call	This is a function that returns a value of type CHAR.
:char_host_object	This is the name of a previously declared object of type CHAR or of a type that can be implicitly converted to type CHAR.
‖	The symbol ‖ is the concatenation operator. The result of concatenating string1 with string2 is a character string that contains string1 followed by string2.

Keyword and Parameter Description for Date Expression

Keyword or Parameter	Description
date_literal	This is a string literal that contains a valid date.
date_variable	This is the name of a previously declared variable or constant of type DATE or of a type that can be implicitly converted to type DATE.
date_function_call	This is a function call that returns a value of type DATE or of a type that can be implicitly converted to type DATE.
:date_host_object	This is the name of a previously declared object of type DATE or of a type that can be implicitly converted to type DATE.
NULL	The keyword NULL represents a NULL. When used in a date_expression, the result is always a NULL.

Usage Notes

The operations occur in their predefined order of precedence. From first to last (top to bottom), the default order of operations is as follows:

- Parentheses
- Exponents
- Unary operators
- Multiplication and division
- Addition, subtraction, and concatenation

PL/SQL evaluates multiple operators of equal precedence in an undefined order.

When parentheses surround an expression that is part of a larger expression, the expression within the parentheses is evaluated first. The result is then used as a single value in the larger expression.

In a plsql_expression, you can use only values having datatypes that are compatible with (or convertible to) each other.

Related Topics

Assignment Statement, Conditions, Variables and Constants

FETCH Statement

The FETCH statement retrieves the next row of data from the active set (those rows that satisfy the query associated with a cursor). The data is stored in variables that correspond to the columns selected by the query.

Syntax

```
fetch_statement ::=
FETCH <cursor_name> INTO variable_namelist ¦ record_name ,... ;
variable_namelist ::= {variable_name};
```

Keyword and Parameter Description

Keyword or Parameter	Description
cursor_name	This parameter names an explicitly declared and currently open cursor.
INTO variable_name	INTO variable_name defines the scalar variables that will store the retrieved data. All variables in the variable_name list must have been declared.
INTO record_name	This parameter indicates that retrieved data is stored in a record variable declared using the %ROWTYPE attribute or explicitly.

Usage Notes

In PL/SQL, a SELECT INTO statement should return only one row. If no rows are returned, the predefined exception NO_DATA_FOUND is raised. If more than one row is returned, the predefined exception TOO_MANY_ROWS is raised. You must use either a cursor FOR loop or the FETCH statement to process multirow queries.

Related Topics

Assignment Statement, CLOSE, Cursors, LOOP, %NOTFOUND, OPEN, %ROWTYPE, SELECT INTO

%FOUND Attribute

PL/SQL cursors have four attributes (including %FOUND) that, when appended to the cursor name, let you access useful information about the cursor. Until the SQL statement is executed, %FOUND evaluates to NULL. Thereafter, %FOUND evaluates to TRUE if an INSERT, UPDATE, or DELETE affected one or more rows or a SELECT INTO returned one or more rows. Otherwise, %FOUND evaluates to FALSE.

For multirow queries, you can explicitly declare a cursor to process the rows. After the cursor is open but before the first fetch, %FOUND evaluates to NULL. Thereafter, it evaluates to TRUE if the last fetch returned a row or to FALSE if no row was returned.

Syntax

```
found_attribute ::= <cursor_name>%FOUND
```

Keyword and Parameter Description

Keyword or Parameter	Description
cursor_name	This parameter must be the name of an explicitly declared cursor or the name of the implicit cursor (SQL).

Usage Notes

You can use the %FOUND attribute in procedural statements but not in SQL statements. %FOUND is associated with every explicit cursor. Therefore, you can open multiple cursors, then use %FOUND to tell which cursors have rows left to fetch. If a cursor is not open, referencing it with %FOUND raises INVALID_CURSOR.

When an explicit cursor is opened, the rows that satisfy the associated query are identified and form the active set. Rows are FETCHed from the active set one at a time. If the last fetch returned a row, %FOUND evaluates to TRUE. If the last fetch failed to return a row (because the active set was empty), %FOUND evaluates to FALSE. %FOUND can be applied to the SQL cursor as well, but a SELECT-INTO statement will raise NO DATA FOUND before you can check %FOUND.

Related Topics

CLOSE, Cursors, DELETE, FETCH, INSERT, %NOTFOUND, OPEN, SELECT INTO, UPDATE

Functions

A function is a named program unit that takes parameters and returns a computed value. A function has two parts: a specification and a body. The function specification begins with the keyword FUNCTION and ends with the RETURN clause, which specifies the datatype of the result value. Argument declarations are optional. Functions that take no arguments are written without parentheses.

The function body begins with the keyword IS and ends with the keyword END followed by an optional function name. The function body has three parts: a declarative part, an executable part, and an optional exception-handling part (just like a block).

The declarative part contains declarations of types, cursors, constants, variables, exceptions, and subprograms. These objects are local and cease to exist when you exit the function. The executable part contains statements that assign values, control execution, and manipulate Oracle data. The exception-handling part contains exception handlers, which deal with exceptions raised during execution.

Syntax

```
function_specification ::=
FUNCTION <function_name> [(argument,...)] RETURN type_name ;
function_declaration ::=
function_body
function_body ::=
FUNCTION <function_name> [(argument,...)] RETURN type_name IS
    [{variable_declaration; | cursor_declaration;
    | exception_declaration; | record_declaration; |
    plsql_table_declaration; | procedure_declaration; |
```

```
   function_declaration;},...]
BEGIN seq_of_statements [EXCEPTION exception_handler;,...]
   END [function_name] ;
argument ::=
<argument_name> [{IN | OUT | IN OUT}] type_name
   [{:= | DEFAULT} value]
```

Keyword and Parameter Description

Keyword or Parameter	Description
function_name	This identifier names a function.
variable_declaration	This construct declares variables and constants.
cursor_declaration	This construct declares an explicit cursor.
exception_declaration	This construct declares exceptions.
record_declaration	This construct declares user-defined records.
plsql_table_declaration	This construct declares PL/SQL tables.
procedure_declaration	This construct declares a procedure.
function_declaration	This construct declares a nested function.
seq_of_statements	This represents a sequence of statements.
exception_handler	This construct associates an exception with a sequence of statements, which is executed when that exception is raised.
IN, OUT, IN OUT	These parameter modes define the behavior of formal parameters. The IN parameter mode lets you pass values to the subprogram being called. An OUT parameter lets you return values to the caller of the subprogram. An IN OUT parameter lets you pass initial values to the subprogram being called and return updated values to the caller.
DEFAULT or :=	This keyword or assignment operator allows you to initialize IN parameters to default values.
RETURN	This keyword introduces the RETURN clause, which specifies the datatype of the result value.
type_name	This specifies the datatype of a formal argument or result value.

Usage Notes

Every function must contain at least one RETURN statement. Otherwise, PL/SQL raises the predefined exception PROGRAM_ERROR at run time.

Inside a function, an IN parameter acts like a constant. Therefore, it cannot be assigned a value. An OUT parameter acts like an uninitialized variable. Therefore, its value cannot be assigned to another variable or reassigned to itself. An IN OUT parameter acts like an initialized variable. Therefore, it can be assigned a value, and its value can be assigned to another variable.

Avoid using the OUT and IN OUT modes with functions. The purpose of a function is to take zero or more arguments and return a single value. It is poor programming practice to have a function return multiple values. Also, functions should be free from side effects, which change the values of variables not local to the subprogram. Thus, a function should not change the values of its actual parameters.

You can write the function specification and body as a unit, or you can separate the function specification from its body. That way, you can hide implementation details by placing the function in a package.

You can define functions in a package body without declaring their specifications in the package specification. However, such functions can be called only from inside the package.

Related Topics

Cursors, Exceptions, Packages, PL/SQL Tables, Procedures, Records

GOTO Statement

The GOTO statement branches to a labeled statement or PL/SQL block unconditionally. The label must be unique within its scope and must precede an executable statement or a PL/SQL block. When executed, the GOTO statement transfers control to the labeled statement or block.

Syntax

```
Label_name_declaration ::=
<<label_name>>
goto_statement ::=
GOTO label_name ;
```

Keyword and Parameter Description

Keyword or Parameter	Description
label_name	This is an undeclared identifier that optionally labels a statement or block to which you want to transfer control.

Usage Notes

Some possible destinations of a GOTO statement are illegal. In particular, a GOTO statement cannot branch into an IF statement, LOOP statement, or subblock.

From the current block, a GOTO statement can branch to another place in the block or into an enclosing block, but not into an exception handler. From an exception handler, a GOTO statement can branch into an enclosing block, but not into the current block.

If you use the GOTO statement to leave a cursor FOR loop prematurely, the cursor is closed automatically. The cursor is also closed automatically if an exception is raised inside the loop.

IF Statement

The IF statement lets you execute a sequence of statements conditionally. That is, whether the sequence is executed or not depends on the value of a condition.

Syntax

```
if_statement ::=
IF plsql_condition THEN seq_of_statements
[ELSIF plsql_condition THEN seq_of_statements ,...]
[Else seq_of_statements] END IF;
```

Keyword and Parameter Description

Keyword or Parameter	Description
plsql_condition	This is a condition associated with a sequence of statements, which is executed only if the condition evaluates to TRUE.
seq_of_statements	This represents a sequence of statements.
THEN	This keyword associates the condition that precedes THEN with the seq_of_statements that follows. If the condition evaluates to TRUE, the associated seq_of_statements is executed.
ELSIF	This keyword introduces a condition to be evaluated if the condition following IF and all the conditions following any preceding ELSIFs evaluate to FALSE or NULL.
ELSE	No condition follows this keyword. If control reaches the keyword ELSE, the seq_of_statements that follows is executed.

Usage Notes

There are three forms of IF statements: IF-THEN, IF-THEN-ELSE, and IF-THEN-ELSIF. The simplest form of IF statement associates a condition with a sequence of statements enclosed by the keywords THEN and END IF. The sequence of statements is executed only if the condition evaluates to TRUE. If the condition evaluates to FALSE or NULL, the IF statement does nothing. In either case, control passes to the next statement.

The second form of IF statement adds the keyword ELSE followed by an alternative sequence of statements. The sequence of statements in the ELSE clause is executed only if the condition evaluates to FALSE or NULL. Thus, the ELSE clause ensures that a sequence of statements is executed.

The third form of IF statement uses the keyword ELSIF to introduce additional conditions. If the first condition evaluates to FALSE or NULL, the ELSIF clause tests another condition. An IF statement can have any number of ELSIF clauses; the final ELSE clause is optional. Conditions are evaluated one by one from top to bottom. If any condition evaluates to TRUE, its associated sequence of statements is executed and control passes to the next statement. If all conditions evaluate to FALSE or NULL, the sequence in the ELSE clause is executed.

Related Topics

Conditions

INSERT Statement

The INSERT statement adds new rows of data to a specified database table or view.

Syntax

```
insert_statement ::=
INSERT INTO table_reference [(column_name,...)]
{VALUES (sql_expression, ...) | select_statement} ;
table_reference ::=
[schema.] {table | view} [@dblink]
```

Keyword and Parameter Description

Keyword or Parameter	Description
table_reference	The table or view specified by table_reference must be accessible when you execute the INSERT statement, and you must have INSERT privileges.
alias	This is another (usually short) name for the referenced table or view and is typically used in the WHERE clause of the subquery.
column_name	This identifier names a column in the table or view into which data is inserted. Column names must not be specified more than once in the column_name list and need not appear in the order in which they were defined by CREATE TABLE or CREATE VIEW. If a column_name list does not include all the columns in a table, the excluded columns are set to NULL or to a default value specified in the CREATE TABLE statement.

Keyword or Parameter	Description
VALUES (sql_expression, sql_expression, ...)	This clause assigns the values of sql_expressions in the VALUES list to corresponding columns in the column list. If no column list is supplied, the first value is inserted into the first column defined by CREATE TABLE, the second value is inserted into the second column, and so on. An sql_expression is any expression valid in SQL.
select_statement	This is a query that returns a set of values for insertion into a database table (or view). As many rows are added to the table as are returned by select_statement. The query must return a value for every column in the column list or for every column in the table if no column list is supplied.

Usage Notes

All character and date literals in the VALUES list must be enclosed by single quotes ('). Numeric literals are not enclosed by quotes.

An INSERT statement might insert one or more rows, or it might insert no rows. If one or more rows are inserted, the following things occur:

- SQL%NOTFOUND evaluates to FALSE.
- SQL%FOUND evaluates to TRUE.
- SQL%ROWCOUNT returns the number of rows inserted.

If no rows are inserted, the following things occur:

- SQL%NOTFOUND evaluates to TRUE.
- SQL%FOUND evaluates to FALSE.
- SQL%ROWCOUNT returns the number 0.

%ISOPEN Attribute

PL/SQL cursors have four attributes (including %ISOPEN) that, when appended to the cursor name, let you access useful information about the cursor.

There are two kinds of cursors: implicit and explicit. PL/SQL implicitly declares a cursor for all SQL data manipulation statements, including single-row queries. Oracle automatically closes the SQL cursor after executing its associated SQL statement, so %ISOPEN always evaluates to FALSE.

For multirow queries, you can explicitly declare a cursor to process the rows. %ISOPEN evaluates to TRUE if the cursor is open; otherwise, %ISOPEN evaluates to FALSE.

Syntax

```
isopen_attribute ::=
<cursor_name>%ISOPEN
```

Keyword and Parameter Description

Keyword or Parameter	Description
cursor_name	This identifier designates the implicit SQL cursor or names an explicitly declared cursor.

Usage Notes

You can use the %ISOPEN attribute in procedural statements but not in SQL statements. %ISOPEN is associated with every explicit cursor. Therefore, if you are unsure of a cursor's status, use the %ISOPEN attribute to see if the cursor is open. However, with the implicit SQL cursor, %ISOPEN always evaluates to FALSE.

Related Topics

CLOSE, Cursors, DELETE, FETCH, INSERT, OPEN, SELECT INTO, UPDATE

Literals

A literal is an explicit numeric, character, string, or Boolean value not represented by an identifier. The numeric literal 135 and the string literal 'Tom & Jerry' are examples.

Syntax

```
numeric_literal ::=
[{+ | -}] {integer | real_number}
integer ::=
digit,...
real_number ::=
{integer [.integer] | .integer | integer.} [ {E | e}
   [{+ | -}] integer]
character_literal ::=
{'char' | ''''}
string_literal ::=
' {char | ''},... '
boolean_literal ::=
{TRUE | FALSE | NULL}
```

Keyword and Parameter Description

Keyword or Parameter	Description
integer	This is an optionally signed whole number without a decimal point.
real_number	This is an optionally signed whole or fractional number with a decimal point.
digit	This must be one of the numerals 0 .. 9.
char	This is a member of the PL/SQL character set.
TRUE, FALSE	This is a predefined Boolean value.
NULL	This is a predefined nonvalue, which stands for a missing, unknown, or inapplicable value.

Usage Notes

Two kinds of numeric literals can be used in arithmetic expressions: integers and reals. Numeric literals must be separated by punctuation. Space characters can be used in addition to the punctuation.

A character literal is an individual character enclosed by single quotes (apostrophes). Character literals include all the printable characters in the PL/SQL character set: letters, numerals, spaces, and special symbols. PL/SQL is case-sensitive within character literals. Therefore, for example, PL/SQL considers the literals 'Q' and 'q' to be different.

A string literal is a sequence of zero or more characters enclosed by single quotes. The NULL string ('') contains zero characters. To represent an apostrophe within a string, write two single quotes. PL/SQL is case-sensitive within string literals; for example, PL/SQL considers the literals 'white' and 'White' to be different.

Unlike the nonvalue NULL, the Boolean values TRUE and FALSE cannot be inserted into a database column.

Related Topics

Variables and Constants

LOCK TABLE Statement

The LOCK TABLE statement lets you lock entire database tables in a specified lock mode so that you can share or deny access to tables while maintaining their integrity.

Syntax

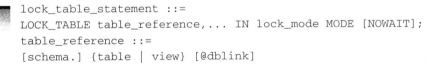

```
lock_table_statement ::=
LOCK_TABLE table_reference,... IN lock_mode MODE [NOWAIT];
table_reference ::=
[schema.] {table | view} [@dblink]
```

Keyword and Parameter Description

Keyword or Parameter	Description
table_reference	The table or view specified by table_reference must be accessible when you execute the LOCK TABLE statement.
lock_mode	This parameter specifies the lock mode. It must be one of the following: ROW SHARE, ROW EXCLUSIVE, SHARE UPDATE, SHARE, SHARE ROW EXCLUSIVE, or EXCLUSIVE.

Keyword or Parameter	Description
NOWAIT	This optional keyword tells Oracle not to wait if the table has been locked by another user. Control is immediately returned to your program so it can do other work before trying again to acquire the lock.

Usage Notes

If you omit the keyword NOWAIT, Oracle waits until the table is available; the wait has no set limit. Table locks are released when your transaction issues a COMMIT or ROLLBACK.

Related Topics

COMMIT, DELETE, INSERT, ROLLBACK, SAVEPOINT, UPDATE

LOOP Statement

A LOOP statement executes a sequence of statements multiple times. The loop encloses the sequence of statements that is to be repeated. PL/SQL supports four types of loops:

- Basic loops
- WHILE loops
- Numeric FOR loops
- Cursor FOR loops

The simplest form of LOOP statement is the basic (or infinite) loop, which encloses a sequence of statements between the keywords LOOP and END LOOP. With each iteration of the loop, the sequence of statements is executed, then control resumes at the top of the loop.

The WHILE-LOOP statement associates a condition with a sequence of statements enclosed by the keywords LOOP and END LOOP. Before each iteration of the loop, the condition is evaluated. If the condition evaluates to TRUE, the sequence of statements is executed, then control resumes at the top of the loop. If the condition evaluates to FALSE or NULL, the loop is bypassed and control passes to the next statement.

Whereas the number of iterations through a WHILE loop is unknown until the loop completes, the number of iterations through a FOR loop is known before the loop is entered. Numeric FOR loops iterate over a specified range of integers. The range is part of an iteration scheme, which is enclosed by the keywords FOR and LOOP.

A cursor FOR loop implicitly declares its loop index as a %ROWTYPE record, opens a cursor, repeatedly FETCHes rows of values from the active set into fields in the record, and closes the cursor when all rows have been processed.

Syntax

```
loop_statement ::=
[<<label_name>>]
[{WHILE plsql_condition | FOR {numeric_loop_param
    | cursor_loop_param}}]
LOOP seq_of_statements END LOOP [label_name];
numeric_loop_param ::=
index IN [REVERSE] integer_expr .. integer_expr
cursor_loop_param ::=
record_name IN {cursor_name [(parameter,...]
    | (select_statement)}
```

Keyword and Parameter Description

Keyword or Parameter	Description
label_name	This is an undeclared identifier that optionally labels a loop. If used, label_name must be enclosed by double angle brackets and must appear at the beginning of the LOOP statement. Optionally, label_name can also appear at the end of the LOOP statement.
seq_of_statements	This represents a sequence of statements to be repeated.
WHILE plsql_condition	WHILE loop condition.
FOR numeric_loop_param	This identifier names a loop index.
integer_expr	This parameter is an expression that evaluates to an integer. The expression is evaluated only when the loop is first entered.

Keyword or Parameter	Description
REVERSE	By default, iteration proceeds upward from the lower bound to the higher bound. However, if you use the keyword REVERSE, iteration proceeds downward from the higher bound to the lower bound. After each iteration, the loop index is decremented.
record_name	This identifier names an implicitly declared record.
cursor_name	This identifier names a previously declared cursor.
parameter	This identifier names a formal cursor parameter.
select_statement	This is a query associated with an internal cursor unavailable to you. PL/SQL automatically declares, opens, fetches from, and closes the internal cursor.

Usage Notes

You can use the EXIT WHEN statement to exit any loop prematurely. If the condition in the WHEN clause evaluates to TRUE, you exit the loop immediately.

When you leave a cursor FOR loop, the cursor is closed automatically even if you use an EXIT or GOTO statement to leave the loop prematurely. The cursor is also closed automatically if an exception is raised inside the loop.

Related Topics

CLOSE, Conditions, Cursors, EXIT, FETCH, OPEN, %ROWTYPE

%NOTFOUND Attribute

PL/SQL cursors have four attributes (including %NOTFOUND) that, when appended to the cursor name, let you access useful information about the cursor.

There are two kinds of cursors: implicit and explicit. PL/SQL implicitly declares a cursor for all SQL data manipulation statements, including single-row queries. Until the SQL statement is executed, %NOTFOUND evaluates to NULL. Thereafter, %NOTFOUND evaluates to FALSE if an INSERT, UPDATE, or DELETE affected one or more rows or a SELECT INTO returned one or more rows. Otherwise, %NOTFOUND evaluates to TRUE (0 rows raises the NO_DATA_FOUND condition).

For multirow queries, you can explicitly declare a cursor to process the rows. After the cursor is open but before the first fetch, %NOTFOUND evaluates to NULL. Thereafter, it evaluates to FALSE if the last fetch returned a row or TRUE if no row was returned.

Syntax

```
notfound_attribute ::=
<cursor_name>%NOTFOUND
```

Keyword and Parameter Description

Keyword or Parameter	Description
cursor_name	This identifier designates the implicit SQL cursor or names an explicitly declared cursor.

Usage Notes

You can use the %NOTFOUND attribute in procedural statements but not in SQL statements. %NOTFOUND is associated with every explicit cursor. Therefore, you can open multiple cursors, then use %NOTFOUND to see which cursors have rows left to fetch. If a cursor is not open, referencing it with %NOTFOUND raises INVALID_CURSOR.

When an explicit cursor is opened, the rows that satisfy the associated query are identified and form the active set. Rows are fetched from the active set one at a time. If the last fetch returned a row, %NOTFOUND evaluates to FALSE. If the last fetch failed to return a row (because the active set was empty), %NOTFOUND evaluates to TRUE.

Related Topics

CLOSE, Cursors, DELETE, FETCH, %FOUND, INSERT, OPEN, SELECT INTO, UPDATE

NULL Statement

The NULL statement explicitly specifies inaction; it does nothing other than pass control to the next statement. In a construct allowing alternative actions, the NULL statement serves as a placeholder.

Syntax

```
null_statement ::=
NULL;
```

Usage Notes

The NULL statement improves readability by making the meaning and action of conditional statements clear. It tells readers that the associated alternative has not been overlooked, but that indeed no action is necessary.

Each clause in an IF statement must contain at least one executable statement. The NULL statement meets this requirement. Therefore, you can use the NULL statement in clauses that correspond to circumstances in which no action is taken.

Do not confuse the NULL statement with the NULL value; they are unrelated.

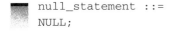

OPEN Statement

The OPEN statement executes the query associated with an explicitly declared cursor. It also allocates resources used by Oracle to process the query and identifies the active set, which consists of all rows that meet the query search criteria. The cursor is positioned before the first row in the active set.

Syntax

```
open_cursor_statement ::=
OPEN <cursor_name> [(input_parameter,...)];
```

Keyword and Parameter Description

Keyword or Parameter	Description
cursor_name	This identifier names an explicitly declared cursor that is not currently open.
input_parameter	This identifier names a formal cursor parameter and is typically referenced in the WHERE clause. If formal parameters are declared, actual parameters must be passed to the cursor. The values of actual parameters are used when the cursor is OPENed. Their datatypes must be the same as or convertible to the datatypes of corresponding formal parameters.

Usage Notes

Generally, PL/SQL parses an explicit cursor only the first time it is OPENed and parses an SQL statement (thereby creating an implicit cursor) only the first time the statement is executed. All the parsed SQL statements are cached. An SQL statement must be reparsed only if it is bumped out of the cache by a new SQL statement.

Therefore, although you must CLOSE a cursor before you can reOPEN it, PL/SQL need not reparse the associated SELECT statement. If you CLOSE and then immediately reOPEN the cursor, a reparse is definitely not needed.

Rows in the active set are not retrieved when the OPEN statement is executed. The FETCH statement retrieves the rows. With a FOR UPDATE cursor, the rows are locked when the cursor is OPENed.

Related Topics

CLOSE, Cursors, FETCH, LOOP

Packages

A package is a database object that groups logically related PL/SQL types, objects, and subprograms. Packages usually have two parts, a specification and a body, although sometimes the body is unnecessary. The specification is the interface to your applications; it declares the types, variables, constants, exceptions, cursors, and subprograms available for use. The body fully defines cursors and subprograms and so implements the specification.

Syntax

```
package_specification ::=
PACKAGE <package_name> IS
{variable_declaration; | cursor_specification; |
   exception_declaration; | record_declaration; |
   plsql_table_declaration; | procedure_specification; |
   function_specification;}
END [package_name] ;
package_body ::=
PACKAGE BODY <package_name> IS
{variable_declaration; | cursor_body; | exception_declaration; |
record_declaration; | plsql_table_declaration; | procedure_body; |
   function_body;}
END [package_name] ;
```

Keyword and Parameter Description

Keyword or Parameter	Description
package_name	This identifier names a package.
variable_declaration	This construct declares variables and constants.
cursor_declaration	This construct, which cannot contain a RETURN clause, declares an explicit cursor.
cursor_specification	This construct declares the interface to an explicit cursor.
exception_declaration	This construct declares exceptions.
record_declaration	This construct declares user-defined records.
plsql_table_declaration	This construct declares PL/SQL tables.
procedure_specification	This construct declares the interface to a procedure.
function_specification	This construct declares the interface to a function.
cursor_body	This construct defines the underlying implementation of an explicit cursor.
procedure_body	This construct defines the underlying implementation of a procedure.
function_body	This construct defines the underlying implementation of a function.
seq_of_statements	This represents a sequence of statements.

Usage Notes

Packages cannot be embedded in a PL/SQL block or subprogram. However, you can define packages using any Oracle tool that supports PL/SQL.

To become available for general use, packages must be CREATEd and stored in an Oracle database. You can issue the CREATE PACKAGE and CREATE PACKAGE BODY statements interactively from SQL*Plus or SQL*DBA and from an Oracle precompiler host program.

Related Topics

Cursors, Exceptions, Functions, PL/SQL Tables, Procedures, Records

PL/SQL Tables

PL/SQL tables are objects of type TABLE, which are modeled after (but are not the same as) database tables. PL/SQL tables use a primary key to give you arraylike access to rows. Like the size of a database table, the size of a PL/SQL table is unconstrained. That is, the number of rows in a PL/SQL table can increase dynamically. PL/SQL tables must be declared in two step: You define a TABLE type, then declare PL/SQL tables of that type.

Syntax

```
plsql_type_type ::=
TYPE <type_name> IS TABLE OF {column_type | table.column%TYPE}
    [NOT NULL] INDEX BY BINARY_INTEGER;
plsql_table ::=
<plsql_table_name> plsql_table_type;
```

Keyword and Parameter Description

Keyword or Parameter	Description
type_name	This identifier names a user-defined type specifier, which is used in subsequent declarations of PL/SQL tables.

Keyword or Parameter	Description
column_type	This specifies the datatype of the column in a PL/SQL table. It can be any scalar (not composite) datatype.
table.column	This refers to a table and column that must be accessible when the declaration is elaborated.
INDEX BY BINARY INTEGER	The primary key of a PL/SQL table must belong to type BINARY_INTEGER, which can represent signed integers of any practical size. The magnitude range of a BINARY_INTEGER value is $-2^{31} -1 .. 2^{31} -1$ ($-2147483647 .. 2147483647$).
plsql_table_name	The identifier names an entire PL/SQL table.

Usage Notes

You can declare TABLE types and PL/SQL tables in the declarative part of any block, subprogram, or package. PL/SQL tables can have one column and a primary key, neither of which can be named. The column can belong to any scalar type, but the primary key must belong to type BINARY_INTEGER. You can use the %TYPE attribute to specify a column datatype.

Unlike an array, a PL/SQL table is unconstrained (not of fixed size) because its primary key can assume any value in the range of values defined for BINARY_INTEGER. As a result, you cannot initialize a PL/SQL table in its declaration. The first reference to a row in a PL/SQL table must be an assignment. Otherwise, the predefined exception NO_DATA_FOUND is raised.

PL/SQL tables follow the usual scoping and instantiation rules. In a package, they are instantiated when you first reference the package and cease to exist when you exit the application or end the database session. In a block or subprogram, the tables are instantiated when you enter the block or subprogram and cease to exist when you exit the block or subprogram.

Like scalar variables, PL/SQL tables can be declared as the formal parameters of procedures and functions. The restrictions that apply to scalar parameters also apply to PL/SQL tables.

Related Topics

Assignment Statement, Functions, Procedures, Records

Procedures

A procedure is a named PL/SQL block that can take parameters and be invoked. Generally, you use a procedure to perform an action.

A procedure has two parts: a specification and a body. The procedure specification begins with the keyword PROCEDURE and ends with the procedure name or a parameter list. Parameter declarations are optional. Procedures that take no parameters are written without parentheses.

The procedure body begins with the keyword IS and ends with the keyword END, followed by an optional procedure name. The procedure body has three parts: a declarative part, an executable part, and an optional exception-handling part.

The declarative part contains declarations of types, cursors, constants, variables, exceptions, and subprograms. These objects are local and cease to exist when you exit the procedure. The executable part contains statements that assign values, control execution, and manipulate Oracle data. The exception-handling part contains exception handlers, which deal with exceptions raised during execution.

Syntax

```
procedure_specification ::=
PROCEDURE <procedure_name> [(parameter,...)] ;
procedure_declaration ::=
procedure_body
procedure_ body::=
PROCEDURE <procedure_name> [(parameter,...)] IS
   [{variable_declaration; | cursor_declaration;
   | exception_declaration; | record_declaration;
   | plsql_table_declaration; ]
```

Keyword and Parameter Description

Keyword or Parameter	Description
procedure_name	This identifier names a procedure.
variable_declaration	This construct declares variables and constants.
cursor_declaration	This construct declares an explicit cursor.
exception_declaration	This construct declares exceptions.

Keyword or Parameter	Description
record_declaration	This construct declares user-defined records.
plsql_table_declaration	This construct declares PL/SQL tables.
procedure_declaration	This construct declares a nested procedure.
function_declaration	This construct declares a function.
seq_of_statements	This represents a sequence of statements.
exception_handler	This construct associates an exception with a sequence of statements, which is executed when that exception is raised.
parameter_name	This identifier names a formal parameter, which is a variable declared in a procedure specification and referenced in the procedure body.
IN, OUT, IN OUT	These parameter modes define the behavior of formal parameters. The IN parameter mode lets you pass values to the subprogram being called. An OUT parameter lets you return values to the caller of the subprogram. An IN OUT parameter lets you pass initial values to the subprogram being called and return updated values to the caller.
type_name	This specifies the datatype of a formal parameter. Unlike the datatype specifier in a variable declaration, the datatype specifier in a parameter declaration must be unconstrained.

Usage Notes

At least one statement must appear in the executable part of a procedure. The NULL statement meets this requirement. A procedure is called as a PL/SQL statement.

You can write the procedure specification and body as a unit. You can also separate the procedure specification from its body. That way, you can hide implementation details by placing the procedure in a package. You can define procedures in a package body without declaring their specifications in the package specification. However, such procedures can be called only from inside the package.

Procedures can be defined using any Oracle tool that supports PL/SQL. To become available for general use, however, procedures must be CREATEd and stored in an Oracle database. You can issue the CREATE PROCEDURE statement interactively from SQL*Plus or SQL*DBA or from the precompilers.

Related Topics

Cursors, Exceptions, Functions, Packages, PL/SQL Tables, Records

RAISE Statement

The RAISE statement stops normal execution of a PL/SQL block or subprogram and transfers control to the appropriate exception handler. Normally, predefined exceptions are raised implicitly by the run-time system. However, RAISE statements can also raise predefined exceptions. User-defined exceptions must be raised explicitly by RAISE statements.

Syntax

```
raise_statement ::=
RAISE [exception_name] ;
```

Keyword and Parameter Description

Keyword or Parameter	Description
exception_name	This identifier names a predefined or user-defined exception.

Usage Notes

PL/SQL blocks and subprograms should RAISE an exception only when an error makes it impractical or impossible to finish processing. You can code a RAISE statement for a given exception anywhere within the scope of that exception.

When an exception is raised, if PL/SQL cannot find a handler for it in the current block or subprogram, the exception propagates. That is, the exception reproduces itself in successive enclosing blocks until a handler is found or there are no more blocks to search. In the latter case, PL/SQL returns an "unhandled exception" error to the host environment.

Omitting the exception name in a RAISE statement—allowed only in an exception handler—reraises the current exception. When a RAISE statement with no parameters executes in an exception handler, the first block searched is the enclosing block, not the current block.

Related Topic

Exceptions

Records

Records are objects of type RECORD. Records have uniquely named fields that can store data values of different types. Records must be declared in two steps: You define a RECORD type, then declare user-defined records of that type.

Syntax

```
record_type ::=
TYPE <type_name> IS RECORD (field_name datatype [NOT NULL],...) ;
datatype ::=
{field_type | table.column%TYPE}
record ::=
record_name record_type;
```

Keyword and Parameter Description

Keyword or Parameter	Description
type_name	This identifier names a user-defined type specifier, which is used in subsequent declarations of records.
field_name	This identifier names a field in a user-defined record.
field_type	This specifies the datatype of a field in a user-defined record. It can be any datatype including RECORD and TABLE.
table	This refers to a table that must be accessible when the declaration is elaborated.
table.column	This refers to a table and column that must be accessible when the declaration is elaborated.
NOT NULL	This constraint prevents the assigning of NULLs to a field. Trying to assign a NULL to a field defined as NOT NULL raises the predefined exception VALUE_ERROR.
record_name	This identifier names a user-defined record.

Usage Notes

You can declare RECORD types and user-defined records in the declarative part of any block, subprogram, or package. Furthermore, a record can be initialized in its declaration.

Instead of assigning values separately to each field in a record, you can assign values to all fields at once. This can be done in two ways. First, PL/SQL lets you assign one record to another if they belong to the same datatype. Note, however, that even if their fields match exactly, a user-defined record and a %ROWTYPE record belong to different types. Second, you can assign a list of column values to a record by using the SELECT or FETCH statement. Just make sure the column names appear in the same order as the fields in your record.

Related Topics

Assignment Statement, Functions, PL/SQL Tables, Procedures

RETURN Statement

The RETURN statement immediately completes the execution of a subprogram and returns control to the caller. Execution then resumes with the statement following the subprogram call. In a function, the RETURN statement also sets the function identifier to the result value. (Do not confuse the RETURN statement with the RETURN clause, which specifies the datatype of the result value in a function specification.)

Syntax

```
return_statement ::=
RETURN [plsql_expression] ;
```

Keyword and Parameter Description

Keyword or Parameter	Description
plsql_expression	This is an arbitrarily complex expression. It is evaluated when the RETURN statement is executed.

Usage Notes

A subprogram can contain several RETURN statements, none of which need be the last lexical statement. Executing any of them completes the subprogram immediately. However, it is poor programming practice to have multiple exit points in a subprogram.

In procedures, a RETURN statement cannot contain an expression. The statement simply returns control to the caller before the normal end of the procedure is reached.

However, in functions, a RETURN statement must contain an expression, which is evaluated when the RETURN statement is executed. The resulting value is assigned to the function identifier. Therefore, a function must contain at least one RETURN statement. Otherwise, PL/SQL raises the predefined exception PROGRAM_ERROR at run time.

The RETURN statement can also be used in an anonymous block to exit the block (and all enclosing blocks) immediately, but the RETURN statement cannot contain an expression.

ROLLBACK Statement

The ROLLBACK statement is the inverse of the COMMIT statement. It undoes some or all database changes made during the current transaction.

Syntax

```
rollback_statement ::=
ROLLBACK [WORK] [TO [SAVEPOINT] savepoint_name] [COMMENT 'text'];
```

Keyword and Parameter Description

Keyword or Parameter	Description
ROLLBACK	When a parameterless ROLLBACK statement is executed, all database changes made during the current transaction are undone.
WORK	The keyword WORK is optional and has no effect except to improve readability.

Keyword or Parameter	Description
ROLLBACK TO savepoint_name	The ROLLBACK TO statement undoes all database changes (and releases all locks acquired) since the SAVEPOINT identified by savepoint_name was marked. The identifier savepoint_name names a SAVEPOINT that was marked earlier in the current transaction using the SAVEPOINT statement.
SAVEPOINT	This keyword is optional and has no effect except to improve readability.
COMMENT	The keyword COMMENT specifies a comment to be associated with the current transaction and is typically used with distributed transactions. The text must be a quoted literal <50 characters long.

Usage Notes

All savepoints marked after the SAVEPOINT to which you roll back are erased. However, the SAVEPOINT to which you roll back is not erased. For example, if you mark savepoints A, B, C, and D, in that order, then ROLLBACK TO SAVEPOINT B, only savepoints C and D are erased.

An implicit SAVEPOINT is marked before executing an INSERT, UPDATE, or DELETE statement. If the statement fails, a ROLLBACK to the implicit SAVEPOINT is done. Normally, just the failed SQL statement is rolled back—not the whole transaction. However, if the statement raises an unhandled exception, the host environment determines what is rolled back.

When a distributed transaction fails, the text specified by COMMENT helps you diagnose the problem. If a distributed transaction is ever in doubt, Oracle stores the text in the data dictionary along with the transaction ID.

Related Topics

COMMIT, SAVEPOINT

%ROWCOUNT Attribute

PL/SQL cursors have four attributes (including %ROWCOUNT) that, when appended to the cursor name, let you access useful information about the cursor.

There are two kinds of cursors: implicit and explicit. PL/SQL implicitly declares a cursor for all SQL data manipulation statements, including single-row queries.

Until the SQL statement is executed, %ROWCOUNT returns a NULL. Thereafter, %ROWCOUNT returns the number of rows affected by an INSERT, UPDATE, or DELETE or returned by a SELECT INTO. %ROWCOUNT returns a zero if an INSERT, UPDATE, or DELETE affected no rows or a SELECT INTO returned no rows.

For multirow queries, you can explicitly declare a cursor to process the rows. When you open its cursor, %ROWCOUNT is zeroed. Before the first fetch, %ROWCOUNT returns a zero. Thereafter, it returns the number of rows fetched so far. The number is incremented if the latest fetch returned a row.

Syntax

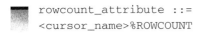

```
rowcount_attribute ::=
<cursor_name>%ROWCOUNT
```

Keyword and Parameter Description

Keyword or Parameter	Description
cursor_name	This identifier designates the implicit SQL cursor or names an explicitly declared cursor.

Usage Notes

You can use the %ROWCOUNT attribute in procedural statements but not in SQL statements. %ROWCOUNT is associated with every explicit cursor. Therefore, you can open multiple cursors, then use %ROWCOUNT to see how many rows have been fetched so far. If a cursor is not open, referencing it with %ROWCOUNT raises INVALID_CURSOR.

If a SELECT INTO returns more than one row, the predefined exception TOO_MANY_ROWS is raised and %ROWCOUNT is set to 1, not the actual number of rows that satisfy the query.

Related Topics

CLOSE, Cursors, FETCH, INSERT, OPEN, SELECT INTO, UPDATE

%ROWTYPE Attribute

The %ROWTYPE attribute provides a record that represents a row in a table (or view). The record can store an entire row of data selected from the table or fetched by a cursor. Columns in a row and corresponding fields in a record have the same names and datatypes.

You use the %ROWTYPE attribute in variable declarations as a datatype specifier. Variables declared using %ROWTYPE are treated like those declared using a datatype name.

Syntax

```
rowtype_attribute ::=
identifier%ROWTYPE
```

Keyword and Parameter Description

Keyword or Parameter	Description
identifier	This identifier names a previously declared cursor.

Usage Notes

The %ROWTYPE attribute lets you declare records structured like a row of data in a database table. The column values returned by the SELECT statement are stored in fields. To reference a field, you use dot notation. In addition, you can assign the value of an expression to a specific field.

There are two ways to assign values to all fields in a record at once. First, PL/SQL allows aggregate assignment between entire records if their declarations refer to the same table or cursor. Second, you can assign a list of column values to a record by using the SELECT or FETCH statement. The column names must appear in the order in which they were defined by CREATE TABLE or CREATE VIEW. Select-list items fetched by a cursor associated with %ROWTYPE must have simple names or, if they are expressions, must have aliases.

Related Topics

Cursors, FETCH, Variables and Constants

SAVEPOINT Statement

The SAVEPOINT statement names and marks the current point in the processing of a transaction. With the ROLLBACK TO statement, savepoints let you undo parts of a transaction instead of the whole transaction.

Syntax

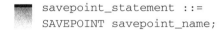

```
savepoint_statement ::=
SAVEPOINT savepoint_name;
```

Keyword and Parameter Description

Keyword or Parameter	Description
savepoint_name	This is an undeclared identifier that names the current point in the processing of a transaction.

Usage Notes

When you roll back to a savepoint, any savepoints marked after it are erased. However, the savepoint to which you roll back is not erased. A simple ROLLBACK or COMMIT erases all savepoints.

If you mark a savepoint within a recursive subprogram, new instances of the SAVEPOINT statement are executed at each level in the recursive descent. However, you can only ROLLBACK to the most recently marked savepoint.

Savepoint names can be reused within a transaction. This moves the savepoint from its old position to the current point in the transaction.

An implicit savepoint is marked before executing an INSERT, UPDATE, or DELETE statement. If the statement fails, a ROLLBACK to the implicit savepoint is done. Normally, just the failed SQL statement is rolled back—not the whole transaction. However, if the statement raises an unhandled exception, the host environment determines what is rolled back.

Related Topics

COMMIT, ROLLBACK

SELECT INTO Statement

The SELECT INTO statement retrieves data from one or more database tables, then assigns the selected values to variables.

Syntax

```
select_into_statement ::=
SELECT select_list_item [alias] ,... INTO {variable_name |
    record_name},... FROM table_reference,...
    rest_of_select_statement;
table_reference ::=
[schema.] {table | view} [@dblink]
```

Keyword and Parameter Description

Keyword or Parameter	Description
select_list_item	This parameter retrieves a value for each select_list_item in the select list, then assigns the values to corresponding variables in the variable_name list or to corresponding fields in record_name.
INTO variable_name	This parameter defines which scalar variables will store the retrieved data. All variables in the variable_name list must be previously declared.
INTO record_name	This parameter indicates that retrieved data is stored in a record variable declared using the %ROWTYPE attribute.
table_reference	The table or view specified by table_reference must be accessible when you execute the SELECT statement.
alias	This is another (usually short) name for the referenced column, table, or view and can be used in the WHERE clause.
rest_of_select_statement	This parameter is anything that can legally follow the FROM clause in a SELECT statement.

Usage Notes

The implicit SQL cursor and the cursor attributes %NOTFOUND, %FOUND, %ROWCOUNT, and %ISOPEN let you access useful information about the execution of a SELECT INTO statement.

When you assign values to variables using a SELECT INTO statement, the SELECT must return only one row from the table. If more than one row is returned, the following things occur:

- The predefined exception TOO_MANY_ROWS is raised.
- SQLCODE returns –1422 (Oracle error code ORA-01422).
- SQLERRM returns the Oracle error message "single-row query returns more than one row."
- SQL%NOTFOUND evaluates to FALSE.
- SQL%FOUND evaluates to TRUE.
- SQL%ROWCOUNT returns the number 1.

If no rows are returned, the following things occur:

- The predefined exception NO_DATA_FOUND is raised unless the SELECT called a SQL group function.
- SQLCODE returns +100 (Oracle error code ORA-01403).
- SQLERRM returns the Oracle error message "no data found."
- SQL%NOTFOUND evaluates to TRUE.
- SQL%FOUND evaluates to FALSE.
- SQL%ROWCOUNT returns the number 0.

Related Topics

Assignment Statement, FETCH, %ROWTYPE

SET TRANSACTION Statement

The SET TRANSACTION statement establishes a read-only transaction, which lets you query multiple tables while other users update the same tables.

Syntax

```
set_transaction_statement ::=
SET TRANSACTION READ ONLY;
```

Keyword and Parameter Description

Keyword or Parameter	Description
READ ONLY	This parameter is required. If a transaction is set to READ ONLY, subsequent queries see only changes committed before the transaction began. The use of READ ONLY does not affect other users or transactions.

Usage Notes

The SET TRANSACTION statement must be the first SQL statement in a read-only transaction and can only appear once in a transaction. Furthermore, only the SELECT, COMMIT, and ROLLBACK statements are allowed in a read-only transaction. For example, including an INSERT or DELETE statement raises an exception.

Related Topics

COMMIT, ROLLBACK, SAVEPOINT

SQL Cursor

Oracle implicitly opens a cursor to process each SQL statement not associated with an explicitly declared cursor. PL/SQL lets you refer to the most recent implicit cursor as the "SQL" cursor. The SQL cursor has four attributes: %NOTFOUND, %FOUND, %ROWCOUNT, and %ISOPEN. When appended to the cursor name (SQL), these attributes let you access information about the execution of INSERT, UPDATE, DELETE, and SELECT INTO statements.

Syntax

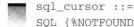

```
sql_cursor ::=
SQL {%NOTFOUND | %FOUND | %ROWCOUNT | %ISOPEN}
```

Keyword and Parameter Description

Keyword or Parameter	Description
%NOTFOUND	%NOTFOUND evaluates to TRUE if an INSERT, UPDATE, or DELETE affected no rows or a SELECT INTO returned no rows. Otherwise, %NOTFOUND evaluates to FALSE. If a SELECT INTO fails to return a row, the predefined exception NO_DATA_FOUND is raised, whether you check %NOTFOUND on the next line or not. However, a SELECT INTO that calls a SQL group function never raises the exception NO_DATA_FOUND. This is because group functions such as AVG and SUM always return a value or a NULL. In such cases, %NOTFOUND always evaluates to FALSE.
%FOUND	%FOUND is the logical opposite of %NOTFOUND. %FOUND evaluates to TRUE if an INSERT, UPDATE, or DELETE affected one or more rows or a SELECT INTO returned one or more rows. Otherwise, %FOUND evaluates to FALSE.
%ROWCOUNT	%ROWCOUNT returns the number of rows affected by an INSERT, UPDATE, or DELETE or returned by a SELECT INTO.
%ISOPEN	Oracle automatically closes the SQL cursor after executing its associated SQL statement. As a result, %ISOPEN always evaluates to FALSE.

Usage Notes

You can use cursor attributes in procedural statements but not in SQL statements. Before Oracle opens the SQL cursor automatically, the implicit cursor attributes evaluate to NULL.

The values of cursor attributes always refer to the most recently executed SQL statement, wherever that statement appears. It might be in a different scope;

therefore, if you want to save an attribute value for later use, you should assign it to a Boolean variable immediately.

Related Topics

%FOUND, %NOTFOUND, %ISOPEN, %ROWCOUNT

SQLCODE Function

The function SQLCODE returns the number code associated with the most recently raised exception. SQLCODE is meaningful only in an exception handler. Outside a handler, SQLCODE always returns zero.

For internal exceptions, SQLCODE returns the number of the associated Oracle error. The number SQLCODE returns is negative unless the Oracle error is "no data found," in which case SQLCODE returns +100. For user-defined exceptions, SQLCODE returns +1 unless you used the pragma EXCEPTION_INIT to associate the exception with an Oracle error number, in which case SQLCODE returns that error number.

Syntax

```
sqlcode_function ::=
SQLCODE
```

Usage Notes

You cannot use SQLCODE directly in a SQL statement. Instead, you must assign the value of SQLCODE to a local variable, then use the variable in the SQL statement.

Related Topics

Exceptions, SQLERRM

SQLERRM Function

The function SQLERRM returns the error message associated with its error-number argument or, if the argument is omitted, with the current value of SQLCODE. SQLERRM with no argument is meaningful only in an exception handler. Outside a handler, SQLERRM with no argument always returns the message "ORA-0000: normal, successful completion." For internal exceptions, SQLERRM returns the message associated with the Oracle error that occurred. The message begins with the Oracle error code.

For user-defined exceptions, SQLERRM returns the message "User-Defined Exception," unless you used the pragma EXCEPTION_INIT to associate the exception with an Oracle error number; in that case, SQLERRM returns the corresponding error message.

Syntax

```
sqlerrm_function ::=
SQLERRM [(error_number)]
```

Keyword and Parameter Description

Keyword or Parameter	Description
error_number	This argument must be a valid Oracle error number.

Usage Notes

You can pass an error number to SQLERRM, in which case SQLERRM returns the message associated with that error number. The error number passed to SQLERRM should be negative. Passing a zero to SQLERRM always returns the message "ORA-0000: normal, successful completion." Passing a positive number to SQLERRM always returns the message "User-Defined Exception," unless you pass +100, in which case SQLERRM returns the message "ORA-01403: no data found."

You cannot use SQLERRM directly in an SQL statement. Instead, you must assign the value of SQLERRM to a local variable, then use the variable in the SQL statement.

Related Topics

Exceptions, SQLCODE

 ## %TYPE Attribute

The %TYPE attribute provides the datatype of a variable, constant, or database column. You use the %TYPE attribute in variable and constant declarations as a datatype specifier. Variables and constants declared using %TYPE are treated like those declared using a datatype name.

Syntax

```
type_attribute ::=
{variable_name | [owner.] table.column} %TYPE
```

Keyword and Parameter Description

Keyword or Parameter	Description
variable_name	This identifier names a variable or constant previously declared in the same scope.
owner.	This identifier names the owner of a table (or view) that must be accessible when the declaration is elaborated.
table.column	This refers to a table and column that must be accessible when the declaration is elaborated.

Usage Notes

The %TYPE attribute is particularly useful when declaring variables that refer to database columns. You can reference a table and column, or you can reference an owner, table, and column. And, a %TYPE declaration can include an initialization clause. However, the NOT NULL column constraint does not apply to variables declared using %TYPE.

Related Topics

%ROWTYPE, Variables and Constants

UPDATE Statement

UPDATE changes the values of specified columns in one or more rows in a table or view.

Syntax

```
Update_statement ::=
UPDATE table_reference SET {column_name = {sql_expression |
    one_val_set_stmt)},... | (column_name,...) =
    (select_statement)},... [WHERE {search_condition
    | CURRENT OF cursor_name}] ;
table_reference ::=
[schema.] {table | view} [@dblink]
```

Keyword and Parameter Description

Keyword or Parameter	Description
table_reference	The table or view specified by table_reference must be accessible when you execute the UPDATE statement, and you must have UPDATE privileges.
alias	This is another (usually short) name for the referenced table or view and is typically used in the WHERE clause.
column_name	This parameter is the name of the column (or one of the columns) to be updated. It must be the name of a column in the referenced table or view. The column names must not be repeated in the column_name list. They need not appear in the UPDATE statement in the order they appear in the table or view.

Keyword or Parameter	Description
SET column_name = sql_expression	This parameter assigns the value of the sql_expression to the column called column_name. The term sql_expression can be any valid SQL expression.
SET column_name = one_val_sel_stmt	This clause assigns the value retrieved from the database by the one_val_sel_stmt to the sole column in the column_name list.
SET (column_name) = select_statement	This clause assigns the values retrieved from the database by select_statement to the columns listed in the column_name list.
WHERE search_condition	The search_condition conditionally chooses the rows in table_reference to be updated. Only rows that meet the search_condition are updated. If you omit search_condition, all rows in the table are updated.
WHERE CURRENT OF cursor_name	This parameter refers to the latest row processed by the FETCH statement associated with cursor_name. The named cursor must have been declared using the FOR UPDATE clause and must be open and positioned on a row. If the cursor is not open, using the CURRENT OF clause results in an error. If the cursor is open, but no FETCH has been done or the last FETCH returned no rows, the predefined exception NO_DATA_FOUND is raised.

Usage Notes

The UPDATE ... WHERE CURRENT OF statement can be used after a FETCH from an open cursor, provided the associated query was declared with a FOR UPDATE clause. The UPDATE ... WHERE CURRENT OF statement updates the current row.

The implicit SQL cursor and the cursor attributes %NOTFOUND, %FOUND, %ROWCOUNT, and %ISOPEN let you access useful information about the execution of an UPDATE statement.

An UPDATE might update one or more rows, or it might update no rows. If one or more rows are updated, the following things occur:

■ SQL%NOTFOUND evaluates to FALSE.

■ SQL%FOUND evaluates to TRUE.

■ SQL%ROWCOUNT returns the number of rows updated.

If no rows are updated, the following things occur:

■ SQL%NOTFOUND evaluates to TRUE.

■ SQL%FOUND evaluates to FALSE.

■ SQL%ROWCOUNT returns the number 0.

Variables and Constants

You can declare variables and constants in the declarative part of any PL/SQL block, subprogram, or package. Declarations allocate storage space for a value, specify its datatype, and name the storage location so the value can be referenced. They can also assign an initial value and add the NOT NULL constraint.

Syntax

```
variable_declaration ::=
<variable_name> [CONSTANT]
{type_name | identifier%TYPE | identifier%ROWTYPE} [NOT NULL]
   [{:= | DEFAULT} plsql_expression];
```

Keyword and Parameter Description

Keyword or Parameter	Description
variable_name	This names a variable or constant.
CONSTANT	This denotes the declaration of a constant. You must initialize a constant in its declaration using a plsql_expression. Once initialized, the value of a constant cannot be changed.
type_name	This specifies the datatype of a variable or constant.
%TYPE	The %TYPE attribute provides the datatype of a variable, constant, or database column.
%ROWTYPE	The %ROWTYPE attribute provides a record that represents a row in a database table. Columns in a row and corresponding fields in a record have the same names and datatypes.

Keyword or Parameter	Description
NOT NULL	This prevents the assigning of NULLs to a variable or constant. Trying to assign a NULL to an object defined as NOT NULL raises the predefined exception VALUE_ERROR. In variable declarations, the constraint NOT NULL must be followed by an initialization clause.
plsql_expression	This is an arbitrarily complex expression. It is used to initialize a variable or constant.

Usage Notes

Variables and constants are initialized every time a block or subprogram is entered. By default, variables are initialized to NULL. Therefore, unless you expressly initialize a variable, its value is undefined.

Whether public or private, variables and constants declared in a package specification are initialized only once per session.

A plsql_expression is required when declaring NOT NULL variables and when declaring constants. If a plsql_expression is not included in a variable declaration, the variable is assigned a NULL by default.

Related Topics

Assignment Statement, Expressions, %ROWTYPE, %TYPE

APPENDIX C

Oracle Call Interface (OCI) Quick Reference

This appendix describes the ground rules for using the Oracle Call Interface functions and each function in the OCI C language library.

Using OCI Functions

This section describes the conventions and rules for the OCI function definitions and how to use these functions in an OCI application program.

Datatypes

The datatypes used in the C examples in this section are defined in the file ORATYPES.H. This is a system-specific file; the online location of this file can also be system-specific. Refer to the Oracle installation or user's guide for the location of ORATYPES.H on your system.

Parameter Names

The parameter names used in each function description are six or fewer characters long and contain only alphanumeric characters. In your OCI C programs, however, you can use longer, more descriptive parameter names that contain nonalphanumeric characters.

Parameter Datatypes

Parameters used in the OCI functions can be of five datatypes:

- **sword** signed word or natural integer
- **byte integer** signed (**sb1**) or unsigned (**ub1**)
- **byte integer** signed (**sb2**) or unsigned (**ub2**)
- **byte integer** signed (**sb4**) or unsigned (**ub4**)
- **pointer** address of a character or integer program variable

Integer
When a literal is passed to an OCI function, you should cast the literal to the datatype of the parameter. For example, the **oparse** function has the following prototype, using ANSI C notation:

```
oparse (struct cda_def *cursor, text *sqlstm, sb4 sqllen,
        sword defflg, ub4 lngflg);
```

If the **oparse** function is called with the following parameters:

```
oparse (&cda, "select sysdate from dual", -1, 1, 2);
```

the C compiler might issue warning messages to the effect that the datatype conversions are nonportable. A better way to call **oparse** would be as follows:

```
oparse (&cda, (text *) "select sysdate from dual", (sb4) -1,
        (sword) 0, (ub4) 2);
```

The typecasts in this example ensure that each argument is converted to the proper type before being passed to the function. It is important to distinguish signed and unsigned short integers (**sb2** and **ub2**) from natural integers (**sword**) and signed and unsigned long integers (**sb4** and **ub4**).

Pointers

Be careful to pass all pointer parameters as valid addresses. When a null pointer (0) is passed to an OCI function, Oracle recommends that you cast it to the appropriate datatype.

When a pointer is passed as a parameter, storage must be allocated in the OCI program for the data indicated by the pointer. OCI routines never allocate storage for program objects.

String literals can be passed to an OCI function where the parameter datatype is **text ***, as shown in the previous example with the call to the **oparse** function.

Parameter Classifications

There are three classifications of parameters in the OCI function descriptions: required, optional, and unused.

Required Parameters

Required parameters are used by Oracle to process the OCI function. The OCI program must supply valid values for each required parameter.

Optional Parameters

The use of optional parameters depends on the requirements of the OCI program. Square brackets ([ ]) are used to indicate optional parameters.

Optional parameters that are not used must still have parameters passed for them. A value of –1 should be passed for unused integer parameters, and a null pointer (0) should be passed for unused pointer parameters.

Unused Parameters

Unused parameters are not used by Oracle, at least for the C language. Unused parameters exist so that the OCI functions are consistent across all language definitions. For example, some parameters that would be used by OCI functions written in COBOL would not be used by OCI functions written in C. From C, these parameters should be passed the same way as optional parameters.

Parameter Modes

Parameters for the OCI functions are described in terms of their datatype and their mode. Parameters can have one of the following modes:

■ **IN**   A parameter that passes data to the OCI function

■ **OUT**   A parameter that outputs data from the OCI function on this or a subsequent function call

■ **IN/OUT**   A parameter that passes data to the OCI function and outputs data on this or a subsequent function call

Function Return Value

When called from a C program, OCI functions return an integer value. A return value of zero indicates that the function completed without error. A nonzero return value indicates that an error occurred. When an error occurs, you should check the return code field in the cursor data area (CDA) to get the error number. The function **oerhms** can be called to get the error message text associated with the number.

OCI Function Definitions

This section describes each OCI function available in the Oracle run-time library. The descriptions consist of:

■ The purpose of the function

■ The prototype that defines the function name and its parameter list

■ A table describing each parameter

■ Notes on how the function is used (with examples, where applicable)

■ Related functions that affect or are used with the function

The functions are described in alphabetical order for easy reference.

obndra

The purpose of this function is to associate the address of a program variable or array with a placeholder in an SQL statement or PL/SQL block. The bind variable will be used in place of a PL/SQL table in the block.

Prototype

```
obndra(struct cda_def *cursor,
       text *sqlvar,
       [sword sqlvl,]
       ub1 *progv,
       sword progvl,
       sword ftype,
       <sword scale,>
       [sb2 *indp,]
       [ub2 *alen,]
       [ub2 *arcode,]
       [ub4 maxsiz,]
       [ub4 *cursiz,]
       <text *fmt,>
       <sword fmtl,>
       <sword fmtt>);
```

Table C-1 describes the parameters for **obndra**.

Parameter	Mode	Description
cursor	IN/OUT	A pointer to the cursor data associated with the SQL statement by the **oparse** call.
sqlvar	IN	Specifies the address of a character string containing the name of a placeholder (including the preceding colon) in the SQL statement.
sqlvl	IN	The length of the character string sqlvar, including the preceding colon. If the placeholder name is a null-terminated character string, this parameter can be omitted (passed as –1).

TABLE C-1.   *obndra parameter descriptions*

Parameter	Mode	Description
progv[1]	IN/OUT[2]	A pointer to a program variable or array of program variables from which input data will be retrieved, or into which output data will be placed, when **oexec** is executed.
progvl	IN	The length, in bytes, of the program variable or array element. Since **obndra** might be called only once for many different progv values on successive execute calls, progvl must contain the maximum length of progv.
ftype	IN	The external datatype of the program variable in the user program. Oracle converts the program variable from external to internal format before it is bound to the SQL statement.
scale	IN	Only used for PACKED DECIMAL variables, which are not normally used in C. Set this parameter to –1.
indp[1]	IN/OUT[2]	A pointer to an indicator parameter, or array of indicator variables if progv is an array. As an array, indp must contain at least the same number of elements as progv.
alen[1]	IN/OUT[2]	A pointer to an array of elements containing the length of the data. This is the effective length of the bind variable element, not the size of the array. If arr is an IN parameter, each element in alen should be set to the length of the data in the corresponding element in the arr array before the execute call. If arr is an OUT parameter, the length of the returned data appears in alen after the PL/SQL block is executed. Once the bind is done using **obndra**, you can change the data length of the bind variable without rebinding. However, the length cannot be greater than that specified in alen.

TABLE C-1.   *obndra parameter descriptions (continued)*

Parameter	Mode	Description
arcode[1]	OUT[3]	An array containing the column-level error return codes. This parameter points to an array that will contain the error code for the bind variable after the execute call. The error codes that can be returned in arcode are those that indicate that data in progv has been truncated or that a null occurred on a SELECT or PL/SQL FETCH. If **obndra** is being used to bind an array of elements, then arcode must point to an array of at least equal size.
maxsiz	IN	The maximum size of the array being bound. Values range from 1 to 32,512, but the maximum size of the array depends on the datatype. The maximum array size is 32,512 divided by the internal size of the datatype. If **obndra** is being used to bind a scalar, set this parameter to zero. A value of 1 means an array one element long.
cursiz	IN/OUT[2]	A pointer to the actual number of elements in the array. If progv is an IN parameter, set the cursiz parameter to the size of the array being bound. If progv is an OUT parameter, the number of valid elements being returned in the progv array is returned after the SQL statement or PL/SQL block is executed. If **obndra** is being used to bind a scalar, set this parameter to the null pointer ((ub4 *) 0).
fmt	IN	Not normally used in C.
fmtl	IN	Not normally used in C.
fmtt	IN	Not normally used in C.

Notes:

1. If maxsiz > 1, must be an array with cardinality at least as great as maxsiz.

2. IN/OUT parameter used or returned on the execute or fetch call.

3. OUT parameter returned on the fetch call.

TABLE C-1.   *obndra parameter descriptions (continued)*

Usage Notes

The function **obndra** can be used in place of **obndrv** to bind scalar variables in an OCI program to placeholders in an SQL statement or a PL/SQL block. The **obndra** function has a parameter, *alen,* that allows you to change the size of the bound variable without actually rebinding the variable.

When you bind arrays in a program to PL/SQL tables, you must use **obndra**. This function provides additional parameters that allow you to control the maximum size of the table and to retrieve the current table size after the block has been executed.

The **obndra** function must be called after a call to **oparse** to parse the statement containing the PL/SQL block and before calling **oexn** or **oexec** to execute it.

Once you have bound a program variable, you can change the value in the variable and length of the variable and reexecute the block without rebinding.

However, if you must change the datatype of the variable, you must reparse the statement or block and rebind the variable before reexecuting.

Related Functions

obndrv, **oparse**, **oexec**, **oexn**

obndrn

The purpose of this function is to associate the address of a program variable with the specified placeholder in the SQL statement. The placeholder is identified by number.

Prototype

```
obndrn(struct cda_def *cursor,
       sword sqlvn,
       ub1 *progv,
       sword progv1,
       sword ftype,
       <sword scale,>
       [sb2 *indp,]
       <text *fmt,>
       <sword fmt1,>
       <sword fmtt>);
```

Table C-2 describes the parameters for **obndrn**.

Parameter	Mode	Description
cursor	IN/OUT	A pointer to the CDA associated with the SQL statement by the **oparse** call.
sqlvn	IN	A placeholder in the SQL statement referenced by the cursor by number. For example, if sqlvn is an integer literal or a variable equal to 2, it refers to all placeholders identified by :2 within the SQL statement.
progv	IN/OUT[1]	A pointer to a program variable or array of program variables from which input data will be retrieved, or into which output data will be placed, when **oexec**, **oexn**, or **oexfet** is executed.
progvl	IN	The length, in bytes, of the program variable or array element. Since **obndra** might be called only once for many different progv values on successive execute calls, progvl must contain the maximum length of progv.
ftype	IN	The external datatype of the program variable in the user program. Oracle converts the program variable from external to internal format before it is bound to the SQL statement.
scale	IN	Only used for PACKED DECIMAL variables, which are not normally used in C. Set this parameter to –1.
indp	IN/OUT[1]	A pointer to an indicator parameter, or array of indicator variables if progv is an array. As an array, indp must contain at least the same number of elements as progv.
fmt	IN	Not normally used in C.
fmtl	IN	Not normally used in C.
fmtt	IN	Not normally used in C.

Note:

   1. If the SQL statement is an anonymous PL/SQL block that assigns to the bind variable, progv and indp will be set by the **oexec** call.

TABLE C-2. *obndrn parameter descriptions*

Usage Notes

obndrn is used just like **obndrv**, except the placeholders in the SQL statement are numbers rather than names. The same four pieces of information are passed: the address of the bind variable, the address of an associated indicator variable, the length of the bind variable, and the external datatype of the variable. An SQL statement that could be used for **obndrn** would be

```
select * from employee
  where state = :1
  and pay_rate = :2
```

while a statement for **obndrv** would be

```
select * from employee
  where state = :b_state
  and pay_rate = :b_pay_rate
```

Related Functions

odescr, **oexec**, **oexfet**, **oexn**, **oparse**

obndrv

The purpose of this function is to associate the address of a program variable with the specified placeholder in the SQL statement. The placeholder is identified by name.

Prototype

```
obndrv(struct cda_def *cursor,
       text *sqlvar,
       [sword sqlvl,]
       ub1 *progv,
       sword progv1,
       sword ftype,
       <sword scale,>
       [sb2 *indp,]
       <text *fmt,>
       <sword fmt1,>
       <sword fmtt>);
```

Table C-3 describes the parameters for **obndrv**.

Parameter	Mode	Description
cursor	IN/OUT	A pointer to the CDA associated with the SQL statement by the **oparse** call.
sqlvar	IN	A placeholder in the SQL statement referenced by the cursor by number. For example, if sqlvn is an integer literal or a variable equal to 2, it refers to all placeholders identified by *:2* within the SQL statement.
sqlvl	IN	The length of the string pointed to by sqlvar. If sqlvar points to a null-terminated string, this parameter can contain –1.
progv[1]	IN/OUT	A pointer to a program variable or array of program variables from which input data will be retrieved, or into which output data will be placed, when **oexec**, **oexn**, or **oexfet** is executed.
progvl	IN	The length, in bytes, of the program variable or array element. Since **obndra** might be called only once for many different progv values on successive execute calls, progvl must contain the maximum length of progv.
ftype	IN	The external datatype of the program variable in the user program. Oracle converts the program variable from external to internal format before it is bound to the SQL statement.
scale	IN	Only used for PACKED DECIMAL variables, which are not normally used in C. Set this parameter to –1.
indp[1]	IN/OUT	A pointer to an indicator parameter, or array of indicator variables if progv is an array. As an array, indp must contain at least the same number of elements as progv.
fmt	IN	Not normally used in C.
fmtl	IN	Not normally used in C.
fmtt	IN	Not normally used in C.

Note:

   1. If the SQL statement is an anonymous PL/SQL block that assigns to the bind variable, progv and indp will be set by the **oexec** call.

TABLE C-3.   *obndrv parameter descriptions*

Usage Notes

obndrv is the most commonly used bind function. It is called after **oparse** and before **oexec** or **oexfet**. During the bind, the address of the buffer, the external datatype, the length of the buffer, and the address of an associated indicator variable are passed to the database. This is true regardless of the bind function used. To change any of this information, you must rebind by issuing the **obndrv** call again. Note that you can change the contents of the buffer and/or the indicator without rebinding, since the addresses of these quantities won't change.

The value of the bind variable (contents of the buffer pointed to by progv) is examined when the statement is executed via **oexec** or **oexfet**.

Related Functions

odescr, oexec, oexfet, oexn, oparse

obreak

This function is the only OCI function that can be called while another function is executing. Its purpose is to interrupt the currently executing function.

Prototype

```
sword obreak(struct cda_def *lda);
```

Parameter	Mode	Description
lda	IN	Address of a logon data area (LDA) in your program

Usage Notes

obreak is not available on all operating systems. To work successfully, the operating system needs to be able to interrupt the currently running program. This is the only way **obreak** can be called since an OCI function must be executing on the connection indicated by the LDA passed to it.

The following program, from the *Programmer's Guide to the Oracle Call Interfaces*, illustrates the use of **obreak**. The program must be linked "two-task" to work properly. Two-task linking is the default on most systems and means that a separated process is started when the program connects to the database. This *shadow* process communicates with the user process as the program runs. Note the use of the SIGNAL.H header file and the signal and alarm built-in functions. These functions are standard on UNIX and VAX/VMS systems but are not available under Windows.

This program does not have complete error handling or details for the other OCI functions. Its purpose is to demonstrate an application of the **obreak** function.

```c
#include <stdio.h>
#include <signal.h>
#include <ocidfn.h>

#define ANSI_C
#include <ocidem.h>

Lda_Def lda;
Cda_Def cda;

void sighandler(void);
void (*old_sig)();
void err(void);

main() {
  text *uid = "scott";
  text *pwd = "tiger";
  ub1 hda[256];
  text name[10];

  /* Connect to Oracle. Program must be linked two-task. Note
     that this is the default on UNIX and Windows systems. */
  if (orlon(&lda, hda, uid, -1, pwd, -1, 0)) {
    printf("Cannot connect as %s\n", uid);
    exit(1);
  }

  if (oopen(&cda, &lda, 0, -1, -1, 0, -1)) {
    printf("Cannot open cursor data area");
    exit(1);
  }

  /* Save pointer to the current signal-handler function. */
  old_sig = signal(SIGALRM, sighandler);

  /* Parse a query statement. */
  if (oparse(&cda, "select ename from emp", -1, 0, 2))
    err();

  /* Define the output variable. */
  if (odefin(&cda, 1, name, sizeof(name), 1, -1, (sb2 *) 0,
             (text *) 0, 0, -1, (ub2 *) 0, (ub2 *) 0))
    err();
```

```
   if (oexec(&cda))
     err();

   /* Set the timeout to 6 seconds. This will fire the signal
      handler. */
   alarm(6);

   /* Begin the query. */
   for (;;) {
     if (ofetch(&cda)) {
       /* Break if no data found. Should never happen, since the
          alarm should interrupt first. */
       if (cda.rc == 1403)
         break;
       /* When the alarm is signaled and obreak is called, you
          should get ORA-1013 at this point. */
       err();
     }
     printf("%10.10s\n", name);
     /* Make sure you won't finish before the alarm. */
     sleep(1);
   }

   printf("Unexpected termination.\n");
   err();
}

/* Define the new alarm function. This is where obreak will
   be called. */
void sighandler(void) {
   sword rv;
   fprintf(stderr, "Caught alarm!\n");
   /* Call obreak */
   if (rv = obreak(&lda))
     fprintf(stderr, "Error %d on obreak\n", rv);
   else
     fprintf(stderr, "obreak performed\n");
}

void err(void) {
   text errmsg[512];
```

```
    sword n;
    n = oerhms(&lda, cda.rc, errmsg, sizeof(errmsg));
    fprintf(stderr, "Oracle error %.s\n", errmsg);
    oclose(&cda);
    ologof(&lda);
    exit(1);
}
```

Related Function
orlon

ocan

This function cancels a query, which frees resources associated with the query. It
does not free memory associated with the cursor itself.

Prototype

```
sword ocan(struct cda_def *cursor);
```

Parameter	Mode	Description
cursor	IN/OUT	Address of CDA in your program

Usage Notes
ocan should be called after you have fetched the last row from a cursor. After **ocan**,
you can no longer fetch unless the query is reexecuted or a new statement is parsed
with **oparse** in the same CDA. **oparse** will cancel the current statement before
beginning the parse. The *cancel* parameter of **oexfet** calls **ocan** after the data has
been fetched.

Related Functions
oexfet, **oparse**

oclose

This call frees all resources associated with a cursor.

Prototype

```
sword oclose(struct cda_def *cursor);
```

Parameter	Mode	Description
cursor	IN/OUT	Address of a CDA in your program

Usage Notes

oclose should be the last call made for a CDA. Any resources allocated for this CDA by **oopen** are freed by **oclose**. Before the CDA can be used again, it must be reopened with **oopen**. If the current statement has not been canceled, **oclose** will call **ocan** first.

A cursor should be opened once (with **oopen**) and closed once (with **oclose**). You can execute several statements in the same cursor simply by parsing another SQL statement. It is not necessary to close and reopen the cursor to process another statement in it.

Related Functions

oclose, **oopen**

ocof

This function turns autocommit off.

Prototype

```
sword ocof(struct cda_def *lda);
```

Parameter	Mode	Description
lda	IN/OUT	Address of an LDA in your program

Usage Notes

ocof turns the autocommit feature off. This is the default. Autocommit will issue a commit after every SQL statement issued by your program, which can significantly affect performance. **ocon** turns autocommit back on. The **ocom** function commits the current transaction.

Related Functions

ocom, **ocon**

ocom

This function commits the current transaction.

Prototype

```
sword  ocom  (struct cda_def *lda);
```

Parameter	Mode	Description
lda	IN/OUT	Address of an LDA in your program

Usage Notes

ocom should be called after each transaction in your program. To roll back a transaction, use the **orol** function. Note the difference between **ocom** and **ocon**—**ocom** issues a single commit, while **ocon** turns autocommit on.

Related Functions

ocon, orol

ocon

This function turns autocommit on.

Prototype

```
sword ocon (struct cda_def *lda);
```

Parameter	Mode	Description
lda	IN/OUT	Address of an LDA in your program

Usage Notes

With autocommit on, a commit will automatically be issued after every SQL statement. This will affect performance and will greatly reduce the benefits of transactions. Thus, **ocon** should be used with care, if at all. **ocof** turns autocommit off (the default). Note the difference between **ocom** and **ocon**—**ocom** issues a single commit, while **ocon** turns autocommit on.

Related Functions

ocof, ocom, orol

odefin

odefin is similar to **obndrv** except that **odefin** is used for output variables (the define operation), while **obndrv** is used for input variables (the bind operation). It is valid only for queries and should be called after **obndrv** but before **oexec** or **oexfet**.

Prototype

```
sword odefin(struct cda_def *cursor,
             sword pos,
             ub1 *buf,
             sword bufl,
             sword ftype,
             <sword scale>,
             [sb2 *indp],
             <text *fmt>,
             <sword fmtl>,
             <sword fmtt>,
             [ub2 *rlen],
             [ub2 *rcode])
```

Table C-4 describes the parameters for **odefin**.

Usage Notes

odefin is similar to **obndrv**. Both functions pass the same four pieces of information about variables in your program: the address of the variable, the length of the variable, the external datatype to be associated with the variable, and the address of an associated indicator variable. The difference is that the define operation passes this information about output variables, while the bind operation does the same for input variables.

If the SQL statement is not a query, calling **odefin**, **odescr**, **ofetch**, or **ofen** will result in an error. For nonqueries, only the parse, bind, and execute steps need to be performed. For a query, after the execute, the define and fetch steps are necessary. The define step is done via **odefin**.

If buf points to an array, then a batch fetch is done. Use **oexfet** or **ofen** to specify the number of rows in the array. **odefin** is used to pass information about each element of the array only.

Related Functions

oparse, obndrv, oexec, oexfet, ofetch, ofen

Parameter	Mode	Description
cursor	IN/OUT	Address of a CDA in your program. This CDA should already have a statement parsed in it (via **oparse**).
pos	IN	Position in the select list. The first select-list item is at position 1, the next at 2, and so on. **odefin** is usually called in a loop, with this parameter increased by 1 each time. The loop ends when **odefin** returns ORA-1007: variable not in select list.
buf	IN/OUT[1]	Address of the output buffer in which the data will be written. This parameter can also point to an array.
bufl	IN	Length of the output buffer. If buf is an array, bufl should be the length of each element.
ftype	IN	External datatype to be associated with this output variable. Oracle will convert the select-list item from its internal datatype into the external datatype given by this parameter.
scale	IN	Not normally used in C. Pass as –1.
indp	IN/OUT[1]	Address of an indicator variable. If buf points to an array, indp should point to an array of two-byte integers. If an indicator variable isn't desired, pass as null.
fmt	IN	Not normally used in C.
fmtl	IN	Not normally used in C.
fmtt	IN	Not normally used in C.
rlen	IN/OUT[1]	Pointer to a buffer in which Oracle will place the actual length of the output data. Note that the bufl parameter won't change. If buf points to an array, then rlen should also point to an array of ub2's. If this information isn't desired, pass as null.

Note:

1. These parameters aren't written to by the **odefin** call but by the **oexfet**, **oexec**, or **ofen** call.

TABLE C-4.   *odefin parameter descriptions*

odescr

This call implements the describe operation. This is valid only for queries and is optional. The purpose of the describe is to return information about the select list of the query. Based on this information, the define operation can be performed.

Prototype

```
sword odescr(struct cda_def *cursor,
             sword pos,
             sb4 *dbsize,
             sb2 *dbtype,
             sb1 *cbuf,
             sb4 *cbufl,
             sb4 *dsize,
             sb2 *prec,
             sb2 *scale,
             sb2 *nullok);
```

Table C-5 describes the parameters for **odescr**.

Usage Notes

The describe is usually done in the same loop as the define operation. The loop can be structured as follows:

```
for (pos = 1; pos < MAX_NUMBER_OF_ITEMS; pos++) {
  rv = odescr(&cda, pos, ...);
  if (rv == 1007) break;
  if (rv < 0)
    handle_error(&cda);
  /* Based on values returned by odescr, determine the
     appropriate type for the output buffer. */
  odescr(&cda, pos, ...);
}
```

If the statement is not a query, it is an error to perform a describe. If the parse has been deferred, it is performed at the time of **odescr**. Thus, **odescr** will always cause a network round trip. Table C-6 shows the values for the *dbsize* parameter.

Related Functions
oparse, odefin

Parameter	Mode	Description
cursor	IN/OUT	A pointer to a CDA in your program. This context area should contain a query that has been parsed via **oparse**.
pos	IN	Position within the select list. The first select-list item is at position 1, the next at position 2, and so on. This corresponds to the pos parameter of **odefin**. If pos is greater than the actual number of select-list items in the query, the error ORA-1007: variable not in select list is returned.
dbsize[1]	OUT	A pointer to a buffer in which the maximum size of the select-list item will be written. This size comes from the data dictionary; some valid values are given next in Table C-6.
dbtype[1]	OUT	A pointer to a buffer in which the internal datatype of the select-list item will be written.
cbuf[1]	OUT	A pointer to a buffer in which the name of the select-list item will be written. This is the name of the column, expression, or alias at this select-list position. Note that this value is not null-terminated.
cbufl	IN/OUT	Before the call to **odescr**, cbufl should contain the maximum length of cbuf. After the call, cbufl will contain the actual length of cbuf.
dsize[1]	OUT	A pointer to a buffer in which the maximum display size of the select-list item will be written. This can be different from the dsize value—for example, when the TO_CHAR or SUBSTR function is used.
prec[1]	OUT	A pointer to a buffer in which the precision of numeric select-list items will be written. If the select-list item is not a number, then this value is not relevant.[2]
scale[1]	OUT	A pointer to a buffer in which the scale of numeric select-list items will be written. If the select-list item is not a number, then this value is not relevant.[2]

TABLE C-5.   *odescr parameter descriptions*

Parameter	Mode	Description
nullok[1]	OUT	A pointer to a buffer that will contain 0 if the select-list item cannot be null and nonzero if nulls are permitted for the select-list item.

Note:

1. If the information given by these parameters isn't desired, pass null for them.

2. *prec* and *scale* are useful in determining whether the select-list item can fit into an integer or floating-point variable.

TABLE C-5.   *odescr parameter descriptions (continued)*

odessp

odessp is used to describe stored procedures. It returns information about the parameters to procedures, whether they are stored in a package or not.

Prototype

```
sword odessp(struct cda_def *lda,
             text *objnam,
             size_t onlen,
             ub1 *rsv1,
             size_t rsv1ln,
             ub1 *rsv2,
             size_t rsv2ln,
             ub2 *ovrld,
             ub2 *pos,
             ub2 *level,
             text **argnam,
             ub2 *arnlen,
             ub2 *dtype,
             ub1 *defsup,
             ub1* mode,
             ub4 *dtsiz,
             sb2 *prec,
             sb2 *scale,
             ub1 *radix,
```

```
        ub4 *spare,
        ub4 *arrsiz);
```

Table C-7 describes the parameters to **odessp**.

Usage Notes

odessp is especially useful when your program dynamically creates an anonymous PL/SQL block to call a stored procedure. The procedure may not be known until run time, so **odessp** provides the necessary information about the procedure or function's parameters. Based on this information, you can provide the appropriate external datatypes for the bind variables. This process is very similar to the **odescr/odefin** process. Unlike **odescr**, however, only one call to **odessp** is necessary.

Internal Type Given by dbtype	Value Returned by dbsize	Comments
CHAR, VARCHAR2, RAW	Length of the column in the table	This is the only case in which the dbsize value is variable.
NUMBER	22	Although numbers are actually of variable lengths, this parameter is returning the maximum length. A NUMBER will take up at most 22 bytes.
DATE	7	All dates are exactly 7 bytes long.
LONG, LONG RAW	0	The maximum length of a LONG or LONG RAW column is 2 gigabytes.
ROWID	System-dependent	On UNIX systems, ROWIDs are usually 13 bytes long. This is the length of the internal format of a ROWID, not the external format, which is always an 18-character string.

TABLE C-6.   *values for the dbsize parameter*

Parameter	Mode	Description
lda	IN/OUT	A pointer to a valid logon data area in your program, which has been established with **orlon**. Note that this is an LDA, not a CDA.
objnam	IN	Name of the object to describe, including the schema if desired. The object can be standalone or in a package. If a synonym is passed here, it will be translated.
onlen	IN	Length of objnam. If objnam is a null-terminated string, pass as –1.
rsv1	IN	Reserved for future use. Pass as null.
rsv1ln	IN	Reserved for future use. Pass as 0.
rsv2	IN	Reserved for future use. Pass as null.
rsv2ln	IN	Reserved for future use. Pass as 0.
ovrld[1]	OUT	An array indicating whether the procedure is overloaded. If not, 0 is returned. Otherwise, 1..n is returned for a procedure overloaded n times. Information about each overloaded procedure is returned, with a different value of ovrld for each.
pos[1]	OUT	An array indicating the parameter's position in the parameter list. The first parameter is at position 1. If pos = 0, it is describing the return type of a function.
level[1]	OUT	For scalar parameters, level returns 0. For a record, each level of nesting increases level by 1. A PL/SQL table has one element at level 0 (the table itself) and one element at level 1 (the type of the table).
argnam[1]	OUT	A pointer to an array of strings. Each element will hold the name of the corresponding parameter in the parameter list of the function. The strings are not null-terminated, and the maximum length of each string is 30.
arnlen[1]	OUT	The length in bytes of the corresponding element of argnam.

TABLE C-7. *odessp parameter descriptions*

dtype[1]	OUT	The Oracle internal datatype for each parameter. If the parameter is a record, 250 is returned. If it is a table, 251 is returned. A value of 0 indicates the procedure has no parameters.
defsup[1]	OUT	If 0, the corresponding parameter has no default value. If 1, a default value was supplied in the procedure or function specification.
mode[1]	OUT	If 0, the corresponding parameter is an IN parameter. If 1, the parameter is OUT. If 2, the parameter is IN/OUT.
dtsiz[1]	OUT	The maximum size of the datatype, in bytes. This parameter returns the same values as **odescr**. See Table C-6 for more information.
prec[1]	OUT	The precision of the corresponding parameter. This is only valid if the parameter is numeric (dtype = 2).
scale[1]	OUT	The scale of the corresponding parameter. This is only valid if the parameter is numeric (dtype = 2).
radix[1]	OUT	The radix of the corresponding parameter. This is only valid if the parameter is numeric (dtype = 2). This parameter is seldom, if ever, used.
spare[1]	OUT	Reserved for future use. Unlike the rsv* parameters, however, this needs to be allocated as an array of ub4's.
arrsiz	IN/OUT	The number of elements in each of the previous arrays. On input, this should be set to the maximum size of the arrays. On output, it will be set to the actual number of values filled in.

Note:

1. All of these parameters are arrays. They should be allocated prior to the call to **odessp**. Each array element provides information about one parameter to the procedure or function. The size of each array is passed via the *arrsiz* parameter. All the arrays should be the same size—if not, use the smallest cardinality for the *arrsiz* value.

TABLE C-7.   *odessp parameter descriptions (continued)*

Related Functions
orlon, **odescr**

oerhms

oerhms is used for error handling.

Prototype

```
sword oerhms(struct cda_def *lda,
             sb2 rcode,
             text *buf,
             sword bufsiz);
```

Table C-8 describes the parameters for **oerhms**.

Usage Notes
Unlike most of the other OCI functions, **oerhms** will usually return a nonzero value. It returns the length of the string written to *buf*. The message text is the same as that returned by the **sqlglm** function with embedded SQL. The maximum length of an error message is 512 bytes. A typical use of **oerhms** is with an error-handling function, such as the following:

Parameter	Mode	Description
lda	IN/OUT	Address of an LDA in your program. The message text appropriate for the database to which this LDA points will be returned. If it points to a V6 database rather than V7, some of the error message texts may be different. V7 also has more error codes than V6.
rcode	IN	Contains the error code for which you want the text. This is usually the rc field of another LDA or CDA.
buf	OUT	Buffer into which the error message text will be written. The message text will be null-terminated.
bufsiz	IN	Initial size of buf.

TABLE C-8. *oerhms parameter descriptions*

```
void handle_error(struct cda *lda, struct cda *cda) {
  sword BufferSize;
  text MessageBuffer[512];

  BufferSize = oerhms(lda, cda->rc, MessageBuffer,
    sizeof(MessageBuffer);
  printf("OCI Error!\n");
  printf("%s\n", MessageBuffer);
}
```

Related Function
orlon

oexec

This function executes the statement. It is called after **oparse** and **obndrv**. If the statement is a query, the data is then fetched with **ofen** or **ofetch**.

Prototype

```
sword oexec(struct cda_def *cursor);
```

Parameter	Mode	Description
cursor	IN/OUT	Pointer to a CDA in your program that contains a parsed statement

Usage Notes
Note that the only parameter of **oexec** is the CDA. This points to the context area that contains all the necessary information to execute the statement. If the statement is not a query, after **oexec**, processing is complete. If the statement is a query, the bind variables are examined during the execute. The active set is also determined, then retrieved via the fetch operation. The execute and fetch can be combined using the **oexfet** function. **oexec** is equivalent to the EXEC SQL OPEN embedded SQL command.

    oexec isn't used for array processing. If a batch operation is desired, you should use **oexn** instead. **oexec** is equivalent to **oexn** with *iters* set to zero.

Related Functions
oexn, ofetch, ofen, oexfet

Parameter	Mode	Description
cursor	IN/OUT	A pointer to a valid CDA in your program. This context area should point to a parsed and bound statement.
nrows	IN	The number of rows to fetch. This is used for a batch fetch. If nonzero, then arrays should have been passed in the **odefin** call rather than scalars.
cancel	IN	If nonzero, **ocan** is called after this batch of rows. After the query is canceled, no further rows can be returned.
exact	IN	If nonzero, **oexec** will return an error if the number of rows in the active set is not equal to nrows. This is similar to the SELECT_ERROR precompiler option. If it is nonzero, a cancel of the query is always performed regardless of the setting for cancel.

TABLE C-9. *oexfct parameter descriptions*

oexfet

oexfet executes a query and fetches the data in one call. It can also cancel the query in the same operation.

Prototype

```
sword  oexfet(struct cda_def *cursor,
              ub4 nrows,
              sword cancel,
              sword exact);
```

Table C-9 describes the parameters for **oexfet**.

Usage Notes
oexfet is preferred to calling **oexec**, **ofen**, and then **ocan**, since it requires only one network trip for all three operations. If there are more than *nrows* rows to fetch, **ofen** can be called (usually in a loop) to fetch the remaining rows. It is an error to call **oexfet** for a nonquery; use **oexn** instead.

Related Functions
oexec, **ofen**, **ocan**, **odefin**, **ofetch**

oexn

oexn is used to execute nonquery statements using the Oracle array interface. It should be called after **oparse** and **obndrv**.

Prototype

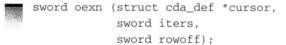

```
sword oexn (struct cda_def *cursor,
            sword iters,
            sword rowoff);
```

Table C-10 describes the parameters for **oexn**.

Usage Notes
oexn should be used instead of **oexec**. **oexec** is equivalent to **oexn** with *iters* set to zero. If an error occurs during execution of the statement, processing stops at the offending row. The rows processed count in the CDA (*rpc* field) can be used to determine the row that failed; rowoff can then be set to start with the next row. In this manner, only the correct rows will be inserted.

Related Functions
oexec, **oexfet**

Parameter	Mode	Description
cursor	IN/OUT	Address of a CDA in your program.
iters	IN	Total size of the arrays. The arrays should have been passed via the **obndrv** call. This is where you specify the number of rows—**obndrv** just included information on each element.
rowoff	IN	Zero-based offset within the arrays at which to start. If no error occurs, **oexen** will process (iters −rowoff) elements of the arrays.

TABLE C-10.   *oexn parameter descriptions*

ofen

ofen is used to fetch rows using the Oracle array interface (batch fetch). It should be called after the parse, bind, define, and execute operations. It is illegal to use **ofen** for nonqueries.

Prototype

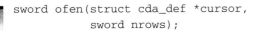

```
sword ofen(struct cda_def *cursor,
           sword nrows);
```

Table C-11 describes the parameters for **ofen**.

Usage Notes

ofen is preferred to **ofetch** since it can return more than one row at a time. If there are fewer than *nrows* rows remaining in the active set, then ORA-1403: no data found is returned.

   oexfet should be used rather than **oexec** and **ofetch** or **oexec** and **ofen**, since it will combine the calls to the database and result in increased performance.

Related Functions
ofetch, oexec, oexfet, odefin

ofetch

ofetch is used to return a single row from a query. It is valid after the parse and the define.

Parameter	Mode	Description
cursor	IN/OUT	A pointer to a valid CDA in your program. This context area should point to a query that has been parsed and executed.
nrows	IN	Number of rows to fetch. If > 1, then arrays should have been passed to **odefin** rather than scalars.

TABLE C-11.   *ofen parameter descriptions*

Prototype

```
sword   ofetch(struct cda_def *cursor);
```

Parameter	Mode	Description
cursor	IN/OUT	A pointer to a CDA containing a query that has been parsed, executed, and defined

Usage Notes

ofetch should be called after **oexec**. It will return one row of data into the buffers that have been passed by **odefin**. Each call to **ofetch** requires a trip to the database, so **ofetch** is usually combined with **oexec** via the **oexfet** call. This is significantly more efficient.

Related Functions

oexec, **ofen**, **oexfet**

oflng

oflng is used to fetch LONG or LONG RAW data in more than one piece. This avoids the necessity of allocating contiguous memory for the entire row.

Prototype

```
sword oflng(struct cda_def *cursor,
            sword pos,
            ub1 *buf,
            sb4 bufl,
            sword dtype,
            ub4 *retl,
            sb4 offset);
```

Table C-12 describes the parameters for **oflng**.

Usage Notes

Unless you have explicitly stored the length of LONG or LONG RAW data in another column in the table, there is no way to know the length of the column before the fetch. The maximum length of LONG or LONG RAW data is 2 gigabytes, which is impossible to allocate in one memory area. **oflng** allows you to fetch the data in more manageable chunks, or *blobs* (binary large objects). Note that this functionality is not available with Pro*C.

Parameter	Mode	Description
cursor	IN/OUT	A pointer to a valid CDA in your program. This context area should point to a query that has been executed and at least one row has been fetched.
pos	IN	Position within the select list of the LONG or LONG RAW column.
buf	OUT	Address of a buffer to hold the fetched piece.
bufl	IN	Length of buf, in bytes. This can change over successive calls to **oflng**, resulting in different-size pieces, if desired. The maximum length is 65,535.
dtype	IN	External datatype associated with this piece. This is usually LONG (8), LONG RAW (24), LONG VARCHAR (94), or LONG VARRAW (95).
retl	OUT	Actual number of bytes returned.
offset	IN	Zero-based offset within the data at which the piece starts. Data from byte offset to byte (offset + bufl) will be returned.

TABLE C-12.   *oflng parameter descriptions*

It is more efficient to retrieve the data starting from the beginning of the row and advancing toward the end than randomly or starting at the end. See the Oracle example CDEMO3.c for an example of how to use the **oflng** function.

Related Functions
ofetch, oexfet, odefin

ologof

This function disconnects from the database.

Prototype

```
sword ologof(struct cda_def *lda);
```

Parameter	Mode	Description
lda	IN/OUT	A pointer to a valid logon data area in your program. This LDA became valid via the **orlon** call.

Usage Notes

ologof should be the last OCI call made by your program. It will disconnect you from the database, similarly to the RELEASE qualifier of COMMIT and ROLLBACK. If there is a transaction pending when **ologof** is called, it is rolled back. Therefore, you should commit or roll back all transactions explicitly before calling **ologof**.

Related Functions

orlon, **ocom**, **orol**

oopen

oopen establishes a CDA for use.

Prototype

```
sword oopen (struct cda_def *cursor,
             struct cda_def *lda,
             text *dbn,
             sword dbnl,
             sword arsize,
             text *uid,
             sword uidl);
```

Table C-13 describes the parameters for **oopen**.

Usage Notes

The only two parameters of **oopen** that are still meaningful are the CDA and LDA. After the call, this context area is ready to have an SQL statement parsed in it via **oparse**. **oclose** will free any resources allocated by **oopen**.

Normally, cursors are only opened and closed once. You can execute many SQL statements in the same CDA without closing it.

Related Functions

orlon, **oclose**, **oparse**

Parameter	Mode	Description
cursor	OUT	A pointer to a CDA in your program. After the call, this CDA will be ready for use.
lda	IN/OUT	A pointer to a valid logon data area in your program, established via **orlon**.
dbn	IN	Included for version 2 compatibility. Pass as null.
dbnl	IN	Included for version 2 compatibility. Pass as –1.
arsize	IN	Not used in Oracle 7. This corresponds to the area size of the context area, which is no longer necessary. Pass as –1.
uid	IN	String containing the username and password, separated by a /. This parameter is not normally used; pass as null.
uidl	IN	Length of uid. Since uid is normally unused, pass as –1.

TABLE C-13. *oopen parameter descriptions*

oopt

This call is used to set run-time options for the CDA.

Prototype

```
sword oopt(struct cda_def *cursor,
           sword rbopt,
           sword waitopt);
```

Table C-14 describes the parameters for **oopt**.

Usage Notes
oopt is included only for compatibility with prior versions of Oracle. For new programs, there is little or no use for it.

Related Function
oopen

Parameter	Mode	Description
cursor	IN/OUT	A pointer to a valid CDA in your program.
rbopt	IN	Flag indicating whether the row or the transaction will be rolled back upon a nonfatal error. This flag is no longer valid in Oracle 7—only the row is rolled back.
waitopt	IN	If set to 4, an error will be returned if a resource is not available. If set to 0 (the default value), the program will wait for the resource.

TABLE C-14.   *oopt parameter descriptions*

oparse

oparse takes an SQL statement as input and parses it. The parse can optionally be deferred.

Prototype

```
sword oparse(struct cda_def *cursor,
             text *sqlstm,
             sb4 sqllen,
             sword defflg,
             ub4 lngflg);
```

Table C-15 describes the parameters for **oparse**.

Usage Notes

Table C-16 describes the *lngflg* parameter's values. Note that if *lnglfg* is set to 2, the program must connect to a Version 7 database.

During the parse, the execution plan for the statement is determined. The database will also check to see if the statement is in the shared pool. If so, the parsed representation already in the pool will be returned. If not, the statement is parsed and stored in the shared pool for future use.

DDL statements are executed immediately upon the parse, unless the parse is deferred. In the latter case, an **oexec** call is required to execute the statement. The statement can be any valid dataq definition, control, or manipulation statement or an anonymous PL/SQL block.

Parameter	Mode	Description
cursor	IN/OUT	A pointer to a valid cursor data in your program.. The context area became valid via the **oopen** call.
sqlstm	IN	String containing the SQL statement. Note that there is no trailing semicolon in the string unless it is an anonymous PL/SQL block.
sqllen	IN	The length of sqlstm. If the string is null-terminated, pass as –1.
defflg	IN	If nonzero, the parse is deferred until the describe or the execute, whichever comes first. If zero, the parse is executed immediately.[1]
lngflg	IN	Flag that determines the behavior for the statement. Valid values are listed in Table C-16. This flag is similar to the DBMS precompiler option.

Note:

1. The application needs to be linked in deferred mode for the parse to be deferred. This is the default on most platforms. If the application is linked in deferred mode, the bind and define operations are also deferred.

TABLE C-15. *oparse parameter descriptions*

Related Functions
oopen, obndrv, oexec

Value of lngflg	Behavior
0	Version 6 behavior. The database can be Version 6 or later.
1	Normal behavior for the database to which you are connected, which can be Version 6 or 7.
2	Oracle 7 behavior. The database version must be at least 7.0.

TABLE C-16. *values for the lngflg parameter*

orlon

orlon establishes a connection to the database.

Prototype

```
sword orlon(struct cda_def *lda,
            ub1 *hda,
            text *uid,
            sword uidl,
            text *pswd,
            sword pswdl,
            sword audit);
```

Table C-17 describes the parameters for **orlon**.

Parameter	Mode	Description
lda	IN/OUT	A pointer to a valid logon data area in your program.
hda	IN/OUT	A buffer allocated by your program. It should be at least 256 bytes. On 64-bit platforms, the HDA should be 512 bytes.
uid	IN	Oracle username to which to connect. This string can also consist of the username and the password, separated by a slash(/). A connect string can follow the password, separated by a @ character. See the following section for valid examples.
uidl	IN	Length of uid. If uid is a null-terminated string, pass as −1.
pswd	IN	Password for the Oracle userid. If uid contains the password as part of the string, can be passed as null. See the following section for valid examples.
pswdl	IN	Length of pswd. If pswd is null-terminated, pass as −1.
audit	IN	No longer used; pass as −1.

TABLE C-17.   *orlon parameter descriptions*

Usage Notes

orlon should be the first OCI statement executed by your program. It establishes the connection to the database, similar to EXEC SQL CONNECT for Pro*C. The userid and password are specified by *uid* and *pswd*, and valid values for these parameters are:

uid	pswd
scott	tiger
scott/tiger	null
scott/tiger@newyork	null
scott@newyork	tiger

Related Functions
ologof, **sqllda**

orol

This call rolls back the current transaction.

Prototype

```
sword orol(struct cda_def *lda);
```

Parameter	Mode	Description
lda	IN/OUT	Address of an LDA in your program

Usage Notes

orol will roll back the current transaction and end the transaction as well. **ocom** will commit the current transaction.

Related Function
ocom

sqllda

This function is used to obtain a valid LDA based on a connection made via embedded SQL.

Prototype

```
void sqllda(struct cda_def *lda);
```

Parameter	Mode	Description
lda	IN/OUT	A pointer to an LDA in your program. After the call, this LDA will be valid for the same connection made via EXEC SQL CONNECT.

Usage Notes

sqllda is used when you want to have both embedded SQL and OCI calls use the same connection. They will also be in the same transaction. It should be called immediately after the EXEC SQL CONNECT statement and returns a valid LDA for that connection. Note that no HDA is necessary.

```
/* Establish connection 1. */
EXEC SQL CONNECT :username IDENTIFIED BY :password;
sqllda(lda1);

/* Establish connection 2. */
EXEC SQL CONNECT :username2 IDENTIFIED BY :password2
  AT db2 USING :connect_string;
sqllda(lda2);
...
EXEC SQL COMMIT WORK RELEASE;
EXEC SQL AT db2 COMMIT WORK RELEASE;
```

The connection should be terminated via embedded SQL, *not* by **ologof**.

Related Functions
ologof, orlon

sqlld2

sqlld2 provides a valid LDA when the connection is made from the XA interface using a TP monitor.

Prototype

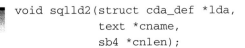

```
void sqlld2(struct cda_def *lda,
            text *cname,
            sb4 *cnlen);
```

Table C-18 describes the parameters for **sqlld2**.

Usage Notes

sqlld2 should only be used in an XA environment. Establish the connection with the TP monitor, then call **sqlld2** to get a valid LDA for this connection. **sqlld2** works similarly to **sqllda**.

Related Function

sqllda

Parameter	Mode	Description
lda	OUT	A pointer to an LDA. The call will initialize the LDA for future use. No HDA is required.
cname	IN	The name of the connection, as indicated in the XA open string. If not specified, the default connection is used.
cnlen	IN	A pointer to the length of cname. If passed as 0, the default connection is used regardless of cname.

TABLE C-18.   *sqlld2 parameter descriptions*

APPENDIX D

Reserved Words and Keywords

This appendix contains the reserved words and keywords for the Oracle Server, Pro*C, and PL/SQL.

Oracle Reserved Words

Table D-1 lists the words that are reserved by the Oracle Server and Pro*C. They have a special meaning to Oracle and cannot be redefined. You cannot use them to name database objects such as columns, tables, or indexes.

ACCESS	DEFAULT	INTEGER	OPTION	SQLBUF
ADD	DELETE	INTERSECT	OR	START
ALL	DESC	INTO	ORDER	SUCCESSFUL
ALTER	DISTINCT	IS	PCTFREE	SYNONYM
AND	DROP	LEVEL	PRIOR	SYSDATE
ANY	ELSE	LIKE	PRIVILEGES	TABLE
ARRAYLEN	EXCLUSIVE	LOCK	PUBLIC	THEN
AS	EXISTS	LONG	RAW	TO
ASC	FILE	MAXEXTENTS	RENAME	TRIGGER
AUDIT	FLOAT	MODE	RESOURCE	UID
BETWEEN	FOR	MODIFY	REVOKE	UNION
BY	FROM	NOAUDIT	ROW	UNIQUE
CHAR	GRANT	NOCOMPRESS	ROWID	UPDATE
CHECK	GROUP	NOT	ROWLABEL	USER
CLUSTER	HAVING	NOTFOUND	ROWNUM	VALIDATE
COLUMN	IDENTIFIED	NOWAIT	ROWS	VALUES
COMMENT	IMMEDIATE	NULL	SELECT	VARCHAR
COMPRESS	IN	NUMBER	SESSION	VARCHAR2
CONNECT	INCREMENT	OF	SET	VIEW
CREATE	INDEX	OFFLINE	SHARE	WHENEVER
CURRENT	INITIAL	ON	SIZE	WHERE
DATE	INSERT	ONLINE	SMALLINT	WITH
DECIMAL				

TABLE D-1. *Oracle reserved words*

Oracle Keywords

Table D-2 lists keywords that have special meaning to Oracle but are not reserved words. These words could be redefined, but it is highly recommended that it not be done. Some of these words might eventually become reserved words.

ADMIN	DEC	LINK	OBJNO
AFTER	DECLARE	LISTS	OFF
ALLOCATE	DISABLE	LOGFILE	OLD
ANALYZE	DISMOUNT	MANAGE	ONLY
ARCHIVE	DOUBLE	MANUAL	OPCODE
ARCHIVELOG	DUMP	MAX	OPEN
AUTHORIZATION	EACH	MAXARCHLOGS	OPTIMAL
BACKUP	ENABLE	MAXDATAFILES	OWN
BECOME	END	MAXINSTANCES	PACKAGE
BEFORE	ESCAPE	MAXLOGFILES	PARALLEL
BEGIN	EVENTS	MAXLOGMEMBERS	PCTINCREASE
BLOCK	EXCEPT	MAXTRANS	PCTUSED
BODY	EXCEPTIONS	MAXVALUE	PLAN
CACHE	EXECUTE	MIN	PRIMARY
CANCEL	EXPLAIN	MINEXTENTS	PRIVATE
CASCADE	EXTENT	MINVALUE	PROCEDURE
CHANGE	EXTERNALLY	MOUNT	PROFILE
CHARACTER	FLUSH	NEXT	QUOTA
CHECKPOINT	FREELIST	NEW	RBA
CLOSE	FREELISTS	NOARCHIVELOG	READ
COMMIT	FORCE	NOCACHE	REAL
COMPILE	FOREIGN	NOCYCLE	RECOVER
CONSTRAINT	FUNCTION	NOMAXVALUE	REFERENCES
CONSTRAINTS	GROUPS	NOMINVALUE	REFERENCING
CONTENTS	INCLUDING	NONE	RESETLOGS
CONTINUE	INDICATOR	NOORDER	RESTRICTED
CONTROLFILE	INITRANS	NORESETLOGS	REUSE
CYCLE	INSTANCE	NORMAL	ROLE
DATABASE	INT	NOSORT	ROLES
DATAFILE	KEY	NUMERIC	ROLLBACK
DBA	LAYER	ONLY	SAVEPOINT

TABLE D-2.   *Oracle keywords*

SCHEMA	STATEMENT_ID	TEMPORARY	UNLIMITED
SCN	STATISTICS	THREAD	UNTIL
SEGMENT	STOP	TIME	USE
SEQUENCE	STORAGE	TRACING	USING
SHARED	SWITCH	TRANSACTION	WHEN
SNAPSHOT	SYSTEM	TRIGGERS	WRITE
SOME	TABLES	TRUNCATE	WORK
SORT	TABLESPACE	UNDER	

TABLE D-2. *Oracle keywords* (continued)

PL/SQL Reserved Words

Table D-3 lists words that are reserved by PL/SQL. They have a special syntactic meaning to PL/SQL and thus cannot be used as identifiers for program objects, such as datatypes, constants, variables, cursors, PL/SQL tables, records, procedures, functions, or packages.

ABORT	ASSIGN	CHAR_BASE	CRASH
ACCEPT	AT	CHECK	CREATE
ACCESS	AUTHORIZATION	CLOSE	CURRENT
ADD	AVG	CLUSTER	CURSOR
ALL	BEGIN	CLUSTERS	CURVAL
ALTER	BETWEEN	COLAUTH	DATABASE
AND	BINARY_INTEGER	COLUMNS	DATA_BASE
ANY	BODY	COMMIT	DATE
ARRAY	BOOLEAN	COMPRESS	DBA
AS	BY	CONNECT	DEBUGOFF
ASC	CASE	CONSTANT	DEBUGON
ASSERT	CHAR	COUNT	DECLARE

TABLE D-3. *PL/SQL reserved words*

DECIMAL	GROUP	OF	ROWID
DEFAULT	HAVING	ON	ROWLABEL
DEFINITION	IDENTIFIED	OPEN	ROWNUM
DELAY	IF	OPTION	ROWTYPE
DELETE	IN	OR	RUN
DELTA	INDEX	ORDER	SAVEPOINT
DESC	INDEXES	OTHERS	SCHEMA
DIGITS	INDICATOR	OUT	SELECT
DISPOSE	INSERT	PACKAGE	SEPARATE
DISTINCT	INTEGER	PARTITION	SET
DO	INTERSECT	PCTFREE	SIZE
DROP	INTO	POSITIVE	SMALLINT
ELSE	IS	PRAGMA	SPACE
ELSIF	LEVEL	PRIOR	SQL
END	LIKE	PRIVATE	SQLCODE
ENTRY	LIMITED	PROCEDURE	SQLERRM
EXCEPTION	LOOP	PUBLIC	START
EXCEPTION_INMAXT		RAISE	STATEMENT
EXISTS	MIN	RANGE	STDDEV
EXIT	MINUS	RAW MLSLABEL	SUBTYPE
FALSE	MLSLABEL	REAL	SUM
FETCH	MOD	RECORD	TABAUTH
FLOAT	NATURAL	RELEASE	TABLE
FOR	NEW	REM	TABLES
FORM	NEXTVAL	RENAME	TASK
FROM	NOCOMPRESS	RESOURCE	TERMINATE
FUNCTION	NOT	RETURN	THEN
GENERIC	NULL	REVERSE	TO
GOTO	NUMBER	REVOKE	TRUE

TABLE D-3. *PL/SQL reserved words* (continued)

GRANT	NUMBER_BASE	ROLLBACK	TYPE
UNION	VALUES	VIEW	WHILE
UNIQUE	VARCHAR	VIEWS	WITH
UPDATE	VARCHAR2	WHEN	WORK

TABLE D-3. *PL/SQL reserved words* (continued)

APPENDIX E

Errors and Warnings

This appendix describes the errors and warnings that may occur in the following environments:

- Pro*C precompiler
- Oracle run-time library
- Oracle Server
- PL/SQL

Each error's number, accompanying message, probable cause, and corrective action are described.

Pro*C Precompiler Errors and Warnings

The Pro*C precompiler issues errors that consist of a prefix, severity code, and sequence number. The prefix *PCC* indicates that the error is issued by the Pro*C precompiler. There are four severity codes; Table E-1 lists their meanings.

To help diagnose, find, and fix errors, the object names and numbers are inserted into some error messages. In this appendix, these names and numbers are represented by *"X"* and *N*, respectively. For example, the error message listed as

PCC-0032:   Invalid option "X"

might actually appear as

PCC-U-0032:   Invalid option "MADE"

The following error messages might be issued at precompile time by the Pro*C precompiler.

PCC-0001:   Unable to open file "X"

Cause: The precompiler was unable to open a temporary file for internal use. There might be insufficient disk space, too many open files, or read-only protection on the output directory.

Action: Make sure there is enough disk space, that the limit for open files is set high enough (check with your system manager), and that protection on the directory allows opening a file for writing.

PCC-0002:   Invalid syntax at column N in line N of file "X"

Code	Meaning
W	Warning—despite an error, a compilable output file was created.
S	Severe error—despite an error, an output file was created. However, it might not be compilable.
F	Fatal error—no output file was created because of an internal problem or because a resource (such as memory) was unavailable or was exceeded.
U	Unrecoverable error—no output file was created because an input requirement was not met.

TABLE E-1. *Pro*C error severity codes*

Cause: There is a syntax error in an EXEC statement, or the statement is not properly terminated.

Action: Correct the syntax of the EXEC statement. If the error occurred at the end of the input file, make sure the last EXEC statement is properly terminated.

PCC-0003:   Invalid SQL Identifier at column N in line N of file "X"

Cause: The symbol in a conditional precompilation statement (such as EXEC ORACLE IFDEF) is invalid, or the name of an SQL descriptor, statement, or cursor is invalid or was not properly declared.

Action: Check the statement syntax and your spelling of the identifier, and make sure you did not use a reserved word. If necessary, define the identifier in a variable declaration or DECLARE statement ahead of the line in error.

PCC-0004:   Mismatched IF/ELSE/ENDIF block at line N in file "X"

Cause: There is an EXEC ORACLE ELSE or EXEC ORACLE ENDIF statement without a matching EXEC ORACLE IFDEF statement.

Action: Add the missing EXEC ORACLE IFDEF statement, or delete or move the EXEC ORACLE ELSE or EXEC ORACLE ENDIF statement.

PCC-0005:   Unsupported datatype in line N of file "X"

Cause: A host variable defined in the DECLARE section has an unsupported datatype or has a scale or precision outside the supported range.

Action: Redefine the host variable using a supported datatype. Make sure the scale and precision of a numeric variable are in the accepted range.

PCC-0007:   Invalid WHENEVER condition at column N in line N of file "X"

Cause: A condition other than SQLERROR, SQLWARNING, or NOT FOUND was specified in an EXEC SQL WHENEVER statement, or one of these was used but spelled incorrectly.

Action: Correct the spelling of the WHENEVER condition, or use a host-language IF statement to test the special condition.

PCC-0008:   Invalid WHENEVER action at column N in line N of file "X"

Cause: An action other than CONTINUE, GOTO, or STOP was specified in an EXEC SQL WHENEVER statement, one of these was spelled incorrectly, the host language does not allow the action (STOP is illegal in Pro*Pascal programs), or a GOTO label is invalid.

Action: Make sure your host language allows the specified WHENEVER action. If necessary, correct the spelling of the WHENEVER action or correct the GOTO label.

PCC-0009: `Invalid host variable at column N in line N of file "X"`

Cause: A host variable used in an EXEC SQL statement was not declared in the DECLARE section or has an unsupported datatype.

Action: Declare the host variable in the DECLARE section, making sure it has one of the supported datatypes.

PCC-0010: `Statement out of place at line N in file "X"`

Cause: An EXEC statement was not placed properly in the host program. For example, there might be a data manipulation statement in the DECLARE section. In a Pro*COBOL program, the DECLARE section might be outside the WORKING-STORAGE section.

Action: Remove or relocate the statement.

PCC-0011: `Already in a DECLARE section at line N in file "X"`

Cause: A BEGIN DECLARE SECTION statement was found inside a DECLARE section.

Action: Remove the extra BEGIN DECLARE SECTION statement.

PCC-0012: `Not in a DECLARE section at line N in file "X"`

Cause: An END DECLARE SECTION statement without a matching BEGIN DECLARE SECTION statement was found. Either the BEGIN DECLARE SECTION statement is missing or misspelled, or the END DECLARE SECTION statement is an extra.

Action: Add or correct the BEGIN DECLARE SECTION statement, or remove the extra END DECLARE SECTION statement.

PCC-0013: `Unable to open INCLUDE file "X" at line N in file "X"`

Cause: The precompiler was unable to open the input file specified in the INCLUDE statement. Some possible causes are:

- The filename is misspelled.
- The file does not exist.
- The search path to the file is incorrect.
- You have insufficient file-access privileges.
- Another user has locked the file.
- There is not enough disk space.
- There are too many open files.

Action: Make sure the file exists, that the search path to the file is correct, that you have sufficient privileges to access the file, and that it is not locked by another user. Also make sure there is enough disk space and that the limit for open files is set high enough (check with your system manager).

PCC-0014:   Undeclared SQL identifier "X" at line N in file "X"

Cause: The name of a descriptor, statement, or cursor was not declared or is misspelled.
Action: Add or correct the descriptor, statement, or cursor declaration.

PCC-0015:   Unrecognized host language syntax ignored at line N in file "X"

Cause: The host language syntax used to define a host variable in the DECLARE section is incorrect.
Action: Check the syntax and your spelling, then correct the declaration.

PCC-0016:   Unable to open a cursor at line N in file "X"

Cause: The syntax in an SQL statement is faulty. The precompiler was expecting a host variable but found something else.
Action: Check the syntax and your spelling, then correct the SQL statement.

PCC-0017:   Unable to parse statement at line N in file "X"

Cause: There is a syntax error in an array declaration. The precompiler was expecting a right bracket (]) but found something else.
Action: Check the syntax, then correct the array declaration.

PCC-0018:   Expected "X", but found "X" at line N in file "X"

Cause: The syntax in an SQL statement is faulty. The precompiler found an unexpected or illegal token.
Action: Check the syntax and your spelling, then correct the SQL statement.

PCC-0019:   Unable to obtain bind variables at line N in file "X"

Cause: The precompiler was unable to find information about an input host variable (bind variable) used in an SQL statement.
Action: Make sure the input host variable is declared in the DECLARE section and used properly in the SQL statement.

PCC-0020:   Unable to obtain define variables at line N in file "X"

Cause: The precompiler was unable to find information about an output host variable (define variable) used in an SQL statement.

Action: Make sure the output host variable is declared in the DECLARE section and used properly in the SQL statement.

PCC-0021:   ORACLE Error: N

Cause: An Oracle error occurred.
Action: Look up the Oracle error number in the *Oracle 7 Server Messages and Codes Manual,* then take the recommended action.

PCC-0022:   Out of space - unable to allocate N bytes

Cause: The precompiler process ran out of memory.
Action: Allocate more memory to the process, then retry.

PCC-0023:   Unable to log off ORACLE

Cause: An Oracle connection error occurred while the precompiler was trying to log off, probably because Oracle has been shut down.
Action: Make sure Oracle is available, then retry.

PCC-0024:   Indicator variable "X" has wrong type or length at line N in
             file "X"

Cause: An indicator variable was not declared in the DECLARE section as a two-byte integer.
Action: Redefine the indicator variable as a two-byte integer.

PCC-0025:   Undeclared indicator variable "X" at line N in file "X"

Cause: The name of an indicator variable used in an SQL statement was not declared in the DECLARE section or is misspelled.
Action: Add or correct the indicator variable declaration.

PCC-0026:   Undeclared host variable "X" at line N in file "X"

Cause: The name of a host variable used in an SQL statement was not declared in the DECLARE section or is misspelled.
Action: Add or correct the host variable declaration.

PCC-0027:   Redeclared SQL identifier "X" at line N in file "X"

Cause: The name of an SQL descriptor, statement, or cursor was redeclared (that is, declared twice).
Action: Check your spelling of the identifier, then, if necessary, remove the extra declaration.

PCC-0028:   Option "X" not legal as EXEC ORACLE OPTION

Cause: A precompiler option was specified inline in an EXEC ORACLE statement instead of on the command line. Some options, such as INAME, can be specified only on the command line.

Action: Respecify the precompiler option on the command line instead of in an EXEC ORACLE statement. To see an online display of the precompiler options, enter the precompiler command (with no options) at the operating system prompt.

PCC-0029:   Ambiguous option "X"

Cause: The name of a precompiler option was abbreviated ambiguously. For example, MAX= might refer to MAXLITERAL or MAXOPENCURSORS.

Action: Respecify the full option name or an unambiguous abbreviation. To see an online display of the precompiler options, enter the precompiler command (with no options) at the operating system prompt.

PCC-0031:   Invalid value given for option "X"

Cause: A precompiler option has an invalid operand, probably because the operand value is misspelled (LTYPE=HORT, for example) or illegal (PAGELEN = –55, for example).

Action: Check the operand, making sure it is spelled correctly and within the legal range.

PCC-0032:   Invalid option "X"

Cause: The precompiler found an invalid precompiler option name. Some possible causes are:

- The option name is misspelled.

- The specified option does not exist.

- The equal sign (=) between the option name and operand is missing or has space around it.

- The name of the input file was not preceded by INAME=.

Action: Make sure the option exists and that its name is spelled correctly. To see an online display of the precompiler options, enter the precompiler command (with no options) at the operating system prompt. Make sure there is an equal sign between the option name and operand.

PCC-0033:   Missing operand for option "X"

Cause: No operand was specified for a precompiler option. Either the operand is missing or there is a space around the equal sign (as in LTYPE =SHORT).

Action: Make sure each option has an operand and that there is no space around the equal sign.

PCC-0035:   No host language specified

Cause: The precompiler was unable to determine the host language of the input file. If you use a nonstandard input file extension when specifying the INAME precompiler option, you must also specify the HOST option. However, most operating systems are set up to prevent this error (by automatically specifying the HOST option when a precompiler is invoked).

Action: Either add the standard input file extension or specify the HOST option. If the operating system is supposed to prevent this error, call Oracle customer support for assistance.

PCC-0036:   No input file name specified

Cause: The input file was not specified on the command line.

Action: Use the INAME command-line option to specify the input file.

PCC-0037:   Unable to log on to ORACLE with "X". ORACLE error number: N

Cause: The precompiler was unable to log on to Oracle with the specified username and password. An Oracle error with given number occurred when the logon was attempted.

Action: Look up the Oracle error number in the *Oracle 7 Server Messages and Codes Manual,* then take the recommended action.

PCC-0038:   Unable to open a cursor

Cause: This is an internal error message and is not normally issued.

Action: Call Oracle customer support for assistance. If your application does not require syntactic or semantic checking of SQL statements and does not use PL/SQL, specify SQLCHECK=NONE on the command line.

PCC-0039:   Unable to open input file "X"

Cause: The precompiler was unable to open the input file specified by the INAME precompiler option. Some possible causes are:

■ The filename is misspelled.

■ The file does not exist.

■ The search path to the file is incorrect.

- You have insufficient file-access privileges.

- Another user has locked the file.

- There is not enough disk space.

- There are too many open files.

Action: Make sure the file exists, that the search path to the file is correct, that you have sufficient privileges to access the file, and that it is not locked by another user. Also make sure there is enough disk space and that the limit for open files is set high enough (check with your system manager).

PCC-0040:   Unable to open listing file "X"

Cause: The precompiler was unable to open the listing file specified by the LNAME precompiler option. Some possible causes are:

- The filename is misspelled.

- The file does not exist.

- The search path to the file is incorrect.

- You have insufficient file-access privileges.

- Another user has locked the file.

- There is not enough disk space.

- There are too many open files.

Action: Make sure the file exists, that the search path to the file is correct, that you have sufficient privileges to access the file, and that it is not locked by another user. Also make sure there is enough disk space and that the limit for open files is set high enough (check with your system manager). If you do not need a listing file, specify LTYPE=NONE on the command line.

PCC-0041:   Unable to open output file "X"

Cause: The precompiler was unable to open the output file specified by the ONAME precompiler option. Some possible causes are:

- The filename is misspelled.

- The file does not exist.

- The search path to the file is incorrect.

- You have insufficient file-access privileges.

- Another user has locked the file.

- There is not enough disk space.

- There are too many open files.

Action: Make sure the file exists, that the search path to the file is correct, that you have sufficient privileges to access the file, and that it is not locked by another user. Also make sure there is enough disk space and that the limit for open files is set high enough (check with your system manager).

PCC-0042:   Must include SQLCA file when MODE=ANSI and WHENEVER SQLWARNING
            used

Cause: When MODE={ANSI | ANSI14}, you tried to use the WHENEVER SQLWARNING statement without declaring the SQLCA. When MODE={ANSI | ANSI14}, declaring the SQLCA is optional, but to use the WHENEVER SQLWARNING statement, you must declare the SQLCA.
Action: Remove all WHENEVER SQLWARNING statements from your program, or declare the SQLCA by hardcoding it or by copying it into your program with the INCLUDE statement.

PCC-0044:   Array size mismatch in INTO/USING. Minimum is: "X"(N:N)

Cause: The size of an array variable in an INTO/USING clause is too small for the number of rows processed.
Action: Declare all array variables in the INTO/USING clause to have at least the minimum dimension given.

PCC-0045:   "X" clause inappropriate at line N in file "X". Ignored

Cause: There is a misplaced clause at the end of an EXEC SQL statement (an AT clause at the end of a SELECT statement, for example), or the action specified in a FOR clause is invalid (for example, FOR :loop INTO ...).
Action: Check the statement syntax, then relocate or correct the misplaced or invalid clause.

PCC-0047:   Unterminated comment/string constant beginning near line N in
            file "X"

Cause: A string constant is missing an ending quote, or a comment is missing an ending delimiter.
Action: Make sure all comments are delimited and all string constants are enclosed by quotes.

PCC-0048:   PRO* configured without ORACLE. INLINE=NO ignored

Cause: Currently the Oracle precompilers generate inline code, not access modules. Thus, the INLINE=NO command-line option is ignored. However, future versions of the Oracle precompilers will be able to generate access modules.
Action: Do not specify the INLINE option.

PCC-0050:   Unable to generate descriptor in program unit ending line N in
             file "X"

Cause: Part of a descriptor was generated incorrectly, or the precompiler was unable to generate a descriptor in a program unit terminated by an end-of-file.
Action: Call Oracle customer support for assistance.

PCC-0051:   Size of VARCHAR "X" at N is larger than 65533 at line N in
             file "X"

Cause: The declared size of a VARCHAR host variable exceeds the precompiler limit of 65,533 bytes.
Action: Check the DECLARE section, making sure the size of each VARCHAR variable does not exceed 65,533 bytes.

PCC-0053:   FOR variable "X" is invalid type at line N in file "X"

Cause: The count variable in a FOR clause has the wrong datatype. The datatype must be NUMBER or LONG (or compatible with NUMBER or LONG).
Action: Check the declaration and make sure the count variable has a datatype of NUMBER or LONG (or a compatible Oracle or host-language datatype).

PCC-0054:   Expected end-of-statement at column N in line N of file "X"

Cause: The precompiler expected to find a statement terminator at the end of an EXEC statement but found something else. This can happen if you embed tabs in your source code (because the precompiler has no way of knowing how many spaces a tab represents).
Action: If you find tabs embedded in the source code, replace them with spaces. Check the statement syntax and make sure each EXEC statement has a terminator. For embedded CREATE {FUNCTION | PROCEDURE | PACKAGE} statements and for embedded PL/SQL blocks, make sure the statement terminator is END-EXEC.

PCC-0055:   Array "X" not allowed as bind variable at line N in file "X"

Cause: A host array was used as a bind (input) variable in the WHERE clause of a SELECT statement. This is not allowed.

Action: Remove the host array or replace it with a simple host variable.

PCC-0056: FOR clause not allowed in SELECT statement at line N in
           file "X"

Cause: This message warns that the FOR :loop SELECT ... construct will eventually be disallowed.

Action: Keep in mind that code containing this construct will eventually have to be modified.

PCC-0060: Both CURSOR and STATEMENT have AT clauses at line N of file "X"

Cause: Two AT clauses, one in a DECLARE STATEMENT statement, the other in a DECLARE CURSOR statement, pertain to the same SQL statement. You can specify the AT clause with either DECLARE STATEMENT or DECLARE CURSOR, but not both.

Action: Remove the AT clause from one of the statements.

PCC-0061: Error at line N, column N. PLS-N: "X"

Cause: The precompiler found a syntax error while parsing an embedded SQL statement or PL/SQL block. If the error was found in a PL/SQL block, the PL/SQL error message code and text are given.

Action: Correct the syntax error. For more information about a PL/SQL syntax error, look it up in the *Oracle 7 Server Messages and Codes Manual*.

PCC-0062: Must use option SQLCHECK=SEMANTICS when there is embedded PL/SQL

Cause: The precompiler tried to parse an embedded PL/SQL block when SQLCHECK={SYNTAX | NONE}. PL/SQL blocks can be parsed only when you specify SQLCHECK=SEMANTICS.

Action: Remove the PL/SQL block or specify SQLCHECK=SEMANTICS.

PCC-0063: Reached end of file "X" before end-of-statement at line N

Cause: The precompiler encountered an end-of-file while parsing a PL/SQL block.

Action: Add the appropriate statement terminator (;) or end-of-block statement (END;) to the PL/SQL block.

PCC-0064: All uses of a given host variable must use identical indicator
           variables

Cause: Two or more occurrences of a host variable in an EXEC SQL statement are associated with different indicator variables. This is not allowed.

Action: Rename the indicator variables so that each occurrence of the host variable is associated with the same indicator variable.

PCC-0065:   USERID required, but not specified

Cause: You specified the SQLCHECK=SEMANTICS option but failed to specify the USERID option on the command line.

Action: Specify USERID=username/password, enter a username and password when prompted, or specify SQLCHECK={SYNTAX | NONE}.

PCC-0066:   USERID only used when SQLCHECK=SEMANTICS, USERID ignored

Cause: You specified the USERID option when SQLCHECK={SYNTAX | NONE}. This is unnecessary.

Action: Specify the USERID option only when SQLCHECK=SEMANTICS.

PCC-0067:   IRECLEN exceeded. Line N in file "X" truncated

Cause: While reading the input file, the precompiler found a line longer than IRECLEN.

Action: Either shorten the input line or specify a larger IRECLEN value on the command line.

PCC-0068:   Host and indicator variables may not have the same name

Cause: In an EXEC SQL statement, an indicator variable has the same name as a host variable. The names of a host variable and its associated indicator variable must be different. Also, an indicator variable cannot be used as a host variable.

Action: Rename the host or indicator variable.

PCC-0069:   Host variable "X" has unsupported datatype at line N in file "X"

Cause: A host variable has an unsupported datatype. For a list of supported datatypes, see your *Supplement to the Oracle Precompilers Guide.*

Action: Redefine the host variable in the DECLARE section, giving it a supported datatype.

PCC-0070:   Illegal syntax. Exponential value in SQL statement: "X"

Cause: The precompiler found a syntax error while parsing a number coded in scientific notation. The precompiler expected to find a signed integer following the exponentiation indicator (E) but found something else.

Action: Reformat the number correctly.

PCC-0072:   Input file name length exceeds 14 characters

Cause: On some platforms, the maximum length of a filename is 14 characters. The filename you specified exceeds the maximum length.
Action: Use a filename of 14 or fewer characters.

PCC-0073:   Cursor is declared but never OPENed at line N in file "X"

Cause: You DECLAREd a cursor but did not code an OPEN statement for it. This is only an informational message.
Action: Remove the cursor declaration, or code an OPEN statement for the cursor.

PCC-0074:   FIPS warning: Multiply defined host variable in line N of file "X"

Cause: You used an Oracle extension to the ANSI/ISO SQL standard. Specifically, you reused the name of a global host variable to declare a local host variable. This message is only a warning issued by the FIPS flagger when FIPS=YES.
Action: None required, but for ANSI/ISO compliance, do not reuse the names of global host variables to declare local host variables.

PCC-0075:   ":" expected before indicator variable

Cause: An indicator variable is not prefixed with a colon as required.
Action: Prefix a colon to the indicator variable in question.

PCC-0076:   DISPLAY type must be SIGN LEADING SEPARATE

Cause: This message is normally issued only by Pro*COBOL. DISPLAY SIGN LEADING SEPARATE is the only DISPLAY type supported by Pro*COBOL.
Action: Check your spelling of the variable declaration. If necessary, remove the reference to the unsupported DISPLAY type.

PCC-0077:   Colon usage with numeric label in WHENEVER statement is not
             ANSI

Cause: You used an Oracle extension to the ANSI/ISO SQL standard. Specifically, a numeric WHENEVER ... GOTO label was prefixed with a colon. For example, you might have coded EXEC SQL WHENEVER SQLERROR GOTO :99; This message is only a warning issued by the FIPS flagger when FIPS=YES.
Action: None required, but for ANSI/ISO compliance, prefix alphanumeric (but not numeric) WHENEVER ... GOTO labels with a colon.

PCC-0078:   FIPS warning: Invalid ANSI SQL identifier

Cause: You used an Oracle extension to the ANSI/ISO SQL standard. Specifically, the name you gave to a host variable meets one of the following conditions:

- It is longer than 18 characters.
- It does not begin with a letter.
- It contains consecutive or trailing underscores.

This message is only a warning issued by the FIPS flagger when FIPS=YES.

Action: None required, but for ANSI/ISO compliance, change the host variable name so that it is <=18 characters long, begins with a letter, and does not contain consecutive or trailing underscores.

PCC-0079:   ANSI requires colon on label in WHENEVER statement

Cause: You used an Oracle extension to the ANSI/ISO SQL standard. Specifically, an alphanumeric WHENEVER ... GOTO label was not prefixed with a colon. This message is only a warning issued by the FIPS flagger when FIPS=YES.

Action: None required, but for ANSI/ISO compliance, prefix alphanumeric (but not numeric) WHENEVER ... GOTO labels with a colon.

PCC-0080:   TYPE identifier already TYPEd

Cause: The identifier being TYPEd in an EXEC SQL TYPE statement appeared in a previous EXEC SQL TYPE statement. A given identifier can appear in only one EXEC SQL TYPE statement.

Action: Check your spelling of the identifiers. Use different identifiers in the EXEC SQL TYPE statements, or remove one of the EXEC SQL TYPE statements.

PCC-0081:   Scale specification not allowed for given datatype

Cause: The Oracle external datatype referenced in an EXEC SQL VAR or EXEC SQL TYPE statement does not allow a scale specification.

Action: Check the precision specification and remove the scale specification.

PCC-0082:   Length and scale specifications must be an integer

Cause: You used a floating-point number or a nonnumber to specify a length or scale. Only integers can be used.

Action: Correct or remove the length and/or scale specification.

PCC-0083:   Bind and define variables not allowed in CREATE statement

Cause: Host variables cannot appear in a CREATE statement. If the makeup of a CREATE statement cannot be known until run time, you must use dynamic SQL to execute it. That is, your program must accept or build the CREATE statement at run time, store it in a host string, then EXECUTE it.

Action: Correct or remove the erroneous CREATE statement.

PCC-0085:   Error writing to file "X"

Cause: The precompiler was unable to write to the named output file. Some possible causes are:

■   You have insufficient file-access privileges.

■   Another user has locked the file.

■   There is not enough disk space.

■   There are too many open files.

Action: Make sure you have sufficient privileges to access the file and that it is not locked by another user. Also make sure there is enough disk space and that the limit for open files is set high enough (check with your system manager).

PCC-0086:   Source file "X" has zero length

Cause: The source file you specified on the command line contains no code. Consequently, there is nothing for the precompiler to process.

Action: Specify a valid source file containing embedded SQL statements.

PCC-0087:   EXEC SQL TYPE statement not allowed for this host language

Cause: You used the EXEC SQL TYPE statement with a host language that does not support user-defined datatype equivalencing. This feature is available only in Pro*C and Pro*Pascal.

Action: Remove the offending EXEC SQL TYPE statement.

PCC-0088:   User defined type identifier expected

Cause: The user-defined datatype name in an EXEC SQL TYPE statement is missing or misspelled, is a reserved word, is not a legal identifier in your host language, or conflicts with a base datatype in that language.

Action: Check your spelling of the user-defined datatype name. If necessary, declare a valid user-defined datatype. User-defined datatype equivalencing is available only in Pro*C and Pro*Pascal.

PCC-0089:   Invalid ORACLE TYPE specification

Cause: The Oracle external datatype name in an EXEC SQL TYPE or EXEC SQL VAR statement is missing or misspelled.
Action: Check your spelling of the external datatype name. If necessary, supply the missing datatype name.

PCC-0090:   Precision/scale specification must be given for DECIMAL
            datatype

Cause: You omitted a precision and/or scale specification for the Oracle external datatype DECIMAL in an EXEC SQL TYPE or EXEC SQL VAR statement.
Action: Add the precision and/or scale specification to the EXEC SQL TYPE or EXEC SQL VAR statement.

PCC-0091:   TYPE statement requires format specification for this ORACLE
            datatype

Cause: You omitted a length, precision, and/or scale specification for an Oracle external datatype in an EXEC SQL TYPE or EXEC SQL VAR statement.
Action: Add the length, precision, and/or scale specification for the external datatype to the EXEC SQL TYPE or EXEC SQL VAR statement.

PCC-0092:   Length and/or scale incompatible with specified ORACLE datatype

Cause: You specified an invalid length or scale for an Oracle external datatype in an EXEC SQL TYPE or EXEC SQL VAR statement.
Action: Make sure to specify a length that is large enough to accommodate the external datatype. If you specify a scale, make sure it lies in the range –84 .. 99.

PCC-0093:   Invalid or obsolete option, ignored

Cause: The precompiler found an option available in a prior version or different host language, but not in your version or host language.
Action: Remove the option specification.

PCC-0094:   Array length for char[n] datatype must be => 2

Cause: When MODE={ANSI | ANSI14}, you specified a length of less than two characters for a char[n] host variable. When MODE={ANSI | ANSI14}, the length must be at least two characters. This message is issued only by the Pro*C precompiler.
Action: Correct the declaration so that it specifies a length of at least two characters.

PCC-0095: Missing PROGRAM, SUBROUTINE, FUNCTION, or BLOCK DATA statement

Cause: FORTRAN source files are expected to have at least one PROGRAM, SUBROUTINE, FUNCTION, or BLOCK DATA statement, which the precompiler uses to detect the beginning of a routine or compilation unit.

Action: Add one of these statements to the source file.

PCC-0096: Array FETCH not allowed for MODE=ANSI14

Cause: When MODE=ANSI14, you attempted an array SELECT or FETCH. However, array operations are not allowed when MODE=ANSI14.

Action: If you must specify MODE=ANSI14, place the SELECT or FETCH statement in a host-language loop instead of using the array interface.

PCC-0097: Use of DECIMAL and DISPLAY types allowed only for COBOL and PLI

Cause: You used the DECIMAL or DISPLAY external datatype in an EXEC SQL VAR statement with an Oracle precompiler other than Pro*COBOL or Pro*PL/I. These external datatypes are available only in Pro*COBOL and Pro*PL/I.

Action: Remove the reference to the DECIMAL or DISPLAY external datatype from the EXEC SQL VAR statement.

PCC-0098: Scale specification cannot be used in this context

Cause: In a Pro*C, Pro*FORTRAN, or Pro*Pascal program, you cannot specify scale in an EXEC SQL TYPE or EXEC SQL VAR statement in the current context.

Action: Remove the scale specification from the EXEC SQL TYPE or EXEC SQL VAR statement.

PCC-0099: Length cannot be given for types ROWID and DATE

Cause: You specified a length for the ROWID or DATE external datatype in an EXEC SQL TYPE or EXEC SQL VAR statement. This is unnecessary because those types are fixed-length.

Action: Remove the length specification from the EXEC SQL TYPE or EXEC SQL VAR statement.

PCC-0100: Non integer label is not ANSI

Cause: You used an Oracle extension to the ANSI/ISO SQL standard. Specifically, a noninteger WHENEVER ... GOTO label was in a Pro*Pascal program. This message is only a warning issued by the FIPS flagger when FIPS=YES.

Action: None required. However, for ANSI/ISO compliance, use only integer WHENEVER ... GOTO labels in a Pro*Pascal program.

PCC-0101:   Lower case 'e' in floating point number is not ANSI

Cause: You used an Oracle extension to the ANSI/ISO SQL standard. Specifically, a lowercase *e* was used in scientific notation. This message is only a warning issued by the FIPS flagger when FIPS=YES.

Action: None required. However, for ANSI/ISO compliance, use an uppercase *E* in scientific notation.

PCC-0102:   FOR UPDATE is an Oracle extension

Cause: You used an Oracle extension to the ANSI/ISO SQL standard. Specifically, the FOR UPDATE OF clause was used in a cursor declaration. This message is only a warning issued by the FIPS flagger when FIPS=YES.

Action: None required. However, for ANSI/ISO compliance, do not use the FOR UPDATE OF clause.

PCC-0103:   AT clause is an Oracle extension

Cause: You used an Oracle extension to the ANSI/ISO SQL standard. Specifically, the AT <db_name> clause was used in an SQL statement. This message is only a warning issued by the FIPS flagger when FIPS=YES.

Action: None required. However, for ANSI/ISO compliance, do not use the AT <db_name> clause.

PCC-0104:   FOR clause is an Oracle extension

Cause: You used an Oracle extension to the ANSI/ISO SQL standard. Specifically, the FOR clause was used in an array-processing SQL statement. This message is only a warning issued by the FIPS flagger when FIPS=YES.

Action: None required. However, for ANSI/ISO compliance, do not use the FOR clause.

PCC-0105:   Keyword WORK required here by ANSI

Cause: You used an Oracle extension to the ANSI/ISO SQL standard. Specifically, the keyword WORK was not used in a COMMIT or ROLLBACK statement. This message is only a warning issued by the FIPS flagger when FIPS=YES.

Action: None required. However, for ANSI/ISO compliance, use the keyword WORK.

PCC-0106:   RELEASE is an Oracle extension to the COMMIT and ROLLBACK
             statements

Cause: You used an Oracle extension to the ANSI/ISO SQL standard. Specifically, the parameter RELEASE was used in a COMMIT or ROLLBACK statement. This message is only a warning issued by the FIPS flagger when FIPS=YES.

Action: None required. However, for ANSI/ISO compliance, do not use the parameter RELEASE.

PCC-0107:   The CONNECT statement is Oracle implementation dependent

Cause: You used an Oracle extension to the ANSI/ISO SQL standard. Specifically, the CONNECT statement was used to log on to Oracle. This message is only a warning issued by the FIPS flagger when FIPS=YES.

Action: None required.

PCC-0108:   This statement is not supported by ANSI

Cause: Requirement was not met. You used an Oracle extension to the ANSI/ISO SQL standard. Specifically, a nonconforming SQL statement such as PREPARE was used. This message is only a warning issued by the FIPS flagger when FIPS=YES.

Action: None required. However, for ANSI/ISO compliance, do not use the nonconforming SQL statement.

PCC-0109:   Dynamic SQL and PL/SQL are an Oracle extensions to ANSI SQL

Cause: You used an Oracle extension to the ANSI/ISO SQL standard. Specifically, dynamic SQL or embedded PL/SQL was used. This message is only a warning issued by the FIPS flagger when FIPS=YES.

Action: None required. However, for ANSI/ISO compliance, do not use dynamic SQL or embedded PL/SQL.

PCC-0110:   Oracle extension to the WHENEVER statement

Cause: You used an Oracle extension to the ANSI/ISO SQL standard. Specifically, a nonconforming keyword such as NOTFOUND, STOP, RAISE, or DO was used in the WHENEVER statement. (Note that NOT FOUND is ANSI-compliant.) This message is only a warning issued by the FIPS flagger when FIPS=YES.

Action: None required. However, for ANSI/ISO compliance, do not use the nonconforming keyword.

PCC-0111:   SQLCHECK value in EXEC ORACLE statement exceeds command line
             value

Cause: You entered the SQLCHECK option inline, specifying a level of checking higher than the level you specified (or accepted by default) on the command line. This is not allowed. For example, if you specify SQLCHECK={SYNTAX | LIMITED} on the command line, you cannot specify SQLCHECK={SEMANTICS | FULL} inline. This message is only a warning; the precompiler ignores the inline value and continues processing.

Action: Revise the EXEC ORACLE statement, or specify a lower level of checking on the command line.

PCC-0112:   Datatype not supported by ANSI

Cause: You used an Oracle extension to the ANSI/ISO SQL standard. Specifically, a pointer or nonconforming datatype such as VARCHAR was used. This message is only a warning issued by the FIPS flagger when FIPS=YES.

Action: None required. However, for ANSI/ISO compliance, do not use pointers or nonconforming datatypes.

PCC-0113:   Value of DBMS option invalid with given value of MODE option

Cause: When MODE={ANSI14 | ANSI13}, you specified DBMS=V7, or, when MODE=ANSI, you specified DBMS=V6. These option settings are incompatible. Note that the DBMS option is available only with version 1.5 of the Oracle precompilers.

Action: With DBMS=V7, instead of MODE={ANSI14 | MODE=ANSI13}, you can specify MODE={ANSI | MODE=ORACLE}. With DBMS=V6, instead of MODE={ANSI14 | MODE=ANSI13}, you can specify MODE={ANSI14 | MODE=ANSI13 | ORACLE}, but MODE=ORACLE is recommended.

PCC-0114:   Length spec required in EXEC SQL VAR statements for VARxxx
              types

Cause: In an EXEC SQL VAR statement, a VARCHAR or VARRAW external datatype was specified without a length. Unlike other types, the VARCHAR and VARRAW types have a two-byte field followed by a variable-length data field. Therefore, you must specify the maximum length of the data field.

Action: Add a length specification to the EXEC SQL VAR statement.

PCC-0115:   Array required here

Cause: In an ARRAYLEN statement, you failed to specify the name of a previously declared host array. The first host variable in an ARRAYLEN statement must be an array; the second host variable, which specifies an array dimension, must be a four-byte integer. The correct syntax is

```
EXEC SQL ARRAYLEN host_array (dimension);
```

The ARRAYLEN statement must appear in the DECLARE section along with, but somewhere after, the declarations of **host_array** and **dimension**.

Action: Check your spelling of both identifiers in the ARRAYLEN statement. If necessary, supply the missing host array name.

PCC-0116:   This array already given in an ARRAYLEN statement

Cause: You specified the same host array in two different ARRAYLEN statements. You cannot reference a given host array in more than one ARRAYLEN statement.

Action: Check your spelling of the host array names in both ARRAYLEN statements. Change one of the names so that they refer to different host arrays, or remove one of the ARRAYLEN statements.

PCC-0117:   Invalid ARRAYLEN length variable type

Cause: In an ARRAYLEN statement, you failed to specify a valid array dimension. You must specify the array dimension using a previously declared four-byte, integer host variable, not a literal or expression.

Action: Supply a valid array dimension. If necessary, declare a four-byte, integer host variable for use in the ARRAYLEN statement.

PCC-0118:   Use of host variable initialization not supported by ANSI SQL

Cause: You used an Oracle extension to the ANSI/ISO SQL standard. Specifically, you initialized a host variable in its declaration. This message is only a warning issued by the FIPS flagger when FIPS=YES.

Action: None required, but for ANSI/ISO compliance, do not initialize host variables in their declarations.

PCC-0119:   Value of const variable in INTO clause will be modified

Cause: You used a constant instead of an output host variable in the INTO clause of a SELECT statement. The SELECT INTO statement retrieves a value for each item in the select list, then assigns the values to corresponding variables in the INTO clause. Since the values of constants are fixed, you cannot use them as output host variables.

Action: Check your spelling of all identifiers in the INTO clause. If necessary, change the constant declaration to a variable declaration.

PCC-0120:   File I/O error during code generation

Cause: This is an internal error message not normally issued.

Action: Call Oracle customer support for assistance.

PCC-0121:   Arrays of VARCHAR pointers are not supported

Cause: You tried to declare an array of pointers, which is not allowed. However, pointers to scalar types are allowed. With Pro*C, declare pointers to char[n] and VRCHAR[n] variables as pointers to char or VARCHAR (with no length specification).
Action: Correct or remove the declaration.

PCC-0122:   Input file name and output file name are identical

Cause: On the command line, you mistakenly specified the same path/filename for INAME and ONAME, which designate the precompiler input and output files, respectively.
Action: Change one of the path/filenames.

PCC-0123:   Entire VARCHAR declaration must be on same line

Cause: In a Pro*C program, a VARCHAR declaration spans more than one line, which is not allowed.
Action: Revise the declaration so that it uses only one line.

PCC-1200:   You are not authorized to run Pro*C

Cause: Your authorization or license to run the Pro*C precompiler has expired.
Action: Call Oracle customer support for assistance.

PCC-1201:   Your Pro*C authorization is about to expire

Cause: Your authorization or license to run the Pro*C precompiler is about to expire.
Action: Call Oracle customer support for assistance.

Oracle Run-time Library Errors and Warnings

The following error messages might be issued at run time by the Oracle run-time library. The error code prefix RTL stands for "run-time library."

RTL-2100:   out of memory (i.e., could not allocate)

Cause: The Oracle run-time library was unable to allocate enough memory to execute your program.

Action: Allocate more memory to your user session, then rerun the program. If the error persists, call Oracle customer support for assistance.

RTL-2101:   Inconsistent cursor cache (UCE/CUC mismatch)

Cause: The precompiler generates a unit cursor entry (UCE) array. An element in this array corresponds to an entry in the cursor cache (CUC). While doing a consistency check on the cursor cache, the Oracle run-time library found that the unit cursor entry or cursor cache entry for an EXEC SQL statement is missing.

Action: The unit cursor entry must be regenerated, so rerun the program. If the error persists, call Oracle customer support for assistance.

RTL-2102:   Inconsistent cursor cache (no CUC entry for this UCE)

Cause: The precompiler generates a unit cursor entry (UCE) array. An element in this array corresponds to an entry in the cursor cache (CUC). While doing a consistency check on the cursor cache, the Oracle run-time library was unable to find a cursor cache entry in the UCE array. This happens only if your program runs out of memory.

Action: Allocate more memory to your user session, then rerun the program. If the error persists, call Oracle customer support for assistance.

RTL-2103:   Inconsistent cursor cache (out-of-range CUC ref)

Cause: The precompiler generates a unit cursor entry (UCE) array. An element in this array corresponds to an entry in the cursor cache (CUC). While doing a consistency check on the cursor cache, the Oracle run-time library found that the UCE array contains an ordinal value that is either too large or less than zero. This happens only if your program runs out of memory.

Action: Allocate more memory to your user session, then rerun the program. If the error persists, call Oracle customer support for assistance.

RTL-2104:   Inconsistent cursor cache (no CUC available)

Cause: No cursor cache is available. The Oracle run-time library was unable to allocate enough memory to execute your program.

Action: Allocate more memory to your user session, then rerun the program. If the error persists, call Oracle customer support for assistance.

RTL-2105:   Inconsistent cursor cache (no CUC entry in cache)

Cause: While doing a consistency check on the cursor cache, the Oracle run-time library found that an entry in the cursor cache was missing. This happens only if your program runs out of memory.

Action: Allocate more memory to your user session, then rerun the program. If the error persists, call Oracle customer support for assistance.

RTL-2106:   Inconsistent cursor cache (invalid ORACLE cursor number)

Cause: While carrying out an SQL operation, the Oracle run-time library found an invalid Oracle cursor number.

Action: This is an internal error message not normally issued. Call Oracle customer support for assistance.

RTL-2107:   Program too old for runtime library; please re-precompile it

Cause: Your program was precompiled by an older-version Oracle precompiler that is not compatible with the Oracle run-time library.

Action: Precompile the program using a newer-version Oracle precompiler.

RTL-2108:   Invalid descriptor passed to runtime library

Cause: While carrying out an SQL operation, the Oracle run-time library found an invalid descriptor.

Action: This is an internal error message not normally issued. Call Oracle customer support for assistance.

RTL-2109:   Inconsistent host cache (out-of-range SIT ref)

Cause: The Oracle run-time library found an SIT reference that is either too large or less than zero. This usually happens when your program runs out of memory.

Action: Allocate more memory to your user session, then rerun the program. If the error persists, call Oracle customer support for assistance.

RTL-2110:   Inconsistent host cache (invalid SQI type)

Cause: The Oracle run-time library found an SQI type value that is either too large or less than zero. This usually happens when your program runs out of memory.

Action: Allocate more memory to your user session, then rerun the program. If the error persists, call Oracle customer support for assistance.

RTL-2111:   Heap consistency error

Cause: After dynamically allocating or freeing memory, the run-time library found an error while doing a consistency check on the heap. This usually happens when your program runs out of memory.

Action: Allocate more memory to your user session, then rerun the program. If the error persists, call Oracle customer support for assistance.

RTL-2112:   SELECT..INTO returns too many rows

Cause: When you tried to SELECT into a host array, the number of rows returned by the query was larger than the dimension of the host array.

Action: Either specify a larger array dimension, or declare a cursor for use with the FETCH statement.

RTL-2114:   Invalid SQL Cursor usage: trying to close a closed cursor

Cause: You tried to CLOSE a never OPENed or already CLOSEd cursor, or you misspelled the cursor name. Only a currently open cursor can be CLOSEd.

Action: Check your spelling of the cursor name, and make sure the cursor is open before you try to CLOSE it.

RTL-2115:   Code interpretation problem -- check COMMON_NAME usage

Cause: With Pro*FORTRAN, this error occurs if you specify the precompiler option COMMON_NAME incorrectly. With other Oracle precompilers, this error occurs when the precompiler cannot generate a segment of code.

Action: With Pro*FORTRAN, when you're using COMMON_NAME to precompile two or more source modules, make sure to specify a different common name for each module. With other Oracle precompilers, if the error persists, call Oracle customer support for assistance.

RTL-2116:   FATAL ERROR: Reentrant code generator gave invalid context

Cause: The code generator assigned an invalid value to a system-specific parameter.

Action: This is an internal error message not normally issued. Call Oracle customer support for assistance.

RTL-2117:   Invalid SQL Cursor usage: trying to open an opened cursor

Cause: When MODE={ANSI | ANSI14 | ANSI13}, you tried to OPEN an already open cursor. However, you can reOPEN an already open cursor only when MODE=ORACLE.

Action: When MODE={ANSI | ANSI14 | ANSI13}, make sure you CLOSE a cursor before trying to reOPEN it. If you want to reOPEN an already open cursor to avoid reparsing, specify MODE=ORACLE.

RTL-2118:   Invalid row for a WHERE CURRENT OF operation

Cause: You tried to reference a nonexistent row using the CURRENT OF clause in an UPDATE or DELETE statement. This happens when no FETCH has been executed or when FETCH returns a "no data found" error that your program fails to trap.

Action: Make sure the last cursor operation succeeded and that the current row of the cursor is valid. You can check the outcome of a cursor operation in two ways: implicit checking with the WHENEVER statement or explicit checking of SQLCODE in the SQLCA.

RTL-2122:   Invalid OPEN or PREPARE for this database connection

Cause: You tried to execute an OPEN or PREPARE statement using a cursor that is currently open for another database connection and therefore cannot be used for this connection.

Action: Close the cursor to make it available for this connection, or use a different cursor for this connection.

Oracle Server Errors and Warnings

The following errors may be returned from the Oracle Server when you are accessing a database from an application program.

User Program Interface: 01000-01099

This section lists messages generated when you use the User Program Interface (UPI) to access the Oracle Server. Pro*C, OCI, SQL*Forms are examples of products that use the UPI.

ORA-01000   maximum open cursors exceeded

Cause: A host language program attempted to open too many cursors. The maximum number of cursors per user is determined by the initialization parameter OPEN_CURSORS.

Action: Modify the program to use fewer cursors. If this error occurs often, shut down Oracle, increase the value of OPEN_CURSORS, and restart Oracle. OPEN_CURSORS should be greater than or equal to MAXOPENCURSORS + 6.

ORA-01001   invalid cursor

Cause: Either a host language program call specified an invalid cursor, or the values of the AREASIZE and MAXOPENCURSORS options in the precompiler command were too small. All cursors must be opened (using the OOPEN call) before being referenced in any of the following calls: SQL, DESCRIBE, NAME, DEFINE, BIND, EXEC, FETCH, and CLOSE. The Logon Data Area (LDA) must be defined by using OLON or OLOGON. If the LDA is not defined, this message is issued for the following calls: OPEN, COM, CON, ROL, and LOGOFF.

Action: Check the erroneous call statement. Specify a correct LDA area, or open the cursor as required. If there is no problem with the cursor, it may be necessary to increase the AREASIZE and MAXOPENCURSORS options before precompiling.

ORA-01002   fetch out of sequence

Cause: In a host language program, a FETCH call was issued out of sequence. A successful parse-and-execute call must be issued before a fetch. This can occur if an attempt was made to fetch from an active set after all records have been fetched. This may be caused by fetching from a SELECT FOR UPDATE cursor after a commit. A PL/SQL cursor loop implicitly does fetches and may also cause this error.

Action: Parse and execute an SQL statement before attempting to fetch the data.

ORA-01003   no statement parsed

Cause: A host language program call referenced a cursor with no associated parsed SQL statement. An SQL call (for example, OSQL3) must be used to pass an SQL statement to Oracle and to associate the statement with an open cursor. A cursor must already have an associated SQL statement if referenced in a DESCRIBE, NAME, DEFINE, BIND, EXECUTE, or FETCH.

Action: Do the SQL call (for example, OSQL) to pass the required SQL statement before referencing the cursor.

ORA-01004   default username feature not supported; logon denied

Cause: An attempt was made to use automatic logon on a system not supporting this feature.

Action: Specify the complete username and password to log on to Oracle.

ORA-01005   null password given; logon denied

Cause: An invalid password was given when logging on.

Action: Provide a valid password.

ORA-01006   bind variable does not exist

Cause: A program issued a BIND call for a variable not listed in the associated SQL statement. Only those variables prefixed by either a colon (:) or ampersand (&) in the SQL statement may be referenced in a BIND call (OBIND or OBINDN). This error may also be caused by a mismatch between a precompiler program and the related library (SQLLIB).

Action: Modify the BIND call to reference one of the substitute variables specified in the associated SQL statement.

ORA-01007   variable not in select list

Cause: A reference was made to a variable not listed in the SELECT clause. In OCI, this can occur if the number passed for the position parameter is less than 1 or greater than the number of variables in the SELECT clause in any of the following calls: DESCRIBE, NAME, or DEFINE. In SQL*Forms or SQL*Report, specifying more variables in an INTO clause than in the SELECT clause also causes this error.

Action: In OCI, specify a position number between 1 and the number of variables in the SELECT clause. In SQL*Forms or SQL*Report, specify an equal number of variables in the SELECT and INTO clauses.

ORA-01008   not all variables bound

Cause: An SQL statement containing substitution variables was executed without all variables bound. All substitution variables must have a substituted value before the SQL statement is executed.

Action: In OCI, use an OBIND or OBINDN call to substitute the required values.

ORA-01009   missing mandatory parameter

Cause: A host language program call did not pass all required parameters. The syntax and parameter description for each call is given in the *Programmer's Guide to the Oracle Precompilers*.

Action: Check the syntax for the call and enter all required parameters.

ORA-01010   invalid OCI operation

Cause: This is an internal error message not normally issued.
Action: Contact Worldwide Customer Support.

ORA-01011   Cannot use ORACLE7 compatibility mode with an ORACLE Version 6
            server

Cause: An attempt was made to use Oracle 7 compatibility mode when accessing Oracle version 6.

Action: Do not use Oracle 7 compatibility mode when accessing Oracle version 6.

ORA-01012   not logged on

Cause: A host language program issued an Oracle call (other than OLON or OLOGON) without being logged on to Oracle. This can occur when a user process attempts to access the database after the instance it is connected to terminates, forcing the process to disconnect.

Action: Log on to Oracle (by calling OLON or OLOGON) before issuing any Oracle calls. When the instance has been restarted, retry the action.

ORA-01013   user requested cancel of current operation

Cause: The user interrupted an Oracle operation by entering CTRL-C or another canceling operation. This forces the current operation to end. This is an informational message only.

Action: Continue with the next operation.

ORA-01014   ORACLE shutdown in progress

Cause: A user tried to log on to Oracle while an instance shutdown was in progress. Oracle logons are disabled while Oracle is being shut down.

Action: Wait until Oracle is brought back up before attempting to log on.

ORA-01015   logon called recursively

Cause: This is an internal error message not normally issued.

Action: Contact Worldwide Customer Support.

ORA-01016   This function can be called only after a fetch

Cause: The cursor is in an invalid state.

Action: Ensure the appropriate OCI/UPI function is called after the fetch and prior to the offending function.

ORA-01017   invalid username/password; logon denied

Cause: An invalid username or password was entered in an attempt to log on to Oracle. The username and password must be the same as specified in a GRANT CONNECT statement. If the username and password are entered together, the format is *username/password*.

When Trusted Oracle is configured in OS MAC mode, this error may occur if you are attempting to query a table/view in a secondary database when the username was not created or granted the CREATE SESSION privilege in the secondary database.

When Trusted Oracle is configured in DBMS MAC mode, this error may occur if you were granted the CREATE SESSION system privilege at a higher label than that attempted at logon.

Action: Enter a valid username/password combination in the correct format.

For Trusted Oracle users, if the cause of this error is that the username was either not created or not granted the CREATE SESSION system privilege in a secondary database, ask the database administrator to authorize the username to access the secondary database. Alternatively, if the cause of this error is that the username is granted the CREATE SESSION system privilege at a higher level than that of the attempted logon, either logon at that higher level or ask the database administrator to regrant the privilege at the appropriate level.

ORA-01018   column does not have a LONG datatype

Cause: An attempt was made to fetch data using the LONG fetch option, but the specified column was not LONG.

Action: Reexecute the fetch without the LONG fetch option, or create the table with a LONG column.

ORA-01019   unable to allocate memory in the user side

Cause: The user side memory allocator returned an error.
Action: Increase the process' heap size.

ORA-01020   unknown context state

Cause: This is an internal error message not normally issued.
Action: Contact Worldwide Customer Support.

ORA-01021   invalid context size specified

Cause: An invalid value was entered for the initial context area size. The initialization parameter CONTEXT_AREA specifies the context area size, which must be between 1,024 and 131,07 2 bytes.
Action: Specify an initial context area size between 1,024 and 131,07 2 bytes.

ORA-01023   cursor context not found (Invalid cursor number)

Cause: The cursor number is not a valid open cursor.
Action: Make sure that the cursor is open.

ORA-01024   invalid datatype in OCI call

Cause: An OCI program call specified an invalid datatype. In OCI calls, Oracle datatypes are specified as numbers between 1 and 7. Datatypes are described in the *Programmer's Guide to Oracle Precompilers*.
Action: Check the datatype description and enter the correct number for the datatype.

ORA-01025   UPI parameter out of range

Cause: An integer parameter to a UPI function is out of range. This is an internal error message not normally issued.
Action: Contact Worldwide Customer Support.

ORA-01026   multiple buffers of size > 2000 in the bind list

Cause: There is more than one long buffer in the bind list.
Action: Change the buffer size to be less than 255 for the bind variable bound to a normal column.

ORA-01027   bind variables not allowed for data definition operations

Cause: An attempt was made to use a bind variable in an SQL data definition statement. For example, suppose you have a CREATE TABLE AS SELECT statement in which the SELECT's WHERE clause refers to a variable.
Action: Remove the bind variable; then reexecute the SQL statement.

ORA-01030   SELECT ... INTO variable does not exist

Cause: The SELECT ... INTO specified in the bind call does not correspond to a variable in the SQL statement.
Action: If it is not possible to correct the statement, call Worldwide Customer Support.

ORA-01031   insufficient privileges

Cause: An attempt was made to change the current username or password without the appropriate privilege. This error also occurs if you are attempting to UPDATE a table with only SELECT privileges, attempting to CONNECT INTERNAL, or attempting to install a database without the necessary operating system privileges.
When Trusted Oracle is configured in DBMS MAC, this error may occur if the user was granted the necessary privilege at a higher level than the current logon.
Action: Ask the database administrator to perform the operation or grant the required privileges.

For Trusted Oracle users getting this error although granted the appropriate privilege at a higher level, ask the database administrator to regrant the privilege at the appropriate level.

ORA-01032   no such userid

Cause: This is an internal error message related to Export/Import.
Action: Contact Worldwide Customer Support.

ORA-01033   ORACLE startup or shutdown in progress

Cause: An attempt was made to log on while Oracle is being started up or shut down.
Action: Wait a few minutes; then retry the operation.

ORA-01034   ORACLE not available

Cause: Oracle was not started up. Possible causes are

■ The SGA requires more space than was allocated for it.

■ The operating system variable pointing to the instance is improperly defined.

Action: Refer to accompanying messages for possible causes, and correct the problem mentioned in the other messages. Retry after Oracle has been initialized. If Oracle has been initialized, verify that Oracle was linked correctly. Also, refer to the installation or user's guide for additional information about this error.

**ORA-01035   ORACLE only available to users with RESTRICTED SESSION
               privilege**

Cause: Logons are disallowed because an instance started in restricted mode. Only users with the RESTRICTED SESSION system privilege can log on.
Action: Request that Oracle be restarted without the restricted option, or obtain the RESTRICTED SESSION system privilege.

ORA-01036   illegal variable name/number

Cause: Unable to find bind context on user side.
Action: Make sure that the variable being bound is in the SQL statement.

ORA-01037   cannot allocate sort work area cursor; too many cursors

Cause: The maximum number of cursors for the program has been exceeded.
Action: Retry the operation using fewer open cursors.

ORA-01038   cannot write data file version ver with ORACLE
             Version ver

Cause: An attempt was made to write data file headers in an old format. The new format cannot be used until after the database has been verified as being compatible with this software version.

Action: Open the database to advance to the new file formats, then repeat the operation. If the operation is required before the database can be opened, then use the previous software release to do the operation.

ORA-01039   insufficient privileges on underlying objects of
             the view

Cause: An attempt was made to explain the query plan on another user's view without the necessary privileges on the underlying objects of the view.

Action: Obtain the necessary privileges or do not perform the offending operation.

ORA-01040   invalid character in password; logon denied

Cause: There are multibyte characters in the password, or some characters in the password are not in the US7ASCII range.

Action: Resubmit password with valid characters.

ORA-01041   internal error. HOSTDEF extension does not exist

Cause: The pointer to the HSTDEF extension in HSTDEF is NULL.

Action: Report as a bug to Worldwide Customer Support.

ORA-01042   detaching a session with open cursors not allowed

Cause: An attempt was made to detach a session that has open cursors.

Action: Close all the cursors before detaching the session.

ORA-01043   user side memory corruption [num], [num], [num], [num]

Cause: The application code corrupted some of the user memory.

Action: Make certain that the application code is not overwriting memory. Contact Worldwide Customer Support.

ORA-01045 user name lacks CREATE SESSION privilege; logon denied

Cause: An attempt was made to connect to a userid that does not have CREATE SESSION privilege.

Action: If required, GRANT the user the CREATE SESSION privilege.

ORA-01046   cannot acquire space to extend context area

Cause: Oracle could not extend the current area any further because the operating system would not supply any more space. A system-specific message should appear following this message.
Action: Close some cursors and try again, or check operating system quotas to allow use of more virtual memory.

ORA-01050   cannot acquire space to open context area

Cause: Oracle could not open a new context area because the operating system would not supply any more space. A system-specific message should appear following this message.
Action: Close some cursors and try again, or check operating system quotas to allow use of more virtual memory.

ORA-01053   user storage address cannot be read

Cause: A bind variable or other user area could not be read by Oracle.
Action: Check that binds are done correctly on valid user buffers, then retry the operation.

ORA-01054   user storage address cannot be written

Cause: A define (FETCH ... INTO or SELECT ... INTO) variable or other user area could not be written to by Oracle.
Action: Check that INTO variables and indicators are correctly specified; then retry the operation.

ORA-01057 invalid or ambiguous block.field reference in user exit

Cause: The reference to a block.field identifier in a user exit is incorrect or ambiguous, probably because it is misspelled or incomplete.
Action: Check syntax and identifier spelling; then correct the reference.

ORA-01070   Using an old version of Oracle for the server

Cause: An attempt was made to run an older, obsolete Oracle 7 Server.
Action: Upgrade the server.

ORA-01071   cannot perform operation without starting up ORACLE

Cause: An attempt was made to perform an operation before Oracle was started.
Action: Start up Oracle; then retry the operation.

ORA-01072   cannot stop ORACLE; ORACLE not running

> **Cause:** An attempt was made to stop Oracle, but Oracle was not running.
> **Action:** No user action is required.

ORA-01073   fatal connection error: unrecognized call type

> **Cause:** An illegal internal operation was attempted. This is an internal error message not normally issued.
> **Action:** Contact Worldwide Customer Support.

ORA-01074   cannot shut down ORACLE; inside a logon session
            - log off first

> **Cause:** An attempt was made to shut down Oracle inside a logon session.
> **Action:** Log off before shutting down Oracle.

ORA-01075   currently logged on

> **Cause:** An attempt was made to log on while already logged on.
> **Action:** No user action is required.

ORA-01076   multiple logons per process not yet supported

> **Cause:** Oracle does not support multiple logons per process.
> **Action:** No user action is required.

ORA-01077   background process initialization failure

> **Cause:** A failure occurred during initialization of the background processes.
> **Action:** Refer to the diagnostic information in the accompanying message stack or in the trace file, and take appropriate action.

ORA-01078   failure in processing initialization parameters

> **Cause:** A failure occurred during processing of the initialization parameters during system startup.
> **Action:** Refer to the diagnostic information in the accompanying message stack, and take appropriate action.

ORA-01079   ORACLE database was not properly created,
            operation aborted

> **Cause:** There was an error when the database or control file was created.

Action: Check the message signaled when the database was first created or when the control file was recreated. Take appropriate actions to recreate the database or a new control file.

ORA-01080   error in shutting down ORACLE

Cause: A failure occurred during system shutdown.
Action: Refer to the diagnostic information in the accompanying message stack, and take appropriate action.

ORA-01081   cannot start already-running ORACLE -
             shut it down first

Cause: An attempt was made to start Oracle while it was already running.
Action: Shut down Oracle first, if you want to restart it.

ORA-01083   value of parameter var is inconsistent with that
             of other servers

Cause: The value of the given initialization parameter is required to be the same for all servers in the parallel configuration.
Action: Change the value in the initialization parameter file to match that of the other control files.

ORA-01086   savepoint 'name' never established

Cause: An attempt was made to roll back to a savepoint that was never established.
Action: No user action is required.

ORA-01087   cannot start up ORACLE - currently logged on

Cause: An attempt was made to start up Oracle by a user who is currently logged on.
Action: Log off; then issue the STARTUP command.

ORA-01088   cannot shut down ORACLE while active processes exist

Cause: Users are still logged on to the instance.
Action: Either wait for all users to log off, or issue the SHUTDOWN IMMEDIATE command to force the users off the system. Alternatively, issue the SHUTDOWN ABORT command to shut down the database without waiting for users to be forced off.

ORA-01089   immediate shutdown in progress - no operations
             are permitted

Cause: The SHUTDOWN IMMEDIATE command was used to shut down a running Oracle instance, terminating any active operations.

Action: Wait for the instance to be restarted, or contact the database administrator.

ORA-01090   shutdown in progress - connection is not permitted

Cause: The SHUTDOWN command was used to shut down a running Oracle instance, disallowing any connects to Oracle.

Action: Wait for the instance to restart, or contact the database administrator.

ORA-01091   failure during startup force

Cause: Unable to destroy the old SGA.

Action: Manually remove the old SGA (see the installation or user's guide for instructions); then reissue the STARTUP command.

ORA-01092   ORACLE instance terminated. Disconnection forced.

Cause: The instance connected to was terminated abnormally, probably due to a SHUTDOWN ABORT. The current process was forced to disconnect from the instance.

Action: Contact the database administrator to determine when the instance is restarted. Attempt to reconnect after the instance is running again.

ORA-01093   ALTER DATABASE CLOSE only permitted with no
             sessions connected

Cause: There is at lease one more session (other than the current one) logged in to the instance. ALTER DATABASE CLOSE is not permitted when other sessions are active.

Action: Find the other sessions and disconnect them. Then resubmit the ALTER DATABASE CLOSE command. Also, issue the SHUTDOWN IMMEDIATE command to force users off the system, or issue the SHUTDOWN ABORT command to shut down the database without waiting for users to be forced off.

ORA-01094   ALTER DATABASE CLOSE in progress. Connections
             not permitted

Cause: An attempt was made to connect while the database is being closed with the ALTER DATABASE CLOSE command.

Action: Attempt to connect again when the database is open. Contact the database administrator to find out when the database will be open.

ORA-01095   DML statement processed zero rows

Cause: A DML cursor from the OTEX( ) call processed 0 rows when executed.
Action: Caller can either do a rollback or ignore the message and execute the rest of the cursors in the cursor array.

```
ORA-01096    program version (num) incompatible with
             instance (num)
```

Cause: The program was linked with a different version of the server than the instance it is attempting to connect to.
Action: Relink the program against the same version of Oracle as the instance, or restart (use the command startup force) the database using the program's version of the SERVER.

```
ORA-01097    cannot shutdown while in a transaction
             -commit or rollback
```

Cause: An attempt was made to shut down the database while a transaction was in progress.
Action: Either commit or roll back the current transaction, then attempt to shut down the database.

```
ORA-01099    cannot mount database in SHARED mode if started in
             single process mode
```

Cause: An attempt was made to mount a database in parallel mode with the initialization parameter SINGLE_PROCESS set to TRUE.
Action: Either mount the database in EXCLUSIVE mode, or set the initialization parameter SINGLE_PROCESS to FALSE before starting the instance in parallel (shared) mode.

Oracle Files: 01100-01250

This section lists messages generated when files are accessed by the Oracle Server.

```
ORA-01100    database already mounted
```

Cause: An attempt was made to mount a database with the name of a currently mounted database.
Action: No user action is required.

```
ORA-01101    database being created currently mounted by some
             other instance
```

Cause: An attempt was made to create a database with the name of a currently mounted database.
Action: Either change the database name or shut down the other instance.

ORA-01102   cannot mount database in exclusive mode

Cause: An instance tried to mount the database in exclusive mode, but some other instance has already mounted the database in exclusive or parallel mode.
Action: Either mount the database in parallel mode, or shut down all other instances before mounting the database in exclusive mode.

ORA-01103   database name 'name' in control file is not 'name'

Cause: The database name used does not match that in the control file.
Action: Ensure the correct control file and database name are used.

ORA-01104   number of control files (num) does not equal num

Cause: The number of control files used by this instance disagrees with the number of control files in an existing instance that is accessing the same database.
Action: Make sure all control files are listed in the initialization parameter CONTROL_FILES, then retry the operation.

ORA-01105   mount is incompatible with mounts by other instances

Cause: An attempt was made to mount the database, but another instance has already mounted a database by the same name, and the mounts are not compatible. Additional messages will accompany this message to report why the mounts are incompatible.
Action: See the accompanying messages for the appropriate action to take.

ORA-01106   database must be closed before dismounting

Cause: An attempt was made to dismount a database before it was closed.
Action: Close the database, then retry the operation.

ORA-01107   database must be mounted for media recovery

Cause: An attempt to perform media recovery was made, but the database is not mounted.
Action: Mount the database, then retry the operation.

ORA-01108   media recovery active on file name

Cause: Media recovery is actively being applied to the given file. The file cannot be used for normal database access or crash recovery.

Action: Wait for media recovery to complete, or cancel the media recovery session.

ORA-01109   database not open

Cause: An attempt was made to perform an operation on an unopened database.
Action: Open the database, then retry the operation.

ORA-01110   data file name: 'str'

Cause: This message reports the filename involved with other messages.
Action: See the associated messages for a description of the problem.

ORA-01111   name for data file name is unknown - rename
             to correct file

Cause: The data file was missing from a CREATE CONTROLFILE command, or backup control file recovery was done with a control file that was saved before the file was created.
Action: Rename the missing file to the name of the real file.

ORA-01112   media recovery not started

Cause: An attempt was made to continue media recovery, but media recovery had not been started.
Action: No user action is required.

ORA-01113   file name needs media recovery

Cause: An attempt was made to open a data file that is in need of media recovery.
Action: First apply media recovery to the data file identified in the message, then retry the operation.

ORA-01114   IO message writing block to file name (block # num)

Cause: The device on which the file resides is probably offline.
Action: Restore access to the device, then retry the operation.

ORA-01115   IO message reading block from file name (block # num)

Cause: The device on which the file resides is probably offline.
Action: Restore access to the device, then retry the operation.

ORA-01116   `message in opening data file name`

Cause: Usually the file is not accessible.
Action: Make sure the data file is in the expected location and can be accessed properly, then retry the operation.

ORA-01117   `adding file 'name' with illegal block size num,`
             `limit is num`

Cause: An attempt was made to add a data file with a block size that is greater than the maximum block size allowed.
Action: Retry the operation with a smaller block size.

ORA-01118   `cannot add any more data files: limit of num exceeded`

Cause: An attempt to add a data file failed because the limit for such files had already been reached.
Action: If more database space is required, export the database and re-create it with a higher limit for data files (and perhaps increased file size).

ORA-01119   `message in creating data file 'name'`

Cause: Insufficient space on device.
Action: Decrease the size of the requested file, or allocate a file on another device with more available space. If a file size was not specified in the statement, then specify a file size smaller than the available space on the device.

ORA-01120   `cannot remove online data file name; database`
             `is open or mounted parallel`

Cause: An attempt to remove an online data file failed because the file was not closed, or was opened in parallel mode. This message can occur when trying to drop a tablespace. A tablespace cannot be dropped while users are accessing its data, index, rollback, or temporary segments, or while the database is mounted in parallel mode.
Action: Shut down Oracle and mount the database in exclusive mode to drop a tablespace. To prevent users from opening the tablespace, take it offline, or put the instance in restricted access mode.

ORA-01121   `cannot rename data file name - file is in use`
             `or recovery`

Cause: An attempt to rename an online data file failed because the file was not closed or was being recovered. Either the file is online and the data file is open to some instance, or another process is currently performing media recovery on the file.

Action: Close the file, or shut down Oracle and mount the database in exclusive mode. End all recovery sessions. To prevent users from opening the file, take its tablespace offline, or put the instance into restricted mode.

```
ORA-01122    data file name - failed verification check
```

Cause: The information in the data file is inconsistent with information from the control file. This could be because the control file is from a time earlier than the data files, or the data file size does not match the size specified in the control file, or the data file is corrupted.

Action: Make certain that the data files and control files are the correct files for this database, then retry the operation.

```
ORA-01123    cannot start online backup; media recovery
             not enabled
```

Cause: An attempt to start backup of an online tablespace failed because archiving was not enabled.

Action: Enable archiving and retry the operation.

```
ORA-01124    cannot recover online file 'name' - must be offline
             to recover
```

Cause: An attempt was made to recover an online file.

Action: Take the file offline before recovery.

```
ORA-01125    cannot disable media recovery - file name has
             online backup set
```

Cause: An attempt to disable media recovery encountered an online recovery still in progress.

Action: Wait for the recovery to finish before retrying the operation.

```
ORA-01126    database must be mounted exclusive and not open for
             this operation
```

Cause: An operation failed because the database was not mounted in exclusive mode.

Action: Shut down Oracle and mount the database in exclusive mode.

```
ORA-01127    database name 'name' exceeds size limit of
             num characters
```

Cause: The specified database name is too long.

Action: Shorten the database name to eight characters or fewer, then retry the operation.

ORA-01128   cannot start online backup - file name is offline

> **Cause:** A file to be backed up in the online backup is offline.
> **Action:** Either bring the file online for the online backup, or do an offline backup.

ORA-01129   user's default tablespace does not exist

> **Cause:** A user's default or temporary tablespace was dropped.
> **Action:** Recreate the tablespace that was dropped, or change the user's default or temporary tablespace.

ORA-01130   data file version num incompatible with
                 ORACLE Version num

> **Cause:** The named data file was created under an incompatible version of Oracle, or the file is invalid or nonexistent.
> **Action:** Shut down and restart the correct version of Oracle, or check the references to the data file and make sure it exists.

ORA-01131   DB_FILES files initialization parameter value num
                 exceeds limit of num

> **Cause:** The specified value of the initialization parameter DB_FILES is too large.
> **Action:** Reduce the value of the DB_FILES parameter and retry the operation.

ORA-01132   length of data file name 'name' exceeds limit of
                 num characters

> **Cause:** The specified data filename is too long.
> **Action:** Shorten the filename and retry the operation.

ORA-01133   length of logfile name 'name' exceeds limit
                 of num characters

> **Cause:** The specified redo log filename is too long.
> **Action:** Shorten the filename and retry the operation.

ORA-01134   database mounted exclusive by another instance

> **Cause:** An attempt to access a database failed because it is mounted in exclusive mode by another instance.
> **Action:** Either shut down the other instance, or wait for the other instance to either close the database or mount it in parallel mode, before retrying the operation.

ORA-01135   file name accessed for DML/query is offline

Cause: A query failed because it referenced a data file that belongs to an offline tablespace. An offline tablespace must be brought online to access its data.
Action: Wait until the tablespace is brought online before executing the query.

```
ORA-01136    specified size of file num (num blocks) is less
             than original size of num blocks
```

Cause: An attempt was made to specify a size in the AS clause of the ALTER DATABASE CREATE DATA FILE command that is smaller than the size needed.
Action: Issue the statement again using the correct size for the file.

```
ORA-01137    data file name is still in the middle of going offline
```

Cause: It was not possible to get the lock for a file that is offline when attempting to bring it online. The most likely cause is that the lock is still held by the instance that is took it offline.
Action: Wait for the other instance to release the lock on the file.

```
ORA-01138    database must either be open in this instance or not
             at all
```

Cause: The requested operation cannot be done when the database is mounted but not opened by this instance, and another instance has the database open.
Action: Execute the operation in the open instance, open the database in the current instance, or close the database in the other instances.

```
ORA-01139    RESET LOGS option only valid after an incomplete
             database recovery
```

Cause: The RESET LOGS option was specified in an ALTER DATABASE OPEN statement, but there has been no incomplete recovery session.
Action: Reexecute the statement without specifying RESET LOGS.

```
ORA-01140    cannot end online backup - all files are offline
```

Cause: All the files were offline when you attempted to end an online backup.
Action: None. Online backup does not need to be ended for this tablespace.

```
ORA-01141    message renaming data file name - new file 'name'
             not found
```

Cause: An attempt to change a data file's name in the control file failed because no file was found with the new name.
Action: Make sure that the data file has been properly renamed by the operating system, then retry the operation.

ORA-01142 `cannot end online backup - none of the files are`
`in backup`

Cause: None of the files was found to be in the online backup when you attempted to end the online backup.

Action: None. Online backup does not need to be ended for this tablespace.

ORA-01143 `cannot disable media recovery - file name is offline`

Cause: An attempt to disable media recovery found a file that needs media recovery, thus media recovery cannot be disabled.

Action: Recover the offending file or drop the tablespace to which it belongs, then retry the operation.

ORA-01144 `file size (num blocks) exceeds maximum of num blocks`

Cause: The specified file size is larger than the maximum allowable size.

Action: Specify a smaller size.

ORA-01145 `offline immediate disallowed unless media`
`recovery enabled`

Cause: ALTER TABLESPACE ... OFFLINE IMMEDIATE or ALTER DATABASE DATA FILE ... OFFLINE is only allowed if database is in ARCHIVEREDO LOG mode.

Action: Take the tablespace offline normally, or do a shutdown abort before attempting the required operation. It is worthwhile reconsidering the backup strategy for the database. The attempted operations can be done if ARCHIVEREDO LOG mode is enabled.

ORA-01146 `cannot start online backup - file name is already`
`in backup`

Cause: An attempt was made to start an online backup, but an online backup was already started for one of the data files.

Action: End the first backup before beginning another.

ORA-01147 `SYSTEM tablespace file name is offline`

Cause: A file belonging to the SYSTEM tablespace has been marked offline by the database administrator. The database cannot be started until all SYSTEM tablespace files are online and can be opened.

Action: Bring the file online.

ORA-01148 `database must be mounted exclusive for this operation`

Cause: Database was not mounted in exclusive mode.
Action: Mount the database in exclusive mode and retry the operation.

ORA-01149   cannot shutdown - file name has online backup set

Cause: A normal shutdown was attempted while online backup is in progress.
Action: End the online backup then shut down.

ORA-01150   cannot offline tablespace - file name has online
             backup set

Cause: Tablespace cannot be taken offline when online backup is running.
Action: End the online backup then take the tablespace offline.

ORA-01151   use media recovery to recovery block, restore backup
             if needed

Cause: Crash recovery or instance recovery could not apply a change to a block because it was not the next change. This can happen if the block was corrupted then repaired during recovery. This message is usually accompanied by ORA-01172.
Action: There is additional information for ORA-01172. Perform a RECOVER DATA FILE for the file containing the block. If this does not resolve the problem, then restore the file from a backup and recover it again.

ORA-01152   file name was not restored from a sufficiently
             old backup

Cause: An incomplete recovery session was started, but an insufficient number of redo logs was applied to make the database consistent; this file is still in the future of the last redo log applied. The most likely cause of this message is forgetting to restore the file from backup before doing incomplete recovery.

NOTE
This message cannot always be caught.

Action: Apply additional redo log files until the database is consistent, or restore the data files from an older backup and repeat recovery.

ORA-01153   an incompatible media recovery is active

Cause: An attempt was made to start an incompatible media recovery or open and reset the redo log files during media recovery. Media recovery sessions are incompatible if they attempt to recover the same data file. Incomplete media recovery or OPEN RESETLOGS is incompatible with any media recovery.

Action: Wait for the completion of, or cancel, the other media recovery session.

ORA-01154   database busy. Open, Close, mount, and dismount
             not allowed now

Cause: Some operation is in progress that expects the state of the instance to remain open or mounted.

Action: Wait for the operation to complete and try again. If attempting a normal database shutdown, try SHUTDOWN ABORT.

ORA-01155   the database is being opened, closed, mounted,
             or dismounted

Cause: The attempted operation will not succeed while the instance is in one of the states mentioned in the message.

Action: Wait for the open, close, mount, or dismount to complete and try again. If attempting a normal database shutdown, try SHUTDOWN ABORT.

ORA-01156   recovery in progress may need access to files

Cause: Either media or instance recovery is in progress. The recovery may need access to the files that the attempted operation tried to use.

Action: Wait for the recovery to complete and try again.

ORA-01157   cannot identify data file name - file not found

Cause: The background process was not able to find one of the data files. The database will prohibit access to this file, but other files will be unaffected. However, the first instance to open the database will need to access all online data files. Accompanying messages from the operating system will describe why the file was not found.

Action: Make the file available to database. Then either open the database or do ALTER SYSTEM CHECK DATA FILES.

ORA-01158   database name already mounted

Cause: Another instance has a database by this name mounted.

Action: Find and shut down the instance that has this database mounted before issuing the CREATE CONTROLFILE statement.

ORA-01159   file name is not from same database as previous files

Cause: Not all of the files specified in the CREATE CONTROLFILE statement are from the same database.

Action: Check the list of files specified in the CREATE CONTROLFILE statement, and remove files that are not part of the same database.

ORA-01160   file name is not a str it is of type str

Cause: The file in the DATA FILE or LOGFILE section of the CREATE CONTROLFILE statement is not of the type listed in the command line.

Action: Check the file and determine its type. Enter the command again using the correct type for the file.

ORA-01161   database name name in file header does not match
             given name of name

Cause: The database name given at the command line does not match the database name found in the file header. The database name specified at the command line is incorrect.

Action: Enter the command again with the correct name for the database.

ORA-01162   block size num in file header does not match
             DB_BLOCK_SIZE (num)

Cause: CREATE CONTROLFILE discovered that the block size for this file is incompatible with the initialization parameter DB_BLOCK_SIZE used to allocate cache buffers. If this is not the first file, then there is a mixture of block sizes, or the file is corrupt.

Action: If this is the first file in the command, then correct DB_BLOCK_SIZE to match the file and restart the instance. If it is not the first file, find the correct version of the file.

ORA-01163   file size in header num (bytes) does not match
             SIZE num (bytes)

Cause: File size specified at CREATE CONTROLFILE does not match the size stored in the header. Most likely the specification is wrong.

Action: Restore the file from a backup and issue the statement again.

ORA-01164   MAXLOGFILES may not exceed num

Cause: The value for MAXLOGFILES specified on the command line is greater than num.

Action: Resubmit the command with a value of MAXLOGFILES that is num or less.

ORA-01165   MAXDATAFILES may not exceed num

Cause: The value for MAXDATAFILES specified on the command line is greater than num.

Action: Resubmit the command with a value of MAXDATAFILES that is num or less.

ORA-01166   file number num is larger than num (num)

Cause: In the CREATE CONTROLFILE statement, the file mentioned has a file number that is larger than that specified in MAXDATAFILES or MAXLOGFILES, or the file number is larger than the maximums specified in the initialization parameter, DB_FILES.

Action: Increase the values of MAXLOGFILES, MAXDATAFILES, or the parameter DB_FILES.

ORA-01167   two files are the same file/group number or the
            same file

Cause: There is an overlap of file numbers in the files specified on the command line, or the same file is specified twice. If they are not exactly the same file, then one is likely to be a backup of the other. If they are two members of the same redo log, they must be specified together in a group file spec.

Action: Confirm that the file mentioned is not a repeat of a file already mentioned in the command. If they are different files, then omit the earlier backup. If they are members of the same redo log, ensure they are in the same group file specification.

ORA-01168   physical block size num does not match size num of
            other members

Cause: The file is located on a device with a different physical block size than the other members in the group.

Action: Use a physical device with matching block size.

ORA-01169   DATA FILE number 1 not found. Must be present

Cause: Data file number 1 was not specified in a CREATE CONTROLFILE statement.

Action: Locate data file number 1 and resubmit the CREATE CONTROLFILE statement, making certain to include data file 1 on the command line.

ORA-01170   file not found 'name'

Cause: A file specified in the CREATE CONTROLFILE statement was not found. All data files (and all redo log files, if NORESETLOGS was used) must be accessible by the process that issues the CREATE CONTROLFILE statement.

Action: Check the statement for a typing mistake in the filename, and check for the existence of all files. Then issue the statement again after correcting the filenames.

ORA-01171   data file string is going offline due to message
             advancing checkpoint

Cause: The checkpoint in the file header could not be advanced. See accompanying messages for the reason. The data file will be taken offline the same as for a write message of a data block.

Action: See accompanying messages for details. Restore access to the file, do media recovery, and bring it back online.

ORA-01172   recovery of thread num stuck at block num
             of file name

Cause: Crash recovery or instance recovery could not apply a change to a block because it was not the next change. This can happen if the block was corrupted then repaired during recovery.

Action: Perform a RECOVER DATA FILE for the file containing the block. If this does not resolve the problem, then restore the file from a backup and recover it again.

ORA-01173   data dictionary indicates missing data file from
             system tablespace

Cause: Either of the following:

- The database is recovered to a point in time in the future of the control file.

- A data file from the system tablespace is omitted from the issued CREATE CONTROLFILE statement.

Action: Either of the following:

- Recover the database from a more recent control file.

- Recreate the control file, ensuring all data files are included for the system tablespace in the command line.

ORA-01174   DB_FILES is num but needs to be num to be compatible

Cause: The maximum number of data files supported by this instance is not the same as for the other instances. All instances must be able to open all the files any instance can open.

Action: Change the value of the DB_FILES initialization parameter to be compatible.

ORA-01175   data dictionary has more than the num files allowed
             by the instance

Cause: The data dictionary has more files than the instance can support.

Action: Increase the value of the initialization parameter DB_FILES, then shut down and restart the instance.

ORA-01176   data dictionary has more than the num files allowed
             by the controlfile

Cause: After a CREATE CONTROLFILE statement, the data dictionary has more data files than supported by the control file.

Action: Recreate the control file with a larger value for MAXDATA FILES.

ORA-01177   data file does not match dictionary - probably
             old incarnation

Cause: When comparing the control file with the data dictionary after a CREATE CONTROLFILE or OPEN RESETLOGS, it was noted that this data file was inconsistent with the dictionary. Most likely the file is a backup of a file that was dropped from the database, and the same file number was reused for a new file. It may also be that an incomplete recovery stopped at a time when this file number was used for another data file.

Action: Do a CREATE CONTROLFILE with the correct file or none at all.

ORA-01178   file name created before last CREATE CONTROLFILE,
             cannot recreate

Cause: An attempt was made to use the ALTER DATABASE CREATE DATA FILE to recreate a data file that existed at the last CREATE CONTROLFILE command. The information needed to recreate the file was lost with the control file that existed when the file was added to the database.

Action: Find a backup of the file, and recover it. Perform incomplete recovery to the time before the file was originally created.

ORA-01179   file name does not exist

Cause: During data file recovery, a file was listed that was not part of the database.

Action: Recheck the filename. Remember to use double quotes at the SQL*DBA command line and remember that the filename is translated in the environment of SQL*DBA.

ORA-01180   can not create data file 1

Cause: Data file 1 cannot be created with the ALTER DATABASE CREATE DATA FILE command.
Action: Either recover the file from a backup, or recreate the database.

ORA-01181   file name created before last RESETLOGS, cannot
             recreate

Cause: An attempt was made to use the ALTER DATABASE CREATE DATA FILE command to recreate a data file that existed before the last time the database was opened using the RESETLOGS option.
Action: Find a backup of the file and recover the backup file. Perform incomplete recovery to a time before the file was originally created.

ORA-01182   cannot create data file name - file is in use or
             recovery

Cause: An attempt was made to use the ALTER DATABASE CREATE DATA FILE command to recreate a data file that is currently online in an open instance or is currently being recovered.
Action: Close the database to all instances, or end all recovery sessions, then take the file offline and retry the operation.

ORA-01183   cannot mount database in parallel mode

Cause: The database is mounted in exclusive mode by another instance. It is not possible to mount a database in parallel mode if it is mounted in exclusive mode by another instance.
Action: Shut down the other instance and try again.

ORA-01184   logfile group num already exists

Cause: An ALTER DATABASE ADD LOGFILE command specified a log number for the new redo log which is already in use.
Action: Specify a different redo log file number, or let the database choose an unused value.

ORA-01185   logfile group number num is invalid

Cause: An ALTER DATABASE ADD LOGFILE command specified a redo log number for the new redo log which is too large.
Action: Specify a valid redo log file number.

ORA-01186   verification tests failed on file name

Cause: The data file did not pass the checks to ensure it is part of the database. See the accompanying messages for the reason the verification did not succeed.
Action: Make the correct file available to database. Then either open the database, or do ALTER DATABASE CHECK.

ORA-01187   cannot read from file name because it failed
             verification tests

Cause: The data file did not pass the checks to ensure it is part of the database. Reading the file is not allowed until it is verified.
Action: Make the correct file available to database. Then either open the database, or do ALTER DATABASE CHECK.

ORA-01188   block size num in header does not match
             physical block size

Cause: A redo log file member given to CREATE CONTROLFILE is on a physical device that has a different block size than the device originally used to create the redo log.
Action: Move the file to a device with the correct block size, or use the RESETLOGS option to CREATE CONTROLFILE.

ORA-01189   file is from a different RESETLOGS than previous files

Cause: In a CREATE CONTROLFILE command either this file or all previous files were backups from before the last RESETLOGS. This may also occur if this is a file that is offline and has been offline since before the last RESETLOGS.
Action: If the file was taken offline (normally) before the last RESETLOGS and is still offline, omit it from the CREATE CONTROLFILE command. Rename the file and put it online after the database is open. Otherwise find the version of the mentioned file consistent with the rest of the data files and resubmit the command.

ORA-01190   control file or data file name is from before
             the last RESETLOGS

Cause: An attempt was made to perform media recovery when the redo log reset information in a data file did not match the control file. Either the data file or the control file must be a backup that was made before the most recent ALTER DATABASE OPEN RESETLOGS.

Action: Restore the file from a more recent backup.

ORA-01191   file name is already offline - cannot do a
             normal offline

Cause: An attempt was made to take a tablespace offline normally, but the file named in the message is already offline.
Action: Bring the data file online first, or use the IMMEDIATE option when taking the tablespace offline.

ORA-01192   must have at least one enabled thread

Cause: At least two redo log files from at least one thread must be specified in the CREATE CONTROLFILE command line.
Action: Find the missing redo log files, and resubmit the command with the newly found redo log files included in the command line.

ORA-01193   file name is not the same file seen at start
             of recovery

Cause: An attempt was made to perform media recovery on a file, but a different copy of the file now exists since the last media recovery. Perhaps an invalid backup of the file was resorted.
Action: Find the correct version of the file, then retry media recovery.

ORA-01194   file name needs more recovery to be consistent

Cause: An incomplete recovery session was started, but an insufficient number of redo logs was applied to make the file consistent. The named file was not closed cleanly when it was last opened by the database. The most likely cause of this message is forgetting to restore the file from a backup before doing incomplete recovery.
Action: The file must be recovered to a time when it was not being updated. Either apply more redo logs until the file is consistent, or restore the file from an older backup and repeat recovery.

ORA-01195   online backup of file name needs more recovery
             to be consistent

Cause: An incomplete recovery session was started, but an insufficient number of redo logs was applied to make the file consistent. The reported file is an online backup which must be recovered to the time the backup ended.
Action: Either apply more redo logs until the file is consistent, or restore the file from an older backup and repeat recovery.

ORA-01196   file name is inconsistent due to a failed
             media recovery session

Cause: A media recovery session failed while the named file was being recovered. The file is in an inconsistent state, and no more recovery was successfully completed on this file.

Action: Either apply more redo logs until the file is consistent, or restore the file from a backup again and repeat recovery.

ORA-01197   thread num only contains one log

Cause: During a CREATE CONTROLFILE statement, all threads represented in the redo logs must be represented by at least two redo logs: a "last redo log" and a second redo log. The named thread does not contain two redo logs.

Action: Either find more redo logs from the named thread, or remove all references to redo logs from that thread, then resubmit the command.

ORA-01198   must specify size for file 'name' if RESETLOGS

Cause: File sizes must be given for all redo log files if you are doing a CREATE CONTROLFILE with the RESETLOGS option.

Action: Resubmit the command with the appropriate redo log file size.

ORA-01200   actual file size of num is smaller than correct
             size of num blocks

Cause: The size of the file, as returned by the operating system, is smaller than the size of the file as indicated in the file header and the control file. Somehow the file has been truncated.

Action: Restore a good copy of the data file from a backup and perform recovery as needed.

ORA-01201   file size num in header does not match size num
             in control file

Cause: The file sizes in the control file and in the file header do not match. One of the files is probably corrupted.

Action: Replace the corrupted file with a good copy and perform recovery as needed.

ORA-01202   wrong incarnation of this file - wrong creation time

Cause: The creation time in the file header is not the same as the creation time in the control file. This is probably a copy of a file that was dropped.

Action: Restore a current copy of the data file and perform recovery as needed.

ORA-01203   wrong incarnation of this file - wrong creation SCN

Cause: The creation change number in the file header is not the same as the creation change number in the control file. This is probably a copy of a file that was dropped.

Action: Restore a current copy of the data file and perform recovery as needed.

ORA-01204   wrong file - file number is num rather than num

Cause: The file number in the file header is not correct. This is probably a restored backup of the wrong file, but from the same database.

Action: Restore a copy of the correct data file and perform recovery as needed.

ORA-01205   not a data file - type number in header is num

Cause: The file type in the header is not correct for a data file. This is probably a redo log file or control file.

Action: Restore a copy of the correct data file and perform recovery as needed.

ORA-01206   file is not part of this database - wrong database id

Cause: The database ID in the file header does not match the database ID in the control file. The file may be from a different database, or it may not be a data file at all. If the database was rebuilt, this may be a file from before the rebuild.

Action: Restore a copy of the correct data file and perform recovery as needed.

ORA-01207   file is more recent than control file -
            old control file

Cause: The control file change sequence number in the data file is greater than the number in the control file. This implies that the wrong control file is being used.

NOTE
If this message occurs repeatedly (by opening the database many times), the message may stop occurring without the problem being corrected. Every attempt to open the database will advance the control file change sequence number until it is great enough.

Action: Use the current control file or perform cancel-based recovery to make the control file current. Be sure to follow all restrictions on performing a cancel-based recovery.

ORA-01208   data file is an old version - not accessing
            current version

Cause: The checkpoint in the file header is less recent than in the control file. If opening a database that is already open by another instance, or if another instance just caused this file to be placed online, then the database is probably looking at a different version of the file. Otherwise, a backup of the file was probably restored while the file was still in use.

Action: Make the correct file available to the database. Then either open the database or do ALTER DATABASE CHECK.

ORA-01209   data file is from before the last RESETLOGS

Cause: The reset redo log data in the file header does not match the control file. If the database is closed or the file is offline, this is an old backup that was taken before the last ALTER DATABASE OPEN RESETLOGS command. If you are opening a database that is already open by another instance, or if another instance just brought this file online, then you are probably looking at a different version of the file. Otherwise a backup of the file was probably restored while the file was in use.

Action: Make the correct file available to the database. Then either open the database, or issue an ALTER DATABASE CHECK statement.

ORA-01210   data file header is media corrupt

Cause: The file header block is internally inconsistent. The beginning of the block has a header with a checksum and other data for ensuring the consistency of the block. It is possible that the last disk write did not operate correctly. The most likely problem is that this is not a data file for any database.

Action: Make the correct file available to the database. Refer to any trace file generated after this message for more information. If the trace file indicates that the checksum is wrong, restore the file from a backup and perform media recovery.

ORA-01211   Version 6 data file is not from conversion to ORACLE7

Cause: The file is not a copy of the file last used under version 6. When you convert a database from version 6 to Oracle 7, the conversion utility must be run the last time the database is opened under version 6. Only the data files that were current when the conversion was done may be accessed by Oracle 7. This data file is either a backup taken from before the conversion, or the database was opened by version 6 after the conversion.

Action: Have the operating system make the correct data file available to the database, or repeat the version 6 to Oracle 7 conversion.

ORA-01212   MAXLOGMEMBERS may not exceed num

Cause: The value specified for MAXLOGMEMBERS is too large.
Action: Resubmit the command with a smaller value for MAXLOGMEMBERS.

ORA-01213   MAXINSTANCES may not exceed num

> **Cause:** The value specified for MAXINSTANCES is too large.
> **Action:** Resubmit the command with a smaller value for MAXINSTANCES.

ORA-01214   MAXLOGHISTORY may not exceed num

> **Cause:** The value specified for MAXLOGHISTORY is too large.
> **Action:** Resubmit the command with a smaller value for MAXLOGHISTORY.

ORA-01215   enabled thread num is missing after
             CREATE CONTROLFILE

> **Cause:** A CREATE CONTROLFILE command did not list all of the enabled threads for the database.
> **Action:** Issue the CREATE CONTROLFILE command again, and include all of the enabled threads.

ORA-01216   thread num is expected to be disabled after
             CREATE CONTROLFILE

> **Cause:** A thread specified in the CREATE CONTROLFILE command was enabled, but the data files indicate that the thread should be disabled. This is probably due to the fact that the redo log files supplied to the CREATE CONTROLFILE command are from a time before the thread was disabled.
> **Action:** This thread is not required for the operation of the database. Resubmit the command without specifying the thread. If desired, the thread can be recreated after the database has been opened.

ORA-01217   logfile member belongs to a different redo log
             file group

> **Cause:** A member of a redo log file group specified in the CREATE CONTROLFILE command is not part of the same group as the previous members.
> **Action:** Group together the correct members of the redo log file group for the CREATE CONTROLFILE command.

ORA-01218   logfile member is not from the same point-in-time

> **Cause:** A member of a redo log file group specified in the CREATE CONTROLFILE command is from a different point in time from the previous members. One of the members specified may be an older (possibly a backup copy) version of the redo log.
> **Action:** Find the correct version of the redo log, or leave it out of the CREATE CONTROLFILE command.

ORA-01219　database not open: queries allowed on fixed
　　　　　　　tables/views only

Cause: A query was issued against an object not recognized as a fixed table or fixed view before the database was opened.

Action: Rephrase the query to include only fixed objects, or open the database.

ORA-01220　file based sort illegal before database is open

Cause: A query issued against a fixed table or view required a temporary segment for sorting before the database was open. Only in-memory sorts are supported before the database is open.

Action: Rephrase the query to avoid a large sort, and increase the SORT_AREA_SIZE parameter in the initialization parameter file to enable the sort to be done in memory.

ORA-01221　data file name is not the same file to a
　　　　　　　background process

Cause: When the database writer opens the data file, it is accessing a different physical file than the foreground doing the recovery. The time-stamp set in the file header by the foreground was not found by the background. It may be that the background process could not read the file at all.

Action: Look in the DBWR trace file for the message it received when attempting to read the file header. Reconfigure the operating system as needed to have the filename successfully access the same file when opened by a background process.

ORA-01222　MAXINSTANCES of num requires MAXLOGFILES be at
　　　　　　　least num, not num

Cause: You attempted to create a database or control file that does not have room for at least two redo logs per thread of redo. A thread of redo must have two online redo logs in order to be enabled. It does not make sense to allow more redo threads than can be supported by the logs.

Action: Either reduce the MAXINSTANCES argument or increase MAXLOGFILES.

ORA-01223　RESETLOGS must be specified to set a new
　　　　　　　database name

Cause: The SET database name option was specified to CREATE CONTROLFILE, but RESETLOGS was not specified. The database name can only be changed when you open the database with RESETLOGS.

Action: Either add the RESETLOGS option, or drop the SET option to CREATE CONTROLFILE.

ORA-01224   group number in header name does not match GROUP name

Cause: Group number specified at CREATE CONTROLFILE does not match the group number stored in the header. Most likely the specification is wrong.
Action: Omit the GROUP option or give the correct one.

ORA-01225   thread number num is greater than MAXINSTANCES num

Cause: The redo log is for a thread greater than the MAXINSTANCES arguments.
Action: Increase the value for MAXINSTANCES and resubmit the command.

ORA-01226   file header of redo log member is inconsistent
            with other member

Cause: The redo log file member in the accompanying message is for the same group as the previous members, but other fields in the header are different. Either a file header is corrupted, or some file is a member of a deleted redo log.
Action: Correct the redo log member or omit this member from the command.

ORA-01227   log name is inconsistent with other log

Cause: The redo log file in the accompanying message is inconsistent with the contents of other redo logs given in the CREATE CONTROLFILE command. Either a file header is corrupted, or some file is an old copy rather than the current version. The problem may not be with the redo log listed, since all that can be detected is that there is an inconsistency. All redo log files listed in the command must be the current versions of the online redo logs.
Action: Find the correct online redo logs, or use the RESETLOGS option.

ORA-01228   SET DATABASE option required to install seed database

Cause: The SET DATABASE option was not included in the CREATE CONTROLFILE command during installation of a seed database. The database does not have a database ID because it is intended to be installed at multiple sites, and each site needs to be a different database with its own database ID. Both the SET DATABASE and RESETLOGS options must be specified to create the control file for this database.
Action: Command with the SET DATABASE and RESETLOGS options.

ORA-01229   data file name is inconsistent with logs

Cause: The data file in the accompanying message is inconsistent with the contents of the redo logs given in the CREATE CONTROLFILE command. The most likely cause is that one or more of the online redo logs was missing from the command. It is also possible that one or more of the redo logs is an old copy rather than the current version. All online redo log files must be listed in the command and must be the current versions of the online redo logs.

Action: Correct the online redo logs or use the RESETLOGS option.

SQL Execution: 01400-01489

This section lists messages generated during SQL execution.

ORA-01400   primary key or mandatory (NOT NULL) column is missing
             or NULL during insert

Cause: During insertion or updating of rows, a value for a column defined as NOT NULL was not specified.

Action: Specify a value for each NOT NULL column, or modify the table definition to allow NULL values in columns now defined as NOT NULL.

ORA-01401   inserted value too large for column

Cause: The value entered is larger than the maximum width defined for the column.

Action: Enter a value smaller than the column width, or use the MODIFY option with ALTER TABLE to expand the column width.

ORA-01402   view WITH CHECK OPTION where-clause violation

Cause: An INSERT or UPDATE statement was attempted on a view created with the CHECK OPTION. This would have resulted in the creation of a row that would not satisfy the view's WHERE clause.

Action: Examine the view's WHERE clause in the dictionary table VIEWS. If the current view does not have the CHECK OPTION, then its FROM clause must reference a second view that is defined using the CHECK OPTION. The second view's WHERE clause must also be satisfied by any INSERT or UPDATE statements. To insert the row, it may be necessary to insert it into the underlying table rather than through the view.

ORA-01403   no data found

Cause: In a host language program, all records have been fetched. The return code from the fetch was +4, indicating that all records have been returned from the SQL query.

Action: Terminate processing for the SELECT statement.

ORA-01404   ALTER COLUMN will make a concatenated index too large

Cause: Increasing the length of a column would cause the combined length of the columns specified in a previous CREATE INDEX statement to exceed the maximum index length (255). The total index length is computed as the sum of the width of all indexed columns plus the number of indexed columns. Date fields are calculated as a length of 7, character fields are calculated at their defined width, and numeric fields are length 22.

Action: The only way to alter the column is to drop the affected index. The index cannot be recreated if to do so would exceed the maximum index width.

ORA-01405   fetched column value is NULL

Cause: In an OCI program, a FETCH operation returned a NULL column value. The column buffer in the program remained unchanged, and the cursor return code was +2.

Action: Include program processing for this condition. This is only a warning.

ORA-01406   fetched column value was truncated

Cause: In a host language program, a FETCH operation was forced to truncate a character string. The program buffer area for this column was not large enough to contain the entire string. The cursor return code from the fetch was +3.

Action: Increase the column buffer area to hold the largest column value, or perform other appropriate processing.

ORA-01407   cannot update mandatory (NOT NULL) column to NULL

Cause: An attempt was made to update data in a NOT NULL column to a NULL value.

Action: Specify a value for the column, or modify the table definition to accept NULL values in that column.

ORA-01408   such column list already indexed

Cause: A CREATE INDEX statement specified a column that is already indexed. A single column may be indexed only once. Additional indexes may be created on the column if it is used as a portion of a concatenated index (that is, if the index consists of multiple columns).

Action: Do not attempt to reindex the column; it is unnecessary. To create a concatenated key, specify one or more additional columns in the CREATE INDEX statement.

ORA-01409   NOSORT option may not be used; rows are not
             in ascending order

Cause: An index was created with the NOSORT option when rows were not ascending. For nonunique indexes the ROWID is considered part of the index key. Therefore, if you create an index NOSORT and two of the rows in the table have the same key and are stored in ascending order—but get split across two extents where the data block address (dba) of the first block in the second extent is less than the data block address of the last block in the first extent—then the create index NOSORT may fail.

Action: Create the index without the NOSORT option, or ensure that the table is stored in one extent.

ORA-01410   invalid ROWID

Cause: A ROWID was entered incorrectly. ROWIDs must be entered as formatted hexadecimal strings using only numbers and the characters A through F. A typical ROWID format is '0001.000001F8.0006'.

Action: Check the format, then enter the ROWID using the correct format.

ORA-01411   cannot store the length of column in the indicator

Cause: Oracle tried to fetch a column more than 64K long and couldn't store the length of the column in the given indicator size of two bytes.

Action: Use the new bind type with callbacks to fetch the long column.

ORA-01412   zero length not allowed for this datatype

Cause: The length for datatype 97 is 0.

Action: Specify the correct length for the datatype.

ORA-01413   illegal value in packed decimal number buffer

Cause: The user buffer bound by the user as a packed decimal number contained an illegal value.

Action: Use a legal value.

ORA-01414   invalid array length when trying to bind array

Cause: An attempt was made to bind an array without either a current array length pointer or a zero maximum array length.

Action: Specify a valid length.

ORA-01415   outer-join (+) may not be applied to the
             label pseudo column

Cause: The user specified an outer join (+) following a reference to the label pseudocolumn.

Action: Work around the problem by defining a view on the table, and perform an outer join on the view column corresponding to a label.

ORA-01416   two tables cannot be outer-joined to each other

Cause: Two tables in a join operation specified an outer join with respect to each other. If an outer join is specified on one of the tables in a join condition, it may not be specified on the other table.

Action: Remove the outer-join specification (+) from one of the tables, then retry the operation.

ORA-01417   a table may be outer joined to at most one other table

Cause: A table in a join operation specified an outer join to more than one other table. A table may specify an outer join to only one other table.

Action: Specify only one outer join (+) to this table, then retry the operation.

ORA-01418   specified index does not exist

Cause: An ALTER INDEX, DROP INDEX, or VALIDATE INDEX statement specified the name of an index that does not exist. Only existing indexes can be altered, dropped, or validated. Existing indexes may be listed by querying the data dictionary.

Action: Specify the name of an existing index in the ALTER INDEX, DROP INDEX, or VALIDATE INDEX statement.

ORA-01419   datdts: illegal format code

Cause: During a date-to-character conversion, the internal representation of the conversion format was invalid. This is an internal message not normally issued.

Action: Contact Worldwide Customer Support.

ORA-01420   datstd: illegal format code

Cause: During a character-to-date conversion, the internal representation of the conversion format was invalid. This is an internal message not normally issued.

Action: Contact Worldwide Customer Support.

ORA-01421   datrnd/dattrn: illegal precision specifier

Cause: During a date truncate or round operation, the internal representation of the date precision was invalid. This is an internal message not normally issued.

Action: Contact Worldwide Customer Support.

```
ORA-01422    exact fetch returns more than requested
             number of rows
```

Cause: More rows were returned from an exact fetch than specified.
Action: Rewrite the query to return fewer rows or specify more rows in the exact fetch.

```
ORA-01423    message encountered while checking for extra rows
             in exact fetch
```

Cause: A message was encountered during the execution of an exact fetch. This message will be followed by more descriptive messages.
Action: Take the appropriate action for the messages that follow.

```
ORA-01424    missing or illegal character following the
             escape character
```

Cause: The character following the escape character in LIKE pattern is missing or not one of the escape characters '%' or '_'.
Action: Remove the escape character or specify the missing character.

```
ORA-01425    escape character must be character string of length 1
```

Cause: Given escape character for LIKE is not a character string of length 1.
Action: Change it to a character string of length 1.

```
ORA-01426    numeric overflow
```

Cause: Evaluation of a value expression has caused an overflow, or possibly, an underflow.
Action: Rewrite the expression as a series of expressions with fewer operands than the "overloaded" expression.

```
ORA-01427    single-row query returns more than one row
```

Cause: The outer query must use one of the keywords ANY, ALL, IN, or NOT IN to specify values to compare, because the subquery returned more than one row.
Action: Use ANY, ALL, IN, or NOT IN to specify which values to compare, or reword the query so only one row is retrieved.

```
ORA-01428    argument num is out of range
```

Cause: An illegal value for a mathematical function argument was specified. For example:

SELECT SQRT(–1) "Square Root" FROM DUAL;

Action: Refer to Chapter 4 of the *Oracle 7 Server SQL Language Reference Manual* for valid input and ranges of the mathematical functions.

ORA-01430   column being added already exists in table

Cause: An ALTER TABLE ADD statement specified the name of a column that is already in the table. All column names must be unique within a table.
Action: Specify a unique name for the new column, then reexecute the statement.

ORA-01431   internal inconsistency in GRANT command

Cause: An internal message occurred while attempting to execute a GRANT statement.
Action: Contact Worldwide Customer Support.

ORA-01432   public synonym to be dropped does not exist

Cause: The synonym specified in DROP PUBLIC SYNONYM is not a valid public synonym. It may be a private synonym.
Action: Correct the synonym name, or use DROP SYNONYM if the synonym is not public.

ORA-01433   synonym to be created is already defined

Cause: A CREATE SYNONYM statement specified a synonym name that is the same as an existing synonym, table, view, or cluster. Synonyms may not have the same name as any other synonym, table, view, or cluster available to the user creating the synonym.
Action: Specify a unique name for the synonym, then reexecute the statement.

ORA-01434   private synonym to be dropped does not exist

Cause: A DROP SYNONYM statement specified a synonym that does not exist. Existing synonym names may be listed by querying the data dictionary.
Action: Specify the name of an existing synonym in the DROP SYNONYM statement.

ORA-01435   user does not exist

Cause: This message is caused by any reference to a nonexistent user. For example, it occurs if a SELECT, GRANT, or REVOKE statement specifies a username that does not exist. Only a GRANT CONNECT statement may specify a new username. All other GRANT and REVOKE statements must specify existing usernames. If specified in a SELECT statement, usernames must already exist.

Action: Specify only existing usernames in the SELECT, GRANT, or REVOKE statement, or ask the database administrator to define the new username.

ORA-01436   CONNECT BY loop in user data

Cause: The condition specified in a CONNECT BY clause caused a loop in the query, where the next record to be selected is a descendent of itself. When this happens, there can be no end to the query.
Action: Check the CONNECT BY clause and remove the circular reference.

ORA-01437   cannot have join with CONNECT BY

Cause: A join operation was specified with a CONNECT BY clause. If a CONNECT BY clause is used in a SELECT statement for a tree-structured query, only one table may be referenced in the query.
Action: Remove either the CONNECT BY clause or the join operation from the SQL statement.

ORA-01438   value larger than specified precision allows
             for this column

Cause: When you inserted or updated records, a value was entered that exceeds the column width.
Action: Enter a smaller value, or use the MODIFY option to increase the column width.

ORA-01439   column to be modified must be empty to
             change datatype

Cause: An ALTER TABLE MODIFY statement attempted to change the datatype of a column containing data. To alter a column's datatype, the column must only contain NULL values.
Action: To alter the datatype, first set all values in the column to NULL.

ORA-01440   column to be modified must be empty to decrease
             precision or scale

Cause: An ALTER TABLE MODIFY statement attempted to decrease the scale or precision of a numeric column containing data. To decrease either of these values, the column must contain only NULL values. An attempt to increase the scale without also increasing the precision will also cause this message.
Action: Set all values in the column to NULL before decreasing the numeric precision or scale. If attempting to increase the scale, increase the precision in accordance with the scale, or set all values in the column to NULL first.

ORA-01441   column to be modified must be empty to decrease
             column length

Cause: An ALTER TABLE MODIFY statement attempted to decrease the size of a character field containing data. To decrease the maximum size of a character column, the column must contain only NULL values.
Action: Set all values in column to NULL before decreasing the maximum size.

ORA-01442   column to be modified to NOT NULL is already NOT NULL

Cause: An ALTER TABLE MODIFY statement attempted to change a column specification unnecessarily, from NOT NULL to NOT NULL.
Action: No user action is required.

ORA-01443   internal inconsistency; illegal datatype in
             resultant view column

Cause: An internal message occurred in referencing a view.
Action: Contact Worldwide Customer Support.

ORA-01444   internal inconsistency; internal datatype maps to
             invalid external type

Cause: This is an internal error message not normally issued.
Action: Contact Worldwide Customer Support.

ORA-01445   cannot select ROWID from view of more than one table

Cause: A SELECT statement attempted to select ROWIDs from a view derived from a join operation. Because the rows selected in the view do not correspond to underlying physical records, no ROWIDs can be returned.
Action: Remove ROWID from the view selection clause, then reexecute the statement.

ORA-01446   cannot select ROWID from view with DISTINCT,
             GROUP BY, etc.

Cause: A SELECT statement attempted to select ROWIDs from a view containing columns derived from functions or expressions. Because the rows selected in the view do not correspond to underlying physical records, no ROWIDs can be returned.
Action: Remove ROWID from the view selection clause, then reexecute the statement.

ORA-01447   ALTER TABLE does not operate on clustered columns

Cause: An ALTER TABLE MODIFY statement specified a column that is used to cluster the table. Clustered columns may not be altered.

Action: To alter the column, first recreate the table in nonclustered form. The column's size can be increased at the same time.

ORA-01448   index must be dropped before changing to desired type

Cause: An ALTER TABLE MODIFY statement attempted to change an indexed character column to a LONG column. Columns with the datatype LONG may not be indexed, and hence the index must be dropped before the modification.

Action: Drop all indexes referencing the column before changing its datatype to LONG.

ORA-01449   column contains NULL values; cannot alter to NOT NULL

Cause: An ALTER TABLE MODIFY statement attempted to change the definition of a column containing NULL values to NOT NULL. The column may not currently contain any NULL values if it is to be altered to NOT NULL.

Action: Set all NULL values in the column to values other than NULL before ALTERING the column to NOT NULL.

ORA-01450   maximum key length exceeded

Cause: The combined length of all the columns specified in a CREATE INDEX statement exceeds the maximum index length. The maximum index length varies by operating system. The total index length is computed as the sum of the width of all indexed columns plus the number of indexed columns. Date fields have a length of 7, character fields have their defined length, and numeric fields have a length of 22.

Action: Select columns to be indexed so the total index length does not exceed the maximum index length for the operating system.

ORA-01451   column to be modified to NULL cannot be modified
             to NULL

Cause: The column may already allow NULL values, the NOT NULL constraint is part of a primary key or check constraint, or an ALTER TABLE MODIFY statement attempted to change a column specification unnecessarily, from NULL to NULL.

Action: If a primary key or check constraint is enforcing the NOT NULL constraint, then drop that constraint.

ORA-01452   cannot CREATE UNIQUE INDEX; duplicate keys found

Cause: A CREATE UNIQUE INDEX statement specified one or more columns that currently contain duplicate values. All values in the indexed columns must be unique, by row, to create a UNIQUE INDEX.

Action: If the entries need not be unique, remove the keyword UNIQUE from the CREATE INDEX statement, then reexecute the statement. If the entries must be unique, as in a primary key, then remove duplicate values before creating the UNIQUE index.

ORA-01453   SET TRANSACTION must be first statement of
             transaction

Cause: A transaction was not processed properly because the SET TRANSACTION statement was not the first statement.

Action: Commit or roll back the current transaction before using the statement SET TRANSACTION.

ORA-01454   cannot convert column into numeric datatype

Cause: A nonnumeric value could not be converted into a number value.

Action: Check the value to make sure it contains only numbers, a sign, a decimal point, and the character *E* or *e*, then retry the operation.

ORA-01455   converting column overflows integer datatype

Cause: The converted form of the specified expression was too large for the specified datatype.

Action: Define a larger datatype, or correct the data.

ORA-01456   may not perform insert/delete/update operation
             inside a READ ONLY transaction

Cause: A non-DDL INSERT/DELETE/UPDATE or SELECT FOR UPDATE operation was attempted.

Action: Commit or roll back the current transaction, then retry the operation.

ORA-01457   converting column overflows decimal datatype

Cause: The converted form of the specified expression was too large for the specified type. The problem also occurs in COBOL programs when using COMP-3 in the picture clause, which is acceptable to the Pro*COBOL precompiler and to COBOL but results in this error.

Action: Define a larger datatype, or correct the data.

ORA-01458   invalid length inside variable character string

Cause: An attempt was made to bind or define a variable character string with a buffer length less than the two-byte minimum requirement.
Action: Increase the buffer size or use a different type.

ORA-01459   invalid length for variable character string

Cause: The buffer length was less than the minimum required (two bytes) or greater than its length at bind time minus two bytes.
Action: None. Buffer length is set correctly by Oracle at fetch time.

ORA-01460   unimplemented or unreasonable conversion requested

Cause: The requested format conversion is not supported.
Action: Remove the requested conversion from the SQL statement. Check the syntax for the TO_CHAR, TO_DATE, and TO_NUMBER functions to see which conversions are supported.

ORA-01461   can bind a LONG value only for insert into
             a LONG column

Cause: An attempt was made to insert a value from a LONG datatype into another datatype. This is not allowed.
Action: Do not try to insert LONG datatypes into other types of columns.

ORA-01462   cannot insert string literals longer than
             2000 characters

Cause: The longest literal supported by Oracle consists of 2,000 characters.
Action: Reduce the number of characters in the literal to 2,000 characters or fewer, or use the VARCHAR2 or LONG datatype to insert strings exceeding 2,000 characters.

ORA-01463   cannot modify column datatype with
             current constraints

Cause: An attempt was made to modify the datatype of a column which has constraints which only allow changing the datatype from CHAR to VARCHAR or vice versa.
Action: Remove the constraint(s) or do not perform the offending operation.

ORA-01464   circular grant (granting to grant ancestor) of
             table or view

Cause: The user in the TO clause of the GRANT statement has already been GRANTed privileges on this table.

Action: Do not GRANT privileges on a table to the user who originally GRANTed privileges on that table. The statement in error is probably unnecessary.

ORA-01465   invalid hex number

Cause: In an UPDATE statement following a SELECT FOR UPDATE, part of the ROWID contains invalid characters. ROWID must be expressed in the proper and expected format for ROWID, and within single quotes.
Action: Enter the ROWID just as it was returned in the SELECT FOR UPDATE.

ORA-01466   unable to read data — object definition has changed

Cause: This is a time-based read-consistency error for a database object (such as a table or index). Either of the following occurred:

■ The query was parsed and executed with a snapshot older than the time the object was changed.

■ The creation time-stamp of the object is greater than the current system time.

This happens, for example, when the system time is set to a time earlier than the creation time of the object.
Action: If the cause is an old snapshot, then commit or roll back the transaction and resume work. If the cause is a creation time-stamp in the future, then ensure the system time is correctly set.
If the object creation time-stamp is still greater than the system time, then export the object's data, drop the object, recreate the object (so it has a new creation time-stamp), import the object's data, and resume work.

ORA-01467   sort key too long

Cause: A DISTINCT, GROUP BY, ORDER BY, or SET operation requires a sort key longer than that supported by Oracle. Either too many columns or too many group functions were specified in the SELECT statement.
Action: Reduce the number of columns or group functions involved in the operation.

ORA-01468   a predicate may reference only one outer-joined table

Cause: A predicate in the WHERE clause has two columns from different tables with "(+)".
Action: Change the WHERE clause so that each predicate has a maximum of one outer-join table.

ORA-01469 PRIOR can only be followed by a column name

Cause: An invalid column name was specified after the PRIOR keyword.
Action: Check syntax, spelling, use a valid column name, and try again.

ORA-01471 cannot create a synonym with the same name as object

Cause: An attempt was made to create a private synonym with the same name as the object to which it refers. This error typically occurs when a user attempts to create a private synonym with the same name as an object that he/she owns.
Action: Choose a different synonym name, or create the synonym under a different username.

ORA-01472 cannot use CONNECT BY on view with DISTINCT, GROUP BY, etc.

Cause: CONNECT BY cannot be used on a view where there is not a correspondence between output rows and rows of the underlying table.
Action: Remove the DISTINCT or GROUP BY from the view, or move the CONNECT BY clause into the view.

ORA-01473 cannot have subqueries in CONNECT BY clause

Cause: Subqueries cannot be used in a CONNECT BY clause.
Action: Remove the subquery, or move it to the WHERE clause.

ORA-01474 cannot have START WITH or PRIOR without CONNECT BY

Cause: START WITH and PRIOR are meaningful only in connection with CONNECT BY.
Action: Check the syntax for the SQL statement, and add a CONNECT BY clause if necessary.

ORA-01475 must reparse cursor to change bind variable datatype

Cause: After a statement was executed, an attempt was made to rebind a bind variable with a datatype different from that of the original bind.
Action: Reparse the cursor before rebinding with a different datatype.

ORA-01476 divisor is equal to zero

Cause: An expression attempted to divide by zero.
Action: Correct the expression, then retry the operation.

ORA-01477 user data area descriptor is too large

Cause: This is an internal error message not normally issued.
Action: Contact Worldwide Customer Support.

ORA-01478   array bind may not include any LONG columns

Cause: An attempt was made to use array bind on a column whose maximum size is greater than 2,000 bytes. This is not permitted.
Action: Do not use array bind for a LONG column. Use an ordinary bind instead.

ORA-01479   last character in the buffer is not Null

Cause: A bind variable of type 97 does not contain NULL at the last position.
Action: Make the last character a NULL.

ORA-01480   trailing null missing from STR bind value

Cause: A bind variable specified as type SQLT_STR is not terminated with an ASCII NULL (0) character.
Action: Check maximum lengths and contents of string bind variables.

ORA-01481   invalid number format model

Cause: An invalid format parameter was used with the TO_CHAR or TO_NUMBER function.
Action: Correct the syntax, then retry the operation.

ORA-01482   unsupported character set

Cause: The second or third parameter to the CONVERT function is not a supported character set.
Action: Use one of the supported character sets.

ORA-01483   invalid length for DATE or NUMBER bind variable

Cause: A bind variable of type DATE or NUMBER is too long.
Action: Check the installation or user's guide for the maximum allowable length.

ORA-01484   arrays can only be bound to PL/SQL statements

Cause: You tried to bind an array to a non-PL/SQL statement.

ORA-01485   compile bind length different from
             execute bind length

Cause: You bound a buffer of type DTYVCS (VARCHAR with the two-byte length in front), and at execute time the length in the first two bytes is more than the maximum buffer length (given in the bind call). The number of elements in the array and the current number of elements in the array cannot be more than the maximum size of the array.

ORA-01486   size of array element is too large

Cause: You tried to bind a data value which was either too large for the datatype (for example, NUMBER) or was greater than 2,000 bytes (for example, VARCHAR or LONG).

ORA-01487   packed decimal number too large for supplied buffer

Cause: A conversion request cannot be performed because the buffer is too small to hold the result.
Action: Increase the size of the buffer.

ORA-01488   invalid nibble or byte in the input data

Cause: A conversion request cannot be performed because a digit was invalid.
Action: Fix the number and retry.

ORA-01489   result of string concatenation is too long

Cause: The result of a string concatenation was larger than the maximum length of a string (2,000 characters).
Action: Reduce the size of one or both of the strings to be concatenated. Make certain the total length of the concatenation result is less than 2,000 characters.

Miscellaneous, ANALYZE, SQL Parsing, Execution: 01490-01499

This section lists miscellaneous messages generated by among others, the ANALYZE command, SQL parser, and during the execution of Oracle commands.

ORA-01490   invalid ANALYZE command

Cause: The syntax of the ANALYZE command was incorrect.
Action: Check the syntax and enter the command using the correct syntax.

ORA-01491   CASCADE option not valid

Cause: The CASCADE option should be used only for tables or clusters.

Action: Do not use the CASCADE option in this manner. Check the syntax of the statement then retry.

ORA-01492   LIST option not valid

Cause: The LIST option can only be used for tables or clusters.

ORA-01493   invalid SAMPLE size specified

Cause: The specified SAMPLE size is out of range.
Action: Specify a value within the proper range.

ORA-01495   specified chain row table not found

Cause: The specified table either does not exist, or the user does not have the proper privileges to access it.
Action: Specify an existing table, or obtain the privileges to access the desired table.

ORA-01496   specified chain row table form incorrect

Cause: The specified table does not have the proper field definitions.
Action: Check the spelling of the table name, and specify the correct table to use.

ORA-01497   unable to initialize statistics scan -
             see trace file.

Cause: The first block checked in the object from the ANALYZE ... STATISTICS command was found to be corrupted.
Action: Check the trace file for more descriptive messages about the problem. Correct these messages. The name of the trace file is operating system-specific (for example, ORAxxxx.TRC), and it is found in the directory specified by the initialization parameter USER_DUMP_DEST. If USER_DUMP_DEST is not set, trace files are not created. It may be necessary to recreate the object.

ORA-01498   block Check Failure - see trace file

Cause: A message occurred while checking a block with the ANALYZE command.
Action: Check the trace file for more descriptive messages about the problem. Correct these messages. The name of the trace file is operating system-specific (for example, ORAxxxx.TRC), and it is found in the directory specified by the initialization parameter USER_DUMP_DEST. If USER_DUMP_DEST is not set, trace files are not created. It may be necessary to recreate the object.

ORA-01499   table/Index Cross Reference Failure - see trace file

Cause: A message occurred during validation of an index or a table by use of the ANALYZE command. One or more entries do not point to the appropriate cross-reference.

Action: Check the trace file for more descriptive messages about the problem. Correct these messages. The name of the trace file is operating system-specific (for example, ORAxxxx.TRC), and it is found in the directory specified by the initialization parameter USER_DUMP_DEST. If USER_DUMP_DEST is not set, trace files are not created. It may be necessary to recreate the object.

PL/SQL Errors and Warnings

The following is a list of error messages issued by PL/SQL. To help diagnose, find, and fix errors, PL/SQL embeds object names, numbers, and character strings in some error messages. These embedded variables are represented by name, num, and str, respectively. For example, the error message listed as:

PLS-00388:   undefined column 'name' in subquery

might actually appear as:

PLS-00388:   undefined column 'AMPNO' in subquery
PLS-00102:   parser stack overflow because nesting is too deep

Cause: The parser, which checks the syntax of PL/SQL statements, uses a data structure called a stack; the number of levels of nesting in your PL/SQL block exceeded the stack capacity.

Action: Reorganize your block structure to avoid nesting at too deep a level. For example, move the lowest-level subblock to a higher level.

PLS-00103:   found 'str' but expected one of the following: 'str'

Cause: This error message is from the parser. It found a token (language element) that is inappropriate in this context.

Action: Check previous tokens as well as the one given in the error message. The line and column numbers given in the error message refer to the end of the faulty language construct.

PLS-00104:   empty argument list in call of procedure 'name'
              must be omitted

Cause: In a subprogram call, the name of the subprogram was followed by an empty parameter list. For example, procedure P was called as P( ). This is not allowed.

Action: Remove the empty parameter list. In the example, change the procedure call to P.

PLS-00105:   at most one forward declaration of type 'name'
              is permitted

Cause: Not in Release 2.0.

PLS-00108:   declarative units must be a single
              variable declaration

Cause: While checking a declarative unit (a top-level declare block without the BEGIN...END), PL/SQL found that there was more than one item declared, or that the item was not a variable declaration. A table is a common variable declaration at the unit level. To define a TABLE, you can compile a DECLARE compilation unit, but only one at a time is allowed.

Action: Declare variables in separate declarative units.

PLS-00109:   unknown exception name 'name' in
              PRAGMA EXCEPTION_INIT

Cause: No declaration for the exception name was found within its scope.

Action: Make sure the pragma follows the exception declaration and is within the same scope.

PLS-00110:   bind variable 'name' not allowed in this context

Cause: A bind variable, that is, an identifier prefixed with a colon, was found in an inappropriate context.

Action: Remove the colon or replace the bind variable with the appropriate object.

PLS-00111:   end-of-file in comment

Cause: A comment had a comment initiator (/*), but before the comment terminator (*/) was found, an end-of-file marker was encountered.

Action: Remove the comment initiator or add a comment terminator. The line and column numbers given in the error message refer to the beginning of the last legal token before the comment initiator.

PLS-00112:   end-of-line in quoted identifier

Cause: A quoted identifier had a beginning quote ("), but before the ending quote (") was found, an end-of-line marker was encountered.

Action: Remove the beginning quote or add the ending quote. The line and column numbers given in the error message refer to the beginning of the quoted identifier.

```
PLS-00113:   END identifier 'name1' must match 'name2'
             at line num, column num
```

Cause: Following the keyword END, which terminates some language constructs (such as loops, blocks, functions, and procedures), you can optionally place the name of that construct. For example, at the end of the definition of loop L you might write **END L**.

This error occurs when the optional name does not match the name given to the language construct. It is usually caused by a misspelled identifier or by a faulty block structure.

Action: Make sure the spelling of the END identifier matches the name given to the language construct and that the block structure is correct.

```
PLS-00114:   bind variable 'name' exceeds implementation length
```

Cause: The name of a PL/SQL variable is longer than 30 characters. Legal identifiers (including quoted identifiers) have a maximum length of 30 characters. You might have mistakenly enclosed a string literal in double quotes instead of single quotes, in which case PL/SQL considers it a quoted identifier.

Action: Shorten the name to 30 or fewer characters, or if you are using a string literal, replace the double quotes with single quotes.

```
PLS-00115:   this PRAGMA must follow the declaration of 'name'
```

Cause: The pragma refers to a PL/SQL object that was not declared or is not within the scope of the reference. Identifiers must be declared before they are used in a pragma; forward references are not allowed.

Action: Check your spelling and declaration of the identifier. Also confirm that the declaration is placed correctly in the block structure.

```
PLS-00116:   duplicate WHERE clause in table expression
```

Cause: Two or more WHERE clauses were found in a DELETE, SELECT, or UPDATE statement. The WHERE clause specifies a condition under which rows in a table are processed. The condition can contain several logical expressions connected by AND or OR, but a statement can contain only one WHERE clause.

Action: Remove one of the WHERE clauses and, if necessary, connect logical expressions by AND or OR.

PLS-00117:   duplicate CONNECT BY clause in table expression

Cause: Two or more CONNECT BY clauses were found in a SELECT statement. The CONNECT BY clause defines a relationship used to return rows in a hierarchical order. The relationship can contain two expressions separated by a relational operator (such as = or !=), but a statement can contain only one CONNECT BY clause.

Action: Remove one of the CONNECT BY clauses and, if necessary, separate expressions by a relational operator.

PLS-00118:   duplicate GROUP BY clause in table expression

Cause: Two or more GROUP BY clauses were found in a SELECT statement. The GROUP BY clause lists column expressions used to form a summary row for each group of selected rows. The list can contain several column expressions separated by commas, but a statement can contain only one GROUP BY clause.

Action: Remove one of the GROUP BY clauses and, if necessary, separate column expressions by commas.

PLS-00119:   duplicate HAVING clause in table expression

Cause: Two or more HAVING clauses were found in a SELECT statement. The HAVING clause specifies a condition under which groups of rows (formed by the GROUP BY clause) are included in the result. The condition can include several logical expressions connected by AND or OR, but a statement can contain only one HAVING clause.

Action: Remove one of the HAVING clauses, and, if necessary, connect logical expressions by AND or OR.

PLS-00120:   inappropriate argument in OPEN statement

Cause: The cursor_name parameter in an OPEN statement is misspelled or does not refer to a legally declared cursor.

Action: Check your spelling of the cursor_name parameter. Make sure the cursor was declared properly.

PLS-00123:   program too large

Cause: PL/SQL was designed primarily for robust transaction processing. One consequence of the special-purpose design is that the PL/SQL compiler imposes a limit on block size. The limit depends on the mix of statements in your PL/SQL block. Blocks that exceed the limit cause this error.

Action: The best solution is to modularize your program by defining subprograms, which can be stored in an Oracle database. Another solution is to break your program into two subblocks. Have the first block INSERT any data the second block needs into a temporary database table. Then have the second block SELECT the data from the table.

PLS-00124:   name of exception expected for first argument
              in EXCEPTION_INIT pragma

Cause: The first argument passed to the EXCEPTION_INIT pragma was something other than an exception name. The first argument must be the name of a legally declared exception.

Action: Replace the first argument with the name of a legally declared exception.

PLS-00201:   identifier 'name' must be declared

Cause: You tried to reference an undefined variable, exception, procedure, function, or other object. Either you failed to declare the identifier, or it is not within the scope of the reference.

Action: Check your spelling and declaration of the identifier. Also confirm that the declaration is placed correctly in the block structure. Check to see if a privilege was granted via a role, inside a stored procedure.

PLS-00202:   type 'name' must be declared

Cause: You tried to reference an undefined type. Either you failed to declare the type identifier, or it is not within the scope of the reference.

Action: Check your spelling and declaration of the type identifier. Also confirm that the declaration is placed correctly in the block structure.

PLS-00203:   function DECODE must be called with at least 3
              non-Boolean arguments

Cause: Fewer than three arguments were passed to the built-in function DECODE. Though DECODE takes a variable number of (non-Boolean) arguments, you must pass it at least three.

Action: Call DECODE with three or more arguments.

PLS-00204:   function or pseudocolumn 'name' may be used inside
              a SQL statement only

Cause: A pseudocolumn or proscribed function was used in a procedural statement. The SQL pseudocolumns (CURRVAL, LEVEL, NEXTVAL, ROWID, ROWNUM) can be used only in SQL statements. Likewise, certain functions such as DECODE and the SQL group functions (AVG, MIN, MAX, COUNT, SUM, STDDEV, VARIANCE) can be used only in SQL statements.

Action: Remove the pseudocolumn reference or function call from the procedural statement, or replace the procedural statement with a SELECT INTO statement.

PLS-00205:   aggregate not allowed here

Cause: An aggregate, that is, a parenthesized list of values such as *(7788, 'SCOTT', 20),* was found in an inappropriate context.
Action: Remove or relocate the aggregate.

PLS-00206:   %TYPE must be applied to a variable or column,
              not 'name'

Cause: The program object declared using the %TYPE datatype attribute is not of the appropriate class. It must be a variable, column, record component, subprogram formal parameter, or other object to which values can be assigned.
Action: Declare an object of the appropriate class, or define the datatype in another way (for example, use %ROWTYPE).

PLS-00207:   identifier 'name', applied to implicit cursor SQL,
              is not a legal cursor attribute

Cause: An identifier that is not a cursor attribute was applied to the identifier SQL. For example, this error occurs if the cursor attribute is misspelled.
Action: Check your spelling of the cursor attribute name. Make sure the attribute is one of these: %NOTFOUND, %FOUND, %ROWCOUNT, %ISOPEN.

PLS-00208:   identifier 'name' is not a legal cursor attribute

Cause: An identifier not declared as a cursor attribute was applied to an identifier declared as a cursor. For example, this error occurs if the cursor attribute is misspelled.
Action: Check your spelling of the cursor attribute name. Make sure the attribute is one of these: %NOTFOUND, %FOUND, %ROWCOUNT, %ISOPEN.

PLS-00209:   table 'name' is not in FROM clause

Cause: In a query, a table referenced by the select list is not named in the FROM clause.
Action: Check your spelling of the table names, make sure each column in the select list refers to a table in the FROM clause, then reexecute the query.

PLS-00210:   an OTHERS clause is required in this CASE statement

Cause: Not in Release 2.0.

PLS-00211:   CASE labels or ranges must not be duplicated in
              different WHEN clauses

Cause: Not in Release 2.0.

PLS-00212:   could not obtain enough memory to compile
              CASE statement

Cause: Not in Release 2.0.

PLS-00213:   package STANDARD not accessible

Cause: The PL/SQL compiler could not find package STANDARD in the current Oracle database. To compile a program, PL/SQL needs package STANDARD.
Action: Make sure that package STANDARD is available in the current Oracle database, then retry the operation.

PLS-00214:   BEGIN...END block nesting is too deep

Cause: The number of levels of nesting in your PL/SQL block is too large. You can nest blocks up to 255 levels deep, depending on the availability of system resources such as memory.
Action: Reorganize your block structure to avoid nesting at too deep a level. For example, move the lowest-level subblock to a higher level

PLS-00215:   string length constraints must be in range
              (1 .. 32767)

Cause: When declaring a character variable, you specified a length that is outside the legal range.
Action: Change the length constraint, making sure that it lies in the range 1 .. 32,767.

PLS-00216:   NUMBER precision constraint must be in range
              (1 .. 38)

Cause: You declared a NUMBER variable with a precision that is outside the legal range. Declarations such as N NUMBER(800) or N NUMBER(123,10) are not supported.
Action: Change the illegal NUMBER precision constraint, making sure that it lies in the range 1 .. 38.

PLS-00217:   NUMBER scale constraint must be in range
              (-84 .. 127)

Cause: You declared a NUMBER variable with a scale that is outside the legal range. Declarations such as N NUMBER(10,345) or N NUMBER(10,–100) are not supported.

Action: Change the illegal NUMBER scale constraint, making sure that it lies in the range –84 .. 127.

```
PLS-00218:    a variable declared NOT NULL must have an
              initialization assignment
```

Cause: In general, variables that have no initialization clause in their declaration are automatically initialized to NULL. This is illogical for NOT NULL variables, and therefore an initialization clause is required.

Action: Add an initialization clause to the variable declaration.

```
PLS-00219:    label 'name' reference is out of scope
```

Cause: A block or loop label was used to qualify a variable (as in outer_block.date) that was not declared or is not within the scope of the label. The variable name might be misspelled, its declaration might be faulty, or the declaration might be placed incorrectly in the block structure.

Action: Check your spelling and declaration of the variable name. Also confirm that the declaration is placed correctly in the block structure.

```
PLS-00220:    simple name required in this context
```

Cause: A qualified name such as A.B or A.B.C is not permitted here.

Action: Use a simple name such as A instead.

```
PLS-00221:    'name' is not a procedure or is undefined
```

Cause: The named identifier is being referenced as a procedure, but the identifier was not declared or actually represents another object (for example, it might have been declared as a function).

Action: Check your spelling and declaration of the identifier. Also confirm that the declaration is placed correctly in the block structure.

```
PLS-00222:    no function with name 'name' exists in this scope
```

Cause: The named identifier is being referenced as a function, but the identifier was not declared or actually represents another object (for example, it might have been declared as a procedure).

Action: Check your spelling and declaration of the identifier. Also confirm that the declaration is placed correctly in the block structure.

PLS-00223:   parameterless procedure 'name' used as function

Cause: The named identifier is being referenced as a parameterless function, but the identifier actually represents a procedure.

Action: Check your spelling and declaration of the identifier. Also confirm that the declaration is placed correctly in the block structure. If necessary, change the declaration of the identifier, or change the reference so that it does not require a return value.

PLS-00224:   object 'name' must be of type function or array to
             be used this way

Cause: The named identifier is being referenced as a function or an array, but the identifier actually represents an object (a number or date, for example) that cannot be referenced in this way.

Action: Check your spelling and declaration of the identifier. Also confirm that the declaration is placed correctly in the block structure.

PLS-00225:   subprogram or cursor 'name' reference is out
             of scope

Cause: A subprogram or cursor references a variable that was not declared or is not within the scope of the subprogram or cursor. The variable name might be misspelled, its declaration might be faulty, or the declaration might be placed incorrectly in the block structure.

Action: Check your spelling and declaration of the variable name. Also confirm that the declaration is placed correctly in the block structure.

PLS-00226:   package 'name' used as variable reference

Cause: A package was referenced in an expression as if it were a variable or function. Either the name of the variable or function is misspelled, or the reference is not fully qualified. For example, to call the function my_function, which is stored in package my_package, you must use dot notation as follows:

... my_package.my_function ...

Action: Correct your spelling of the variable or function name, or use dot notation to reference the packaged variable or function.

PLS-00227:   IN formal parameter 'name' not allowed in
             this context

Cause: When declaring the formal parameters of a subprogram, you used one parameter to initialize another, as in

PROCEDURE my_proc (j NUMBER, k NUMBER := j) IS ...

The first parameter has no value until run time, so it cannot be used to initialize another parameter.

Action: Remove the illegal formal parameter reference.

PLS-00229:   attribute expression within SQL expression

Cause: You used an attribute expression such as SQL%NOTFOUND in an SQL statement, but attribute expressions are allowed only in procedural statements.

Action: To work around this limitation, assign the value of the attribute expression to a variable, then use the variable in the SQL statement.

PLS-00230:   OUT and IN OUT formal parameters may not have
              default expressions

Cause: When declaring the formal parameters of a procedure, you initialized an OUT or IN OUT parameter to a default value. However, only IN parameters can be initialized to default values.

Action: Remove the illegal default expression.

PLS-00231:   function 'name' may not be used in SQL

Cause: You used a proscribed function in an SQL statement. Certain functions such as SQLCODE and SQLERRM can be used only in procedural statements.

Action: Remove the function call from the SQL statement, or replace the function call with a local variable. However, you can assign the values of SQLCODE and SQLERRM to local variables, then use the variables in the SQL statement.

PLS-00232:   nested packages not permitted

Cause: You declared a package inside another package, but package declarations are allowed only at the top level. In other words, you cannot nest packages.

Action: Move the package declaration outside the enclosing package.

PLS-00233:   function name used as an exception name in
              WHEN clause

Cause: The WHEN clause in an exception handler contains a function call instead of an exception name. A valid exception handler consists of a WHEN clause, which must specify an exception, followed by a sequence of statements to be executed when that exception is raised.

Action: Check your spelling of the identifier in the WHEN clause, then replace the function call with an exception name.

PLS-00302: `component 'name' must be declared`

Cause: In a reference to a component (for example, in the name A.B, B is a component of A), the component was not declared. The component might be misspelled, its declaration might be faulty, or the declaration might be placed incorrectly in the block structure.

Action: Check your spelling and declaration of the component. Also confirm that the declaration is placed correctly in the block structure.

PLS-00303: `qualifier 'name' must be declared`

Cause: In a name such as A.B, A is a qualifier and B is a component of the qualifier. This error occurs when no declaration for the qualifier is found. The qualifier might be misspelled, its declaration might be faulty, or the declaration might be placed incorrectly in the block structure.

Action: Check your spelling and declaration of the qualifier. Also confirm that the declaration is placed correctly in the block structure.

PLS-00304: `cannot compile body of 'name' without its specification`

Cause: The compiled package specification needed to compile a package body could not be found. Some possible causes are:

- The package name is misspelled.

- The package specification was never compiled.

- The compiled package specification is not accessible.

You must compile the package specification before compiling the package body, and the compiler must have access to the compiled specification.

Action: Check your spelling of the package name. Compile the package specification before compiling the package body. And, make sure the compiler has access to the compiled specification.

PLS-00305: `previous use of 'name' conflicts with this use`

Cause: While looking for prior declarations of a cursor, procedure, function, or package, the compiler found another object with the same name in the same scope.

Action: Check your spelling of the cursor, procedure, function, or package name. Also check the names of all constants, variables, parameters, and exceptions declared in the same scope. Then remove or rename the object with the duplicate name.

PLS-00306: `wrong number or types of arguments in call to 'name'`

Cause: This error occurs when the named subprogram call cannot be matched to any declaration for that subprogram name. The subprogram name might be misspelled, a parameter might be of the wrong datatype, the declaration might be faulty, or the declaration might be placed incorrectly in the block structure. For example, this error occurs if you call the built-in square root function SQRT with a misspelled name or with a parameter of the wrong datatype.

Action: Check your spelling and declaration of the subprogram name. Also confirm that its call is correct, its parameters are of the right datatype, and, if it is not a built-in function, that its declaration is placed correctly in the block structure.

PLS-00307:   too many declarations of 'name' match this call

Cause: The declaration of a subprogram name is ambiguous because there was no exact match between the declaration and the call, and more than one declaration matched the call when implicit conversions of the parameter datatypes were used. The subprogram name might be misspelled, its declaration might be faulty, or the declaration might be placed incorrectly in the block structure.

Action: Check your spelling and declaration of the subprogram name. Also confirm that its call is correct, its parameters are of the right datatype, and, if it is not a built-in function, that its declaration is placed correctly in the block structure.

PLS-00308:   this construct is not allowed as the origin of
              an assignment

Cause: The construct or expression does not designate a value that can be assigned to a variable. For example, the datatype name NUMBER cannot appear on the right-hand side of an assignment statement as in X := NUMBER.

Action: Correct the illegal assignment statement.

PLS-00309:   with %LAST attribute, 'name' must be a variable
              of an enumerated type

Cause: Not in Release 2.0.

PLS-00310:   with %ROWTYPE attribute, 'name' must name a
              cursor or table

Cause: The %ROWTYPE attribute must be applied to an identifier declared as a cursor or table. This error occurs when %ROWTYPE follows some identifier that has not been so declared.

Action: Change the declaration or do not apply the %ROWTYPE attribute to the identifier.

PLS-00311:   the declaration of the type of 'name' is
              incomplete or malformed

Cause: This occurrence of the identifier cannot be compiled because its datatype has not been properly defined.

Action: Correct the faulty datatype declaration.

PLS-00312:   a positional parameter association may not follow
              a named association

Cause: When passing a list of parameters to a subprogram or cursor, if you use both positional and named associations, you must place all positional associations in their declared order and before all named associations, which can be in any order.

Action: Reorder the parameter list to meet the requirements, or use named associations only.

PLS-00313:   'name' not declared in this scope

Cause: There is no declaration for the given identifier within the scope of reference. The identifier might be misspelled, its declaration might be faulty, or the declaration might be placed incorrectly in the block structure.

Action: Check your spelling and declaration of the identifier. Also confirm that the declaration is placed correctly in the block structure.

PLS-00314:   TABLE declarations are not allowed as PL/SQL
              local variables

Cause: In a precompiled program, you mistakenly used the DECLARE TABLE statement inside an embedded PL/SQL block. If an embedded PL/SQL block refers to a database table that does not yet exist, you can use the DECLARE TABLE statement to tell the precompiler what the table will look like. But DECLARE TABLE statements are allowed only in the host program.

Action: Move the DECLARE TABLE statement outside the embedded PL/SQL block. If you want a variable that can store an entire row of data selected from a database table or fetched by a cursor, use the %ROWTYPE attribute.

PLS-00315:   PL/SQL TABLE declarations must currently use
              BINARY_INTEGER indexes

Cause: In the INDEX BY clause of a PL/SQL table declaration, you specified a datatype other than BINARY_INTEGER. PL/SQL tables can have one column and a primary key. The column can belong to any scalar type, but the primary key must belong to type BINARY_INTEGER.

Action: Change the datatype specifier to BINARY_INTEGER.

PLS-00316:   PL/SQL TABLE declarations must currently use
              a single index

Cause: In the INDEX BY clause of a PL/SQL table declaration, you specified a composite primary key. PL/SQL tables must have a simple, unnamed primary key of type BINARY_INTEGER.
Action: Change the faulty clause to INDEX BY BINARY_INTEGER.

```
PLS-00319:   subquery in an IN or NOT IN clause must contain
             exactly one column
```

Cause: You used an invalid expression such as:

IN (SELECT x, y, z FROM ...)

When a [NOT]IN clause is used with a subquery, it does not test for set membership. The number of expressions in the [NOT]IN clause and the subquery select list must match. Therefore, in the preceding example, the subquery must specify at most one column.
Action: Change the subquery to select only one column.

```
PLS-00320:   the declaration of the type of this expression
             is incomplete or malformed
```

Cause: In a declaration, the name of a variable or cursor is misspelled, or the declaration makes a forward reference. Forward references are not allowed in PL/SQL. You must declare a variable or cursor before referencing it in other statements, including other declarative statements.
Action: Check your spelling of all identifiers in the declaration. If necessary, move the declaration so that it makes no forward references.

```
PLS-00321:   expression 'str' is inappropriate as the left hand
             side of an assignment statement
```

Cause: The expression does not designate a variable that can have a value assigned to it.
Action: Correct the illegal assignment statement.

```
PLS-00322:   declaration of a constant 'name' must contain an
             initialization assignment
```

Cause: A constant declaration is lacking the assignment of the constant value. For example, in the following declaration, := 3.14159 is the initialization assignment:

pi CONSTANT NUMBER := 3.14159;

Action: Correct the constant declaration by supplying the missing initialization assignment.

PLS-00323: `subprogram 'name' is declared in a package`
`specification and must be defined in`
`the package body`

Cause: You placed a subprogram specification in a package specification, but neglected to place the corresponding subprogram body in the package body. The package body implements the package specification. Therefore, the package body must contain the definition of every subprogram declared in the package specification.

Action: Check your spelling of the subprogram name. If necessary, add the missing subprogram body to the package body.

PLS-00324: `cursor attribute may not be applied to`
`non-cursor 'name'`

Cause: This error occurs when a cursor attribute (%FOUND, %NOTFOUND, %ROWCOUNT, or %ISOPEN) appears following an identifier not declared as a cursor. It occurs, for example, if the variable name my_cur in my_cur%FOUND was not properly declared as a cursor, or if the variable declaration was placed incorrectly in the block structure.

Action: Check your spelling and declaration of the identifier. Also confirm that the declaration is placed correctly in the block structure.

PLS-00325: `nonintegral numeric literal num is inappropriate`
`in this context`

Cause: A nonintegral numeric literal was used in a context that requires an integer (a number with no fractional part).

Action: Replace the inappropriate literal with an integral literal.

PLS-00326: `IN clause must contain same number of expressions`
`as subquery`

Cause: The number of expressions in an IN clause did not equal the number of expressions in a corresponding subquery select list.

Action: Check the number of expressions in each set, then revise the statement to make the numbers equal.

PLS-00328: `a subprogram body must be defined for the forward`
`declaration of 'name'`

Cause: You declared a subprogram specification, but failed to define the corresponding subprogram body. You can write the subprogram specification and body as a unit, or you can separate the specification from its body, which is necessary when you want to define mutually recursive subprograms or group subprograms in a package.

Action: Check your spelling of the subprogram name. If necessary, supply the missing subprogram body.

```
PLS-00341:    declaration of cursor 'name' is incomplete
              or malformed
```

Cause: A cursor declaration is improper, or an identifier referenced in the cursor declaration was not properly declared. You might have specified a return type (%ROWTYPE) that does not refer to an existing database table or previously declared cursor.

Action: Check your spelling and declaration of the cursor name and any identifiers referenced in the cursor declaration. Also confirm that the declaration is placed correctly in the block structure. If you specified a return type, make sure that it refers to an existing database table or previously declared cursor.

```
PLS-00351:    not logged on to database 'name'
```

Cause: You tried to access an Oracle database without being logged on. Probably, an invalid username or password was entered.

Action: Log on to Oracle with a correctly spelled username and password before trying to access the database.

```
PLS-00352:    unable to access another database 'name'
```

Cause: You tried to reference an object in a database other than the current local or remote Oracle database.

Action: Correct your reference and make sure the object is in the current Oracle database.

```
PLS-00353:    'name' must name a user in the database
```

Cause: This error occurs when the username was misspelled or when the user does not exist in the database.

Action: Check your spelling of the username, and make sure the user exists.

```
PLS-00354:    username must be a simple identifier
```

Cause: A qualified username such as **scott.accts** is not permitted in this context.
Action: Specify a simple username such as **scott** instead.

```
PLS-00356:    'name' must name a table to which the user
              has access
```

Cause: The named table is not accessible to the user. This error occurs when the table name or username was misspelled, the table and/or user does not exist in the database, the user was not granted the necessary privileges, or the table name duplicates the name of a local variable or loop counter.

Action: Check your spelling of the table name and username. Also confirm that the table and user exist, that the user has the necessary privileges, and that the table name does not duplicate the name of a local variable or loop counter.

PLS-00357:   table, view or sequence reference 'name' not
              allowed in this context

Cause: Reference to database table, view, or sequence was found in an inappropriate context. Such references can appear only in SQL statements or (excluding sequences) in %TYPE and %ROWTYPE declarations.

Action: Remove or relocate the illegal reference.

PLS-00358:   column 'name' exists in more than one table;
              use qualifier

Cause: Your statement is ambiguous because it specifies two or more tables having the same column name.

Action: Precede the column name with the table name (as in **emp.deptno**) so that the column reference is unambiguous.

PLS-00359:   assignment target in 'str' must have components

Cause: An assignment target was not declared to have the required components. For example, this error occurs if you try to assign a row of column values to a variable instead of a record.

Action: Check your spelling of the names of the assignment target and all its components. Make sure the assignment target is declared with the required components and that the declaration is placed correctly in the block structure.

PLS-00360:   cursor declaration without body needs return type

Cause: A cursor declaration lacks either a body (SELECT statement) or a return type (%ROWTYPE). If you want to separate a cursor specification from its body, you must supply a return type, as in

CURSOR c1 RETURN emp%ROWTYPE;

Action: Add a SELECT statement or return type to the cursor declaration.

PLS-00363:   expression 'str' cannot be used as an
              assignment target

Cause: You mistakenly used a literal, constant, IN parameter, loop counter, or function call as the target of an assignment.

Action: Correct the statement by using a valid assignment target.

PLS-00364:   loop index variable 'name' use is invalid

Cause: A reference to a loop counter was found in an inappropriate context.

Action: Change the loop range expression so that it does not reference the loop counter. If you want to refer in the range expression to another variable with the same name as the loop counter, change either name or qualify the variable name with a label.

PLS-00365:   'name' is an OUT parameter and cannot be read

Cause: You tried to assign the value of an OUT parameter to another parameter or variable. Inside a procedure, an OUT parameter acts like an uninitialized variable; therefore, its value cannot be read.

Action: Use an IN OUT parameter instead of the OUT parameter. Inside a procedure, an IN OUT parameter acts like an initialized variable; therefore, its value can be read.

PLS-00366:   subtype of a NOT NULL type must also be NOT NULL

Cause: Not in Release 2.0.

PLS-00367:   a RAISE statement with no exception name must be
              inside an exception handler

Cause: A RAISE statement not followed by an exception name was found outside an exception handler.

Action: Delete the RAISE statement, relocate it to an exception handler, or supply the missing exception name.

PLS-00368:   in RAISE statement, 'name' must be an exception name

Cause: The identifier in a RAISE statement is not a valid exception name.

Action: Make sure the identifier in the RAISE statement was declared as an exception and is correctly placed in the block structure. If you are using one of the PL/SQL predefined exception names, check its spelling.

PLS-00369:   no choices may appear with choice OTHERS
              in an exception handler

Cause: A construct of the form

WHEN excep1 OR OTHERS =>

was encountered in the definition of an exception handler. OTHERS must appear by itself as the last exception handler in a block.

Action: Remove the identifier that appears with OTHERS, or write a separate exception handler for that identifier.

```
PLS-00370:    OTHERS handler must be last among the exception
              handlers of a block
```

Cause: One or more exception handlers appear after an OTHERS handler. However, the OTHERS handler must be the last handler in a block or subprogram because it acts as the handler for all exceptions not named specifically.

Action: Move the OTHERS handler so that it follows all specific exception handlers.

```
PLS-00371:    at most one declaration for 'name' is permitted in
              the declaration section
```

Cause: A reference to an identifier is ambiguous because there are conflicting declarations for it in the declaration section of a block, procedure, or function. At most one declaration of the identifier is permitted in a declaration section.

Action: Check your spelling of the identifier. If necessary, remove all but one declaration of the identifier.

```
PLS-00372:    in a procedure, RETURN statement cannot contain
              an expression
```

Cause: In a procedure, a RETURN statement contains an expression, which is not allowed. In functions, a RETURN statement must contain an expression because its value is assigned to the function identifier. However, in procedures, a RETURN statement simply lets you exit before the normal end of the procedure is reached.

Action: Remove the expression from the RETURN statement, or redefine the procedure as a function.

```
PLS-00373:    EXIT label 'name' must label a LOOP statement
```

Cause: The statement with the named label is not a loop. An EXIT statement does not require a label operand, but if you specify one (as in EXIT my_label), it must be the label of a loop statement.

Action: Make sure the label name is spelled correctly and that it refers to a loop statement.

PLS-00374:   illegal EXIT statement; it must appear inside the
              loop labeled 'name'

Cause: An EXIT statement does not require a label operand, but if you specify one (as in EXIT my_label), the EXIT statement must be inside the loop designated by that label.

Action: Make sure the label name is spelled correctly, placed properly, and refers to the appropriate EXIT statement.

PLS-00375:   illegal GOTO statement; this GOTO cannot branch
              to label 'name'

Cause: The line and column numbers accompanying the error message refer to a GOTO that branches from outside a construct (a loop or exception handler, for example) containing a sequence of statements to a label inside that sequence of statements. Such a branch is not allowed.

Action: Either move the GOTO statement inside the sequence of statements, or move the labeled statement outside the sequence of statements.

PLS-00376:   illegal EXIT statement; it must appear inside a loop

Cause: An EXIT statement was found outside of a loop construct. The EXIT statement is used to exit prematurely from a loop and so must always appear within a loop.

Action: Either remove the EXIT statement, or place it inside a loop.

PLS-00377:   internal type PLS_INTEGER is not included in
              this release of PL/SQL

Cause: In a declaration, you mistakenly specified the obsolete datatype PLS_INTEGER, which has been replaced by the datatype BINARY_INTEGER.

Action: Specify the datatype BINARY_INTEGER instead of PLS_INTEGER.

PLS-00378:   invalid compilation unit for this release of PL/SQL

Cause: A compilation unit is a file containing PL/SQL source code that is passed to the compiler. Only compilation units containing blocks, declarations, statements, and subprograms are allowed. This error occurs when some other language construct is passed to the compiler.

Action: Make sure the compilation unit contains only blocks, declarations, statements, and subprograms.

PLS-00379:   CASE statements are not included in this release
              of PL/SQL

Cause: The unit being compiled contains a CASE statement. However, the current release of PL/SQL does not support CASE statements.

Action: Remove the CASE statement from the compilation unit.

```
PLS-00381:    type mismatch found at 'name' between column and
              variable in subquery or INSERT
```

Cause: The datatypes of a column and a variable do not match. The variable was encountered in a subquery or INSERT statement.

Action: Change the variable datatype to match that of the column.

```
PLS-00382:    expression is of wrong type
```

Cause: The given expression variable is of the wrong datatype for the context in which it was found.

Action: Change the datatype of the expression. You might want to use datatype conversion functions.

```
PLS-00383:    type mismatch found at 'name' inside an IN or
              NOT IN clause
```

Cause: In a test for set membership such as X NOT IN (SELECT Y ...), the expressions X and Y do not match in datatype, and it is unclear which implicit conversion is needed to correct the mismatch.

Action: Change the expressions so that their datatypes match. You might want to use datatype conversion functions in the select list.

```
PLS-00384:    type mismatch found at 'name' in UPDATE's SET clause
```

Cause: The column to the left of the equal sign in the SET clause of an UPDATE statement does not match in datatype with the column, expression, or subquery to the right of the equal sign, and it is unclear which implicit conversion is needed to correct the mismatch.

Action: Change the expressions so that their datatypes match. You might want to use datatype conversion functions in the SET clause.

```
PLS-00385:    type mismatch found at 'name' in SELECT...INTO
              statement
```

Cause: The expressions to the left and right of the INTO clause in a SELECT...INTO statement do not match in datatype, and it is unclear which implicit conversion is needed to correct the mismatch.

Action: Change the expressions so that their datatypes match. You might want to use datatype conversion functions in the select list.

PLS-00386:   type mismatch found at 'name' between FETCH cursor
             and INTO variables

Cause: An assignment target in the INTO list of a FETCH statement does not match in datatype with the corresponding column in the select list of the cursor declaration, and it is unclear which implicit conversion is needed to correct the mismatch.

Action: Change the cursor declaration or change the datatype of the assignment target. You might want to use datatype conversion functions in the select list of the query associated with the cursor.

PLS-00387:   INTO variable cannot be a database object

Cause: An item in the INTO list of a FETCH or SELECT statement was found to be a database object. INTO introduces a list of user-defined variables to which output values are assigned. Therefore, database objects cannot appear in the INTO list.

Action: Check your spelling of the INTO list item. If necessary, remove the item from the INTO list, or replace it with a user-defined output variable.

PLS-00388:   undefined column 'name' in subquery

Cause: A subquery contains a column name that was not defined for the specified table.

Action: Change the expression to specify a column that was defined.

PLS-00389:   undefined column 'name' in left-hand-side expression

Cause: A left-hand-side expression in an SQL statement refers to an undefined column.

Action: Check your spelling of the column name, then change the expression so that it refers only to defined columns.

PLS-00390:   undefined column 'name' in INSERT statement

Cause: An INSERT statement refers to a column not defined for the table or view into which data is being INSERTed.

Action: Check your spelling of the column name, then revise the statement so that it refers only to defined columns.

PLS-00391:   undefined column 'name' in UPDATE statement

Cause: An UPDATE statement refers to a column not defined for the table or view being UPDATEd.

Action: Check your spelling of the column name, then revise the statement so that it refers only to defined columns.

`PLS-00392:    type mismatch in arguments to BETWEEN`

Cause: In a comparison such as X BETWEEN Y AND Z, the expressions X, Y, and Z do not match in datatype, and it is unclear which implicit conversion is needed to correct the mismatch.

Action: Change the expressions so that their datatypes match. You might want to use datatype conversion functions.

`PLS-00393:    wrong number of columns in SELECT...INTO statement`

Cause: The number of columns selected by a SELECT...INTO statement does not match the number of variables in the INTO clause.

Action: Change the number of columns in the select list or the number of variables in the INTO clause so that the numbers match.

`PLS-00394:    wrong number of values in the INTO list of a FETCH`
`               statement`

Cause: The number of variables in the INTO clause of a FETCH statement does not match the number of columns in the cursor declaration.

Action: Change the number of variables in the INTO clause or the number of columns in the cursor declaration so that the numbers match.

`PLS-00395:    wrong number of values in VALUES clause of INSERT`
`               statement`

Cause: The number of columns in an INSERT statement does not match the number of values in the VALUES clause.

Action: Change the number of items in the column list or the number of items in the VALUES list so that the numbers match.

`PLS-00396:    INSERT statement's subquery yields wrong number of`
`               columns`

Cause: The number of columns in an INSERT statement does not match the number of columns in a subquery select list.

Action: Change the number of items in the column list of the INSERT statement or the number of items in the select list so that the numbers match.

`PLS-00397:    type mismatch in arguments to IN`

Cause: In a test for set membership such as X IN (Y, Z), the expressions X, Y, and Z do not match in datatype, and it is unclear which implicit conversion is needed to correct the mismatch.

Action: Change the expressions so that their datatypes match. You might want to use datatype conversion functions.

```
PLS-00398:    wrong number of columns in UNION, INTERSECT,
              or MINUS expression
```

Cause: The SELECT clauses to the left and right of a UNION, INTERSECT, or MINUS expression do not select the same number of columns.

Action: Change the select lists so that they contain the same number of items.

```
PLS-00399:    different types of columns in UNION, INTERSECT,
              or MINUS expression
```

Cause: The select lists to the left and right of a UNION, INTERSECT, or MINUS expression select at least one column that is mismatched in datatype.

Action: Change the select lists so that they match in datatype. You might want to use datatype conversion functions in the select list of one or more queries.

```
PLS-00400:    different number of columns between cursor SELECT
              statement and return value
```

Cause: In a cursor declaration, you specified a return type (such as RETURN emp%ROWTYPE), but the number of returned column values does not match the number of select-list items.

Action: Change the cursor return type or the select list so that the number of returned column values matches the number of select-list items.

```
PLS-00401:    different column types between cursor SELECT
              statement and return value found at 'name'
```

Cause: In a cursor declaration, you specified a return type (such as RETURN emp%ROWTYPE), but a returned column value and its corresponding select-list item belong to different datatypes.

Action: Change the cursor return type or the select list so that each returned column value and its corresponding select-list item belong to the same datatype.

```
PLS-00402:    alias required in SELECT list of cursor to avoid
              duplicate column names
```

Cause: A cursor was declared with a SELECT statement that contains duplicate column names. Such references are ambiguous.

Action: Replace the duplicate column name in the select list with an alias.

PLS-00403: `INTO list of FETCH statement contains illegal`
`assignment target`

Cause: A FETCH statement was unable to assign a value to an assignment target in its INTO list because the target is not a legally formed and declared variable. For example, the following assignment is illegal because *'Jones'* is a character string, not a variable:

FETCH my_cur INTO 'Jones';

Action: Check your spelling and declaration of the assignment target. Make sure you followed the rules for forming variable names.

PLS-00404: `cursor 'name' must be declared with FOR UPDATE to`
`use with CURRENT OF`

Cause: The use of the CURRENT OF 'name' clause is legal only if 'name' was declared with a FOR UPDATE clause.
Action: Add a FOR UPDATE clause to the definition of the cursor, or do not use the CURRENT OF 'name' clause.

PLS-00405: `subquery not allowed in this context`

Cause: A subquery was used in an inappropriate context. Subqueries are allowed only in SQL statements.
Action: You can get the same result by using a temporary variable.

PLS-00406: `length of SELECT list in subquery must match number`
`of assignment targets`

Cause: A query select list is not the same length as the list of targets that will receive the returned values.
Action: Change one of the lists so that they contain the same number of items.

PLS-00407: `'*' not allowed here; a list of columns is required`

Cause: An asterisk (*) was used as an abbreviation for a list of column names. However, in this context the column names must be written out explicitly.
Action: Replace the asterisk with a list of column names.

PLS-00408: `duplicate column 'name' not permitted in INSERT`
`or UPDATE`

Cause: An UPDATE or INSERT statement has a column list that contains duplicate column names.
Action: Check your spelling of the column names, then eliminate the duplication.

PLS-00409:   duplicate variable 'name' in INTO list is
             not permitted

Cause: The same variable appears twice in the INTO list of a SELECT or FETCH statement.

Action: Remove one of the variables from the INTO clause.

PLS-00410:   duplicate fields in record or table are not allowed

Cause: When declaring a user-defined record, you gave the same name to two fields. Like column names in a database table, field names in a user-defined record must be unique.

Action: Check your spelling of the field names, then remove the duplicate.

PLS-00412:   list of values not allowed as argument to this
             function or procedure

Cause: A parenthesized list of values separated by commas (that is, an aggregate) was used in the wrong context. However, an equal sign can take a list of values and a subquery as left- and right-hand-side arguments, respectively.

Action: Rewrite the expression.

PLS-00413:   identifier in CURRENT OF clause is not a cursor name

Cause: The identifier in a CURRENT OF clause names an object other than a cursor.

Action: Check your spelling of the identifier. Make sure that it names the cursor in the DELETE or UPDATE statement and that it names the cursor itself, not a FOR-loop variable.

PLS-00414:   no column 'name' in table

Cause: A table name or alias was used to qualify a column reference, but the column was not found in that table. Either the column was never defined, or the column name is misspelled.

Action: Confirm that the column was defined, and check your spelling of the column name.

PLS-00415:   'name' is an OUT parameter and cannot appear
             in a function

Cause: When declaring the formal arguments of a function, you specified the OUT or IN OUT parameter mode. Procedures can take IN, OUT, and IN OUT parameters, but functions can take only IN arguments.

Action: Remove the OUT or IN OUT argument from the formal argument list, or redefine the function as a procedure.

PLS-00450:   a variable of this private type cannot be
             declared here

Cause: Not in Release 2.0.

PLS-00483:   exception 'name' may appear in at most one
             exception handler in this block

Cause: The same exception appears in two different exception handlers within the same EXCEPTION section. That is not allowed.
Action: Remove one of the duplicate exception handlers.

PLS-00484:   exceptions 'name' and 'name' have same ORACLE
             error number and must appear in same
             exception handler

Cause: Using PRAGMA EXCEPTION_INIT, you initialized different exceptions to the same Oracle error number, then referred to them in different exception handlers within the same EXCEPTION section. Such references conflict.
Action: Remove one of the exceptions or initialize it to a different Oracle error number.

PLS-00485:   in exception handler, 'name' must be an
             exception name

Cause: An identifier not declared as an exception appears in an exception handler WHEN clause. Only the name of an exception is valid in a WHEN clause.
Action: Check your spelling of the exception name, and make sure the exception was declared properly.

PLS-00486:   SELECT list cannot be enclosed in parentheses

Cause: In a SELECT statement, the select list was enclosed in parentheses. Parentheses are not needed because the keywords SELECT and FROM delimit the select list.
Action: Remove the parentheses enclosing the select list.

PLS-00487:   invalid reference to variable 'name'

Cause: A variable was referenced in a way that is inconsistent with its datatype.
Action: Check your spelling of the variable name. Make sure the variable was declared properly and that the declaration and reference are consistent with regard to datatype.

PLS-00488:   invalid variable declaration: object 'name' must
              be a type or subtype

Cause: The datatype specifier in a variable declaration does not designate a legal type. When declaring a constant or variable, to provide the datatype of a column automatically, you must use the %TYPE attribute. Likewise, when declaring a record, to provide the datatypes of a row automatically, you must use the %ROWTYPE attribute.

Action: Make sure the datatype specifier designates a legal type. Remember to use the %TYPE and %ROWTYPE attributes when necessary.

PLS-00489:   invalid table reference: 'name' must be a column
              in this expression

Cause: In a query, a select-list item refers to a table in the FROM clause but not to a database column.

Action: Check your spelling of the column names, make sure each column in the select list refers to a table in the FROM clause, then reexecute the query.

PLS-00503:   RETURN <value> statement required for this
              return from function

Cause: In a function body, you used a RETURN statement that contains no expression. In procedures, a RETURN statement contains no expression because the statement simply returns control to the caller. However, in functions, a RETURN statement must contain an expression because its value is assigned to the function identifier.

Action: Add an expression to the RETURN statement.

PLS-00504:   type 'name'_BASE may not be used outside of
              package STANDARD

Cause: In a declaration, you mistakenly specified (for example) the datatype NUMBER_BASE. The datatypes CHAR_BASE, DATE_BASE, MLSLABEL_BASE, and NUMBER_BASE are for internal use only.

Action: Specify (for example) the datatype NUMBER instead of NUMBER_BASE.

PLS-00505:   user-defined types may only be defined as PL/SQL
              tables or records

Cause: You tried to define a datatype derived from some base type other than RECORD or TABLE. User-defined types must be derived from the RECORD or TABLE type.

Action: Remove the faulty type definition, or define a RECORD or TABLE type.

PLS-00506: user-defined constrained subtypes are disallowed

Cause: You tried to define a subtype (a subtype associates a base type with a constraint and so defines a subset of values). User-defined subtypes are not allowed in this release of PL/SQL. However, future versions of PL/SQL will allow you to define subtypes.

Action: Remove the illegal type definition.

PLS-00507: PL/SQL tables may not be defined in terms of records or other tables

Cause: In a TABLE type definition, you mistakenly specified a composite datatype (RECORD or TABLE) for the column. The single, unnamed column must belong to a scalar datatype such as CHAR, DATE, or NUMBER.

Action: Remove the TABLE type definition, or replace the composite datatype specifier with a scalar datatype specifier.

PLS-00700: PRAGMA EXCEPTION_INIT of 'name' must follow declaration of its exception in same block

Cause: A PRAGMA EXCEPTION_INIT was not declared in the same block as its exception. They must be declared in the proper order in the same block, with the PRAGMA EXCEPTION_INIT declaration following the exception declaration.

Action: Place the PRAGMA EXCEPTION_INIT declaration directly after the declaration of the exception referenced by the pragma.

PLS-00701: illegal ORACLE error number num for PRAGMA EXCEPTION_INIT

Cause: The error number passed to a PRAGMA EXCEPTION_INIT was out of range. The error number must be in the range –9999 .. –1 (excluding –00) for Oracle errors or in the range –20000 .. –20999 for user-defined errors.

Action: Use a valid error number.

PLS-00702: second argument to PRAGMA EXCEPTION_INIT must be a numeric literal

Cause: The second argument passed to a PRAGMA EXCEPTION_INIT was something other than a numeric literal (a variable, for example). The second argument must be a numeric literal in the range –9,999 .. –1 (excluding –100) for Oracle errors or in the range –20,000 .. –20,999 for user-defined errors.

Action: Replace the second argument with a valid error number.

PLS-00703: multiple instances of named argument in list

Cause: Two or more actual parameters in a subprogram call refer to the same formal parameter.

Action: Remove the duplicate actual parameter.

PLS-00704:   'name' must be declared as an exception

Cause: The exception_name parameter passed to PRAGMA EXCEPTION_INIT is misspelled or does not refer to a legally declared exception, or the pragma is misplaced; it must appear in the same declarative section, somewhere after the exception declaration.

Action: Check your spelling of the exception_name parameter. Then check the exception declaration, making sure the exception name and the keyword EXCEPTION are spelled correctly. Also make sure the pragma appears in the same declarative section somewhere after the exception declaration.

PLS-00705:   exceptions not allowed in an expression

Cause: You mistakenly referred to an exception within an expression. Exceptions have names but not values and therefore cannot contribute values to an expression.

Action: Check your spelling of the identifiers in the expression, then rewrite the expression so that it does not refer to an exception.

PLS-00900:   can't find body of unit 'name'

Cause: At run time, the body of a program unit could not be found. This happens, for example, if you reference a procedure for which a specification but no body exists. (No compile-time errors were generated because the specification exists.)

Action: Define a body for the program unit.

PLS-00901:   the datatype of column 'name' of table 'name' is
              not supported

Cause: A column in a database table belongs to a datatype that is not supported by the current release of PL/SQL.

Action: Remove the offending column from the table, or copy the desired columns to another table.

PLS-00902:   a read-only bind variable used in OUT or
              IN OUT context

Cause: A host variable that is protected from update was used in a context that allows an update.

Action: Check the context and change your use of the host variable, or assign the value of the host variable to a PL/SQL local variable, then use the local variable instead.

PLS-00904:   insufficient privilege to access object 'name'

Cause: You tried to operate on a database object without the required privilege. This error occurs, for example, if you try to UPDATE a table for which you have only SELECT privileges.

Action: Ask your DBA to perform the operation or to grant you the required privilege.

PLS-00905:   object 'name' is invalid

Cause: You referenced an invalid package specification or stored subprogram. A package specification or stored subprogram is invalid if its source code or any database object it references has been DROPped, REPLACEd, or ALTERed since it was last compiled.

Action: Find out what invalidated the package specification or stored subprogram, then make sure that Oracle can recompile it without errors.

PLS-00995:   unhandled exception # 'num'

Cause: An exception was raised for which no handler was found. If it cannot find a handler for a raised exception, PL/SQL returns an unhandled exception to the host environment. The number embedded in the message is an Oracle error code listed in the *Oracle 7 Server Messages and Codes Manual.*

Action: Fix the condition that raised the exception, write an appropriate exception handler, or use the OTHERS handler. If there is an appropriate handler in the current block, the exception was raised in a declaration or exception handler. (An exception raised in a declaration or exception handler propagates immediately to the enclosing block.) You can avoid unhandled exceptions by coding an OTHERS handler at the topmost level of every PL/SQL block and subprogram.

PLS-00996:   out of memory

Cause: A request from PL/SQL for more memory failed.

Action: Make sure that you are not referencing the wrong row in a PL/SQL table and that your program is not recursing too deeply.

Index

B

C

D

J

O

P

T

W

X

Y

Z

The NEW CLASSICS

ORACLE DBA HANDBOOK

by Kevin Loney
Every DBA can learn to manage a networked Oracle database efficiently and effectively with this comprehensive guide. Oracle Magazine columnist Kevin Loney covers everything a DBA needs to manage Oracle, from architecture to layout considerations to supporting packages. A command reference and configuration guidelines are included as well as scripts and tips. The **Oracle DBA Handbook** is the ideal support and resource for all new and existing DBAs.

Price: $34.95 U.S.A.
Available Now
ISBN: 0-07-881182-1
Pages: 704, paperback

TUNING ORACLE

by Michael J. Corey, Michael Abbey, and Daniel J. Dechichio, Jr.
Learn to customize Oracle for optimal performance and productivity with this focused guide. Michael Corey, president of the International Oracle Users Group, and Michael Abbey and Daniel Dechichio, recognized Oracle experts, teach strategies and systems to help administrators avoid problems, increase database speed, and ensure overall security. For a powerful and versatile database, **Tuning Oracle** is your ultimate resource for making Oracle reach its full potential.

Price: $29.95 U.S.A.
Available Now
ISBN: 0-07-881181-3
Pages: 336, paperback

ORACLE WORKGROUP SERVER HANDBOOK

by Thomas B. Cox
Take full advantage of the power and flexibility of the new Oracle Workgroup Server with this comprehensive handbook. Thomas Cox helps users master the intricacies of this relational database management system, including creating a database, developing queries, and using SQL as well as explaining and defining declarations, referential integrity, and more. Perfect for both users and administrators, the **Oracle Workgroup Server Handbook** is the one authoritative book.

Price: $34.95 U.S.A.
Available Now
ISBN: 0-07-881186-4
Pages: 320, paperback

ORACLE® *Oracle Press*™

Driving Your Information Systems for Optimal Performance

BC604SL